THE GAME BIRDS OF INDIA, BURMAH, AND CEYLON.

THE GAME BIRDS OF INDIA, BURMAH, AND CEYLON.

HUME AND MARSHALL

IN THREE VOLUME

VOLUME III

GYAN

Published by

Gyan Publishing House
5, Ansari Road
Daryaganj, New Delhi-110002
Phone: 011-47034999, 9811692060
E-mail: books@gyanbooks.com

Distribution Network
gyanbooks.com
India, USA, Canada, UK, Australia, France

ISBN : 978-81-212-9207-8 (Set)
978-81-212-9204-7 (PB)
First Published, 1881

2nd Impression 2023

Printed at: Gyan Press, Delhi.

THE GAME BIRDS OF INDIA, BURMAH, AND CEYLON (VOL. III)
Author:HUME AND MARSHALL

THE

GAME BIRDS

OF

INDIA, BURMAH, AND CEYLON.

HUME AND MARSHALL.

VOLUME III.

CONTENTS.

1. Wrongly *cinerea* on Plate.
2. ,, *ferus* on Plate.
3. ,, *minutus* on Plate.
4. ,, *Sarkidiornis melanotus* on Plate.
5. ,, *Nettapus coromandelicus* on Plate.
6. ,, *arcuata* on Plate.
7. Wrongly *major* on Plate.
8. ,, *vulpanser* on Plate.
9. ,, *Casarca* on Plate.
10. ,, *boschas* on Plate.
11. ,, *æcilorhyncha* on Plate.
12. ,, *Anas* on Plate.
13. ,, *Anas* on Plate.

14. Wrongly *glocitans* on Plate.
15. " *Anas* on Plate.
16. " *Mareca gibberifrons* on Plate.
17. " *Branta* on Plate.
18. " *Aythya* on Plate.
19. " *glaucion* on Plate.
20. Wrongly *castor* on Plate.
21. " *Scalopax* on Plate.
22. " *stenura* on Plate.
23. " *scolopacinus* on Plate.
24. " *Totanus* on Plate.
25. " *rufa* on Plate.

GRUS ANTIGONE

THE SARUS.

Grus antigone, *Linné.*

Vernacular Names.—[Sarus, *passim;* Sirhans, (Hindee); Gyo-gya, *Arakan;* Gyo-gya, Jo-ja, *Pegu.*]

THE Sarus is found, *in suitable localities*, throughout the Central Provinces (including Bustar and the other Feudatory States), the Madras Presidency, north of the Gódávari, (and perhaps between the Kistna and Gódávari), Chota Nagpur, Lower Bengal, the North-Western Provinces and Oudh, Rajputana (except the more western portions), Cutch, Káthiáwár, the eastern portions of Sind and the Punjab, and in the Bombay Presidency north of the Nerbudda, and along the Coast, at any rate, as far south as the Tapti, and the southern talukas of the Surat District. But Mr. Mulock, the Collector of Tanna, a good sportsman who knows the district thoroughly, says that he has never once met with the Sarus in that district, although as it is found (but even there as a rare visitor) in the adjoining Surat Talukas, it may, occasionally, occur in the Tanna Collectorate also. In Khandesh Major Probyn, who has been stationed in that district for years, says that he has only thrice seen it, so that there also it can only be a very rare straggler. As regards the Deccan, Mr. J. Davidson, C.S., tells me that he has "never seen or heard of its being found there."

Eastwards it extends far up into the valley of Assam, being common in Darrang, and occurring, though more sparingly, in Lakhimpur.

Again it occurs in Arakan, in Pegu, and in those few portions of Tenasserim where there are wide plains, as in the valleys of the Attaran and the Sitang.

Mr. Oates remarks that it is "common and a constant resident throughout the flat, swampy plains of Lower Pegu; it breeds during July, August and September. The bird is becoming less common every year, and will probably be entirely driven away in a few years."*

---

* Mr. Davis also writes :—

"The Sarus is common on the extensive swampy plains, between the mouths of the Irrawaddy and Salween Rivers, but they are most numerous on the Thatone plain opposite the village of Theinzeik."

The Sarus is very rare in Sind, even east of the Indus; and, so far as I know, does not occur west of this river at all. Burnes remarked that he had occasionally seen it on the Indus, but never in Afghanistan.

In the Punjab it is found in the Dehli, Gurgaon, Kurnál, Umballa, Gurdaspur and Lahore Districts, in fact as far west as the Ravee, but not, so far as I know, in the Rohták, Hissar, Sirsa or Ferozpur districts, nor south of Ferozpur, anywhere between the Satlej and the Indus, nor west of the Indus. Its distribution southwards is not at present well defined. It does not seem to occur at all in Mysore* nor in any of the Madras districts south of this, nor has it ever been recorded from Ceylon. Probably a line drawn from Damaun on the west, to Masulipatam on the east coast, would approximately indicate the southern limits of its range in the Indian Peninsula.

It does not normally ascend the mountains, but in places, as in the valley of Nepál, has been introduced. In Kulu also Mr. Graham Young says it used to breed, but is now, he believes, extinct. Into Kulu likewise it must have been introduced.

Dr. Anderson obtained† this species in Upper or Independent Burma; but, with this exception, it is not as yet *known* to occur outside the limits of our Indian Empire, though it may prove to extend to Siam (as Blyth asserts,‡ but without quoting any authority,) and South-western China.

THE SARUS is essentially a bird of widely-extended and well-watered plains. Hilly and broken country on the one hand, and sandy, waterless tracts (like many portions of North-western Rajputana) on the other, it equally eschews. It much prefers the neighbourhood of cultivation; but it may be found far away from this in places where wide level plains are watered by streams or rivers, or dotted about with ponds or lakes.

Water in some abundance it must have; and, though not in any degree normally migratory in India, it will, in years of great drought, desert whole districts where it is ordinarily plentiful.

---

* Major Charles Mc. Inroy says (writing from Mysore) :—

"As far as my knowledge goes—and I know Mysore pretty well—the Sarus *never* comes down here, nor did I ever see or hear of it south of the Gódávari. North of the Nirmul jungle, and thence towards Kamptee, is the furthest southerly point at which it occurs to my knowledge."

† Dr. Anderson obtained specimens at Tsit Kaw. He is also of opinion that he saw huge flocks of this Crane (Zool. Yunan Exp. 684) flying overhead when he was encamped at Ponsee. This is remarkable, as this species is not known to be migratory, nor even, when in large parties, to fly in V-shaped flocks, as he describes those seen by him to have done.

‡ Blyth also mentions that Cantor procured it in Wellesley Province. If so, it must have been a domesticated specimen. We have explored, not only Wellesley Province, but the native states all round, without ever even hearing of the bird, of which the Malays, who are keenly observant of birds, would have been *sure* to speak and tell stories, did it really ever occur there.

Its habits vary somewhat, both according to season and to locality. In most places it feeds during the day, in fields or open plains, and in the forenoon, at some hour, and again in the evening, comes down to water, where it mostly spends the night. Some, however, live entirely in swamps and about large lakes, and rarely leave the immediate neighbourhood of these at any time.

During the dry weather they are concentrated in the few localities where water is available, but during the rains they are more equally distributed over the country. But whether in large or small numbers, they are always in pairs, each pair acting independently of the other pairs, though necessarily their habits and the hours they keep at the same locality in the same season, being identical, they often move together, and thus to a certain extent seem to keep, at times, in flocks. During the autumn and cold season most of the pairs are accompanied by one, two, or rarely three, young ones, over whom they watch with great solicitude.

They certainly pair for life, and palpably exhibit great grief for the loss of their mate, keeping for weeks, at times, about the locality where their partner was killed, and calling constantly. Generally, after a week or ten days, the survivor disappears, and, it is to be hoped, finds consolation elsewhere with a new mate; but on two occasions I have actually known the widowed bird to pine away and die; in the one case my dogs caught the bird in a field, where it had retreated to die, literally starved to death; in the other, the bird disappeared, and a few days later we found the feathers in a field, where it had obviously fallen a prey to jackals. In both these cases I had killed the birds by accident, shooting at other things with a rifle; but I confess, with sorrow, that in my younger, thoughtless days, I have often purposely killed them, simply for practice. If absolutely required for food, (and the liver is very good eating, and many of the lower castes of natives will eat the bodies) or as specimens, of course they may be shot (though even then I share the native prejudice that it is best to kill the pair), but otherwise it is, I think, a sin to kill them.

I say this, because, including them amongst the "Game Birds," it might be thought that we look upon them as fit objects of sport. But the fact is that two of our Cranes are really this, and we have only included the Sarus and the Snow-Wreath Crane, in order that our account of the several Indian species of the genus might not be incomplete.

Where not shot at, they are extremely tame, and unsuspicious of men, especially of natives, often allowing these to pass within twenty yards without taking wing, and in parts of India, as in Rajputana and the Central India Agency, where the natives, although not attaching to them the religious reverence which they do to Pea-Fowl and Blue-Rock Pigeons, yet object to their being interfered with, I have myself watched them from distances of forty or fifty yards without attracting their attention.

When the young are still only half grown, say up to the end of the year, both old birds may often be observed to seize some morsel and call one of the young to eat it; and again, when down by the water, they may be seen pluming and adjusting the toilette of their progeny. Later, though the young often keep with them as late as March, they do not, I think, feed them, though they still call to them, and warn them if any suspicious object appears. Later again in the spring, the pair may be seen standing, side by side, in the shallow water, pluming and fondling each other most affectionately; and, though in captivity and in a semi-domesticated state, they seem to be rather ill-conditioned, spiteful birds, where men, and especially children and dogs, are concerned, pecking savagely at the eyes of these without provocation, in their wild state, amongst themselves, they appear to be most gentle loving creatures.

They rise off the ground with some little difficulty, always taking a run of some yards before actually getting on the wing the heavy strokes of their powerful pinions resounding meanwhile far and wide. But when once off, their flight is very strong; and though, from the noise attending it, it seems laboured, it is continued at times, without apparent effort and voluntarily, for several miles, but never, so far as my experience goes, at any great height above the ground. In March and April, one year, in Etawah, a pair that I got to recognize from meeting them constantly at different points along their course, used to come down every day about 8 o'clock in the morning to the banks of the Jumna from high ground (about five miles distant) which, during some months of the year, contained a large piece of water, and during some months more, a daily diminishing swampy pool. Throughout this long flight, I do not believe that they ever rose above twenty yards from the ground. I do not think that they *ever*, in India, rise high in air, and circle round and round as other Cranes do, even the Australian "Native Companion," which, in most other respects, so closely resembles our Indian bird.

Their food is very varied—frogs, lizards and all small reptiles, insects of all kinds, snail and other land and water shells, seeds, grains and small fruits of various kinds, green vegetable matter, and the bulbous roots of various species of aquatic plants—all contribute to their nutriment; and they seem to feed indifferently in wet and dry fields, on dry grassy uplands, on the margins and in the shallows, of rivers, broads and swamps.

They walk alike on land and in water fully eighteen inches deep, easily and gracefully, but withal in a slow, stately manner, lifting each leg deliberately and rather high. The land, or land and water, seem more to their taste than the air, and they never venture into the latter, I think, except on business. Unlike most other birds they never fly for pleasure, but only to escape a possible or threatened danger, or when the quest of food or water requires them to move rapidly to a considerable distance. I have often watched a pair walk deliberately one, or even two, miles down to the waters' edge over a grassy plain or meadow, or wide level, free from banks and hedges, carpeted with springing wheat, instead of flying down, as they could have done, in one-tenth of the time. If trees and banks and other cover intervene, they *will* fly, but only I think because they do not feel certain that some enemy may not be lurking behind these, and therefore, get on the wing so as to enable themselves to keep a better look-out as they proceed.

Their call is very loud and sonorous, and may be heard at great distances. It is sounded at all seasons, and is uttered alike on the ground and during flight, but is most often repeated during the night and in the mornings and evenings. They always call when alarmed, both before and after rising, and during the night they seem to call continually. Whether, when darkness shrouds them from each other, they thus make sure that their mates are not playing truants, or, whether prowling wolves or jackals alarm them, I cannot say; but in many parts of the plains of Upper India, if you are encamped within a couple of miles of any good-sized sheet of water, you are sure to hear their clear trumpet-like call, re-echoing at intervals, through the stillness, throughout the live-long night.

From Burma, Mr. Davis sends me the following interesting note:—

"In last August (1879) I saw several flocks of these birds every day in the *Khendans*, or rising ground opposite Theinzeik, which is twelve miles north of Thatone. The flocks varied in size, from parties of 8 or 10 to fully 60. As a rule, these birds live in pairs, and I was unable to ascertain the cause of their thus congregating, especially at this season. The flocks consisted of both sexes, and included young birds of the previous year.

"I have found numbers of their nests about the end of August. Some of the young cannot fly, even as late as December, and I have often caught them by chasing them on foot. They are very cunning, and take advantage of the slightest shelter, but when run down in the open, bury their heads in the short grass, and make no further attempts to escape. They remain perfectly quiet even when lifted up.

"They feed a great deal on the young paddy plant, and sometimes do considerable damage in the nurseries. I have never myself noticed them feeding on anything else, though probably they do also eat other green shoots, grasshoppers, and frogs, and perhaps young fry, left stranded in the fields, but I do not think they catch live fish, although the young, when domesticated, are often fed by the Burmans on small fish and shrimps.

"With us the Sarus is shy and difficult to shoot, except from a bullock cart, or during the rains from a canoe. From the latter, especially, they are easily killed.

"The female calls at daylight, during the time of incubation, standing on the top of her nest, and any one desirous of finding a nest should go out in a canoe to a likely place before daylight, and watch from a high "*tai*," or paddy grower's hut, with binoculars.

"The Burmans have many legends illustrative of the strong affection borne by these birds for their mates, and are rather averse to their being shot."

Taking the facts noted by Mr. Davis of the appearance of these birds in large flocks early in August about Thatone, in connection with what Dr. Anderson tells us of seeing large flocks passing over head at Ponsee, in Upper Burma, apparently migrating, the suggestion naturally arises whether it may not happen that in Burma this species is, to a certain extent, migratory, numbers of the Upper Burman birds coming south to near the Gulf of Martaban to breed. The point is one well worthy the observation of sportsmen in Burma, where, by the way, Mr. Davis tells me he often used to shoot and send them to friends at Moulmein, "who considered them a great luxury." *De gustibus*, &c. But people *are* very hard put to for meat in many parts of Burma.

THE SARUS breeds freely over the whole of the North-West Provinces, Oudh, and Upper Bengal, and more rarely in the Punjab, Cis-Satlej, the eastern and southern portions of Rajputana, and parts of the Central Provinces.

Captain Butler and Mr. Davidson found numbers of nests in Guzerát, north of the Nerbudda. Ramsay obtained the eggs near Tounghoo, Oates in Lower Pegu, and generally, I believe, we may say that the species is a strictly resident one, and breeds wherever it occurs at other seasons of the year.

They lay in different parts of the country from July to November, in which latter month Mr. Davidson has taken fresh eggs in Guzerát.

In Upper India they breed in July and August,* some few laying in some seasons as late as the middle of September. Soon after the first burst of the rains, *i.e.*, towards the close of June, the old birds begin to construct their nest. These are in nine cases out of ten on some firm spot in the midst of the largest jhíl or swamp that they can find; not always an island, for they often build on sites completely overflowed, but some spot that would be an island if the water fell eight or ten inches.

---

* Occasionally however they certainly breed also in the spring. Quite recently Mr. Chill wrote to me from near Delhi:—"Last month (April) my men brought me in a young Sarus about 20 days old, so it must have been hatched about the end of *March!* It is quite a new thing to me to find this bird breeding in the spring."

The nest is a huge heap, a broad truncated cone, composed of reeds and rushes and straw, varying much in size according to situation and circumstances. At top it is about two feet in diameter, with a central depression from four to eight inches deep for the eggs. If, as is commonly the case, the nest is placed in water, the bottom of the egg cavity will be from eight to twelve inches above the surface of the water, and there may be six inches to two feet of nest below water. On more than one occasion, when in sudden and heavy falls, such as we get in India, six and eight inches of rain falling within twelve hours, the jhíls were rising very rapidly, I have seen the birds very busy raising their nests. One nest that had thus been raised, I measured a couple of months later, when the ground on which it stood was dry, and found it to be fully nine feet in diameter at base, and three feet in height, and it must have lost at least a foot by settling. When built on land, surrounded, but not overflowed with water, the nest is a much less pretentious affair, perhaps five feet in diameter at base and a foot only in height. Occasionally, apparently where they could not get a large enough piece of water to secure, as they considered, their safety, I have found them seeking this in concealment. As a rule, the nest is out in the open, visible from all directions at a mile's distance. In the few cases to which I refer I have found it in dense beds of bulrush and reed so lofty that, even when standing on its nest, the bird was only to be seen by climbing a neighbouring tree. In these cases the rushes and reeds, where they were thickest, had been bent and trampled down across and across, so as to form a platform five or six feet in diameter, and on this a comparatively slight nest had been constructed.

Two is certainly the normal number of eggs, but I have twice (out of more than one hundred nests) found three, and I have also occasionally seen three young birds in company with an old pair.

I remember one day, as I was coming home from Rahun, I saw in a sheet of rain-water, some distance off the road, a Sarus sitting on her nest, and the male standing beside her. I rode as near the place as I could, and then sent my syce to get the eggs. As he commenced wading towards the nest, the male began to dance about, flapping his wings and trumpeting most bravely; but when the man got within a few yards and landed safely on the patch of dry ground on which the nest rested, the male put his head down and ran off very crest-fallen to a ridge in the water some fifty yards distant, whence he began, with loud cries, to encourage his lady not to allow "that black rascal" to take any liberties. She sat quite still, neither moved nor cried, only as the man came close to her made such vigorous pokes and drives at him that he got frightened and was picking up a great dry branch to strike her with, when I called out to him to flap her in the face with his waist-cloth. This he did vigorously, and this being more than she could endure, she reluctantly crept off the nest, now complaining loudly, and joined the male. There was only one egg: this the man brought, but before he could reach me, the female had regained the nest, and after minutely examining it and making certain that the egg was gone, she stood up on the top, and with bill, legs, and feet commenced throwing the straw about in the air in the most furious manner as if beside herself with rage. Then the male came up trumpeting vigorously, but directly he came near she flew at *him*, and he scrambled off half-running half-flapping through the water, and making more noise than ever. By this time I had received the egg, and found the point of the young one's bill protruding, so sent the man back with it sharp. As he approached, the female ran off, but she must have seen what he was at, for before (having gently laid the egg in the disordered nest, which he smoothed a little), he could get off the island, the female was down upon the egg, sitting as if nothing had happened, but uttering a low chuckling sound such as I had never heard before. But the real joke was to see the male; the moment he perceived that the coast was clear and that his mate was again sitting, he came back to the nest and paraded round and round, his wings extended, his head in the air, trumpeting *a ne pouvoir plus*, clearly wishing her to believe that it was all his doing.

I have heard many stories of these birds showing fight in defence of their *penates*, but this was the nearest approach to anything of the kind I ever witnessed, and, as a rule, both birds run away directly you get within twenty yards of the nest.

With dogs it is different, and I have seen a large water-retriever so buffeted, scratched, and cut in two minutes that he was fain to make off at his best pace, howling and yelping, and I have no doubt that foxes or jackals would fare equally ill.

Capt. Butler says:—"The hen bird, if sitting, leaves the nest when disturbed, very reluctantly, first raising her body gradually into an upright position, and then with head lowered almost to the ground walks in a half-crouching attitude slowly away from the nest. In the breeding season the two old birds may often be seen engaged in a kind of "nautch" which is very amusing to watch. They spread their wings and lower their necks until they look like two game cocks about to fight; then all of a sudden they raise themselves and begin to dance, trumpeting loudly all the time. Then one, or both, spring high into the air, descending again to perform the same absurd antics."

I have often seen this "nautch," as also the similar, but even more remarkable, one of the *Loha-sarung*, (*Xenorhynchus asiaticus.*)

These birds occasionally lay a second time in their nests after these have been robbed, and Captain Butler notes that "a single egg, which I took on the 19th of September, was laid by a bird whose nest I had robbed of two eggs on the 24th of August, and in the same nest, while another egg that I took on the 23rd of September was laid in a nest (not the one already referred to) out of which I had also taken a single fresh egg on the 19th September."

The eggs are invariably elongated ovals, and are usually a good deal pointed towards one end; but long, cylindrical varieties, narrower and more elongated than even similar varieties of the Great Bustard, are not uncommon. The shell is very hard and strong, very rarely almost devoid of gloss, *generally*, fairly, and sometimes highly glossy. The shell is in most eggs pitted with small pores, set rather wide apart, and in some specimens very conspicuous owing to the bottoms of the pores being colored differently to the rest of the shell of the egg, and thus producing a speckled effect. Usually, however, the pits are only noticeable on close inspection, and not uncommonly they are so fine and minute as to be scarcely noticeable at all.

The ground colour varies,—in some it is pure white, in some clear pale sea green, in others a sort of pinky cream colour, and numerous intermediate shades are observable.

Some few eggs are entirely spotless and devoid of markings, but they are commonly more or less profusely studded with blotches and clouds of pale yellowish brown, purple, or purplish pink. Sometimes the markings are all large; in others,—but more rarely,—they are small and speckly. As a rule, the markings are, I think, most numerous at the large end. In some they are conspicuously so, and in some they are entirely confined to that part of the egg. As I noticed when speaking of the eggs of the Great Bustard, the eggs of this species very frequently exhibit pimples, warts, creases, and wrinkles; indeed, after examining a large series, I should say that not one in twenty was entirely free from such imperfections, but of the hundreds of specimens that I have at one time or another taken of this bird's eggs, I have never met with one anything like so richly coloured as those of the Common Crane (*Grus communis.*)

The eggs vary excessively in size, in length from 3·6 to 4·48, and in breadth from 2·35 to 2·75; but the average of fifty-one eggs is 3·96 by 2·56.

THE MALES average larger than the females; they measure:—

Males.—Length, 56·0 to 60·0; expanse, 94·1 to 102·0; wing, 24·0 to 27·0 (to end of longest primaries, the tertiaries extend during the breeding season from 5 to 8 inches beyond these);

tail from vent, 10·0 to 12·5; tarsus, 13·0 to 14·0; bill from gape, 6·0 to 7·0; mid-toe and claw, 5·87; weight, 16lbs. 12 ozs. to 20lbs.

Females.—Length, 53·0 to 55·0; expanse, 90·0 to 94·0; wing, 23·5 to 24·5; tail from vent, 10·0 to 11·0; tarsus, 11·0 to 13·0; bill from gape, 6·0 to 6·87; mid-toe and claw, 5·5; weight, 15 lbs. 1 oz. to 17lbs. 6 ozs.

The bill is pale green, dusky towards the tip; the legs and feet are dull pinkish red; the irides orange to orange red.

THE PLATE is an unfinished sketch, and by no means satisfactory. I need not tell Indian readers that, excepting the broad white neck collar, and the somewhat elongated tertials, (greatly exaggerated in the plate,) the rest of the plumage is not greyish white, as depicted by Mr. Neale, but a full grey blue. In this and other cases dealing with accomplished artists and gentlemen, we have trusted to them, (being unable in India to supervise work at home), to supply us with really good plates. It is a source of regret to us that this trust has, in some instances, been but ill requited.

The white collar, immediately below the crimson papillose skin of the neck, is, as Blyth correctly pointed out a quarter of a century ago, a seasonal ornament, assumed, as part of the nuptial plumage, about April. At this same time the crimson above this becomes brighter, as does the red of the legs, and the tertiaries and longer scapulars become whiter and more or less elongated, though never to the extent observable in the Common Crane.

The young birds have the heads and necks covered with pale rusty feathers, (which gradually drop off during the latter part of their first cold season,) and not bare as in the adults.

$\frac{1}{5}$

GRUS LEUCOGERANUS

THE SNOW-WREATH OR SIBERIAN CRANE.

Grus leucogeranus, *Pallas.*

Vernacular Names.—[Kare-Khur, Care-Kur, (Hindee) *N. W. Provinces;* Tunhi, *Oudh;* Chini Kulung, *Hansi;* Syakbal, *Cabul.*]

A WINTER migrant only, to India, the range within our limits of this magnificent species is as yet quite undefined.

I know of its occurrence now as a pretty regular visitant to several districts in Oudh, and to many districts of the N.-W. Provinces, north and east of the Jumna, and Mr. Forsyth observed a flock at Dehree-on-Soane. It has occurred once, at any rate, at the Najafgurh Jhíl, or lake, south of Delhi, and Jerdon wrote to me that he had met with it in 1864 near Kurnál, and ascertained its occurrence near Hansi. I observed it in two places in Northern Sindh, west of the Indus, and Mr. Doig has seen it on the Eastern Narra, east of that river.

But it occasionally, at any rate, wanders much further south, as Colonel McMaster records having killed one at Koohee, twenty miles south-east of Kampti (near Nagpur) on the 3rd of February. This is in about 21° north latitude, about the same parallel as Surat.

On *passage* both Mr. Wilson and myself have met with it at lakes far in the interior of the Himalayas.

Beyond this I possess no certain information; and, though Jerdon remarks that it has been said to occur in the Punjab and Rajasthan, I have heard of it nowhere in the former, except in the extreme eastern portions, in the places above mentioned, and nowhere at all in the latter.

Outside our limits it occurs in Afghanistan, Eastern Turkestan, in various parts of Siberia, Mongolia, Manchuria, and Japan, and very rarely in Northern China.

Prjevalsky saw a flock in October at the Kokonor, obviously on passage, and in Eastern Turkestan also it is probably only a passing migrant, as indeed appears to be the case in Eastern Russia, where it is regularly seen on the spring migration.

It is said to have been seen near St. Petersburg and in one or two other localities in Central Russia, and Colonel Drummond Hay observed it once in Macedonia.*

As a rule, the Snow-Wreath does not, I think, put in an appearance even in the Sub-Himalayan tracts before the middle of October, and they are at least a week later further south, as at Etáwah, but in 1879 one was shot somewhere near Kurnál on the 3rd, and Mr. W. Forsyth notes having seen a large flock at Dehree-on-Soane on the 6th of October.

The distribution of this species in India must be, to a great extent, governed by its peculiar habits. It affects only good sized sheets of water, large portions of which are shallow, and which contain a considerable growth of the rushes and aquatic plants on which it seems to feed exclusively. Necessarily, therefore, the localities in which it can occur in India, and especially in Northern and North-Western India, (and we have no reason to suppose that it ever goes far south,) are comparatively limited in number ; and, though I can name a good many tracts of country which are yearly visited by small flocks or parties, still, taking Upper India as a whole, they are excessively rare birds, and I should greatly doubt as many even as five thousand birds of this species yearly visiting India Proper. We gather that during the summer they are more or less abundant over incredibly vast tracts of Northern Asia, and it is pretty certain that they do not winter in Turkestan, Kashgar, or Tibet, but only a very small portion of those that migrate from the north can be accounted for in India, and it seems to me probable that they will prove to go further east, and that when we know more of the fauna of these tracts, we shall find that they occur in Assam, Yunan, the Shan States, Independent Burma, &c., wherever broads and lakes suited to their peculiar habits exist.

No plate, that has ever been given of this species, does any justice to its extreme elegance of form, or to the dense, snowy, Swan-like character of its plumage. To judge by the pictures, Gould's, Dresser's, our own, the bird appears a gaunt, gawky, ill-proportioned creature, whereas, in reality, it is the lily of birds, and stand in what position it may, the entire outline of its form presents a series of the most graceful and harmonious curves.

No one else appears ever to have watched these birds carefully, or to have recorded anything about their habits, haunts, or food, and I myself have seen but little of them for the last ten years, so that I am constrained to reproduce, with a few verbal alterations, the account I published of this species in the *Ibis* for 1868.

---

* *Ibis*, 1870, p. 333.

Many years have now elapsed since I first shot one in Ládakh. This was late in September, and the birds were doubtless on their way to the plains of India. They arrived at a small fresh-water lake, near the Tso-khar, in the Ley District, beside which I was encamped, towards nightfall; and though after I had fired at them and secured a specimen they again (contrary to their usual custom) settled at some little distance, I did not molest them further. They remained there all night, and I saw them again up to nine o'clock, but they had left the place when I went down to the lake again about noon.

After this, though constantly shooting both in the Himalayas and many parts of the North-Western Provinces, I did not again meet with this species until 1859, when I succeeded in shooting one out of a flock of some five and twenty, which I found in a large jhíl in the north of the Etáwah District.

Later again, during the winters of 1865-66 and 1866-67, I procured numerous specimens, and had opportunities of watching the habits of the species rather closely. The locality in which, during these two winters, I saw and procured, comparatively, so many of these beautiful birds, is somewhat peculiar. A broad straggling belt of Dhák (*Butea frondosa*) jungle, some ten miles in width, at one time doubtless continuous, but now much encroached upon and intersected in many places by cultivation, runs down through nearly the whole of the "Doab," marking, possibly, an ancient river course. Just where the northern and southern boundaries of the Etáwah and Mynpoorie Districts lie within this belt, the latter encloses a number of large shallow ponds or lakes ("jhíls" as we call them), which, covering from two hundred acres to many square miles of country each, at the close of the rainy season, are many of them still somewhat imposing sheets of water early in January, and some few of them of considerable extent, even as late as the commencement of March. Mohree-Sonthenan, Mamun, Sirsai-Nawur, Kurree, Beenan, Soj, Hurrera, Suman, Kishnee, Phurenjhee, are some of the largest of these rain-water lakes, many of which abound with rushes and sedges, and as the waters gradually dry up or are drawn off for irrigating purposes, become successively the favorite haunts of the White Crane.

There will always be, at any particular time, two or three "jhíls," that for the moment they particularly affect, and these are, as a rule, just those that then happen to average about eighteen inches to two feet in depth, and that have a good deal of rush (*Scirpus carinatus* amongst others) somewhere in the shallower parts.

To this tract of country they make their way as early as the 25th of October (and possibly sooner, though this is the earliest date on which I have observed them), and there they remain at least as late as the end of March, or perhaps a week or two longer. During the whole of our cold season they stay in this neighbourhood; and, though growing more and more wary (if possible) each time they are fired at, and disappearing for a day or two from any "jhíl," where an attempt has been made to kill or capture them, they never seem to forsake the locality until the change of temperature warns them to retreat to their cool northern homes. Week after week I have noticed and repeatedly fired at, sometimes even slightly wounded, particular birds, which have nevertheless remained about the place their full time—nay, I have twice now killed the young bird early in the season, and the parents, one by one, at intervals of nearly a couple of months.

The Buhelias, a native caste of fowlers, (and, I fear I must add, thieves) of whom there are many in the neighbourhood, and who are keen observers of all wild animals, assured me that, as far back as any of them could remember (namely, for at least the previous fifty years), parties of the White Crane, or as they call them "*karekhurs*"* have been in the habit of yearly spending their winters in the same locality.

Though occasionally seen in larger flocks, it is usual to find either a pair of old ones accompanied by a single young one, or small parties of five or six, which then, as far as I can judge, consist exclusively of birds of the second year.

The fully adult birds are even, when they first arrive, of snowy whiteness, and each pair is, almost without exception, accompanied by a young one, which, when first seen, is of a sandy or buffy tint throughout, and very noticeably smaller than its parents. The males are considerably larger and heavier than the females, the adults of the former weighing up to 19lbs., but of the latter only, as far as my experience goes, to about 16lbs.

---

* Professor Max Muller justly ridicules the excessive length to which what he denominates the "bow-wow theory" of the origin of words, has been pushed by some comparative etymologists; but, in the case of the Cranes, the Hindu names in use, in this portion of Northern India, clearly owe their origin to the cries of the several birds. Thus *Grus communis* is called "*Kooroonch*," or "*Koorch*," *Anthropoides virgo*, "*Kurrkurra*," and *G. leucogeranus*, "*Karekhur*," each of these names, when pronounced by a native, conveying to my idea an appreciable imitation of the cry of the particular species it serves to designate. Not so, however, thinks Mr. Brooks. He says:—"With regard to the notes of *Grus leucogeranus* how the native can imagine that their name 'Karekhur,' or, as I should call it, 'Carecur,' expresses any one of them, I cannot conceive. The notes are all simply whistles, from a mellow one to a peculiar feeble shrill shivering whistle, if I may so express it. No written word will express the note of this species, nor give the faintest idea of it. I watched a flock of these fine birds for a long time, yesterday, as they fed in a marsh, in company with about a dozen of *G. antigone* and three of *G. cinerea*. I found it impossible to get within shot of the White Cranes, nor could I get them driven over me as I sat in ambush; for, as soon as they take wing, they immediately begin to soar, and circle round and round till they attain a height far above the reach of any shot; they then fly straight away, uttering their peculiar whistle, which, though weak, compared with the call of other Cranes, can still be heard a mile off, or even more. It is a magnificent bird, and I think, the most graceful of the group in its attitudes. The species is abundant, being found in large flocks; and the eggs might be obtained from Russian sources. The plumage is so very compact and Swan-like that it must go very far north to breed, where perhaps its snowy plumage harmonizes with the still unmelted snow as it sits upon its nest."

Of the young birds, however, when they first arrive, the males do not exceed about 10lbs. in weight, and the females 9lbs., though generally very fat and well cared for by the parents.

When we first see them, they cannot, I estimate, be more than six months' old. The testes and ovaria of adults, examined on the 20th of March, were still, if I may use the term, quite dormant; and allowing for the "passage home," the pairing season, and incubation, they can scarcely hatch off before the middle of May.

They never appear to have more than one young one with them; but it does not at all follow that they do not lay more than one egg. The Sarus, which usually lays two, and sometimes, though rarely, three eggs, and which has no long or arduous journey to perform, constantly fails to rear more than one young one.

The watchful care and tender solicitude evinced by the old birds for their only child is most noticeable. They never suffer the young one to stray from their side; and, while they themselves are rarely more than thirty yards apart, and generally much closer, the young, I think, is invariably somewhere between them. If either bird find a particularly promising rush tuft, it will call the little one to its side, by a faint creaking cry, and watch it eating, every now and then affectionately running its long bill through the young one's feathers. If, as sometimes happens, the young only be shot, the old birds, though rising in the air with many cries, will not leave the place, but for hours after keep circling round and round high out of gun or even rifle shot, and for many days afterwards will return apparently disconsolately seeking their lost treasure.

Like the Sarus, these birds pair, I think, for life; at any rate a pair, whose young one was shot last year, and both of whom were subsequently wounded about the legs, so as to make them very recognizable, appeared again this year, accompanied by a young one, and were at once noticed as being our wary friends of the past year, by both the native fowlers and myself. I was glad to see they were none the worse for their swollen, crooked, bandy legs, and this year at least they have got safe home, I hope, with their precious charge.

Throughout their sojourn here, the young remain as closely attached to their parents as when they first arrived, but doubtless by the time the party return to their northern homes, the young are dismissed, with a blessing, to shift for themselves.

Long before they leave, the rich buff or sandy colour has begun to give place to the white of the adult plumage, and the faces and foreheads, which (as in the Common Crane) are feathered in the young, have begun to grow bare. This, I notice, seems to result from the barbs composing the vanes of the tiny feathers falling off, and leaving only the naked hair-like shafts. Even when they leave us, however, there is still a good deal of buff about the head, upper back, lesser and median wing-coverts, longer scapulars, and tertials of the young, while the dingy patch along the front of the tarsus is still well marked.

Each year several small parties of birds are noticeable, unaccompanied by any young ones, and never separating into pairs. These, when they first come, still show a few buff feathers, and have a dingy patch on the tarsus; and, though before they leave us, they become almost as purely white, and have almost as well-coloured faces and legs as the old ones that are in pairs, they never seem to attain to the full weight of these latter. From these facts I am disposed to infer that these parties, which include individuals of both sexes, consist of birds of the second year; that our birds do not either breed or assume their perfect plumage till just at the close of their second year; and that, like Pigeons and many others, they do not attain their full weight until they have bred once at least.

Unlike the four other species of Crane with which I am acquainted, the Snow-Wreath never seems to resort during any part of the day or night to dry plains or fields in which to feed, and unlike them, too, as far as my experience goes, it is exclusively a vegetable eater. I have never found the slightest traces of insects or reptiles (so common in those of the other species) in any of the twenty odd stomachs of these White Cranes that I have myself examined.

Day and night they are to be seen, if undisturbed, standing in the shallow water. Asleep, they rest on one leg, with the head and neck somehow nestled into the back, or they will stand like marble statues, contemplating the water with curved necks, not a little resembling some white Egret on a gigantic scale; or, again, we see them marching to and fro, slowly and gracefully feeding amongst the low rushes.

Other Cranes, and notably the common one and the Demoiselle, daily pay visits in large numbers to our fields, where they commit great havoc, devouring grain of all descriptions, flower, shoots, and even some kinds of vegetables. The White Crane, however, seeks no such dainties, but finds its frugal food, rush-seeds, bulbs, corms, and even leaves of various aquatic plants, in the cool waters where it spends its whole time.

Without preparations by me for comparison I hardly like to be too positive on this score; but I am impressed with the idea that the stomach in this species is much less muscular than in any of the others with which I am acquainted. The enormous number of small pebbles that their stomachs contain is remarkable. Out of an old male I took very nearly sufficient to fill an ordinary-sized wine-glass, and that, too, after they had been thoroughly cleansed and freed from the macerated vegetable matter which clung to them. These pebbles were mostly quartz, (amorphous and crystalline,) greenstone, and some kind of porphyretic rock; the largest scarcely exceeding in size an ordinary pea, while the majority were not bigger than large pins' heads.

I have found similar pebbles in the stomachs of the Common and Demoiselle Cranes, but never in anything like such numbers as in those of the present species.

When not alarmed, the White Cranes' note is what, for so large a bird, may be called a mere chirrup; and even when most alarmed, and circling and soaring wildly round and round, looking down upon the capture of wounded offspring or partner, their cry (a mere repetition of the syllables *karekhur*) is very feeble as compared with that of any other of the Cranes (including even *Balearica pavonina)* whose notes I have myself never heard.

An examination of the trachea of a fine male that I dissected on the 22nd of February 1867, at once explained this feebleness. Instead of a convolution entering and running far back into the sternum, there is merely a somewhat dilated bend just where the windpipe enters the cavity of the body; and it is only after the pipe has divided, which it does symmetrically into two very nearly equal tubes, about three inches before entering the lungs, that the rings are at all strongly marked, or that the tube impresses one as at all powerful.

I have already noticed that it is not easy to get at these birds (possibly due in part to a keen sense of hearing, accompanying their large ear-orifices); and, as far as my experience goes, there is only one way of shooting them with a shot gun. With a rifle it is not difficult to get within two-hundred and fifty to three-hundred yards of them, at which distance, with a heavy ·442 match rifle, one ought to knock them over every time. The melancholy fact, however, is, that habitually one only succeeds in missing them, and thoroughly scaring them with a rifle; so nothing remains but to have recourse to a long single eight-bore with B. B. wire cartridge. This will easily knock them down up to seventy, or, if a shot tells well in the neck, up to eighty yards; but getting within eighty or even a hundred yards of them can only be managed, as a general rule, in one way. You obtain from one of the native fowlers the loan of a trained buffalo, and enter the water a good quarter of a mile, away from the birds, under cover of the quadruped. It has, as usual, a string run through the nostrils, and tied tightly together behind the horns. You hold this string where it lies across the cheek with the left hand; your extended left arm is hidden behind the neck; your whole body is bent, so that your head and neck are covered by the buffalo's shoulders, your body and the greater part of your legs, by its body. Only your legs to a little above the knees show close to the hind legs; and, as far as possible, you always keep the beast up to his belly in water. Thus covered you slowly sidle up towards the Cranes, making the buffalo, now put his head up, nose in air, now stop and lower his head to the water, and generally dawdle and meander about with apparently no fixed idea in his head, according to the natural manners and customs of a free and independent buffalo. With a little practice it is easy thus to get within shot. You softly let the cheek string go, and at once fire below the buffalo's neck. Before your gun is well off, your sporting companion, who has a marked distrust of Europeans and white faces, and has been incessantly endeavouring to kick you throughout your whole promenade, knocks you head over heels, and rushes off towards his dusky owner, bellowing as if he, and not you, were the injured party. This is first-rate sport; but, after trying it once or twice, nearly catching my death of cold, losing a powder flask, and realizing a stock-in-trade of bruises enough to last the rest of my natural life, I have preferred sitting quietly on the bank and allowing my native coadjutors to shoot the birds I wanted.

When shot they were worth nothing as food, which, considering their purely vegetable diet, is surprising.

I ought not to omit to notice that, out of more than twenty specimens of the White Crane that I have procured (between October and the middle of March), none had the tertials at all conspicuously elongated; and in no instance did these, when the wings were closed, exceed the tail feathers or longest primaries (which usually reach just to the end of the tail) by more than 3 inches. It is possible that at the breeding season the tertials may be *much* more developed; but such is not the case with the Sarus, nor, I fancy (to judge from the magnificent trains of plumes with which we here shoot them in the spring,) with the Common Crane.

The feathers of the hind head and nape are somewhat lengthened, so as to form a full and broad, though short, subcrest, very noticeable when a wounded bird is defending itself against dogs or other assailants. It is a brave bird, and fights to the last, striking out powerfully, at times with bill, legs, and wings, but most generally defending itself chiefly with its bill, with which it inflicts, occasionally, almost serious wounds.

NOTHING absolutely seems as yet to be known of its nidification.

IN THIS species also the males are considerably larger than the females.

Males.—Length, 52 to 56; expanse, 90 to 99·5; wing, 23 to 26; tail from vent, 8·0 to 9·5; tarsus 11·0 to 12·0; bill from gape, 7·75 to 8·0; weight, 16 lbs to 19 lbs.

Females.—Length, 48·0 to 53·0; expanse, 83·0 to 92·0; wing, 22·5 to 24·0; tail from vent, 7·75 to 8·25; tarsus, 10·5 to 11·5; (one female had the tarsus only 9·0); bill from gape, 6·75 to 7·65; weight, 12·5 lbs to 16 lbs.

The legs and feet are dull pale reddish pink, (dullest in the young), varying to dull red, somewhat brighter on the feet. In all but quite old birds the front of the tarsus, the ridges of the toes, and the bare portions of the tibia in front are tinged (the first strongly, the others faintly) with dark brown, which, on the front of the tarsus, sometimes takes the form of a black mottling; claws blackish or dark horny brown.

The irides are a bright very pale yellow; the colour does not vary with age, but in some birds the iris is almost silvery, and in others there is a pinkish tinge.

The bill is umber brown; the membrane of the nasal groove red, much the same colour as the naked skin of the forehead, lores and cheeks; all are duller coloured in the less mature birds.

THE PLATE is coarsely and carelessly executed. No one can doubt Mr. Neale's capacity. Some of the plates of the Sand-Grouse show how *well* he *can* draw when he choses, but this plate and that of the Sarus are quite unworthy of his pencil.

In the young there is no bare space about the face; the whole head and upper half of the neck are of a somewhat rusty buff; the space destined later to become bare, however, is, in the youngest specimens that I have seen, well defined, its clothing feathers being of a browner and dingier hue than those of the rest of the head, and sitting much closer to the skin. The buff is clearest and deepest on the cheeks, and the top and back of the head, and very pale on the chin and throat. The rest of the plumage, when we first see the young birds, may (excepting the primaries and their greater coverts and the winglet) be described as buff, in some places brighter and more rufous, in others duller and sandier, with white everywhere beginning to peep through it.

By February, though still much varied by buff, the white predominates in the body plumage. At this time many of the feathers of the back of the neck and upper back are still pure buff, and many others are more or less tinged with this colour; many of the longer scapulars and tertials and the hindermost of the secondaries are also buff, while the upper tail-coverts and most of the lesser and median wing-coverts are tipped with it, and the patch of coverts just above the winglet is usually entirely ferruginous. There is a very faint tinge of buff on some of the feathers of the breast; and many of the thigh-coverts are wholly rusty.

By the end of March, when the birds are nine or ten months old, the face has begun to grow bare; and, though there is still some buff on the parts above mentioned, it has become markedly less in extent and feebler in tint.

1/8

GRUS CINEREA

THE COMMON CRANE.

Grus communis, *Bechstein.*

Vernacular Names.—[Kooroonch, Koorch, (Hindee), *N. W. Provinces;* Kullung. (Oordoo) *Upper India;* Kallam, *Deccan;* Kulungi, (Telegu); Wainu, *Munipur.*]

A WINTER migrant to our Empire, the range of the Common Crane has yet to be accurately defined. It has been recorded from most of the districts of the Deccan, becoming rarer towards the south. How much further south it wanders I have been unable to ascertain. Mr. Albert Theobald seems never to have met with it anywhere in the Madras Districts south of Mysore, but Major Campbell, of the 26th M. N. I., writes from Quilon, that it is not uncommon in Travancore. It has never as yet, I believe, been recorded from Ceylon.

Northwards it extends through the northern portions, at any rate of the Nizam's Dominions, Khandesh, Berar, the Central Provinces, Guzerát, the Central India Agency, Cutch, Káthiáwár, Sind, Rajputana, the North-West Provinces and Oudh and the Punjab, being far more common towards the north than towards the south of this vast tract. On the east I have no *record* of its occurrence south of the Mahanadi. North of this it is found in the Tributary Máhals, Chota Nagpur, and the whole of Western Bengal and Behar. I do not know whether it occurs in the deltaic districts of Bengal, but it is common in the Sikhim Terai and the Dúars, and probably extends up to the easternmost extremity of the valley of Assam, as Col. Graham writes that it is very common in the Darrang and Lakhimpur Districts. South and east of the Brahmaputra again I have no record of its occurrence ;* but Mason, whether on any sufficient grounds or not I cannot say, includes it without remark in his list of the Birds of Burma.†

Outside our limits it may be broadly said to occur throughout Europe right up to the North Cape, and Northern Africa as

---

* Mr. Inglis of Dilkoosha, Cachar, tells me that in all the years he has been there, sportsman and somewhat of an ornithologist to boot as he is, he has never seen or heard of a Crane in that district.

† Mr. Oates has never met with it in Pegu.

far south as Nubia, the majority wintering in the southern and summering in the northern portions of their range, though some breed as far south as Spain. In Palestine, Asia Minor, the countries about the Caspian, Persia, Afghanistan, and Beluchistan, Eastern Turkestan, Siberia, Kashgar, and China, this species is found, as in Europe, wintering for the most part in the more southern countries it visits.

Whether Japan should really be included in the range of this species I do not know; the Japanese form has been separated as *longirostris*, and is said to differ in the greater amount of white about the face and in having a bill six inches in length at front (from margin of feathers) against 4·6, which is a maximum for the bill similarly measured in our Indian birds.

Blyth, it may be remembered, at one time announced that our Indian bird was *longirostris;* but Mr. Gurney has kindly measured for me the bills of eight specimens of the European bird (two of them killed in England), and has found those of adults (measured as above) to vary only from 4·05 to 4·7, which dimensions cover those of every Indian specimen that I have examined, and I have no doubt, therefore, that I have correctly referred our bird to *communis.*

I HAVE never myself observed this species in Upper India before the 3rd of October, and, as a rule, the majority do not seem to arrive during the latter half of that month. From Central India and the Deccan, the majority disappear by the middle of March, in the Doab they remain a fortnight later, and further north and west they are still in great force in some years in the middle of April. But though the majority thus leave, a certain proportion, almost invariably, I believe, young birds that will not breed that year, remain behind from a fortnight to three weeks later than the rest of their comrades, so that I have shot them in Etáwah as late as the 20th of April, and at Jhilum, as the 3rd of May.

In Sind they seem to arrive earlier. Doig says: "Large flocks of this Crane begin to come in, in the month of August; they are generally seen flying very high, and are apparently going far south, probably towards Cutch. By the month of November the rice fields are swarming with them. The latest date on which I have seen this Crane, in the Nara Districts, was the 4th May, on which date I shot two out of a small flock of five. They feed on the rice fields usually in the early morning, retiring to lonely plains or swamps during the day time."

The Common Crane, like most waders, passes much of its time by the water side, often standing asleep in the noonday sun, in the water itself. Where large rivers are near, at least if their banks are sandy and shelving, it certainly resorts to them in preference to tanks, and may be found in or near the water at almost any hour of the day and night, except, perhaps, between sun-rise and 9 A.M., when it is usually feeding inland. Where no large river invites them, they may be met with in large tanks and jhíls, but this is, I think, the exception in their case and that of the Demoiselle Crane. *Per contra*, the White Crane, as far as I have observed, frequents jhíls alone, and the Sarus prefers these to rivers.

They feed regularly in the early mornings, chiefly in grain fields, in this country—wheat, gram, pulse, and rice being those most resorted to; but they may often be seen feeding at the waters' edge during the day, and both during the day and night they not unfrequently pay one or two other short visits to the fields.

They sleep on one leg,* with the neck and head nestled into the feathers of the back, are pretty quiet during the heat of the day, when most of them are asleep, and very noisy during the night, and at other times also when flying.

Often, especially in the afternoon, they collect together in great numbers on one of those vast, white, sandy flats which abound in the beds of the Jumna, Ganges, and other large rivers in Northern India, and there stalk about majestically, apparently taking an airing. They certainly are not feeding, though now and then to aid digestion they pick up small pebbles, and beyond some crusty individual, dealing an ill-natured poke with his strong bill at some passer-by who incontinently trots off, with comical haste, with wings half extended, trumpeting his disgust at such bad manners, there is certainly little play. Every now and then a small party, who perhaps have been lately picking up minute shells or insects on the sand, march down to the water side to drink, lifting their heads very high after two or three gulps, much like Geese.

Further south more than twenty are, I believe, rarely seen together; but in the Upper Provinces, flocks of from one to three

* The story of Frederic the Great's cook really deserves to be remembered. This cook rejoiced in a most *exigeant* mistress, who would never be satisfied unless she had some portion of every dish sent up to the king. One day the *piece de resistance* happened to be a Crane, and the cook abstracting one leg dished up the remainder. By chance the king noticed the mutilation. Sending for the cook he said. "Rascal, is it not sufficient that you devour everything that leaves my table? nay—forsooth, you must make a meal off the dishes before they leave the kitchen. What has become of the other leg of that Crane?" "Other leg," replied the cook; "why, everyone knows that Cranes never *have* more than one leg." "Do you dare to trifle with me?" said the king; "here bring him along," and Frederic stalked out of the window to the adjoining aviary in which several tame Cranes were confined. Now it chanced that this was but little after midday, the Cranes had been fully fed, and they stood asleep in a row, each showing only a single leg. "Thanks be to the saints," exclaimed the cook unctuously, "who thus vindicate the right and protect the poor and slandered; Your Majesty can now see for yourself that it is even as I said." The king gave an angry stamp, the Cranes awoke with a start, and down came the second leg of each. "How now thou thief about Cranes having only one leg?" roared the king. "Sire," said the cook, "you are all powerful; doubtless had you stamped like that, when the roast Crane came on table, even that dead bird would have put out a second leg to gratify Your Majesty." *N. B.*—This story has been told in a variety of ways, about a number of different persons, but the above version is quite as authentic as any other!

hundred are not uncommon, and ten or a dozen may be secured at one time by shots fired out of a boat which has been allowed to drift softly down alongside the sand bank they are occupying.

On returning from feeding in the fields they fly round and round high in the air, apparently examining carefully the place at which they intend to alight, all the while trumpeting loudly. Sometimes they will descend rapidly, all turning and twisting, almost like wild Geese, but generally they come down with long sweeps gracefully and gently, their long legs hanging down ready to touch the ground some time before they actually reach it.

Their note is a fine, clear, trumpet-like call, not so loud as that of the Sarus, but clearer and more musical *I* think. It can be heard distinctly when the bird is a mere speck in the sky. Especially after having been surprised and shot at, and several killed, flocks will rise in a body to an extraordinary height, and there keep trumpeting, circling round and round, almost out of sight, but well within hearing, for a considerable time. This is particularly the case when there are several wounded birds on the ground which are being chased.

A winged bird runs very well, and I have often seen a couple of boatmen pretty well out of breath before they could come up with one, and then when they did, fairly non-plussed by the vigorous darts that the fugitive, once at bay, made at them with his strong beak. A pretty severe wound may be received by incautiously closing with a wounded bird, but a slight blow on the side of the neck, with ever so thin a walking stick or cane, finishes the struggle at once. When thus pursued they will occasionally take to the water and swim, not gracefully, indeed, much like a Flamingo, jerking their long necks with each stroke, but with greater ease and rapidity than could have been expected. Even when overtaken thus swimming they will make a desperate resistance.

The force with which a dead Crane falls at times is surprising. I had crossed the Jumna, late one evening, after some Geese which we saw sitting on the opposite bank, but they were too wise to await my arrival ; then I saw another flock browsing on the young wheat some little distance from the shore, and as it was getting dusk and you can at that time get nearer Geese on land than at any other, I trudged wearily after them, but before I could reach the place it had become pitch dark, and we heard them go off cackling without being able to get a shot. As we walked back to the boat, we became aware that an enormous flock of Cranes, that had been trumpeting all the while, were directly over our head. I wanted to unload my big gun, and so fired at random straight up. I had hardly recovered from the recoil of the old cannon, as my friends christened it, when a peculiar rushing sound caught my ear (luckily the sound out-sped the bird). I just started back to listen, when with a "scrush" a dead Crane plopped on to the ground at my feet precisely where I had stood. It was a minute or two before we quite realized what had happened; the ground was the stiff, clayey, river soil, damp, so far that one sank about three to four inches into it in walking; the Crane had fallen *back* downwards, the shoulders first striking the ground, and was firmly bedded in the clay. We pulled it out and found the basin-like depression, as far as I could judge in the dark, *feeling* the place carefully, fully eight inches deep in the deepest part. I had only a thin grey tweed smoking cap on, and had I not started back that step, I fancy that our Cranes would have had to find another historian.

When feeding they are wary birds, almost always posting sentinels and rarely to be approached within gun shot, without a careful stalk; but like all long-necked birds a single shot in the neck drops them, and in parts of the country, as in many places in the Punjab and Rajputana, where they have not recently been shot at, you may, with a native blanket over your head, approach within sixty or seventy yards, by walking as if you meant to pass them, when a heavy duck gun, with wire cartridge and very large shot, will generally drop three or four out of the flock as they rise. I have killed as many as seven with one shot thus. As a rule, however, on the land, a small-bore rifle is to be preferred, and they often stand so thick that a single bullet secures two or even three.

But when you approach them by water, drifting down on them in a small native boat, such as they continually see passing, you and every one in the boat lying quiet, and only one man wading behind the boat, guiding it and hidden by it, you may get as close as you like to the outermost files, fire your big gun into the densest patch distant from fifty to seventy yards, and knock over three or four more of the closer ones with your ordinary doubles.

I have thus killed in one day out of five flocks in a length of about seven miles of the Jumna, just below its junction with the Chambal, thirty-two, besides Geese and Ducks. It may seem mere butchery, but the Mahomedans eat all whose throats are cut, and all Hindoos, but Brahmins and Bhugguts, the rest, and when you have a large camp, and want to keep people healthy and happy, it is well never to pass Deer, Crane or Geese.

Very different opinions are often expressed as to the edibility of Cranes—some laud them to the skies, some abuse them as fishy, stringy brutes, unfit to eat, and marvel greatly when they read in old books that in England our ancestors reckoned them great dainties. The fact is, that both their laudators and depreciators generalize too hastily. A Crane recently arrived before there is grain, or young juicy shoots to crop, and that is, perforce, feeding chiefly on insects, worms, small frogs, and even fishes, *is* no doubt very indifferent eating, but the same bird four months later, when for six weeks it has been gorging itself daily with gram, wheat, rice, pulses, and peas of various kinds, almost to the exclusion of animal food, is as fat, tender, and well tasted a bird as can be found, and when *properly* cooked well merits any praises that our forefathers, who chiefly saw grain-fed birds, may have bestowed on them.

All depends upon the locality and food. In parts of the country where no large rivers offer them pure air and water, and where, when not feeding elsewhere, they haunt the marshes and morasses, they are never, even though fat, *very* good, but where these advantages are available, and (as in so many parts of the Doab during the three first months of the year) the fat of the land is theirs to revel in at will, they emerge superior to the common run of comestibles, and furnish, unless betrayed by the malevolent stupidity of the ordinary native cook, a truly royal dish.

Here, in India, the Crane, undoubtedly *prefers* grain of all kinds—wheat, gram, rice and pulses, together with tender young shoots of all these, while they are yet young—to all other food. Perhaps of all things they most love the young pods of an arborescent pulse, the Urhur or Dál as it is often called, (*Cajanus indicus*,) and in the low alluvial lands of our larger rivers in which this grows into miniature trees, six and seven feet (or even more) in height, you may at times, after watching a flock settle, push your way through the scented golden-blossomed thicket, and enjoy the luxury of knocking over a brace right and left as they rise, flustering noisily and clumsily out of the heavy cover. Not only do they eat the young pods at such times, but also quantities of the yellow pea-like flowers, and at other times, too, flower buds seem not to come amiss to them, and Jerdon mentions one he examined that had fed exclusively on the buds of the safflower.

Vegetables also attract them, and in China Swinhoe says that they feed chiefly at one time on the so-called sweet potato, which I need hardly say is no more a potato than a horse-chestnut is either a horse or a chestnut. But the strangest article of diet for birds of this kind is the one in which they so greedily indulge in parts of the Punjab. As children, we read with mingled incredulity and wonder the fable of the fox and the grapes, and it is not until we have travelled far east that we begin to realize that foxes and jackals are really passionately fond of grapes, and I can well fancy European friends who have known Cranes only in their northern homes receiving, with similar feelings, the statement that these huge waders are devoted to *Watermelons!* But such is the case; in the sandy plains of Ferozpore, Sirsa, Hissar and other parts of the Punjab, the husbandmen when sowing the giant and bulrush millets, sow watermelons largely, and when the millets have been reaped, the otherwise bare stubbles resemble some deserted battle field, thickly strewed with balls of all sizes from a 3-pounder (represented by countless wild colocynth fruits) up to a 13-inch shell. The watermelons grow by millions; there is no sale for them; any passer-by may pluck and eat unchallenged, provided only he spares the particular fruits that the owner has shaded from the sun for greater enjoyment during the noontide glare. On these descend the Cranes. When first I noticed a field where they had fed, it seemed as though some malevolent Mrs. Gamp had patrolled the place, viciously digging the point of her huge umbrella two or three times into each melon. The people told me that the offenders were Cranes, but with truly national contempt for facts, not verified by one's self, I disbelieved the fact. Later, however, I repeatedly watched them in the act, and from their mode of lifting their heads when at work, and from the examination of scores of injured fruit, I came to the conclusion that, though they did eat small portions of the interior part of the fruit, and some of the seeds, they attacked the melons chiefly for drinking purposes, water being in most cases far distant.

I myself believe the Common Crane to be by preference, mainly a vegetarian; but at all times a small admixture of animal food may be traced in the stomachs of *some* birds, and when their favourite food is scarce, they eat water-crickets and other insects, slugs and worms, small shells, both land and water, and I have found the remains of small fish occasionally in their gizzards. Of course these latter contain, like those of all such birds, quantities of small pebbles, mostly quartz, some as large as peas, a few at times even larger.

At night they prefer to roost—if I may use the expression of birds so persistently noisy during hours of darkness that none but very old and deaf individuals can possibly sleep a wink—on some sandbank entirely surrounded by a good breadth of water; whether as a protection against nocturnal beasts, or why, I cannot say.

Dr. Jerdon tells us that this species is sometimes hawked with Peregrines, and gives a fine chase. I have seen it tried on more than one occasion without success. Once from a high perpendicular cliff of the Jumna we flew one at a flock, immediately below us, that rose as we appeared on the edge of the cliff. This was, I suppose, about 100 feet high, and the Cranes may have been 200 from the base of the cliff. The Falcon went down into the flock with one swoop. How it happened it was impossible to see, but the Cranes flew off uninjured, and the Peregrine floated, breast upwards and stone dead, down the river. When recovered, both wings were broken, the head was smashed in, and the back and backbone were completely broken in. On other occasions, when flown from below, I have seen Peregrines and Shaheens, either refuse the chase, or after vigorous efforts fail to get above the Cranes. But I have seen a pair of Bonelli's Eagles come down on a solitary, winged Crane, on a sandbank, and kill it at the first swoop, and try hard, but without success, to carry it off as the boatmen approached.

THIS CRANE does not of course breed with us, but it breeds in many parts of Europe, from Spain to Lapland, in Turkestan, Mongolia and Siberia.

Formerly it used to breed in England, and there was in old times a fine of twenty pence (then no small sum) for every Crane's egg taken or destroyed; but these good old days have long since past away, and the Crane, like the great Bustard, is scarcely ever now seen in Great Britain even as a chance visitor. The nest, like that of the Sarus, is seldom, if ever, concealed in any way; but, unlike that of its Indian congener, is a comparatively slight affair of sedges and grass or small twigs twenty to thirty inches across, and only a few inches in thickness. It is usually placed in the open in some marsh, moss, or morass. The birds lay from the latter part of April to well into June, according to locality; as a rule two, occasionally, as is the case also with the Sarus, three eggs.

The eggs vary in colour from a rich brownish to a pale greyish olive, and are blotched, smeared, streaked, and spotted, more or less thinly, never densely, with primary markings of varying shades of brownish red and reddish brown, and secondary subsurface-looking spots and clouds of pale brown, varying to grey.

In length they vary from 3·6 to 4·0 inches, and in width from 2·3· to 2·6, but the average of fifteen is 3·9 by 2·4.

I HAVE not many measurements recorded of this species, and what I have do not bring out any constant difference in the size of the sexes, although, if my memory is to be trusted, the males do run larger and heavier than the females. The following were the dimensions of four females and three males:—

Length, 43 to 48; expanse, 79 to 91; wing to end of longest primaries, 20·5 to 24·0; tail from vent, 7·0 to 9·12; tarsus, 8·25 to 9·9; bill from gape, 4·3 to 4·8; weight, 9·5 lbs to 13 lbs.

The irides are deep reddish, orange red, reddish brown, dingy orange, and in the young salmon coloured to very pale yellow; the legs and feet black; the soles brown to fleshy.

The bill is dingy horny green, or greenish brown or pale plumbeous with a greenish tinge, varying a good deal in shade, and yellowish horny towards the tip; in the young the bill is lighter coloured, and the base of the upper mandible and the membrane in which the nares are set, pale yellowish brown. In the adult the lores, forehead, crown, and occiput are destitute of feathers; the skin blackish or dark plumbeous in front and at the top of the head, and dingy red, or in some, orange red, mingled with greenish yellow on the occiput; the whole featherless space, in some sparsely, in some very thickly, clad with coarse black hairs, a few of which are also generally to be seen on either side of the lower mandible at its base.

THE PLATE is unsatisfactory. In the first place the artist having chosen to place the birds against a sun-set sky, has been compelled to show them as altogether browner and smokier, and less of a bluish grey than they commonly appear. No doubt against a sun-set sky they would look somewhat of the colour represented, but in ordinary daylight, with the sun falling on them, they look altogether greyer and bluer. I think most people would be dissatisfied with an artist who painted their portraits as they would look behind a green glass window, and our birds (*and subscribers*) have equal cause for dissatisfaction with Mr. Neale in the present case.

Then the colours of the legs, bill, and irides are all alike wrongly given. The red patch on the head is far too bright, *and ought to commence where the artist has made it end*; it is occipital and not coronal. Lastly, the plate fails to distinguish between the bare and feathered portions of the head.

A YOUNG bird, shot on the 25th December, had no portion of the face or head bare. The portions bare in adults were densely clothed with small feathers, blackish on the lores, forehead, and over the eyes, and pale sandy on the middle of the crown and occiput. The feathers had very short more or less disintegrated webs; the shafts of all black and bristle-like, projecting beyond the ends of the webs. The webs appeared a good deal abraded, and if entirely worn away, would leave their bristle-like shafts exactly as in the adult. The whole nape and upper part of the back of the neck were sandy brown, and there were traces of the same colour on the cheeks and ear-coverts. There was no white anywhere about the head and neck, and of the dark, in some almost blackish, slatey, so conspicuous in the adult, no trace was visible except on the foreneck. The tertiaries were scarcely elongated, and only reached in the closed wing to the ends of the primaries, whereas in adults, at the same season, they exceed these latter by from five to eight inches.

Although even in the cold season the adults of this species exhibit trains, and although these become very fine by the end of March, I have never seen an Indian-killed specimen with so large and fine a train, or of so pure a blue grey, or with quite so much white on the neck, as is exhibited by a male killed in Finland in June.

ANTHROPOIDES VIRGO.

THE DEMOISELLE CRANE.

Anthropoides virgo, *Linné.*

Vernacular Names.—[Karkarra, (Hindee) *N. W. Provinces;* Ghanto, *Nepal;* Kúrkúrchi, (Mahrathi) *Satara;* Kallam, *Deccan* (of many); Karkoncha, (Canarese); Parvuth-akee (Canarese), *Mysore and North of Coimbatore District;* Wada-koraka, (Telegu); Shuck duruck, *Cabul;*]

THE Demoiselle Crane is another species, of which the Indian range is still very ill-defined. I am quite unable to ascertain its limits towards the east and north-west. To the south, I know of its extending on the west to the southernmost portions of the Deccan, not, however, occurring in the Southern Konkan or on the Malabar Coast.

In the central portion of the Peninsula, Mr. Albert Theobald writes, that he has only *seen* it in the neighbourhood of Collegal, in the north of the Coimbatore District and northwards of this, but that he has *heard*, from reliable persons, that it has occurred as far south as Tinnevelli. Even if it does stray at times further south than Collegal, it must (as Mr. Theobald has been for many years shooting and collecting in all the southernmost districts of the Peninsula and has never yet seen it there), be an extremely rare visitant to this part of the Empire. To Ceylon there is no record of its having ever wandered.

In both Mysore and the Nizam's dominions it does occur, though it is probably, even in these, far from common.

On the east no one records it from any of the Madras Districts, nor does Ball include it in his list from the "Ganges to the Gódávari." It does not seem to occur at all in Lower Bengal, or in the districts east of the Brahmaputra, or in any part of Burma. But it certainly occurs in the Népal and Sikhim Tarais, and the Dúars, and as I gather from Colonel Graham's remarks, in the valley of Assam, north of the Brahmaputra, at least, as far east as the Darrang District.

On migration it is often met with in the valleys of the Himalayas, and occasionally at the lakes far in the interior. Thus Hodgson says that it is seen as a passenger, halting for a week or so to rest in the valley of Népal in April and early in May, and again in the latter part of September and the earlier portions of October. Mr. Young informs me that in Kullu, it is often similarly seen, some few being occasionally met with there at other times during the winter. One was shot on the 22nd of May (!) on a small lake between Hanle and the Tso-mourari—a solitary bird that must have dropped out of a flock.

So far as ascertained, therefore, the normal range of this species within our limits would appear to be the plains portions of the whole Bombay Presidency, excluding the sub-ghát littoral, but including Cutch, Káthiáwar and Sind, in the latter of which, however, it is rare Trans-Indus, Berar, the Central India Agency,* the Central Provinces, the Nizam's Territories, Mysore and the northern portions of the Coimbatore District, the North-West Provinces, Behar, and the submontane districts of Bengal and Assam, as far east as Darrang, Oudh, Rajputana and the Punjab, where it seems rare in the more north-westerly portions, and the Central and Eastern Himalayas generally, on passage.

Outside our limits, the Demoiselle occurs regularly in Southern and South-Eastern Europe (stragglers having been shot in the British Isles, Scandinavia, &c.), and in suitable localities in Africa, as far south as Natal. A migrant like the Common Crane, it goes much farther south, and does not extend nearly so far north in Europe.

It is found in Asia Minor, in all the countries about the Caspian, in Eastern Turkestan, Afghanistan, Southern and South-Eastern Siberia, Dauria, Mongolia and Western China, and Prjevalsky saw a flock at the Kokonor on the 28th of February.

A COLD weather visitant to India, the Demoiselle Crane arrives in Guzerat, and I believe the northern portions of the Deccan very early in October, and, so far as I can ascertain, a little *later*, and not earlier, in Upper India. The earliest date that I have found noted for it in the North-West Provinces is the first week in October by A. Anderson; but, as a rule, my own experience leads me to think that from the 10th to the 15th is the usual period, at which it arrives in the Dún and other districts of the Doab.

Moreover, this species never occurs, I think, in Upper India, in the same numbers that it does in the Deccan and Guzerat and Káthiáwar. You see enormous flocks no doubt—flocks, one of which I once estimated† to contain fully 2,000 individuals,—

* Not uncommon on tanks about Oojein and Ooneil—*Captain W. J. Heaviside*, R.E.

† I counted carefully with a glass the birds occupying one section of a bank, and estimated by subsequent measurement, careful landmarks having been taken, the proportion that this section bore to the entire area occupied. The birds were in one uniform dense belt along the water's edge. From a post to a small promontory was 144 feet in length; this section contained, by actual count, 480 to 500 (three separate persons counted them, and hardly a bird moved the whole time.) They were 8, 9 and 10 deep. The birds looked to be touching, but this gives nearly six square feet to each bird. The flock extended 120 feet left of the post, and 376 right of the promontory, and except at the extreme ends was perfectly uniform in

but you see very few of them, compared to what you see in the Deccan, or to what you see of the Common Crane. Being much rarer than this latter, I was always much more eager in their pursuit, and when you do see them, they may be equally certainly killed either in high urhur, or from a boat, and yet I have not killed, in either the North-West Provinces or the Punjab, one Demoiselle for every ten of the Common Crane.

Again, they seem to remain much later in parts of the Deccan than thay ever do in Upper India. Burgess says: "I saw a large flock of this species on the Seena River near Waterphul, as late as the 24th May, and was told that one had been brought into the Cantonments of Ahmednugger as late as the 12th of June;" and I have two or three other records of their having been obtained in other parts of the Deccan well into May. I have never known one killed in any part of Upper India later than the 20th April* ; the majority leave the Doab, by the end of March, and the rivers of the North-West Punjab by the 10th April, and in some years earlier.

It is a pure hypothesis I admit, but these facts have led me to suspect that the birds of Western India come mostly to us like the small Flàmingo from Africa, while those of Upper India cross the Himalayas to us from the uplands of Central Asia. The latter migration I have myself twice witnessed when in the interior of the Himalayas; once near Petoragurh and once near Chini in the Satlej valley, both times early in October, (unfortunately I did not record dates), and Beavan noted that he had seen large flights passing over head at Mount Tongloo in 1862. There is no possibility of mistaking their harsh grating cry, so that neither Beavan nor myself could have confounded them with the Common Crane which, no doubt, migrates along the same line and at nearly the same season.

In the far south I may notice they arrive much later; thus Mr. Theobald writes, "that about Collegal they appear towards the latter part of December, *viz.*, about harvest time, and leave by the end of February or early in March."

As a general rule the Demoiselle greatly prefers the shelving shores and sandbanks of the larger rivers to lakes and tanks, but I have seen them on many occasions about these latter, and Captain Butler, writing of Northern Guzerat, remarks:—

"The Demoiselle Crane occurs in immense flocks all over the plains in the cold weather, arriving about the first week in October. Dr. Jerdon remarks that 'it never betakes itself to tanks or jhíls during the day.' This is an erroneous impression, as I have seen tanks fringed with a blue margin of

distribution. This would give fully 2,000 to the whole flock. This was on a huge sandbank in the Jumna near Beejhulpore in the Etáwah district. The entire flock was standing *in* the water, the rearmost birds close to the edge, where it may have been 3 inches, and the outermost birds about 20 feet from the margin, where it was about 7 inches deep. There was a fair breeze blowing down stream, and all the birds stood, head to wind, their bodies parallel to the shore.

* See, however, the Postscript, page 40.

these birds at least sixty yards wide, and extending over several acres of ground, over and over again."*

I have seen *comparatively* so little of this species that I cannot speak positively about it as I can of the Common Crane; but I should say that in Upper India its habits were much like those of the latter. They feed in fields in the early mornings, come down to the river or to large tanks about 9 o'clock, and spend a good part of the day there, though generally paying a second visit late in the afternoon to their feeding grounds, and return to the water about sunset to pass the night upon some bare, low, sandbank, whence their harsh cries ceaselessly resound till they again leave about or just before dawn. I have not observed them so perpetually on the wing, as Mr. Vidal, whose remarks I quote below, tells us it is their habit to be in the Deccan, nor have I found them one whit more wary or difficult to shoot than the Common Crane. More noisy they certainly are, and the uproar that arises when after a successful drift you have fired into one of the enormous flocks, such as I have already described, is alike indescribable, and to any one who has had no personal experience of it, incredible. Thousands of mighty pinions, almost convulsively beating the air at the same moment, and, thousands of powerful windpipes all simultaneously grating out the harsh kurr-kurr-kurr, &c., some shriller, some baser, each single voice amongst the multitude capable of making itself heard for two miles. Scream as you will, it will be a couple of minutes before you can make a man close beside you hear a syllable you say.

They run well, but not nearly so swiftly as the Common Crane; and though when dropping in the water they will try to swim, the few I have seen attempt it made but little way, and were captured at once.

On the ground they will fight fiercely, but they have nothing like the power of the Common Crane, and the boatmen would close with them and seize their bills in a way they never could with the other bird, and return in triumph to the boat, holding them by these, but carefully at arms' length, as they can give a very nasty cut with their claws.

I have never happened to have the chance of hawking this species, but I know that it is often successfully done, though even the Demoiselle is frequently too much for the best Falcons. Jerdon says that this species never makes use of its beak in self-defence, but is very apt to injure the Falcon with its sharp inner claw, and that a well-trained Peregrine, therefore, always strikes this Crane on the back and not on the head. He adds, that the mate of a stricken quarry often turns and comes to its companion's rescue. I can well believe this, for when winged birds are being pursued on the sands, others

---

* This passage is wrongly quoted by Dresser in the "Birds of Europe" as mine. It is Captain E. A. Butler's.

continually come down recklessly within easy shot, and once when having fired at a flock high over head, on the plain near the Bhurtenan Railway Station, one bird dropped suddenly after the flock had gone on two or three hundred yards, a second one dashed down along with it, and seemed, as we ran up, to be endeavouring to rouse its lifeless mate. Despite the natural shyness of these birds, this faithful comrade did not take wing till we were within twenty yards, and even then, though the rest of the flock were out of sight, hung high in air, circling and calling above us for a long time. It struck me at the moment that had these been Common Cranes the flock would *not* have gone on, but would have remained circling over head, at any rate until the second bird had been shot or had rejoined the party; and I was led to suspect, though it is idle generalizing from a solitary case, that in this species possibly the domestic ties are stronger and the tribal ones weaker than in the Common Crane. Certainly I can say this, that in Upper India this latter species keeps for the whole cold season in much the same flocks; while of the Demoiselle, the flocks are constantly splitting up and re-uniting, so that where you see 2,000 one day, there are only perhaps fifty the next, and five hundred the third, and so on; whereas for months together you recognize, or fancy you do, the parties of the Common Cranes by their size. Moreover, these latter more habitually and persistently (even though repeatedly shot at) frequent the same neighbourhood, whereas the Demoiselle is as inconstant as her name implies, and rarely remains attached to the same locality for many weeks running.

Though I have found animal food similar* to that devoured by the Common Crane in the gizzards of the present species, it has always been in small quantities, and the great bulk of the food in all the specimens I have examined has always proved to be grain and green vegetable matter, and I may add that most of those I have eaten, killed on rivers, proved just as good eating as the Common Crane. They leave us in the Doab, as a rule, before the 1st of April, and I have no record of any specimen having been killed later than the 20th of April, and that was near Jhilum.

Their habits and food vary a good deal in different parts of the country. Mr. G. Vidal writes:—

"The Demoiselle Crane is abundant in Sattara in the valleys of the Krishna, Nira and Yerla Rivers, and further east. They avoid the vicinity of the Sahyadri Ghάts, and are *never* found in the Southern Konkan. They arrive in large flocks usually in December, and for the first few weeks of their arrival spend nearly all their time on the wing, seldom, except perhaps at night, alighting on the fields. They descend usually to the

* Except fishes; I have never found these in the stomachs of this present species.

river banks to drink, both morning and evening. At this time of the year they are almost impossible to approach.

"When the crops have been reaped they grow less wild, and may generally be found feeding in the stubbles in the early morning from sunrise to 8 A.M., when they again take wing, mostly soaring in large circles at a great height till evening. Their favourite food, *par excellence*, in this district, is the '*karda*' or safflower oil seed (*Carthamus tinctorius*) which is sown in alternate rows with linseed. They roost sometimes on bare, open plains in a long single line, with sentinels posted on all sides, and sometimes on the banks of large tanks, congregating in vasts flocks by night, and separating into smaller parties of from twenty to hundred birds as they go afield at early dawn.

"They are at all times very wary birds, and will seldom allow a sportsman to get within eighty yards of them on open ground. They can, however, sometimes be stalked when feeding close to high standing crops. Cornstacks also afford occasional ambushes. Walking by the side of a country cart or a led horse is also a good plan; and like black buck they are sometimes partially deceived by this innocent device. But as I have found, by long experience, *the* best way to make sure of a shot is to walk boldly up to the flock without concealment, and immediately the first bird flaps his wings preparatory to taking flight, to *run* as fast as ever you can, straight at them. Cranes are very slow, indeed, in getting under weigh, and if you have any breath left in you, after a short spurt of sixty or seventy yards, you are almost certain of a shot at the fag end of the flock within killing distance. I have practised this myself systematically for years, and with almost invariable success. A moderate turn of speed, and to know the exact moment to stop, which is when you can get no nearer, is all that is required. This plan, however, will not perhaps commend itself to staid and elderly sportsmen of a corpulent habit, and for such the country cart has its advantages.

"These Cranes are by far the most suspicious and un-get-overable birds in existence. The Phansi Pardis, who can circumvent most birds with their gut nooses and cunning ways, fail entirely when they think to catch a Demoiselle. I have had a party of these ne'er-do-weels near my camp, for days vainly trying to entrap a few of the thousands of Cranes which daily congregated on the shores of a large irrigation reservoir; but not one bird was ever simple-minded enough to entrust its leg within the fatal noose, however deftly concealed."

"The Cranes leave the district by the first week in March."

Mr. J. Davidson again says:—

"This bird is very common in the Sholapur and Sattara Districts. It feeds morning and evening principally on "kurda," a kind of oil seed sown in almost all the jowari fields and which bears a bright yellow flower. In the middle of the day they either rest on a sandbank in one of the larger rivers or on the bank of a large tank. They are then very difficult to approach from the shore, though oddly enough they will allow a sailing vessel to pass quite near them. They arrive about the beginning of November and leave in March.

"I never saw 'Kalam' either in Tumkur (Mysore) or in the Pánch Máhals."

In Upper India, the native fowlers capture and bring in many, catching them sometimes in nets* as they do Geese and other Water Fowl, and sometimes with snares, as in the case of Bustard. I have never seen the birds caught, but have often seen them carried about for sale. The fowlers sew the eyelids together very lightly, and they will then allow themselves to be carried about unresistingly, motionless, and as if mesmerized. If fed and kept for some days in a dark place after their eyelids have been unclosed, they soon become tame, and if their wings are clipped, may be safely let loose. They will wander about the garden, and sometimes associate with the poultry, (always if there be Geese amongst these), and come back at night to their cells as though they had been tame-bred fowl. They *seem* very gentle, graceful beings, but like their namesakes, are not always reliable, are very spiteful at times, especially where any, that they consider rivals in your affections, children or dogs, are concerned, and can scratch terribly when out of temper.

Generally they seem to pine away during the hot weather, but the Maharajah of Jeypore and other native princes have, I know, succeeded in keeping them for many years. They are, however, mostly kept by natives as quarries on which to train Falcons.

No sort of sanctity attaches to these or the Common Crane in Northern India, but in the south it would seem to be different.

---

* Mr. W. N. Chill writes from near Delhi :—

"The Demoiselle Crane is caught in the very same way as are the Bustard and the large White and Common Crane, *viz.*, in slip nooses made out of the tendons obtained from the tarsi of large birds. These nooses, a caste of people known here as *Bawaryas*, who catch both birds and animals, use most dexterously. On discovering their game they choose a favourable spot, lay their nooses, which are attached to little pegs which they drive into the ground, and then veer round towards the birds outflanking them with the assistance of a buffalo, the best animal used for this purpose. They approach closer and closer, then suddenly when coming very near to the game, they hasten the pace of the buffalo, thus consequently forcing the birds to walk faster. In their confusion some generally entangle their feet in the nooses and are thus captured :—

"The Demoiselle Crane (but not any of the other larger birds above enumerated) is also netted by a caste called *Kalbuts*, real fowlers. These men, on observing localities frequented by these birds, go and lay their nets there, taking great care to cover them over with grass to prevent suspicion, and after scattering grain about the ground that the nets will cover when sprung, go off and hide in some adjacent spot, taking with them of course the strings of the nets. When the birds arrive as usual, and finding, as they soon do, the grain, commence devouring it greedily, the strings are pulled, the nets rise suddenly, and some of the birds get enclosed within them, though many always escape."

Mr. Theobald writes (from Collegal) :—

"They chiefly affect cultivated rice fields, and feed on paddy. The Brahmins here and in Mysore consider them sacred, and with their usual hazy conceptions of geography say that they come from a high mountain near Kashi (Benares), called in Sanskrit *Himovuth Parvuttum*, or snowy mountain. Some *rayats* leave small patches of paddy uncut for these birds to feed on. A naturalist runs some risk in shooting one of these birds near a Brahmin village here. In the north of India it is, I hear, the Sarus which is considered a sacred bird, but not this one. The Brahmins about here confound, I suppose, the one with the other."

WE HAVE not many details of the nidification of this species which, however, breeds probably in Spain, and certainly in the Dobrudscha, the Steppes of Southern Russia, Southern Algeria, the countries about the Caucasus, Southern and South-Eastern Siberia, Dauria and Mongolia. One writer (Artzibascheff) says that it "does not (near Sarepta) take the trouble to make a a nest, but scratches a hole in the ground in which it deposits about the middle of April one or two eggs."

Dybowski says that in Dauria "it nests on the rocky banks of rivers and rarely on bare mountains. The nest is made of small stones fitting close to each other ; the surface of the nest is flat or deepening somewhat towards the centre ; it chooses sometimes a place which is a few inches higher than the surrounding ground, and fills up all the crevices and openings with stones. We have seen eggs in June, and till the middle of July."

These seem no doubt rather abnormal nests for Water Birds like Cranes, and Nordmann says they build nests like the Common Crane, but it must not be forgotten that Cranes are closely allied to Bustards, and that these latter lay their eggs on the bare ground, and that the eggs of both the Common Crane and the present species present a certain superficial resemblance to those of the Great Bustard.

Many writers notice the dances in which this species indulges just prior to, or at the commencement of, the breeding season. We see nothing of this, of course, in India, but they appear to be similar to those already described of the Sarus, with this exception, that the Sarus, keeping always in pairs and not in flocks, you see amongst them only two performers on the stage at once, while in the case of the Demoiselles you have a whole flock amusing themselves simultaneously.

Von Nordmann says : "They dance and jump towards each other, bowing themselves in a most burlesque manner, bending their necks forward, extending the plumes on the neck and depressing their wings ; others again in the meanwhile run races, and on arrival at the gaol, return striding along gravely and quietly, whilst the rest of the assembly greet them with reiterated cries, inclinations of the head, and other demonstrations."

I have never seen the eggs of this species, and *authentic* eggs are uncommonly rare. Dresser says that they are, as a rule, smaller, darker, and more clearly marked than those of the Common Crane which I have already fully described, and that they vary from 3·05 to 3·55 in length, and from 2·02 to 2·2 in breadth.

I DO not find that the sexes in this species differ in any way in size. I have recorded the measurements of sixteen adults, and find that some males are as large, and some as small, as any female, and *vice versâ*.

Length, 31·0 to 35·6; expanse, 66·0 to 73·0; wing, 18·0 to 21·0; tail from vent, 6·0 to 7·5; tarsus, 6·25 to 7·8; bill from gape, 2·7 to 3·05; weight, 5 lbs to 6·75 lbs.

The tertiaries project from 4·0 to 6·0 inches beyond the primaries in birds killed in March; perhaps during the breeding season they are somewhat more elongated.

The irides in the adult are red, varying from crimson to vermilion; in the young they are brown, and every intermediate shade occurs in more or less immature birds. The bill varies a good deal; it is generally greenish, with a reddish tinge at tip; in some I have noted it sea green at base, yellowish towards the middle, and pink at tip; in another yellowish at tips, greenish horny at base; the legs and feet are normally black, but I shot one specimen, a large male, but probably a sickly bird, in which they were only a dusky slate colour, and in this bird, though it was certainly an adult, the irides were orange red.

THE PLATE very fairly represents our bird, and is most creditable to a comparative novice like Miss Herbert.

The young bird differs from the old in having the sides of the head, chin, and throat, grey instead of black as in the adult; the ear tufts are very little developed, and are grey; the pectoral plumes are very little developed, and only the central ones blackish brown; the tertials are not developed at all.

CRANES, subdivided by ornithologists into several genera, are distributed pretty well over the whole of the world, but appear to avoid, to a great extent, the smaller islands. In Asia, besides those already noticed, we have *G. viridirostris*, like the Snow-Wreath, but with a green bill and black legs; *G. vipio*, of a slatey grey, with the nape and entire back of neck white, and red legs; and *G. monachus* of a dark brownish slatey colour, with the head and upper part of the neck all round, white, and brownish green legs, all of which seem to belong to Japan and

Eastern Siberia, and more or less of Northern China, Manchuria and Mongolia.

In Australia, there is the Sarus-like, native companion, *G. australasianus*. In Southern Africa we have the somewhat aberrant *G. carunculatus*, *Anthropoides paradisea*, and the Southern Crowned-Crane (*Balearica regulorum*), and in the north, extending perhaps to some of the Islands of the Mediteranean, the Crowned-Crane (*B. pavonina.*) Lastly, America has three, or possibly four, species of true Crane.

POSTSCRIPT.—Long after the above had been in type, Captain FitzHerbert, of the Rifle Brigade, favoured me with the following note :—"Yesterday, August the 25th, a native brought in two specimens of the Demoiselle Crane, which he said had been killed at the Sohan River near this station, Rawulpindee." Were these accidental lingerers, like the Swans (p. 44,) seen in July? More probably they were early arrivals, and since the Common Crane appears in Sindh in August, (p. 22,) perhaps this species also returns to the extreme western and north-western portions of the empire in that month.

CYGNUS FERUS
⅓
CYGNUS OLOR.
W. Foster.

THE MUTE SWAN.

Cygnus olor, *Gmelin.*

Vernacular Names.—[Penr, *N. W. Punjab;* Koday, (Turki,) *Yarkand.*]

THIS species may be considered a pretty regular, though somewhat rare, cold-weather visitant to the Peshawer and Hazára Districts, and an occasional straggler to the Kohát and Rawal Pindi Districts and to the Trans-Indus portions of Sind. It has also, *perhaps,* occurred on the Runn of Cutch.

Outside our limits, this species has been seen in the Kábul River near Jellalabad, and is known to visit Northern Afghanistan pretty regularly. It is abundant on the Caspian.* It occurs and breeds in Western Turkestan and Central Siberia, and is found also in Kashgar, where it is said to be plentiful at Aksu, and further east at the Lob series of lakes. But specimens from this latter locality have yet to be compared, and it is not impossible that these eastern birds, as well as Radde's and Prjevalski's supposed *olor* from South-east Siberia and South-east Mongolia, may really prove to have belonged to the more eastern species with *feathered* lores and orange-red bill and feet named by Swinhoe, *C. davidi.*

The present species is also found pretty well throughout Europe, but becomes very rare towards the north, and in Great Britain never seems to occur in a truly wild state. It extends in winter to Northern Africa, Egypt and Asia Minor.

THIS IS the tame Swan of Europe, so well known to all that it is needless to quote, from European writers, accounts of its habits which, here in India, I have never had any opportunity of observing in a wild state.

This species has been, however, so seldom *recorded* as killed in India that it may be well to enumerate every instance of this which has come to my knowledge.

---

* In 1877 Captain Butler learnt from some of the telegraph officers in the Persian Gulf that Swans had been occasionally seen about the head of that gulf and the mouths of the Euphrates. It is impossible to say to what species these birds may have belonged.

The first occurrence of this species, of which I have a record, was near Peshawer, in 1857, when a small flock were seen, and one shot and placed in the Peshawer Museum, whence it was sent to me by Sir F. Pollock in, I think, 1867.

This Swan was shot by W. Mahomed Oomer Khan, who wrote to me about it as follows :—

"In the month of January 1857, I shot this Swan in the Peshawer District on the Shah Alum River, about a mile and a half on this side of the Kábul River. Neither before nor after have I seen other Swans, but a few years after I killed it, I heard from the shikaris of Hashtnagar (also in the Peshawer District) that they had recently seen five of these birds in the Agra (?) village lake, in this same district, but had failed to shoot any."

The specimen had been so entirely ruined by exposure and insects that I could not, at the time, decide positively to which species it belonged, but from what remains of the bill and head I have since satisfied myself that it was *C. olor.*

In 1871 Captain Unwin, of the 5th Goorkhas, sent me the skins of a pair of young Swans of this species with the following extract from his diary, under date 17th January 1871 :—

"To-day, while Duck-shooting on the Jubbee Stream, on the border of the Hazára and Rawal Pindi Districts, during a short halt for breakfast on the banks of the nullah, I was attracted by seeing two large white birds flying over the stream some 250 yards lower down. The Jubbee has here a wide stony bed, with a small stream in the centre, forming occasional pools, in one of which the birds seemed inclined to alight. Changing their intention, however, they came flying up, and passed me at a distance of about 60 yards ; to my surprise and delight I recognised in them most undoubted wild Swans. Firing with loose shot at that distance was useless, so I watched in the hope that they would settle in some of the pools higher up the stream, and thereby afford a stalk, but they continued their slow, heavy, flight until I lost sight of them in the distance.

"Concluding that they would not stop until they reached the Indus, some 20 miles off, I was returning to my breakfast, a sadder and a wiser man, when, in taking a last look in their direction, I saw them returning. I hastily got into the centre of the nullah, in their line of flight, and as they rose slightly, to avoid me, fired both barrels, No. 3 shot, at the leader. She (for it proved to be the female) staggered, but went on, slowly sinking, till she settled in a large pool, about 400 yards off, accompanied by her mate, which alighted close beside her.

"The pool, being commanded by a high bank, offered an easy stalk, and getting round into a favorable position, I found the Swans within 20 yards of me. A crowd of Gadwall (*C. streperus*), which was close by, took flight on seeing me, but the male Swan stuck nobly by his mate, and paid dearly for his fidelity, and shortly I had the satisfaction of landing them both.

"The villagers who collected to see the birds gave the local name as "penr" (pronounced with a nasal *n*), and told me that the birds came there occasionally once in every three or fours years."

I may here notice that in other parts of Upper India this name "*penr*" is usually applied to Pelicans.

In the cold weather of 1871-72, Dr. Stoliczka, when in Cutch, thought he saw Swans there. He says, J. A. S., B., 1872, 229:—

"While crossing the Runn from Kachh to Pachain early in November (1871), I noticed several Swans, but at too great a distance for it to be possible to form an idea as to the species the birds belonged to."

Until recently I had always considered (S. F., IV., 33) that Stoliczka, being very short-sighted, had mistaken Pelicans (the white *P. crispus* abounds there) for Swans; but the recent occurrence of Swans in Sind renders it not improbable that Stoliczka was right after all, and if so they would almost certainly have belonged to the present species.

Between 1872 and 1876 I received notices of Swans being killed on three occasions, on the Swat and Kábul Rivers, in the Peshawer District and in Kohát near one of our salt mines, in November, January and February. In one case a pair, in another three, and in the last case five, were seen, one being shot in each case, but none preserved. All would seem, from what was noted of the tails and colours of the bill, to have been *olor*.

During the cold season of 1877-78 Swans were numerous in the far North-West. One was killed near Attock on the 17th of January by Lt. Hill, of the Rifle Brigade, and I heard of two others being killed in the Peshawer District in February, and of many others being seen.

On the 12th of February, Mr. H. E. Watson killed three Swans in the Sehwan District in Sind.

He first saw birds of this species in January, at the Manchhar Lake, and later saw five, and actually procured three, in a small broad in the same district. He writes:—

"I shot three Swans this morning. As far as I can judge they are identical with the English species" (that is the tame Swan); "there were five on a small 'dhand' or tank, about half a mile or less in length by a quarter of a mile or less in breadth. I went to shoot Ducks, but seeing these large white birds, I went after them and recognized them to be the same as those I had seen on the Manchhar. They let a boat get pretty close and I shot one. The other four flew round the tank a few times and then settled on it again. I went up in the boat and fired again, but without effect. They flew round and then settled again. The third time I shot another; the three remaining again flew round and settled, and the fourth time I fired I did not kill. Exactly the same thing happened the fifth time, the birds flew round and settled close to me, and I shot a third. The remaining two flew a little distance, and settled, but I thought it would be a pity to kill them. I considered that there would be more than I could skin myself (for I have no one that can do it for me) so I began to shoot Ducks, and then the two remaining Swans flew by me, one on the right and one on the left, so that I could easily have knocked them over with small shots. However I spared them and came home with three."

These specimens proved, as surmised by Mr. Watson, to belong to the present species and to be adults—a noteworthy fact—it being almost exclusively birds of the year that visit India.

But the most remarkable instances have yet to be noticed.

On the 3rd of June 1878 Major Waterfield telegraphed to me from Peshawer that a Swan had just been shot.

Later he wrote: "The Swan was killed on the Ojca Jhíl on the 3rd of June; there were a pair, but the other flew away. The bird that I have had preserved for you measured exactly 5 feet in length and 7 feet 5 inches in expanse. The feet and legs were black; the upper mandible is reddish white; its edge, lores, and lower mandible black."

A few days later Mr. D. B. Sinclair wrote to say that he had killed another Swan, a male, on the 1st of June at the Gulabad Jhíl, 12 miles north-east of Peshawer, and on the 7th July he wrote to say that there was still at least one Swan left on this same jhíl.

The specimen sent by Major Waterfield proved to be a nearly mature *C. olor*, but Mr. Sinclair's bird, unfortunately imperfectly preserved, decayed so rapidly in the hot weather that then prevailed, (the temperature was over 100° Far. in the shade at 10 A.M., in Peshawer at the time,) that it shortly grew a mass "to make men tremble who never weep;" and though, from what was said, I believe it also to have been *olor*, I cannot be certain.

What *could* possibly keep a number of Swans down in the middle of June in one of the hottest places in India, I cannot pretend to say.

Looking to the uncertainty that exists at present as to the number of species that visit us, and to the difficulty apparently experienced by many (a difficulty in which until I had studied the group I fully shared) in discriminating the young birds, it is very desirable that sportsmen should preserve every specimen they shoot, and submit them for examination to some competent ornithologist.

NATURALLY THIS rare and *normally* only winter visitant does not breed with us. Many of us have taken the eggs of tame birds at home, and know well the huge nest that they build of rushes, reeds and coarse aquatic herbage, on the bank of some island or shore of a lake, or in thick reed beds. The nidification of the wild birds in Turkey, South Russia, in Sweden and Denmark, about the Caspian, in Western Turkestan and Central Siberia, what little has been recorded of it, seems to differ in no way from that of their domesticated brethren, except that the wild birds are said by some to breed gregariously, many nests being placed in close proximity to each other. They lay from five to eight eggs, (and the domesticated birds at times as many as eleven,) with but little gloss of a rather coarse texture; in shape rather elongated, very regular, obtuse ended ovals; in colour a dull pale greenish grey or white, and they average nearly four and a half inches in length by nearly three in breadth.

IN THIS SPECIES, individuals of both sexes, even apparent adults, differ very considerably in size, the dimensions probably increasing for some years after they attain their perfect plumage; but still the males, I believe, average somewhat larger than the females. I have never, in India, had the chance of measuring wild specimens of this species myself, and can, therefore, only reproduce dimensions recorded by others.

First, those of three adults, not sexed, which were measured by Mr. H. E. Watson :—

	No 1. feet inches.	No 2. feet inches.	No 3. feet inches.
"Length from tip of bill to end of tail ...	4—10·5	5—2	5—0
Expanse	6—6	7—0	6—10
Wing	1—10	1—11	......
Tail from vent	0—9·75	0—10·25	0—9·75
Bill from gape	0—3·75	0—3·8	......
Tarsus measured on inner side... ...	0—3·8	0—4·2	......
Weight	17½lbs.	19lbs.	17½lbs."

Second, of two immature birds measured by Captain Unwin:—

"*Male*.—Length, 55·5; expanse, 84·37; wing, 23·12; tail from vent, 8·5; bill at front, straight from termination of frontal plumes to tip, 3·5; from anterior angle of eye, 5·15; from gape, 4; tarsus, 4·05; mid toe to root of claw, 5; weight, 15 lbs.

"*Female*.—Length, 53·12; expanse, 82·37; wing, 21·38; bill at front from frontal plumes straight to tip, 3·55; from anterior angle of eye, 4·75; from gape, 3·9; tarsus, 3·8; mid toe to root of claw, 4·8; weight, 13 lbs.

But of the tame birds, old males are said to weigh up to 30 lbs.

In the adult "the nail at the point of the bill, the edge of the upper mandible on each side, its base and lores to the eye, the orifice of the nostrils and the tubercle, are black; the rest of the bill reddish orange; the irides brown, the legs and feet black."

The female, it is to be noted, besides being smaller, has the tubercle smaller, the neck more slender and swims deeper in the water.

In immature birds, such as are most commonly seen in India, the bill exhibits no trace of a tubercle; the feathers of the forehead are prolonged to a point, only very slightly truncated. If from each side of the frontal tongue of feathers, about half an inch from its point, a slightly curving line be drawn to a point on the edge of the upper mandible, about a quarter of an inch from the gape, the whole of the space enclosed by such line between it and the eye is perfectly black. At the extreme point of the frontal feathers again is a black band, about a quarter of an inch wide, which extends right and left over the whole nareal space; the nail is black; the rest of the bill is light grey, fleshy grey, pale fleshy yellow, to pale buff. The legs and feet are greyish black; the irides dark brown.

THE PLATE of the adult of this species, (the right hand figure,) is satisfactory, except that the black patch from the nostril to the tubercle is not shown; in some the anterior portion of the tubercle also is orange.

In the adult the entire plumage is a very pure white with, at times, a creamy or buffy tinge on the crown and back of upper neck, often disappearing in the dry skin.

At the end of October the young are said to have the head, neck, and entire upper surface a nearly uniform sooty greyish brown, and the under surface of a lighter greyish brown; the beak is then (where not blackish) of a light slatey grey, but in the immature birds, as we generally see them, the general colour of the lower surface is a dull white; of the upper whitey-brown; the crown and occiput buffy-brown; the greater portion of the wing, the scapulars and rump are buffy or sandy brown. There is nowhere any trace of a "sooty grey." The brown is essentially a buffy or sandy brown, though here and there, as in the feathers at the base of the neck, a faint greyish shade *is* intermingled.

THIS SPECIES may be distinguished at any age at which we ever see it, from both the other species—known or supposed to have occurred within our limits—first by its black lores, and secondly by the shape of its tail, which is comparatively long and pointed or wedge-shaped, and *not* short and rounded as it is in both *C. ferus* and *C. bewicki.*

THE HOOPER.

Cygnus musicus, *Bechstein.*

Vernacular Names.—[None.]

I HAVE no reason to believe that the occurrence of this species within our limits has ever been satisfactorily ascertained. It was included in this work, because Mr. Brooks, and others, identified the drawing of a Swan obtained in Népal by Mr. Hodgson, (of which the specimen has been lost,) as pertaining to the present species. A most careful examination of this drawing leads me, personally, to believe, (it is of course a mere matter of opinion,) that Hodgson's bird was *bewicki*. My opinion is mainly based on the fact that the black on the bill, as depicted in the drawing, is distributed precisely as in Mr. Yarrell's most accurate figure of the head of this latter species, (Yar., 3rd edition, III, 198), and not at all as in his figure of the head of the present species (*tom cit*, 195.)

But the Hooper is by no means unlikely to occur within our limits, and as we have figured it on the same plate as the preceding species, it may be well to give a brief notice of it.

St. John obtained a young Swan of this species near Teheran in winter. It abounds on the southern parts of the Caspian in winter, and in summer some are found in the more northern portions. It occurs in Western Turkestan, chiefly on passage, though a few breed also in certain districts ; it is found almost throughout Siberia to beyond the 74° North Latitude in summer. In South-east Mongolia it is seen chiefly as a bird of passage, though a few remain to breed, Prjevalsky says, at Lake Hanka and probably about Tsaidam. In winter it is apparently widely spread throughout China and Chinese Tibet, though its southernmost limits are as yet quite undefined, and it also occurs in Japan.

Throughout Europe, (from Iceland and Nova Zembla southwards,) in the Islands of the Mediterranean, and in many places in Northern Africa, this species is met with as a summer or winter visitant or on passage.

ITS HABITS are apparently much those of the Common Swan, though it feeds more, and moves about with greater ease, on land, but it is distinguishable from this at great distances by its loud and musical call, which I have often heard at home, and which, though much resembling the word "hoop," "hoop," repeated many times, has, when uttered by a large flock of birds of different sexes and ages, and mellowed by the winds and waves, a really fine effect.

These Swans are, I fancy, chiefly vegetarians, feeding mostly upon herbs, and their seeds and sometimes flowers, weeds and grasses.

On the whole, this species seems a more northern bird than the Mute Swan, their average distribution being, I think, more northerly. Not only do they live and breed further north, but fewer of them go far south, and the bulk of the species do not, except in excessively severe winters, go anything like as far south as does *C. olor*.

THEY BREED as far north as south Greenland, Iceland, and the more northerly portions of Europe and Asia, and it is believed in Nova Zembla also, and southwards in both continents, where sportsmen or dense population have not banished them, to between the fortieth and fiftieth degrees of North Latitude.

They build in similar situations to the last species, (but solitarily and not in flocks,) a similar, but smaller and less massive nest, and breed from May to July, according to locality, laying from five to seven eggs.

The eggs are described as similar in shape to, but as averaging slightly larger* (4·0 to 4·5 by 2·55 to 2·95,) than, those of the Mute Swan, and they are said to be of an uniform, dull, very pale, dingy buff, or buffy white, not unfrequently with a fair amount of gloss.

OF COURSE we have no measurements of Indian birds.

The following are the dimensions of an adult male and adult female, recorded in England :—

Male.—Length, 60 ; expanse, 95 ; wing, 25·75 ; tail, 7·5 ; bill along culmen, including bare space on forehead, 4·25 ; from tip to eye, 5·16 ; tarsus, 4·16 ; weight, 19 lbs.

Female.—Length, 52 ; expanse, 85 ; wing, 23·5 ; tail, 7·5 ; bill, as above, 4·5 ; to eye, 4·84 ; tarsus, 4·0 ; weight, 16·5 lbs.

The dimensions of this species vary a great deal, and full-plumaged Hoopers are said to range in weight from 13 lbs. to 21 lbs.

The bare space on the forehead and in front of the eyes, and the basal portion of the bill, is yellowish to bright yellow ; the

* They do average, I believe, larger than the eggs of the domesticated *olor*, but not I think than those of the wild birds.

nail and the tip of the bill is black, the black extending upwards as a point along the culmen to within perhaps one inch of the margin of the frontal feathers, while the yellow extends forward along the sides of the upper mandible to within, perhaps, one and a half inches of the point, the two colors meeting in a slanting line on either side of the bill. Part of the base of the lower mandible and the space between the rami yellow ; the rest of the lower mandible, black ; the iris is brown ; the feet and claws black.

THE PLATE, (the left hand figure,) conveys a sufficiently accurate idea of the adult of this species, but the neck is somewhat too long and too gracefully curved. In this species the bird usually holds the neck comparatively stiffly and straight.

A young bird killed in March measured 44 inches in length and weighed 8·25 lbs. The basal portions of the bill were flesh colour instead of yellow ; the irides dusky ; the feet greyish dusky, with a reddish tinge ; the feathers on the forehead and before the eyes dull orange ; the rest of the head and upper neck behind brown ; the underparts white, tinged with rufous ; the lower neck behind, and the rest of the upper parts not already mentioned, ashy grey.

BOTH THE Hooper and Bewick's Swan are, as already noticed, at once distinguished from the Mute Swan by their comparatively short and rounded (not wedge-shaped) tails.

The two former species differ, *birds of the same sex and age being compared*, in the greatly superior size of the Hooper. But young female Hoopers are decidedly smaller than old male Bewick's Swans, so that it will not do to depend blindly on dimensions, without carefully considering the sex and apparent age of the specimen examined, and the surest external diagnosis consists in the far greater amount and somewhat different distribution of the black on the bills of Bewick's bird, which is shown in the plates and fully explained in describing the colours of the soft parts of each species. I may add that in the Hooper the frontal feathers are prolonged into an angle, while in Bewick's Swan they terminate in a semicircle. The internal distinctions, first pointed out by Yarrell, in the different arrangement of the wind-pipe, &c., are even more conspicuous, but do not fall within the scope of a work like the present.

F Walter Chromo Lith 15 Hatton Garden London

CYGNUS BEWICKII.

BEWICK'S SWAN.

Cygnus bewicki, *Yarrell.*

Vernacular Names.—[None.]

THE only instance of the occurrence of this species within our limits, of which we have any record, is the one noted by Mr. Hodgson, by one of whose people a Swan was shot in January 1829, in the valley of Népal. The skin was destroyed by insects, but a large and careful drawing of the fresh bird was made by one of Mr. Hodgson's trained ornithological artists; and, although others have supposed this drawing to represent the Hooper, I myself cannot doubt that it represents a nearly adult bird of the present species. Unfortunately, Mr. Hodgson recorded none of his customary notes as to dimensions, anatomy, &c., which would have set all doubts on the subject (if any such *can* exist,) finally at rest.

In regard to this Swan Mr. Hodgson noted on a copy of his Catalogue which he sent me :—

" The valley of Nepal is sub-tropical, and of course, no habitat for the Swan. The specimen I got was obtained in a winter of very unusual severity. The bird must be a purely accidental straggler, as I could not learn that any like it had ever before been seen in Nepal."

In reply to queries of mine on the subject, Dr. Scully says :—

" I have made enquiries from a number of Nepalese, and I cannot find any one now remaining who ever remembers to have seen a wild Swan in the valley."

In "Asiatic Researches," XVIII, pt. II., 125, Hodgson gives *Cygnus* as one of the *Natatores* which usually pass over the valley, seldom alighting, and then only for a few hours.

At page 127 he adds :—" India, I fancy, is too hot for the taste of the *Natatores*, a great majority of which seem to affect Arctic regions, or at least high latitudes. I throw out the remark for canvas and enquiry, and for fear I should deceive any one by the display of the genus *Cygnus* at the head of my list, I must add that the wild Swan was never seen here (valley of

Nepal), but once in the mid-winter of 1828, when the apparition suggested a new version of the well-known hexameter

'*Rara avis in terris, alboque simillima cygno.*'"

Outside our Empire this species seems to occur on the Caspian and throughout Siberia, to be found in Mongolia, and to be even more widely and generally distributed in winter in China than the Hooper. Like this latter it also occurs in Japan. It has, however, been so constantly confounded with the Hooper that its real area of distribution is still quite undetermined. It inhabits the more northern portions of Europe in summer, migrating southwards in winter, stragglers having occurred as far south as Marseilles. As yet I do not think that it has been observed in Italy or the more eastern portions of the Mediterranean or in Northern Africa.

GENERALLY I gather that Bewick's Swan is even more of a cold region species than the Hooper, and has a somewhat more northerly average range.

This species is in a wild state very shy and difficult of approach, more so if possible than the Hooper; but in captivity it is said to be very gentle, never molesting other Water Fowl as the Mute Swan often does. The call is said by some to be a low deep-toned whistle once repeated, but Naumann represents it by the syllable "kuk," uttered many times. In England they have not unfrequently been mistaken for Geese, and when swimming their carriage is intermediate between that of the Mute Swan and Goose, wanting alike "the grace and majesty" of the former. On the land, however, where by choice they spend much of their time, they show to greater advantage, and winged birds will run well and fast. It seems on the whole to be more of a marsh and narrow water species and less of an open water bird than the Hooper. Their food, like that of the other Swans, seems to consist of seeds, stems, and corms of rushes, and various kinds of aquatic herbs, together with, *perhaps*, worms and larvæ of insects.

Like the other species this Swan seems to migrate both by day and night.

I HAVE met with no reliable details of the nidification of this species, though recently Messrs. Seebohm and Harvey-Brown brought home eggs from the Petchora, which they consider to belong to this bird. What Naumann and Thienmann give of their breeding in Iceland refers really to the Hooper. Doubtless they pair for life, as is I believe the case with the other species, and construct a large nest of rushes, grass and aquatic herbage, in similar situations to those of the Mute Swan. Like the Hooper they probably repair an old nest in preference to building a new one; they lay (if S. and H.-B. are correct,) in May and June, probably five to seven eggs, smaller than those of the Hooper, and dull white and glossless.

THE FOLLOWING are dimensions, &c., of a male of *C. bewicki*:—

Length, 45; expanse, 74; wing, 20·5; tarsus, 5·5; bill along culmen from margin of frontal feathers, 3·5; to eye, 4·41; tarsus, 3·75.

The females are smaller, but some males are said to be larger than the dimensions above given, and to measure nearly, if not quite, 50 inches in length.

Naumann's dimensions, however, (converted from the Leipzig foot he uses) for the two sexes are: *Male*—Length, 42·2; expanse, 75·8; wing, 19·5. *Female*.—Length, 39·8; expanse, 73·0; wing, 18·6.

In the adults in this species the greater part of the bill is black, which colour generally extends on the culmen, right up to the frontal plumes, but the bare space in front of the eyes is bright yellow, as is also the basal portion of the upper mandible, the colour extending forwards in a curve, towards, but not reaching to, the nostrils; the feet black; the irides brown.

In the young the portions of the bill that are yellow in the adult are yellowish fleshy. The irides are dusky, and the feet more of a reddish dusky colour.

THE PLATE represents fairly both the adult and very young bird, but the less said of the blue smudge in the back ground the better. In the young of a somewhat more advanced age, the plumage is a darker or lighter grey, bluer in some parts, browner elsewhere, paler on the lower surface, and almost white on the abdomen and lower tail-coverts.

SWANS EXTEND over the whole world. Besides those already mentioned, a fourth at any rate, the Polish Swan, is admitted to occur in Europe. In Asia we have *C. davidi* of Swinhoe, and possibly a second species. In America four, or possibly five, species, and in Australia the well-known Black Swan. Some of these are separated by many ornithologists under distinct genera—*Coscoroba*, *Chenopsis*, &c.—but though they do differ to a certain extent, I am, as at present informed, disposed to think that they may all be properly retained under the one genus—*Cygnus*.

ANSER CINEREUS

THE GREY LAG-GOOSE.

—— o ——

Anser cinereus, *Meyer*.

—— o ——

Vernacular Names.—[Sona,* (Hindee) *N. W. Provinces;* Hans, Raj-hans, Kurria-sona, *Upper India;* Kallauk, ?; Kar-hans, *Bhagulpore;* Mogala, Mogala-buttuk, *Nepal Terai;* Kângnai, *Manipur;* Ghaz, *Kashghar;*]

—— o ——

THE Grey Lag-Goose is a cold-weather visitant to pretty well the whole of Continental India. I have notices of its occurrence in all suitable localities throughout Upper India, from Peshawer to Sadiya, and it extends southwards,† but in greatly diminished numbers to about the 22° North Latitude. South of this *it may* extend as a straggler, but the lower course of the Nerbudda on the west, and the Subanreeka on the east, are the two very most southern points where I have as yet *known* this species to be killed. Eastward it is not uncommon in the neighbourhood of Calcutta, and has been occasionally seen east and south of this in the Sunderbans. It occurs in the Dacca‡ District and right up the valley of the Brahmaputra to Sadiya, but I know hardly anything of its distribution south of the Gáro, Khási, and Naga Hills, and east of the Brahmaputra in Cachar, Chittagong, Tipperah, &c.

Mr. Damant writes:—" This bird is common in the Rungpore District on both banks of the Brahmaputra, and also in Manipur."

---

* This name is often given as that of *Anser indicus*, but all the oldest and best skikarrees and falconers say that it is the Grey Goose that is the true "*Sona.*"

† Writing from Eastern Sind Mr. Doig says:—"The Grey Lag appears about the end of October, and goes away again by the end of March and beginning of April. It is the only Goose I have seen in the Eastern Nara Districts, and principally confines itself to the larger tracts of swamps during the day. As evening approaches they go to feed in the rice fields or young wheat fields."

‡ Mr. Cripps writes:—

"In the Dacca District I on one occasion came upon a huge flock of this species. It was on a large chur on the "Megna" river opposite Boyd Bazar. The river at that season (January) had fallen a great deal, leaving a good large sheet of water in the centre of the chur. Round the edges of this water was a strip of paddy, about 100 yards in breadth, which afforded concealment not only to the birds but to a sportsman. I managed to creep through it unobserved, and get a couple of shots; there were about 200 of *A. cinereus* and about 50 of *A. indicus*. I never again noticed the Grey Lag-Goose in that district."

It does not appear to extend into any part of British Burma.

This species is not confined to the plains, or even the sub-montane tracts; in the cold season it is at times seen in suitable places in the interior of the Himalayas, up to elevations of from four to six thousand feet, as in Nepal, Kullu and Kashmir.

This species is not uncommon during the winter in Afghanistan. In Western Turkestan it breeds commonly, and some winter there. In Kashghar, it breeds freely, especially about Maral Bashi, but does not winter in the country. It is found in summer throughout Eastern Siberia, except in the extreme north. I do not find it recorded from Northern China, but it winters apparently in those portions of the empire, south of the Yang-tse-kiang. Prjevalsky met with them breeding in South-eastern Mongolia, the upper valley of the Hoangho, and as far south as Lake Kokonor, where, he says, they were rather common in the latter part of March. He adds that this species arrives in South-eastern Mongolia, about the middle of March, or perhaps earlier, and in Tsaidam about the 18th of February. This species has not been reported from Japan, nor as yet from Persia, Asia Minor, Palestine, or North-eastern Africa, though further west as near Tangier and in Algeria, it is found in Northern Africa.

It occurs throughout Europe, except in the extremest north, for the most part, in the south in winter and (though some breed as far south as Bulgaria and Spain) in the north during the summer.

A great deal has still to be done in working out the distribution of this species in Asia, if not in Europe also. For long it was confounded with the very distinct species *albifrons* and *brachyrhynchus*, and even now I rather suspect that two recognizably distinct species are included under the name Grey Lag-Goose.

THIS SPECIES rarely appears in Upper India before the last week in October, and further south the first week in November is, I think, the earliest time for their arrival. In some years they are a good week or ten days later. Everywhere many, I believe, leave the country during the first week in March, but many may be met with in the north until quite the end of that month; and I have shot them once as late as the 10th April, on the Jhelum, a little below the station of that name. The early date on which Prjevalsky observed them in Tsaidam will have been noticed, and Scully says, that in Kashghar he got his first specimen on the 28th of February, and that during the early part of March they were often seen flying over the fort at Yarkand and going straight north.

Where Geese are much shot at, they feed in the meadows and fields exclusively during the hours of darkness, but where comparatively unmolested, you will find them grazing in the young wheat till nine o'clock in the morning and back again at their pastures by 4 P.M.

When not out feeding they spend their time dozing or daudling about on the margin of some lake or the bank of some river, always by preference choosing some island in these for their noon-tide siesta. Unless disturbed, they very rarely take to the water; where you see a flock swimming about in mid stream of one of our larger rivers or in the open water of some broad, between the hours of ten and three, you may generally safely conclude that they have been recently fired at, or frightened in some way.

They feed exclusively, so far as my experience goes, on tender shoots of grass, young corn, and other spring crops, and on grain of all kinds—gram, when nearly ripe, being a great attraction to them. Generally they are pretty well on the alert when feeding inland, but in parts of the country where the people have no guns, and there are no native or European sportsmen about, they get very bold; and when put up at one end of a field, fluster lazily away and settle a couple of hundred yards away in another field, and give the cultivators a good deal of trouble, since three or four hundred of these birds will clear off an incredible amount of grain in a morning. In such localities you may with a common blanket, donned native-fashion over head and body, walk up to within thirty yards of a flock, and then judiciously startling them get a couple of effective shots into the mass, as it rises. In such cases never fire until they have risen, and are about the level of your face. A shot on the ground, amongst the crops, with an ordinary twelve bore may yield three, generally only two, often only one; the same shot fired when the flock is on the wing, and about gun level, will account for from five to eight. I have often got ten, and once or twice more, with two barrels in such cases.

Where, however, they have been once thus shot at, you will not get near them again for some time without further precautions, but even where on the alert, you may often stalk them behind a horse and get to within forty or fifty yards. In such cases it is best to make sure of your one or two birds on the ground with the first shot, as you will seldom have time for more than one shot after they rise.

Although they rise rather awkwardly and slowly, with violent and noisy flappings of their wings, they fly very strongly and easily when once well off, and I do not know a more beautiful sight than the sudden and rapid descent of a large flock from high in the air to some sandbank. The flock comes along in sober state, circles round decorously once or twice, and then suddenly, as though all hands had been piped to skylark, down they come with incredible rapidity, twisting and turning, with an ease and grace for which no one could at other times have given them credit. They swim well, no doubt, and dive when hard pressed fairly well, though they cannot keep long under water; but neither in walking nor swimming (though in both less awkward, for they are less paunchy birds than the domestic Goose) do they show to any great advantage.

When moving any considerable distance they fly high and usually in a single line, or in a V, with the point foremost; but when merely changing ground, they often fly in an irregular flock.

They are met with in parties of all sizes, from a single pair to more than a thousand, but flocks of from thirty to a hundred are most commonly seen in Upper India. All our Geese prefer rivers to tanks and lakes, but of all the species the Grey Lag is least rarely seen about these latter.

Geese, Crane, and Mallard, shy and wild as they are as a rule inland, are easily killed on all our larger rivers. During the hotter parts of the day they are, as already mentioned, generally found in larger or smaller parties, dozing in the sun, on some sandbank, at the water's edge, or, in the case of the Cranes, standing asleep in the water near some such bank. Directly such a party is sighted, you take a small boat, and with the aid of a couple of experienced men, row or punt noiselessly down to within two or three hundred yards of the birds, when, if the water intervening is shallow enough to allow it, (and the boatmen seem to know this by instinct) one man gets quietly out of the boat behind, and while you and your companion in the boat lie down out of sight, he, stooping so as to be entirely concealed by the boat, pushes it down gently and noiselessly, aided by the stream, towards the flock. In this way you may approach, if all is well managed, to within twenty yards of even Cranes. You make some arrangement at the bows, (I had a false gunwale screwed on with suitable holes pierced in it,) so as to admit of peeping and shooting, without raising your head into view, and when you get to what you consider the right distance, knock over as many you can sitting, with the first shot, and as many more as you have time for, before they get out of shot, after they rise. Everything depends on judging rightly the distance for the first shot, with reference to your bore and charge. A little too far, you wound a score, without perhaps bagging one; a little too near, and you kill one or two outright, and though you perhaps get two or three more as they rise, that is all; but if you use a good heavy duck gun, say No. 8 bore, with two ounces of A. A., and fire at about fifty yards, you will rarely get less than eight out of a good large flock of Geese (and I have got as many as sixteen) with the first shot, besides a brace or so more, with green cartridge, as they rise.

In England, where the Wild Geese are so wary, it seems odd enough that these birds should have been selected as types of stupidity; but here when thus worked they are the tamest of all Water Fowl, and allow a boat to drift almost on to them before they move. When still about a hundred yards off, the flock is seen to be grouped in a dense mass ; fully half are asleep, a few are standing at the water's edge drinking slowly, raising the head at each gulp, and the rest are standing gazing listlessly about ; as the boat approaches, a general low cackling takes place, a good many of the sleepers get up and begin to look about, and a few of those already on their legs begin to waddle away from the water's edge. As you approach nearer, all begin to walk slowly away, and, as a rule, if you persist in coming within twenty yards, and coming on quicker than they can walk, they rise and fly ; or if you stand up in the boat or make any sudden noise, they will equally take the wing ; but if you drift quietly down on them, they will let you come within twenty or thirty yards without quitting the bank. The first gun fired, the din that rises from a flock of 300 or 400 (and I have carefully counted and estimated, glass in hand, flocks containing fully treble the latter number,) is incredible ; their cries, mingled with the flappings of their wings, render it impossible to make one's-self heard for a brief space until they get well on the wing. Then they will circle round and round over head whilst the dead are being picked up, and the winged, which always take the water, swim well, and dive fairly, are being hunted down, uttering the most clamorous cries, and not unfrequently returning within shot.

A tremendous chase a slightly wounded bird will often lead you—your boat, a rough native affair, square or nearly so at both ends, and propelled by two crazy paddles, which are always giving way some where, whenever you want the *rowers* to give way. If the bird heads up stream and you have the wind against you also, you may have to give the chase up for the time, but later in the afternoon, when the wind has dropped, as it almost always does in the cold weather towards evening, you are sure to find your friend sitting somewhere solitary a mile or so up-stream by the water's edge, unless he has been made away with *en-route* by some Crocodile or Eagle. Once, and once only, I saw a "Mugger," or snub-nosed Crocodile, engulf a wounded Goose in its huge jaws and disappear ; but both Bonelli's Eagle and the Ring-tailed Fishing Eagle (*Haliaëtus leucoryphus*) constantly carry off wounded birds even of this large species. The Ring-Tail is by far the most troublesome in this repect. If anywhere he spy a wounded Goose, or other water bird, he is down on him, or after him, in a moment. The bird, even if only slightly wounded, and flying more or less well when the Eagle takes up the chase, drops at once into the water. Down swoops the Eagle, its long legs extended to the utmost, and just as his claws are within a yard of the victim's head, down dives the Goose, only to rise when its pursuer has swept past ; round comes the Ring-Tail again, down dives the Goose ; again and again these manœuvres are repeated, and at last either the Eagle gives up the chase, or the Goose, (and this, I think, is most generally the case) diving a little too slowly, gets caught by the long legs (which are each time dashed their whole length into the water) before it has got deep enough down, and the Eagle then flies slowly to the shore, bearing its prey in its talons. An Indian Grey Goose will weigh on the average 7lbs., but I have repeatedly seen good-sized Grey Geese carried off in the claws of one of these Eagles, the bird flying slowly and low over the surface of the water, but still quite steadily.

Even in lakes and broads they are very tame birds if properly handled, and a man who knows what he is about, by moving backwards and forwards slowly, can walk a flock of *Anser cinereus* before him up to any point he pleases, where some hidden comrade awaits their advent.

Provided the driver never walks *at* them, but always as if passing by them, and does not walk quicker than they can swim along lazily, and especially if he has a buffalo with him, the entire herd will progress slowly in the required direction with very little regard to wind, and, strange to say, with very little hesitation though repeatedly fired at in the same way. On one of the large jhils in the Etáwah District (Sarsai-Nawur) lived a shikarree who killed on the average a Goose a day as long as the water lasted. Every two or three days he used to lay up with his old match-lock at some convenient point, get his boy to drive the Geese, fire his shot and kill his one, two, three or more. His whole secret was, that he *never showed* himself ; he crawled away through the rushes as soon as the flock had flown away, and let the boy, after a time, work his way to where the dead birds were and pick them up. Wounded birds he never chased, (indeed one year I got a boat and shot eleven of his winged birds that had accumulated since the beginning of the season), and the herd never knew how they were shot or by whom, and I doubt not concluded that it was an inevitable dispensation of Providence. I shot six Geese I think this way, on two occasions, but gave it up as you had to lay in water and mud some three inches deep at least an hour before firing, and at least five minutes afterwards, and had a ten minutes wet crawl to and from the shooting point.

The cackling of a frightened flock is a perfect Babel of discords, but, on the other hand, the cackle of a large flock flying over head at night, high in air, is most sonorous and musical, and there are few sportsmen through whose hearts it does not send a pleasant thrill. To me it comes ever "like the odour of brine from the ocean," redolent with memories of happy boyish days, when before Drainage Commissioners and Steam Mills, Wild Geese were common enough in winter upon our East Norfolk "ronds and ma'shes."

Geese of this species tame very readily, and are often kept in captivity by natives. A broken-winged bird will be on good terms with you and the whole poultry yard within a fortnight after its capture. They stand the hot weather perfectly, and constantly breed and lay in captivity, but the young, though often hatched, rarely, if ever, reach maturity.

This species is probably the original stock from which most of the domestic Geese of Europe, as also some of our tame Geese in Northern India, have descended ; but in other parts of India the domestic Geese appear to have been derived either entirely from the Northern and Eastern Asiatic Goose, *A. cygnoides*, (no wild specimen of which has as yet been recorded within our limits, though I suspect its occurrence in North-east Assam), or to be, as Blyth says, a prolific hybrid between the derivatives of the two species. Certainly in the Calcutta market I have seen some birds that, but for a somewhat coarser and paunchier look, could not have been distinguished from wild *A. cygnoides*.

Some Wild Geese are *very* good eating, some quite unfit for the table. As I remarked in the case of the Common Crane, much depends upon how they have been living for six weeks or two months previous to being shot. Birds recently arrived from northern climes are, as a rule, not worth cooking ; even fat grain-fed birds that have been spending their days in marshes and broads are often very indifferent. Again, even grain-fed birds that have been spending their days on the banks of some pure river, like the Chambal, are not always equally good. It is well to select for yourself, when distributing the day's spoils to the camp followers, the birds of the year, weighing 6lbs. or so, and all white underneath, the old, heavy ones much marked below, though fat and well flavoured are too often tough and hard. As a rule, under like conditions, the Barred-headed or Indian Goose is better eating than the Grey Lag.

I DO not think that this species breeds within our limits. Adams, no doubt, in one of his papers says that it breeds on the Ladákh Lakes, but I have never seen it there, and in another paper he says it is the Barred-headed Goose (of which thousands do breed on these lakes) and the White-fronted Goose, (which, however, I have never seen there) that breed in Ladákh.

In more northern regions, where they do breed, Dresser tells us that " the nest is placed on the ground, and is rather loosely constructed of grass, dried flags, &c., &c., is tolerably well shaped ; but soon after the eggs are deposited, becomes trampled down out of shape. It is without any true lining until the eggs are deposited, when the female plucks down off her breast to cover the eggs, until her breast is almost denuded of its soft covering. When the nest is well cushioned with down, it is a tolerably sure sign that incubation has commenced ; and as she sits she keeps continually plucking and adding down to what is already there so that towards the end of the incubation term there is much more down there, than previously. The eggs vary in number from six to twelve, and are not rough in texture of shell, but dull and without gloss, dull yellowish white in colour when fresh, with the faintest tinge of green. In early seasons the eggs are deposited early in March; but otherwise they are frequently not laid until May; and in Finland I generally obtained them from the 1st to the 15th of June. Eggs in my collection vary in size from 3·4 by 2·25 to 3·62 by 2·38 inches. When the young are hatched they remain about a day in the nest, and are then conducted by the mother to the water; and when the nest is near the water, which is not always the case, they return to the nest every evening, and are covered during the night by the old bird."

The only Indian eggs of this species, that I have seen, were laid in captivity, early in May 1869, by the female of a pair of pinioned wild birds in the possession of Ruttun Singh, of Juggernathpur, Zillah Etáwah. The previous year the same bird had laid and hatched a single egg, and had succeeded in rearing the young one till it was destroyed by a snake when about three months old.

The two eggs laid in 1869 are moderately long ovals, the broadest portion in the centre and the two ends sloping away thence pretty equally. The shell is glossless, and of a compact, but not a very fine, texture. The eggs are spotless white, with a faint creamy or ivory tinge, and when held up against the light, seem pale pinkish yellow. They measured 3·4 and 3·55 by 2·25 and 2·45.

"When in Kashgar," Scully writes, "two eggs of *Anser cinereus* (laid by a captive bird with cut wings) were obtained on the 1st and 12th June. They are spotless white, with an ivory tinge, glossless or faintly glossy in parts, and of a compact texture. In shape they are moderately long ovals, broadest about the centre, and measure 3·37 by 2·33 and 3·21 by 2·21."

THIS SPECIES varies very much in size and weight, chiefly, I think, according to age, the birds not acquiring their full growth until the third year. The males, too, *average* larger than the females, but many of the latter are quite as big as many of the former; and all we can say is, that the very smallest are always young females, and the very largest, old ganders.

The following is a *resumé* of the measurements of nearly fifty specimens:—

Length, 30 to 35; expanse, 58 to 68; wing, 15·75 to 19·0; tail from vent, 5·75 to 7·0; tarsus, 2·5 to 3·2; bill from gape, 2·5 to 3; weight, 5 lbs. 12 ozs. to 8 lbs. 14 ozs.

As for weight, I have weighed several hundred and never yet met with one that weighed quite 9 lbs., whereas Naumann gives the weight of the *smallest* of the European orange-billed form (*vide infra*) as over 9 lbs. English, and says that they commonly weigh nearly 11 lbs., at times exceed 12 considerably, and are said to have been obtained up to 16½ lbs.

The irides are always brown; the nail of the bill sullied white, generally yellowish or pinkish white; the bill, legs, and feet vary from creamy white with only, in places, a faint tinge of pink, though pale, somewhat livid fleshy pink, to a dingy livid purplish red, and very often the bill is of one shade, the legs and feet of another. Never in any of the innumerable specimens that I have examined in India have the bills had any orange or yellow tint about them.

Season has nothing to do with the changes of colour above referred to, for I have got specimens of all types of colouring on the same day; nor could I make out that these variations were dependent on age. They seem to me to be a matter of individual complexion, and certainly often coincide with differences in the general tone of plumage.

THE PLATE is an extremely good one, but it was drawn from an European and *not* an Indian specimen, and it shows the barrings on the lower neck and breast as far more pronounced than they ever are in Indian birds, and it exhibits the bills as a more or less orange yellow, which they never are in our birds. But some European birds do apparently have the lower surface very much banded and the bills orange yellow, and these are the birds that Naumann figures as the present species, or as the Common Grey (or Grey Lag) Goose. His accuracy is unimpugnable, and he says distinctly—"bill orange, without black, naked eyelids and feet pale flesh colour." The birds are of much the same dimensions, but the yellow-billed birds weigh up to considerably over 12 lbs. English.*

Macgillivray gives the bill as yellowish orange. Yarrell, however, gives it a pink flesh colour, and this is the colour of the bill of the Lincolnshire specimen, figured by Dresser, which, in every respect, perfectly represents the birds so common in Upper India. I may say pretty positively that with us the orange-billed form does not occur. I have shot some *thousands* of Geese in India, and I have never met with any Goose of this type, with the bill coloured otherwise than as above described. It may be that there are two distinct species; if so the name *cinereus* applies to the orange-billed race, for Meyer says, "bill pale orange red." On the other hand our pinky-billed species, *rubrirostris* of Hodgson, is the *Anser vulgaris* of Pallas, who says, "bill, feet, and eyelids reddish."

Whether the two forms are specifically distinct, I cannot say; but it must be clearly borne in mind that the form we get in

---

* 12 Leipsig Pfund are equal to about 12·4 lbs. Avoirdupois.

India is *not* the one figured, but that which is less barred below and has the pinky or reddish bill.

The plumage of our birds varies a good deal. In some, which I take to be the young, the lower breast and the whole abdomen to vent are pure white; in many they are strongly tinged with sandy or orange; in others very thickly and conspicuously mottled with brownish black. The head and neck vary from pale ashy or earthy brown to dark clove brown; in most there is a mingled white and orange patch on the forehead. In some there is a similar spot at the base of the upper mandible on each side, just above the gape. Often in birds killed just before they leave us in March or April, most of the feathers of the head and cheeks are obscurely tipped with orange, and traces of this are seen on the whole neck. I note that most of our birds have a tiny patch of white on the centre of the chin.

In some specimens the breast and abdomen are so closely blotched and mottled with black or blackish-brown, and pale rusty buff, (the former predominating,) as to leave no other colour visible. The black markings will sometimes continue to within an inch of the vent, the pale rust colour to 2½ inches beyond this. In some specimens the gathering of the feathers of the upper neck into parallel longitudinal ridges is most marked; in others it is quite wanting. In some the cap and back of the upper neck are conspicuously darker; in some they are absolutely uniform in colour with the rest of the neck. Generally the whole tone of the plumage varies much more than it usually does in wild birds, or than it does in any other Goose with which I am acquainted; and though the brownest is never so brown as either *segetum*, *brachyrhynchus*, *albifrons* or *minutus*, and the greyest never so grey as *indicus*, still some are very much darker and browner, and some very much paler and greyer than others.

AS SOME difficulty is experienced by sportsmen in discriminating the different species of Geese, I subjoin a short table which may be useful, although I should hope that our plates will, as a rule, prove sufficient:—

Name.	Colour of nail of Bill.	Colour of rest of Bill.	Colour of legs and feet.	Wing.	Bill at front from margin of feathers to tip of nail.
The Grey Lag. (*A. cinereus.*)	White or whitish.	Varies from creamy white through fleshy pink to dingy livid purplish red.	Varies as does that of the bill.	15·75 to 19·0	2·4 to 2·8

Name.	Colour of nail of Bill.	Colour of rest of Bill.	Colour of legs and feet.	Wing.	Bill at front from margin of feathers to tip of nail.
The White-fronted Goose. (*A. albifrons*)	White or yellowish white.	Varies from livid fleshy to yellow in either case, with more or less of an orange tinge	Bright orange, sometimes tinged reddish.	15·0 to 17·0	1·7 to 1·9
The Dwarf Goose. (*A. erythropus.*)	Whitish.	Varies from reddish to livid fleshy (? at times from yellow to orange.)	Fleshy red or pink (? at times orange.)	13 2 to 14·1	1·3
The Bean Goose. (*A. segetum*, and *allied subspecies.*)	Black.	Black, combined with orange or orange yellow in varying proportions.	Varies from yellow to orange.	16 5 to 19·5	2·0 to 2·45
The Pink-footed Goose. (*A. brachyrhynchus.*)	Black.	Black, with pink varying to red with a somewhat orange tinge.	Varies from pink and orange pink to fleshy red.	15·5 to 17·5	1·65 to 18 5
The Barred-headed Goose. (*A. indicus.*)	Blackish or black.	Orange, greenish towards nostrils.	Bright orange.	16·0 to 19·0	1·8 to 2·1

¼
ANSER SEGETUM

THE BEAN GOOSE.

Anser segetum, *Gmelin.*

Vernacular Names.—[None.]

I HAVE never seen an Indian-killed specimen of a Bean Goose,* but I have been on several occasions assured of late years of the occurrence of this species, by people whom I believe able to recognize it, or at any rate the sub-group to which it belongs; and Blyth distinctly states, (*Ibis*, 1868) that Mr. Gould has a skin of the Common Bean Goose, procured in the Deccan.

I say sub-group advisedly, because, so far as I can judge, there are several Bean Geese with orange feet, and orange and black bills, differing in size, tone of colour, size and shape of bill, amount and distribution of black on the bills, *viz.*, *arvensis*, *segetum*, *obscurus*, *serrirostris*, *middendorffi*, &c., of which the first, second, and fourth, at any rate, are very easily separable.

Our artist has figured *arvensis* (commonly confounded by English writers with *segetum*). The true *segetum* has much more of the bill black—in fact all black, but a broad orange band across it, not unlike in position, but rather larger than the pink or red band on the bill of *brachyrhynchus*.

I have heard of Bean Geese from Sind, Oudh, and the Central Provinces, and Blyth, as above noticed, says, the Deccan also; but as I have seen no specimen, and as even in Europe the different species of this sub-group have not been generally discriminated, I cannot give any exact details of distribution here or elsewhere, and can only say that the distribution in Europe, Northern Africa and Northern and Central Asia of the Bean Geese as a group, seems to be very much the same as that of the Grey Lag Geese.

In Norfolk we used often to get a Bean Goose in autumn and winter, and birds of this sub-group are pretty abundant visitors at these seasons to many parts of the British Isles, where, however, they are not known to breed. There is no country in Europe where Bean Geese do not occur on passage or during

---

* It would be interesting to learn how David and Oustalet (Ois. d. l. Chine, 491 have ascertained that this species "*est fort commune dans l'Inde.*"!

the winter; and in the northernmost portions of Norway, Sweden, and Russia they breed. They occur in Iceland on the one hand, in Madeira on the other and throughout Northern Africa, but they have not apparently been observed in Egypt on the North-East, though, as they occur in Asia Minor and Palestine, they will probably, sooner or later, be met with in Lower Egypt also. They are found on the Caspian and in Turkestan, (where Severtzoff separated the particular large form he met with as *middendorffi*,) throughout Siberia, (in the northern portions of which they breed), in China (where Père David says, they are the commonest species of Goose that visits that country,) and in Japan.

OF THE habits of this species we can say little. Those of the sub-group do not differ appreciably elsewhere from those of the Grey Lags, and as for any peculiarities in the particular species or sub-species that visits India, we have yet to find out which this is. Dresser, who treats them all as one species, says:—

"Except that this Goose is said to affect more inland localities, it differs but little in habits from its allies. With us in England it appears in the late autumn, and remains on our coast for the winter, usually flying tolerably far inland to feed, and returning to the coast in the evening. These birds are extremely cautious, and carefully examine the surrounding country before they alight; and even then they post a sentinel, who gives notice directly there is the least sign of any danger. They usually feed in large open fields or pastures, and eat tender grass, young wheat, and other plants, as well as grain and the roots of various sorts of grasses.

"The Bean Goose swims with ease, and sits buoyantly on the water; but it rises on the wing rather heavily, and its flight is not very swift, though direct and steady. Its cry, though harsh when uttered close to one, is by no means unpleasant when heard at a distance, and does not differ much from the call of the other Geese. It not unfrequently flies and feeds at night; but, as a rule, it prefers to feed at early dawn."

SO TOO of the nidification we can say nothing precise. Dresser remarks:—

"This Goose certainly breeds in North Finland, but I never succeeded in finding its nest. A forester, who had taken its eggs, told me that it does not in the least differ from the Grey Lag in breeding habits, and, like that species, makes its nest in some marshy locality. Mr. Aschan found it breeding in Northern Savolax, and says, that on the 15th June he came across a brood of six or seven young ones with the two old birds, on a small brook in a forest above Hankalampi Träsk, and caught two of the former, which he reared. Late in July these birds were nearly full-feathered, and early in August they could fly. They became very tame, and would follow any one so soon as they got accustomed to see people.

"Von Middendorff saw the first on the Bogonida (in 70° North Latitude) on the 14th April (O. S.); and they settled down for nidification on the tundras of Taimyrland. He found a nest containing eggs on the 1st July; and on the 17th of that month the Bean Geese began to moult on the Taimyr. In South-east Siberia he saw the first near Anginsk on the 23rd April; and the return migration commenced on the 30th August on the south coast of the Sea of Ochotsk. It breeds, he adds, in the Stanowoi Mountains and on the Great Schantar Island. Von Middendorff says, that the nest he found on the Taimyr was in the hollow in the top of a high tussock close to the river, about two fathoms above the water, and was a mere lining of old grass bents and a little down to the hollow.

"I have eggs of the Bean Goose which are like those of the Grey Lag Goose, but rather smaller in size, and slightly less rough in grain of shell."

Which sub-species these several quotations may refer to, (assuming, as I do, that there probably are two or more such) it is impossible now to decide.

AS TO DIMENSIONS I will reproduce those given by Naumann of *arvensis* and *segetum*, by Macgillivray of his *segetum* (probably *arvensis*), by Swinhoe of *serrirostris*, the sub-species most likely to visit us, and by Severtzoff of *middendorffi*.

	Naumann.		Macgillivray.	Swinhoe.	Severtzoff.
	arvensis.	*segetum.*	*segetum.*	*serrirostris.*	*middendorffi.*
Length ...	30·6 to 32·0	25·0 to 28·0	31	31·5	33·42 to 34·33
Expanse ...	59·3 to 63·0	59·3 to 66·6	64	...	64·0 to 64·58
Wing ...	17·25 to 19·5	16·7 to 17 7	18·5	18·5	....
Tail ...	5·2 to 5·65	4·9 to 5·1	5·5	7·0	....
Tarsus ...	3·1 to 3·3	2·8	3·17	3·4	....
Bill from gape	... ...	......	...	2·6	....
Culmen ...	2·3 to 2·45	2·0 to 2·28	2·33	...	....
Weight ...	7lbs. to 10lbs.	5·28lbs to 9lbs	...	...	10lbs to 10·5lb.

In very old specimens of *arvensis* the bill is black and orange as shown in our plate; but in younger specimens of this larger form there is more black on the sides and on the base of the bill, but never, Naumann affirms, nearly so much as in *segetum*, in which the black is distributed much as in our plate of *brachyrhynchus*, only that the coloured ring is orange, not carmine, and is a little further back on the bill.

In all the Bean Geese the legs and feet are a more or less orange yellow, paler in the young, more orange in the old; the claws blackish brown; and the irides deep brown.

THE PLATE is a very fair representation of one of the Bean Geese. These may be distinguished at once from the Grey Lags by their black and orange bills; but, as already mentioned, the particular species figured is, I think, *arvensis* and not the true *segetum*, which is smaller, besides having much more black on the bill. It may be that, as Bechstein says, the older and more mature birds lose a good deal of the black on the bill, and so become *arvensis*; but this is not Naumann's view, and Naumann, who studied every species carefully in life, is rarely in error in such matters.

ANSER BRACHYRHYNCHUS

THE PINK-FOOTED GOOSE.

Anser brachyrhynchus, *Baillon.*

Vernacular Names.—[?]

THE Pink-footed Goose is so extremely rare in this country that it can at present only be accounted a rare winter straggler to the northern portions of Continental India.

Blyth mentions having seen a picture, undoubtedly of this species, taken from a specimen obtained in the Punjab. Colonel Irby records having seen a specimen of this species, which had been killed at the Alumbágh, (near Lucknow,) in January 1858. In January 1864 I saw a pair of this species on a sandbank in the Jumna, in the midst of a huge flock of Grey Lags, amongst which, as I looked down on them from a cliff above, they were conspicuous by their smaller size, clove-brown colour (that is what they looked at a distance) and very pink feet. I went across the river, and after much trouble succeeded in shooting the pair, which proved to be the Pink-footed Goose, with which I had been familiar at home. Colonel Graham assures me that this species is not uncommon on the Brahmaputra in Assam.

We have no other record of its occurrence in India.

Elsewhere its range is extremely ill-defined, it having been long confused with other species. It is a pretty abundant visitant to the British Isles, breeds in Iceland and Spitzbergen,* and occurs throughout Northern Europe. It probably extends to Central Europe and Northern Asia, but no reliable information exists on this subject ; all we do know for certain is, that it occurs in Japan.

THE HABITS of this species do not differ, so far as we know, from those of the Grey Lag Geese. No one has observed them in this country, nor do I find anything worthy of notice recorded of them by European writers, except that their voice

* "In Spitzbergen the Pink-footed Goose has been met with in Wide Bays, Latitude 79°35″ north, and it probably occurs all along the West Coast. It is most numerous in Ice Sound."—*Newton.*

differs from that of the Bean Goose in being sharper in tone, the note being also more rapidly repeated.

AS TO ITS nidification, Dresser remarks: "Of its breeding habits but little, comparatively speaking, is known, and it is only known with certainty to breed in Iceland and Spitzbergen. Professor Malmgren, who obtained its eggs in the latter Island, says that it is exceedingly shy and wary. In the early summer it is to be seen in small flocks on moss-covered lowlands near the sea, or on rocky precipices, where there is vegetation here and there; but in the breeding season it is seen in pairs. When moulting, it frequents fresh-water swamps, and later on, when collected in flocks, it is to be met with near the coast.

"Its nest is placed in prominent situations on high rocks, or platforms on steep cliffs, often close to a river, or in some grass-covered place, and sometimes on high cliffs close to the sea on the inner fiords. The nest is so situated that the bird can have an uninterrupted view from it of the country round, and can readily see if an intruder approaches or danger threatens. Hence it is difficult to shoot this shy bird even at its nest, for the gander is extremely watchful, and directly any one approaches warns his mate by uttering a clear whistling cry. In June the female lays four or five eggs, which are hatched about the 10th to the 15th July, and both parents assist in taking care of the young. I possess a single egg of this Goose, obtained on the Swedish Expedition to Spitzbergen, which is pure white, resembling the egg of *Anser cinereus*, but is rather smaller, and the grain of the shell is somewhat smoother."

UNFORTUNATELY I neither measured, nor preserved my specimens. After my large collections and Library had been destroyed in the Mutiny in 1857, I did not recommence collecting until 1866. So I can only quote dimensions from European authors:—

Length, 26 to 30; expanse, 58 to 62; wing, 15·5 to 17·5; tail, 5 to 6; tarsus, 2·3 to 2·55; bill from gape, 1·65 to 1·85; weight, old males, 6 lbs.; females, 5 lbs.; young, 4·5 to 4·75 lbs.

Bill black or blackish at base and tip, including the nail; the intermediate portions pink to bright carmine, and sometimes more or less orange. When this latter is the case the colouration approaches that of the true *segetum*, but the much smaller and conspicuously narrower bill of the present species would distinguish it at any time. The legs and feet are fleshy to purplish pink, again at times with an orange tinge; the claws blackish, paler at base; irides hazel.

THE PLATE conveys, on the whole, a very fair idea of the species, but the banding about the base and sides of the neck and breast, instead of being so conspicuous as in the figure, is often little more than indicated.

P Walter Chromo Lith. Hatton Garden London

ANSER ½ ALBIFRONS.

THE WHITE-FRONTED OR LAUGHING GOOSE.

Anser albifrons, *Scopoli.*

Vernacular Names.—[ ]

THOUGH doubtless a rare species, the White-fronted or Laughing Goose is still a regular and certain cold-season visitant to the submontane tracts of Continental India, straggling occasionally further south.

I know now of its occurrence, in several rivers of the Punjab, near Attock, Jhelum, Wazirabad, and Gurdaspur ; in the Ganges and Jumna in the Sahâranpur and Moozuffernugger Districts ; in the north of Oudh, and Col. Graham says that they are found right up the valley of Assam.

I shot three specimens on the Jhelum below Shahpur, and I saw a pair on the Indus betwein Sehwan and Kotree. I have a specimen killed a few miles south of Lucknow.

Outside our limits this species seems to range throughout Northern and Central Asia. We hear of it on the Caspian, in Western Turkestan, Yárkand, Siberia, Mongolia, China, and probably Japan, but it has not as yet been recorded from Afghanistan, Beluchistan, or Persia beyond the littoral of the Caspian.

Westwards, it is common in parts of Asia Minor and in Egypt, and North-east Africa, of course as a winter visitant only, and it occurs more or less throughout Europe and Northern Africa, as a summer or winter visitant or on migration, according to situation.

In Greenland probably, and throughout North America—and it has been asserted in Japan also—a barely separable race of this species (distinguished as *A. gambeli)* occurs, which scarcely appears entitled to specific rank.

Admitting the specific identity of the two forms, then the range of this species might be roughly indicated as the Northern Hemisphere from about the Tropic of Cancer* to the Arctic Circle, and in Asia, at any rate, well inside this latter.

* Dresser remarks that V. Heuglin surmises that this species scarcely crosses the *Equator !* Heuglin, I submit, says, nothing of the kind. He uses the word "Wendekreis," which here means the *Tropic of Cancer.*

DURING THIRTY years I have, myself, only twice met with this species, and I have only once shot it.

On the 27th of November 1874, when boating down the Jhelum, and when about half way between Shahpur and Jhang, I caught sight of three Geese on a sand bank on the river, which, looking somewhat like Grey Lags, yet struck me as being both browner and smaller than this species. This was about 8 A.M. I took a small boat and worked from up-stream very carefully down on to the party, and succeeded in getting to within about fifty yards, when they rose, and I knocked two down with loose No. 3 shot out of the right barrel of a long double No. 10 bore, and the third, with a green (wire) cartridge, No. 2 shot, with the left. When I first saw them, the three were seated close together at the water's edge ; no other Geese were near ; but a small knot of Mallard were feeding on the brink about fifty yards lower down. The Geese were very wary ; rose to their feet as soon as my skiff got within ninety or hundred yards, and walked away inland from the water's edge as I drew nearer. It was only by extreme care that I was able to get within shot.

Although I had knocked all three down, before I could load again or land to secure them, one flapped away, along the sand for some distance, and finally got on the wing and flew heavily, barely rising two yards above the surface of the water, across an arm of the river to the mainland ; where it gradually sank in a bare field. I got my glasses and saw that it was lying with its wings outspread and head down, and concluding that it was dead, I sent a boatman to retrieve it. He got up to within a few yards of it, when it suddenly stood up and flew off apparently all right. Away it flew, quite out of sight down the river. I marked the direction, followed it up, and after a long search, I found it in the water in a side arm of the river. I worked up to it most cautiously, but it rose at about hundred yards and flew off very low across the river. Following the direction, I also crossed the river, and striking inland found it, about half a mile from the river, walking about slowly amongst some bare sandhills. There was no cover, but I was able to crawl on hands and knees to within about 80 yards, beyond which the sand stretched perfectly bare and level. The moment I emerged our Goose started to rise, I fired a wire B. B. cartridge at him, the pellets of which cut the sand up all round him and rattled against his feathers, but did not impede his progress. He now flew stronger than ever, and went away inland for a good mile, but I ran to the top of a sandhill, and getting my glasses to bear, marked him down precisely between three small trees. It was by this time past midday, and very hot ; all my people were tired of plodding through the loose sand ; all objected to going further after this Goose. In the first place they declared he had flown away altogether out of sight ; in the second place they said

I might have killed a dozen Geese during the time I had wasted over this one wounded bird, which was, moreover, a very small one. There was almost a mutiny, but I had marked the bird precisely and insisted on going up to the spot. When we got there, there was no Goose—a great triumph for the men. I looked about for a few minutes; the men said, "there, we told you it flew out of sight." I said, "I know it *did* alight here just at the foot of this tree," and I turned to go back to the boats, when, as I passed the tree in question, suddenly from under a little overhanging sandcrest, not five yards from my feet, out flustered the Goose. I let him get away a suitable distance and then rolled him over, dead *at last*. This, I regret to say, is all I know of the species, and except that the note is rather more harsh and cackling than that of the Grey Lags, I do not find one single fact worthy of note recorded by European writers in regard to their habits, food, and the like.

Though I have seen so little of this species, I have had reason to believe that it is not so very rare in the sub-montane districts, especially those of the North-West Punjab; but making very allowance, I do not suppose that one bird of this species visits this Empire for every thousand of Grey Lags, or every five thousand of the Barred-headed Geese. Elsewhere it is different. Shelley says: "This is the most abundant Goose in Egypt, where it may usually be met with in flocks, but does not remain in the country later than March. When on the wing, they fly in a wedge-shaped flock, and frequently utter a loud, harsh cry, which may be heard at a considerable distance. They are generally on the move just before sunrise and sunset, and as they are very regular, taking the same line of flight and feeding at the same spot each day, they may be most readily obtained by lying in wait for them. If once fired at, the flock generally leaves the neighbourhood altogether."

We cannot say certainly when this species arrives in India or when it leaves us, but probably early in November and towards the end of March. The specimens I killed had fed entirely on some species of wild rice and on tender green shoots of some grass or grain.

IN SIBERIA, Middendorff found it breeding up to the 74° North Latitude, and this is about the only authentic account we have of its nidification except in Greenland, where probably it is the slightly larger-billed American form that occurs.

They seem to lay, much like other Geese, five to seven eggs, thickly bedded in and covered with down, (which the female gradually accumulates about them as incubation proceeds,) in a good sized nest, placed on the ground near inland waters.

The eggs are said to be yellowish white, and vary from 3·0 to 3·2 in length, and from 1·95 to 2·1 in breadth.

THE DIMENSIONS of my three birds, measured in the flesh, were as follows :—

Length, 26 to 27·75 ; expanse, 52 to 55·5 ; wing, 15 to 15·75 ; wings, when closed, reached exactly to the end of tail ; tail from vent, 5·2 to 6 ; bill at front, including nail, 1·7 to 1·75 ; from gape, 1·87 to 2·0 ; tarsus, 2·45 to 2·75 ; weight, 4 lbs 5 ozs. to 5 lbs 2 ozs.

Legs and feet bright orange ; nails pinky or greyish white ; bill pale livid fleshy, in one tinged orange on the culmen, in another similarly tinged on the nares and base of lower mandible ; nail whitish or pale yellowish white ; irides pale brown.

European specimens, that I possess, seem to be larger, the wings running to 17 inches.

THE PLATE, taken from two of the Jhelum specimens, is admirable ; *O si sic omnes* !

Specimens, however, vary a good deal ; one, which appears to be an adult male, has the whole chin white, as is also the broad band on the forehead and on each side of the upper mandible. A female has only one single feather white at the point of the chin, and the white band at each side of the upper mandible is much parrower ; a third, also a female, but as I take it a young one, has the head and neck much paler brown, no white at all on the chin, and the band, both on the forehead and at the sides of the upper mandible, very narrow. The lower surface, too, varies very much ; in one it is pale greyish white, with only a few comparatively small black mottled patches on the abdomen ; in another, the mottled patches are so numerous and large that the black decidedly preponderates over the greyish white ; in a third, there is scarcely anything but black. In one specimen, which I have from Oudh, the white frontal band is 1·15 broad ; in the adult male above-mentioned, it is 0·85 broad ; in the adult female it is 0·6, and in the young female only 0·3. In all these it is a band stretching straight across the whole forehead, not running up on to the crown in a broad longitudinal band as it does in the Dwarf Goose.

1/4
ANSER MINUTUS

THE DWARF GOOSE.

Anser erythropus, *Linné.*

Vernacular Names.—[?]

THIS species is so rare a straggler to India, that I have never myself seen a living wild specimen.*

Colonel Irby tells us that, on the 24th of October 1859, he killed two and saw a third Dwarf Goose near Seetapore, in Oudh. Mr. A. Anderson obtained specimens near Hurdui (Oudh) and Futtehpur (North-West Provinces). Dr. Bonavia gave me a specimen procured near Lucknow. Mr. Chill sent me three specimens shot by him on the 3rd, 12th, and 29th March 1879, near Sultanpore, some 30 miles south of Delhi. We have no other record of its occurrence within our limits.

In Europe it is recorded from the more northern and central portions of that continent, extending into Turkey, Greece, the Caspian, Siberia up to its northernmost point, Mongolia, China, and Japan. It has never yet been observed in the British Isles. I do not find it recorded from Northern Africa, but towards the north-east it does occur, as Heuglin says, that there is no doubt that it occasionally strays into Lower Egypt. Mr. J. H. Gurney, junior, exhibited a specimen killed at Damietta at a meeting of the Zoo, (2nd May 1876), and Dresser mentions a specimen shot by Mr. Cavendish Taylor in Upper Egypt. It has not been recorded from any part of Turkestan.

There is no doubt that the distribution of this species is very imperfectly known at present, it having for long been confounded with *albifrons*, to which it bears a strong resemblance, and of which it is almost a perfect minature, but from which it is distinguishable at a glance, by its smaller size, its *tiny* bill, its darker general tone of plumage and much darker brown rump, and also, in adults, by the much greater distance

---

* Dresser quotes, as referring to this species, the remarks recorded by me in S. F., I., 259, in regard to *Anser albifrons*. I called it *A. erythropus* then, no doubt, but *erythropus* of Fleming, which is *albifrons* (a name I also quoted,) and not *erythropus* of Linné. Moreover I distinctly called it the White-fronted and *not* the Dwarf Goose, and gave dimensions !

to which the white on the forehead extends backwards on to the crown in the Dwarf.

VERY LITTLE seems known about the habits of this species. Here also the extraordinary discrepancies in the alleged colouring of the soft parts, as stated by various authorities, might lead some to suspect that two species have been confounded.

However, assuming that Naumann's Dwarf Goose with yellow bill and legs is the bird we get here in India, (even though it may not prove to be the veritable *erythropus*,) we learn that this species (which is about the size of a Brahminy Duck, though with a much smaller bill and head) is much bolder and less shy than the other Geese. With its proportionally longer and more pointed wings it flies much faster, twisting and turning far more rapidly. It is less noisy than the other species, with one or other of which it often keeps company, not indeed joining parties, but keeping near them, and maintaining the same interval of separation whether flying or on the ground. Perhaps, too, this species spends more of its time in the water, and less on land, than its larger congeners already noticed. The food seems to be similar to that of the other Geese—grain and green shoots.

IT CERTAINLY breeds in Lapland, where Wolley, Dann and others have taken the eggs, from nests of the usual Goose-nest type. They lay five to seven or eight eggs, of the usual broad regular oval shape, glossless, of a dull creamy white colour, and averaging about 2·9 in length by 2·0 in breadth.

THE FOLLOWING are the dimensions, taken from the skin of my Lucknow specimen:—

Length, (*about*) 21·5; wing, 14·05; tail from vent, 4·7; tarsus, 2·2; bill from gape, 1·41.

To judge by their present appearance, the bill has been orange, tinged with carmine; its nail whitish, and the legs and feet orange yellow.

Of Mr. Chill's birds, the dimensions (taken from the skins) are:—

Sex.	Length	Wing.	Tail.	Tarsus.	Bill from gape.	Bill at front from margin of feathers.
♂	24·23	14·91	4·2	2·48	1·59	1·36
♂?	21·5	14·55	3·8	2·49	1·56	1·26
♀	21·75	14·0	3·9	2·39	?	1·16

Of the first male, the bill appears to have been red, the legs and feet orange; of the second, (which I suspect may have been missexed), bill, legs and feet pale yellow; of the female, bill yellow, legs and feet red.

But from dry specimens, no safe conclusions as to colours of soft parts can ever be drawn. According to Linné's original description, the bill should be dingy flesh colour, the feet sanguineous. Gerbe and Degland give both bill and feet as a grey reddish, or flesh colour, but notice that some authorities describe the bill as yellowish, and the feet as orange yellow, and surmise that these differences may be due to age.* But Naumann does not lead this to be inferred, at any rate where the feet are concerned. He says :—"The colour of the bill is in the young, before the first autumn moult, a reddish grey; the nail blackish; later this latter becomes greyish white, and the bill pale orange yellow; in old birds the bill is lively reddish yellow or orange; the nail yellowish reddish white. There is never any trace of black upon the bill.

"The naked edges of the eyelids are dirty yellow in the young, orange in the old; the irides are dark brown.

"The feet are in the young a pale dirty yellow, tending towards orange; in the old a lively orange yellow or almost orange red. The claws pale horn colour, dark brown towards the tips."

He gives the following dimensions :—

"Length, 19·5 to 21·0; expanse, 39·0 to 42·5; wing, 13 to 14·1; tail, 2·85 to 3·25; tarsus, 2·3 to 2·4."

In some younger birds the dimensions are even smaller than these.

Never having seen a freshly-killed specimen of the species, and really knowing nothing about it, I must leave it to future observers to settle whether two species are here confounded, or whether the differences in the colours of the soft parts are due to age, or what is more likely, to *season*. Linné got the birds in Lapland, &c., in the breeding season. Naumann and others have obtained them only in the winter.

THE PLATE is fair, but the specimen figured is only just adult, and consequently shows only a narrow band of white on the forehead. According to Naumann, the young birds entirely want this white band, which gradually develops with age, and extends upwards and backwards on to the crown as a more or less longitudinal band, the very old birds having nearly the whole anterior half of the head white.

---

* Since this was written, Dresser's article on this species has appeared. In this he gives, "bill dull white, with a flesh tinge; nail pale horn colour; legs and edge of eyelids orange yellow." But he has not worked out the Geese in the exhaustive manner in which he has dealt with some other groups; he does not seem to have noticed that there are either a number of recognizable sub-species, or that there are very marked seasonal differences in the colours of the soft parts, which require notice and explanation.

$\frac{1}{4}$ ANSER INDICUS

THE BARRED-HEADED GOOSE.

Anser indicus, *Latham.*

Vernacular Names.—[Birooa, Kureyee-Hans, Ráj-hans (Hindee), *Doab, North-West Provinces;* Paria, *Nepal Terai;* Nang-pa (Ladakhi), *Ladakh;* Dod Sarle hake,* (Canarese) *Mysore;* Neer-bathoo, *Coimbatore;* Kangnai, *Munipur;* Badi-hans; *Chittagong;*]

THE Barred-headed or Indian Goose appears to occur as a regular cold-weather visitant in most parts of Continental India, and as an occasional straggler to many parts of Peninsular India; but its exact distribution is still very uncertain.

As far as I can ascertain, it occurs, *in suitable localities*, throughout the Punjab, (to the extreme North-West at Murdan, where I myself obtained a specimen), Rajputana, the North-West Provinces and Oudh, and Bengal† west of the Brahmaputra, Chota Nagpur, Ganjam (at the Chilka Lake in which it is extremely abundant) and the Central Provinces, where, close to Kamptee, Colonel McMaster obtained it.

I have no record as yet of its occurrence in Tippera or any part of Assam, but it must surely occur there, as Godwin-Austen obtained it at the Logtak Lake in Munipur, and Mr. Damant says, it is common in the latter, and Mr. H. Fasson tells me that it occurs in large flocks in salt marshes along the Chittagong Coast.

---

* This name which merely means, Major Mc. Inroy tells me, "large Duck," is, he says, indiscriminately applied to all the Geese and larger Ducks.

† Of its distribution in Bengal, I am by no means certain. I have observed it everywhere along the course of the Ganges and in several places in the neighbourhood of Calcutta.

Mr. Rainey notes it from Jessore, where it is rare. Tickell says:—"They supply in Bengal the place of the Grey Lag, and are met with well within the influence of the tides. I have seen numbers of them at the mouth of the Hooghly, below Diamond Harbour."

Cripps records it from Dacca and Faridpur, and I have a specimen from Purneah; but Tickell says, "all along Tirhoot, Chupra, and the Terai, they appear to be unknown, and Hodgson does not mention this Goose amongst his Birds of Nepal."

This may be partially correct, but as it certainly occurs in Goruckpur and the Nepal Terai, and everywhere along the Ganges, it must occur in Chupra, and I shall be much surprised if it does not also occur in Tirhoot.

In Sind, where it is much rarer than the Grey Lag, it is almost confined to the course of the Indus, and Doig says, he never met with it on the Eastern Narra. I have no record of its occurrence in Cutch, Káthiáwar, Gujarat, the Konkan, or the Deccan. Even in the southern part of the Central Provinces, it seems rare, and south of this it is, as a rule, extremely rare. But Major Mc.Inroy tells me, that it occurs in large numbers in the Chitaldroog District of Mysore, and he has heard that it is also found along the banks of the Kaveri, south-east of Mysore, while Mr. Theobald has shot it in Coimbatore.* Though it has not, I believe, ever been procured in Ceylon, Jerdon in his first Catalogue, (Madr. J. of Science, &c., 1840, 218,) remarks:—"This Goose is not so common in Southern India as it appears to be in Bengal and the more northern provinces; but *I have seen it in pairs in August, within a few miles of Cape Comorin,* and once or twice in flocks of fifteen or twenty in large tanks, on the central table land." The passage italicised is inexplicable, as before August, every Barred-Goose has left India for more temperate climes; but Jerdon's subsequent statement, in the Birds of India, "that he had seen *a pair* at the southern extremity of the continent," and that these were perhaps wounded birds, may help to explain the matter.

During the cold weather these birds occur, not only in the plains, but far up into the Himalayas in the valleys of the large rivers, often to elevations of 4,000 and 7,000 feet, in the lakes of Cashmere, &c., &c.

I am not aware that this species has been observed in any part of British Burma (Tickell says it is quite unknown in Arakan); but Dr. Anderson tells us, that "occasionally large flocks of this bird were observed at various parts of the Irrawaddy above Mandelay, and on the sandbanks in the Tapeng, and on the old rice flats behind the village."

This species occurs and breeds in all the lakes of Tibet in the eastern portions of Western Turkestan, and in Yárkand. Major Biddulph writes to me: "I saw one on the small Pamir Lake on our way back in May, and also all along the Aktash Stream in the same month."

It was obtained at Lake Baikal by Dybowski, (and probably occurs throughout Central and Southern Siberia), and in the Kokonor in Chinese Tibet by Prjevalski.

---

* Mr Albert Theobald says:—"I have not seen this Goose south of Coimbatore. I have shot them in the Collegal Taluq only; they come at the end of November or early in December, and leave about February or March—a few stragglers being found in April in the Agaroram tank about 3 miles from Collegal. They are far from common, only a few, ten to twenty, being found in a flock.

"During the day they keep floating idly in the centre of some tank or river, and as soon as it gets dusk, they all leave it and go to the paddy fields to pick up the fallen grain after harvesting, and even pick the grain off the standing crop. They return to the tanks or river at 6 or 7 in the morning."

The latter remarks :—"As far as we can judge from our observations, the northern limit of the distribution of this bird is formed by the Kokonor basin and the river Tetunga ; and the same localities are probably also the eastern boundary, as this species does not occur in China proper."

Of course Lake Baikal is a thousand miles north of the Kokonor, but what Prjevalski's researches seem to show, is, that from the Kokonor it neither goes eastwards into China nor north-eastwards into Mongolia.

Broadly speaking, we may define the distribution of this species as India and Independent Burma in the winter, and Central Asia, due north of these up to about the 55° North Latitude in summer.

I CANNOT remember ever seeing the Barred-headed Goose in the Doab before the 15th of October* and in the North-West Provinces the majority do not arrive until quite the close of that month. In the North-West Punjab they appear a little earlier I believe, and further south they are later.

In the Doab, the great majority leave by the end of March, but I have shot them in Etáwah as late as the 10th of April, and near Jhelum on the 20th of that month. Further south they leave a good deal earlier.

Their movements are, I apprehend, a great deal governed by the harvest ; as soon as all the crops are cut and carried, and the stubbles have been pretty well gleaned, they disappear.

Taking Upper India as a whole, this species enormously outnumbers all the other species of Geese put together. I think that at least five of the Barred-heads visit India to every one of the Grey Lags, and as for all the rest of the Geese they are apparently so rare that when one comes to consider numbers, they are not worth speaking about.

---

* According to Tickell they reach Bengal too about this time. I rather doubt their getting to Diamond Harbour, where he says he saw so many, as early as this, but his remarks are interesting and I reproduce them. He says :—"They are first noticed in Bengal about the middle of October, flying like the Crane in single diagonal (or echelon) lines, or in two lines, forming an acute angle. At such times their mingled voices sound like ill-blown clarionets, each emitting a single note. As they wend along in the air the leading bird is seen every four or five minutes to drop to the rear, its place being immediately filled by the next one, who is in turn relieved by the next, and so on. This movement is to be seen amongst Cranes, Pelicans, Spoonbills, Swans, and other birds which perform long migratory voyages ; from which it would seem that the leading bird meets with greater resistance from the air than do the succeeding files, and thus requires to be relieved after a certain time from his post.

"When about to settle, the line breaks up, and the birds mingling together sweep round in circles, approaching nearer and nearer to the earth, till, with a great flapping of wings, they settle. When on the ground they preserve something like order, keeping one or more sentries on the look-out while the rest are grazing. The flight of this bird is like that of some of the larger Ducks, with a stiffly outstretched neck ; but its larger flapping wings, moved with slower strokes, serve readily to distinguish it at any distance. During the day they repose near the water's edge, on sand-flats ; and in such open situations it is vain to attempt approaching them, unless in a native *dinghee*, which must be so managed as to appear to be passing heedlessly."

Compared with the Grey Lags, this species is far more essentially a river, or very large lake bird. I do not mean to say that you never find them in swamps or moderate-sized broads; on the contrary, I have repeatedly seen them in such, but I mean that for one that you meet with in these, you will meet with hundreds on or near the banks of rivers.

Very few people have any idea of the truly countless myriads of this species that visit Upper India, because very few people, now-a-days, boat steadily along our larger rivers. Indeed, they rarely see these except in the neighbourhood of some large town, or where they are crossed by some regular line of traffic, and of course in such places few Geese are to be seen.

In a length of ten miles on the Jumna, immediately below its junction with the Chambal at Bhurey, I have seen more than ten thousand Geese in a morning. Large flocks of from one to five hundred or more on one or other bank, or on some sandbank, every quarter of a mile at least. One must boat steadily down one of the larger rivers in the Punjab or the North-West Provinces in December, January, or February, in order to realize the vastness of the multitudes of the Barred-headed Geese that yearly visit us.

Their habits are similar to those of the Grey Lags. Where frequently disturbed, they feed inland only at night; where rarely molested, they will be found feeding up to eight or nine in the morning and again long before sunset. The day, or at all events the warmer hours of this, they pass by the water's side. They feed in fields, preferentially in those in the immediate neighbourhood of the larger rivers, browsing on the young wheat or waddling awkwardly amongst the heavy clods, amidst which the gram grows, to devour the young shoots, or later the ripening pods of this vetch. All vetches, lentils, grain, tender grasses, and herbs, seem equally to suit their taste, and so long as these are available they eat nothing else, and by the end of December (thin and poor as they usually are when they first arrive), they are generally in fine condition.

All I said as to the edibility of the Crane and the Grey Goose applies equally to this species. You will find them good or bad eating according to their condition and antecedents. Here, too, you should always select for the table the young birds, which, though quite fat, do not weigh above 5 ℔s. at the outside.

As for shooting, they afford any *quantity* of this when attacked by water in the manner which I have fully explained when treating of the Grey Lag. I have bagged 44 of this species, besides Grey Lags, Cranes, Ducks, &c., in a single day on the Jumna just below its junction with the Chambal. But the *quality* of the sport afforded is a matter of opinion, and some soon come to consider it monotonous. To me this river shooting is always a delight. I float luxuriously over the glittering water fanned by the fresh cool breeze, always blowing along the valleys of our larger rivers. Around me are all my little luxuries; in my lips the peaceful pipe—guns of various sizes ranged orderly at hand. Now an old Pea Fowl or a Ravine Deer, an Otter, a Crocodile or a big Turtle on the banks, offers a fascinating if difficult rifle shot; now a little swampy bend, certain to harbour a few Snipe, or a tempting gram patch, just under the cliffs, a sure find for two or three brace of Grey Partridges, invite one to land for a few moments. Ever and anon a flock of Cranes, or a knot of Fowl of one kind or another, afford scope for careful circumventing, and whenever nothing else appears, there is always a flock of Geese to work judiciously. And, simple as it may seem, it takes much practice and a good deal of judgment to make the most out of a flock; any one may knock over two or three, but to get ten to sixteen with the first shot, requires a careful appreciation of distance, whilst still in a reclining position, an accurate perception of the exact moment at which to fire, attention to the slope and set of the ground and to a dozen other minor points, all of which deprive this sport of the purely mechanical character it may at first sight seem to assume, while the subsequent chase after the winged birds adds a not unpleasant additional element of excitement, especially, when towards noon, the wind rises and careful management of the clumsy native "*doonga*" is necessary to avoid a ducking.

On land again, whilst feeding, they may be stalked just like, but more easily than, the Grey Lag Goose, and Mr. Reid (who clearly knows nothing of river-shooting) writes to me enthusiastically of another method of killing these Geese. He says:—

"The Barred-headed Goose is unquestionably the most abundant of all, and is met with all over the Lucknow Division, generally in fairly-sized and frequently in immense flocks. During the night, like the Grey Goose, they collect in countless numbers on their favourite feeding grounds, and break up into companies as they leave them in the morning for the larger jhils or rivers where they repose during the day.

"The number of sportsmen in this country who waste their energies and powder in unsuccessful attempts to shoot this and the Grey Goose in the day time, is sufficiently large to justify some general observations on the subject.

"At the best of times, and under the most favourable circumstances, it is unprofitable work* to attempt to shoot Geese during the day. In the early morning, when leaving their feeding grounds, which they generally do when the villagers commence to knock about, they may be intercepted and shot as they fly leisurely along, at no great height, to the large jhils or rivers to which they invariably resort for the day, and where, in spite of duck guns and punts, they will tease and worry the gunner.

* Quite so, if you don't know how to do it—A. O. H.

"The best plan of all is undoubtedly to shoot them after dusk, or by moon-light. To be successful, it is necessary to ascertain beforehand where they go to feed at night. The villagers will readily give this information, but it is just as well to know that shallow, weedy jhils, with a foreshore of mud and slush, are favourite resorts, especially if the corn fields around them are nice and green. Having taken up his position on the mud at sunset (their foot-prints and feathers will indicate the spot where they generally settle) all the sportsman has to do is to await their arrival patiently. They will soon put in an appearance, and as gang after gang arrives and hovers above him within easy shot, he will only have himself to blame if he does not massacre them right and left. In this way, with an ordinary gun, I have shot as many as thirty between sunset and 7-30 P.M."

Prjevalski indicates yet another method by which these Geese may be shot, which I confess never occurred to me, though I have attracted Black Buck in this way. He says:—

"This Goose is also very curious, and I several times shot it by performing the following manœuvre.—As soon as I noticed a pair flying, I at once lay down on the ground and commenced waving my hat at them. The Geese came usually quite close to me then. Altogether it is very tame; but when pursued much by men, it gets very shy."

Indian sportsmen who try this plan will oblige me greatly by reporting the results.

The note of the Barred-headed Goose is quite distinct from that of the Grey Lag. It is sharper, harder, less sonorous, and more strident. I hardly know how to put it in words, but it is so distinct that you can never doubt, even when the flock is passing over head high in air, during the night, to which species it belongs. The two species never mingle companies; you may see half a dozen of the one, along with a flock of the other, but whether feeding, sleeping, swimming, or flying, the parties keep a little apart.

Like the Grey Lag this present species rarely takes to the water unless disturbed, but whether flying, walking, or swimming, it is a lighter built, more graceful and more active bird than the other; and though perhaps easier to stalk, it is much more difficult to drive, or walk up to a given spot, than the Grey Lag.

I have often had them in captivity; but although at the Delhi Gardens and at one are two other places I have known them to live for years, they do not stand the heat so well as the Grey Goose, and they never, I think, become quite so tame as these latter, which, once they get to know you, will trot about awkwardly at your heels like a lap-dog. None of the Geese of this species that I have ever had, have laid in captivity.

My late, much lamented friend, Mr. Damant, drew attention to the curious habit, which I have already noticed in the case of the Grey Lag, that these Geese have of skylarking, when descending to the water after feeding. He said :—

"In Manipur, I have often watched them returning from their feeding grounds to the lake where they intend to pass the day; their cry is heard before they can themselves be seen ; they then appear flying in the form of a wedge, each bird keeping his place with perfect regularity; when they reach the lake they circle round once or twice, and, finally before settling, each bird tumbles over in the air two or three times precisely like a tumbler pigeon. After they have once settled they preserve no regular formation."

THIS SPECIES breeds in thousands at the Tso-mourari Lake, and other sweet-water and salt lakes in Ladákh, and equally in all the innumerable lakes of the Thibetan Plateau.

I have never had the good fortune to obtain the eggs ; perhaps I might have found a late nest had I thought of hunting for it, but hundreds of goslings were already about, by the latter end of June, and at that time I concluded that I was too late for eggs. Drew, however, writing of an Island in the Tso-mourari, says :—

"The *island* is about half a mile from the shore, near mid-way in the length of the western side—it may be 100 yards from corner to corner in one direction and 60 yards in another ; it is of gneiss rock, rising only nine or ten feet above the water ; the soundings before given show that there is about 100 feet of water between the island and the near shore. This little place, being ordinarily undisturbed by man, is a great resort of the Gull, which in Ladákhi is called *Chagharatse ;* the surface was nearly all covered with its droppings, and there were hundreds of the young about ; most of these must have been hatched near the beginning of July. Having heard that it was a matter of interest with some ornithologists to learn about the nidification of the Wild (Barred-headed) Goose, I was on the look-out for information concerning it, and I found that this island is one of the places where it lays its eggs. I was told by the Chámpás that they find the eggs there just before the ice breaks up—say the beginning of May ; after that they have no means of reaching the island. I myself found there a broken egg, but at the time I was on the island (the last week in July), the young had all been hatched. A few days later, I followed the same inquiry in the valley of the Salt Lake, and on an earthy island in the fresh-water lake called Panbuk, I found a nest where the mother was sitting with some goslings and two eggs, one just breaking with the chick ; the other egg I measured and found to be 3¼ inches by 2¼, and very nearly elliptical in form. The nest was a slight hollow, lined with first, a few bits of a soft herb, then with feathers. I was told that these Goose eggs are found also at the edge of the Salt Lake itself."

Again Prjevalsky say :—

"We found this beautiful Goose at Lake Kokonor where the first migrants appeared on the 5th of March; and in the course of the whole month small flocks of from five to twelve in number are to be seen frequently. Also at the sources of the river Tetunga we saw some *A. indicus*, which were breeding there; and a female, which we killed on the 6th of April, was already laying.

"In spring the male chases the female on the wing, and occasionally makes peculiar darts, resembling those of our Common Raven, and when the female is shot, the male usually flies long about its dead mate, until it shares the same fate."

I HAVE measured and weighed a very large series of this species. The males average appreciably larger than the females of the same age, but they take some years to attain their maximum dimensions and weight, and many females are, therefore, as large or larger than many males, and it seems therefore useless to give the dimensions of the two sexes separately. Apparent adults varied as follows :—

Length, 27·25 to 33·5; expanse, 56 to 66; wing, 16·0 to 19·0; tail from vent, 5·0 to 7·0; tarsus, 2·5 to 3·3; bill from gape, 1·8 to 2·3; weight, 4 lbs. to 6 lbs. 14 ozs.

I have weighed I find more than a hundred; but I have never obtained one weighing quite 7 lbs.; yet Jerdon gives the weight as 7 lbs. to 8 lbs. Only two of my specimens exceeded 6 lbs. 8 ozs. The great majority are less than 6 lbs.

The legs and feet are bright orange, sometimes paler, occasionally only yellow; claws horny black; the irides deep brown; the bill orange yellow to orange, rarely only pale, lemon yellow often paler or greenish towards the nostrils; the nail black or blackish.

There is a prominent tubercle nearly half an inch long in old males, just below the carpal joint, varying in size according to sex and age, but always more prominent than in the Grey Lag, and other Geese already mentioned.

THE PLATE, though a little coarse, and on the whole rather too brown, is good, though the bill is generally more orange. The bird in the foreground is a gosling about three months old obtained in September in Tibet. This has never been figured before, and is so unlike the adult that it may be well to subjoin a description.

It differs from the adult altogether in the head and neck markings. The bill is, as in the adult, yellow, but with the nail deep brown; the legs and feet appear to have been a brownish orange; the forehead is brownish white, a little tinged with rusty ; there is a dusky line through the lores to the eyes ; the whole crown, occiput, and nape is a sooty or dusky black ; below this the back of the neck is wood brown, and the sides and front of the lower part of the neck a pale dusky greyish, mottled with whitish, this being the colour of the tips of the feathers ; most of the feathers of the breast and abdomen and lower parts generally have a pale, rusty or fulvous tinge towards the tips ; the conspicuous dark banding of the flanks is almost entirely wanting, only one dark greyish brown feather on each side having as yet made its appearance.

There is no trace of either the two distinct black head-bars or of the conspicuous white neck streak, so that the head and neck look strangely unlike those of the adult.

The tail is rather browner than in the old bird. The rest of the plumage is very similar to that of the adult, but perhaps everywhere less pure in colour.

BESIDES THE six species of Geese above enumerated, it is very probable that other species of true Geese occur within our limits.

First there is *Anser* (*Bernicla*) *ruficollis*, of which I subjoin* a description, and of which Mr. Blyth remarked :—"This is probably the species of which four were seen near Nagpur, one of which was procured—(Bengal Sporting Magazine for April 1836, p. 247.")

Then there is the large *Anser cygnoides*, very like the tame Goose of Lower Bengal, (but wanting the tubercle on the bill)—with a black bill, and orange fleshy legs and feet ; top and back of the head and neck very deep brown, and the whole upper plumage darkish brown, the feathers narrowly margined with white, and the upper tail-coverts pure white—which I have had reason to suspect occurs in Assam. But it seemed useless to

* *Anser* (*Bernicla*) *ruficollis*.

"*Adult Male in breeding-dress.*—Entire crown of head, extending from the forehead far on the back of the neck, black ; entire throat, fore-part of cheeks and a band encircling the eye, and joining the crown, also black ; a large loral patch, a spot under the eye, and a broad stripe extending backwards from the hinder part of the eye, on to the sides of the neck, and another stripe extending downwards on to the neck, and then proceeding backwards and joining the sides of the neck, pure white ; a very large auricular patch deep chestnut, entirely surrounded by the before-mentioned white line ; on the throat the black narrows in the centre of the lower portion ; the whole of the fore-part of the chest, and sides of the neck extending far backwards and forming an interrupted collar, deep brick-red ; a narrow white band encircling the whole of the fore-part of the body margined on both sides with black ; rest of the body glossy black with slight greenish reflections, excepting the edges of the wing-coverts which are greyish white, and the rump, abdomen, and sides of the body which are pure white ; the flanks are banded slightly with black ; under tail-coverts white ; under wing-coverts black ; bill and feet black ; iris dark brown. Total length 20 inches ; culmen, 1·0 ; wing, 14·5 ; tail, 6·0 ; tarsus, 2·1.

"*Female.*—In general similar to the male, but the colours very much duller." (*Dresser's Birds of Europe.*)

figure either of these until we obtained more certain information as to their occurrence within our limits.

GEESE OF ONE type or another [and there are three marked sub-divisions of these, the true Geese, to which belong all the species which we have figured, the Barnacle Geese (*Branta or Bernicla)*, and the Upland Geese (*Cereopsis*), the two former divided customarily into numerous sub-genera,] occur all over the world, and are too numerous and concern Indian readers too little to call for separate enumeration.

4

SARKIDIORNIS MELANOTUS

THE NUKHTA OR COMB DUCK.

—o—

Sarcidiornis melanonotus, *Pennant.*

—o—

Vernacular Names.—[Nukhta, *Upper India, Pánch Máhals, Deccan, &c.*; Nakwa, *Chota Nagpur*; Toopee-heydeggey, (Kole); Jutu chilluwa, (Telegu); Do'd sarle haki, (Canarese) *Mysore*; Neer-koli, *Coimbatore*; Tan-bay, (Burmese), *Pegu*; Bowkbang, (Karen).]

—o—

AT one season or another, the Nukhta* is found throughout the greater portion of the Empire. But it does not ascend the hills anywhere, and does not occur in Kashmir, Kullu, Kumaon or Nepal. I do not know of its occurrence in the Punjab, Trans-Sutlej, or in Sind, except as a rare straggler to the easternmost portions. I have no record of its appearance in Sylhet, Cachar, Tippera, Chittagong or Arakan.† It does not, to the best of my belief, extend, at present, to any part of Tenasserim† proper, and it seems doubtful whether it is found, except perhaps as a rare and accidental straggler, in the Western Sub-Ghát littoral, *viz.*, the South Konkan, the Malabar Coast, and Travancore.

In Ceylon and the entire Peninsula‡ east of the Western Ghâts, in the Central Provinces, Gujarat, Cutch, Káthiáwar,

---

* Jerdon calls this the "Black-backed *Goose*;" but it is a *Duck* and not a Goose, and I therefore reject his name which is calculated to create erroneous conceptions.

† Tickell however says: "The Knobbed Goose is tolerably common off the alluvion in Bengal, throughout the central provinces of India, and in *Arakan*, Burma, and *Tenasserim.*

In Aracan it very likely does occur, and in Tonghoo, a district of Pegu, *now* included in Tenasserim, we know that it does occur; but we have never obtained a trace of it in any part of Tenasserim proper, in fact in any part of what was Tenasserim when Colonel Tickell knew the province. Yet Tickell distinctly says, "I found them in *Tenasserim*, but nowhere numerous; also in Burma and Aracan;" and we can only surmise that during the 30 odd years that intervened between his and our ornithological explorations of Tenasserim, the bird has ceased to visit this province.

‡ Note however that in the southernmost districts of Madras, in fact those south of Mysore, it would seem to be rare. Mr. Albert Theobald has shot over and collected in most of these for years, but he writes:—

"I have only seen this Duck in this Collegal Taluq of Coimbatore, and not to the best of my belief further south. It comes here about December, and leaves again in February or March. It is very rare here, only four or five pairs coming in every year.

"It is generally found in any small lake or jhíl during the day time, but at nights they are only found in paddy fields where they go to feed on the grain, returning early to the lakes, where they keep near the reeds growing at the borders of the water. They are not wary birds and are easily shot.

in Rajputana (except in the north-western portions,) in the Punjab, Cis-Sutlej, the North-Western Provinces and Oudh, the Central India Agency, Chota Nagpur, Bengal, west of the Brahmaputra, (excluding perhaps the Sunderbans, Jessore and one or two others of the deltaic districts), the valley of Assam right up to Sadiya, and the northern two-thirds at any rate of Pegu,* it is more or less common, at one season or another, *in suitable localities.*

It is not as yet known to visit any country outside our limits, but I should expect it to be found hereafter in Upper or Independent Burma.

WITHIN THE limits above assigned there are many more or less extensive tracts where this species has never been observed, and where probably it does not occur, except accidentally. Only certain localities suit its habits, and of these many only suit it during particular portions of the year. It is not, strictly speaking, migratory; but while in some few districts it really is a permanent resident, and may be there found commonly throughout the year, in many it is only a seasonal visitant. Thus it almost entirely deserts the North-Western Provinces, Eastern Rajputana, Cutch, and the Deccan, during the dry hot season, though it is abundant in these during the rains, and in a lesser degree during the cold weather. On the other hand it is chiefly during the hotter and drier parts of the year that it is found in the damper low-lying deltaic districts of Bengal.

It is a good deal of a tree Duck, often perches on trees, generally lays in holes of trees, and it much prefers well-wooded tracts, not dense forest like the White-Winged Wood-duck, but well-wooded, level, well-cultivated country. It is a lake bird too, one that chiefly affects rush and reed-margined broads, not bare edged pieces of water like the Sámbhar Lake, and it is *comparatively* rarely met with on our larger rivers. I have shot them alike in the Ganges and the Jumna during the cold season, but it is far more common to find them in jhíls and bhíls. I have never found it in hilly ground, and very rarely in *small* ponds. Fairly large pieces of water, fringed and dotted about with rushes and aquatic herbage, in level, well-cultivated country, boasting a good sprinkling of large mango groves are its favourite haunts, and with these tastes and predilections it will readily be understood that many minor portions of the provinces and territorial sub-divisions, which have been above included in its range, are more or less unsuited to it, and that in some of these it will be rare, and in others practically unknown. Of course in the case of birds like these, which on the first burst

* Mr. Oates says that this species is "a constant resident in Pegu; common in the Eugmah swamp in Upper Pegu, but not found in any quantities elsewhere. It is not discriminated apparently by the natives from the Pintail; at any rate both go by the same name, '*tan-bay*' or Jungle Duck."

of the monsoon, and just before they breed, wander about to a marvellous extent, a straggler might turn up in the most unexpected and apparently unsuitable place.

Just when the rains first set in, they seem to be on the wing at all hours of the day, and almost wherever you go in the North-West Provinces you see them moving about, always in pairs, the male, as a rule, in front, conspicuous by its much larger size and huge nasal protuberance, distinguishable against the clear sky at a great distance.

They never, so far as I have observed, and certainly very rarely,* associate in *flocks*. There may be half a dozen pairs about a broad in the rains, or half a dozen families, each consisting of two old and from four to ten young birds, during the early part of the cold season ; but I have never seen them congregate in flocks as most Geese and so many of the Ducks do.

Their flight is powerful and fairly rapid ; they fly better, rise quicker on the wing, swim more rapidly, and dive longer and far more adroitly than any of the Geese, though the male, at any rate, weighs quite as much as the majority of Barred-headed Geese.

They spend little of their time dozing on banks, but keep mostly to the water, generally when leaving this, perching on trees, where, I am inclined to think, they spend a good deal of the night. At any rate, under certain local conditions, they feed a great deal by day, and cannot, therefore, in such places, feed as continuously by night as many other Ducks, and most of the Geese do.

Their food consists chiefly of tender shoots and seeds of aquatic herbage, worms, larvæ of water insects, small shells, fresh-water crustaceans and occasionally a tiny fish or two. They do not visit, as a rule, or rob our fields much in Upper India : I have never found any grain, but wild rice seed, in their stomachs, and only once or twice have I seen them browsing on the turf near the water's edge.

Compared with most other Water Fowl they are rather tame. Except in quite out-of-the-way places, they will not, as a rule let you walk up within shot, and pot them as they swim about unconcernedly on the water, from a distance of thirty to forty yards as both the Shoveller and the Common Teal often will ; but during the rainy season, especially, they habitually fly past you within easy shot. On the water, too, it is much easier to work up to them in a punt than to most other Water Fowl.

Sometimes, however, a family is very difficult to get near owing to their associating with one or two pairs of Brahminies,

* Jerdon says that they are occasionally seen in flocks of above a hundred, and Mr. George Reid remarks : "The Nukhta is common in the Lucknow division on all grassy jhíls, and is easily stalked and shot, being far from a wary bird. In the early morning it may frequently be seen in recently-flooded paddy fields and in swamps among the rushes. I have never seen it in large flocks, but parties of from four to ten and from twenty to thirty are common enough."

or Ruddy Shieldrakes (almost the only Ducks with which they ever do closely associate) who, ever on the alert, effectually prevent any surprise of their comrades.

They tame very readily, and will live well in captivity, becoming very gentle, docile birds, and I do not understand why they have not been domesticated, since, although not by any means first-rate eating, they are quite as good, when well fed in the poultry yards, as the Muscovy Duck (*Cairina muschata*) of Central America, and would probably like this* produce very fine hybrids with the common domestic Duck.

Jerdon correctly says that this bird is generally little esteemed for the table, and I must say I think justly so. If roasted, when in good condition, with nice sage and onion stuffing, and served with a good gravy made from other things and Indian apple sauce (*i.e.*, the fruit of the Papaw with lime juice), they are of course nice enough, though rather hard, and if you are very hungry you will not grumble, let them be cooked as they may; but, judging them impartially on their own merits, the old birds are never worth cooking when any of the better migratory Ducks are available, and even the young, in November and December, though often as fat and tender as possible, have almost invariably a certain faint, marshy flavour, which it needs a good sauce to correct and conceal.

My personal knowledge of this species has been mainly acquired in the North-Western Provinces; elsewhere their habits and haunts may be different, and I gladly quote Colonel Tickell's account of the species, partly because his experience seems to contradict mine on many points, and partly for the sake of an anecdote he tells of what befell him once when after a Comb Duck.

He says: "I have met with these birds chiefly about West Burdwan, Bankoora, Singhbhoom, and Chota Nagpur, in open, uncultivated, bushy country, on a gravelly soil scattered over with small clear ponds or tanks, where they may be found in parties of four or five, resting during the heat of the day on the clean pebbly or sandy margins, and flying off, if disturbed, to the next piece of water. The scenery of Chota Nagpur is remarkable for the number of huge, dome-like granite rocks which start in isolated masses from its plains, and in places project from the soil in the shape of huge slabs, covering perhaps two or three acres of ground. These are often hollowed into pools of pellucid water, forming natural baths, so clean and refreshing as to tempt the most fastidious to a dip. These rocky ponds are much frequented by the "nukwas," especially at Bhandra, where I met with greater

* In the Straits, people habitually raise for the table hybrids between the Muscovy and Common Duck, which combine the size of the former with the delicacy of flavour of the latter. These hybrids are infertile. They lay quantities of eggs, (which are pale sea green, unlike those of either parent) but these never hatch.

numbers of these birds than in any other locality. But where-ever found they appear to prefer clear water with a gravelly or stone bottom, and are never seen in shallow, muddy jhíls or marshes, which attract such hosts of other kinds of Wild Fowl. In this respect they resemble *Casarca rutila* (the Brahminy or Ruddy Goose). They are very wary, and, as they take to wing generally at a long shot distance, and have both skin and plumage exceedingly thick, it is difficult to kill them with an ordinary fowling piece; and if winged on the water, they dive so incessantly as to require the help of several people, even in small ponds, to catch them.

"At Bhandra, in January 1840, I had an odd adventure while stalking a fine gander nukwa, which was swimming on one of the rocky pools I have above described. The ground was entirely composed of great horizontal slabs and fields of granite, garnished everywhere with jujube or "bair" bushes; and about two hundred yards behind me rose a mass of towering perpendicular rocks, which cast a cool grey shade over the pretty little tarns or "lakelets" spread at their feet. Now "Bandra pahar," as these rocks are termed, is, or was, a notorious stronghold or refuge for all the vagabond bears in the vicinity, who, after roaming the livelong night over the country, repaired, as dawn broke, in twos and threes, to the fissures and caves within these huge boulders. As evening drew on, these nocturnal marauders would creep stealthily out of their fastnesses, and as darkness increased sally out into the surrounding plain. And thus it came to pass that on the day, aforesaid, as I drew warily towards the "nukwa" a bear, which had emerged from a black crevice in the rock behind me, followed in my wake—with no evil intentions, I believe, for I do not think he spied me for a considerable time, but simply in pursuit of his usual evening meal of bairs and white ants, for which he scratched and snuffed in the manner peculiar to these beasts. The noise he made soon caused me to be aware of his propinquity; and ere long I began to feel in that condition which the natives of India designate as "do dil" (two hearts), or, as we should say, of two minds—whether to continue advancing to the attack of the Goose, or turn to cover my rear from that of the bear. Those were not the days of breech-loaders, when I could have shot the first, and then, whipping in a ball cartridge, have so disposed of the second. *Hinc illæ lachrymæ*—"hence my quandary." I looked at the bear as he dug and grubbed and approached, and then cautiously at the "nukwa" with his snowy-white breast reflected on the pool. The sight of the latter was irresistible. I was nearly within shot, and continued my insidious approach, determined that if the bear charged me, I would let him come close, bang both barrels of shot at his eyes, and then take to my scrapers. So, like a red Indian in the forest, I stole quietly on towards a screening rock which margined the pond, the pig-headed bear still following, as if there were no ants nor berries save in my footsteps. When I had gained the rock, I do not think he was above fifty yards from me. With the sensation of a headlong rush impending upon my rear, I was obliged to be as cool, cautious, and circumspect as if nothing but the Goose and I *(par nobile fratrum !)* were at issue. But I gained my point. I rounded the rock, and, standing revealed on the edge of the pond, fired just as *Sarkidiornis melanonotus* spread his pinions to fly, and then dropped writhing on the water. Almost simultaneously with the report, a prodigious roaring bark or shout arose behind me. I turned quickly, and had brought the remaining barrel into position, when, not a little to my relief, the bear, after a short rush forward, wheeled abruptly round, and, like a great black bundle, went off pitching and tearing through the jungle back to his den. * * * * * * *

"The young are on the wing by October, and for two or three months keep with the parents. I have placed their eggs under hens and domestic ducks, and hatched and reared the young birds easily, but they never became thoroughly tame, and escaped on the first opportunity, though they had, up to the time of their flight, fed readily with the poultry in the yard. They ran and walked freely, and could perch on anything that did not require to be *grasped;* but they took to water much less frequently than the goslings of *Nettapus coromandelianus* (the Teal Goose), or *Dendrocygna javanica* (the Whistling Teal), of which I bred several in my farmyard in Singhbhoom.

"It is an exceedingly silent bird; indeed, I have never heard it utter any sound. They repose chiefly on gravel beaches by the side of clear still water, and when on the wing can be readily distinguished at a long distance by their flight, which is between the heavy flagging of the Wild Goose and the rapid beats of the smaller Wild Fowl. The gander is always conspicuous, appearing nearly double the size of the others in the flock. Their flight is high and well sustained, and after being shot at once or twice, they continue on their course till out of sight, though almost sure to be found on the same pond the next day. Like many other Water Fowl, they appear to have certain tanks or ponds in which to feed, and others for sleeping in. At night they roam over the paddy stubble, and I have found their stomachs full of rice during the harvest."

Clearly the habits of the birds do differ widely in different parts of the country. I can only hope that between the two somewhat discrepant accounts, we may have fairly exhausted the peculiarities of this species.

I have not habitually shot these birds, because I hardly think them worth the powder and shot, when other better

Water Fowl are about ; but just at the commencement of the rains, when they are all over the country, and before they begin to lay, they afford, in some parts of the North-Western Provinces, in combination with the Whistling and Cotton Teal, a few days' very pretty shooting.

It is only during the first burst of the monsoon, and before they commence to lay, that it is right to shoot any of these three species. The way in which some men go on shooting them throughout the rains, whilst they have nests and helpless young about, is much to be regretted.

THE NUKHTA lays in the North-West Provinces, where alone I have taken its nest, in July, August, and occasionally the first-half of September. I have received no detailed accounts of its nidification elsewhere, but Major Mc.Inroy tells me that it breeds to his knowledge, in the Bagriodkere Tank in the Chittaldoog district, and in some other disricts in Mysore, and Mr. J. Davidson writes :—"In the Pánch Máhals, it was very fairly common, a pair inhabiting nearly every one of the small tanks which are scattered about everywhere. They breed in the latter part of the rains ; the only nest I took contained thirteen eggs, and was in the hollow top of a dead mango tree, but I saw the young in very many places." Ramsay says that it breeds in Tonghoo in July and August. In Ceylon it is said to breed from January to March.

According to my experience, it generally nests in some mango grove bordering a jhíl or broad, placing its nest, which is composed of sticks, a few dead leaves, grass, and feathers, at no great height from the ground, either in some large hole in the trunk, or in the depression between three or four great arms, where the main stem, (as it so often does in mango trees,) divides at a height of from six to ten feet from the ground.

I have found numerous nests thus situated. Once, and once only, I found a nest in a regular swamp at one end of a jhíl in amongst a thick growth of sedge and rush, and in this case no sticks had been used, but the whole nest, which was a foot in diameter, and five or six inches in depth, was composed of reeds and rushes, lined with a little dry grass and a few feathers ; this nest had a good deep cavity, I dare say fully four inches in depth, while those found in trees had central depressions barely half this depth. Twelve is the largest number of eggs that I have found, and I believe seven or eight to be the usual complement, but in regard to this and other points I may quote the following interesting remarks by the late Mr. A. Anderson. He says :—

"This curious and handsomely-colored Duck deposits its eggs in holes of old deciduous trees, and never, I should say, in grass by the sides of tanks, &c., as stated by Jerdon. The male bird assists the female in the selection of a site. I have frequently watched both birds flying into trees together, the male uttering a harsh, grating noise, while his mate is left behind on inspection duty.

"Although the Nukhtas nest by preference in trees, I have known them to lay in holes of old ruined forts; as a general rule, they select localities in close proximity to water.

"I have no actual proof of their appropriating old nests, as is frequently done by the Whistling Teal; but it is worth mentioning that a nest of *Haliaëtus leucoryphus*, which I had examined last winter for the eggs of *Ascalaphia bengalensis*, and which was at the time tenanted by this Owl, actually contained seven or eight rotten eggs, which were, in my opinion, referable to this Duck.

"The number of eggs seems to vary considerably; fifteen and twenty have been brought to me from one nest, the advanced state of incubation clearly indicating that in all cases the full complement had been laid. I was present, however, at the capture of a female Nukhta on her nest, which yielded the extraordinary number of forty eggs! Of course it is just possible, though highly improbable, that this may have been the joint produce of two birds; but the emaciated condition of the one captured, coupled with the fact that one egg was an abnormally small one, and evidently her last effort, do not favor such a supposition.

"The tree selected was an ancient Banyan (*Ficus indica*), which overlooked a large sheet of water, several miles in circumference; the nest-hole was at an elevation of some twenty feet, three feet deep, and two in circumference.

"The eggs (incubation was barely commenced) were laid several tiers deep, and those at the bottom were a little soiled from resting on the damp wood. It is highly probable that a large proportion of these eggs are never hatched, and that they all become discoloured as the process of incubation progresses."

Captain G. F. L. Marshall says:—"I took one egg on the 20th July from a mulberry tree. I found an egg of this species in a nest of *Dissura episcopa*, with three eggs of the latter bird; this is, I believe, an unusual occurrence."

The eggs are regular ovals, only slightly more pointed at one end than the other. The texture of the shell is wonderfully close and compact, and, when fresh, the eggs, both in colour and appearance, seem made of polished ivory. As incubation proceeds a good deal of the gloss disappears, and the delicate ivory white becomes stained and sullied, but even to the last they are amongst the smoothest eggs to the touch that I know.

The eggs vary in length from 2·22 to 2·58, and in breadth from 1·65 to 1·78; but the average of forty-five eggs is 2·41 by 1·72.

A FINE adult *male* measured :—

Length, 31·5 ; expanse, 55 ; wing, 15·37 ; tail from vent, 6·5 ; tarsus, 2·87 ; bill from gape, 2·8 ; weight, 5 lbs. 12 ozs.

A *female*, apparently nearly adult, measured :—

Length, 26·4 ; expanse, 46 ; wing, 11·3 ; tail from vent, 4·0 ; tarsus, 2·2 ; bill from gape, 2·21 ; weight, barely 3 lbs.

Three males of the year shot on the 24th December measured :—

Length, 28·5 to 29·0 ; expanse, 51·75 to 53·5 ; wing, 13·37 to 14·5 ; tail from vent, 5·25 to 6·0 ; tarsus, 2·62 to 2·75 ; bill from gape, 2·5 to 2·75 ; weight, 4 lbs. 4 ozs. to 5 lbs. 2 ozs.

In the adult male, the irides were a moderately dark brown ; bill and comb black, paler on the lower mandible, and fleshy towards the base of this latter.

In the young males the irides were dark brown ; the legs and feet delicate pale plumbeous ; the upper mandible black ; the nail bluish towards the tip ; the lower mandible pinkish, and its nail a somewhat pinkish white.

THE PLATE is extremely good, except that it does not sufficiently bring out the metallic colours on the back of the male (the specimen figured was not, I fear, quite in full plumage), and that it hardly sufficiently exhibits the difference in the size of the sexes.

Most unfortunately the female is actually made to float higher in the water in proportion to her size, whereas of course from anatomical causes she floats much deeper, is not in fact so buoyant ; the under tail-coverts are correctly shown to be pure white. This, so far as I can remember, has been the colour of these feathers in every specimen I have examined, and this is their colour in every specimen in our museum, but Dr. Sclater figures them, (P. Z. S. 1876, p. 6, LXVII.) as bright gamboge yellow, and this from living specimens in the Zoo !

In the cold season the comb of the male (the females of this species never have any comb) shrinks up almost to nothing, while in the height of the breeding season it is from 2·3 to nearly 2·5 in length at the base, and almost as high.

The young are dull earthy brown above, and dirty white below.

THE GENUS *Sarcidiornis* is, as Sclater grandiosely designates it, a " truly tropicopolitan one."(!)

Besides the present species, a nearly allied form, *S. carunculatus*, is found in tropical America, and there is a third species (*S. africanus*) also closely allied to our bird, the distinctness of which some ornithologists seem to doubt ; *non vidi.*

F. Waller Chromo-Lith. 18, Hatton Garden, London

NETTAPUS COROMANDELICUS

THE COTTON TEAL.

Nettopus coromandelianus, *Gmelin.*

Vernacular Names.—[Girri, Girria, Girja, (Hindustani, Mahrathi); Gur-gurra, *Etawah;* Ghangariel, Ghangani (Bengali); Bullia-hans, *Dacca, Faridpur, Sylhet;* Lerreget-perriget, Merom-derebet, (Kole); Ade, Adla, *Ratnagiri;* Chick sarle haki (for all small ducks), *Mysore;* Neer-akee (Water-fowl) *Coimbatore;* Karagat, *Arakan.*]

IF we exclude Sind, Cutch, Kashmir and the Himalayas, all but the eastern portions of Rajputana and the Punjab, and the Nicobars, the Cotton Teal is found in suitable situations throughout the rest of the Empire, including Ceylon and the Andamans.

But it is comparatively rare towards the west, and in Káthiáwar, the westernmost district to which it is as yet known to extend, has only been observed at Lake Bullol, east of Limree, while even in Gujarat it is not common, and in the Deccan as a whole, Mr, J. Davidson says, it is decidedly rare. In the Southern Konkan, which they visit apparently only during the cold season, Mr. G. Vidal says that, though they have been shot both in Ratnagiri itself and Chiplun, they are decidedly uncommon. In Malabar* they possibly do not occur at all, but they are not uncommon in the rest of the southern Madras Districts, and both Major Campbell, 26th M. N. I., and Mr. C. B. Sherman, report them from Travancore.

It affects a particular class of localities, and even well within its range there are large tracts unsuited to its tastes, and in which, therefore, it is never seen. Moreover in the drier parts of the country, such as the Deccan, parts of the North-Western Provinces, and the eastern portions of the Punjab and Rajputana, it is to a great extent migratory. It is more or less common in these during the rainy season, and to be met with there, though in diminished numbers, during the winter, but during the hot season it is never, or scarcely ever, seen.

It is in the Deltaic Districts of Bengal that it has its head-quarters, and there it simply swarms.

---

* Mr. Albert Theobald writes :—

"I have seen them in the Coimbatore, Salem, and Tinnevelly Districts, *but not in Malabar.* I don't think they leave this part of the country during the dry weather. They breed on trees in any suitable locality."

Right through the year, summer and winter, this little Goose or Cotton Teal abounds in the Calcutta market. In number, even in January, it exceeds all the other Ducks put together. Two or three hundred is not at all an uncommon number to come in, in one morning. I have known over 500 to be brought. Where all these birds come from is a perfect mystery to *me*. The limits within which the people assure me that all their birds are captured, (*very* few are shot,) *cannot*, it seems to me, supply the requisite number of a resident species like this. In the case of migratory species, it matters less; you may clear off one area this year, but next year a new set of migrants will restock it; but in the case of a non-migratory species, I cannot understand how persecution like this, (fully 20,000 must be caught during the year,) does not exterminate it. Of this, however, I see no signs. It is more than ten years since I first began to watch this market; I notice a manifest falling-off in the numbers of the migratory Ducks, none in those of the Cotton Teal.

The Deltas of the Ganges and Brahmaputra appear to be its home, and thence it spreads in all directions, on the whole growing rarer as we get further and further away, though here and there, specially favourable conditions have, even in localities far removed from its original habitat, greatly encouraged its multiplication. So far as I know, it does not occur at any elevation inside the Himalayas; it has not been recorded from any of the Kashmir Lakes. Mr. Young does not include it in his Kullu list, and I have never seen it in any of the lakes or ponds further west up to the borders of Nepal. It is included in Hodgson's "List of the Birds of Nepal," but Dr. Scully never saw it there, and the notes on Hodgson's drawings show that all his specimens came up from the Terai below.

Outside our limits we have observed this species in the northern portions of the Malay Peninsula, and possibly it may occur to the extreme south, though we have not yet met with any suitable localities there.*

It is said to occur in Java and the Philippines, though I am not aware that any specimens have been procured in recent years in any of these islands, and the fact seems to require verification. Pére David tells us that it visits Central China in small numbers during the summer, and breeds there.

Although there is no record of the fact, I have reason to believe that it occurs both in Siam and Independent Burma.†

---

* Davison, however, writing from Singapore says: "I saw a couple of Cotton Teal yesterday morning in one of the ponds in the Public Gardens here, and Mr. Merton, the Superintendent, tells me that they are wild birds that made their way *suo motu* to the Gardens."

† We found it common in Central Tenasserim and the plains country west of the Sitang, and Mr. Oates says that it is "excessively common throughout the year all over the province of Pegu," so that my information, as to its occurrence in Siam and Upper Burma, is very likely to be correct.

MODERATE-SIZED pieces of water, much overgrown with Singhara, (*Trapa bispinosa*,) and other water plants, and more or less surrounded by trees, are the favourite haunts of the Cotton Teal. Tame and familiar little birds, village ponds, at any rate where Singhara are grown, seem to be just as much affected as more secluded pieces of water. You may often see half-a-dozen dabbling about in the water and weeds within ten yards of the spot where the village washerman is noisily thrashing the clothes of the community, *more suo*, on large stones or ribbed slabs of wood, as if his one object in life was to knock every thing into rags at the earliest possible moment. Even the loud half-grunt, half-groan, with which he relieves his feelings after each mighty thwack, has no terror for these little birds, nor for the Water Pheasants (*Hydrophasianus chirurgus*), the Dab-Chicks (*Podiceps fluviatilis*), or the Whistling Teal (*Dendrocygna javanica*) —all so habitually seen in the same ponds as the Cotton Teal.

Fire a shot and they disappear like the Dab-Chicks for a minute, but only to reappear and continue paddling about and feeding as if nothing had happened, apparently, in most places where I have met with them, confident that no attack on *them can* be contemplated. No doubt in parts of the country where they are habitually shot at they grow wilder and warier, but in the North-West Provinces people so seldom shoot at them, that you may often clear a large pond of other Water Fowl, firing a dozen shots or more, and yet see the Cotton Teal swimming about, quite at their ease and unalarmed, within thirty yards of you. And it seems almost a pity to shoot them; they are by no means particularly good eating; there is very little on them, and they are such pretty bright little birds, and, as a rule, so confiding that to pot them at five and twenty or thirty yards distance, as I have occasionally seen done, is a down-right shame. In Lower Bengal, however, where they are both wilder and much more numerous, they afford, at times, fairly good sport. I mean where you can get them beaten and driven, and for perhaps a quarter of an hour you have them dashing past you, eight or ten per minute, in ones and twos, in all directions, and at all angles. They fly very fast when well on the wing, and while nothing is easier than to shoot them just as they have risen, I have seen them missed, time after time, as they flashed by over head, or in front or behind one, at distances of from thirty to fifty yards. As a rule they fly *low*, but when thoroughly routed up at some long frequented jhíl, though they cling to this latter persistently, they fly high enough. They are hardy, densely-plumaged birds, and will carry away a good deal of shot.

Their call is quite peculiar, a sort of sharp, short, chuckling cackle, which they sometimes utter very frequently, at others very seldom. I never quite understood this; alike when at their ease, when chased by dogs, when shot at and whirring bewildered round and round their invaded sanctuary, when all is peace, and when warring men and dogs appear "*in penetralia hostes*," in the winter and during the breeding season, in the finest and the wettest weather, I have found them both noisy and silent. No doubt, as a rule, they always chuckle incessantly as they fly about after having been disturbed, but yet, at times, I have noticed party after party swish by without uttering a sound. When quite undisturbed, they are more commonly silent, or at most call only occasionally, but I have watched parties, which nothing whatsoever was meddling with or threatening, and which were yet chattering with one consent, like ladies at a tea-fight.

During the cold season and spring where at all numerous they are commonly seen in flocks of from ten to thirty; in the breeding season (though there may be fifty about the same pond) they always keep distinctly in pairs, and during the latter portion of the summer and autumn they are in families which do not, I think, coalesce into flocks before the middle of November, or even later.

Though they rise rather awkwardly, they fly, as already noticed, with great rapidity and ease, turning and twisting with a facility unequalled, I think, by any of our other Water Fowl. I have seen Peregrines (wild and tame) strike almost every kind of Duck and Teal that we get commonly in Upper India, but I never saw one get the better of a Cotton Teal. More than once I have seen these Falcons swoop at them, under conditions which would have ensured the capture of even a Common Teal (and these are pretty sharp flyers also); but the little Girri, twisted out of the way, as easily as an unwearied Hare from before a Greyhound, and long before the Peregrine could recover itself, was down on and *under* the water.

They swim pretty rapidly, though rather jerkily, but they dive like Dab-Chicks. On land they seldom venture, though I have seen them occasionally feeding or resting on small grassy islands; but, as Blyth long ago remarked, they cannot *walk* at all, they only wabble along, shuffling as if their bodies were too heavy for their legs, yet when on trees—and it is on these that they pass almost the whole of their time not spent on the water or on the wing—they stand firm enough, and betray no weakness in the lower extremities.

They feed chiefly during the hours of daylight, sleeping usually on trees, where I have repeatedly seen them go to roost about dusk, but on bright moonlight nights I have occasionally seen them in the water with other Wild Fowl.

Their food consists of rice grains, especially the seed of the wild rice known as "*Pasaie*" in Upper India, and of the shoots of various kinds of aquatic plants, worms, water insects, and their larvæ. Once or twice I have found what I believed to be the remains of minute fishes and fresh-water crustaceans in their stomachs, but of this I could not be quite certain.

Tickell remarks:—

"In large sheltered sheets of water they seldom shift their quarters, but pass the time frolicking about the clear spaces between the beds of the water lily and other aquatic weeds, or taking their insect food from the floating leaves, at night resting securely amid the tangle and coarse herbage matting over the centre of the pool. When off their feed these birds are at times very frolicksome, flying rapidly round and round the pond, the male making a singular drumming, quacking, which has been correctly enough compared to the words "Fix baggonets! fix baggonets!" and has gained the bird that familiar cognomen amongst our soldiers in India. The Koles and Oorias have named it from its cry, "Lerreget-perreget," also "Merom-derebet," the word "merom" amongst the Koles meaning goat, the bleat of which animal is not unlike the voice of this Goslet.

"When fired at, the Girras, after a circle or two round the tank or pond, will frequently alight again, and allow of a second or even a third shot. If the sheet of water be broad, they will then usually settle in the middle, and there remain out of range, in spite of yells and shouts, and splashing with sticks, and pelting with stones—devices to which, with the aid of the neighbouring villagers, the young sportsman must have recourse, unless a canoe be procurable, in which to invade the birds in their fastnesses. If the water be not capacious enough for the Girras to settle out of shot, they will fly off to a neighbouring pond, but never to a great distance. Their flight is exceedingly swift, but low, just clearing the tops of the trees or skimming over the surface of the water, and they afford very pretty practice at single shots as they come, sweeping over a bank or a mango grove, to alight on the pond where the gunner has taken his stand.

"This pretty little miniature Goose—or, as Jerdon terms it, Goslet—from its comparative tameness and numbers, is amongst the first objects to attract the notice of the young sportsman anxious to try his hand at "Duck-shooting." But it is also, alas! the not unfrequent innocent cause of death to its too ardent pursuers. There have been too many instances of soldiers and other Europeans, especially amongst new arrivals, who have been miserably drowned in swimming far into tanks and jhíls to pick up the bodies of these birds which they have just shot. The pond appears so small, the water so clear, the little Duck with its plump white breast floating upwards so tempting—so in goes a stout young fellow, and in a dozen strokes is up with his prize, when the deadly weeds, which he had not seen from the bank, but which in such spots spread like a net some two or three feet beneath the surface, lap round his legs and close upon him in a gentle but irresistible embrace. In vain to kick and plunge; each effort involves the swimmer more. In vain to cry for help, with none but one or two timid or apathetic natives on the shore, who from dread or stupidity, or perhaps dislike to the sufferer, do not move a finger to his rescue. But, indeed, in such situations, without ropes, or long bamboos, or floats of some description, what can be done? To follow empty-handed a person into such a trap, exposed not only to the tenacious grasp of the weeds, but to the desperate clutch of the drowning man, is but to ensure the death of two instead of one!"

I HAVE only found the eggs of this species in July and August, and towards the end of the latter month the young are to be seen about everywhere. I have seen many nests, all in mango trees, in or at the edge of swamps or ponds, in hollows of large decayed branches, and with very little or no lining (except crumbling fragments of decayed wood); but it would appear from the remarks of others quoted below, that these are by no means the only situations they affect for nesting. I have never found more than twelve eggs, and from eight to ten appear to me to be the usual full complement.

Mr. F. R. Blewitt, writing from Jhansi, says of this species:—

"It breeds in July and August.

"Just above the village of Buragaon is a large lake from which several eggs of this Goslet were brought. The eggs were collected in the two months on different occasions. It makes a semi-floating nest on the water, among the rushes or lotus leaves, of weeds, grass, &c., all mixed together and piled up several inches above the water level."

Dr. Jerdon says:—"It breeds generally in holes in old trees, often at some distance from water, occasionally in ruined houses, temples, old chimneys, and the like, laying eight or ten (sometimes, it is stated, as many as fifteen) small white eggs."

Mr. A. Anderson remarks: "This species nests in holes of trees and old ruins, and never, according to my experience, in old nests or on the ground.

"I once had an opportunity of watching a pair in the act of selecting their habitation. They invariably flew into the tree together; and while the female used to enter the hole, to reconnoitre as it were, the male sat on a bough watching for her exit. No sooner did she make her appearance than they both flew away together, giving utterance to a peculiar cackling sound, which has been pronounced to be like the words "Fix bayonets." Their visits used to be repeated at intervals of every fifteen or twenty minutes. The Drake never went into the hole; and I am, therefore, inclined to believe that he does not lend his aid in the performance of the duties of incubation.

"The greatest number of eggs laid by the Goslet, of which I have a record, is twelve. This nest was taken by Mr. Spry at Budaon in August last. The hole occupied was at no great height; but it was three and a half feet deep, and only large enough to admit of ingress and egress. The contents had to be removed by means of an iron spoon, something like a soup ladle with an extra long handle."

Mr. Cripps writes :—

"Very common in the districts of Dacca, Sylhet and Faridpur during the rainy season, when they are found in the paddy fields and 'bhils' in pairs and small parties. In all those districts they breed in July and August, and invariably in cavities in trees, and holes in buildings, making a rough pad nest of fine grasses and twigs with feathers for a lining. I have seen a nest in a hole of a date tree, only seven feet off the ground, and alongside of a ryot's house, and I have taken the eggs out of a niche in a factory chimney about 40 feet off the ground. Eight is the greatest number of eggs that I have found in one nest; these birds never nest at any distance from water."

In the northern parts of Ceylon this species also is said to breed from January to March.

The eggs are oval, scarcely more pointed at one end than the other. They are miniatures of those of the preceding species, of a delicate ivory white colour, very smooth to the touch, but scarcely so glossy as those of the Nukhta, and, as a rule, much less liable to become soiled during incubation than those of this latter species.

In length the eggs vary from 1·54 to 1·75, and in breadth from 1·17 to 1·38; but the average of twenty-six is 1·7 by 1·29.

THE MALES are rather larger than the females, and in both sexes full-plumaged birds vary somewhat in size, probably according to age.

Males.—Length, 12·62 to 13·5; expanse, 20·5 to 24·0; wing, 6·25 to 6·75; tail from vent, 2·82 to 3·25; tarsus, 1·0 to 1·06; bill from gape, 1·08 to 1·25; weight, 8 ozs to nearly 11·0 ozs.

The irides vary from dark brown to crimson, the latter, I believe, in the breeding season; the legs and feet from light yellowish to dirty sap green, with the webs and claws black; the bill in the breeding season black, at other times dark grey above, yellowish on the lower mandible, and more like that of the female.

Females.—Length, 12·5 to 12·75; expanse, 21·0 to 22·0; wing, 6·25 to 6·37; tail from vent, 2·8 to 3·0; tarsus, 1·0 to 1·1; bill from gape, 1·04 to 1·2; weight, 6·5 ozs. to 9·0 ozs.

The irides are dark brown. I do not know whether they ever become red in this sex. The legs and feet dirty green; webs and claws black. I have no record of these parts being yellowish, as they often are in the male, but perhaps they also become so; upper mandible dark greenish brown, lighter at the sides; lower mandible dull yellow, brownish pink towards the sides.

THE PLATE is an extremely satisfactory one, and represents the male in breeding plumage. Its only fault is, that neither on land nor in water do the birds ever stalk about with their legs visible below them. As already mentioned, it is only when resting on branches of trees that they are ever seen standing erect on their legs. The chicks, with their funny little brush tails, are correctly figured, but there is not generally the fulvous tinge on the sides of the face and neck depicted in the plate. As a rule these parts are white.

During the latter part of the autumn, the winter and the early part of the spring, the males lose the collar round the neck, which is replaced by irregular banding similar to that on the neck of the female; the lower mandible becomes yellow, and generally the entire plumage closely resembles that worn by the female at all seasons; but the male still retains the conspicuous white patch on the primaries, which is entirely wanting in the female, as also to a certain extent the metallic green on the secondaries and coverts.

The young male of the year is almost precisely like the female and wants the white patch on the primaries, and is only to be distinguished from the female, I think, by dissection, though, perhaps the lower mandible is never so yellow as in the female.

TWO OTHER closely-allied species, *pulchellus* and *albipennis*, of Gould (the latter differing from our bird only, I believe, in its larger size) are known from Australia; a third somewhat different species, generically separated by some authors, *N. auritus* is found in Madagascar and the adjacent regions of South Africa.

4

DENDROCYGNA ARCUATA

THE WHISTLING TEAL.

Dendrocygna javanica, *Horsfield.*

Vernacular Names.—[Saral, Shareil, *Lower Bengal;* Soreil, Harrili-hans, *Eastern Bengal;* Silli. Silháhi (Hindustani); Chihee, *Etawah;* Ade, Adla (Mahrathi); Yerra Chilluwa, (Telugu); Yerrundi (Malayalum), *Quilon, Travancore;* Sisalee, Sessilli (Burmese), *Pegu, Tenasserim;* Tingi, *Munipur;*]

EXCEPT the north-western portions of Rajputana and the Punjab, there is scarcely any suitable locality within the limits of the Empire, including Burma,* Ceylon, the Andamans, and Nicobars, in which the Whistling Teal does not occur, either as a permanent resident or a seasonal visitant.

In many parts of the country it is almost entirely the latter. Thus in Sind it is very rarely seen, except from the end of April to October. In the Deccan its occurrence is nearly confined to the rainy and cold seasons; in the drier portions of the North-Western Provinces it is ten times as numerous in the rains as it is between January and the commencement of the latter.

Again Mr. Cripps says:—"In the Faridpur District this species is a permanent resident, but in Dacca it is seen only during the rainy season in pairs and small parties. In the cold season large flocks of these birds are met with in the tract of swampy country which forms the central southern portion of the district of Sylhet; in some of these swamps, I have come across flocks numbering thousands, and although I have seen them in Faridpur in winter, when they go about in flocks of twenty and thirty, my opinion is that the greater number of the birds which scatter over Eastern Bengal during the monsoon, retire to Sylhet in the cold weather."

I do not think it occurs, except perhaps as a straggler, in the Himalayas. It has not been recorded from Kashmir nor from Kullu, nor have I met with it in any part of the Himalayas west of Nepal. Hodgson includes it in his "List of the Birds of Nepal," and he seems to have obtained one specimen from the Residency

* *We* found it common throughout Tenasserim, and Mr. Oates writes that it is "very abundant all the year round in the swamps of Lower Pegu, though I have never observed it in the Engmah swamp where so many other kinds abound."

pond (perhaps one introduced there), but the rest of his specimens came from the Terai, and Scully did not observe it in Nepal.

It is not, I think, a hill bird, and nowhere, I believe, ascends the hills to any considerable elevation. Fairbank observed it at Mahableshwar, but it has not been noticed at Abú or Ooty, or on the Pulneys.

Outside our limits it occurs in Independent Burma and Siam, throughout the Malay Peninsula, in Sumatra, Java, and Borneo. A specimen, said to differ only from this species in the length of the tarsus, is in the British Museum, brought by Clapperton and Denham, from Lake Tchad in Central Africa, but I am not prepared, without further information, to accept this latter as a habitat of the present species.

THE WHISTLING TEAL is essentially a tree Duck; it must have trees as well as water, and hence its entire absence from some pieces of water, in treeless parts of Rajputana for instance, where other species of Ducks abound during the cold season. Generally it is more common in well-wooded than in comparatively bare, open country. Yet it prefers level or fairly level tracts to very broken hilly country, and again, though in some places, *e.g.*, at Tavoy, it may be met with in rivers in enormous flocks, it, as a rule, prefers moderate-sized lakes and ponds to rivers.

Owing to these preferences, there are many tracts, as for instance, portions of the Deccan, where it is extremely rare. In the Southern Konkan it is almost unknown. Mr. Vidal tells me that he has only once seen it in the Ratnagiri District, and that was in February on the Washishti River near Chiplun.

I have already alluded to its migratory habits. I may add that it seems to be altogether a permanent resident only in well-watered, well-wooded, and *well-drained*, districts; in the drier districts the majority are only monsoon visitants; in the more swampy tracts the majority come only for the dry season. But although the majority gad about like fashionable folks; spending one season here and the other there, a few seem to be everywhere (except in the western portions of the range of the species), truly permanent residents. Of course this must depend upon the supply of food available, but we know too little as yet of the details of such matters to be able to trace this partial migration to its exact causes.

It is about weedy tanks and swamps that one mostly meets with the Whistling Teal, in pairs during the breeding season, but in flocks of from twenty to two thousand (according to the size of the swamp or broad which they inhabit), during the cold season and spring. Like the Cotton Teal—and both species are commonly seen in the same tanks—they are very tame and familiar birds, frequenting village ponds, and living on the trees surrounding such, even on trees growing inside the enclosures of cottages. They are rather dull birds, slow on the wing and easily shot, and they have a habit of circling round and round the gunner, when one of their number has been shot, that often proves fatal to the greater portion of the flock, when it unfortunately falls under the tender mercies of "butchers." When absolutely required for food, a pair or so may be shot, but they are indifferent eating, and fly so poorly that they really afford no sport. Indeed in many places they are so tame that they sit unconcernedly on some overhanging branch looking down at the gunner, who has to throw stones at them, before they will give him a chance of a flying shot.

They swim and dive extremely well. Indeed a winged bird in a good large pond, full of holes, into which the pursuers plump without warning, will afford admirable exercise and amusement to a dozen beaters while you smoke a sympathetic cigar on the bank in the cool shade of some huge peepul. They are not very often seen, I think, on land, but they walk far better than the Cotton Teal. I have seen them feeding like Geese on short fine grass, and Mr. Cripps says :—"This species is often seen on freshly-ploughed paddy fields, evidently feeding on the grains of paddy that have been left above ground after sowing."

Certainly when not on the wing they are more commonly either feeding in the water or resting on trees. There are differences in their habits, however, according to season and locality. During the breeding season they spend much more of their time in trees, at any rate where they breed on these, than at other times, the female, either sitting on the eggs or at the edge of the nest on the alert against crows and other robbers, and the male on some neighbouring branch with one eye on the water and the other on his mate, whom he is always ready to assist against all, but human, assailants. I once saw a good large half-wild village Cat spring down on a Duck, which was sitting on her nest, in a broad four-pronged fork of a mango-tree. The Duck did not whistle in the usual manner; she positively screamed; in a second, the Drake dashed at the Cat, and to my surprise down came a Black Crow (*C. macrorhynchus*), not as any one would have thought to steal the eggs during the confusion, but to assail the Cat with claws and beak as if his own homestead had been attacked. In less time than it takes to describe, the Cat was squalling in her turn, and fled up one of the branches pursued closely by the Drake and Crow, who were immediately joined by another Crow, and the three made it so hot for pussy that she sprung down to the ground, where my Dogs, aroused by the uproar above, (the noise those two Crows made was astounding) were awaiting her, and before I could interfere, and before she quite recovered the jump of some 35 or 40 feet, killed her outright. But the strangest part of the business was, that the villagers assured me that this nest was the Crow's *own* nest, and that they *lent it every year* after their young had flown to the Whistling Teal. I should have verified this the next spring, but left the Mynpooree District and never again had the chance of revisiting the spot.

Where the Whistling Teal lives in moderate-sized tanks, and where it is tame and fearless, it feeds, I believe, almost exclusively in the water and during the day, chiefly in the fore and afternoons, resting in trees during the middle of the day and roosting on these at night. I have continually seen them going up to roost about sunset, alighting first on the outside twigs of some large branch, and presently sidling up well inside the tree and nearer to the trunk. But where they are wilder, and where they frequent rivers, they feed at night like other Ducks, and may be seen about sunset leaving the river in large flocks to feed in the neighbouring paddy fields and swamps.

They are chiefly, I think, vegetarians, and devour rice especially, wild and cultivated, most greedily, but they also feed on all kinds of seeds, rushes and other water plants, and on the herbage, bulbs and corms of these and on grass, and at times, small shells, worms and a variety of insects are found in their stomachs. Once I shot one that disgorged, as it fell, a tiny silvery fish about two inches in length. But, as a rule, (and I have dissected many), they feed principally, I believe, on vegetable substances, and I am therefore at a loss to account for the peculiar, faint, half-muddy, half-fishy taste, that their flesh always seems to have, and which, to me, makes them unpalatable even when disguised with sauces in a stew.

Their call is a double hissing whistled note, uttered always when they are alarmed, or when they are about to fly, and often repeated during flight, but more seldom heard when they are at rest and at their ease, either on the water or on trees. Only when the female is sitting inside a hole where the male cannot see her, the pair keep up a pretty continuous conversation.

OF FEW SPECIES does the nidification vary so much according to local circumstances as that of our present bird.

In one place it lays almost exclusively in stick nests, (of its own building, or else old ones of Crows, Cormorants or Paddy Birds slightly furbished up), fairly high up on large trees ; in another in hollows between the huge branches of ancient trees, such as a Wood Owl would use, or deep in holes in the trunks of these, such as a Nukhta would select. In other places it nests on low palms, small thorny bushes, or dense clumps of bulrush and reeds, or again on the ground in thick grass or on the water on floating patches of tangled water weeds.

The laying season also varies in most places from the middle of June until quite the middle of October, but in

Northern Ceylon and other southern localities where the N. E. Monsoon rains are heavy, it breeds after the close of these, viz., from December or January to March.

I myself have only seen its nests in the Etáwah District, in Mynpooree, Cawnpore, Muttra, Allyghur, and Meerut.

I have found its eggs in two situations,—in hollows in trees, or between the larger branches of these, either unlined or slightly lined with grass and feathers,—or in old Crow's and Kite's nests, which it lines in a similar fashion. In all cases the trees in or on which I have found it nesting have been in the immediate proximity of water. This, however, is not at all the rule elsewhere.

With us it lays in July and August, and a few eggs may be found even during the first-half of September, but the majority have, I think, hatched off by the first of that month. Twelve is the maximum number of eggs that I have seen in any nest, and ten or eleven are, I think, the usual complement.

Captain G. F. L. Marshall remarks that "this species builds in trees a nest of sticks, and lays about seven to ten eggs.

"A nest, found on the 25th of July near Bolundshahr, contained only one egg, on which both the parent birds were sitting. It was a tolerably compact structure of twigs in a Keekur tree at the edge of a jhíl about eight feet from the road ; it was at the side of a metalled road near a large town. I shot the male, but missed the female with the left barrel. When I returned next day, there was a pair of birds on the nest again, so that the female had apparently provided herself with a fresh mate in that short interval. In another case the nest was swarming with ants and maggots."

Mr. A. Anderson says:—"Jerdon could never have found a full clutch of the eggs of the Whistling Teal, or he would not have limited the number to "six or eight" (BIRDS OF INDIA, Vol. III, p. 790). Ordinarily this Duck lays fully a dozen eggs ; but I am indebted to my friend, Mr. Fynes-Clinton, for two clutches of twelve and fourteen respectively, which he took from the same nest ; whether these were laid by one or two birds must of course remain an open question.

"On the 29th June 1872, Mr. Clinton flushed a bird from the top of a low Date Palm, (*Phœnix dactylifera*), and found the first-mentioned lot (twelve) ; on the 13th July he happened to visit the same locality, and to his surprise found the second clutch in exactly the same situation ; the Duck was on her eggs. Now the dates are so coincident that, supposing these twenty-six eggs to be the produce of two different females, the second one must have laid her first egg the very day after the removal of the first batch.

"As to situation, the choice may be mentioned in the following order :—

(*1st*).—Depression at the fork of the lower branches of large-limbed trees ;

(*2nd*).—Old nests, particularly those belonging to Crows, Herons, &c.; and

(*3rd*).—Thorny scrub or grass on the edge of swamps."

Capt. Butler writes from Deesa: "On the 24th of August 1876, I found a nest of this species containing ten eggs, slightly incubated; it was placed in a tussock of grass growing out of a dead stick fence that had become submerged from the height of the water. It was well concealed, and consisted of a quantity of dry grass and sedge trodden down into a good thick pad. The old bird sat close, and when I looked into the tussock of grass, flapped off the nest into the water like a wounded bird, swam 5 or 6 yards, and then dived. In about five minutes both birds (♂ and ♀) returned on the wing, and after flying uneasily round and round in circles close to me for a few seconds, settled in some short grass on the bank about 10 yards from me, and tried to draw me away from the nest by cackling and running, or rather waddling through the grass as if wounded. A day or two latter, I found several young broods about a week old, and in two instances amalgamated broods numbering about twenty-two young birds and two old Ducks."

Again writing from Sind he says:—

"Mr. Doig took a nest containing ten fresh eggs in the Eastern Nara, Sind, on the 22nd June 1878, and later on, during the last week of July, in another part of the district where the water had risen later, he and I found a few more nests containing eight to ten fresh eggs. At that season of the year large dhunds are filled with water by the overflow of the Indus, and large tracts of thickly wooded country, which are dry in the hot weather, become converted into huge lakes, dotted all over with trees, and patches of partly submerged tamarisk jungle. Many of these trees are overgrown with a dense green creeper, and on these trees, in a little arbour in the middle of the creeper, at heights varying from 3 to 8 feet above the surface of the water, we invariably found the nests. The birds were very plentiful, and of course all in pairs, and the nests were not difficult to discover as the old birds were quite tame, and as a rule were sitting on the tree, one generally on the nest, the other outside keeping guard. The nest consisted of a moderate-sized pad of green twigs, plucked from the creeper in which it was built, which, becoming moist from the bird's feet, usually caused the eggs to become more or less marked with green stains."

Mr. Doig himself notes that "the Whistling Teal breeds in great numbers on the Nara, (Hyderabad, Sind,) earlier in some portions than in others. At one place, on the 23rd of June, I found a nest containing 10 fresh eggs. The nest was simply composed of leaves of the large bulrush trodden down, so as to make a platform, and was on the top of a clump of these bulrushes at about 10 feet from the ground. On 24th June I found another nest similarly situated, but containing nothing but egg shells—the chicks had felt the nest. At another place, about 25 miles further north, where the birds were very numerous, they were building their nests in July, and did not begin to lay till towards the end of July and beginning of August. Here in nearly every instance the nest was in a tamarisk bush which had been covered over with a small green creeper, the eggs being laid on a mass of the creeper inside the bush, and having generally a lot of the creeper forming an arch over head."

Mr. Brooks tells me that "on one occasion" he "took a nest of this species out of a broken tree stump about four feet high, which was hollow in the centre. The nest was about an arm's length down in the stump, and the old bird allowed herself to be lifted off the eggs when she was set free."

Mr J. Davidson, C.S., writes: "This was a rare Duck, and only met with in the cold weather in Sholapur and other parts of the Deccan. In Mysore it was also rare, though pairs evidently going to breed were scattered among the weedy tanks. In the Pánch Máhals they were nearly as common in the rains and cold weather, (I did not spend a hot weather there) as the Cotton Teal, and bred in September and October. All the nests I found myself were in tufts of grass which formed islands in the middle of weedy tanks; one clutch of eggs was, however, brought to me, said to have been taken from a stick nest built in a bush, 6 or 7 feet high, standing in water."

Mr. J. R. Cripps says: "This species breeds to my knowledge in Faridpur, Dacca, and Sylhet on trees in the vicinity of water, as well as in '*sun*' grass fields; when in these latter the nest is placed on the ground. The nest when built on trees is of twigs, with a slight lining of grass, but when on the ground, it is made exclusively of 'Sun' grass. July and August are the principal months for their laying. I have never found more than 9 eggs in any nest; the nest when on trees is never very high up, 20 feet from the ground being the maximum according to my experience."

In Pegu, Mr. Eugene Oates records that he has "found nests from the 6th July to the 29th August, twice with six and once with seven eggs. The nest is apparently always placed on thick matted canebrakes in paddy fields or on the ground in thick grass. I have never seen any indications of nests on trees. In all the three nests I have found, the above number of eggs was the full complement, for the female in each instance, on dissection, contained no mature eggs."

Writing from Singapore Davison says:—

"The Whistling Teal breeds freely on an island in the big pond in the public gardens here. This island is almost entirely covered and overshadowed by a huge fig tree, on which I should have expected the birds to nest; but Mr. Merton, the

Superintendent, assures me that he has repeatedly seen their nests, and that these are here invariably on the ground and close to the water's edge. Of course on this island there is absolute protection from man and beast."

I have dwelt already, I fear some will think, at too great length on the nesting habits of this species ; but I must still add a most curious fact recorded by Mr. H. Kemp. Writing from the Futtehpur District on the 13th July, he says : "Last evening I saw a pair of Whistling Teal settle high up on a large peepul tree. One went into a hollow and the other sat outside near its mouth. This other one I shot ; it proved to be the male. After a moment's pause the female flew out and made away to a sheet of water about 300 yards distant. While I was walking towards her, a man, close over whom the bird flew, in telling me where it had settled, added that it had an egg in its claw. I disbelieved this and took no notice of it, but when I shot the bird, my servant in bringing it out of the water found an egg on a narrow ridge where the bird was standing when shot. There was no nest, nor had the ground any signs of having been sat upon.

"I then sent a man up the peepul tree and he found one more egg of the same kind in the hollow out of which the bird flew. There was no prepared nest in the hollow, but only decayed and crumbled chips."

Strange as this may seem, it is confirmed by the fact that the Duck similarly transports the young, to the water, in her claws. I have *heard* of their being seen flying down to the water with ducklings on their backs, but I have twice *seen* them carrying these in their claws. On one of these occasions, between 8 and 9 A.M., I saw a Duck carry down her whole brood of seven, one at a time, from a hole in a huge mango to the water, she passing each time within three yards of my face as I sat at the water's edge. The first time the Drake came down with her, and then he remained with the ducklings, whilst she went backwards and forwards fetching the rest. Natives say that when the weather is stormy the old birds carry the young *back* to the nest, and that may be so, but on this particular occasion, I returned at sunset and saw both old birds and the brood swimming about ; and, though I waited till it was quite dark, saw nothing of their returning to the tree. Next morning I was there before daylight, but as soon as it was light, I made out the party. I had the place watched, and am satisfied that that brood never returned to the nest. But then the weather, though there was plenty of rain, was not stormy or windy, and I must leave it to future observers to determine whether they *ever* carry their young on their backs, or in their bills, and whether, once they have launched their young, they *ever* carry them again back to the nest's dry dock.

The eggs of this species are usually very broad ovals, often slightly compressed towards one end. In texture they differ much from those of the Black-backed Goose and Goose Teal already described. They lack the exquisite smoothness and satiny feel of these latter, and instead of the delicate ivory white, they are, when fresh, nearly pure white,* becoming no doubt yellowish or brownish, and sullied, as incubation proceeds. Here and there one may exhibit a slight gloss, but as a rule, this is almost entirely wanting.

In length the eggs vary from 1·72 to 2·0, and in breadth from 1·4 to 1·6; but the average of forty-four is 1·86 nearly by 1·49.

THE BIRDS vary a good deal according to age, but not apparently according to sex, though the head of the male is rather larger and the plumage on it fuller. Speaking merely from memory, I should have said that the males were larger, but a comparison of a large series of measurements of both sexes in the flesh shows that this is not the case.

Length, 16·0 to 17·45; expanse, 27·25 to 30·3; wing, 7·0 to 8·04; tail from vent, 2·3 to 3·02; tarsus, 1·6 to 1·92; bill from gape, 1·7 to 2·06; weight, 1 lb. to 1 lb. 4 ozs.

The irides are deep brown; the eyelids bright yellow to pale golden; the legs and feet generally dark, at times somewhat pale, plumbeous blue, often dusky in patches and on the webs, and claws blackish; bill plumbeous to pale dull blue at the base, shading to black at the tip, the bill in some having a greater extent of plumbeous, in others of black; the membrane between the rami of the lower mandible is generally pinkish.

THE PLATE only tolerably represents the species, and is everywhere too brightly coloured and too orange. In reality the wing-coverts are a deep maroon; the edgings to the feathers of the back dingy fulvous chestnut; and the lower breast and abdomen a rather light but dull chestnut. The legs of the standing bird are unfortunately wrongly drawn. Both legs are on the off side, and the tibial portion of the leg, which when the bird is thus standing, shows out very conspicuously, on the near side, is ignored. There should be more plumbeous at the base of the bill.

The young, when just able to fly, do not differ very much from the adult, but are everywhere duller coloured. The margins to the feathers of the interscapulary region are inconspicuous and dingy fulvous, and the entire lower surface a rather pale, dull fulvous brown.

---

* The lining membrane of the egg which is of a delicate salmon pink, gives at times a faint rosy tinge to *perfectly* fresh unblown eggs.

DENDROCYGNA MAJOR

THE LARGER WHISTLING TEAL.

Dendrocygna fulva, *Gmelin.*

Vernacular Names.—[Murghabi (*i.e.*, Duck), *Lower Bengal;* Badak (*i.e.*, Duck), (Mahrathi), *Deccan;* ? Yerrinda, (Malayalum), *Travancore;* Silli, (Hindustani); Sisalee, (Burmese), *Pegu.*]

VERY little is as yet known of the exact distribution of the larger Whistling Teal within our limits.

In Sind I only know of its occurring as a rare visitant about the larger lakes and canals during the monsoon. In the Punjab and Rajputana I have only heard of its occurrence in Bhawulpur. In the Doab of the North-West Provinces I have only known it to be found in the submontane districts. In parts of Rohilkhand, Oudh, and Gorakhpur and Basti it is not uncommon in the rains, but whether it is a permanent resident in any of these districts, I cannot say. In the Central Provinces, I have only heard of its occurrence in the Jhansi and Saugor Districts during the monsoon.

In Cutch Col. Palin says it occurs, but is not common. In Káthiáwar and Gujarat, though stragglers may occur there during the rains, it has not been observed, nor has it been recorded from Khandesh or the Central India Agency. In the rest of the Bombay Presidency it occurs occasionally, but only as a rare straggler. Fairbank obtained it once near Ahmednagar. Wenden shot several at Nulwar. Vidal found it "uncommon" in Sattara, and has never seen it at Ratnagiri. Just outside the Bombay Presidency, at the north-west corner of the Nizam's Territories, Jerdon found it tolerably abundant at Jalna. Holdsworth does not record it from Ceylon, nor is there, that I can discover, a single record if its occurrence anywhere in Travancore,* Mysore, or any part of the Madras Presidency, except near Nellore, where Jerdon occasionally procured it.

---

* Note however that C. B Sherman, Esq., Ex.-Engineer, writing from Travancore, affirms that it is very common in the north of that state; that it is generally only seen from October to April, but that some stay and breed as he has seen them with young in August. Major Campbell, of the 26th M. N. I., on the other hand writing from Quilon, says, that it is the common and not the larger Whistling Teal that occurs in Travancore, and as *no* one else notes the larger species from Travancore, it seems probable that Mr. Sherman has confounded the two species. However I have given his remarks, and hope that the point will be verified.

Ball excludes it from his list of birds found between the Ganges and the Gódávari. In the Deltaic Districts of Bengal, particularly in the neighbourhood of Calcutta, and in Jessore, it is fairly common, extending up the Ganges to Purneah, and, *I believe*, to the Sikhim and Nepal Terai, (though Hodgson never procured it there).

No one has noticed it from any part of Assam, Sylhet, Cachar, Tippera, Chittagong or Aracan. But it *is* found in Burma. Mr. Oates remarks:—"It occurs sparingly in the plains of Lower Pegu, while in the Engmah swamp it is a common bird; indeed it seems to occupy Upper, as the smaller Whistling Teal does Lower, Pegu." Ramsay also found it, though less common, on the Tonghoo side of the Pegu Yoma, but so far as we know it occurs nowhere in Tenasserim proper.

I am far from wishing it to be understood that it occurs in none of the localities where it has not as yet been observed. On the contrary I should confidently expect it to be found in Assam, Cachar, &c.; all I can do is to expose our existing ignorance of its distribution and leave it to future observers to work this out.

Outside our limits it is not *known** to occur anywhere in Asia, but it certainly occurs in Madagascar, and Messrs. Sclater and Salvin state that there exist no tangible grounds for separating our Indian bird from the species, *(non vidi,)* that occurs in sub-tropical America, north and south, *viz.*, throughout Mexico on the one hand, and Southern Brazil, Paraguay, Buenos Ayres, and Monte Video on the other.

This, be it observed, is somewhat similar to its distribution in the old world, with one head-quarters as it were near Calcutta, corresponding in latitude with the Mexican one, and another in Madagascar, corresponding similarly with the Southern American range.

There are few, if any, species whose distribution is so remarkable. It inhabits, apparently, four isolated blocks of country—one block in Asia and one in North America, both just under the Tropic of Cancer; one block in Africa, and one in South America, and both these just under the Tropic of Capricorn.

IT is only in the neighbourhood of Calcutta, and specially at some weedy ponds a few miles from Port Canning, that I have had any opportunities of observing this species. There I found them much less tame than their congener, with a decidedly stronger and somewhat more rapid flight; like them perching a good deal on trees, but far more often seen on land, on which they walk fairly well and upright with a very Goose-like gait.

* I have had reason to believe that it is found in both Upper or Independent Burma, and in Siam. But I have failed hitherto to procure specimens from either locality, and rough descriptions, by persons who have paid no attention to birds, cannot be relied on to identify species like this.

Their food during the cold season, when alone I have procured them, consisted apparently mainly of rice, but they are very miscellaneous feeders, and I have found in their stomachs, not only all kinds of aquatic seeds, bulbs, leaf-shoots, and buds, grass, and rush, but small shells, insects, worms, and larvæ, and on one occasion a tiny frog. Still in the case of those I examined, grains of rice, wild and cultivated, constituted the bulk of their food.

Their note is much like that of the smaller species, but rather louder and more of a chuckling whistle, and I have only heard it when the birds were alarmed, were about to rise, or were on the wing.

They are wilder and more difficult to get at, afford better sport, and are to my taste decidedly better eating than the Common Whistling Teal. I found them invariably in parties of from six to twenty, but on one or two occasions, the parties were dispersed all about the pond, and instead of rising at once when the first shot was fired, as they usually do, they kept rising in one's and two's out of the rushes as I pushed through these in a dug-out, just as I have often seen the Marbled and White-eyed Ducks do, thus affording numerous good, though all rather long, shots.

My experiences, however, of this species are very limited.

OF THE nidification of the larger Whistling Teal but little seems to be known. So far as it has been observed it is similar to that of its smaller congener. I have never myself found a nest, and the only eggs I possess were sent me years ago with the parents from Saugor.

The nest was found on the 15th August; it was a large hollow in an old tree overhanging a large piece of water, rather liberally lined with a few twigs, a good deal of grass, and some feathers. It contained seven eggs, a good deal incubated.

The eggs, except for size and a somewhat superior smoothness, are precisely like those of the Common Whistling Teal; very broad, regular ovals, moderately smooth to the touch, but with no perceptible gloss, and of a dull slightly yellowish white colour. Probably, when first laid, the eggs were pure white.

In length they vary from 2·12 to 2·25; and in breadth from 1·65 to 1·75.

THE MALES average a little larger and heavier than the females.

The following are the dimensions of a fine pair* :—

Male.—Length, 20·1; expanse, 36·75; wing, 9·2; tail from vent, 2·9; tarsus, 2·5; bill from gape, 2·4; weight, 1lb. 12 ozs.

The legs and feet pale leaden blue; webs dusky; bill dusky bluish at base; irides brown.

* Last year in Calcutta I carefully recorded all these particulars of over twenty specimens, expressly for this work, but unfortunately the paper cannot be found.

Female.—Length, 19·5 ; expanse, 36·0 ; wing, 8·75 ; tail from vent, 3·0 ; tarsus, 2·3 ; bill from gape, 2·35 ; weight, 1lb. 10 ozs.

The legs and feet pale leaden lavedner ; webs dusky ; bill dusky leaden, paler at base ; irides brown.

The bills, legs, and feet vary a good deal in shade in both sexes ; in some they are more dusky ; in others markedly paler and bluer.

THE PLATE is on the whole fair, but the rufous portions are throughout too orange, and should be more of a dull chestnut on the belly, and of a warm brown elsewhere. There is never the faintest trace of the black lunules, that the artist has indicated on the sides of the breast. Further I regret to notice that here too there has been a mistake in the drawing of the legs.

BESIDES the two species already referred to, both of which as will have been seen, have a very wide distribution, other members of this genus occur in various parts of the world. First, the species commonly known as *D. vagans* of Eyton, but which is the species [*vide* S. F., VI., 488], figured by Horsfield under Cuvier's M.S.S. name *arcuata*, which name has precedence, from Java, the Philippines, Celebes, Timor, and throughout the Archipelago to Australia where it occurs at any rate as far south as Sydney. *D. eytoni* from Australia, *D. guttata*, Müller, from Celebes, Bouru, Gillolo, &c., *D. viduata* widely distributed in Africa and South America, *D. autumnalis* of America, from Demerara to Texas, and *D. arborea* from the West Indies. Very possibly there is another African species, and one or two others from elsewhere. The genus is a "tropicopolitan" one, though its range extends here and there a little north and south of the Tropics.

¼

CASARCA RUTILA

THE RUDDY SHELLDRAKE* OR BRAHMINY DUCK.

Casarca† rutila, *Pallas.*

Vernacular Names.—[Surkhab, (Hindustani); Chakwa, *(male)*, Chakwi *(female)*, (Hindee); Lall, (many boatmen on Jumna); Boogri, (Bengali); Mungh, *Sind;* Sarza, (Mahrathi), *Poona, Sattara;* Neer-bathoo, Neer-kolee, *S. Peninsula;* Bassana Chilluwa, (Telegu); Hin-tha, *Pegu;* Surkhed, *Cabul;* Hangat, (Turki), *Yarkand.*

COUNTLESS myriads of the Brahminy yearly visit India during the cold season, and there are few places in the Empire where they may not be met with. Still they are not found, I believe, on the mainland in Tenasserim, South of the Gulf of Martaban, (Davison believes he saw one straggler on Kolan Island in the Mergui Archipelago), nor have they yet been recorded from Travancore,‡ Malabar or the Southern Konkan,§ while in Tinnevelly, Salem, Coimbatore‖ and the southern portions of Mysore they are rare.

In the North-east of Mysore and the northern half of the Madras Presidency, and thence northwards in the Deccan, the Nizam's Dominions, and so on through the whole Empire to the Hubb River and Shabkadr on the extreme west, and Dibrugarh, Munipur, and Northern Tenasserim on the extreme east, the

---

* The derivation of this name is doubtful, and it is spelt in a variety of ways, Shelldrake, Shieldrake, &c. I suspect that the original name was that by which it still goes in the north, *viz.*, *Skeldrake*, or *Skel goose*.

† It is very doubtful whether *Casarca* should be recognized as a genus, and whether it would not be better to re-unite it with *Tadorna*, the type of which is the common Shell or Shieldrake. As separated, *Tadorna* has the sexes alike, the bills broader and red or yellow; and the culmens markedly concave, while in *Casarca* the sexes differ more or less in plumage, and the bills are less concave on the culmen and black.

‡ Though extremely rare there, it *has* occurred in Ceylon.

§ Mr. G. Vidal writes :—

"The Ruddy Shelldrake is common in the cold weather in Poona, Sattara, &c., on the Bhima, Nira, and Yerla Rivers, and perhaps also the Krishna, though I have never found it there. *It is unknown in Ratnagiri.* They are found sometimes in small flocks, sometimes in pairs, and sometimes solitary. They are late in leaving, individuals or pairs being frequently seen in March and April, and perhaps even in May."

‖ Mr. Albert Theobald says :—

"I have shot them in the Salem, Tinnevelly, and Coimbatore Districts. They come in about November and leave about March. I have shot them in the Collegal Taluq *as late as June;* this was in 1869. They are not common, seldom more than 2 or 4 in a batch."

Ruddy Shelldrake is more or less common in all suitable localities. Naturally, however, in desert, riverless country like so much of Rajputana, they are seldom seen,* and in certain similar tracts in Sind, and again in Cutch and Káthiáwar, they are rare.

In Cachar too, according to Mr. Inglis, they are rather rare, but throughout the Assam Valley and in Munipur† they are very common and so they seem to be in Mymensing and Chittagong, so that their alleged scarcity in Cachar is rather unaccountable.

They are not confined to the plains, but are to be met with equally in the earlier and later parts of the cold season, (they are scarcer in mid-winter,) throughout the lower outer ranges of the Himalayas, in the lakes of the Kashmir, the Kullu and Sutlej Valleys—indeed in the valleys of all our larger Himalayan rivers, the valley of Nepal, and generally up to elevations of six or seven thousand feet, while in the summer they are found breeding at elevations of 12,000 feet and upwards, in the valleys of the Indus and Shyok, at the Tso-mourari, Tso-khar, Pangong, and other lakes, and again in the higher Sikhim ranges,‡ &c.

Outside our limits, I do not think that they extend to any part of the Malay Peninsula, nor have they been recorded from Siam, though they must needs occur in the northern portions, at any rate, of that kingdom ; but they are common in Independent Burma, and Anderson records finding them in the Sanda valley and on the sandbanks of the Taipeng River.

This species appears to be common in winter on inland waters pretty well throughout China, and extends to Japan where some

---

* Its non-occurrence in Arabia (if that *be* a fact) while occurring in India, Persia, Mesopotamia, Palestine, and Egypt, may be due to this same cause.

† My late lamented friend, Mr. Damant, sent me the following interesting note about this species:—"The Brahminy occurs generally throughout Lower Bengal and Assam, and it is *very* common in Manipur. In the day time it is generally found on sand-banks in the larger rivers ; it goes out early in the morning to feed in the rice fields, and is then sometimes found in small flocks, rarely, however, numbering more than twenty birds. It is hardly worth shooting as it is very fishy in taste.

"The great resort of all Water Fowl in Manipur is the Logtak Lake, a large sheet of water lying some twenty miles to the south of the capital. In the cold weather this is about seven miles in length by three or four in width. A leading feature of this lake is the floating islands with which it is studded ; they are composed of masses of vegetation so densely matted together that in some instances fisherman's huts have been built on them. They drift about the lake, and form excellent hiding places for birds.

"In the cold weather this lake is literally covered with Wild Fowl, their numbers far exceeding any thing I have seen elsewhere. I have killed the following species there:—Grey Lag and Barred-headed Geese, Cotton and Whistling Teal, Brahminy Duck (which are very numerous), Shoveller, Grey Duck, Gadwall, Pintail Duck, Common and blue Winged Teal, Red-headed Pochard and Tufted Duck, and I have seen the Pink-headed Duck.

"Of these the Cotton and Whistling Teal and Grey Duck breed in large numbers, the remainder (except perhaps the Pink-headed Duck) are migrants, appearing generally about the end of October and going away about the end of March."

‡ Where Hooker observed it and Blandford also says:—

"A pair were seen on the lake Bidan, near the Jelep-lá in the Chola Range, and one was shot by Capt. Elwes."

breed. It is very common in Mongolia, where it is chiefly a summer visitant, (though some winter in the valley of the Hoang-ho,) as it is likewise to Southern Siberia, and the whole of Central Asia (Turkestan) to the Caspian. It is not a northern bird, and in Asia does not seem, even in summer, to range much north of the 52nd parallel.

Westwards it is common in Afghanistan, Beluchistan and many parts of Persia; in Mesopotamia, Asia Minor, and Palestine, and the entire northern portions of Africa, to which many are, however, only winter migrants.

In Europe it is nowhere common at any season except in the basin of the Black Sea. In the rest of Southern Europe it is rare, (some few breeding, it is said, in Spain,) while to Northern Europe, in most countries of which, (as in Great Britain,) its occasional occurrence has been recorded, it is a mere straggler.

THE BRAHMINY is first seen in the Kashmir Lakes, the Nepal valley and other places in the lower southern ranges of the Himalayas, about the end of September or the beginning of October. By the end of the latter month they are generally pretty well distributed through the whole of Northern India, and during November they arrive in the Deccan and further south.

The majority leave Southern India before the 1st of April, and Northern India by the first week in May, but Messrs. Davidson* and Wenden both say that some remain in the Deccan until late in the hot weather; others in Upper India have noticed individual birds of this species late in May, and it may be that some of the later hatched broods do not breed in their first year, and that these are the laggards.

This is in India, as a rule, essentially a fresh-water Duck; it is rare to find them on the sea-coast or even in estuaries where the water is salt, but Jerdon says he has seen thousands on the Chilka Lake, which is, I believe, mainly sea water.

They arrive in flocks, and before leaving in April gather again into these, but during the winter they are almost invariably seen in pairs. Often several pairs may be found congregated in the same place, but even then each pair comes out distinct on any alarm, and acts on its own behoof and without reference to the others.

It is in the broad beds of our Indian rivers, where clean sandbanks break the river into many channels, that the Ruddy Shelldrake most especially delights, and in such

* Thus Davidson says:—Common along the sandy islands and banks of all the largish rivers in the Deccan, arriving in November and *remaining till very late in the hot weather*; rare in Tumkur, Mysore, and only seen in two or three instances on the larger tanks; not noticed in the Pánch Mahals, but doubtless found along the Mahi River. (*See also Mr. Theobald's remarks, ante, note, bottom of p.* 123.)

places each separate bank will often be found to be the home of several pairs, each however, as a rule, keeping to its own particular portion of the bank and river frontage. In almost every river, however, large and small, they are to be met with dotted in pairs every half mile or so along its course. It is rare to see them in the plains, where the river banks and bed are rocky, still rarer to find them in small ponds or tanks ; but most large lakes are the resort of a few pairs throughout the winter, and in March and April, when gathering into flocks, preparatory to their departure, large flocks are far more commonly seen on the more extensive broads and lakes than on any river.

On such extensive pieces of water, I have often seen parties numbering many hundreds of birds, but I cannot recollect ever noticing more than thirty or forty Brahminies congregated in any one spot on a river.

No object is more familiar in river scenery in India than a pair of these Ducks, standing or squatting, side by side, on the banks, or on some chur ; no sounds are more perpetually heard as one floats lazily down with the stream, than their loud warning notes, repeated more earnestly as one draws nearer and nearer, and followed by the sharp patter of their wings as they rise on the approach of the boat. Very wary they are, and yet not at all afraid of men so long as these keep just out of gun-shot. At Allahabad, at the sacred junction of the Jumna and Ganges, I noticed during a great fair, which is held on the spit of sand, at whose apex the rivers meet, two pair of these Ducks, placidly performing their own ablutions just opposite where some 200,000 people, densely packed, were bathing. The hum, the roar, I should say, of the mighty multitude sounded a mile off, like the surge of wind and waves in stormy weather on a rock-bound coast—scores of boats conveying the richer pilgrims to a shallow of special sanctity, a hundred yards below the point, were ceaselessly plying backwards and forwards, crowded and crammed with human beings,—hundreds of gaudy flags were fluttering from the topmost points of gigantic bamboos planted near the water's edge,——yet, totally regardless of sounds and sights that might have startled the boldest bird, the old Brahminies dawdled about the opposing bank of the Ganges, distant barely 300 yards here from the clamorous struggling rainbow-coloured mass, as though these vagaries were no concern of theirs and signified no more than a convocation of ants.

And it is not that any sanctity here guards them ;—you may see them constantly exposed for sale in the market,—nor that they are unmolested ; for Allahabad is one head quarters of E. I. Railway, and numbers of Europeans are constantly shooting about this very place in boats and favouring the Brahminies, as well as all other feathered things, with " sky" shots.

It seems to be that thoroughly confident in their own ceaseless watchfulness, and quite aware of the range of shot-guns, they are too wise to take the trouble of moving until this becomes really needed.

Everywhere the same thing is to be noticed, and there is hardly a bridge of boats or much-frequented ferry on any of our larger rivers, close to which a pair, at least, of these handsome wide-awake birds may not be found during the cold season. Other Ducks and Geese mostly shun the busy haunts of men, but these seem only to search for spots that suit them (nice *sandy* and not muddy, or rocky banks are what they like), and then "men may come and men may go," but there they are as persistent as their beloved river.

A philosophical contempt for everything and every one well outside gun range, and a rooted determination to allow no one to approach within this, equally characterize these birds; and though they mostly keep by and to themselves, yet where other Water Fowl are numerous, they are necessarily near some of these, and in such cases become veritable *bêtes noirs* to sportsmen.

Not only do they carefully provide for their own safety, but they seem positively to take a malicious pleasure in spoiling all sport. You are working down on a lump of Fowl—a few minutes more and you will be within range. Suddenly the loud call of the Brahminy sounds, and rising out of a hollow in the sand where they have been squatting, you see a pair waddling to the water's edge. Again and again the pair call and answer, (side by side, as they are, one would think that save out of sheer spite they need not shout at each other thus,) then with a rapid chuckle off they go, their wings clattering as they rise like a train on an iron culvert, and with them of course go all the Fowl. Further on are a lot of Geese; you work towards them—vain hope. The ruddy wideawakes have alighted near these now, and duly put them up before you are within a hundred yards, and sometimes a pair will thus persecute you for a couple of miles, before they finally turn up stream to return to their proper beat. As Mr. Reid truly remarks:—

"Sportsmen, as a rule, detest the Brahminy Duck. It not only keeps a sharp look-out on its own account, but will fly along the jhíl side before the gunner, uttering its warning note and putting every bird on the *qui vive.* In fact, it is almost impossible to get up to a flock of Ducks if there is a Brahminy amongst them, or, I may add, any where near them."

Still it is possible to come to an understanding even with them. Keep a small bore express rifle; they offer superb shots, and knock over as many as you can at 150 yards and upwards. After being at this game a few days, and killing five or six, not a Brahminy in the neighbourhood will let you approach within a quarter of a mile, and thenceforth they give you so wide a birth that they interfere very little with fowling. Geese *won't* get up in our rivers when they are comfortable, while there is nothing in sight within a quarter of a mile, let the Brahminies preach never so wisely and long before you are within range the Shelldrake's vaticinations have all been forgotten, and the, whole flock is asleep again.

Although it starts with much noise, as if it had great difficulty in rising, its flight, when once on the wing, is easy and rapid, far more so than it at first appears, which leads to its being continually missed, or hit behind, when crossing at long ranges.

It swims perfectly; few birds look better on the water, and when wounded dives and turns under water (though it cannot keep under *long*) with great ease; but it is essentially a *shore* rather than a *water* bird, and spends the great majority of its time on land at and near the water's edge.

It walks well, quite as well as the Barred-headed Goose, but like this, when undisturbed, is very slow and deliberate in its movements. In walking it holds itself more erect than most of the Ducks.

Although I have on rare occasions noticed them far inland grazing with Geese, and more often paddling about in flooded fields, still it is not, according to my experience, their *habit* to wander far from the water's edge in search of food; certainly they do not with us *regularly* visit distant fields as Geese and many Ducks do. Often encamped on the banks of rivers, I have had a pair continuously within sight or hearing for several days.

No doubt they will graze on young grass and corn when this comes down to the water's edge, and in jhíls gobble up various kinds of water weeds and seeds, but tiny fry of fish, shrimps, and all kinds of small land and water shells have proved the chief food of most that I have examined. On the Jumna I continually found their stomachs half full of small spiral univalve shells. Tame ones I had were dead upon tiny frogs, and though they are decidedly omnivorous, and do at times eat grain and green shoots of all kinds, I think that, in India at any rate, the animal element predominates in their diet.

It has long been charged against them that they feed on carrion also. With Jerdon, I confess, I have always doubted this. In the Ganges and Jumna, where for many years I have watched them, corpses, especially in a sickly season like the last, are not rare, but I have never once *seen* them in close proximity to any dead body. Mr. Reid however says:—"I cannot say that I have ever actually seen it eating carrion, though I have seen it associating with vultures under very suspicious circumstances." And Mr. H. J. Rainey writes:—"I have heard from several sportsmen that it is a very foul feeder, and I myself on one occasion, in 1868, actually *saw* it eating carrion."

We must, therefore, I suppose, admit that it does sometimes, on very rare occasions, thus disgrace itself; but it is certainly quite exceptional, and in Upper India I should say that they may be quite safely eaten, if necessary, without any qualms as to their previous diet.

When better Ducks are procurable, of course, no one would eat them, as the flesh is rather hard and dry, and cooked in the ordinary way, they have a nasty, rank, somewhat fishy taste; but it may be useful to mention that if *skinned* before cooking, this taste disappears, (it is not in the flesh, but in the skin and fat which adheres to this,) and they then form a very tolerable addition to a stew.

Their note is a very clear loud one, of two syllables, which Pallas, Elliot, and others represent by the syllables *à-oung.** It seems with us during the cold season to be only uttered as an alarm, or call to vigilance, and is heard not only during the day but much more frequently during the night, throughout which it resounds at intervals—a very pleasing and inspiriting call to my ear, despite its piled-up associations of lost labour and sport spoiled.

Jerdon gives us the classical native legend that the souls of erring lovers, who have loved not wisely but too well, pass into the forms of these Ducks, condemned thenceforth to pass the night, the season of their transgressions, apart, on opposite banks of some stream, each ever praying the other for permission to rejoin them, and each ever compelled sternly to refuse.

"Chakwa, shall I come?" "*No* Chakwi!" "Chakwi, shall I come?" "*No* Chakwa!"

This story, however, I fear belongs to a more poetical age than the present, and I myself have never met with a native in Upper India who knew of it except from Europeans. Perhaps too the world is more virtuous, or celestial vigilance less keen, for certain it is that in these degenerate days, except in the case of very narrow rivers like the Hindon in Meerut, alike by day and night, Chakwa and Chakwi *are* to be found both on the *same* side of the water.

As the pairs seem most tenderly attached to each other, even throughout the winter or non-breeding season, one rarely straying 100 yards from the other, and both being generally within a circle of twenty paces, we may conclude that they pair for life. This being so, and they being as we know from captive birds anything but quarrelsome, it is difficult to believe that in the breeding season the males often fight and even attack Drakes of other species. Such, however, Prjevalsky asserts to be the case in Mongolia, and I can only suppose that it is the young birds who have not yet mated, or chance widowers, who thus seek to display their prowess.

In India, though perhaps natives, like Europeans, have some feeling against killing them, owing to their manifest affection for,

* The Turks call it "au-gout."—(*Elwes and Buckley—Ibis*, 1870, *p.* 339.)

and constancy to, each other, no sacred reverence attaches to them. It is otherwise in Buddist countries. "It is," says Mr. Oates, "the sacred and national bird of the Burmese, and the native name of the Rangoon District is derived from it." "In Mongolia," says Pére David, "it is the object of a religious respect on the part of the Lamas," and Prjevalsky too says that "the Mongols consider the bird sacred."

THE RUDDY SHELLDRAKE breeds, within our limits, only in the high central portion of the interior of the Himalayas. It nests always in these hills, in holes, in cliffs overhanging, or at any rate in more or less close proximity to, streams, lakes, or pools, at an elevation of not less than 12,000, and often as high as 16,000 feet.

In other countries, though cliffs are favourite resorts everywhere, they also nest in all kinds of queer places.

Prjevalsky says:—"They build in holes or clefts in the ground, and sometimes even in the fireplaces of the villages deserted by the Mongols, and in the latter places the females while hatching get almost quite black with soot." Messrs. Elwes and Buckley say, that in the Dobrudscha, where it is very common, "the nest is very difficult to find, as it is always in a hole, *sometimes in the middle of a corn field*, and the male bird keeps watch near by to call the female off her eggs when any one approaches."

In parts of Southern Russia and Dauria, it lays in holes in trees and even of fallen logs, and in deserted nests of birds of prey. Tristram found it breeding in a cliff in Northern Galilee amongst Griffon Vultures in May, and in the Eastern Atlas associating with the Raven, the Black Kite and Egyptian Vulture.

So too in Ladákh its nests have been found associated with one of the Tibetan Raven.

So far as I can ascertain it lays with us from early in May to near the end of June, according to situation and season.

The nest holes contain usually a thick pad of down and feathers, chiefly those of the bird itself, but at times mixed, the natives aver, with those of the Barred-headed Goose.

The number of the eggs are variously stated by natives at from 6 to 12, but Dybowsky says, writing of them in Dauria, that they lay from 12 to 16 eggs.

I have seen the old birds with crowds of ducklings on several of the Tibetan Lakes towards the end of June or early in July, but this was in old days, when I cared for none of these things, and I never climbed up to examine a nest-hole, of which many have been pointed out to me in the cliffs, conspicuous by the droppings of the birds. But I am quite certain that the generality of the broods did not contain above eight young ones, and even if they ever do lay 16 eggs, I am quite sure that they very seldom here hatch off this number.

In the account of the first Yárkand Mission we say, that "this species was first noticed at the hot springs above Gokra, at an elevation of 16,000 feet. Then they were seen on small lakes that are dotted about on the Salt Plain and all along the Karakash River. The young were at that time—July—scarcely able to fly; when approached, the mother made them all dive by swimming and flapping on to each of them as soon as it showed itself above water. The mother also pretended to be wounded, and lay on the water every now and then with wings spread out as if unable to fly. All along the Karakash Valley, and also on the high table-land, wherever there was water overhung by cliffs, there numbers of Brahminy Ducks with broods of young ones were seen, and holes in these cliffs plastered over with droppings were pointed out by the Kirghiz as the places in which they had bred."

Mr. F. R. Mallet remarks *in epistolâ*:—"As to the Brahminy Ducks, I first observed them in Tibet north of the Niti Pass, at an elevation of about 14,000 feet, on a shallow stagnant pond. There were the old pair and eight young ones unable to fly. I bagged all the latter, but the old parties did not see the fun of it at all and kept out of range. This year I first saw a solitary one in Spiti on a small shallow pond at about 13,000 feet.

"In neither of these cases was there much vegetation; in fact, almost none. Afterwards we saw perhaps two dozen old and young in the streams flowing into the *Indus* in Ladákh. These streams are rapid but smooth, and bordered by coarse grassy plains; from a mile to two miles wide, marshy near the middle. They contain plenty of small fish, and the Ducks I shot near the Niti had a very fishy taste.

"These streams are about 14,000 to 15,000 feet above the sea, and there were lots of Geese on one of them.

"I never saw 'Brahminies' on the rough streams and torrents, except *north* of the first high ranges of the Himalayas, at elevations of 13,000 to 15,000 feet.

"They are not found in summer in the outer high ranges of the Himalayas themselves, but in Tibet, Ladákh, &c."

At the Tso-mourari, the cliffs in which they breed, are far from the water; yet the tiniest ducklings are to be seen swimming about in the lake. Tristram notices the same thing in the Eastern Altas. "At Bow Guizdem," he says, "I captured some half dozen nestlings of various ages in the downy state, some of them scarcely more than a day old, and yet the only place where they could possibly have bred, and where we had procured a nest three days previously, was a range of cliffs more than twelve miles distant." Of course the old birds *carry* the nestlings; but how? The Ládakhis say *in their feet*, and this *may* be so, but it would seem more likely that they carried them on their backs, as their feet are not so well suited for grasping things as are those of the Whistling Teal.

The Drake takes no part, we are told, in incubation; but whilst the female is sitting, always mounts guard close at hand to call her off the eggs should any cause for alarm appear, and once the young are in the water, keeps with them, and watches over them closely as I can testify.

Dr. Scully says: "The Ruddy Shieldrake was observed in the plains of Kashgharia in the beginning of winter, and from March to August it was exceedingly plentiful in the lakes and swamps of Sughuchak, near Yárkand. I met with many young birds, unable to fly, usually swimming about with the old female bird. In July, I saw a party of about ten of these Ducks amongst some rushes; they had a sentinel bird placed at some little distance from the main flock, and on seeing me approach he gave a sort of warning cry which seemed to put his party on the alert. When I got a few steps nearer, the watcher gave a loud scream and flew up, followed by the rest of the party. This bird seems to walk very easily on dry land and always in a curiously erect manner. The Yárkandis say that this species migrates to India in winter, and that the eggs are laid in some dry place away from water; as soon as the young bird emerges from the egg, the mother seizes it and puts it into the water."

I have never obtained an egg from the Himalayas; most sportsmen, owing to the difficulty of crossing the passes so early, reach their breeding haunts too late; eggs sent from Southern Russia are moderately broad ovals, slightly pointed towards one end, creamy or ivory white in colour, rather thin and very smooth-shelled.

They vary from 2·4 to 2·7 in length, and from 1·7 to 1·9 in breadth. Probably a good series would show greater variations.

THESE BIRDS vary much in size and even more in weight according to age, but age for age the males are always larger and heavier than the females.

The following is a *resumé* of many measurements of, apparently, full grown birds:—

Males.—Length, 24·5 to 27·0; expanse, 48·0 to 52·5; wing, 14·25 to 15·5; tail from vent, 5·4 to 6·3; tarsus, 2·3 to 2·7; bill from gape, 2·2 to 2·4; weight, 3 lbs. to 4lbs. 4 ozs.

Females.—Length, 21·75 to 24·0; expanse, 42·5 to 47.75; wing, 12·36 to 14·0; tail from vent, 5·06 to 6·0; tarsus, 2·12 to 2·4; bill from gape, 2·0 to 2·3; weight, 2 lbs. 1 oz. to 3 lbs. 5 ozs.

The irides are deep brown, almost black at times; the bill is black, at times leaden dusky; the legs and feet are most commonly entirely black (at times the webs with a purplish tinge) not unfrequently, however, they are only blackish brown, and in a good many birds of both sexes, which I take to be not fully adult, they vary from pale plumbeous to leaden dusky, the joints being generally darker than the intermediate spaces, and the webs and claws always *much* darker; the webs, however, are often quite light coloured just along the junction with the toes.

In both sexes the wings have a conspicuous tubercle; largest in the male, near the carpal joint, which in some old Drakes is close upon half an inch in length.

THE PLATE is fairly good, though what the black-headed *lusus naturæ* flying in the right hand corner of the back ground may be, it would puzzle any ornithologist to decide.

Neither Jerdon nor any single European writer who has dealt with this species seem to have been aware of the fact that the black collar on the male's neck is purely seasonal, has, as a rule, disappeared by the 15th November, and is rarely reassumed before the 15th of March.

Specimens obtained, when the birds first arrive, prior to the 15th November, very commonly show faint traces of the black ring; but I have only met with one specimen killed during the latter half of November that exhibited this, and I have never seen a single bird killed in December, January or the first-half of February that showed any short of traces of it.

Once or twice I have seen male birds, shot towards the end of February, which were beginning to assume the ring; but it is quite the middle of March before the generality show it clearly, and many are only just assuming it at the close of that month.

Besides the want of the ring and the smaller size, the female birds differ in having, (at any rate during the cold season,) the whole anterior portion of the head pure white, while in the males this part is shaded with orange buff like the rest of the head.

It is a mistake to suppose that the females, as a body, are normally duller coloured than the males. I have many females now before me just as richly coloured as *any* males. But the tone of plumage in *both* sexes varies to an extraordinary (and to me, at present, inexplicable) extent.

In some birds the plumage is precisely of the tint shown in the plate; in some it is rather deeper coloured, especially on the lower parts; in some it is considerably lighter. Again in a great many birds killed at all periods during the cold season, some or all of the feathers of the lower neck all round, interscapulary region, breast and abdomen, are more or less broadly fringed at the tips with pale orange buff, in some cases so pale as to be little more than buffy white. In some specimens, a sort of barred appearance is this produced on all the parts above referred to, while in some, where the pale tippings are very broad, the colour of the bird seems altogether washed out. The result is a very great difference in the appearance of specimens. This pale tipping cannot be an invariable seasonal change, as we have many pale or pale mottled birds killed at the same time and place as fully coloured ones, nor can it, I think, be solely due to differences in age, since during December and January, the birds showing more or less of the pale tippings greatly predominate, while they are comparatively rare in March. The point is one that requires investigation.

Very commonly the white wing-coverts are entirely overspread in the *male* with a paler or deeper, richer or duller, orange buff shade. Indeed I have no male killed before the 1st of April in which *traces* of this are not visible, and in one or two birds it is so strongly marked that the wing-coverts are unicolorous with the breast (in all these examples, itself very pale.) But in the *female*, killed during the same months, the wing-coverts are more generally nearly pure white; still a good many even of the females show traces of the orange buff shade on the coverts, and I have one specimen in which they are nearly as richly coloured as in any male.

In some birds the speculum is a deep green, in almost all lights; in others it is almost always a deep purplish bronze.

In some birds the paler colour of the head and upper neck is abruptly defined all round against the richer tint of the lower neck, while in some the one colour passes by insensible degrees into the other.

I may add that in the majority of birds the feathers of the lower abdomen are deeper coloured and more of a chestnut than the rest of the lower plumage, forming a large and often very conspicuous patch; but in some, probably the birds of the year, there is no trace of this.

A nestling brought from the Tso-mourari is mostly white, marked on the upper surface with blackish brown, and with here and there a fulvous tinge.

TO THE RESTRICTED genus or sub-genus *Casarca* (as indicated, *note* p. 123,) belong three other fine species—*C. cana*, long confounded with our bird, from South Africa, *C. tadornoides* from Tasmania, Southern and South Western Australia, and *C. variegata* from New Zealand, perhaps the handsomest of all.

1/3
TADORNA VULPANSER

THE SHELLDRAKE OR BURROW-DUCK.

Tadorna cornuta, *S. G. Gmelin.*

Vernacular Names.—[Shah-chakwa, Sufaid-surkhab, *Upper India;* Niraji, *Sind;* Mekaz (♂), Alikaz (♀), Shah Moorgabee, *Kábul;*]

THE Common Shelldrake or Shieldrake is a somewhat rare visitant to many parts of our Empire, north of the 22nd parallel of North Latitude. I have it from the mouths of the Indus, the Coasts of the Gulf of Cutch, from near Nowanugger, Káthiáwar, and from close to Calcutta, and Mr. H. Fasson writes that it occurs in Chittagong. I have no record as yet of its occurring anywhere southwards of these localities.

Northwards, it has been observed in Sind, on the Eastern Nára, at the Manchar Lake, and one or two other of the larger broads. It occurs occasionally, chiefly on the larger pieces of water, almost throughout the Punjab, the North-West Provinces and Oudh, and has been observed in several of the districts of Lower Bengal. But it has never been recorded from any part of Assam, Chota Nagpur, the Central Provinces, the Central India Agency, or Rajputana, though it may not improbably prove to straggle into one or all of these, especially Assam. For, though it is not found in the Central or Western Himalayas,* Hodgson notices it as a rare visitant, on passage, to the Nepal Valley.

Outside our limits it occurs in Eastern Tibet, and throughout Mongolia as a summer visitant, and again on the Chinese Coast (whence Swinhoe notices it from Amoy, Formosa, Takoo, and Pekin), and in Japan, as a winter migrant. It does not range far north in Asia or beyond the southern portions of Dauria. It has not been recorded from Yárkand, but breeds throughout Eastern Turkestan, and is common on the Caspian. It is not rare about Kábul and Kandáhar, and has been seen once or twice in Beluchistan, of course as a winter visitant only, as it

* Strange as it may seem, it being common in Kábul, no one has ever yet observed it in any of the Kashmir Lakes, nor have I seen or procured it in or from any part of the Himalayas west of Nepal.

is likewise to Northern Persia and Asia Minor. In Europe it has occurred in most countries, ranging as far north as the Faroes, and in Scandinavia as the 70° North Latitude; but it does not get nearly so far north in Russia. It used to be extremely common on the Coasts of the British Isles, but has been exterminated in many places, and only exists, in greatly diminished numbers, in others.

Again in the north of Africa it is found, but not crossing southwards of the Tropic of Cancer.

As a whole it is essentially a bird of the Temperate Zone of the Old World; nowhere approaching the Arctic Circle, except at the extreme west of its range, and nowhere straggling into the tropics except in the easternmost portions of this.

IN EUROPE pre-eminently a sea coast bird, it is only in Sind, Cutch, and Káthiáwar that it is met with, so far as I know, about our Indian Coasts.* This may be, partly, because most of our coast line is too far south for it, and partly because most of what does occur within its range is too muddy. It likes a *sandy* coast, or at any rate clean soil and not mud. I have never known of its occurrence in any of our rivers, grand reaches of fine sands as these afford, but only in large lakes and broads, and always about those portions where the shores were most sandy, or at any rate, free from mud.

They seem to arrive late and leave pretty early. I have no record of ever seeing one before about the middle of November, or after the middle of April, at which latter period I once saw one in the Calcutta Bazar.

Like the Brahminies they are essentially shore birds; until disturbed, I never once saw one swimming about in the open water. They are either prowling about on the land near to the water's edge, or else paddling in the shallows close to this latter.

With us they are always seen in pairs or in small parties of three to five in number; never in considerable sized flocks.

They walk with more ease than the Mallard, more like the Barred-headed Goose, but less pompously, and with quicker steps. They rise and fly more like other Ducks, with less noise and more rapid beats of the wing than either the Bar-head or Brahminy. As for swimming, I have seen them so seldom out of even *their* depths that I really can say nothing. Naturally I have never seen them dive, though doubtless, if wounded, they would dive, as I have seen them when feeding in shallow water, keeping their heads under, and only the tail halves of their bodies above water, quite as long at a stretch as any of the true Ducks.

All those that I have examined had fed chiefly on land and water shells, and fresh water shrimps of kinds, but the stomachs,

---

* It may occur on the Chittagong Coasts, parts of which are hard and sandy.

which I noted as very strong and muscular, also contained some green vegetable matter and a quantity of coarse sand.

"Their note," says Yarrell, "is a shrill whistle." According to Dresser, "the call note of the male is a deep *korr, korr*, but the female utters a loud quacking sound like that of many other Ducks. The "*korr*" note is probably only uttered during the breeding season; I have never heard it. With us both sexes, when undisturbed, emit a harsh quack, recognizably distinct from that of all other Ducks with which I am acquainted, and *both* sexes, most commonly when suddenly surprised, give forth a note of alarm, which might perhaps be called a whistle.

These birds are, as a rule, so very shy in India that it is difficult to learn anything of their habits, and I never once had any opportunity of watching them at close quarters. The only point I noticed was, that on two occasions I saw birds washing and sluicing themselves with an energy and persistence that I have rarely seen equalled in any other species. *Standing* in water five or six inches deep, the bird kept ducking under from bill to tail, fluffing up all the body feathers, and vibrating its half opened wings for such a time that, on the first occasion, I thought something must be wrong. But no sooner had I put down the glasses, and commenced working up cautiously in a grey gun punt, (in which almost any other Fowl would have allowed me to approach within sixty or seventy yards, against the wind, as I then was,) than the bather pulled himself into shape in an instant, gave a couple of waves of his pointed wings, sounded a call to attention to his mate, (hidden from me by some rushes,) and away went the pair, straight off, to Mongolia for all I know, and were out of sight in five minutes. For a fortnight afterwards, I had a man watching the place, but they never returned, and by that time the hot weather was on us.

No bird is more conspicuous amongst Wild Fowl than the Shelldrake, the brilliant whiteness of so much of its plumage catching the eye at long distances, so that it is never likely to be overlooked, and yet every Indian fowler that I have consulted agrees with me that they have very rarely met with it. It is widely spread; you *may* meet with it any year, anywhere within the limits above indicated, but it visits us in very small numbers and very irregularly.

The real secret of this is, I fancy, that they are by preference sea-coast birds; and that though they will halt for a day or so here and there, they do not willingly make a winter home on our fresh-water broads. There are just a few *very* large pieces of water like the Manchar Lake in Sind, or the Najjafgarh Jhíl in the old predrainage days, where a few pairs would spend the whole winter, but, as a rule, they are only to be seen for a day or two at a time at any jhíl, leaving the place for good, for that season at any rate, after a gun has once been fired there.

They are at once perhaps the most showily plumaged and

the least palatable of all our Ducks. Even skinning these birds before cooking them fails to free them from a rank fishy taste; though in a highly seasoned stew this may be nearly smothered.

THE SHELLDRAKE does not breed in India. In Europe, where it breeds on our British Coasts and those of Sweden, Norway, Denmark, Holland, and Northern France, &c., it nests during May and June in some deserted burrow, generally that of a Rabbit, occasionally that of other animals, such as Foxes and Badgers. Sometimes, it is said, that it may be found nesting without molestation in a burrow, stiil occupied by one of these latter animals.

It lays normally from eight to sixteen eggs, but in parts of Holland, where large numbers exist in an only half wild state, and where the peasants prepare nest holes artificially for it, and make a regular and profitable business of robbing the nest both of eggs and of the fine down in which the bird deposits them, *it will* lay up to thirty eggs. The nest from six to twelve feet from the entrance of the hole is composed of dry grass and the like, and is densely lined with the bird's own down.

The eggs vary a good deal in shape; some are very round, some only moderately broad ovals. In texture the shell is very close and smooth, very like that of the Nukhta's egg. In colour they vary from nearly pure white to a pale cream colour, sometimes showing the greenish tinge of the Mallard's eggs.

In length they vary from 2·45 to 2·75; and in breadth from 1·75 to 1·95.

The young are hatched in from 28 to 30 days, and are immediately led to the sea by the old ones.

THE SEXES are alike,—except that the male is rather brighter coloured, and has in life, (it nearly disappears in skins,) a considerable knob at the base of the culmen which the female wants,—but the males are markedly larger than their mates.

I have only recorded the dimensions of five birds of each sex, so that I fear that the following measurements will hardly sufficiently exhibit the limits within which this species varies :—

Males.—Length, 23·5 to 25·25; expanse, 41 to 46; wing, 12·5 to 13·6; tail from vent, 4·75 to 5·5; tarsus, 2·1 to 2·3; bill from gape, 2·2 to 2·4; weight, 2 lbs. 6 ozs. to 2 lbs. 14 ozs.

Females.—Length, 20·8 to 22; expanse, 39 to 42; wing, 11·75 to 12·4; tail from vent, 4·2 to 4·9; tarsus, 1·95 to 2·07; bill from gape, 2·1 to 2·2; weight, 2 lbs. to 2 lbs. 2 ozs.

In adults the bills are deep red; the nail dusky; the irides brown; and the legs and feet fleshy pink to fleshy red, often more or less creamy on the front of toes and tarsi.

When we first get them in November, the birds are duller coloured than later in the spring, owing to the greyish edgings of the freshly-moulted feathers wearing off during the winter months.

Young birds, as we see them, only differ in being smaller and duller coloured, and in having the bills duller and paler coloured, and the legs and feet a sort of bluish fleshy.

THE PLATE, which represents birds in the full brightness of the April plumage, is very good, except that the bills are too much of a brick-dust and not enough of a carmine red, and that the feet should be a fleshy pink or red, and not tile red as the artist has depicted.

THE RESTRICTED genus *Tadorna* (*vide* note p. 123,) contains, so far as I know, only one other species. *T. radjah* of Lesson from Northern and Eastern Australia, and several of the Islands of the Archipelago.

$\frac{2}{3}$

SPATULA CLYPEATA

THE SHOVELLER.

Spatula clypeata, *Linné*.

Vernacular Names.—[Tidari, Punana, Tokurwalla, (Hindustani), *North-West Provinces and Oudh;* Punta-mookhi, (Bengali); Dhobaha Sankhar (♂), Khikheria Sankhar (♀), *Nepal;* Alipat, *Sind;* Kachack-nol, Aleeput, *Kabul;* Kanak-aurdak (Turki), *Yarkand;*]

I HAVE no record, as yet, of the occurrence of this species anywhere in British Burma, or in the Andamans or Nicobars, but it occurs elsewhere *throughout** the Empire from Ceylon to Kashmir on the west, and Munipur† and Sadiya in Assam, on the east.

In Upper or Independent Burma Anderson found it not uncommon in suitable localities, but, as already mentioned, it has not yet been recorded from any portion of British Burma; we have not met with it in the Malay Peninsula, nor has it been noticed in Siam. Northwards, it is common in winter in Southern China, Formosa, and Japan, and breeds in Northern China, Mongolia, South-East Siberia and Yárkand (where a few remain all the winter)‡ and Eastern Turkestan. It is

* Except perhaps Chittagong, where I am not certain of its occurrence. In Dacca, Cachar, Sylhet. and Tipperah, it certainly does occur. Of course in the vast area embraced by its range it is not everywhere equally common. Thus throughout the west coast sub-ghát littoral, the Southern Konkan, the Malabar Coast and Travancore, where there are no big rivers. and very few pieces of water *inland*, it is mostly very rare. So Mr. G. Vidal, writing from Ratnagiri. says :—

"I have only once met with a small flock here. and that was in December 1878, on a little inland river in the Dapuli Sub-division.

"I have not seen it elsewhere in Ratnagiri. I found this one bunch, exceptionally confiding; after I had put them up, they flew backwards and forwards, till six out of a total of eight had been bagged !"

Again it is decidedly *more* common in the Punjab, the North-West Provinces and Oudh than elsewhere.

† As to Munipur, the late Mr. Damant wrote to me :—

"This Duck I have only killed in Munipur, where it is tolerably common. It is generally found on the edges of bhíls in company with Common Teal and Gadwall, and is rarely seen in deep water. I have never seen it in flocks, generally in pairs and sometimes four or five together; it is a good Duck for the table." (!)

‡ Dr. Scully writes :—

"Two specimens of the Shoveller, a female and a male, were preserved at Kashgar in November and December. According to Yarkandi accounts very few of these birds remain in the country during the winter, the vast majority of them migrating to India. They breed during the summer in the north of Kash-

common in winter in suitable places in Afghanistan and Beluchistan, in Persia, in the Caspian provinces at any rate, in Asia Minor, Palestine, and the entire breadth of Northern Africa, extending southwards to Abyssinia, whereof it is said to be a permanent resident. It has occurred in every country in Europe, and is widely distributed throughout Northern and Central America, possibly, just straggling into the North-West Provinces of South America.

In no part of the world does it, broadly speaking, range much north of the 60th parallel of North Latitude, nor much south of the 10th. Specimens *have*, indeed, been obtained (at the great Bear Lake, and the Mackenzie River,) just within the Arctic circle in North America, at Uleaborg (65° North Latitude) in Europe, and Gould says, Bogota (5° North Latitude) in South America, and the same authority asserts that a straggler has even occurred in Australia, but the normal range may be fairly stated as lying within the 10th and 60th parallels of the Northern Hemisphere.

EXCEPT perhaps in Kashmir where Adams asserts that it is common throughout the year* it is elsewhere with us, whether in hills† or plains, only a winter visitant.

With us too it is essentially a fresh water bird, and I have no record of its having ever been observed on the sea coast in India, though in Europe it is not unfrequently seen there.

In the plains I have no record of its appearance before the 22nd of October, and, as a rule, it is not until the middle of November that the great bulk of the birds, (and though apparently thinly‡ distributed immense numbers *do* visit India) arrive. By the end of April all have, as a rule, left the plains country, though in exceptionally cool seasons a few may linger in the Peshawar Valley until nearly the middle of May, and some certainly remain in Kashmir until quite the end of that month.

---

garia, about the neighbourhood of Maralbashi, and are said to collect, for a short time, near Yárkand, when the cold sets in, previous to their migration southwards."

* This, however, needs confirmation. No one has, as *yet*, obtained the eggs there.

† Except in Kashmir, where a good number pass the entire winter, it is in most places in the Himalayas, more of a bird of passage than a winter resident.

Thus Scully says :—

"The Shoveller is a winter visitor to the Nepal Valley, being most common there on its migrations to and from the plains, but especially in October and November. A few birds, however, probably remain in the valley throughout the cold season."

This, too, is much what Mr. A. Graham Young says in regard to Kullu.

‡ Mr. J. Davidson writes :—

"In Sholapur, Deccan, in Tumkur, Mysore, and in the Pánch Máhals, Gujarat, this Duck was widely distributed, without being found in any great numbers in any place. It is an easy Duck to shoot as it is almost invariably found close to the shore feeding behind reeds or other cover."

Although it may be often seen on the banks of rivers, and again on large inland lakes, it is perhaps most commonly found on small pools and ponds. So, too, though it often associates with other kinds of Wild Fowl, it is, owing to its haunting localities that most of these would eschew, more commonly seen by itself or with, at most, a few of the Common Teal in its company. Where it does occur on the larger pieces of water, it is, I think, decidedly more generally associated with Teal and Gadwall than with any other species.

It is a very tame bird. You will meet with it in many parts of the North-West Provinces on every trumpery little village pond, half surrounded by huts, the resort of the washermen, and of the entire population for purposes of ablution, and of the village herds, driven thither twice a day for water. Filthy is quite an inadequate epithet for many of these reeking sinks of pollution, but foul or fair, the Shoveller is equally at home in them, and may be seen at all hours feeding along the very edge, now just in and now just out of water, making no epicurian selection, but feeding on pretty well every organic substance that comes to hand, nice or nasty.

Doubtless in more savoury localities, such as the more aristocratic Ducks frequent, insects and their larvæ, worms, small frogs, shells, tiny fish, and all kinds of seeds and shoots of water grasses, rushes and the like, constitute their food ; but when they take up their abode on one of these village ponds, and the pond is a real dirty one, I can assert, from the examination of many recently killed birds, that it is impossible to say what they will *not* eat.

All Ducks are more or less omnivorous, but no other Duck will, as a rule, frequent the dirty holes in which a pair of Shovellers often pass the entire winter, sticking to their cess-pool, (for it is really, as the season advances, little short of this), so long as a bucketful of liquid filth and mud remains.

At all times their fat has a most rank and unpleasant taste, but if killed off a clean jhíl and *skinned* before cooking, they are not bad, but unless a man is ready to eat Crows and Vultures he ought steadily to abstain from Shovellers that haunt our dirty little village pools.

In such situations, too, they are quite as tame, in many places, as domestic Ducks. You may walk openly up to them, gun in hand ; when within twenty yards they may waddle into the water, and as you approach, swim slowly from the shore, but they will seldom rise until you fire, and even then as often as not will never attempt to leave the pond, but will settle again after a circle or two in the air.

Generally you find a pair, or one male and two females on such ponds. Even on large sheets of water, on which there may be fifty, they are never in flocks, always in small parties, posted at different parts of the shore, and taking no heed, apparently, of each other. And even on these they are still amongst the tamest of all our Ducks, (the Common Teal is almost as tame,) and when after a tremendous fusilade every other Wild Fowl has temporarily quitted the lake, you will still, as you prowl round the shores to clear up the Snipe, continually find Shovellers rising before you from the weedy shallows well within shot.

To the shores they stick; into the open water they never seem to straggle by choice, and if you watch them they are for the most part either dozing on the brink or paddling slowly in the shallows, with their entire bills and more or less of heads and necks under water, their heads working from side to side all the while like a Flamingo's or a Spoonbill's.

They rise heavily and slowly, but when once on the wing attain considerable speed, and as Mr. Reid remarks, "it is not an uncommon occurrence to see an old Drake Shoveller leading a flock of Teal across country at a rattling pace."

They walk much like Gadwall, but with the bodies more erect and less horizontal. They waddle of course, but can nevertheless run for a few paces when some moving delicacy attracts their notice on the shore, more quickly and easily than their habitually sluggish movements would indicate.

They are, to judge from wounded birds that I have pursued, slow swimmers and poor divers. I never saw one diving when unmolested, nor have I ever noticed them feeding upside-down, with only their stern-halves above water, in the way Gadwall, Mallard, and others are so fond of seeking their food.

"On the whole" (to quote my own remarks made many years ago), "though they abound everywhere, and are very easy to get at, they afford no sport, and are not worth eating; and though the Drake, but for his great, clumsy bill, would be handsome, we must, I fear, put them down, all things considered, in the 'cheap and nasty' category."

SO FAR as is yet known this species does not breed within our limits, but I should not be surprised if a few pairs should still prove to nest in one of the Kashmir Lakes. I have known one to be shot, late in May, on the Woollar Lake, and Leith Adams says it is common all the year in Kashmir. In Europe it generally makes its nest by the side of some piece of fresh water, or in some adjoining marsh carefully concealed by aquatic herbage, or some overhanging bush. But in Denmark, at any rate, it also sometimes nests on the coast.

The laying season extends in different localities from the beginning of May to quite the close of July. The nest is a shallow depression in the soil made by the birds, and thinly or thickly lined with dry grass and down. The eggs vary from 7 to 14 in number; and are somewhat elongated ovals as a rule, a good deal pointed towards the small end.

The shell is very fine and compact. The colour a pale delicate greenish stone colour, sometimes greyer, sometimes with a creamy shade.

In size a large series varies from 2·0 to 2·2 in length; and from 1·33 to 1·58 in breadth.

THE MALES, except just after the breeding season, are very differently and far more brilliantly plumaged than the females, and they are also considerably larger and heavier. Those I have measured varied as follows:—

Males.—Length, 19·7 to 21·75; expanse, 29·75 to 32·5; wing, 9 to 9·8; tail from vent, 3·6 to 4·0; tarsus, 1·2 to 1·5; bill from gape, 2·95 to 3·05; weight, 1 lb. 3 ozs. to 1 lb. 14 ozs.

Females.—Length, 18·0 to 19·0; expanse, 27·0 to 29·5; wing, 8·0 to 8·9; tail from vent, 3·5 to 3·85; tarsus, 1·2 to 1·4; bill from gape, 2·65 to 2·87; weight, 1lb. to 1lb 7 ozs.

In the male, in winter, the bill is black, usually with a greyish shade; in some it may be called leaden dusky. In November, when they first arrive, (before they have quite recovered from the temporary eclipse they, like so many Drakes, undergo immediately after the breeding season), and in the case of birds of the year until much later, the bills of the male are like those of the females.

In the female, the upper mandible is dark brown, tinged reddish along the commissure and on the nail, while the lower mandible is dull orange, brownish towards the tip.

The irides vary, as a rule, in the male from yellow to reddish orange, in the female from brown to reddish brown; but I have recorded them as brown in two or three males, and as bright yellow in one female, so that there is only a general, and not a constant, sexual difference in the colour.

The legs and feet vary from orange to Indian or tile red, and are usually brighter coloured in both sexes in the spring, and at the same season, in the male than in the female. The webs are often dusky towards their margins.

THE PLATE is a very good one. But the legs and feet are always more tinged with red than the artist has depicted.

THE GENUS, a very well marked one, is represented almost throughout the Globe; South America (*S. platalea*), South Africa (*S. capensis*), Australia and Tasmania (*S. rhynchotis*), and New Zealand (*S. variegata*), each possess a species peculiar to themselves.

CASARCA LEUCOPTERA

THE WHITE-WINGED WOOD-DUCK.*

Anas leucoptera,† *Blyth.*

Vernacular Names.—[Deo-hans, *Assam.*]

AN ingenuous Frenchman once remarked, "Ce que je sçais, je sçais fort mal, mais ce que j'ignore je l'ignore parfaitement," and similarly I may say that, of the Ducks I know, I have but a very indifferent knowledge, while of those that, like the present species, I do *not* know, my ignorance is quite perfect.

Colonel Graham tells me that this species is rare in Darrang, common in the Lakhimpur district in Assam, and one of my collectors shot a specimen at Dollah, near Sadiya. Godwin-Austen says he got this species on the Dunsiri River, and that he once flushed one in the interior of the Gáro Hills, and that one was killed near Tezpur. Further, specimens have been sent from Tavoy by Briggs, and by Birdmore from Mergui—in both cases, doubtless, obtained from the forests inland.

---

* This species has been commonly classed as *Casarca*, and designated a Shell Drake, but it is certainly not referable to that genus.

Of both *Casarca* and *Tadorna* (though in a lesser degree in the former), the culmens are concave, the bills comparatively short, and the tarsi not much shorter than the mid toe and claw.

In the present species the bill has no perceptible concavity of the culmen ; it is proportionally long, and, whether looked at from above or below, is very close in shape to that of *Anas boscas*. Moreover this species has the tarsus *very much* shorter than the mid toe and claw, just as is the case in *Anas boscas*, and the other members of the restricted genus *Anas*.

Although I think it quite possible that, when we know more of this species, it may be found necessary to remove it from this genus, I think it better for the present to retain it under *Anas*.

Undoubtedly this bird has some curious affinities with *Sarcidiornis*. Whether in the breeding season the male exhibits any comb we do not know. And in fact the only specimen I possess at present was sexed a female. All my enquiries lead me to the belief that it is essentially a forest bird, and as some other name than Shell Drake is needed, I propose to call it a Wood-Duck.

† It is usual, no doubt, to identify this bird with *scutulata*, of Müller, from Java, but I cannot accept this identification. Long ago (*Ibis*, 1867, p. 176) Blyth, after examining Müller's three types in the Leyden Museum, remarked that they were "all abnormally parti-coloured, and having a domesticated appearance unlike the wild race," *i.e.*, the Indo-Malayan species named "*leucoptera*" by himself.

Beyond this nothing certain is known of its distribution within our limits, though it probably occurs almost throughout the well-watered submontane primeval forest tracts of the entire Indo-Burmese section of the Empire, Assam, Cachar, Sylhet, Manipur, Hill Tipperah, Pegu and Tenasserim, and possibly Chittagong and Arakan also.

It is quite true that long ago Dr. Jerdon wrote to me as follows:—

"I have done nothing as yet in the way of collecting; you can't get any birds off a steamer, but I have seen several flocks of *Casarca leucoptera* in the lower part of the Brahmaputra, where it joins the Ganges, not far above Dacca, where, indeed, Simson had seen it. It is very shy, keeps much to the middle of wide rivers, or isolated sandbanks, and is always in flocks of 10 to 30 or 40. I was quite near enough to make them out distinctly."

But although, in justice to Jerdon, who *may* after all have been *right*, I feel bound to put what he said on record, I myself believe that he was entirely *wrong*.

In the first place, these localities have been examined by dozens of people subsequently, several of them specially instructed in that behalf, and no one has since been able to meet with the bird there. In the second place, what Jerdon says is entirely opposed to all that I have been able to ascertain of the habits of this species. I believe that he mistook flocks of *Sarcidiornis melanonotus*, which are yearly met with just where he and Simson thought they saw the Wood-Duck, for this latter species.

Outside our limits we have met with it in the neighbourhood of Poonga, Kussoom and Kopah in the northern portions of the Malay Peninsula, but never towards the south.

It has never been recorded, I believe, from either Borneo or Sumatra; but, as already mentioned, (*note, p.* 147), a nearly allied form, hitherto commonly accepted as identical, *A. scutulata* of Müller, occurs in Java. This is apparently either a distinct species, or possibly a prolific hybrid with some other species, (the Muscovy Duck perhaps,) derived from captive individuals brought by the Dutch from the Malay Peninsula.

Turning to the Leyden Museum Cat. (*Anseres*, 64) it seems to me clear that the Javan bird must, *primâ facie*, be accepted as a distinct species. Our plate, so far as being an accurate *fac-simile* of the specimen I sent to be figured is concerned, is perhaps the best in the whole work. But Professor Schlegel describes the Javan bird as having the entire head and neck pure white, (not white and fulvous, spotted with black as in our bird), omits all reference to the broad conspicuous black band round the base of the neck, and extending to the sides of breast, and says that the rest of the plumage is chocolate brown "*plus ou moins tapiré de* BLANC sur le manteau, le dessous et les couvertures caudales," of which there is not the faintest trace in our bird.

Apparently either the Indo-Malayan form is quite distinct, or the Javan birds are *hybrids*, or a domesticated and much modified race; and, until further light is thrown upon the question, it will certainly be preferable to accept Blyth's name for our species.

In Siam I should expect it to occur.

"THEY ROOST," says Colonel Graham, "on trees, and frequent solitary pools in deep tree jungle. They are always in pairs, and may be heard calling to each other at great distances. They are rare in Darrang, for the forest is not dense enough and extensive enough there as a rule, but in the vast pathless tree jungles of Lakhimpur they are common."

Says Godwin-Austen: "It appears to prefer sluggish streams flowing through forest, like the Dunsiri at Dinapur, and I once flushed it in such a haunt in the interior of the Gáro Hills."

In the northern portions of the Malay Peninsula, where Darling, Davison, and others of my collectors have come across it, it has been entirely confined to still pools in the heart of dense forest, and has always proved too shy and wary to permit of a specimen being secured. It seems to perch more habitually on trees at all seasons than almost any other Indian species.

I have already quoted Jerdon's remarks. Strange that Blyth too says that this species "inhabits the valleys of the great rivers from the Megna at least to Tenasserim." Had he any grounds for this assertion? Is it possible that for a short portion of the year this species comes down in flocks to the great rivers, and at other times lives in pairs far away in the depths of the primeval forests? Such a thing would be possible, but I doubt its being a fact. During the past ten years the valleys of the Megna, the Irrawaddy, the Sitang, the Salween, the Attaran, the Gyne, the Thoungyeen, the Houngthraw, the Tavoy, the Tenasserim and the Pakchan, have been searched (in the case of most of them time after time) by my correspondents and collectors, without any single one of them having ever so much as seen a single bird of this species.

Personally, I believe this great river valley idea to be a pure delusion.

OF THE nidification of this species nothing is known, except that it certainly breeds within our limits. Mr. James, of the Samaguting Police, informed Major Godwin-Austen that it bred on the Dunsiri, and that he had shot the young birds.

THE ONLY specimen that I possess of this species, a female, measures in the skin :—

Length, 27·0; wing, 12·7; tail, 6·8; tarsus, 2·2; bill from gape, 2·58.

The legs and feet, Colonel Graham wrote to me, were dirty yellowish green, and the bill appears to have been yellow, brownish at tip and base. Certainly neither bill, legs nor feet are black, as described by Jerdon, or leaden grey, as figured by our artist.

Of another specimen, a male (as I have good reason to believe) Blyth gave the following particulars :—"Length of wing, 15 ; of bill to gape, 2·75 ; tarsi, 2·25. Bill yellow, with some lateral black specks ; the dertrum darker ; and the feet appear to have been orange."

But later he figured the bird in " Contributions to Ornithology" from live examples, with both bill and feet dingy olive yellow.

THE PLATE, with the sole exception of the colour of the legs and feet, is an admirable representation of my solitary specimen—*a female*. But says Mr. Blyth :—" The male is rather larger than the female, with fewer black spots, and consequently more white on the head and neck ; the back less mottled with dusky, and the underparts much darker than in the female, which last has a strong tinge of the hue of *C. rutila*," *i.e.*, of chestnut. And when he first described the bird, describing what must have been a male, he said :—" General colour black above and below, a little glossy on the back. Head and neck white, with black feathers interspersed, forming more elongated spots than in *Sarcidiornis melanonotus*. Anterior half of the wing white externally," &c., showing that while there is a general resemblance the male is a larger and much darker bird above and below than the female.

It is to be noted that when later Blyth figured a male from a live specimen, he figured those portions of the head and wing that he had *described* as white, as pale dingy fulvous, so that probably, in some seasons or some birds, the white is not pure.

⅓
ANAS BOSCHAS

THE MALLARD.

Anas boscas, *Linné.*

Vernacular Names.—[Nilsir, (Hindustani); Lilgah, Lilg, (*male*), Lilgahi, Lilgé (*female*), *Nepal*; Niroji, *Sindh*; Subz-zurdan, *Cabul*; Sun or Suna Aurdak, (Turki), *Yárkand*;]

ALTHOUGH the Mallard is extremely abundant in Sindh and the North-West Punjab, (to both of which it is only a cold season migrant), and a permanent resident in Kashmir, its range elsewhere within our Empire is very limited. In the Punjab, Cis-Satlej, and in the northern portions of the Doab, Rohilkhand, and Oudh, Gorakhpur, Basti, and Behar, it is not uncommon during the winter, and at the same season is often seen in the valleys of the Himalayas north of these provinces, as in Kullu, Bussahir, Kumaun, and Hodgson tells us (Scully did not meet with it there) in Nepal, up to elevations of five or six thousand feet.

In the rest of the North-West Provinces and Oudh,* it is, on the whole, scarce, and very locally distributed, and very rare in Jhánsi and Bundelkhand. In Cutch, Káthiáwar, and Northern Gujarat it is rare, and I hardly think it normally occurs much south of Surat. It is almost unknown in Rajputana (Adam never obtained it at the Sámbhar Lake), but I have seen it once or twice in the west, in Jodhpore, and the western portions of Oodeypore.

I have no record of its occurrence in the Central India Agency, except of the one Jerdon shot at Mhow, nor in the Central Provinces, though it doubtless occurs, though rarely throughout the former, and in the western portions of the

* Writing from Lucknow Mr. Geo. Reid says:—"Never at any time numerous within the limits of this division, the Mallard may, to a certainty, be found on some of the larger jhíls after seasons of good rainfall; but during the cold weather months of the past two years—years of drought and scanty rainfall—I have not even seen it. The resulting circumscribed area of the jhíls, coupled with the fact that all of them were still further reduced by irrigation long before the really cold weather set in, may account for its absence. In other years I have shot it on some of the larger lakes, though I never at any time saw it in any numbers strictly within the limits of the division, but further north and west in the Hurdui district, and especially on the "Sandi" lake itis fairly common."

latter, as it undoubtedly does in Berar, where Major Mackenzie has observed it. Chota Nagpore and Bengal (excluding Behar and Purneah) appear to be quite out of its range, though individuals may straggle anywhere into both, just as I myself twice (in the course of ten years, however, be it noted) procured examples in the Calcutta market.

As at present informed, I believe that a line drawn from a little north of Bombay to the Bhútan Dúars, would approximately indicate the furthest southern and eastern limits of its normal range in India; and, although I myself procured it (as above) at Calcutta, and Blyth heard of it at Raniganj, and Mr. Inglis assures me that he has obtained it (though it is very rare there) in Cachar, I can at present only regard these occurrences as abnormal, and these localities as quite outside its natural range.*

Broadly speaking, the normal range of this species may be stated as the entire northern hemisphere from the 20th to the 70th degree N. Lat., but practically it may be defined as the northern temperate zone, since comparatively few either go south of the Tropic of Cancer† or enter the Arctic Circle.

Looking, therefore, to its general distribution, it is curious that it should be practically absent from the Deltaic districts of Bengal, Northern Arakan, Chittagong, Sylhet, and above all Assam; and yet from all these localities my correspondents report that they have never seen or heard of it.

It is very common, especially in winter, in Central Asia,‡ and though Kashmir supplies many of our Mallard, doubtless the

---

* From various parts of Southern India, and even from Ceylon, come vague stories of the Mallard having been seen or shot. But I have been unable to ascertain that any specimen has ever been preserved in any of these Southern localities, and equally so to trace out any individual who has *himself* seen or shot the bird there. Of course a straggler of a species like the present *might* turn up *any* where, but up to date there is no valid evidence, I believe, of any Mallard having *actually* thus straggled to either Southern India or Ceylon.

† Rüppell no doubt says it occurs in Abyssinia, but this seems to need confirmation.

‡ Dr. Scully writes:—

"The Mallard occurs in great numbers in Kashgharia during the whole winter, when it is decidedly the commonest of the Duck tribe. In spring and summer it seemed to be less plentiful; but this may perhaps have been because it was cast into the shade by the great variety of other Ducks and Teal then breeding about Yárkand. In winter it was usually found near unfrozen springs and streams, and in summer in lakes and swamps associated with other species of Duck. The condition of a female obtained in April (which contained an egg almost ready for exclusion), and the occurrence of the two young birds preserved in July, prove conclusively that this Duck breeds near Yárkand. The Yárkandis say that of the twenty odd species of Duck, which they discriminate, the Mallard is the only permanent resident in the vicinity of Kashghar and Yárkand; that it lays in April, the number of eggs varying from ten to fifteen; and that the nest is placed amongst *Yekan, i.e.*, rushes.

"A couple of Mallards, kept in confinement in a tank inside the Residency at Yárkand, formed a great friendship with a Red-crested Pochard (*Fuligula rufina*), and a Coot, who were also captives; but they would never associate with tame Ducks, always driving the latter away when they approached."

majority of those that visit the northern portions of Oudh and the North-West Provinces come from Yárkand.

TO THE greater portion of its range, within our limits, the Mallard is a cold weather migrant, appearing towards the close of October ; but in the submontane districts of the Punjab, Oudh, and the North-West Provinces, individuals are often seen much earlier, so much so as to awaken a suspicion that some few may breed near the bases of, as well as in, the Himalayas. I have known adults to be shot near Rawul Pindee, Sialkot, and in the Dún in August, and a recent correspondent to the *Asian* says :—

"A pair of Mallard, (*Anas boscas*, Lin.) were seen by me on the 29th of July, in a large jhíl in the Fyzabad district, and numbers of the same during the past month (August)."

Similarly, although they leave the greater portion of the plains before the 15th of April, and the more southern parts (Etáwah for instance or Sindh) as a rule by the end of March, I have known of several pairs being seen near Attock as late as the 2nd of May.

In India, even in the far North-West and in Sindh, where many hundreds may be met with in a day, the Mallard is rarely seen in large flocks, and is almost invariably in small knots of three to ten in number, or towards the close of the season in pairs. In the North-West Provinces they are usually met with in the larger jhíls and broads, but in the Punjab and Sindh they are equally common on the larger rivers and inland waters.

With us they feed chiefly by night, often changing their ground for this purpose about dusk, though not with the regularity observable in the case of wild fowl at home, while during the day, at any rate between 10 A.M. and 3 P.M., they are, if undisturbed, almost always asleep. On our rivers, you find the party pretty close together, but not huddled into a lump like some other species, snoozing on the bank at the water's edge, while in broads you find them floating motionless in some secluded nook of pellucid water screened in by bulrushes and reeds, and often overhung by tamarisk or other trees.

Compared with many other species they are tame and unsuspicious, or perhaps I *should* say, unwary. With the most ordinary precautions you may always, (where they are not much worried), make sure of some out of every party that you meet with. To quote what I said of this species many years ago :—

"In the North-Western Provinces, compared with other ducks, the Mallard is scarce, and so it is in the Punjab Cis-Satlej ; but, as you proceed further west, its numbers increase, and all down the Jhelum and the Chenab, from Jhelum to Mooltan, it is out-and-out the commonest Duck. I killed from a dozen to twenty daily, and might easily have killed double that number. They were, comparatively speaking, very tame, and I used to drift down on them in a little boat to within thirty or forty yards, as they sat in small parties asleep at the water's edge, bagging two or three as they sat, and knocking over one and sometimes two more, as they rose, with the second barrel. In the Indus, too, they were equally abundant but more wary, as people continually shoot at them from the steamers, and in most of the larger inland waters of Sindh I met with them in great numbers. At first starting, the Mallard lies better, and affords better sport than any of the other Ducks, and when you first go on to a broad that has not previously been shot that season, the Mallard keep continually rising, pretty close to the boat, from under the boughs of water-surrounded tamarisk trees and clumps of rush, affording beautiful shots."

As regards their habits, it is useless attempting to repeat, in probably less accurate language, what Macgillivray, our greatest British field-ornithologist, has already told so admirably; and I shall just quote his remarks, only adding that time after time, both at home and out here, I have verified every word. He says:—

"Marshy places, the margins of lakes, pools and rivers, as well as brooks, rills and ditches, are its principal places of resort at all seasons. It walks with ease, even runs with considerable speed, swims, and on occasion dives, although not in search of food. Seeds of gramineæ and other plants, fleshy and fibrous roots, worms, mollusca, insects, small reptiles, and fishes, are the principal objects of its search. In shallow water, it reaches the bottom with its bill, keeping the hind part of the body erect by a continued motion of the feet. On the water it sits rather lightly, with the tail considerably inclined upwards; when searching under the surface it keeps the tail flat on the water; and when paddling at the bottom with its hind part up, it directs the tail backward. The male emits a low and rather soft cry between a croak and a murmur, and the female a louder and clearer jabber. Both on being alarmed, and especially in flying off, quack; but the quack of the female is much louder. When feeding, they are silent; but when satiated they often amuse themselves with various jabberings, swim about, approach each other, move their heads backward and forward, "duck" in the water, throwing it up over their backs, shoot along its surface, half-flying, half-running, and in short, are quite playful when in good humour. On being surprised or alarmed, whether on shore or on water, they spring up at once with a bound, rise obliquely to a considerable height, and fly off with speed, their hard-quilled wings whistling against the air. When in full flight, their velocity is very great, being probably a hundred miles in the hour. Like other Ducks they impel themselves by quickly repeated flaps, without sailings or undulations."

In this country, where so few sportsmen use or know, or care to know, how to use a punt and swivel gun, there is really little to be *said* about shooting wild fowl. In rivers you either drift on to them in a boat or approach by land under cover of some kind—a very easy matter in narrow rivers with high perpendicular banks. In broads, you similarly creep within shot, or in some native dug-out, push through the rushes, getting many good, but usually mostly long shots, or preferentially (for the first dozen shots generally rouse the majority of the best Ducks,) lie up in some rush bed or some reedy isthmus between two pieces of water and have the fowl driven over you by beaters. This is undoubtedly excellent sport, requiring, if any real success is to be attained, a true aim and a hard-hitting gun, and resulting, to practised hands, in enormous bags.

Butler gives an account of one good day he had. He says:—

"I remember upon one occasion making an extraordinarily good bag upon a tank about 35 miles north of Ahmedabad. There were two of us out, and we took up our stands at about 2-30 P.M. At 5-30 P.M. we discontinued shooting, and sent coolies into the water to collect the dead and wounded. I laid my birds in rows as they were brought out of the water, arranging them according to species, and a more imposing sight I never saw.

"There were eighty birds in all, representing fifteen different species, and every one of them was shot separately and on the wing, that is to say, there was no firing into the brown of big flocks closely packed on the water or mud banks, resulting in the death of half a dozen or so at one shot; the birds, of which there were thousands, were kept constantly on the wing by coolies beating at both ends of the tank, and as they passed our screens, which were erected upon islands in the middle of the tank, we selected single birds to shoot at. We lost a great many wounded birds that dived immediately they fell on the water and were seen no more. My friend shot 47, which, added to mine, made a total of 127 ducks in three hours' shooting—a bag, which I imagine, few sportsmen have beaten."

Very few of these probably were Mallard, but in small gun shooting, the species makes in most cases little difference, while with the punt gun, in which you must get a sitting shot, or one just as the birds rise, the species makes all the difference in the world, and success mainly depends on a thorough knowledge of the manner in which each species of fowl will comport itself on your approach. Some draw together and rise *en masse*, and these should only be taken when a foot above the water; others, though drawing together, rise in succession, and these are best fired at *just* before they rise. Others again separate on any suspicion of danger, and at these a shot, however long, at the first sign that they are on the *qui vive*, is most likely to tell. Then you must be able to tell, from the way they hold their heads and tails, the way they move and face, when they first begin to suspect that there are hostile influences in the neighbourhood ; you must know the exact tone of their calls as suspicion deepens into alarm, and when they resolve to be off. To fire at the exact nick of time is half the battle, and this is only possible after careful study of the behaviour of each species when gradually or suddenly alarmed. I say suddenly, because it will often happen that you can only get a *good* shot, by yourself starting the fowl by a kick on the side of the boat, or a slap with a paddle. You must be exactly in the right place with reference to your bore and size of shot, and you must be able to judge distances extremely correctly, lying flat at the bottom of the boat with your eye only about ten inches above water level. And you must be able to allow for the pitch of the boat, since even in our broads and lakes wavelets of considerable size get up under a stiff breeze. And above all you must have strong arms and wrists and dogged perseverance, to work up dead to windward against a good wind (this is perhaps when the heaviest bags are made,) lying flat, with only your hands over the gunwale just behind the bulge of the boat. I say nothing about the necessity of care as to where exactly your face and arm are with reference to the butt of the gun, but this too is a serious matter ; for stauncheons *will* break, and the long swivel dart back to the stern, and cheek bones and arms suffer if due count of such contingencies has not been taken.

There is more skill, knowledge, and endurance brought into play, and therefore more *sport*, in one day's big gun shooting than in a week of even shooting such as Captain Butler describes ; but punts and swivels, here and at home, have utterly gone out of fashion, and no gentleman now-a-days knows how to use them, (the professional fowlers no doubt stick to them, and with vastly improved and *breech-loading* guns, and only an old fowler knows how much this means), and it is useless playing the part of a *laudator temporis acti*, or saying more of a form of sport which, however glorious, is as much extinct, where my readers are concerned, as falconry and hawking.

Enormous numbers of wild-fowl are yearly captured by natives, and it may be as well to say once for all, something about their *modi operandi*.

I have only seen fowl captured in India, in any numbers, in three* ways :—First by hand. Here the fowler enters the water

* There are two other methods of capturing Wild Fowl, said to be most successful, but which have never succeeded with me. The first is to have a strong but thin cord stretched tightly eight or ten inches above the water, being tied, every ten yards or so, to poles firmly set in the mud below, with their heads projecting, only the

unperceived, with something over his head and shoulders, precisely similar to something that the fowl are accustomed to see floating about, and which thus enables him to move about up to his neck in water, but with his head above this, and yet quite screened from sight. For this purpose they use, in some places, large earthen vessels, (*chatties*, or *gharrahs*,) in some large gourds, in some baskets stuck about with rushes, so as to look like floating lumps of these. In Sindh, as I noted many years ago, they use the skin of a Pelican. I said talking of the Silver-grey or Dalmatian Pelican:—

"This is the Pelican that the fishermen on all the inland waters keep tame. As with the Herons, so with the Pelicans, they generally sew up the eyes, and fasten them, by a string tied to the leg, to the roots of some bunch of rushes, or to a stake driven in below water level. They thus serve as decoys to other water-fowl, who, knowing how wary Pelicans usually are, readily settle where they see one or more of these birds sailing slowly about backwards and forwards, and are thus netted or captured in other ways. These Pelicans serve the fishermen, who are fowlers also, in another way: they skin them carefully, and cutting away the abdomen, in fact the greater portion that would be below water-level in the live bird, line the skin with a frame of thin basket work. They are very clever in mounting the birds, especially in dyeing the pouch and colouring it with turmeric so as to look exactly as in the live bird, and also in imitating the eyes which they manufacture out of lac. When ready, the fisherman places it on his head, gets into the water, and progresses slowly and softly, making the skin, which conceals his head, sail about in the water in the most natural way imaginable, until he reaches the spot where some of his blinded and tethered Pelicans are surrounded

---

required amount above the surface of the water. This line is thickly set with horsehair nooses, at all possible angles, so that a duck can scarcely swim under the line without getting its head through some noose or other. This line is set in one of those jhils in which ducks come to feed at night, and after they have settled, they are gently worked to and fro, backwards and forwards. under the line, never being so pressed as to lead to their rising, only sufficiently to make them swim away. Natives have continually assured me that they have caught hundreds in a night this way, with a really long line. and I believe that there is no doubt that they do thus capture large numbers, but owing to some blundering on my own or my people's part, I have never succeeded in making any hauls this way. It *seems* so reasonable, that I had a beautiful line made fully 500 yards in length with between 30 and 40 thousand nooses on it, and I had it set, time after time (a very troublesome and laborious business, as each noose has to be put in a proper position), and I never caught above a dozen birds in any night, though thousands of fowl must have passed under that line a dozen times at least. Others may manage better.

Another plan is to peg down a strong line along some foreshore where fowls feed at night close to the waters' edge. The line is pegged about every yard. and from each point, where a peg is put down, a thin line, a yard or so long, is led out at right angles into the shallow water. Each line carries two or three strong fish hooks which are baited with worms, large water crickets, small frogs, fish, and the like. The lines and pegs are covered with sand, only the baits are left showing. I have never tried this, but especially on sea coasts, where large bodies of fowl feed regularly in particular spots, it is said to be very effective.

by wild water-fowl which he adroitly pulls under water without in the slightest disturbing the rest. Sometimes, we were told, he drags with him a piece of double rope, twisted, with a stone or weight fastened to it; each bird as it is caught has the neck thrust between the twists of the rope, and thus as many as twenty will be captured at a single trip; some have a light cord fastened round the loins, between which and their bodies they thrust the neck; in either case they kill the duck almost instantaneously by a sharp twist of the neck. I never myself saw the ducks thus caught, but a man put on the Pelican helmet and made it sail about before me in such wise that, even when quite close, it was difficult to believe that it was not a living bird."

In every case the object is to use something which the birds are accustomed to see moving about harmlessly amongst them, and for this purpose, where earthen pots, gourds, &c., are used, a number of these, precisely similar to the one used, are turned adrift in the water a week at least before catching commences, and kept afloat all the season. It is usual, too, in order to facilitate captures, to throw grain daily on the water in a particular spot, where the fowler can most easily work so as to ensure his being able to find birds where there are no dangerous holes and where the water is neither too deep nor too shallow.

Of course a great deal of practice is necessary. Gourds and the like, impelled by the wind, only move in a certain, slow, deliberate manner, and this must be exactly imitated. Any abnormal movement of the helmet would at once excite suspicion, and cause the fowl to disperse. It is difficult too so to pull the birds under, that their fellows do not notice their disappearance. The retreat must be as careful as the advance, and the man, both in getting into and out of the water, must be effectually concealed from view.

Large numbers are captured in this way. One man, a Mahomedan-Bengali, told me that, visiting four tanks on successive days, he caught one day, with another, about a dozen ducks daily throughout the season, and he caught before me every one of a party of seven Gadwall, and that although the last two were obviously getting suspicious, probably on account of the disappearance of their comrades. I have tried this plan myself two or three times, but the cold is trying, and moving as slowly as one has to do, the work is most wearisome; *and* I only once succeeded in capturing a duck (an old Shoveller), and that made such a fuss going under, that it put up all the other fowl, so I very soon gave up the personal practice of this system.

Not so the second plan of the standing net which I worked for years. You make nets of moderately thick English twine, two inch meshes, in pieces, fourteen feet wide, and a hundred yards long. You have, perhaps, six such pieces, and you use one, two, four six, as you require. A thin English cord is run through the upper margin of the net, tied at every fifteen feet, and where tied, it is made into a small loop to receive the head of the pole. For each piece you have twenty-one light, but strong, bamboos, about sixteen feet long. Selecting some large shallow jhíl, where fowl are comparatively scarce during the day, but to which they resort in numbers at night to feed, you run your net about 10 A.M. across part of the water. A little judgment is here required. You have to see where the fowl usually congregate, and in what direction it will be easiest to drive them. You must so plant the net that it shall be invisible at night from that part of the water over which you intend driving the fowl; and it must, therefore, have a dark background, trees, or a high bank. It must be at least eighty yards in from the further shore, or the fowl would (finding they were being driven in too near the shore), rise before they got near the net. The water ought not to be above two feet deep, so that there may be twelve feet of the net above the water. The bamboos should be painted dull lead color, the net (*well tanned* first,) should be dyed with a weak solution of indigo. You run out the one, two, three, or more pieces in a straight line; with six practised men, and a heavy crowbar to make the holes for the butts of the bamboo poles, each piece can be put up in about twenty-five minutes. There are a few yards of spare rope at each end of the net, and this is pegged down about four yards beyond the last pole, with a strong peg, so as to keep the whole line taut. As each piece is set, the net is thrown up over its upper margin, so that, during the day, any fowl there are can swim under it backwards and forwards without even noticing it, as, when properly done, no part hangs down within eight feet of the water. Just at dusk before the fowl arrive, the men silently pull the net down. Then about 8 or 9 P.M., when the fowl have thoroughly settled themselves, and have fed heartily, so that they are averse to flying, you go into the water, and gently drive the fowl towards the net. It is best for every man to be accompanied by a buffalo; in that case you can walk within ten yards of the fowl, and see exactly what there is, and how best to drive them. But this is not necessary. I have often driven fowl without buffaloes, and the only difference is, that you cannot approach the fowl so closely, that you require more men, that the drive takes twice as long, and that you cannot be equally sure of making the best of the haul. You walk backwards and forwards slowly, at right angles to the direction in which the fowl are to go, approaching nearer at each turn, they, all the while, slowly swimming towards the net. The number of men must depend first upon the width of water you have to drive, and upon whether you have cows, buffaloes or ponies with you or not. When the bulk of the fowl are about ten yards from the net, you fire a gun; all the beaters shout, splash, and rush towards the net; the fowl spring up, and many failing to clear the net get entangled in it in the most extraordinary manner, and you rush up and secure as many as possible. Unless you are all very "spry," a good many of those which have been entangled somehow get away. If there are many, it is best to pluck up the poles rapidly, and throw the net down on the water, the fowl undermost; and when you have flushed a little too soon, and the mass of the birds are high in the net, you *must* do this. Not only Wild Fowl, but Geese, Godwit, and Curlew, and all kinds of waders are often found securely meshed. I have had the net completely thrown down by a heavy haul of Geese, (I think we *secured* seventy of them), and I have, on several occasions, bagged over 200 birds of sorts in a single drive. On the other hand, many and many a drive has yielded only half a dozen Teal and Godwit. Most certainly this is very exciting sport, requiring a great deal of skill and organization, and thorough training of your men; and as in a properly chosen jhíl, you ought never to get over the tops of your marsh boots, it has for *you* no drawbacks, but your men must be well fed and have good blankets, and be looked after a good deal, or they will all get fever. It is no use *paying* them well; they will always stint themselves. You must give them free rations, plenty of *gur* and *ghi*, and a sheep now and then, and see they eat it. The same men will manage your nets for fishing, (they should be *Mullahs* and *Kahars*), and make themselves useful in many ways; and, though the "plant" is a little expensive to begin with, (properly taken care of it will last for years,) and you will want at least six and probably ten men, as permanent servants for the five months, you will certainly get your money's worth, if you are marching in a country full of jhíls, and abounding in Water Fowl and Fish.

The third method is by fall nets, set in a place where Fowl habitually feed, and which is regularly baited for them with grain. Natives undoubtedly are very successful with these nets, but I have never been so, and as I have already referred to this plan (*ante* note, p. 37) I need say no more about it now.

Certainly, in my opinion, a Mallard in good condition is the very best Duck for the table that we have in India. The Common Teal and Pintail come next, and Grey Duck, Gadwall and both the Red-headed and Red-crested Pochards are often excellent, but a good Mallard is *facile princeps*.

THE MALLARD breeds in vast numbers in Cashmere, and possibly a few breed elsewhere in the Himalayas, at moderate elevations. Brooks found a pair for instance, in the middle of May, on a small mountain tarn, above Derali in the valley of the Bhagirathi, which very possibly would have bred there, and I have heard of other pairs being met with even later at small secluded lakelets in various parts of the Western Himalayas, at elevations of from 5,000 to 9,000 feet. So too, as already mentioned, it is just possible that here and there a stray pair may remain to breed in swamps about the southern bases of the Himalayas from Hazára to Nepal, but the only locality in which we certainly know of their nesting is Kashmir. There it breeds, not only about most of the lakes in greater or lesser numbers, but even in still reaches of mountain streams, at the edges of water courses, and in rice fields.

The nest is almost invariably placed upon the ground, in thick low cover of grass, rushes, or rice; but the native egg-gatherers report that they have found nests on trees. The nest is always a large, coarse structure, composed of dry grass, rushes, and the like, more or less lined with down and feathers.

It lays in May and the first-half of June. Twelve is the largest number of eggs seen in any nest by my collector (a native), who examined hundreds of them. There is quite a trade in the eggs of this species and *Fuligula nyroca* at Srinugger, and my man went out daily almost for a month in one of the egging boats. The boatmen told him that they *had* found as many as sixteen eggs in one Mallard's nest!

"Frequently in leaving the nest," says Macgillivray, "she covers it rudely with straws and feathers, probably for the purpose of concealing the eggs. The young are hatched in four weeks; and, being covered with stiffish down, and quite alert, accompany their mother to the water, where they swim and dive as expertly as if they had been born in it. The mother shows the greatest attention to them, protects them from birds, feigns lameness to withdraw intruders from them, and, leading them about from place to place, secures for them a proper supply of food."

Mr. Brooks say *in epistolâ*:—"The Mallard's nest I took was amongst rushes in a rather dry spot of one of the Kashmir lakes; it was built of straw and dry rushes, and lined with the bird's own down."

The late Major Cock wrote to me that this species "breeds in large numbers on the Anchar Dall and other lakes in Kashmir during the months of May and June; boat loads of their eggs are brought to the Srinugger bazars for sale, together with the eggs of the Coot and White-eyed Duck. The Mallard breeds near the water in among reeds or high grass, lays six, eight, or more eggs, of a peculiar oil green colour. The nest is formed of dried grass or flag with a little down from the bird's breast, and placed under an overhanging tuft of grass or rush. The female sits close and allows you to come very near before she leaves her eggs." I may add that she will not unfrequently allow herself to be captured by hand on the nest, if the eggs are near hatching.

The eggs of the Mallard vary a good deal in size and colour. In shape they differ little, and are moderately broad, regular ovals, not unfrequently slightly compressed towards one end.

In texture the shell is very fine and smooth, and has a faint gloss. The egg is quite devoid of markings, and when freshly laid, has a dull pale greenish tint; but as incubation proceeds it changes to a very pale drab, or dingy stone colour, and every intermediate shade is observable. In size they differ little from those of the Grey Duck, but the latter are always whiter, and never exhibit the green tinge so conspicuous in the freshly-laid egg of the Mallard.

The eggs vary in length from 2·1 to 2·38, and in breadth from 1·5 to 1·72; but the average of thirty eggs is 2·23 by 1·6.

THE MALES are larger and run much heavier than the females; the former measure:—

Length, 22·5 to 24·5; expanse, 35·0 to 38·0; wing, 10·45 to 11·3; tail from vent, 4·2 to 4·8; tarsus, 1·6 to 1·85; bill from gape, 2·5 to 2·75; weight, if in fair condition, 2 lbs. 8 ozs. to 3 lbs., but I have shot them up to 4 lbs.!

The females measure:—

Length, 20·0 to 21·75; expanse, 33·0 to 35·0; wing, 9·2 to 10·8; tail from vent, 4·1 to 4·7; tarsus, 1·5 to 1·7; bill from gape, 2·47 to 2·63; weight (as above), 1 lb. 10 ozs. to 2 lbs. 10 ozs.

The colours of the soft parts vary. I have found the legs and feet most commonly reddish orange, but also coral and vermilion red, and again pure orange; the claws are black, or dusky, and more or less of the webs are often more or less dusky; the irides are brown, sometimes deep, sometimes comparatively light; the nail of the bill is black; the rest of the bill is normally a rather dingy olive, yellower at base, greener at tip; the lower mandible is generally more or less orange at the base, and I have killed birds, females, with the bills *black* on the culmen and a considerable portion of the upper mandible, and orange yellow elsewhere; others with brown replacing the black, and brownish yellow replacing the orange, and I killed one male with the bill, a distinct orange green, a colour such as I never saw in any other bird.

THE PLATE would be quite satisfactory (though the drawing of the female is rather coarse) had not the bill of the male been drawn rather too short and quite wrongly coloured, and had not that of the female been coloured after an abnormal specimen. The plumage varies a good deal; in many males the head is a deeper and richer green, and the chest a deeper and more maroon chestnut than in our figure. In many the vermicellations of the sides and lower parts are barely discernible; in the specimen figured they happened to be particularly strongly marked. Again, in this and many other species, the entire lower parts are often strongly suffused with an ochraceous buff tint, which has been the subject of much discussion. That this tint is due to iron has been proved, but whether it is absorbed as a dye from ferruginous waters, as some suppose, or secreted from the blood by the feather glands themselves, as others hold, seems to be still quite undecided.

Some females again are considerably less boldly marked than the specimen figured.

I must not omit to notice here the post nuptial plumage that the Drakes of this species, in common with those of many other species, assume—a sad, dull coloured garb, like that of the female. Whether this change is the result of exhausted vigour, the outcome of the male's marital exertions during the breeding season, or whether the less conspicuousness and consequent comparative immunity of the male at the time when the young require his care and protection, has led to the preservation of more young birds of males undergoing this change, and has thus converted an accidental variation into an hereditary characteristic, it were useless here to enquire; but the fact is one of great interest. Waterton, who watched them closely, says: "At the close of the breeding season the Drake undergoes a very remarkable change of plumage. About the 24th of May, the breast and back of the Drake exhibit the first appearance of a change of colour. In a few days after this, the curled feathers above the tail drop out, and grey feathers begin to appear amongst the lovely green plumage which surrounds the eyes. Every succeeding day now brings marks of rapid change. By the 23rd of June scarcely one single green feather is to be seen on the head and neck of the bird. By the 6th of July every feather of the former brilliant plumage has disappeared, and the male has received a garb like that of the female, though of a somewhat darker tint. In the early part of August this new plumage begins to drop off gradually, and by the 10th of October the Drake will appear again in all his rich magnificence of dress."

ANAS PÆCILORHYNCHA

THE GREY OR SPOT-BILL DUCK.

Anas pœcilorhyncha, *Forster*.

Vernacular Names.—[Garam-pai, (Hindustani); Gugral, (Hindi), *North-Western Provinces;* Bata (apud Jerdon); Hunjur, *Sind;* Kara, *Munipur;* Naddun, *Nepal Terai;* Neer-bathoo. (Tamil); Neer-Kolee, (Canarese), for nearly all water fowl, *Madras Presidency;* and Dód-sărlé-hăkí, for all large ducks, *Mysore.*]

A PERMANENT resident and an inhabitant of the major portion of the empire, there are comparatively few places in it, south of the Himalayas, from which the Grey Duck has not been recorded. But to the Himalayas* it does not extend; it has not been noticed in Kashmir, Ladákh, Kullu, Bussahir, &c., Garhwál or Kumaun, except quite at the bases of the Hills, or in Nepal, except in the Terai at their feet. Again it has not been met with in the Southern Konkan, and is extremely rare (if indeed it occurs there at all) in the sub-ghát littoral further south. In Tenasserim I do not believe that it occurs at all, nor is there any reliable record of its occurrence in Pegu. It naturally does not occur in the Andamans, Nicobars or Laccadives, and I cannot ascertain that it has ever been obtained in the extreme north-western corner of the Punjab, Peshawar, Attock, Mardán.

With these exceptions it occurs (rarer in some places, more common in others)† throughout the empire, from Ceylon to Sindh, Sindh to Sealkot, Sealkot to Sadiya, Sadiya to Munipur and southwards to Chittagong (H. Fasson) and Northern Arakan.

Outside our Empire, I only know of its occurrence in Upper or Independent Burma, where Anderson found it not uncommon. It has not been observed westwards in Beluchistan or Afghanistan, and to the east in China and Japan it is replaced

---

* Indeed, so far as my present information goes, it is a bird of the plains, and does not ascend any of our Indian hills to any considerable elevation.

† Thus it is decidedly rare in Jessore and about Calcutta; very common in parts of Mysore, &c.

by a very nearly allied species, (long confounded with our bird,) *A. zonorhyncha*, of Swinhoe, which, even in the adult, has no red patches at the base of the bill.

TO A certain extent the Grey Duck is migratory, and in the drier portions of the North-Western Provinces, the Punjab and Rajputana, is *very* much more abundant during the rainy season and the early part of the cold weather than during the rest of the year. Indeed in the more desert tracts it is scarcely ever seen except during the monsoon.

On the whole this species seems to prefer quiet tanks and small streams in fairly-wooded country; but it may be met with anywhere—in village ponds, on large lakes and on the banks of large rivers. It is a mistake to suppose that they are not found in these latter. I have shot them several times on both the Ganges and Jumna (on both of which, however, they are rare), while on the Jhelum, Chenab and Indus they are quite common.

A rushy weed-margined tank, but with a fair expanse of clear water is, perhaps, their favourite haunt, and in these they commonly keep about the centre, well out of shot, during the day, and feed along, (and often on,) the banks at dusk and during the night. Not that they are very shy birds, or difficult to get near when not much molested; on the contrary they are very like the Mallard in these respects, and can always be worked up to in a punt with certainty. On rivers they will be found commonly on the banks, or asleep alongside these under the shade of some overhanging clifflet, tree or bush. Sometimes too in quanting through beds of rushes you will flush them, or again find them even in broad daylight paddling in the shallows of some mere village pond with a few Teal and a brace of Shovellers.

I do not know whether they absolutely avoid salt water, but I have never met with them anywhere on the sea-coast; and I am inclined to believe that they are essentially fresh-water birds.

Although they rise rather heavily and are as easy to shoot as old hens, when they first fluster up out of the reeds, they fly with very great rapidity when well on the wing—in this respect quite equalling the Mallard; and on the water they both swim and dive more briskly than this latter, as any one who has pursued many winged birds of both species in a native boat will, I am sure, admit.

No bird gives more trouble when wounded, and Captain Butler only does them justice when he says:—"The Grey Duck is one of the most difficult of any of the ducks to catch when wounded, if it once reaches the water, as it dives very freely, and when it rises seldom shows more than its beak above the water, which is by no means an easy object to see amongst weeds or in the rushes. One of the flappers we caught, after diving for a considerable distance, took refuge in a thick mass of weeds at the bottom of the tank (three feet deep) from which moist retreat he was extracted by one of the beaters who accidentally trod on him when walking through the water in search of one of the others."

Many a time have I recovered them, dead under water, firmly fixed to the weeds, and many more I have failed to retrieve even with the help of good dogs.

Their plumage is less dense than that of the Mallard, and to this I attribute the undoubted fact that they are decidedly easier to bring down at long distances.

Their voices, both when chattering to each other, when at rest or feeding, and when uttering their quacks of alarm, closely-resemble those of the Mallard, but may always be distinguished by a somewhat great sharpness; they are not so sonorous, but they seem to be emitted with greater force.

They are very miscellaneous feeders, and I have found worms, small frogs, and insects and their larva in their stomachs; but grain (wild rice by preference), and all kinds of rush, grass and water-plants and their roots constitute the bulk of their food, and I have often examined birds which had fed on vegetable matter only. I have been told that they sometimes have a very fishy flavour, but I have never yet found the remains of fish in any single specimen.

Usually this species is met with in pairs or small parties, but where numerous, they may occasionally be seen in comparatively large flocks. Thus Major Charles McInroy writes: "I have frequently seen at least 100 of these Ducks sitting together on the shores of various tanks in the Mysore Province, and these kept together when on the wing, although it is doubtless more common for the various families to keep to a certain extent separate."

And Mr. George Reid says:—"During the rains it is usually seen in pairs, frequenting small and weedy jhíls or swamps; but in the cold weather it is compelled to resort to the larger lakes, and may then be met with in flocks ranging from 6 to about 30 in number."

Personally I cannot remember ever seeing more than a dozen together; and, though I have often found from fifty to a hundred on a large lake like the Manchar, or the Najafgarh in the pre-drainage time, these have invariably been dotted about the lake in pairs, or in families, (as I take it,) of from three to ten individuals.

They do not consort readily with other fowl, and it is rare to find them mixed up with these; indeed if not quite by themselves, as they usually are, they seem only to associate with Teal and Shovellers.

For the table the Grey Duck is second only to the Mallard and Pintail, and it is such a large fine heavy bird, that, as Captain

Butler says, "I always select this species in a drive to fire at in preference to most of the others."

These ducks are occasionally, but not very often, caught by hand and in nets like other species; and in the south of the Peninsula, Mr. Albert Theobald says, that the *shikaris* make up large bundles of rushes, which they float on the water, and then resting their guns on these, paddle up softly, keeping the bundle between themselves and the ducks, and so get easy and close shots at these ducks, which, as already noticed, are not amongst the more wary and suspicious kinds.

THE GREY DUCK breeds, in suitable situations, pretty well throughout the vast tract above indicated in defining its range; and in the drier portions of this it is only during the breeding season that it is at all common.

This breeding season varies a great deal with locality; in the North-West Provinces, Oudh and the eastern portions of Rajputana and the Punjab, it only breeds, so far as I yet know, once a year, laying during the latter half of July, August and the first-half of September. In Sindh it lays in April and May, and again in September and October. In Gujarat it certainly lays in October, and in Mysore in November and December, though whether in these two last-named provinces also, it has a second spring brood, I have not yet ascertained.

The nest appears to be generally placed upon the ground, and rarely in the fork of some flat branch just above the surface of the ground or water, in low dense cover of grass, rush and the like, to be of the usual duck type and to contain from 6 to 12 eggs.

I have myself only found two nests. The first, which I found on the 1st August at Rahun, was placed on a drooping branch of a tree, which hung down from the canal bank into a thick clump of rushes growing in a jhíl that near the bridge fringes the canal. The nest was about nine inches above the surface of the water, was entirely concealed in the high rushes, and was firmly based on a horizontal trifurcation of the bough. It was composed of dry rush, and had a good deep hollow in which down, feathers, and fine grass were intermingled. The nest was at least a foot in diameter, perhaps more, and I suppose two inches thick in the centre and four inches at the sides. It contained three fresh eggs.

The second nest I found on the 29th August in a large jhíl, half-swamp, half-lake, in front of Moonj, (also in the Etáwah District) on the ground, in a low, thick bed of sedge on an island about two yards square, to reach which a man had to swim. I did not see the nest (though I saw the bird flushed and the eggs taken); but it was described to me much as I have described the nest that I myself examined. The nest contained six fresh eggs.

Captain G. F. L. Marshall writes: "I found a nest in the Muttra District on the 31st August 1871. It was a well-made, cup-shaped nest of grass, fresh plucked, about 9 inches across, 3 inches deep, and the sides fully 2 inches thick; it was sparingly lined with down and feathers from the breast of the parent bird, and contained seven brownish white eggs. It was placed on the ground in a slight hollow amongst thick grass, about 18 inches high, under the trees on the outer side of the canal bank, and about a yard from the edge of a small excavation pit, full of water. The bird was on the nest, and when roused flew with difficulty."

Writing from Sindh, Mr. Doig says: "On the 28th of April I found a nest containing eight eggs, all incubated. I saw the bird fly on to a small island covered with long grass about a foot high, which was out in the middle of the Nárra, so suspecting that there was a nest, I went off in a boat, and after some searching found the nest, the old bird nearly letting me catch her before flying away. The nest was made of grass and lined with feathers from the birds themselves.

"On the 1st of May I found another nest on another island, which had contained ten incubated eggs; but the eggs were scattered all about and broken, only one remaining whole. The nest itself had been pulled to pieces and scattered all about.

"Shortly before getting to the island I noticed a large family of otters playing about on it, who all bolted on seeing me approach in my canoe, so that I have very little doubt that they were the culprits. It could not possibly have been crows, as none of the eggs were pecked, but simply broken; besides if it had been crows, I should have seen them near the place; and, besides, they would be certain to have eaten them. This nest was also in long grass at the foot of a stump of an old tamarisk tree.

"The nest having been disturbed, the bird made another nest about 4 feet from it, and laid again the following day (2nd May). On the 23rd June I observed flappers, just able to fly, in the same locality, and again I caught young birds, not able to fly, on the 8th of November."

Captain Butler remarks: "I found several nests of this species at Langraij between Deesa and Ahmedabad in October 1876. Some contained fresh eggs, some stale eggs—of which a few had been sucked by some kind of animal,—some incubated eggs, and many contained only shells, the young having hatched off. The nests were, in every single instance, placed in long grass, growing either by the side of tanks or else on mounds of earth overgrown with grass, or small islands in the tanks. In some instances, the nests were well concealed under a thick bush or low tree, but in most cases they consisted of a hole scratched in the ground in long grass and lined with grass, the eggs being almost invariably partly or wholly covered with the same material.

"It is not difficult to find the nests, as the old birds are generally in pairs close by, either swimming in the water or sitting on the bank with their long necks raised above the grass; and if flushed, keep flying restlessly backwards and forwards, or round and round in circles about 20 yards high over the nest.

"The greatest number of eggs I took out of one nest was eight, but from the numerous pieces of shell I found in nests which had hatched off, I imagine that they often lay as many as 10 or 11. I found no down in any of the nests I examined.*

"I found five nests on the 12th of October, containing 4 fresh eggs, 8 ditto, 1 ditto, 6 incubated eggs and 7 ditto, respectively, and five more on the 13th, which contained 1, 3, and 5 fresh and 8 and 7 incubated eggs. The latter clutch was stale, and 3 or 4 of the eggs it contained had been sucked.

"Besides these I came upon several nests which had hatched off and had only empty shells in and round them, so that some must have laid early in September."

From Mysore Major McInroy writes: "I cannot say that I have *found* nests, late *or* early in the year, but I have observed flappers in January, and this year on the 5th of February I saw a brood of these, about 10 or 12 in number, still unable to fly, which could not have been hatched before quite the end of December. There was no other kind of Duck in the tank, and no possible mistake about the matter. The parents flew off. Grey Ducks appear to affect particular tanks for breeding purposes, and I cannot personally point to more than half-a-dozen so used—others apparently quite as eligible are never made use of."

The eggs are of the usual broad oval type; in texture compact and smooth, but without the polish and gloss which characterises the somewhat similar eggs of the Comb-Duck. In colour too they are, when fresh, white or greyish white, and never, so far as I have yet seen, exhibit that creamy or ivory tinge already noticed in the case of the *Nukhta* and Cotton Teal.

As incubation proceeds, they become yellowish and sullied, and hard-set eggs are occasionally a very dingy and pale earth brown.

The eggs vary in length from 2·08 to 2·3, and in breadth from 1·65 to 1·8; but the average of fifteen eggs is 2·15 by

---

* In Northern India, the nests always seem to contain a little down and sometimes a good deal.—A. O. H.

1·70. To judge, therefore, from my few specimens, they are shorter and broader than those of the Mallard, and they wholly want the peculiar greenish tint of the eggs of that species.

IN THIS SPECIES the males are only slightly larger than the females. Both sexes measure as follows :—

Males.—Length, 23·8 to 25·9 ; expanse, 34·0 to 38·5 ; wing, 10·6 to 11·2 ; tail from vent, 4·7 to 5·8 ; tarsus, 1·84 to 1·93 ; bill from gape, 2·4 to 2·75 ; weight, 2 lbs. 5 ozs. to 3 lbs. 4 ozs.

Females—Length, 22·0 to 24·0 ; expanse, 32·5 to 36·0 ; wing, 9·2 to 10·7 ; tail from vent, 4·9 to 5·3 ; tarsus, 1·7 to 1·9 ; bill from gape, 2·3 to 2·5 ; weight, 1 lb. 14 ozs. to 2 lbs. 12 ozs.

The legs and feet in the old adult male are the most intense coral to vermilion red ; in the female usually somewhat duller, and more of a tile red. In younger birds of both sexes they are more orange, sometimes quite orange yellow. The claws are black, and there are not unfrequently black or dusky spots or patches on the webs ; the irides vary from light to deep brown ; the bill is black, the base of the upper mandible on the forehead, similarly coloured to the feet and varying as they do ; the terminal one-fourth of the upper mandible, (more or less, it varies in different individuals) except the nail, and also a patch at the tip of the lower mandible, a very bright clear yellow in some, reddish yellow to orange in others.

In the young birds of both sexes the brightly coloured patches at the base of the upper mandible are either wholly wanting or barely indicated, thus recalling the adult of the nearly allied *A. zonorhyncha* of China.

THE PLATE would have been very fair had the median portion of the bill been coloured black, and not pale lead colour, and had the legs been coloured red as those of perfect adults always are, and not orange. The speculum is too dull and pale a green ; it is really a rich emerald green in most lights, a lovely rich blue or purple in others.

The plumage varies a little ;—some birds show much more, others less white on the tertials than in our figures ; in some specimens the spots on the lower surface are smaller, and the ground colour more nearly white ; and in some the brown of the back is everywhere more of a purple chocolate.

DUCKS OF the same type, as the Mallard and Grey Duck, and belonging to the genus *Anas,* as commonly restricted in modern times, are numerous and occur all over the world.

I may take this opportunity of noting that I have no hope even that the manner in which I have arranged our Indian Ducks in genera will be generally approved. Nor am I even prepared to assert that it is correct. The questions of the number of genera that should be accepted amongst the *Anatinæ*, and the manner in which the several species should be distributed amongst these, are very difficult ones, in regard to which no two ornithologists are at all agreed. I have neither had the time, nor have I the materials, for such a study of the group as a whole as would enable me to form any independent opinion on which I could rely, and I have therefore been compelled to follow the views of others, accepting those that seemed to me most to accord with what I know of the limited number of species which occur within our limits. As it is, I have grave doubts as to whether I ought to have accepted the genus *Chaulelasmus*, and I am by no means sure that it would not have been best to retain *streperus* under the generic name *Anas*. I am inclined to suspect that *Anas leucoptera* should become the type of a separate genus, and I think it probable that *Fuligula nyroca* should be generically separated from the rest of the *Fuligulas*. Still I have altered the arrangement over and over again without being able to satisfy myself; and at last, *faute de mieux*, have fallen back on that which I originally adopted, and must crave the indulgence of all who differ from or disapprove this.

♂
ANAS CARYOPHYLLACEA

THE PINK-HEADED DUCK.

Rhodonessa caryophyllacea, *Latham.*

Vernacular Names.—[Sāknāl, (Bengali); Lal-sira, (Hindustani); Doomrar, *Nepal Terai;* Doomar, Domar, *Tirhoot;*]

DESPITE strenuous efforts I have been quite unable to clear up conclusively the question of the distribution of the Pink-headed Duck.

I have no record of its occurrence in Ceylon or the Madras districts south of Mysore, or in this latter, or in the Konkan, Gujarat, Cutch, Káthiáwar, Sindh, Rajputana, the Central India Agency, or Central Provinces.

In the Punjab I only certainly* know of its having been once procured, and that near Delhi, in the easternmost portion of the Province. In the Doab and Rohilkhand, of the North-Western Provinces, it is so excessively rare that during nearly twenty years' fowling I never once saw or heard of it; but Anderson shot one female near Fatehpur, and a writer in the *Asian* professes to have obtained them in the Dún and at Bareilly.† In the western portions of Oudh it is outside the

* Major Alexander Kinloch writes:—"I shot two Pink-headed Ducks on the banks of the canal leading to the Najjafgarh jhíl, near Delhi, during the winter of 1862-63, and a brother officer shot another."

Mr. R. W. Rumsby *thinks* that he once shot it on an exposed jhíl south-west of Umballa, and also in the Gurdaspur district; but on further investigation he is clearly not certain of the species. No one else that I can hear of *thinks* even that they have procured it in the Punjab. Adams never met with it there; neither have I myself, nor any one of the very numerous friends who have collected there for me (some of them for years and most exhaustively), so that I can only (at present), consider it as a rare and accidental straggler during the cold season into the easternmost portions of the Punjab, Cis-Satlej.

† It is impossible to attach much weight to anonymous communications by writers who admit knowing very little of birds. Still I quote what was said, *quantum valeat:*—

"Some time before Christmas, I was out shooting in the Dún, and accidentally came across the very bird, I think, he means. There were only five, and I shot two of them—a male and a female. Had I known that it would have been of any use I would have preserved them, but now alas! they have been eaten, for, as Jerdon says, they are 'excellent eating,' and I knew that. These birds I found in a large pool, formed in the river Asun, made for irrigation purposes. It was a very cold morning, for the night before the water froze in my tent. These Ducks I have come across but seldom in the North-West Provinces, principally about Delhi and Bareilly. At the former place I have often bagged 50 head of Ducks, but it was rarely I found one or two of the pink-headed among the bag. I do not think I can be mistaken in the bird. Although I am not a naturalist, I follow Jerdon's description."

Sal Forests certainly rare; Major Maurice Tweedie, an ardent sportsman, who was for five years stationed in the Kheri district (now Lakhimpur) never so much as heard of it. But Mr. Battie shows* that even in the West it is not very uncommon in the forests, and in the central portions of the Province, though rare, it also occurs. From time to time specimens are netted by fowlers in the neighbourhood of Lucknow; and Mr. Geo. Reid has himself observed it near Mohunlalganj on the Rai Bareilly road during the cold season. In the eastern portions of Oudh it is still rare, but appears to be a *regular*, though scarce, cold weather visitant to the jhíls of the Fyzabad (where Anderson shot it) and Gondah districts. Again it is reported from Gorakhpur and Basti and from the Nepal Terai, but in all these it is scarce; and as far as I can learn, in all but the latter, a cold season visitant only.† It probably occurs in Azimgarh and Ghazipur also, as it certainly does in Arrah, where Mr. Doyle informs me that he shot one on the 22nd of November 1879, at the Bhojpur Jhíl, near the Dumraon Railway Station.

Further east in Behar, Purneah, and Maldah‡ it would seem to be a permanent resident, and in special localities in Tirhoot and Purneah to be comparatively common. Throughout the rest of Lower and Eastern Bengal (except Tipperah and Chittagong, from whence it has not been reported), it occurs, but is everywhere said to be rare. So too both from Sylhet and the entire valley of Assam up to Sadiya, (and in Munipur, where Damant saw it), it is reported by one correspondent or another, but always as a bird very rarely met with.

South of the Ganges, as already mentioned, it is occasionally found at Arrah, and as Ball tells us, in the Rajmehal hills, near Hazáribágh, near Sahibgunge§ on the Ganges, and in Manbhúm of Chota Nagpur.

To the Deccan it is an extremely rare and accidental visitant. Neither Davidson nor Wenden ever met with it there, but Fairbank saw it once near Ahmednagar, Colonel McMaster shot

---

* I shot a Pink-headed Duck this year, in May or June, up in the Sal Forests in the north of the Kheri District. Another was shot some time afterwards in the same jhíl and you often see it in pairs in nullahs in the forests.

"I am told by the natives that this bird breeds in the Sal Forests, but I have never found its nest. I know for a fact however that it stays down in the forests all the year round."—*J. Battie.*

† But too much stress must not be laid upon this, as the question has not been properly worked out, and it may, though rarely, breed in all these as also in Oudh, where Irby says that he saw it three times (apparently the only occasions on which he met with it) towards the close of the rainy season.

‡ Mr. H. Millett kindly informed me, under date the 2nd of May, that Mr. Herbert Reily had then recently "shot four or five specimens of this Duck in the Maldah district;" and that his brother had also previously shot one there.

§ It is nearly opposite Sahibgunge, in the neighbourhood of Caragola (at the south of the Purneah District) that the Pink-headed Duck, to judge from what Mr. F. A. Shillingford, Captain W. T. Heaviside, R.E., and others tell me, is specially abundant.

it once about twenty miles from Secunderabad after the rains had set in, and Jerdon heard of it at Jalna.

But along the east coast it is less rare. It certainly occurs in the Pulicat lake, as I have a specimen shot there, and Jerdon, years previously, had obtained a specimen in the Madras market caught there, and another from Nellore. Again north of Nellore it appears to occur in suitable situations in Vizagapatam* and Ganjam, north of which again in Cuttack, as in the rest of Lower Bengal, it is an occasional straggler.

So far as I yet know, this species does not occur in either Pegu or Tenasserim, but Blyth gives it from Arakan.

Outside our limits I have only heard of its occurrence north of Bhamo, in Independent Burma. It is never found anywhere in the Himalayas, and is therefore not likely to cross them, but *it may* extend *viâ* Assam and Upper Burma into South-western China (Yunan), though as yet this fact has not been ascertained.

Summing up the meagre information at my command, I am disposed to consider Behar and the rest of Bengal north of the Ganges and west of the Brahmaputra as its head-quarters; I include the Nepal and Oudh Terai, the central and eastern portions of Oudh, the Benares division of the North-Western Provinces, the whole of the rest of Bengal, Assam, and Munipur, and the east coast littoral as far south as Madras, within its normal range, throughout which, however, it is, except in certain special isolated localities, very rare. Its occurrence elsewhere in any part of the empire I look upon as quite exceptional and abnormal.

NEVER HAVING myself met with this Duck alive in a feral state, what little I have to say of its habits will be based solely on the reports of others.

Essentially a lake and swamp species, this bird is never seen on any of our large rivers, or indeed, so far as I can learn, on running water of any kind.

Tanks and pools, thickly set with reeds and aquatic plants, swamps dense with beds of bulrushes and the like,

---

* Lieut.-Colonel W. J. Wilson kindly favours me with the following note:—"The Pink-headed Duck used to frequent a piece of water near Condakirla, about 27 miles south of Vizagapatam, and in all probability is still to be found there, as well as at similar places in the Northern Circars, although I do not now remember having actually seen it except at Condakirla.

"The lakes in question are extensive and thickly covered by aquatic plants, so that the birds have plenty of cover, and the only way of shooting them is from a long narrow canoe punted through the weeds.

"These lakes seem to be peculiar to the Circars, and are called '*AWA*' in Vizagapatam, and '*Tumpera*' in Ganjam. They are resorted to by wild fowl of most kinds.

"To the best of my recollection the Pink-headed Duck I shot were killed in November and December. I think I saw about 15 or 20 on each occasion of my visit."

and nullahs and ponds hemmed in by forest, appear to be its favourite, if not its only, haunts. During the cold season it keeps commonly in small parties of from four to eight or ten, but is sometimes seen in flocks of from twenty to thirty. During the breeding season they are found in pairs. Mr. F. A. Shillingford, who has rendered me more assistance than any one else where this species is concerned, writes, that it "may be freely found throughout the year in the southern and western portions of the Purneah district. From November to April they are to be met with in flocks, numbering as many as twenty, along the swamps adjoining the rivers Great Coosee and Ganges; and during the rainy season (June to September) I have observed that they are usually seen in pairs, and are to be met with generally in the higher parts only of the district. Though not to be met with in such numbers as the commoner species, they are not considered at all rare in this district, but they are difficult to get at, remaining, as they do during the cold season, in large swamps fringed with dense jungle."

Mr. J. C. Parker writes:—"Years ago I have fired at them when passing with other Ducks, when out shooting in the *bhils* of Kishnaghur and Jessore. They were easy to distinguish by their beautiful pink heads and salmon-coloured wing-linings. The flight of this Duck is very powerful and rapid."

"Its call," says Mr. Shillingford, "resembles that of the common drake, with a slight musical ring about it."

Hodgson notes:– "Lives and breeds below always. Avoids flowing waters; shy; resides in remote jhíls and feeds at night."

Jerdon says:—"It shows a decided preference for tanks and jhíls well sheltered by overhanging bushes, or abounding in dense reeds; and in such places it may be found in the cold season in flocks of twenty or so occasionally, but generally in smaller parties of from four to eight. During the heat of the day, it generally remains near the middle of the tank or jhíl, and is somewhat shy and wary."

Mr. Shillingford says that the gizzard of one specimen that he examined contained "half-digested water weeds and various kinds of small shells."

Beyond this there is absolutely nothing on record.

MR. F. A. SHILLINGFORD and his brother had found the eggs of this species in former years; but the egg he sent me was so very peculiar that I hesitated to accept it as genuine, and at my request he, and several of his friends, set to work to discover a a nest, and he was soon able to send me the following note:—

"On the 3rd of July Mr. T. Hill, of Jouneah Factory, succeeded in finding a nest of the Pink-headed Duck near the Dabeepoor Factory.

"The nest contained nine much incubated eggs, of which

I send you four. These, as you will observe, are of precisely the same type as the one I formerly sent you.

"The nest was well hidden in tall grass (*Andropogon muricatum*), and both male and female were started from the vicinity of the nest, which was about 400 yards from a *nullah* containing water. The nest was well formed, made of dry grass, interspersed with a few feathers, the interior portion being circular, and about 9 inches in diameter and 4 to 5 inches deep."

To the *Asian* he sent the following further interesting note :—

"During the cold weather, November to March, the Pink-headers remain in flocks, varying from 6 to 30, or even 40 birds, in the lagoons adjoining the larger rivers, and have been observed by myself in considerable numbers in the southern and western portions of this district, that portion of Eastern Bhaugulpore which lies immediately to the north of the river Ganges, and the south-western parts of Maldah. They come up to the central or higher parts of the Purneah district in pairs, during the month of April, begin to build in May, and their eggs may be found in June and July. The nests are well formed, (made of dry grass interspersed with a few feathers,) perfectly circular in shape, about 9 inches in diameter, and 4 or 5 inches deep, with 3 to 4-inch walls, and have no special lining. The nests are placed in the centre of tufts of tall grass, well hidden, and difficult to find, generally not more than 500 yards from water. They lay from 5 to 10 eggs in a nest. Both the male and female have been started simultaneously from the vicinity of the nest; but whether the former assists in incubation is uncertain, though, judging from the loss of weight during the breeding season, the male must be in constant attendance at the nest. The weights of five males, shot between 13th February and 28th June 1880, in consecutive order being—(1), 2 lbs. 3 ozs. (13th February); (2), 1 lb. 14 ozs.; (3), 2 lbs.; (4), 1 lb. 13 ozs.; and (5), 1 lb. 12 ozs., (28th June). When the young are fledged in September and October, the Pink-headers retire with the receding waters to their usual haunts—the jungly lagoons.

"The following account, as indicating their strong attachment to their young, may prove of interest. On the 17th July 1880, whilst searching for Pink-header's nests with T. H. at the northern extremity of Patraha Katal, where nests were reported, we flushed a female Pink-header in the grass jungle on the banks of the Patraha jhíl. T. H. fired with his Miniature Express at a distance of about 300 yards at the bird which had settled at the other end of the jhíl. The ball was seen by both of us to strike the water some distance above, and a little to the left of the bird which did not rise. Upon going up to the spot, to our surprise she fluttered about and dragged herself along with loud quackings. Being closely pursued, she flew along at an elevation of about 6 feet from the ground in a manner that led us to believe that she was badly wounded, and one of her wings damaged, and she fell rather than settled in a patch of grass on dry land. Upon approaching this a similar manœuvre was gone through, and she deposited herself some 100 yards further on. Having decoyed us thus far she flew up into the air with such facility that our old *shikaree* mahout could not help exclaiming *phair jee gya* (it's come to life again), and directed her flight in a direction away from the piece of water. After describing a considerable circuit, she came back to the jhíl on the banks of which we were still standing. Two more bullets were fired at her from the same gun, which only made her rise after each shot, and settle down again some 10 yards further on. Seeing that her tactics had failed in withdrawing us from the vicinity of her young, she again took to the grass jungle, and all endeavours to flush her again proved futile, though she was observed in the same piece of water subsequently."

A great number of ducks and other birds resort to similar artifices to decoy intruders away from the neighbourhood of their nests and young; but in no species is this habit more noticeable than in the Common Lapwing.

The eggs are quite unlike those of any other duck with which I am acquainted. In shape they are very nearly spherical; indeed one is almost a perfect sphere.

The shell is very close and compact, but not particularly smooth or satiny to the touch, and is entirely devoid of gloss.

In colour it is a dull, nearly pure white, with here and there traces of an extremely faint yellowish mottling, probably the result of dirt. Even held up against the light, the shell is white, with a scarcely perceptible ivory tinge.

The five eggs sent me by Mr. Shillingford measure as follows:—1·82 × 1·7; 1·78 × 1·68; 1·8 × 1·62; 1·71 × 1·69; 1·81 × 1·61.

There is no possible doubt, now, that these eggs, taken at two different times by two different persons, are really the eggs of the Pink-headed Duck; but at the same time it must be admitted that they are eggs that no one versed in Oology could, without positive proof, have accepted as pertaining to this species.

I AM very badly off for measurements, &c., of this species. Mr. Shillingford gives the following particulars of two specimens, *sexes not ascertained*:—

"Length, 24, 22; wing, 10·75, 10·0; tail, 4·75, 4·5; tarsus, 2·0, 2·0; bill at front, 2·37, 2·25. Of the second specimen only, expanse, 34·5; weight, 2 lbs. 8 ozs. *Troy!*"

Of the first: "Bill dirty red; cere (?) flesh coloured; irides deep orange red; legs and feet reddish slate. Of the second: "Bill light pink, assuming a purple tint towards gonys; cere*

* I do not understand what is meant by a duck's *cere*.

flesh coloured; irides deep orange; tarsus, web, and nails dark slate, inclining to purple; lower mandible more deeply coloured than upper."

Hodgson gives the following of an ascertained female:—

"Length, 23·0; expanse, 36·0; tail, 4·5; tarsus, (but this is to the sole of the foot) 2·18; weight, 2 lbs.

"Iris yellow brown; bill grey with a rosy tint; legs dusky."

Jerdon says of the male:—

"Bill reddish white, rosy at the base, and faintly bluish at the tip; irides fine orange red; legs and feet blackish, with a tinge of red. Length, 24 inches; wing, 11·5; extent, 39; tail, 4·25; bill at front, 2·25; tarsus, 2·25; mid-toe, 2·37."

This is by no means all that could be desired, and it is to be hoped that all sportsmen who shoot these ducks, for some time to come, will carefully record measurements, weight, and colours of the soft parts; and, after ascertaining the sex of their specimens, favour me with these particulars.

THE PLATE.—The figure in the foreground would be a very fair representation of an adult male, had not the artist chosen to colour the soft parts after the plate in Gray's Ill. Gen. of Birds, and quite wrongly.

But it must be understood that even adult males vary a good deal in plumage, and in a specimen now before me the entire upper and under surface of the body is much darker, and much more nearly black than in the particular specimen figured, while the green of the tertiaries is also much less bright.

In this specimen, too, obtained on the 7th of March, there is a distinct, though short, half-coronal, half-occipital, crest, of a brighter and purer rosy than the pink of the rest of the head.

The figure in the background is said to be that of a young bird just able to fly. I have never seen such a specimen, but the figure was taken, I believe, from one in some museum at home; and except in the matter of the colour of the bill, which was probably grey, is perhaps a fairly correct representation of the young.

Of (I presume) somewhat older birds, Jerdon says:—"The young have the head and neck pale vinous-isabella colour, with the top of the head, nape, and hind neck brown; the whole plumage lighter brown, in some mixed with whitish beneath."

Hodgson figures a female, adult according to him but which is probably not fully so, which has the head, including chin and throat, rosy; the upper neck all round pale whitey brown, with a rosy tinge, and with a brown band down the centre of crown, occiput and nape; the lower neck all round pale brownish white, with large, dark-brown, closely-set roundish spots, and the entire breast and abdomen white or yellowish white, with apparently a moderately broad, brown, shaft-stripe to each feather.

Of the female Jerdon says that she "has the pink of the head somewhat more dull and pale, and the vertex has a brownish spot in some, which is continued faintly down the back of the neck."

I have a female which certainly bears no traces of immaturity, the entire plumage of which, above and below, is duller, paler, and more of a smoky brown than in the male; the pink of the head is dingier and paler, and there is a broad, brown, medial band from forehead over crown and occiput, and (diminishing rapidly in width) on the back of the upper neck. But the most conspicuous difference is that the dull pink of the face runs on, unbroken, over the entire chin, throat, and front of the upper neck, and there is no trace of the dark band along chin, throat, and entire front of the neck so conspicuous in the male.

THERE IS no other species known of this genus which, in most external characters, is very close to restricted *Anas*. Indeed, but for the extraordinary eggs laid by the Pink-headed Duck, I should not have accepted the genus *Rhodonessa*. But it seems to me that such an extraordinary difference in the shape and texture of the eggs must indicate widely different descent and anatomical differences, and constitutes a *primâ facie* ground for generic separation.

It has been suggested that the colouring of this species is very close to that of the Red-crested Pochard, and affinities between the two have been hinted at, based on this.

But this plumage resemblance is purely superficial; it does not extend to the females. The bills are in no way of the same type, and the hind toe of the Pink-headed Duck is long, thin, unlobed, quite of the same type as, though proportionally longer than, those of the Mallard and the Grey Duck, and not at all of the type of that of the Red-crested Pochard.

⅓
ANAS STREPERA

THE GADWALL.

Chaulelasmus streperus, *Linné.*

Vernacular Names.—[Mila, (Hindee), Beykhur, *N. W. Provinces;* Peeing hans, (Bengali); Mail, *Nepal;* Burd, *Sindh;* Syah-dum, *Cabul;*]

HOW far south exactly the Gadwall may wander in India I have been unable to ascertain; but I have no knowledge of its occurrence in Ceylon, or the extreme south of the Peninsula, anywhere south of Mysore. In this province it occurs, though not in great numbers, and everywhere else in India, north of about the 12° N. Lat., in gradually increasing abundance as one proceeds northwards. Eastwards it occurs throughout the Assam Valley to Dibrugárh, and Damant met with it at the Logtag Lake in Manipur; but though common about Calcutta, I have no report of it from the Sunderbans, Tipperah, and Chittagong, though it must needs occur in these if Blyth is correct in saying that it is found in Arakan. In Tenasserim we have not met with it, nor has it been recorded from Pegu, though I should expect it to occur in the northern portions of that province. In the Himalayas it is common during the cold season from Kashmir (whence I have several specimens, though Adams does not include it in his list) to Nepal, up to elevations of about five or six thousand feet.

Outside our limits the range of this species may be described as covering the entire temperate zone of the northern hemisphere. But it is rare in many portions of this vast tract, as in China, Mongolia, Japan, and the British isles. Except in Iceland it does not usually closely approach the Arctic Circle, while both in India and in the West Indies (as in Cuba and Jamaica, &c.,) it straggles well inside the tropics. Still for all practical purposes the species may be defined as essentially one pertaining to the northern temperate zone.

"AS WELCOME," said the late Col. Tickell, "as on the mountains the feet of him who bringeth glad tidings, are the first flights of the Water Fowl, which announce to the nearly exhausted European, the approach of the delicious 'cold season' of India. Riding slowly across the open meadows or the treeless uplands now and then breathing his Arab and his 'long dogs' in a spurt after a 'lomree,' as it returns from its night's rambles to 'earth,' and inhaling with cheered spirits the cold breezes of early morning, the horseman sees across the dappled sky long lines of clamorous Geese or swift-flying Ducks, hurrying up from the horizon and passing over head, as if fraught with messages of comfort and encouragement from the colder regions to the parched torrid zone. Some pass grandly overhead, mere specks and lines far up in the blue vault, bound to distant waters further south; others with a satin rustle of their rapid wings, cleave the air so closely by, that the observer discerns the species as they rush past, and recognises familiar forms associated with recollections of snowy moors and ice-bound ponds 'at home' in far England."

Of all our welcome winter visitants few are earlier, and none come to us in greater numbers than the Gadwall. Further south Wigeon—with us by no means plentiful—are more numerous; but in Upper India there are, as a rule, more Gadwall in the bag after a good day's sport than any other species of duck.

They arrive in the Himalayas during the latter half of September, and gradually extend southwards; few reach the plains (they are earlier in the submontane districts) before the latter half of October; and in Sindh and further south it is usually November before they are seen in any numbers. In the south they leave by the end of March or early in April; further north they are somewhat later (it depends a good deal on the season), and both in Sindh and the Western and North-Western Punjab, they are frequently shot during the first week in May.

They are, I think, essentially fresh-water birds, (I have never seen them really on the sea coast,) but having secured fresh water, they do not seem to have much preference as to locality, and you find them equally in the largest rivers and the smallest hill streams, in huge lakes and small ponds, in open water (as at the Sámbhar lake) where not a weed or rush is to be seen, and in tangled swamps, where there is barely clear water enough to float a walnut.

In rivers and in small pieces of water, the Gadwall commonly occurs in small parties of from three to a dozen, but in large lakes I have seen them in flocks of several hundreds.

On rivers they are generally to be seen snoozing on the bank during the day, and then they commonly leave these towards sunset for feeding grounds inland. In broads they keep, if at all disturbed, well out of gunshot towards the centre, sometimes in clear water, more often skulking in low water weeds; but in unfrequented places, they may, even during the day-time, be found walking on the shore or paddling in the shallows round the edges of the tank, feeding busily with their tail ends bolt upright, and the rest of them hidden by the water.

Audubon by the way says:—"When in this position they are most easily shot, and when hidden at the edge of a piece of water I have often waited until the ducks commenced feeding, and turned ends upwards when I have made a most effectual pot shot amongst them." Let no one be misled by this pernicious doctrine; it is the very worst (and I may add most *cruel*) position in which you *can* shoot at ducks. Of every ten ducks thus wounded not more than three will be disabled, the remainder will fly off, apparently uninjured, to die a lingering death, their intestines riddled with shot holes, but their heads, necks, wings and pectoral muscles untouched. I have a great admiration for Audubon as an artist, but as a sportsman this passage condemns him.

With us their chief staple of food, so long as they can get it, is wild rice, (though in some parts they feed in cultivated rice fields largely), and later the seeds, leaves and flower buds of all kinds of rushes and aquatic plants. Insects and their larva are also largely consumed, and sometimes small worms; but I have never found either frogs or fish in their stomachs, though elsewhere these seem to form, commonly, a portion of their regular diet.

They swim more lightly, and they fly far more easily and rapidly than the Grey Duck or the Mallard. But like the former they spring up with one bound up from land and water, at a rather sharp angle, and usually rise thus for twenty yards before sweeping off in a horizontal course. Their wings are long and pointed, and make in passing through the air a peculiar whistling sound similar to, though louder than, that made by those of the Common Teal, by which they may be recognized as they pass over head in flight shooting.

A great many of the ducks that frequent rivers by day, come inland about dusk to feed in jhíls. Often for some little time one particular piece of water, perhaps not half a dozen acres in extent, attracts the Wild Fowl of the whole country's side; and when you find out such, and do not care, or have not the plant for netting them, you may with three or four guns well posted enjoy an hour's most profitable and exciting sport. Baldwin gives a very good account of this, which I will quote:—

"At other times this lake was a favourite resort of mine in the cold season. It was not far distant from the river Betwah, and about sun down swarms of Wild Fowl, early in the season especially, poured into the jhíl from the river to feed all night. Knowing this habit, I often drove or rode out from Jhánsi of an afternoon to the spot, procured a boat from a village hard by, with a man to guide it, and then made for a creek at the far end of the lake, bordered on each side by high rushes and reeds, and a favourite feeding ground for Wild

Ducks. We hid ourselves at the farthermost point of the creek, overlooking a long strip of open water running down the centre of it, and at the same time facing in the direction of the setting sun, so that in the short eastern twilight we might see the Wild Fowl more clearly as they flew betweeen us and the sky, where the last gleam of day still lingered. Presently they would begin to arrive, and if luck favored us, a goodly flight, after circling around, would prepare to pitch, though not on this occasion to feed, for it was a case of 'first come first served,' and the breech-loader was brought into play. Then the scared Wild Ducks would make off, leaving perhaps one or two of their number behind; but hardly are the fresh cartridges dropped into the barrels when another flight appears on the horizon, to meet with a similar reception; and so the sport continues for perhaps half an hour, when it becomes too dark to see to shoot longer. I have on three or four occasions, in a short space of time, shot over twenty Ducks and Teals in this manner; and one evening, a friend and I, assisted by the light of a brilliant moon, bagged thirty-eight Ducks, besides losing at least half a score more in the darkness."

I must add that to an old Norfolk flight shooter, the best part of the sport commences, when Captain Baldwin and his friends left off, *i.e.*, when in cold cloudy weather, such as we often have about X'mas, it gets pitch dark soon after sunset, and you shoot entirely by the whistle of the wings, and at most catch, just as you fire, the faintest glimpse of a shadow flitting across the gloom above. How the gun cracks at such a time. What a blaze of light it sheds, lightning-like, around for an instant, and then how pleasant, in the midst of the intense darkness that succeeds, to hear the one, two, three, heavy thuds or splashes of the victims, which, in a very few moments, your dogs will lay at your feet. It is just when it *is* too dark to see, and when you have to shoot, judging not only direction and distance, but rate of flight also by ear, that flight-shooting becomes a real sport. But then for this you must not be posted on the far side of the jhíl where the birds will circle, but some distance on the near side, at a place where the birds will certainly pass over with arrowy straightness, if also with arrowy speed. At no time I think does the sportsman feel a greater sense of elation than when standing thus in a clump of bushes, a cold wind and drizzling rain bracing his nerves, he succeeds in making flight after flight, as they swish past unseen, each steadily contribute its quota to his bag. But I suspect that to make any hand of this night work, you must have practised it from childhood, and even then it is, no doubt, uncertain work. Sometimes you cannot hit anything, and sometimes, just as at billiards, you get your hand in, and not a wing can hurtle pass without paying the penalty.

The quack of the Gadwall is very like that of the Mallard,

but weaker and sharper, and more often uttered. They are more talkative birds than either the Grey or Common Wild Duck, and when feeding in undisturbed localities keep up a perpetual chatteration, not unlike that in which the Mallard *occasionally* indulges, but shriller, feebler, and far more incessant.

They are very sociable birds, and may be found in company with every description of Water Fowl ; even amongst Geese, who commonly keep all the smaller Ducks at arms length, I have seen pairs of Gadwall swimming about quite unmolested.

On land it walks extremely well, far more gracefully than do the Mallard or Grey Duck, and may often be seen trotting about on tiny smooth grass patches at the margins of broads, busily devouring grasshoppers, crickets, and (strange though it may seem, it is the fact) small moths and butterflies.

When wounded and pursued, they dive easily, but are much more easily tired out and captured than the Grey Duck, or *á fortiori*, any of the Pochards. Altogether they are lighter, slighter, more agile, more graceful, and withal less robust birds than those that I class under restricted *Anas*, and in most respects are very close to the Teal, differing from these chiefly in the greater elongation of the laminæ of the bill.

For the table the Gadwall is generaly excellent, especially early in the cold weather, when, for a month or so, it has been living chiefly on rice, but occasionally, when vegetable food has been scarce, they have a rather marshy muddy flavour.

SO FAR AS we yet know the Gadwall breeds nowhere within our limits, but as it breeds in Texas nearly as far south as Delhi, I cannot help suspecting that it may yet prove to breed in some of the Kashmir and other comparatively low Himalayan lakes.

In Turkestan, Central and Southern Europe* and North America it breeds in May and June. The nest, a large coarse one of rush and grass, is placed in situations similar to that of the Grey Duck, as a rule, in clumps of low rush and water grass, and often under some overhanging bush or reed tuft. It is lined with finer grass, more or less intermingled with feathers, and as incubation proceeds in northern localities, a good deal of down is added; apparently in Southern Europe there is less of this used.

The number of eggs seems to vary from six to thirteen, but about ten appears to be the average. The eggs are moderately broad, and very regular ovals ; the shell smooth, but without much gloss. In colour they vary from nearly white to a rich creamy yellow, occasionally with a greenish tinge.

---

* And occasionally *very* much farther north, as Procter took a nest of this species in Iceland.

In size they vary from 2·05 to 2·2 in length, and from 1·47 to 1·6 in breadth, but the average of 13 eggs is 2·62 by 1·51.

THE MALES, as usual, are the heavier and larger birds. They measure:—

Length, 19·4 to 21·5; expanse, 33 to 36·75; wing, 10·75 to 11·60; tail from vent, 3·9 to 4·3; tarsus, 1·4 to 1·5; bill from gape, 2·0 to 2·22; weight, (of birds in good condition), 1 lb. 7 ozs. to 2 lbs. 2 ozs.

Of females, I have recorded the following:—

Length, 18 to 20·1; expanse, 30 to 33·75; wing, 9·0 to 10·2; tail from vent, 3·7 to 4·5(!); tarsus, 1·37 to 1·43; bill from gape, 1·94 to 2·1; weight, 1 lb. 1 oz. to 1 lb. 10 ozs.

The irides are brown, sometimes tinged reddish in the male; the legs and feet vary from yellowish brown, through dirty yellow to dull orange, those of the old male being more orange and brighter coloured (though even then rather dull) than those of the female ever are; the webs are always more dusky, sometimes quite dusky, or almost black. In the male the bill is brownish black, or dusky leaden, generally tinged reddish, or even yellow on the lower mandible, and sometimes with this colour encroaching on the sides of the upper mandible. In the female the bill is orange or brownish orange, (sometimes only yellowish brown,) dusky, to almost black on the nail, tip, and culmen; often the yellow or orange portions are irregularly blotched here and there with brown or dusky.

It is probably the result of difference in age and season, or it may be because I have recorded the colours of the soft parts of so many specimens; but certainly the variations in this respect appear to be very considerable in this species.

THE PLATE is fair, but there is in nine cases out of ten a more or less perceptible dusky shade on the webs; the lower mandible of the male almost always shows a yellow or orange tinge (during the time in which we see them) on the lower mandible. The upper mandible of the female always, I think, shows more yellow or orange on the sides of the upper mandible than is depicted in our plate. Then in the male the lunations of the breast are a little too harsh and coarse, and the scapulars should be rather greyer.

In many females the entire face is greyer, and the dark lines much more strongly developed than in the specimen figured.

In the spring, the males develop a very full and silky, but short occipital crest, and acquire a distinct, though dull, green metallic lustre on the sides of the head and nape; moreover many begin to show a fulvous tinge over the base of the neck all round, forming an ill-defined ring, and in some this colour extends over the entire front of the neck, throat, and face.

The female is very like that of the Mallard, but may be distinguished at once by her smaller size, very much smaller bill, and by the conspicuous white speculum (unfortunately not shown in our plate), as opposed to the metallic purplish one of the female Mallard, to say nothing of the black patch above the white, and more or less of chestnut above this, which the Gadwall Duck exhibits, though in a less conspicuous degree, in common with the Drake.

Just when they first come in we get males with the back of the neck and entire interscapulary region light brown, each feather narrowly fringed at the tip with dull white, and with the breast and abdomen covered with small light brown spots. Some of these seem to be young, but many are adults which have not yet emerged from the temporary eclipse, which the Drakes of this species, as well as of the Mallard, undergo towards the close of the breeding season.

I DO not know that there is any other species that can be properly included under the genus *Chaulelasmus*. Some authorities have so included the Marbled Duck ; but after carefully comparing the birds, I think that these range more appropriately with the Teal. Whether it would not be best to drop both *Chaulelasmus* and *Querquedula*, and unite all the species now included under these in the one genus *Anas*, is, to me, still a very moot point.

♂
DAFILA ACUTA.

THE PIN-TAIL.

---o---

Dafila acuta, *Linné*.

---o---

Vernacular Names.—[Sanh, Sink-par, *N. W. Provinces;* Dighons. Sho-lon-cho, *Bengal;* Laitunga, *Manipur;* Taw-bay, Thaw-wom-bay. *British Burmah;* Digoonch, *Nepal;* Kokarali, Drighush, *Sindh;* Ade, Adla. (in common with other species), *Ratnagiri;* Sink-dum, *Cabul;* Chasughsu aurdak, (Turki), *Yarkand;*]

---o---

ONE of the most generally diffused of all our migratory Ducks, there is no district in the Empire, from Ceylon to Kashmir, from Kashmir to Sadiya and Manipur, and so on to Moulmein,* where the Pin-tail does not occur in greater or less abundance, only in the southernmost portions of Tenasserim, it has not yet been observed. It is very common, too, almost throughout the Himalayas. But alike to these and to the plains, it is only a winter visitant.

Outside our limits, it occurs in Northern Siam and Upper Burmah, is excessively common in China, Mongolia, Central Asia, Afghanistan, Beluchistan, and Persia, and generally it may be said to occur almost throughout the entire Northern Hemisphere between the 10th and 70th degrees of North Latitude. It gets a little further south than this in Southern India and Ceylon, and Borneo (where a straggler has recently been observed)† and possibly in South America, where, at any rate, it extends to Panama; and it does not get quite so far south as this in Siam or Tenasserim, or in Eastern or Western Africa. Again, in Asia, at any rate, it probably travels somewhat north of the 70th degree.

It occurs in Japan, Hainan, Formosa, Ireland, Iceland, and several of the West India Islands, but has not been recorded from the Azores, Canaries, Philippines or Sandwich Islands, though these are all apparently within its range.

---

* Davison has now seen several near Moulmein, and Oates writes that this species is "common in the Pegu Province during the cold weather on all large sheets of water. The swamp at Engmah, ten miles north of Poungday, always affords good shooting, this species being particularly abundant there."

† This was at Bintulu, on the north-west coast in about 4° North Latitude.

Its general distribution is not unlike that of the Gadwall, but it covers a wider range, and has a much more northern average breeding zone.

RATHER LATE to arrive the Pin-tail is one of the earliest of our migratory Ducks to leave us. In the Himalayas, as in Kashmir, Kullu and Nepal,* it arrives, no doubt, during September; but it is rarely seen really down in the plains before November, and it very rarely remains there, even in the North-West Provinces, after the 1st of April, while further south it is said to leave, as a rule, early in March. Even in Kashmir and Nepal few, if any, remain at the close of April.

The Pin-tail, though found everywhere in India, is much more restricted in the localities it affects than the Gadwall. It is rare to meet with it on large rivers, and on small streams or ponds, or in mere swamps without any clear water, I do not think I ever saw one in broad daylight. At night they visit all kinds of jhíls, and even rice-fields, but in the day time they are generally only found in considerable pieces of water, sprinkled over with islets of floating weed, amongst the leaves of which they can snooze unnoticed.

Long ago I said, writing from Sindh:—"It is curious how particular ducks affect particular broads, or dhunds as they are called in Sindh. In one dhund, the great mass of the fowl are *Fuligula nyroca;* this will be one much covered with the more or less dry leaves of the lotus. In another, *Q. angustirostris* predominates; here there will be a vast quantity of green rush, making the whole lake look like a meadow; in open, clear-water dhunds of moderate size, *Fuligula ferina* will be in a majority, while, where there is a vast expanse of open water, *Fuligula rufina* and *cristata* will outnumber all the other kinds many fold. Shovellers and Shelldrakes (and precious wary these latter always are) sneak along the edges, while Mallard like to sit round the roots of the tamarisk bushes, thousands of which stand far out into some pieces of water. What the Pin-tail seem to prefer are pieces of comparatively open water, dotted about with small patches of a long-leaved water-plant, a *Sagittaria* I think, which rises about four inches above the surface, in amongst which they sit, completely hidden when asleep, even at a few yards distance, and with their brown and inconspicuous heads, and a little only of their white necks showing when they are looking about them. The Manchar is an epitome of every description of broad, and accordingly in different parts of its huge expanse different species predominate; only the Coots everywhere swarm in

---

* So Dr. Scully reports:—"The Pin-tail is the commonest of the Duck tribe in the Nepal Valley in winter. It is most abundant from September to November and in March and April, but it is to be found in the valley throughout the cold season.

myriads, and make, in rising on the sudden discharge of a gun, a noise like the roaring of mighty waters."

It follows that the Pin-tail is very locally, and, as it seems at first sight, arbitrarily distributed.* You may shoot a beautifully watered tract teeming with many kinds of fowl, and yet not see a Pin-tail; while again elsewhere the whole place swarms with them; and if sportsmen are about, large flocks of them are constantly seen darting by at more than railway speed, high out of shot, over head, conspicuous by their long pointed tails, long necks, and white breasts. In one respect they have the pull over Gadwall. I have repeatedly found them on the sea coast, while I have never seen the Gadwall in India on salt water.

Eminently gregarious, it is unusual to find them in pairs or small parties. Commonly they are in good-sized flocks of from 20 to 200; but I have seen flights far exceeding this latter number even, and once at night a flight passed over me, (and there is no mistaking the low, soft, hissing swish of Pin-tail) which must have numbered thousands.

It is worth noting, because it is a peculiarity almost confined to this species, that during the cold season one continually comes across large flocks consisting entirely of males. I cannot say that I ever noticed similar flocks of females, but this may be because the females do not attract the eye similarly, and are not equally readily discriminated at any distance, but "bull-pic-nics" I have noted, times without number, as a speciality of the Pin-tail.

Their flight is extremely rapid, more so, I think, than that of any species that visits us. They are shy and wary, and leave a jhíl almost at the first shot, or if they do hesitate to change their quarters, circle round and round high out of shot. There is no driving *them* backwards and forwards from one piece of water to another, or one part of a lake to another, over sportsmen concealed behind screens, or in rush clumps. You may kill a brace or so, but directly they begin to find that shooting is going on in earnest, off they go, probably not to alight again for several miles. Then, too, the plumage is very dense, especially on the breast. It is always wrong to fire at fowl coming towards you—you should always let them pass before drawing the trigger—but it is especially so in the case of Pin-tail, whose breast feathers will turn comparatively heavy shot at very moderate distances.

---

* Thus Mr. Davidson writes:—

"The Pin-tail was a rare Duck in the Deccan, though I have shot it on several occasions. In Tumkur, Mysore, it swarmed, and was much the commonest of all the Duck tribe."

So again in the Southern Konkan, it is very rare, and Mr. Vidal can only say of them there, "Pin-tails are to be seen in some years in small parties in the large Duck ground at the junction of the Vashishti and Tagbudi rivers. But they come late and go early."

It is not common, therefore, to make a good bag* of Pin-tail with a small gun. I cannot remember ever bagging a dozen with a shoulder gun in a day. On the other hand, though wary, they *can* be worked up to in a punt; they go in large flocks, and sit close, so that no species yields heavier bags with a swivel. No duck, again, is more readily caught by both fall and standing nets. They are a little troublesome to work up to the latter, being shy and suspicious birds, but they rise less easily, and at a lower angle than Mallard or Gadwall, and can be safely flushed at a greater distance from the net, and there is no *duck* of which you can make as heavy a haul with the standing net as of Pin-tail.

They swim moderately well; they look, perhaps, owing to their long arching necks and raised tails, better than any other species when afloat; but when winged they do not swim rapidly, and are such poor divers that they are very soon tired out and captured.

Feeding, as they commonly do, almost exclusively by night, it is rare to *see* them doing more than nibbling the water weeds around them; but in very unfrequented waters I have, even during the day time, but especially about sunset, repeatedly seen large flocks of them feeding energetically in the shallows, their long tails bent downwards almost parallel to the water, and the whole anterior halves of their bodies invisible, beneath this. I especially noticed that, while every individual of a party of Mallard or Gadwall may be thus seen, head under at the same time, a certain number of Pin-tail always remain on the *qui vive*, whilst the rest are ducking under. Occasionally I have seen a portion of a flock, both early in the morning and towards evening, feeding on the land, on grassy sward close by the margin of some jhíl, the rest of the flock feeding close at hand in the water. They walk very freely, but not so lightly as the Gadwall, and with their necks outstretched in front of them, and their tails raised, are not, in my opinion, thus seen by any means to the best advantage.

Their food is very varied, although, like most of our wild fowl, wild rice, so long as it lasts, is their main staple. But besides this, worms, small shells, both land and water, grass and aquatic plants, bulbous roots and corms, and insects of all kinds, are found in their stomachs. I think that with us they must particularly affect shells, because in no less than three cases (out of twenty-

* Since this was written, I have met with the following remarks by Captain Baldwin, which I quote as being directly opposed to my own experience:—

"A friend and I killed nineteen couple of duck one day off the Lowqua Lake, opposite Tezpoor on the Brahmaputra, and more than half the birds were Pin-tails.

"It is, generally speaking, an easy bird to approach, even when feeding on open pools of water."

All I can say is, that in Upper India I have found it (except when basking, and as it thinks hidden, in a clump of water weeds) the wariest of birds, not only to approach in the ordinary way, but with a regular punt, *secundem artem*.

two) I have noted, "stomach almost entirely full of small fragile fresh-water shells," and in five others I have recorded shells as *amongst* the food found on dissection in the gizzards.

The Pin-tail, when undisturbed, is a silent bird by day, and rarely utters any sound, even when feeding, though I have, when lying up pretty close to them, heard a little low chatteration going on, more like the low clucking of hens than anything else. But when alarmed by day, and pretty constantly by night, they utter their peculiar soft quack,—a note such as one might expect a Mallard, not quite sure whether he meant to speak or not, to emit—quite different from the sharp quack of the Gadwall, softer and less strident than that of the Mallard, but still not at all feeble, on the contrary audible at a great distance.

I could single out the Pin-tail's quack at any time, and yet I am wholly unable to explain, in words, its peculiar and characteristic tone.

On the whole, I think, that next to the Mallard the Pin-tail *is the best* duck for the table in India, for here (it is different at home) I have never come across one with a fishy or unpleasant flavour.

THE PIN-TAIL cannot, I believe, breed with us. Its nidification range is far more northern; and while in many places it breeds well within the Arctic Circle, it rarely breeds, I think, much south of the 50th degree North Latitude.* It lays in May or June according to locality; the nest is placed on the ground generally in marshes, and not on the margins of large pieces of water. It is made of long pieces of bleached grass, rush, twigs or anything that comes to hand, and is lined with down from the mother's breast mingled with a few feathers.

The eggs, from six to nine in number, are rather small for the size of the bird; they are regular ovals, smooth, but with little gloss, with a pale yellowish green tinge. An egg from Finland, collected by Wolley, measures exactly 2·0 by 1·5, and this too Dresser gives as the average of the eggs *he* got in Finland, but he speaks of others from Jutland measuring 2·22 by 1·4.

THIS DUCK varies very widely in dimensions and weight, the former, especially in the case of the males, owing to the different degrees in which the tails are developed.

---

* It breeds in Northern Yárkand about Maralbashi. Dr. Scully says:—

"The Pin-tail Duck was occasionally seen near Yárkand in March, but only one specimen (a female) was obtained. Two experienced Yárkandi bird-catchers gave me the following information about this species:—The male bird is *ala*, *i.e.*, pied black (or dark coloured) and white; it is a seasonal visitant only to Eastern Turkestan, arriving in spring and migrating to Hindostan at the beginning of winter, and it breeds in the neighbourhood of Maralbashi, laying from ten to twelve eggs."

Males.—(All in adult plumage). Length, 22·0 to 29·0; expanse, 32·0 to 37·75; wing, 10·3 to 11·75; tail from vent, 4·8 to 9·4; tarsus, 1·5 to 1·8; bill from gape, 2·0 to 2·45; weight, 1 lb. 10 ozs. to 2 lbs. 12 ozs.

Females.—Length, 20·0 to 22·5; expanse, 32·0 to 34·5; wing, 9·3 to 10·2; tail from vent, 4·2 to 5·5; tarsus, 1·45 to 1·7; bill from gape, 2·1 to 2·35; weight, 1 lb. 2 ozs. to 1 lb. 14 ozs.

In the adult male the bill is plumbeous, light plumbeous or lavender blue, with the entire lower mandible, a broad band along the entire culmen, the angle at the base of the upper mandible, and a strip along the margin of its terminal half, black.

In the adult female (at any rate during the cold season) the bill is generally very similarly but duller coloured; it is blackish dusky, passing to dusky plumbeous on the sides of the upper and rami of lower mandible. Sometimes in apparent adults it is uniform dusky. In young birds the bills are everywhere a nearly uniform blackish dusky.

The irides are deep brown, sometimes with a reddish tinge. The legs and feet are greyish plumbeous, sometimes paler, sometimes darker, often duskier on the joints, and always so on the central portions of the webs, which, in some males, are almost black; the claws blackish dusky. In some apparently adult males (one a very fine bird, length 28·75) I have noted the feet as brownish black, blackish grey, and uniform dusky,* but the normal colouration is as above described.

THE PLATE.—The bills and feet are not typically coloured; usually there is far more blue grey on both. The fulvous buff flank patch of the male is not sufficiently brought out, otherwise the figure of the male is not bad; but in no species is the under surface more commonly tinged with rusty (*vide* ante, p. 162) than in this, and the lower parts in the Pin-tail consequently vary from snow-white to a rich rusty buff. In the female, as figured, the tone of colouration of the upper surface is much too rufous; it should be greyer, and very commonly the whitish margins to the wing coverts are far more conspicuous in this sex than would appear from the plate. The female can always be distinguished from that of all our other species by her sharply pointed tail. Young females have the entire under surface thickly spotted with greyish brown. †

---

* The colour of the legs seems to vary a great deal. I have recorded this in the case of nearly fifty examples, but I have never seen colouration such as Swinhoe met with in a male. "Legs very pale yellowish flesh colour, variegated with shades of purplish brown, darker tint of last on nails and on the web membranes."

† Captain Butler thus describes a young couple of Pin-tails:—"The male had the head dusky, minutely spotted, increasing on to the neck. Tail of 16 feathers with central feathers pointed, but not elongated. There was the pale red bar above the black green speculum with the white edge; tertiaries very broad dark grey, with broad velvet stripe, yellowish edging; back black, with two white bars; and central

This bird, too, towards the close of the breeding season assumes a sober garb resembling that of the female ; and, though I have never obtained a bird in this stage of plumage in India, such must occur in Kashmir and other parts of the Himalayas, and it may be well, therefore, to quote Yarrell's remarks on this subject. He says :—

"The males constantly undergo a remarkable summer change in their plumage which renders them, for a time, more like their females in appearance than any other species in which this change is observed. This alteration commences in July, partly effected by some new feathers, and partly by a change in the colour of many of the old feathers. At first one or more brown spots appear in the white surface on the front of the neck ; these spots increase in number rapidly, till the whole head, neck, breast, and under surface have become brown ; the scapulars, wing-coverts, and tertials, undergo, by degrees, the same change from grey to brown. I have seen a single white spot remaining on the breast as late as the 4th of August ; but generally by that time the males can only be distinguished from females of the same species by their larger size, and their beak remaining a pale blue colour. In the female the bill is dark brown," (*not usually so in Indian birds !*)

"At the annual autumn moult the males again assume, with their new feathers, the colours peculiar to their sex, but the assumption is gradual. White spots first appear among the brown feathers on the front of the neck ; by the end of the second week in October the front of the neck and breast is mottled with brown and white ; at the end of the third week in October a few brown spots only remain on the white."

TWO, if not three, more species, of this genus, occur in South America and the Falkland Islands.

---

tail black, with yellow stripe ; wing-coverts hair brown with white edging ; the flank feathers, as in the female, and not as in the adult male, transversely banded black and white. Length, 24 ; wing, 10½ ; tarsus, 1¾ ; mid-toe, 2¼. Female, with central tail as in young male, but more marked with yellow. Lower plumage altogether more rufous. Length, 20 ; tarsus, 1½ ; mid-toe with claw, 2⅛ ; wing, 9¾."

MARECA ♂♀ PENELOPE

THE WIGEON.

—o—

Mareca penelope, *Linné.*

—o—

Vernacular Names.—[Pea-san, Patári, *N.-W. Provinces;* Cheyun, Chéoon, *Nepal;* Parow, *Sindh;* Ade, Adla. *Ratnagiri;*]

—o—

I AM unable to define the distribution of the Wigeon within our Empire with any degree of accuracy.

In the Himalayas it occurs in winter from Kashmir to Bhútan. Throughout the Punjab, Sindh,* Rajputana, the N.-W. Provinces, Oudh,† Behar and the Deltaic districts of Bengal, it is met with here and there, during the cold season, very locally and capriciously distributed. In Manipur, Godwin-Austen says that it is "very common," but Mr. Damant did not include it in his list, nor does Colonel Graham mention it in his list of the ducks of Darrang or Lakhimpur, nor have I as yet a single notice of its occurrence anywhere in the valley of Assam or in Cachar, Sylhet, Tipperah or Chittagong, though Blyth says it has been sent from Arakan; and if he and Godwin-Austen are correct, it must needs occur in all these.

Mr. Oates does not mention it from Pegu, nor did Captain Feilden, or Wardlaw Ramsay, obtain it there, nor does Blyth include it in his Burmese list; but Mason does, and Colonel McMaster says, "more common in Burmah than in India," so that I suppose it does occur in Pegu. In Tenasserim it does not occur, at any rate normally, though possibly a single bird

---

* As I recorded long ago, the Wigeon is very common on the Manchar Lake, but neither Day, nor myself, nor Watson ever saw it in any of the innumerable dhunds of the Shikarpore Collectorate.

Elsewhere Butler found it far from common, and now Doig writes that even "on the Eastern Narra—" that paradise for aquatic fowl—"it is comparatively rare."

† Writing from the Lucknow Division, Mr. George Reid remarks:—

"The Wigeon is by no means uncommon, though it is, I think, rather erratic in its wanderings, being much more common in some seasons than others. During the past cold weather, for instance, when the jhíls were much below their average size, and many of the smaller ones altogether dry, I did not expect to meet with it; but, as a matter of fact, it was much more common than I had ever known it to be before.

"The result of my experience is, in short, that the Wigeon is fairly abundant in this division in some years, and exceedingly scarce in others."

may some day turn up in the central or northern portions of this Province.

It is common in Káthiáwar, less so in Cutch, not very uncommon in Gujarat, Khandesh, Berar, and the western half of the Central Provinces. It is very common in the Deccan, not uncommon during some seasons in the Konkan,* and the Nizam's Territories, and occurs, in considerable numbers, in some parts of Mysore. But southwards of this my record fails; I cannot find it noted from Ceylon or any of the Madras districts south of Mysore, or from the eastern portions of the Central Provinces or Chota Nagpur, and Ball excludes it entirely in his Conspectus of the Avifauna of the region lying between the Ganges and the Gódavarí.

It is very likely, however, that it may occur in many of these localities the birds of which have never yet been systematically worked out.

Outside our limits it occurs in Independent Burmah, and throughout China, in winter, though there too very locally distributed, extending to Japan, and strange to say, the Pribylov Islands in Behring Sea which are nearer the American than the Asiatic Coast. It has recently been obtained in Borneo. It probably breeds in Mongolia, and throughout Central and Southern Siberia, and Prjevalski saw it on migration at the Koko-Nor and at lake Hanka, where some breed, but none of our explorers have met with it at any season in Yárkand, the true Central Asia. In Western Turkestan Severtzov observed it in winter, and on passage, and it occurs, we know, in the Caspian, in Afghanistan and Beluchistan, and on the coasts of the Persian and Oman Gulfs, also during the winter. It has been found in Armenia, Asia Minor, and Palestine. Throughout the temperate zone in Europe and North Africa it occurs as a summer or winter visitant, and in some few localities perhaps as a permanent resident; and it is said to be not uncommon on the Atlantic Coasts of North America, being elsewhere, on that Continent, replaced by a closely allied species.

---

*Thus Vidal says:—"Wigeon in some years are very abundant on the Vashishti river, congregating in large flocks of five hundred birds or more; but they are not like Common Teal, widely distributed. In 1878-79, after the highest rainfall on record, not a Wigeon was to be found in the district; but in 1879-80, after a year of moderate rainfall, they reappeared again in their usual strength on the Vashishti. Wigeon arrive comparatively late, and usually leave by the end of February. Before the reeds on the mud banks have been cut, very pretty shooting is to be had at the junction of the Vashishti and Tagbudi rivers by stealing up the lagoons in a light and silent canoe. But after the reeds are cut, the Duck get very wild, and cannot be approached by land or water. The only way then is to take up a position in ambush at the edge of some swamp over which they pass and repass on their way from one ground to another, and to have them driven backwards and forwards."

Mr. J. Davidson writes:—"The Wigeon also is a very common duck in the Deccan; it was noticed by me in the Pánch Máhals, but rarely in Mysore (I only remember one largish flock"). But Major Charles McInroy writes that in Mysore "a fair number are seen in some parts."

I HAVE seldom seen the Wigeon anywhere, either in hills or plains before the last week in October; but I once shot one in the Dún on the 21st of that month. In the North-West Provinces I have never shot one as late as April, and further south they leave during the middle of March; but I have a specimen killed in the Peshawur Valley on the 17th of April.

The Wigeon is a very irregular migrant to all parts of the country; all accounts are in accord on this point. "One year we see hardly any; the next perhaps they are specially abundant," is the purport of what correspondents from a dozen different localities have written. Habitually they are far more common during the winter in the south, the Deccan for instance, than in Upper India; but by comparing accounts it would seem that, when they are commonest in the North-West Provinces and Oudh, they are least common in the south, and *vice versâ*, and this may be generally the case, and so not improbably, though very differently distributed in different years, much about the same number yearly find their way to the Empire as a whole.

Where they are abundant you find them, as a rule, in flocks of from twenty to five hundred; where scarce, in pairs or small parties, rarely exceeding seven in number.

Their flight is swift and powerful, but not equal to that of the Pin-tail. On the other hand it is accompanied by a much harsher rustle, which can always be distinguished from that of the other fowl that I know. They spring up more readily than the Pin-tail from the water or the ground, and more perpendicularly than these. In fact, in these respects they are about equal to the Gadwall; and, though they come easily to bait, and are often captured therefore in fall-nets, they must be flushed pretty close to the standing net, or they will clear it.

They swim very well, and when wounded and pursued, give a long chase, diving continually and turning rapidly under water.

Where undisturbed they are seen more on land than most of our ducks, walking about on the turf that often fringes our broads and rivers, and grazing freely.

In Upper India, we habitually meet with them on good-sized pieces of water, some portions of the shores of which are smooth and turfy. They are excessively rare on bare lakes like the Sámbhar. On small ponds I have never once seen them. Nor have I, except very rarely, seen them on our large rivers, but they are not so uncommon in smaller rivers flowing through meadow-like turfy flats. They are common enough on the sea coast however, though generally some little distance up the estuaries and creeks where there is a certain admixture of fresh water.

With us in the North-West Provinces they are more purely grass-eaters than any other duck. Of a large number of specimens that I obtained this last cold season at the Phulpur jhíl, not far from Allahabad, grass had been the chief food, though mingled with this were a few fresh-water shells, insects, and roots, and leaves of rushes and aquatic plants, and a little grain. I have often seen them on land grazing like Geese, but also often feeding in the shallows, with only their stern halves visible, like Mallard or Gadwall. They feed more by day and less by night than the Pin-tail, and do not so constantly change their quarters at sunset as these latter do. I have not found them as wary as the Pin-tail as a whole; and, though Colonel Hawker says that for punt-shooting they are like the fox for hunting, and show the finest sport of anything in England, I can only say that, out here, they are not difficult to work up to if any wind be blowing. No doubt they have a keen scent, and you must work them *on* and not *off* a wind.

Along the coast (and those killed there are very poor eating in my opinion) they feed, I found, on all kinds of shell-fish, shrimps and the like, as well as on vegetable matter (a kind of green sea weed it seemed to me in one case) of various descriptions.

Sometimes they are very reluctant to leave the broad in which you find them, and drive backwards and forwards well, affording very pretty shooting when numerous. They are not robust birds, and drop easily at distances at which, unless you happened to catch him in his long thin neck, a Pin-tail would laugh at you. At other times they are very wild, and go right away at the first shot.

They are, on the whole, rather loquacious birds, and both, when feeding and at rest, when walking, swimming, and flying, often utter a shrill "whew," a sort of whistle, by which you may know them at any distance; it is not a clear full whistle like the Curlew's, but a whistled cry, rather discordant when heard by day, but not without its charms when uttered at night by large numbers, mingled with the calls of many other species, and mellowed by distance and the multitudinous voices of winds and waters.

Very often they are well flavoured enough, and might then rank high as table ducks, but their flesh has not unfrequently a muddy flavour; and those that I have shot on the sea coast have always had such a distinct "odour of brine from the ocean" as to render them very unpalatable. At home in Norfolk we used to consider Wigeons first-rate eating, but out here they must rank as only moderately good on the average.

THERE IS no reason to suppose that this species ever breeds within our limits. It breeds in the highlands of Scotland,*

* Mr. Brooks kindly sends me the following note of a nest of this species that he took in the Highlands :—

"I once took a nest of this Duck, with nine eggs, on one of the small islands in Loch Maddie, which is in Sutherlandshire, and about 20 miles from the North Coast

Iceland, Northern Europe, and Siberia, rarely if ever, I take it, within the Arctic Circle or much south of the 55th degree North Latitude. Dresser says:—"The eggs are deposited late in May or early in June, the locality selected for the purpose of nidification being sometimes close to the water's edge, and at others some distance from it; for Mr. Collett informs me that he found a nest on the fells, not far from the town of Lillehammer, which was under a juniper bush, at least 800 yards from the water. The nest is a mere depression or hole scratched in the ground and well lined with down and a few feathers, intermixed with a little moss or a few grass bents. A nest, which I possess, consists of a little moss matted together with down, the latter being of a dark sooty brown colour, the centre of the down being rather lighter or dark sooty grey; and a few feathers of the bird are interspersed here and there. The eggs are creamy white in colour and oval in shape, tapering slightly towards the smaller end."

Mr. Wolley says that "no other duck is so common as this in Lapland. Wherever there is a still bay or recess in the river, with water-plants and willows, there is sure to be a pair or two of Wigeon; and near the bank they make their nests. In the lakes, too, they are frequently to be found. They are tamer than any of the other ducks, and often let a boat pass quite near, whilst they are constantly swimming about just before houses. The down of the nest is somewhat like that of the Pin-tail, but looser; the same white centres, softened by the transparent grey outside each little tuft; yet the filaments are longer, and their white bars larger and more distinct. A nest is an extremely pretty sight, even when separated from its native bank, and all the accompaniments of flowers, roots, moss, and lichen. The eggs seem to be usually from six to ten in number. When fresh, they are mostly of a rich cream colour; but some are even then quite white."

The eggs are smooth, have a faint gloss, and are rather elongated ovals, measuring from 2·1 to 2·3 in length, by 1·5 to 1·6 in breadth.

THERE IS very little difference in the sizes of the sexes, and though the males average larger, I got one female last year considerably heavier than any male I ever met with.

Males (adults).—Length, 19·0 to 19·5; expanse, 32·75 to 34·5; wing, 10·0 to 10·6; tail from vent, 4·0 to 4·6; tarsus, 1·4 to 1·6; bill from gape, 1·7 to 1·82; weight, 1 lb. 5 ozs. to 1 lb. 10 ozs.

---

of Scotland. The little island, which was rather flat, was overgrown with heather from a foot to eighteen inches high, and at one end of the island was a clump of rather low birch trees on which a number of common Herons had their nests. In walking through the heather one of the boatman who accompanied me put up a Wigeon close by, which almost flew in my face. The nest was at once found among the heather, and was the usual mossy one at the roots of the heather, and lined with the down of the bird. The eggs were quite fresh, and of a fine creamy white."

Females.—Length, 17·8 to 19·25; expanse, 31·5 to 34·0; wing, 9·3 to 10·2; tail from vent, 3·5 to 5·0; tarsus, 1·4 to 1·6; bill from gape, 1·68 to 1·8; weight, 1 lb. 3 ozs., to 1 lb. 12 ozs. (Note that only one female out of 27 exceeded 1 lb. 9 ozs).

The bill is a pale delicate greyish lavender or leaden, rarely a slatey blue, with the nostrils, tip of upper, and all but the basal portions of the rami of the lower mandible, black, and often with a narrow black line along the margins of the upper mandible also. Sometimes only the tip of the lower mandible is black, the rest the same blue as the upper one, but dingier. The irides vary from hazel to deep brown.

The legs and feet vary much; they are (1) pale drab brown with a faint olive tinge, (2) greyish or brownish olive, (3) dusky olivaceous, (4) dusky leaden, (5) plumbeous, (6) plumbeous with an olive tinge, (7) light plumbeous; in all cases the webs are dusky, occasionally almost black, and very often, whatever the colour of the tarsi and toes, they have a dusky shade over the joints.

THE PLATE is good, but the under surfaces of both birds, and the entire shoulder of the male's wing should be of a far purer white. Moreover it is only just as they leave us that the breasts of the males are *nearly* as rich a vinaceous pink as is depicted in the plate, (it is never, I think, *quite* so rich as this). Throughout the cold season the pink is shaded with grey, the result of greyish white tippings to all the feathers, which disappear (wear off I think) just as the breeding season approaches.

The female, what is shown of her, though rather coarsely drawn, may pass. She can always be distinguished from other ducks by her tiny blue, black-tipped bill.

In the males there is generally a conspicuous, broad, more or less speckly, black band, down the middle of the throat, sometimes extending down the whole front of the neck; but I have specimens, apparently otherwise in perfect plumage, showing only the barest trace of this. It is, I believe, the latest sign of complete maturity, the creamy buff *patch* on forehead and crown (it varies much in extent) being the last preceding one.

Very beautiful and interesting specimens of young males are often procured, with the perfect plumage of the adult male, struggling through that of the female—all my specimens in this stage were procured between the 10th November and the 20th December. But I have a specimen procured in January in which, while the plumage is in other respects perfect, a number of brown lunules yet linger amongst the pink of the breast.

I have never seen a bird in India in the "eclipse" stage; but it is well to note that "the adult male birds undergo considerable change in their appearance towards the end of July and the beginning of August, becoming much more uniform in their general colour, and losing some of the most conspicuous external differences which distinguish males from females."

THE WIGEONS are really very close to the Teal, and are scarcely to be separated except by their shorter and rather broader bills *narrowed towards the tips*.

Besides our bird, America has two other species—*americana* from Northern and Central America and Trinidad, and *chiloensis* from Chili, Patagonia, &c., and the Falkland Islands. A third species, to be dealt with hereafter, *gibberfrons* of Australia and the Islands of the Indian Ocean, which we get in the Andamans, is usually classed as a Wigeon, but I am now disposed to class it rather with the Teal.

F. Waller, Chromo Lith. 12 Hatton Garden London.

QUERQUEDULA CRECCA

THE COMMON TEAL.

Querquedula crecca, *Linné.*

Vernacular Names.—[Murghabi, or Chota Murghabi, *India* generally; Kerra, Lohya Kerra, Putari, *North-Western Provinces;* Naroib, Tulsia-bigri, *Bengal;* Baijilagairi, *Nepal;* Kardo, *Sindh;* Killowai, *Madras;* Sorlai haki (Canarese), *Mysore;* Churaka, Jaruka, *Cabul;* Alah bash kurak aurdak, *Yárkand.*]

FEW species, I believe, are more universally distributed throughout the Empire during the cold season, and none probably visits us in greater numbers than the Common Teal. Excepting the Laccadives, the Andamans and Nicobars, Tenasserim, Southern, Central and North-East of the Salween, and *possibly* Malabar, I know of no corner in the Empire, from Ceylon in the south to Ley and the Nubra Valley in the north, and from Soonmeeani Bay and Gilgit on the west to Sadiya, Manipur, and Thatone on the east, in which the Teal is not more or less plentiful.* It is probable that some even remain to breed in the North-West Himalayas, as

---

* I may here reproduce a few of the notes kindly sent me by different friends about this species.

Mr. Vidal says:—"The Common Teal are found everywhere throughout the Ratnagiri, Sattara, and Poona districts in the cold weather, in suitable localities. They arrive in October earlier than any other species, and I think stay later. They are to be found on all the tidal rivers in Ratnagiri both near the coast and in their fresh-water sections inland, as well as in tanks and rice swamps throughout the district. In Sattara and Poona they are also found in moderate numbers on the large rivers and tanks."

Mr. J. Davidson writes:—"Both the Common and Blue-winged Teal are very plentiful in the Sholapur and Sattara districts (Deccan), in Mysore, and in the Pánch Máhals. Both arrive early, the Common Teal, I think, the earliest. It leaves, however, in April, while I have shot the Garganey in the Deccan in the middle of May, and again seen it in October."

Writing from the Lucknow Division Mr. George Reid remarks:—"Generally speaking, the Common Teal arrives in myriads in October, and leaves again by the end of March or beginning of April.

"I have seen flocks of Teal flying about in August, but never succeeded in getting specimens, so that I am uncertain whether it is this species or the next that arrives so early. I think the latter, but probably both come in about the same time.

"The Common Teal is fond of weedy shallow lakes and large or small swamps, with often but little more than a foot or two of water in them; but as these feeding grounds soon dry up, necessity obliges them to resort to the larger jhíls, round the edges of which, often on the mud, sportsmen may slaughter them as they please in the early morning, and continue their operations throughout the day if they care to pick up the stragglers that ever and anon re-visit the shore."

the Mallard does; but though Adams says that they remain all the year round in Kashmir, no one has since confirmed this fact, nor, so far as I know, found the nest within our limits.

Elsewhere, the Teal is common in Independent Burmah, and occurs in Northern Siam,* is plentiful in China, Mongolia, and rather rare in Eastern Turkestan,† in all of which it is mainly a bird of passage or winter visitant. It is found throughout Siberia from Kamschatka to Russia, breeding everywhere, but rarely far inside the Arctic Circle; it occurs in Western Turkestan, in many parts of which it breeds, throughout Persia, Afghanistan, Beluchistan, Mesopotamia, Palestine, and Asia Minor, in which latter a few are said to breed, while to the rest it is only a winter visitant.

It is more or less abundant also, at one season or another, in every part of Europe (where it breeds occasionally as far south, at any rate, as the 40th degree North Latitude), and of North Africa as far south as Abyssinia, and has been recorded from Madeira and the Azores on one of which it breeds. It is very common in Iceland, but in Europe as in Asia does not seem to stray in any numbers, within the Arctic Circle.

Lastly, it straggles to Greenland and the Eastern Coasts of North America, being replaced elsewhere in that region by a barely separable species, *Q. carolinensis.*

IT IS difficult to say when the Common Teal does arrive, as the period varies a good deal in different years, and in different parts of the country. But in the more northern plains portion of the

---

Mr. Oates says:—"The Common English Teal is nowhere met with in the Pegu Province in large quantities. One or two birds may generally be found on large sheets of water in company with the commoner kinds of Teal. It is, of course, only a cold weather visitor."

* In this and many other cases it will be noticed that I have made no reference to Southern Siam, Cambodia, Anam, Cochin China, and Tonquin, though in many cases one or more of these appear to lie within the range of the species referred to. In regard to Northern Siam I have some little information, and hope hereafter to have more; but in regard to Southern Siam, beyond a list of the birds in the Paris Museum kindly prepared for me by Mr. D. G. Elliot, Schomburgk's paper in the *Ibis* (1864), and Gould's list (P. Z. S., 1859), I have *no* information; and in regard to the other provinces mentioned, although I believe that lists have been *printed*, if not published, in Paris, I have utterly failed to procure copies. It must not, therefore, be concluded that any species does *not* extend to one or more of these, because I say nothing about their so doing—on the contrary, this very species most probably occurs in Tonquin—it is simply that I have no information on the subject.

† Henderson says in our Lahore to Yárkand:—"The Common Teal was never seen either on the way to or in Yárkand; the first specimen was met with on the return journey, near the hot springs at Gokra, at an elevation of between 15,000 and 16,000 feet. Later in October they were seen on the Indus, near Lé, and at Kargil, both in Ladákh. Probably this species does not breed so far south as Yárkand, and the birds, seen on the return journey, were doubtless migrating to their winter quarters in Hindostan."

The second Yárkand Mission obtained several there, and in the case of the third Scully writes:—"The Common Teal was only obtained at Kashghar in November; at Sughuchak near Yárkand, by Mr. Shaw, in January; and at Beshkant, in the beginning of February. I was told that it migrated northwards to breed."

Empire, though a few are often seen during the latter half of September, and exceptional cases have been reported of their appearance some weeks earlier even than this, I think we may say that the first heavy flights arrive during the first week of October. Further south and in Sindh they seem to be a little later, but even at Deesa Captain Butler shot them as early as the 27th of September.

Usually they leave most parts of India by the end of April, but they are occasionally seen alike in the south and north well into May; and Mr. Albert Theobald, in a most interesting note which I subjoin,* tells us that they were plentiful near Palamcottah in the Tinnevelli District, (at the extreme south of the Peninsula) on the 15th of May.

Teal occur in flocks of all sizes; and, though perhaps bunches of from ten to thirty are most commonly seen, little parties of two to five are frequently met with on small ponds, and huge flocks, containing many hundreds of birds, occasionally appear. I have never seen gigantic crowds of this species similar to those one sometimes encounters of the Garganey; but still I have seen, I think, at least a thousand birds on several occasions in a single, though rather straggling, flight. I have never, however, seen much above one hundred gathered together on the water in *one* place, and commonly I have observed that, however large the flock that comes in, it alights all about the banks of the lake or river in comparatively small detachments.

You may meet with them anywhere; a pair or two may be seen, where the villagers do not molest them, on any village

---

* Mr. Albert Theobald says:—"I have shot the Common Teal all over Southern India, except in Malabar, where I have not seen them.

"They come in at the beginning of the north-east monsoon about November, and leave again about March and April, when most of the large tanks are dry. I have shot them in Tinnevelli as late as the 15th May 1872. I am inclined to suspect that they may remain throughout the year in well-watered districts. They are common in almost every weedy tank.

"Tanks containing abundance of weeds are their favourite haunts. They feed mainly on the tender shoots of weeds and grasses. The following extract is from some notes made by me in Palamcottah, Tinnevelli district, on the 15th May 1872 *** 'These Teal are found in great abundance in all the large tanks south of Palamcottah;—in one especially they were so tame, that I mistook them for domesticated ones. They were not more than five or six yards from a number of villagers who were having their morning bath, making, as usual, a great noise by dashing their wet clothes on the stones to cleanse them. Even when fired at, they appeared quite unconcerned.

"They were quite playful, chasing each other, sometimes on the water, and sometimes in the air, and then suddenly tumbling into the water. They would frequently turn on their backs, and move about with their wings spread open. At first I fancied they were wounded, but found it was all done in play. The only reason I can give to account for these birds being so tame in this district is, that hardly a native possesses a gun. All were disarmed by Government during the Polligar wars, about 70 or 80 years back, and the villagers are still under the impression that it is illegal to have fire-arms. The few Europeans about here are almost all missionaries, and do not go in for any sort of sport. Elsewhere the natives snare, net and shoot numbers, and all large markets in Southern India are well supplied with them during the season."

pond half or wholly surrounded by houses, in any marshy corner, on the largest lakes, on the banks of rivers and streams of all sizes, alike those gliding sluggishly through the plains, and those foaming and spluttering onwards in the hills.

They are, as a rule, when met with near villages and in densely populated portions of the country, excessively tame—too tame to render shooting them possible, unless you really require them for food. Not only will they let you walk up to them when they are on a village pond, as close as you please, but when you have fired at them, and killed two or three, the remainder, after a short flight, will again settle, as often as not, still well within shot. Nay, at times, though fluttering a good deal, and looking about as if astonished, they will not even rise at all at the first shot, despite the fact of some of their comrades floating dead before them. More than once I have seen them deliberately swim up to their departed brethren, examine them and try to stir them up with their bills, and apparently then only realize the true state of the case, get really alarmed and rise, when their efforts proved unavailing.

But they are not by any means everywhere or always thus tame. Where often molested—and I may say generally in out-of-the-way places, rarely visited by men, and on most large pieces of water—they rise more readily, and where Teal are plentiful, there is no prettier sport, (after the larger ducks have been alarmed and have left,) than shooting round the marshy margins of some large broad, amongst the rushes of which fully half the Teal originally there located will still linger, and whence, as you progress, they will rise in rapid succession usually well within shot.

On the larger rivers and tanks they are constantly met with in good-sized flocks, which fly in such dense bunches that a couple of barrels, well directed, will often secure from a dozen to twenty birds.

About March they swarm in some rivers, (like the Chambal near its junction with the Jumna,) and where the banks are precipitous, so that, having noted where they are, you can always, by walking a few yards inland, approach them unperceived, and suddenly appear immediately above them; they afford wonderfully pretty shooting. They are at this time always in pairs, and there are pairs, or groups of pairs, every fifty or a hundred yards for miles. They rise, when thus startled, very sharply out of the water, and go off at a great pace. Even if you miss one of the pair, or as often happens shoot one of each of two pairs, you are sure to get the other, as they almost invariably return to the rescue of their fallen mates. Indeed, as a rule, Teal seem more attached to each other than any other of the ducks, and this attachment is more specially conspicuous as the spring broadens into summer. In the Chambal the difficulty is recovering the dead birds, because the crocodiles swarm to such a degree that you dare not send in dogs; and, though I never heard of their touching men *there*, still it is not pleasant to run any such risk, and I used to keep a boat two or three hundred yards behind, and men on the bank to watch the birds as they floated, but I lost many birds thus, snapped up by the crocodiles.

There is no duck so easy to net and snare as Teal; and thousands, probably taking the empire as a whole, hundreds of thousands, are yearly captured and sold. Indeed, but for these Teal and Quail, we should many of us fare but poorly during the hot season and early part of the rains in the plains of India.

Tealeries are amongst the greatest of our luxuries, as all who have enjoyed them in out-of-the-way places where butcher's meat was an impossiblity in the hot weather, will, I am sure, allow; and it may be well to say a few words about their construction and management.

Fresh water, and plenty of it, is the first requisite, and to ensure this, the tealery should always be located near the well, and every drop of water drawn thence for irrigating the garden made to pass through it. The site should be, if possible, under some large umbrageous tree, such as we so commonly find near garden wells, and to the east of the trunk, so that the building may be completely protected from the noontide and afternoon sun. You first make a small shallow masonry tank, —twelve feet by eight and ten inches in depth is amply large. Four feet distant from this all round you build a thick mud wall to a height of three feet above the interior. The whole interior surface of this wall and the flat space* between it and the tank must be lined with pukha masonry, and finished off with well-worked chunam. The great points to be aimed at are to have the whole lower parts so finished off as to be on the one hand impregnable to rats, ichneumons, and snakes; on the other to present no crevice in which dirt, ticks, and other insects can lurk. Outside, the walls must be quite smooth, so that no snakes can crawl up them. On the wall you build stout square pillars, four feet high, on which you place a thick pent thatch roof. At the spring of the roof you stretch inside a thin, rather loose, ceiling-cloth to prevent the birds hurting their heads when they start up suddenly, as they will, at first, on any alarm, and especially when the sweeper goes in to wash out the place. The interspaces between the pillars you fill in with well-made cross-work (*jaffri*) of split bamboo, except one of them in which you place a door of similar work made with slips of wood. You must arrange that all the water both enters and leaves the building through gratings impervious to snakes and the like marauders. Two or three feet outside the walls run a little groove, a ditchlet, in which plant, early in the

* This should have a slope of about half an inch in the foot, towards the tank.

year, mulberry cuttings which will form a good hedge round the place, and keep the sun and hot winds off the building ; but this must be kept neatly trimmed inside, or it would interfere with ventilation, and must not be allowed to get higher than the eaves.

Into such a building in February or March you may turn 200 Teal, some Common some Garganey, as you can get them. A few Gadwall and Pin-tail will also do no harm, but they do not thrive so certainly as the Teal; and the Garganey, though very good, is not equal for the table to its smallar congener. The Marbled Teal (*Q. angustirostris*) is not worth eating, and should you chance to obtain the Bronze Cap (*Q. falcata*) or the Clucking Teal (*Q. formosa*,) never dream of putting *them* into a tealery, but skin them carefully, and send the skins *to me*.

In small stations Rs. 2-8 per hundred is a fair price for netted Teal.

Before turning the Teal in, have the place thoroughly washed out two or three times, and cover parts, or the whole of the flat portion, with a thin layer of sand or dry earth. The two ends of the tank should slope down gradually, say, for two feet; the sides may be perpendicular. The water will always remain about two or three inches below the top, so that there will be about seven inches water. Besides the overflow pipe there must be a plug by which the tank can be drained to the last drop; and to ensure this the bottom of the tank should always be a few inches above the surface level of the surrounding ground. Each morning the sweeper who feeds the birds must go in and thoroughly sluice out and cleanse the whole place. He must begin gradually, but in less than a fortnight the ducks will all sit chattering on one side, whilst he sluices on the other, apparently quite unconcerned. Having cleaned the whole place, he lets the water again into the tank, and renews the earth or sand on the margin ; and you have only to watch the birds after he has withdrawn, often before he has finished, to realize how thoroughly *they* appreciate the clean water, &c.

For food, unhusked rice is best. It is usual to buy it just after the rainy season, as you can then purchase several maunds for the rupee, and store it. Give them as much as they will eat. This you must watch yourself, never trusting the key of the door out of your own hands. If, when the man goes in to sweep, you find any appreciable quantity lying about, reduce the allowance ; if, on the contrary, not a grain is to be seen, increase it until there is some little surplus daily apparent. Besides this, bunches of lucerne or fine green grass should be thrown in daily. Many give onions chopped up, others half-boiled dal in small quantities, but I found unhusked rice and lucerne all that was required. As the hot winds begin to blow, get screens (*jhamps*) of grass made to fit all the interspaces, except those on the northern side, and have these put up every day by 8 o'clock in the morning, and removed in the evening. No matter when you go into it, the tealery should always feel cool, and smell *fairly* sweet. If not, there is something wrong, and you must look to it.

Thus managed you may keep Teal, not only all through the hot weather, but right through the rains (when people generally tell you that they become uneatable) as fat as butter, to constitute, when worn out by the climate (as the best of us get more or less by July) one can hardly eat anything, a really delicious meal. I know that many a hot weather through, the partner of my joys and cares, and myself, have dined alternate days on Teal and Quail without ever tiring of them.

Of course you don't want Teal before the middle of April, and it is some expense (though comparatively little) feeding Teal for very long before you want them, so that you should always fill your tealery as late as the circumstances of the district permit.

These vary a great deal, and I have been in places where the people never could catch many after the end of January, as all the jhíls dried up, and the ducks nearly deserted the place, and others in which the heaviest takes were always towards the end of March.

In the wild state, where not molested, they feed equally by day and night, though no doubt at noontide they usually take a siesta. I always, therefore, fed my Teal at sunset and sunrise.

Where habitually shot at they spend the day on some large river or sheet of water, and feed chiefly at night, in wet fields, swamps, and the smaller jhíls, changing their quarters for this purpose about sunset, and there is no species more commonly bagged in flight-shooting.

On the wing they are very swift. I doubt if they are swifter than the Pin-tail, but they are more nimble, and will often escape a Peregrine when the Pin-tail would assuredly have been victimized. They turn and twist in the air with a rapidity second only to the Cotton Teal, and they have a habit after being flushed of dropping suddenly again, which I have not noticed in our other ducks. They swim easily, but not very rapidly, and they cannot dive to much purpose, so that a wounded bird, unless there are weeds near under which it can lie with only the bill above water, has, as a rule, but a poor chance of escape.

On the land, if the ground be fairly smooth, they walk with tolerable ease; but whilst "one foot on land and one on sea" is quite the motto of their lives, the major portion of which, if left to their own sweet wills, they pass in swampy places half-earth, half-water, it is rare to see them as one often sees the Wigeon, well out on the dry sward, walking for pleasure.

Whether it be by night or day, (and that depends upon circumstances beyond their control, poor things) their favourite feeding places are always the swampy margins and weedy shallows of broads or sluggish streams. There they feed on wild rice, grasses of all kinds, and their seeds, and all sorts of tender shoots, roots, corms and bulbs, as well as insects and their larvæ, tiny shells and worms. But this animal food forms but a small proportion of their diet here ; indeed no traces of it have been visible in numbers that I have examined, and in captivity they thrive *à ne pouvoir plus* without it, (which some of the larger ducks do not), and so I am inclined to grade them as essentially vegetarians.

They never dive for food of course, but they in no way disdain the orthodox Mallard upside-down position, and a whole flock will suddenly exhibit to you the reverses of their shields with a want of delicacy that must be truly shocking to those trans-atlantic sisters of ours who put trousers on to piano legs.

The ordinary day call of the Teal is a weak, rather shrill quack, but they have occasionally another note, a distinct whistle, uttered some say only by the male. This is the note most heard at nights, and it is then apt to be confounded with similar calls of Plovers and other water birds; and I have never myself been quite sure of it, though their quack I can tell at any time.

The wild Teal is almost always better than any other duck for the table except Mallard ; but the carefully fed and tended captive Teal is, when rightly cuisined (more than mere cooking is required) the *ne plus ultra* of comestibles.

NO RECORD exists of the Common Teal breeding within our limits, but it breeds generally in suitably secluded spots in Europe and Asia throughout the temperate zone, north of the 40th Degree N. Latitude, and I should not be at all surprised if it bred with us in Kashmir just as the Mallard does. Not only there, but in a small lake not far from Hanle, I have known Teal killed in June and July.

Yarrell says:—"The Teal breeds in the long rushy herbage about the edges of lakes, or in the boggy parts of the upland moors. Its nest is formed of a large mass of decayed vegetable matter, with a lining of down and feathers, upon which eight or ten eggs rest."

Mr. Richard Dann wrote :—"It breeds all over Lapland, both Western and Eastern, and is very abundant in the Dofre Fiel, within the range of the birch trees. The eggs vary in number from ten to fifteen. It breeds also in the cultivated districts in all the mosses and bogs."

Dresser says that in Northern Finland he has repeatedly taken the nests "which he found on the ground amongst the grass, oftenest under some low bush, which served to conceal it, and sometimes at a considerable distance from the water."

The eggs are moderately broad ovals, smooth and with a slight gloss, of a creamy buff or ivory yellow colour, and varied (the few I have measured) from 1·68 to 1·83 in length, and from 1·29 to 1·4 in breadth.

THERE IS not much difference in the sizes of the sexes in this species. The following is a *résumé* of a large number of measurements:—

Males.—Length, 14·5 to 15·85; expanse, 23·0 to 25·25; wing, 7·2 to 8·0; tail from vent, 3·0 to 3·6; tarsus, 1·1 to 1·3; bill from gape, 1·65 to 1·8; weight, 10·5 ozs. to 15 ozs.

Females.—Length, 13·5 to 14·9; expanse, 22·5 to 25·0; wing, 6·5 to 7·4; tail from vent, 2·9 to 3·5; tarsus, 1·0 to 1·2; bill from gape, 1·5 to 1·77; weight, 7·7 ozs. to 12·0 ozs.

In the adult male the bill is black or blackish, brownish on rami of lower mandible; in young males and females the lower mandible, though sometimes only brown, commonly varies from brownish yellow to dull orange, and is generally brownish at tip. The upper mandible also in females is usually rather paler coloured than that of the male, and is often tinged with green or plumbeous green.

The irides are brown, varying in shade from light hazel to almost black.

The legs and feet are commonly grey, with a faint olive tinge (the webs and claws in all cases dusky,) but they vary in shade a little, and at times are bluish grey with a brown shade, and at others distinctly dark slatey grey, sepia grey, brown, greyish brown, olive, greenish olive, dirty greenish plumbeous, or even plumbeous.

THE PLATE is, on the whole, very satisfactory, but the species is a very variable one. In the first place, to begin with the male, the markings or lines on the side of the head, coloured buff in our plate, are often pure white. Sometimes they are quite broad and conspicuous, at others narrow; the line under the green patch is occasionally almost entirely wanting. Sometimes that above it is barely traceable. Generally the base of the back of the neck and upper back is much greyer, and the vermicellations finer than in our plate. Generally, I think, the speculum is greener and less blue.

The ground of the entire under surface varies from pure white to a dark ferruginous. At times the whole breast and upper abdomen are densely spotted; in some specimens they are absolutely spotless. The rufous on the sides of the head varies from the colour figured by us to a dusky chestnut.

The females, as a rule, are greyer and less rufescent than in the plate, and, like the males, they vary below from pure white to ferruginous fulvous.

I find no record of the males of this species undergoing a change of plumage at the close of the breeding season, like that already described in the case of the ducks, and I have myself had no opportunity of learning, by personal observation, whether it occurs in their case or not; but despite the general silence on the subject, I presume that it must.

QUERQUEDULA CIRCIA

THE GARGANEY OR BLUE-WINGED TEAL.

Querquedula circia, *Linné.*

Vernacular Names.—[Chaitwa, Patari, *N. W. Provinces;* Ghang-roib, Giria, *Bengal;* Sitch-dum, *Cábul;* Karak-aurdak, (Turki,) *Yárkand;*]

QUITE as widely distributed throughout the Empire* as the Common Teal, the Garganey is moreover by no means rare about Moulmein in Central Tenasserim. On the other hand, though common in winter in the Himalayas from Kullu to Nepal, it has not, apparently, yet been recorded from Kashmir, though it must surely occur there. As a whole, it visits us in smaller numbers than *crecca*, and in many parts of

---

* It may be useful to quote a few of the notes furnished to me in regard to this species. Writing from Lucknow, Mr. Reid says :—

"I am inclined to think that the Blue-winged Teal is, of all the duck tribe, our earliest cold weather visitor, arriving in countless numbers in September, though it is not before October that they seem to settle down on the jhíls. The majority, however, do not remain long, and early in November appear to go south. From then until they return again in March, the Blue-winged Teal is not by any means as common as *Querquedula crecca*, though it is still far from being scarce. They are shy and wild on their arrival, keeping well to the centre of jhíls, but as the season advances they become more civilized, and may then be found pottering about on the mud or in shallow water, in company with the Common Teal."

Mr J. Davidson tells us that "the Blue-winged Teal is not nearly so plentiful in Khandesh as the common one. but it stays with us much later. I left a flock of 11 or 12 Garganeys upon a tank at Nandurbur on the 8th of May 1880."

Mr. Vidal writes :—

"This species is not so common as *Querquedula crecca*, and as far as my limited experience goes, prefers reedy tanks to rivers. I have found it in Ratnagiri here and there, and in Sattara I came across a good sized flock on the large tank constructed by the Irrigation Department at Maini."

Captain Butler remarks :—

"Bishop shot three Blue-winged Teal on the 1st of September in some irrigated fields at the Hubb River. They had probably remained near the river throughout the year; for the flights of duck were not noticed across the harbour till the middle of September. The Mohanas on the Dunds have all their fowling nets ready, but do not expect the birds in any numbers till after the coming full-moon, November 13th."

And according to Mr. Doig on the Eastern Narra, they only "arrive in December, and leave in April."

Mr. Albert Theobald says :—

"I have shot them in the Salem, North Arcot, Tinnevelli, and Coimbatore

the country is never abundant, and in others only for a short portion of the cold season.

Outside our Empire its distribution in Asia is rather remarkable. It occurs in Independent Burmah and Northern Siam,* but we have never met with any trace of it in Southern Tenasserim or any part of the Malay Peninsula, neither do I find any record of its occurrence in Sumatra or Borneo. But Professor Schlegel says that he has specimens from Java, Celebes, and the Philippines. This must, however, be accepted with hesitation; some mistake may have occurred in regard to the origin or identification of these specimens, since the Marquis of Tweeddale excludes this species from both his Celebes and Philippine lists. In Formosa and Southern China it does occur, and some may possibly breed there, but elsewhere in China it seems rare or non-existent, and I do not find it recorded from Japan. In Yárkand it is common in summer, and breeds there as it does also in South-East Mongolia, and the lakes and marshes of the Hoang-ho; but it does not extend to the Koko-Nor, and in the Ussuri country is, Prjevalsky says, not one-tenth as numerous as the Common Teal. Again it is common in summer, breeding in numberless localities throughout Southern Siberia, and in Western Turkestan.† In winter it is not uncommon in Afghanistan and Beluchistan, and has been procured, during this season, on both the Persian and Arabian coasts of the Gulfs of Oman and Persia. Again it occurs on the Caspian; and probably—though this is not on record, and I have no specimens thence—in suitable localities throughout the interior of Persia. It has been found in Mesopotamia, in the Caucasus, Armenia, Asia Minor (both near the Black Sea and Mediterranean Coasts) in Palestine and Arabia Petræa, and probably extends far south along the Arabian coasts of the Red Sea. It is recorded from all parts of North-East Africa, as far south as the 10th Degree North Latitude, Abyssinia, Nubia, Egypt, and so westwards to Algiers. It may extend to Morocco and Western

---

Districts. They arrive about the early part of December, and leave by March or April, a few stragglers remaining up till May or June. They are common in most large tanks, and keep in flocks.

"Weedy tanks are preferred by these Teal. They live chiefly on the tender weeds and grasses. I have never seen them on paddy fields.

"They are not very hard to shoot, and are easily approached behind a small screen of green boughs. Sometimes a paper kite, made in the shape of a Hawk, and flown over the tanks, keeps the Teal together, and they will not leave the tank though fired at often."

From Pegu Mr. Eugene Oates writes:—

"This Teal is, I think, everywhere rare, much more so than the Common Teal of Europe."

* Note that Schlegel, V. Heuglin and others calmly quote Tickell (or as they spell it Tickel) as an authority for the breeding of this species in Siam. Of course Tickell really wrote about the neighbourhood of Moulmein, but in Europe this place is apparently supposed to be in Siam!

† Stoliczka obtained a specimen, a male, on the 8th of May at Lake Sirikol, near the Pamir (elevation about 13,000) in full breeding plumage.

Africa, but I find no reliable record of this; and it is altogether a less *western* form than *crecca*, and one hears of it neither from the Azores or Madeira, nor from Greenland or the Atlantic coasts of North America. It is also a less northern species, for, though found in summer or winter in most parts of Europe, it does not, except perhaps in Finland, (and in Iceland if it really occurs there) extend either in Europe or Asia much north of the 60th Degree North Latitude.

DESPITE a contrary opinion* recorded by some authors I do not hesitate to say that in the North-West Provinces and Oudh, the Garganey is, as a rule, the earliest of the winter migrants to arrive. Large flights are commonly seen towards the end of August, and I have a special note of having found a flock which I estimated to contain twenty thousand individuals at Rahun, in the Etáwah district, on the 28th of August 1865. Never before or since have I seen so huge a body of fowl of one kind, and I have noted that I bagged 47 of them, besides losing, at the time, many wounded birds (I had no dogs with me) in the thick rushes. I had sent my gun punt (built exactly on the lines of one of our Norfolk boats†) a few days previously out there to see that it was all right for the coming season, and I had taken with me a small but heavy Monghyr-made swivel gun, carrying only 8 ozs. of shot, to try. To my surprise, I found the thickest body of fowl on the open part of the jhíl I had ever seen. I loaded the swivel with No. 4 shot, and worked up quite close to some of them, and within some fifty yards of the main body, when seeing they were all about to start, I fired and knocked over at least 60. I actually secured 47, the largest number I ever got with this small gun at one shot; and a basketful, I forgot to note how many, was brought in the next day by my shikarree who went out with a dog. Not an unwounded bird remained, all had gone straight away at that first shot.

Brooks also writes that he has often seen them in the N.-W. Provinces in August. Anderson says: "This is the first

---

* Thus Captain Baldwin says:—

"This somewhat handsome little Duck is larger than the Common Teal. *It does not arrive so early* as the above mentioned bird; but I have each year noticed that it is about the last to leave the plains of India. I have even seen small flights of this species in the month of May, which is unusually late for migrating wild fowl. This was in the hot season of 1871, in the Lullutpore District. I find a record in my game book that I shot, on May 8th of that year, five Blue winged Teal in a small tank about thirty miles from Lullutpore. Certainly the hot season of 1871 was a mild one; and in the same month of May of that year I killed several snipe—quite as unusual a circumstance, if not more so, than shooting the Garganeys."

† The objection to these boats is their weight, but I had a light platform cart made with two large gun-limber wheels. Four English iron stanchions at each side of the cart with thick girth loops between, on which the boat hung perfectly. A pair of bullocks would run this about *any* where—an essential thing to men in India, who march almost daily during the cold season.

duck to arrive in the country, and has frequently been seen early in August." Mr. Reid's remarks have been already quoted, (*note*, p. 215), and there is no doubt that with us in the north, while some occasionally appear earlier, considerable flights arrive, *as a rule*, towards the close of August or early in September. These, however, generally pass on (even in Calcutta they are in the market early in October), and it is not until the latter part of October in the north, and well into November further south, that the mass of the birds have arrived.

During December, January, and February they are comparatively scarce in Upper India, but they become again plentiful in March, and during the first half of April, owing to the influx of the great bulk of the birds which wandered further south. Shortly after this* the great majority leave us, but in all years, alike in the north and south, a few birds remain well in to May. As I shall notice further on there are grounds for supposing that some few may remain to breed within our limits, but such cases must be quite exceptional.

According to my experience, the Blue-winged Teal almost exclusively frequents good-sized broads and jhíls or wide swamps, containing plenty of aquatic herbage. They are rare even on large lakes, like the Sámbhar, where this is wanting; they are very rare in our large rivers, and still more so on small village ponds.†

I have very seldom seen them in the day feeding in fields, but I know that at nights they come in some parts of the country in such crowds into paddy fields as to destroy acres of

---

* Mr. Cripps, writing from Fureedpore, remarked:—"Swarms in the cold weather in all the small bhíls about the country. During the day they used to remain in the Ganges, and at night come to the interior to feed. The Ganges from my factory was about 20 miles. By the 16th April not a bird was to be seen, all having migrated."

† In this and numberless other cases, I find my experience here utterly at variance with what European writers have recorded. Thus Dresser says, quoting Baron Droste:—

"They frequent the fresh water or salty ponds and rivulets on the islands; and I know no instance of this duck visiting the shores. They are very tame, and soon get accustomed to the sight of human beings, and are satisfied with the smallest sheets of water. When unmolested they can be approached within a few paces without flying up" Now, to render these remarks applicable to India, they must be interpreted, like dreams, by contraries.

They never hardly frequent mere ponds or rivulets, but they are *not* uncommon on the shores. They are never very tame, and I know no instance of their accustoming themselves to the sight of human beings; on the contrary, they persistently shun places which human beings closely frequent. Tiny pieces of water they utterly avoid. Even where no gun has ever been fired, they will not let you walk up within shot openly. You can stalk them easily behind bushes, cattle, &c., but let them see that you are a man, and they certainly will not allow you to get within thirty paces of them.

I do not, for one moment, doubt the correctness of Baron Droste's remarks, *as regards his part of the world*; I only desire equal credence from European writers when, as in many cases has, I find, happened, I have directly traversed the statements of their favourite authorities. I can only say that my remarks are the results of many long years' personal observations here, and that whether in accord with what has been recorded elsewhere, or not, they do represent what are the facts *here*.

crop at one visit. Along the Mekran Coast, and in many places along the Sindh and Bombay Coasts, you find them in secluded salt-water creeks, where they seem just as much at home as in inland waters.

They are not very wild or wary ; it is generally easy enough to get shots at them with a little precaution ; they are easy to work up to in a punt, but they are yet not tame and familiar like the Common Teal, and do not, like this, habitually affect pools, where men constantly come and go, and in close proximity to human habitations. Generally they keep in flocks, rarely less than a dozen are found together, and most commonly from fifty to several hundreds are seen in a bunch. Few fowl sit closer or straggle less, few offer more effective big-gun shots.

Their flight is rapid, though less so than that of the Common Teal, direct and with far fewer sudden turns and twists. They rise rapidly and easily from the water, but not very perpendicularly. I have so seldom seen them on dry land, that I can speak with no certainty about this ; but once when emerging from a dense reed bed through which I had been carefully creeping in order to get a shot at some Shelldrakes that I knew to be paddling about somewhere near the margin, I surprised a party of Garganeys, all asleep, on a patch of turf some ten yards square, almost entirely surrounded by high reeds ; they seemed to me to rise very clumsily, and I made a tremendous bag with two barrels as they flustered up.

They swim well, far more rapidly when pressed than the Common Teal, and dive better. They are altogether, I should say, more *vigorous* and less agile birds.

Their food is chiefly vegetable ; tender shoots and leaves of water-plants, seeds, bulbs and corms, and slender rhizomes of rushes, sedges and the like form the bulk of their diet—to which at times large quantities of rice, wild and cultivated, must be added. Besides this they eat occasionally all kinds of insects and their larva, small frogs, worms, fresh-water shells, and the like ; but, as a rule, this forms inland in India, a very small proportion of their food, and no traces of anything but vegetable matter have been observable in the stomachs of many that I examined. On the sea coast it is different. There I found shrimps, delicate shells, and other animal substances in abundance in their gizzards, and birds shot in such localities are anything but first-rate eating.

Their call is a harsh quack, very loud for the size of the bird ; they are not garrulous, and I have never heard any other note from wild birds ; but in our tealeries, they chatter, like all the other ducks so confined, in a marvellous manner on the least disturbance.

Whether it is only because one habitually meets them in such large flocks, or whether is really peculiar to them, I do not know ; but certainly one associates the over-head flight of this species with a surging hiss, more even, sustained and *rushing* than that of any of our other Ducks. Any one who has stood under heavy round shot fire knows the way in which shots hurtle up to you *crescendo*, and die away as they pass; and just in this way (though the sounds are in a wholly different key) does the swish of a large flock of Garganeys surge up to you in the stillness of the night, and die away as they pass.

For the table I do not rank the Garganey very high; even when in the finest condition in the best kept tealery, they are not equal to their smaller congener, and when wild, despite their vegetarian practice, they are greatly inferior. Even inland the flesh is not always free from a certain marshy twang, and on the coast this is very strongly developed.

DOES THE Garganey breed with us? Years ago Colonel Tickell, writing to Blyth from Moulmein, said that he had then a young one of this species alive, which was brought him just fledged from a pond or small lake about twelve miles off. This would appear conclusive, but since then the neighbourhood has been ransacked by several excellent collectors, without any trace even being obtained of the Blue-winged Teal during the summer. If this species ever bred anywhere in the entire Amherst District, of which Moulmein is the head-quarters, it apparently breeds there no longer. Davison, Bingham, Darling, &c., have all especially looked into this question. All feel sure that this species does not now, at any rate, breed anywhere near Moulmein. Probably (for there has been no marked change here in country or population) Tickell's bird, young as it seemed, was a migrant.

But Colonel Irby tells us (*Ibis*, 1861, 250) that when in Oudh he "caught some young, half-fledged, in the month of September." Now, if he correctly identified the species, these birds *must* have been hatched in Oudh, for "*half*-fledged" birds could hardly migrate. None the less during the last twenty years, during which several ardent oologists and ornithologists have laboured in Oudh, no similar instance has come to notice, and no indication has been discovered of this species breeding there.

Then again from the Mekran Coast, eggs were sent me apparently of this species, of which Captain Butler says:—"The nest was built on the ground in a solitary babool bush, growing on an immense bare tract of salt marsh some seven or eight miles north of Ormarra, called Moorputty, and consisted of a collection of fine twigs interwoven into a very solid pad, without any lining, measuring about eight or nine inches in diameter. The eggs, eight in number, and of a delicate cream colour, were taken on the 19th June 1878."

But the parent birds were not obtained, and there is no certainty that these eggs do belong to the Garganey, though they are like European examples, and though the bird has been killed on this coast late in May.

These eggs are moderately broad obtuse-ended ovals, intermediate in size between those of *D. javanica* and *N. coromandelicus*. The shell is smooth and satiny, and has a perceptible gloss; the colour is an uniform ivory. They vary from 1·8 to 1·9 in length, and from 1·35 to 1·43 in breadth.

But besides all this, though never yet recorded from Kashmir, elsewhere in the Himalayas, the Garganey is continually turning up in out-of-the-way places from elevations of four thousand feet and upwards during the summer. I have repeatedly thus met with them, to the best of my belief, during all the summer months, though, as I never noted the dates, I cannot be quite certain of this now. Other men have also told me of thus seeing them,* and it seems very possible that some few pairs may linger to breed in secluded situations in the Himalayas. Elsewhere they do not appear to breed much south of Sicily and Central Greece, say, approximately the 38th degree North Latitude; but that is in low country, and they may well breed 6 or 8 degrees south of this in our elevated regions. But I confess that I should not expect them to prove to breed normally elsewhere in India; and, if a single nest *should* ever be found anywhere in the plains, I should, in default of evidence to the contrary, consider it as quite an abnormal and exceptional occurrence.

Of their nidification in Europe little need be said, as it precisely resembles that of the Common Teal. Mr. Hoy wrote "from his experience on the continent" (people were vague in those days) that "the Garganey commences laying its eggs about the middle of April. The nest, which is composed of rushes and dried grass, mixed with the down of the bird, is placed upon the ground in low boggy situations, among the coarse herbage and rushes, in marshes, and on the borders of lakes and rivers."

Mr. Benzon, of Copenhagen, tells us that "this Teal breeds here and there in Denmark, in morasses, and inland sheets of water, and is particularly abundant in Jutland, whence I have both the young in down and eggs on which the females have been captured. The number of eggs varies from six to thirteen. The earliest nest contained eleven eggs, and was taken on the

---

* Captain Baldwin also says:—"I met with this bird in the Himalayas several times, first at Nynee Tal, then at Bheem Tal, another lake near the former, where I shot three birds; again on the Pindur river; and, lastly, I shot three more in small patches of water high up in the middle ranges, too close to a tea garden at Gwaldung, and a third at Goomur Tal, on the opposite side of the Pindur river. I do not think these stray birds remained to breed in the out-of-the-way spots I have mentioned, though it is possible, but I am inclined to think that they were merely resting themselves."

29th of April 1865, and the latest, containing seven eggs, on the 21st of May 1864. The largest number (thirteen) in one nest was taken on the 10th of May 1867, and again on the 8th of May 1868. A female with ten young in down was captured on the 25th of June. In Jutland it is generally found breeding earlier than the Common Teal."

The eggs are barely separable, it is said, from those of the Common Teal, but have perhaps a more yellow creamy tinge. Dresser says that eggs in his collection average 1·87 in length by 1·35 in breadth.

THE FOLLOWING is a *résumé* of the measurements, &c., of a great number of adults; the birds of the year are considerably smaller.

Males.—Length, 15·9 to 16·25; expanse, 25·0 to 27·25; wing, 7·4 to 8·1; tail from vent, 3·3 to 3·8; tarsus, 1·0 to 1·3; bill from gape, 1·75 to 1·92; weight, 10 ozs. to 1 lb. (commonly about 13 ozs.)

Females.—Length, 14·8 to 15·5; expanse, 23·0 to 25·5; wing, 7·0 to 7·5; tail from vent, 2·9 to 3·5; tarsus, 1·0 to 1·15; bill from gape, 1·7 to 1·85; weight, 9 ozs. to 14·75 ozs. (commonly about 12 ozs.)

In the adult male the bill is normally blackish above, brownish on the lower mandible, except at the tip, often reddish brown at the gape. In some females the bill is similar, in some, apparently adult, it is blackish plumbeous above, dull plumbeous below. In the young it is horny brown, tinged with greenish plumbeous.

The legs and feet are grey, pale greenish brown, grey with an olive shade, grey slate colour, purplish slate colour, bluish, and, in the young, pale bluish or dirty bluish green, in all cases the webs being more or less dusky, and the claws darker still. The irides are brown, at times pale, at times hazel or reddish.

THE PLATE, which is compiled from some of Mr. Hodgson's drawings, is, on the whole, extremely good. Only the side of the head in the male is somewhat too pink; it should be somewhat browner, a sort of nutmeg brown. The other bird in the foregound is a not fully adult female—in the old female the white tippings to the secondaries and their greater coverts become almost as broad and conspicuous as in the male, forming a double white wing-bar as in his case, and the outer webs of the secondaries get more or less suffused with a dull metallic green, mimicking the emerald speculum of the male. The figure in the background is that of the male in the eclipse stage, assumed towards the close of the breeding season; but it would do perfectly for the adult female (though this is often greyer and less fulvous as a whole) if the wing-coverts were made greyer or less of the light lavender, and the speculum a duller and darker green. Some females seem never to get the green on the speculum, and those that do assume it, get only a dull dark green—never, I think, the light bright green of the males. Some females too have all the coverts a uniform grey like the males ; but in the case of the former it is at most a slatey grey, more or less dull, and never the purer light lavender grey of the latter. In the young female both bill and feet should be lighter coloured, and more leaden.

In this species, as in others, the under surface, normally white, is often strongly tinged with ferruginous.

F. Walter Chromo lith. 16 Hatton Garden London

♂ ♀
QUERQUEDULA GLOCITANS

THE CLUCKING OR BAIKAL TEAL.

Querquedula formosa, *Georgi.*

Vernacular Names.—[None.]

THIS species can, at present, only be considered an extremely rare chance straggler within our limits. Further research may show that it is somewhat less rare than we *now* suppose, but our existing information only justifies its being classed as above.

In 1844 Blyth obtained a single male in the Calcutta Bazaar. So far as I know, it has never subsequently been there procured, although this market has been pretty closely watched from that day to this, by the museum people, several professional taxidermists, Mr. C. J. Parker, myself, and others.

Colonel McMaster, a reliable authority, tells us in his "Vagrancy Acts" that he once obtained a specimen of (he believed) this species in some salt marshes in the Upper Circars.

The only other decently-authenticated record of the occurrence of this species in India, since 1844, until quite recently, is one by Mr. E. James, C.S., who had a water-colour painting of the head of a Teal shot in Sindh, which certainly was male *Q. formosa.*

Lastly, in November 1879, Mr. W. N. Chill procured (and preserved) a male of the Clucking Teal, some thirty miles southwest of Delhi.

Besides this, I have received several statements from different quarters as to *Q. formosa* having been seen or heard (the cry, no doubt, is peculiar) in the Central Provinces on the Nerbudda in May, in the Deccan during the early part of the cold season, &c., and one or two correspondents are *sure* that they have *shot* them. But no specimens have been preserved; and while quite agreeing with the worthy who remarked—"what's hit is history; what's missed is mystery"—I go further, and only acknowledge in the case of most Indian sportsmen, as *history*, species of which specimens have been *preserved.*

Outside our limits, its normal range appears to be Asia, excluding the Mongolian deserts, east of a line drawn from Canton to the mouths of the Yenesay. It is widely diffused throughout China, and has been procured in Formosa and Japan, but to all these localities it is a winter visitant. Further north in North-Eastern Mongolia, Dauria, and South-East Siberia, it is seen in multitudes in the spring on passage ; but the majority later pass on to breed in Central and Northern Siberia, not, however, extending to the extreme north, or much beyond the 70th degree North Latitude.

Prjevalsky says :—

"During migration, in the end of March and the beginning of April, we met with it in large numbers at the Dalai-Nor, but did not find it further west, although it can easily be distinguished from the other ducks by its voice. It also occurs about Lake Baikal, whither it most likely migrates from China Proper, probably crossing the desert in a direct line, or else following its edge.

"At Lake Hanka, it is one of the most plentiful ducks, and arrives there in very large flocks from the 8th to the 15th of March.

"The abundance of this species, on Lake Hanka, continues during all the time of its migration, *i.e.*, all the latter half of March and the first week of April ; but after that time, their numbers decrease quickly, and in the middle of May there is not a single one to be seen."

Dr. Radde tells us that in South-East Siberia "it arrives very early ; and the first specimen was procured as early as 26th March 1856, on the Tarei-Nor. I saw the first specimens in the Bureja Mountains on the 26th March 1858, and on the 4th April met with large flocks on the Uril brook ; and they remained in flocks until the 19th April. On the 24th April only small flocks were observed. After the 7th May this duck was not seen any more. It is generally rare near Lake Baikal, and does not remain there during the summer."

Dybowski also remarks that thay are "pretty common in passage at Kultuk ; they arrive in the spring about the middle of May, but have not been noticed in autumn. In the Darasun regions they are more common, and breed." Clearly, therefore, so far as we can judge, it is never likely to be more than a chance straggler to any part of our Empire, except possibly Eastern Assam.

It is not known to occur, normally, anywhere west of the line I have indicated ; but just as a couple of specimens have been procured in India, a couple have been obtained in France, and stragglers will probably, at rare intervals, appear in other parts of Europe and Central or Western Asia ; but as yet it has never been observed in Central or Western Mongolia, Chinese Tibet, Yárkand, Western Turkestan or even on the Caspian.

OF ITS habits I know nothing, and very little is on record ; the chief characteristic which has attracted notice being its harsh and continuous clucking call, represented as a successive repetition of the syllable "mok," whence Pallas applied to it the specific name "*glocitans*," by which, until of late years, it was most commonly known.

Prjevalsky remarks :—

"When migrating these ducks fly very low, following the plains which abound with lakes; and as soon as one is perceived that is not frozen, especially in cold and stormy weather, they at once settle down on it. The presence of such a flock is always known at a good distance, as the drakes keep calling even when on the wing."

Middendorff says :—

"When in flocks these ducks were very shy, but less so when paired. They make a great noise, as they continually utter their loud clucking note."

Radde too tells us that, "when the waters rose, I often saw both this Duck and the Common Teal sitting in small flocks on the floating ice blocks, and floating down stream on them. *Anas glocitans* is not particular as to its society; and one morning, about the middle of April, I saw, in a small morass above the Udir rivulet, *Anas boschas*, *A. crecca*, *A. glocitans*, *A. clypeata*, *A. acuta*, and a few of *A. penelope* sitting quietly close together after a meal, resting, and I crept close to them under cover."

Of course each species, when you come to know it well, has its characteristic peculiarities; and doubtless when we know more of this one we shall find that it has distinguishing traits in its food, flight, and the like; at present its only recorded speciality is its harsh and oft-repeated clucking call.

IN MANY respects it probably closely resembles the Common Teal; its nest is probably similar, and placed in similar situations. I can find nothing on record about its nidification but the following :—

Dr. Middendorff says :—"Although the commonest Duck on the Boganida (70° North Latitude), it did not occur so far north as the Taimyr River. It was not observed before the 12th June on the Boganida. On the 3rd July we found a nest on the river bank, under a willow bush, containing seven fresh eggs. On the 24th July, the young in down began to exhibit feathers on the head, shoulders, and wings, but were still unable to fly on the 4th August. On the 28th July a male was shot, which had lost its perfect plumage. The latest birds were seen on the 23rd August on the Boganida. This bird was similarly plentiful in the Stanowoj Mountains (Aim River) and at Udskoj-Ostrog, where it arrived during the first days of May.........The eggs are bluish yellow in colour, and small—the smallest* was 1·98 long by 1·4, greatest breadth."

---

* He *says* "*the smallest*;" but to judge from Taczanowski's measurements he may perhaps *mean* "the largest."

And Taczanowski says of a setting of eggs sent by Dybowski from Darasun:—"They are somewhat larger than those of the Garganey; their colour is a pale greyish green, very like that of the eggs of the Mallard. They vary from about 1·8 to 1·9 in length, and from about 1·3 to 1·4 in breadth."

MY SOLITARY Indian specimen, a male obtained by Mr. Chill, measures in the skin:—

Length, 15·8; wing, 8·15; tail, 3·9; tarsus, 1·3; bill at front, 1·5; from gape, 1·92.

No reliable dimensions are on record. Dresser says:—

"*Male.*—Length, 15·5; culmen, 1·5; wing, 8·5; tail, 3·6; tarsus, 1·0."

"*Female.*—Length, 15·0; culmen, 1·45; wing, 7·8; tail, 3·5; tarsus, 0·9"

But these are of course taken from skins. How he has measured the tarsus it is impossible to say; in a fine male from China this is 1·4; in a female, 1·3.

Temminck and Schlegel give the following:—Length, 15·35; wing, 8 5; tail, 3·57; bill at front, 1·62; (in one Chinese male it is 1·6, in a female, 1·53); *tarsus*, 1·28.

Neither Schrenk, Radde nor Middendorff give any dimensions.

Middendorff says that "the bill is a dusky bluish brown; the feet clear grey blue, darker on the webs." Schrenk tells us that in a freshly killed young male "the bill was a dusky greenish black at the base, but lighter coloured, a bluish grey, on the lower mandible and the margin of the upper one; the legs and feet greenish grey, blackish on the joints, and almost quite black on the webs."

Lastly, Swinhoe remarks (*Ibis*, 1867):—A male *Anas glocitans* died in the aviary of a friend. Its iris was chestnut brown; bill deep liver brown; legs and toes pale bluish grey, tinged with brown at the joints, and with deeper brown on the webs and nails."

THE PLATE is on the whole very good, but it must be noted that in fuller-plumaged males the crown is entirely black. not mottled as in the specimen figured. In our Indian specimen the yellow of the face is rather more buffy, and each feather is very narrowly fringed at the tip with brown, thus somewhat obscuring the brightness of the face patches.

In the picture of the female, otherwise very good, there is, I think, to judge from my Chinese birds, one mistake—the anterior of the wing bands should be rufous buff and not white.

The female might perhaps be mistaken for that of *Querquedula crecca*, but it has a much broader bill. In the female of the Common Teal the upper mandible, at its widest point near the tip, does not exceed 0·55; in some specimens it is not above

0·5, while in the present species it exceeds 0·6. The bird is altogether larger, having a wing of about 8·0 against about 7·0 in *crecca*. Then, in this species, to judge from my specimens,* the lower back and rump are a grey brown, nearly uniform, a little darker at the shafts ; while in *crecca* these parts are very dark brown, each feather conspicuously margined with white, greyish white, or buffy white.

The wing specula are very similar, but in *crecca* the tippings of the secondary greater coverts are broader, and are white, only tinged with buff posteriorly. In the present species they are narrower and rufous buff throughout ; again, the white tippings of the secondaries themselves are much broader in this species than in *crecca*.

The male assumes, after breeding, a plumage very similar to that of the female, from which he is only to be distinguished by the darker brownish red tint of the upper breast, and the comparatively uniform colour of the upper back, the feathers of which, in the female, are darker and very conspicuously bordered with reddish buff.

I should add that in the female the black wing bar or speculum is often more or less shaded, especially on the later secondaries with a darker metallic green than in the male ; but in one specimen, perhaps not fully adult, there is no trace of this.

---

* These are purchased and I cannot vouch for the sexing ; they *might* be males in the eclipse stage, but I think not, judging from what Schrenk and Middendorff say, and besides, males in this stage would hardly have been obtained in China.

ANAS ♂ FALCATA

THE CRESTED OR BRONZE-CAPPED TEAL.*

---o---

Querquedula falcata, *Georgi.*

---o---

Vernacular Names.—[None.]

---o---

THE Bronze-capped Teal is another rare winter visitant to the British Asian Empire, but it cannot be so rare as the Clucking Teal, as during the last ten years I have procured no less than five specimens of it, *viz.*, a pair (the male with the tertiaries fully developed) captured by fowlers, near Lucknow, in March, and given me by Dr. Bonavia ; a male shot at Karnal seventy miles north of Delhi, in February, by Major C. H. T. Marshall ; a male procured by myself in the flesh, in the Calcutta market and caught in the immediate neighbourhood in January ; a male obtained by Mr. W. N. Chill, at Sultanpur, thirty miles south-west of Delhi, in February.

I have no other record of the occurrence of this species within our limits.

Outside our limits its range is very similar to that of the Clucking Teal ; but it is, on the whole, a slightly more southern species, and may be expected to occur oftener in India. Like that species it does not appear to occur normally west of the Yenesay, on which river Middendorff heard of one having been once captured in North Latitude 69° 30′ ; but it does not generally get quite so far north as this, and was not observed on the Boganida. Its normal summer range is probably the whole of Siberia east of the Yenesay, and *outside* the Arctic Circle ; and throughout this, including Kamschatka, it breeds, as it does also in Eastern Mongolia and Dauria, and even in the valley of the Hoang-ho. In winter it is found throughout China, including Formosa, as also in Japan. Probably, when we know more of these countries, it will prove to extend to Tonquin at any rate. Anderson actually obtained specimens at Tamilone on the Taipeng River beyond Bhamo, in about 25° North Latitude.

---

* This bird has been commonly called of late years the FALCATED TEAL, but this name I must decline to adopt ; it is not English, and is misleading.

It is not impossible that it wanders, at times, far south of this. Although Sharpe and Dresser, David and Oustalet, and other writers ignore the fact, this is, it seems to me, * *Anas javana* of Boddaërt, founded on plate 930 (and a very fair plate it is of an immature male) of the *Planches Enluminées*, the original of which is explicitly stated to have been received from Java.

To Europe even it has wandered at long intervals, and specimens are said to have been procured in Sweden, Hungary, and near Vienna. But in Asia it has not been observed in Mongolia westward of the valley of the Hoang-ho, or anywhere in Chinese Tibet, Yárkand, Western Turkestan or the Caspian, though I cannot help suspecting it will prove to occur on the latter.

THERE IS little or nothing on record as to the habits and haunts of this species, which may be assumed to be generally very similar to those of the other Teal, Gadwall, &c.

Prjevalski says "that it usually forms flocks with other kinds, but very rarely alone. Its voice is a tolerably loud and piercing whistle."

Schrenk remarks that he has often come unperceived on this species, like the Common Teal, cackling as it fed, carried downwards by the current along the grassy banks of small streams, and that it thus happened to him on the 2nd of October to kill, successively, within a few minutes, three of these Teal without moving from his place.

Radde tells us that the stomachs of some he shot on the 13th of April, just after their arrival, contained nothing but fragments of quartz and a few shoots of plants. He adds that it certainly migrates southwards earlier than the other fresh water fowl, as the migration commences on the first days of September.

A great deal has been written about this species; but I have vainly searched the pages of Latham, Pallas, Brandt, Middendorff, Radde, Schrenk, Bree, Sharpe and Dresser, Taczanowski, David and Oustalet, Prjevalski, Swinhoe's papers, &c., &c., in the hopes of finding some intelligent detailed account of its flight, food, voice, habits, and the like; and it is to be hoped that Indian sportsmen, who may hereafter come across it, will notice and record all they can on these subjects.

THE CRESTED TEAL has decidedly a more southern breeding range than the Clucking Teal. The former nests in the valley of the Hoang-ho and Lake Hanka, where none of the latter ever remain to breed. The latter, on the other hand, breed

* Brandt says that Latham *confounded* the Falcated Teal with the similar Javan form; but Latham was, I think, quite right, and the figure in the *P. E.* is clearly the young male of this species, before it has lost the brown back.

commonly on the Boganida in 70° North Latitude, to which point apparently the Bronze-cap does not extend.

The majority of the Clucking Teal breed north of the latitude of Lake Baikal—the majority of the Crested Teal in the same or even a more southern latitude, the Amoor country being apparently its summer head-quarters. No doubt *some* must breed further north, since Middendorff tells us that it "breeds plentifully in the Stanowoy Mountains, and nearly to the tops of the ranges," and if it breeds high up in these mountains, it must needs breed a good deal further north in the plains.

Dybowski, writing of Western Dauria and the country round the south of Lake Baikal, says:—"The Crested Teal arrives during the latter half of April in great numbers; but few remain to breed in the neighbourhood of Kultuk, but in the Darasun region it is more common. The female makes her nest amidst the bushes of swamps, collecting dry reeds and grass, and lining it thickly with down. At the beginning of June she lays eight eggs, sits closely, and only rises at your feet. They remain in autumn as late as the 27th of September." And Taczanowski, describing eggs collected by Dybowski, says:—"The eggs are decidedly smaller than those of the Mallard, and in colour resemble those of the Gadwall, though the yellow tinge is somewhat more pronounced. They vary from about 2·1 to 2·3 in length, and from about 1·52 to nearly 1·7 in breadth."

Dresser thus describes an egg, taken on the 8th of June at Tolstoi-Mir on the Yenesay River:—"In colour it is pale creamy white, resembling the egg of the Common Wigeon; in texture it is very smooth, and in shape longer and more pointed than the egg of the last named bird. It measures 2·22 by 1·5 inches."

THE FOLLOWING are the dimensions and other particulars of the male that I obtained in the Calcutta bazar:—

Male.—Length, 19·75; expanse, 32·5; wing, 9·5; tail from vent, 3·2; tarsus, 1·5; bill from gape, 2·1; weight, 1 lb. 6 ozs.

Irides deep brown; bill perfectly black; legs and feet drab, with an olive tinge; the webs, except immediately alongside the toes, (where they are unicolorous with these) and claws, dusky black.

A frontal spot ending in a point on the culmen, about 0·4 long and 0·3 wide, pure white.

Of another Indian-killed male, the wing measures also 9·5; of the female, 9·1.

Schrenk gives the following dimensions* of five old males and three old females:—

Males.—Wings, 10·15 to 10·7; tails, 3·39 to 3·85; bills at front, 1·75 to 1·84; tarsi, 1·58 to 1·65.

* He uses the old French foot, inches and lines. I have given the equivalents in English inches and decimals.

Females.—Wings, 9·88 to 10·06; tails, 3·22 to 3·57; bills at front, 1·75 to 1·84; tarsi, 1·46 to 1·62.

Some of these dimensions seem abnormally large. Dresser gives—

Male.—Length, 19·0; wing, 10·0; tail, 3·0; culmen, 1·8; tarsus, 1·35.

Female.—Length, 16·0 (!); wing, 9·0; tail, 3·4; tarsus, 1·2.

Of the soft parts Middendorff says that the female, with a greenish black bill and brown iris, has the same bluish clay-coloured feet, with darker webs, as the male.

THE PLATE is good, and shows the conspicuous white patch on the forehead, which, though ignored in almost every plate I have seen, is conspicuous in every one of the four Indian-killed males that I possess. The feet are not rightly coloured.

In the case of the female the speculum is unfortunately hid.

The female has perhaps often been passed over and mistaken for a female Gadwall. Indeed the two birds are so extremely like each other, and the bills are so very nearly the same size and shape, that this is not to be wondered at. However in the female *falcata*, the whole upper mandible is uniformly dark coloured, whereas in the female Gadwall it is only dark along the culmen. Again the tarsi and toes of the female Gadwall vary from dirty yellow to orange, those of the present species from drab, with an olive tinge to bluish clay colour.

But it is in the speculum of the wing that the difference between the two species is most readily discernible.

In the female Gadwall the entire visible portions of the later secondaries are pure white, the terminal portions of their larger coverts, black.

In female *falcata*, the visible portions of all the later secondaries are black, with more or less of metallic green reflections, narrowly tipped with white, and the terminal portions of *their* greater coverts are white.

Moreover, in the female Gadwall, the upper abdomen is usually pure white, and almost unmarked, whereas in the Bronze-cap, it is fulvous or pale rufescent fawn, or fawny white, thickly set with small, more or less obsolete, brown spots.

As a rule our Indian-killed specimens entirely want the sickle-shaped tertiaries so conspicuous in our plate. Only one of our specimens, obtained in Lucknow, towards the close of March, exhibits these.

In some specimens there is more, and in others less, green at the sides of the head than is shown in the plate. Young birds show nearly the whole back brown like the female, and this after the head has become nearly full plumaged. Most males are greyer everywhere, and rather less fulvous than the Lucknow specimen figured.

In this species also, the male, after the breeding season, assumes a plumage very similar to that of the female; but he may be distinguished from her by a certain amount of green metallic gloss which he retains on the head, and by the whiter or greyer and more spotted under surface. Young birds may probably be obtained in the early part of the season in every intermediate stage of plumage between the male and female.

QUERQUEDULA ANGUSTIROSTRIS

THE MARBLED TEAL.

Querquedula angustirostris, *Ménétries.*

Vernacular Names.—[?]

It is curious that this conspicuously distinct species, and one that visits our Empire in such comparatively large numbers, should have remained unnoticed until my visit to Sindh. Since its first discovery there, however, it has been repeatedly met with—not only there, but in several distant portions of the Empire.

Its normal range with us (it is presumably only a cold weather visitant) appears to be the whole of Sindh, (from every collectorate in which it has been recorded, and where it is extremely common), and Northern Gujerat, the southern half of the Dera Gházi Khan District, and of Bháwalpur, in all three of which it is a regular but less abundant visitant. No doubt it will be met with in Cutch and Northern Káthiáwar, but it has not been thence recorded as yet.

But outside these limits it occurs much further east as a straggler. I have had specimens from Western Oodeypore, and from near Delhi. The late Mr. A. Anderson procured it in the N.-W. Provinces, at Fáttehgarh, and in Oudh near Hurdui; and I myself obtained two freshly-killed specimens in the Calcutta market, the one in December and the other in February, which had been captured about 22 miles south-west, and some 18 miles west, respectively, of the metropolis.

Outside our limits, it occurs in suitable localities (though these are few and far between) in Beluchistan and Southern Afghanistan. From Persia Proper it has not yet been recorded, but it was originally described from Lenkoran, (on the south-west coast of the Caspian in about 39° North Latitude), and there can be no doubt that it will be found in many places in Persia, and probably in Mesopotamia. In Palestine it is very abundant, and breeds. In North-east Africa it seems to be very rare. Tristram has a specimen from Alexandria, and Heuglin himself procured a specimen in the Beni Hasan region; but no other record of its occurrence in Egypt or Nubia is known to me. Heuglin gives it from Tripoli; it is very common in Tunis (in winter) as it is in Algiers and Morocco (in summer), in both of which, as also in the Canaries, it breeds. So it does likewise in Southern Spain, but in none of these latter localities do many appear to remain for the winter. Besides these places it has been occasionally observed in Sardinia, Sicily, the Ionian Islands, and (?) the Albanian Coast.

Its known range is therefore very restricted, and a zone lying between the 20th and 40th degrees North Latitude, and stretching from 20° West, to 95° East Longitude, would entirely cover it, while in fully half this zone it has not as yet been observed.

Favier thinks that this Duck winters in the interior of Africa, and it may do so; but my impression rather is that the migration is east and west, the birds for the most part summering and breeding in the latter and wintering with us in the east.

I DO NOT know exactly when this species arrives. Doig says that they arrive in November and leave in April, but this is on the Eastern Narra, towards the extreme eastern limit of its normal range. In the Shikarpur Collectorate sportsmen and fowlers said that a few might be seen earlier, but that the great bulk appeared during the latter half of October. But at Kurrachee Captain Butler shot a young bird that had clearly only recently left the nest on the 27th of September!

In Sindh, where I had abundant opportunities of observing it, I found the Marbled Teal invariably associated in large parties.

Its favorite haunts were broads, thickly grown with rush, in which it fed and sported, comparatively seldom shewing itself in the open water. As a rule it does not at once rise when guns are fired as the other ducks do; but, if by chance, it is at the moment outside of the rushes or similar cover in the open water, it scuttles into concealment, as a Coot would do, and if in cover already, remains there perfectly quiet, until the boats push within 60 or 70 yards of it; then it rises, generally one at a time, and even though fired at, not unfrequently again drops into the rushes within a couple of hundred yards. When there has been a good deal of shooting on a lake, and almost all the other ducks, and with them of course *some* of these are circling round and round, high in the air, you still keep, as you push through the reeds and rushes, continually flushing the Marbled Teal, and the broad must be small, or the hunting very close and long continued to induce all the Marbled Teal to take wing. Of course where there is little cover (though there you never meet with this duck in large numbers) they rise and fly about with the other ducks; but their tendency in these respects is rather coot-like than duck-like. Individuals may take wing at the first near shot, but the great majority of them stick to cover as long as this is possible; and on two occasions I saw very pretty shooting, boats in line pushing up a wide extent of rush-grown water, and the Marbled Teal rising every minute in front of us at distances of sixty or seventy yards, like Partridges out of some of our great Norfolk turnip fields; here and there a Shoveller or a White-eyed Pochard, both of which, when disturbed, cling a good deal to cover, would be flushed; but there was not one of these to ten of the Marbled Teal.

This species is not amongst first class ducks for the table. It ranks, I should say, little above the Shoveller and the White-eyed Pochard, and after obtaining a goodly array of specimens, we never shot it—first class Ducks, Gadwall, Mallard, and Pintail as well as the Pochard (*Fuligula ferina*) and Common Teal being always available.

The flight of this species, though Teal-like, is less rapid and flexible, (if I may coin an expression to represent the extreme facility with which that species turns and twists in the air) than that of the Common Teal. It more nearly resembles that of the Garganey, but is less powerful, and less rapid even than that of this latter species. There is something of the Gadwall in it, but it wants the ease of this. It flies much lower too, and, as already mentioned, much more readily resettles after being disturbed. I have hardly ever seen them swimming in the open, and in the rushes they make of course slow progress. When wounded, they dive, but for no great distance, and then persistently hold on under water in any clump of rush or weed, with only their bills above water. I have never seen them on land in a wild state, but some captured birds, whose wings had been clipped, walked very lightly and easily; and, though they had been but a few days in confinement, they were very tame and could, I should imagine, be easily domesticated.

In Spain they are described as very wary, and there they seem to frequent open water; here they avoid this latter as a rule, and are, I should say, amongst the tamer of our ducks.

Their food is very varied here. Favier says that in Tangiers they feed on winged insects; in Sindh the major portion of their food consists of leaves, shoots, rootlets, corms and seeds of aquatic plants, intermingled with worms, fresh-water shells, insects of all kinds, and their larvæ. I believe I found a small frog in the stomach of one, but it is not noted on the tickets of any of the specimens now in the Museum, and I cannot be quite sure.

Lord Lilford, an extremely careful observer, says that they utter a low croaking whistle; but I am sure I am correct in saying that they utter also a distinct, but rather hoarse, quack; time after time before a duck has been flushed, amidst the babel of sounds that rises in the rushes as you first begin to push through them on some unfrequented and unpoached broad, I have singled out their note and correctly foretold that in such or such a direction there were a lot of Marbled Teal.

As a whole I consider them poor, rather sluggish ducks, very much disposed to take life easy, and in a *dolce far niente* style, and lacking in every line the vigour and energy that characterize races born and bred within the hardy north.

SO FAR they are not known to breed within our limits, but it has often occurred to me that the supposed eggs of the Garganey, obtained on the Mekran Coast, may quite possibly have really pertained to some laggarts of this species; and the very young bird shot by Captain Butler at Kurrachee gives colour to this idea. Colonel Irby, who found this species breeding in Andalucia (Spain), remarks:—

"The Marbled Duck breeds during the last week in May, nesting in patches of rushes. The nest is like that of a Teal, containing a good deal of the down from the breast of the female, and eleven eggs appear to be the usual complement. The latter much resemble those of the Common Teal, being of a yellowish white colour. Favier states that (near Tangiers) they also nest in rushes during May and June, and that incubation lasts from twenty-five to twenty-seven days."

I find no reliable record of the measurements of the eggs, but they are said to be of the same size as those of the Common Teal.

THE DIMENSIONS of adults of this species are as follow:—

Males.—Length, 18·3 to 19; expanse, 28·5 to 29·5; tail, from vent, 3·6 to 4; wing, 8·1 to 8·5; wings, when closed, reach to within 0·7 to 1·5 of end of tail; bill, at front, including nail, 1·77 to 1·85; tarsus, 1·44 to 1·52; weight, 1 lb. 3 ozs. to 1 lb. 5 ozs.

Females.—Length, 16·9 to 17·5; expanse, 27 to 28; tail, from vent, 2·8 to 3·7; wing, 7·9 to 8·1; wings, when closed, reach to within from 0·5 to 1 of end of tail; bill, at front, 1·6 to 1·75; tarsus, 1·4 to 1·5; weight, 1 lb. to 1 lb. 3 ozs.

The legs and feet are dusky olive or dark horny brown with the claws and webs black; or horny green, with the claws and webs dark grey; the bill bluish grey, black on culmen and tip; or dusky, bounded at the margins of the feathers of the forehead and cheeks with a pale leaden blue line, continued along the margin of both mandibles to near the tip, and a spot of the same colour just above the nail; the irides are brown.

Younger birds are considerably smaller. Anderson gives the following dimensions of a male, clearly a bird of the year:—

Length, 17·3; wing, 7·7; tail from vent, 3·5; tarsus, 1·4; bill straight, 1·7.

Butler, of his quite young bird, a female, recorded the following:—

"Length, 15·75; expanse, 26·5; wing, 7·62; tail from vent, 2·75.

"Legs and feet greenish plumbeous; irides dark brown; bill dusky plumbeous, darkest on the culmen."

THE PLATE, otherwise very fair, ignores the blue grey outer webs (becoming nearly white towards their tips,) of the earlier primaries. There is rather too fulvous a tinge on the head and back of the neck in both birds. The dark eye-patch is scarcely sufficiently brought out, and the colouring of bill, legs, and feet, though approximate, is not quite correct. The throat is always marked like the cheeks; it is never unmarked as might be supposed from the plate.

There is no material difference in the plumage of the sexes, but the female is smaller, and has the eye-patch, and generally all the markings and tints, a trifle duller and less conspicuous.

Captain Butler's young female, already referred to, is, above, extremely like the adult, except that the pale markings are smaller and less conspicuous, the whole upper surface being rather lighter, but the whole of the abdomen, lower tail-coverts, &c., are still tipped with the fluffy fulvous nestling down.

One fine adult has the lower surface tinged with ferruginous; but this appears to be far less common in this species than in many others.

$\frac{1}{3}$

MARECA GIBBERIFIONS

THE OCEANIC TEAL.

Querquedula gibberifrons, *S. Müller.*

Vernacular Names.—[?]

AS yet this species has been procured nowhere within our limits except in the South Andaman Island. We failed to find it in the Northern Island and in the Cocos, and equally in the Nicobars.

Outside our limits it has not yet been observed in the Malay Peninsula, Sumatra, Java, or Borneo ; but it occurs all over the Celebes group, in Timor and Flores ; has been obtained at Port Essington at the extreme north of Australia, near Melbourne at the south, in New Caledonia and New Zealand. On the other hand I cannot find that it has been recorded from the Fiji Islands, the Sooloo Islands, New Guinea, or, in fact, any of the islands except Timor and Flores, lying between the Celebes and Australia, New Caledonia and New Zealand on the one hand, and the Andamans on the other.

This distribution is quite inexplicable, and I can only suppose that, being a bird of retiring habits, it has hitherto escaped observation in many localities where it does occur.

IN THE South Andaman it is a permanent resident, but whatever it may have been in past times, is at present far from common Davison, in our paper on the Islands of the Bay of Bengal, remarked :—" It appears to frequent alike both salt and fresh water. During the day it either perches among the mangroves, or settles down in some shady spot on the bank of a stream ; when wounded it does not attempt at first to dive, but swims for the nearest cover in which it hides itself, but when hard pressed it dives, but does not remain long under water, and appears to get soon exhausted. It feeds by night in the fresh-water ponds, and I was informed that it is to be seen during the rains in small flocks in the morning and evening in the paddy flats about Aberdeen. Sometimes, in going up the creeks, a pair will slip off the bank into the water, and keep swimming about 20 yards ahead of the boat, only rising when hard pressed, but they are more wary when in flocks. I could learn nothing about the breeding of this species. The only note I have heard them utter is a low whistle, and this apparently only at night when they are feeding."

In the day time you commonly see them in pairs, occasionally in flocks of from twenty to thirty, high up in some densely mangrove-bordered creek, where the water is fresh ; but at night they leave these, and, collecting in moderate-sized flocks, resort to fresh-water ponds or paddy fields to feed. When wounded, it sometimes dives most vigorously, not indeed remaining long under water, but by no means getting soon exhausted. On the contrary it will often compel you to fire a second shot before you retrieve it. It swims well and runs through the jungle at a great pace. Its flight appears to be fairly rapid, but they are seldom seen on the wing, except at night, and then it is difficult to judge accurately of this.

They are not, I should say, wild or wary birds ; they do not leave a place at the first shot, and Davison has got as many as eight by successive shots out of the same flock, the birds flying about and settling again at short distances. But they are eminently birds of a retiring habit, and very soon abandon, as a day haunt, any place which civilized or semi-civilized men begin to frequent.

A whole flock is sometimes seen during the day time perched on the mangroves of some salt-water creek ; but they are certainly, by preference, the denizens of forest-embowered fresh water.

VERY LITTLE is as yet known of the breeding of this species. I have only one record of its nidification and a single egg, both of which I owe to Captain Wimberley.

The nest was found in August : it was composed of grass, and was placed in a paddy field near Port Mouat, the only locality, with which we are yet acquainted, in the group, where this species is always to be met with.

The egg is typical, a very perfect broad oval in shape, with a very close-grained smooth shell, devoid of gloss, and of an uniform delicate cream colour.

It measures 1·93 by 1·43.

THE FOLLOWING is a *résumé* of the measurements, &c., of a large number of freshly-killed specimens :—

Males.—Length, 16 to 18 ; expanse, 24·5 to 27 ; tail from vent, 4 to 4·2 ; wing, 7·5 to 8 ; tarsus, 1·3 to 1·4 ; bill at front, 1·4 to 1·5 ; from gape, 1·7 to 1·8 ; wings, when closed, reach to within from 2 to 2·2 of end of tail ; weight, 1 lb.

Females.—Length, 15·0 to 16 ; expanse, 24 to 25·5 ; tail from vent, 3·25 to 3·5 ; wing, 7·1 to 7·4 ; tarsus, 1·25 to 1·35 ;

bill at front, 1·3 to 1·4; from gape, 1·65 to 1·75; wings, when closed, reach to within from 1 to 1·75 of end of tail; weight, 12 ozs.

Legs and feet greenish blue to plumbeous; webs usually darker; claws horny; bill greenish blue, plumbeous or plumbeous blue; nail black; in some the lower mandible tinged with, in one the terminal two-third of this, pink; irides reddish brown to deep brownish red.

THE PLATE very fairly represents the specimens figured, but this species is rather variable. In old adults the eye is always set in a white ring, broader below, narrower above the eye, and the portion of the lores that abuts on the upper mandible is also white. It is quite the exception, however, for a white line to stretch, as shown in the plate, through the eye; but it did so in this particular specimen, a *very* fine male. In the young birds the white eye ring and the white lore patch, or line, are both quite wanting. Old males (and perhaps females, though it is less marked in these) have a very decided and full, though short, occipital crest. The lower surfaces of old birds have generally a sort of vinous fawny tinge, presenting a somewhat paler and greyer appearance than in the specimen figured.

The arrangement of the colours in the wing is so peculiar that I had better describe it in detail. The whole of the earlier secondary greater coverts, and the ends of the later ones, a broad margin to the outer web of the first secondary, and usually a narrow margin to the second, and a more or less broad tipping to all but about the last three secondaries, white, more or less tinged with rufous buff; the rest of the outer webs of the secondaries velvet black with a brilliant longitudinal metallic green band covering the greater part of the visible portions of one, two or three of them—from the seventh to the ninth—smaller and more coppery in the female.

THIS SPECIES has generally, hitherto, been classed as a Wigeon, but the bill is not short enough for that genus, and it is not narrowed towards the tip, but rather broadened as in the Teal.

Teal occur almost throughout the world. America has at least ten species peculiar to it—Africa three that might properly be thus classed. Those found in Europe and Asia have been already discussed. Only in Oceana, Australia, and New Zealand the genus seems to be slenderly represented.

½
FULIGULA FERINA

THE POCHARD OR DUN-BIRD.

Fuligula ferina, *Linné.*

Vernacular Names.—[Boorar nur, Lall-sir, *N. W. Provinces;* Lall muriya, *Bengal;* Cheoon, *Nepal;* Thordingnam, *Manipur;* Rutubāh, *Sindh;* Surkh-sir, Ghotye, *Kábul.*]

THE Pochard* occurs as a cold-season migrant to the northern two-thirds of the Empire, but it is not recorded from Ceylon or Mysore, or any part of the Peninsula south of about the 14th Degree North Latitude. Indeed the southernmost locality at which I *know* of its having been found (very possibly it straggles somewhat further south) is Bellary, where one was killed on the 6th of December by Col. McMaster. It has not been observed in the Southern Konkan, nor has it yet been met with in any part of British Burma.

Moreover in the southern part of the region within which it is known to occur, *viz.*, in the Deccan, the Nizam's Territories, Khandesh, Berar, Gujerat, Cutch and Káthiáwar, the southern portions of the Central India Agency, the Central Provinces, the northern districts of the Madras Presidency and Chota Nagpur it is more or less rare.

Northwards of these it is in suitable localities common alike in hills and plains (except perhaps in Kashmir, whence, strange to say, I have never yet received it,) from Sindh and Peshawur to Sadiya and Manipur; even from Chittagong it is reported by Mr. H. Fasson; only from Tipperah, Sylhet and Cachar no one has noticed it.

Outside our limits this species has by no means a very northern range. It is widely distributed during spring and autumn in China, and Prjevalski observed it in the valley of the Hoang-ho, and at Lake Koko-Nor: a specimen was obtained near Yárkand, and Severtzoff observed it on passage and during winter in Western Turkestan. But northwards it does not go far. Radde found it at Lake Baikal, but neither he, Schrenk nor Middendorff found it elsewhere in Siberia, and

* Jerdon, and following him most Indian sportsmen, call this the *Red-headed* Pochard. But this is the real original Pochard, (Poker as we call them in Norfolk,) and does not require any second qualifying epithet.

Prjevalski says it does not occur at Lake Hanka in the Ussuri country.

Southwards it is not uncommon in Afghanistan and Beluchistan; and, as it has been procured both on the Persian Gulf and on the Caspian, it probably occurs throughout the interior of Persia also.

It has been found in Mesopotamia, is not uncommon in Asia Minor, and extremely common in Palestine and in Lower Egypt, ranging southwards to Nubia. It is equally abundant and breeds in Algiers, while in Morocco it seems to be only a cold weather visitant.

Throughout the greater part of Europe (not however extending much beyond the 60th Degree North Latitude) the Pochard is known either on passage or as a summer or winter visitant, and it breeds in England, Southern Denmark, Germany, Russia (central, and as far north as Lake Ladoga) and many other places.

Its range may well be extended to America, where a variety (*americana*, Eyton), not in my opinion specifically distinct, occurs throughout the whole of North America and more particularly Eastern North America, as well as the Bahamas, and breeds in the Fur countries.

THE POCHARD is rather later, I think, in putting in an appearance than most of our other ducks. I have *never* seen it myself before the 17th of October, and even in the North-West Provinces it is not until the second week in November that it is in full force. Further south it is later still.

What the Pochard really likes is a large broad or mere surrounded by rushes, reeds and aquatic plants, some feet in depth, and with a *considerable* breadth of open water in the centre. Elsewhere you may meet a few, as on the banks of rivers, or in any kind of lake, even the Sámbhar; but in such localities as I have indicated, you will see flocks of several thousands, and many acres of water completely paved over with them. Habitually this species goes about in large flocks, but in places unsuited to its tastes, you will meet with single birds or small parties.

The Pochards are eminently swimming and diving ducks; "their path is o'er the glittering wave, their home is on the deep." They walk badly; indeed it is very seldom one sees them on land, but I have once or twice surprised them feeding in wild rice in the early mornings, and have been struck by the awkwardness of their gait. Their flight is slow and heavy until they get well on the wing, after which it is fairly rapid; but they rise with some little difficulty in perfectly calm weather, and always, if there be a wind against it, if possible. There is no duck of which such an enormous haul may be made in the standing net as of the Pochard ; but the large flocks always frequent waters in which, owing to their depth, it is difficult and troublesome to set the net, and difficult to work the fowl up to it, as you must have canoes, and birds will not work as well in front of these as they will when before men and buffaloes, and then at the flush at least half the Pochards dive (unless the night be very dark); and, though they get meshed, it is a tremendous job getting them out of the net, which, moreover, thirty or forty of them in a lump below water, tear to shreds; so that, though I have twice made gigantic "takes," I generally concluded not to undertake the business, but to stick to shallow jhíls.

They swim very rapidly and gracefully ; as a rule, rather deep in the water, but at times, especially, when a lot are at play together, for a minute or two quite high as if barely resting on the water. They are very playful, and skirmish about together, chasing each other, scuttling along on the surface one moment, out of sight the next. They are grand divers ; like all the Pochards they have the hind toe more webbed (though this is slightly less marked in this species and the White-eye than in the Scaup, &c.) than the true Ducks and Teal have, and it is doubtless partly this which makes them such good divers.

I think that they chiefly feed by night, for which purpose all birds, spending the day in rivers and bare-shored lakes, leave these at night for more suitable feeding grounds, and one often drops a brace or two of "old Pokers" flight shooting. But they feed during the day also when in any of their favourite haunts, and you may see them for an hour together diving for the roots and submerged stems and foliage of all kinds of aquatic plants. With us, in Upper India, their food is, according to my experience, almost entirely vegetable; I have found a few insects, grubs, worms, tiny frogs and a good many shells in their stomachs, but seeds, flower buds, shoots, leaves, stems and roots of water plants, together with fine pebbles and sand, of which there is always a considerable quantity, have always constituted the bulk of the contents of these ; and it is perhaps in consequence of this that, as a rule, when killed inland in India, they are excellent eating. Not so always those killed on the coast. A pair I shot in Kurrachee Harbour turned out rank and far from good eating; and a third, shot a few days later, proved to have fed chiefly on marine plants, small crustacea and mollusca. Occasionally, when in small parties, they are to be seen paddling about in shallow, weedy corners of jhíls, along with and just like Gadwall, Teal and Shovellers ; but normally they keep in large flocks, and feed in pretty deep water when feeding in the day time.

It is difficult to say whether they should be called tame or shy. Naturally I think they are the former. At the Madho Jhíl in Sindh, where no sportsman, European or Native, had previously molested the ducks that season, I rowed into the middle of a flock of this species, several thousands in number, and beyond swimming right and left so as to keep the boat at a distance of some thirty yards, they seemed to take no notice of us ; and, when I halted the boat, and we all remained perfectly still in it, they closed in again, so that scores were swimming within twenty yards of us and many dived under us and popped up here, there and everywhere within a few yards, disappearing under water, however, again instantly as soon as they perceived how close they were.

On the other hand, in meres, where they are a good deal shot at, it is at times extremely difficult to work up to them, even lying on your face in a regular leaden cream-coloured gun punt, in which, if you know how to paddle it, you can get within range of almost any and every fowl in India.

Curiously enough at such times you may often get excellent shots with shoulder guns, by setting a small square sail and sailing past them within shot. Of course, you cannot then use the big gun, as the mast has to be stepped in the stauncheon hole; but you may sail in this way a couple of miles up an open jhíl, full of flocks of the wildest fowl, and if you never stop or alter your course, get shots at from forty to fifty yards every two or three minutes. The killed and wounded you must retrieve as you come back, as lowering the sail and stopping to pick up the spoil would put up every duck within a quarter of a mile, whereas only those quite close to you rise (to settle again within a hundred yards as a rule) from shoulder-gun shots fired from a steadily noiselessly gliding sailing punt. It is a little awkward at first, as you have to steer (with a rudder made to ship for this particular work) by strings attached to your feet* (you *must* keep clear of clumps of floating weed) and fire in a recumbent position between the gunwale or rather wash-board and the lower edge of the sail. But you soon get into the way of it, and you may thus get a heavy bag out of some of the large jhíls, where, as often happens, for reasons best known to themselves, all the fowl are so wild that it is hardly possible to get at them in any other way.

Any small sailing boat will do. Mr. W. Forsyth, writing from Dehree-on-Soane, says :—"There are large flocks in the river here of Pintail, Red-crested and Red-headed Pochards, and very exciting sport they yield, wild as they all are. It is useless trying to approach them in the canoe, in the ordinary way. I think the flash of the paddle frightens them. But on a windy day, you can hoist the sail, bear down rapidly on them, when within range let go the mainsail halyard, throw the half

* This must be by stirrups or some other arrangement, which you are quite sure of being able to slip instantly ; because with the best management and the sharpest look-out all round, sudden gusts do at times come down on these large broads and upset you before you know where you are. This has twice happened to me.

of the paddle (with which you have been steering) below your knee, and quickly swinging the gun up, from your side or between your knees, to the shoulder, secure a brace or more before they are out of range. Even on a calm day I still hoist the sail, and with half the paddle slowly propel until within sixty or seventy yards, when I give one strong stroke, seize the gun and take them as they rise.

"Here the Pochards and Pintail feed in the mornings and evenings over the gravelly parts of the bed of the river, but during the heat of the day they mostly rest on just submerged sandbanks or float over the deep pools."

Of course, with their diving powers, wounded birds give a grand chase; but they are not quite such adepts at disappearing altogether as the White-eye; and, as they are more generally shot in open water, it is less common to lose them.

Their note, rarely heard until they are disturbed, is very like that of the White-eye, but louder and harsher—a kurr, kurr; but their wing rustle is far more characteristic, and I have rarely failed to recognize them by it, when I have shot them at night, before they came to hand.

THERE IS no reason to suppose that this species breeds anywhere within our limits, though it certainly beeds in Algiers in nearly the same latitude as Kashmir. But its nidification is well known, as it breeds, as already mentioned, in several places in England, and many parts of the Continent.

They lay, according to locality, in April, May and June, making their nest either on sedges and rush in the water, or on the ground immediately at the water's edge. The nest in some cases is a regular but slight one, composed of dry flags and sedges wound round into a circular form. In others it is a mere depression in the soil, more or less thinly lined with similar materials. In either case a quantity of the bird's own down gives softness to the nest and more or less covers the eggs.

Professor Newton tells us that in England they usually lay from six to eight eggs in the nest, but that others are not unfrequently found scattered about; but on the Continent they are said, I see, to lay from ten to twelve or even more eggs.

The eggs are very regular broad ovals; the shell smooth but dull and glossless. In colour they are a pale dingy green, or greenish drab, more or less, in most cases, tinged with yellow. They average about 2·4 in length by 1·7 in breadth.

THERE IS very little difference in the size of the two sexes. Half a dozen adults of each sex measured as follows:—

Males.—Length, 18·0 to 18·5; expanse, 29·4 to 32·2; wing, 8·05 to 8·5; tail from vent, 2·35 to 3·2; tarsus, 1·4 to 1·5; bill from gape, 2·15 to 2·27; weight, 1 lb. 13 ozs. to 2 lbs. 5 ozs.

Females.—Length, 17·25 to 18·0; expanse, 28·75 to 31·5; wing, 7·9 to 8·3; tail from vent, 2·2 to 3·1; tarsus, 1·4 to 1·5; bill from gape, 2·0 to 2·19; weight, 1 lb. 5 ozs. to 2 lbs. 4 ozs.

I dare say that, if a really large series were measured, greater variations would be found to exist.

The irides vary; they are generally orange yellow, but I have noted them brown in one, apparently adult female, and lac red in an old male.

The legs and feet are pale bluish, or slatey grey, or dull leaden, often darker on the joints and with the webs black or nearly so. The bills are black and bluish grey or leaden, in varying proportions. In some, the entire bill is black, with only a leaden-coloured crescentic bar on the upper mandible towards the tip, In others, only the tip and the basal portions of the upper mandible to a little beyond the nostrils are black, and the whole intervening portions of this mandible are leaden blue; and between these two extremes the breadth of the blue band or bar varies.

THE PLATE, I think, is very good. I have several birds before me now which match the figure of the male to a nicety; but I notice that in other males the red of the head and neck is a shade browner, the black of the breast less pure and duller, and the mantle a shade greyer. There is not enough black on the bill of the female, and in the fully adult female, the mantle should be greyer, a dull dingy reproduction of that of the male.

Young males, such as we get in November and December, entirely want the black on the breast, &c., so conspicuous in the adults. They have the whole head and neck a dull light chestnut. The mantle greyish or yellowish brown, interspersed with whitish black vermiculated feathers like those of the adult. The lower parts, with the tips of the feathers, rather silky, dingy fulvous or brownish yellow on the breast, yellowish or sordid white on the abdomen, with the dull brown or greyish brown bases of the feathers showing through everywhere; and between this and the perfect plumage every intermediate stage is met with during the cold season.

THE FAMOUS American Canvas-back Duck, (*Fuligula vallisneria*, Wilson), is very closely allied to the Pochard; but there is a certain difference in the plumage of the males, and a marked difference in the shape of the head and bill in both sexes of the two species, fully justifying their separation.

F. Waller Chromo Lith. 18, Hatton Garden, London

BRANTA ♂ RUFINA

THE RED-CRESTED POCHARD.

Fuligula rufina, *Pallas.*

Vernacular Names.—[Lall-chonch, Lall-sir, *N. W. Provinces*; Hero-hans (♂); Chobra-hans (♀), *Bengal*; Doomer (♂), Sunwa (♀) *Nepal*; Rattoba, *Sindh*; Nool-gool, *Kábul*; Kizil-bash aurdak, (Turki) *Yárkand*;]

THE range of this species in India is very similar to that of the Pochard, but it seems to extend normally even less far south than this latter.

Like this it has not yet been reported from Kashmir ; but as it occurs during the cold season from time to time in Kullu, Kumaon and Nepal, it will probably prove to visit the Wooller and other lakes, apparently far better suited to its tastes than any of the other Himalayan localities where it has been procured.

It is more or less common in winter in suitable localities throughout the Punjab, the N. W. Provinces (rarer in the Doab, more common in Bundelkhand and Rohilkhand,) and Oudh, Sindh, Rajputana, the northern portions of the Central India Agency, the northern and eastern portions of the Central Provinces, Chota Nagpur, Bengal, west of the Brahmaputra, the valley of Assam right up to Sadiya, and the Northern Circars, northwards at any rate of Chicacole. It is pretty common in Northern Gujerat and Berar, rare in Cutch, Káthiáwar, Khandesh, the Deccan, the southern portions of the Central Provinces, and the Nizam's Dominions. It has not been recorded from the Southern Konkan, Mysore or any of the Madras districts south of this latter. In Ceylon, too, it has not, so far as I am aware, ever been procured ; but Layard believed that he had seen it there, and not improbably a few individuals of this species may occasionally straggle, not only to Ceylon, but to all the southern portions of the Peninsula. I have no record of its occurrence in Cachar, Sylhet, Manipur, Tipperah, Chittagong or any part of British Burma ; but outside our limits Blyth notes it, I know not on what authority, from Bhamo, in Independent Burma.

The fact is, that in the case of this and the majority of species, the distribution has never been thoroughly worked out. This is the first attempt to do this, and will, it is to be hoped, lead to a far more complete knowledge of the subject.

Hitherto this species has not occurred in China. Prjevalski did not observe it in Mongolia or Chinese Tibet, nor has any one recorded it from any part of Siberia. But our explorers met with it in Eastern Turkestan,* and Severtzoff tells us that in Western Turkestan also it is everywhere common and breeds. In winter it is found in Afghanistan and Beluchistan, and in many parts of Persia, where also it breeds in the neighbourhood of Shiraz, and probably other suitable localities. About the Caspian it is common. It has been sent from the head of the Persian Gulf and from near Bagdad. But it does not seem to have been noticed in Asia Minor or Palestine, and it must be very rare in Egypt, if it really occurs there, for neither Heuglin nor Shelly ever met with it. In Algiers it is not uncommon, and many breed there, and stragglers are occasionally met with at Tangiers; but, beyond this there is no record of its occurrence in Northern Africa. It is found throughout Southern Europe, breeding in Spain, Italy, Sicily and occasionally in the Dobrudscha and Southern Russia. Northwards it becomes rare, though it has occurred occasionally in Belgium, Southern Denmark and England (and once in Scotland), but never apparently in Ireland, Sweden, Norway, Finland or Northern Russia.

The normal range of this species is, therefore, very restricted; and, according to our present information, seems to be little more than Algiers and the countries immediately north of the Mediterranean and Black Seas, the Caspian, Turkestan, (Eastern and Western) Persia, the countries between this and India, and a considerable portion of the latter.

LARGE NUMBERS, compared to what occur in Europe, visit us during the cold season; and, when it is borne in mind that they are fairly common over a belt of country stretching from Kandahar to Sadiya, some 2,000 miles in length and averaging certainly 400 in breadth, and that they do extend (though rarer there) hundreds of miles south of this, there can remain little question that the real head-quarters of this species are India in winter and Turkestan in summer.

They arrive late; the earliest date on which I have seen them in the Doab is the 21st of October; and it is quite the middle of November before the great bulk of them have fairly settled down in the plains of Upper India. They are even later further south, and, on the Eastern Narra, Doig says that they are rarely well in before the first week of December.

---

* Thus Scully says:—"This handsome duck was not observed in winter, but was very common near Yárkand during the summer. It is a fine diver, and has a peculiar manner of emerging from the water with a sharp spring; it carries its head well bent back over its shoulders, and is not easily approached. The bird is only a seasonal visitant to Kashgharia, where it breeds; the nest is said to be placed among rushes growing in marshes, and the eggs are reported to be of a green colour."

I have never shot them after the 8th of April in the North-West Provinces, and further south I believe they have mostly left by the third week in March; but in the submontane tracts and in the Lower Himalayas they arrive earlier and linger somewhat later. Thus I shot a specimen at Nau-koocha Tâl, not very far from Nynee Tal, on the 13th of October, and again I got one in Kullu, in the stream near Juggut-sukh, on the 3rd of May.

Still, deep, waters are what the Red-crested Pochard loves, (though on migration it will halt in any streamlet pool) and deep waters in which grow plenty of weeds. It is chiefly, therefore, in large lakes and broad rivers at points in their course where these are sluggish and plenty of submerged weeds grow near the margin that they are to be met with in any numbers. A stray bird or pair is, however, occasionally met with in apparently most unsuitable localities; and I killed a fine solitary male once, in a small masonry tank, barely one hundred yards square, just outside the walls of Ajeetmul or Oreya, I forget which.

Habitually they keep in moderate-sized flocks of from ten to thirty, but occasionally on very large pieces of water they are seen in thousands.

Mr. George Reid writes:—"Never before or since have I seen so many of these ducks as I saw one December morning on a large jhíl in the Fyzabad district. The whole surface of the lake was literally one moving mass of these lovely ducks."

It was early in December, too, that I saw just such a sight on an immense broad in the north of the Etáwah district. We had had a very heavy and late rainy season, and this *jhíl*, always large, was then immense. All night long, pitched as my tent was on a masonry revetted terrace, rising immediately out of the water, I had heard fowl coming in; and the next morning, before dawn, I was out in my punt, working softly round the margin to the western side, so as to have the fowl, when twilight broke, against the daylight sky. I soon made out by their cries that the mass of the fowl were Pochards, that there were a vast number of them, and that a great number of them belonged to the present species. Day dawned, and I could soon see a dense mass of fowl, but far more distant than I expected, probably fully a quarter of a mile off, and much too far to make anything of, even with glasses, in the dim light and through the wavy curtains of almost impalpable mist that flickered above the water. Lying down I paddled towards them. Very soon a fresh north-east wind (and I was heading that way) sprang up against me; quite a sea rose; I was perpetually grounding (a few months later this whole side of the lake was one waving sea of wheat), and they were swimming away steadily against the wind, so that it was bright sunlight before I got within 200 yards, and then I could see that they were all Red-crests. I had now got into deeper water, and went as hard as I could manage without splashing, but they swam steadily away, and I must have gone fully half a mile before I had gained 100 yards on them. Still they had not shown the smallest signs of suspicion (and I knew their ways well), but were swimming gaily on *en masse*, head to wind as they often will on cold windy mornings. On I went; I had a long heavy English swivel, carrying a pound of shot (No. 1 I had in); there were between two and three thousand of them as closely packed as they could swim. I began to bet with myself that I should not get less than one hundred; never had I had quite such a chance, taking it all round; number of fowl close packing, rumps all towards me, my best gun. I was certainly within seventy yards of the hindermost birds; I calculated to get within about forty yards of these, and fire over their heads into the centre of the flock. They were close packed and backs to me, so that there was little to gain, and possibly a great deal to lose by flushing them. I was within fifty yards when again I grounded; had I even then fired at once, I must have made a very large bag, but I thought I knew that this was only the point of a mound, (a tiny island in most years) and I wasted some precious moments struggling to get over it with the paddles. The nearest birds must have been seventy yards distant, before, seeing I was hard and fast, I snapped an ammunition cap on a little pistol I always carried for the purpose, and raked them as they rose. The next instant there was a whole line of birds fluttering on the water—seven dead, and twenty-one winged. I recovered every one of them, but it was noon before I bagged the last, and if I had had a desperate hard six hours work, I hardly remember any six hours which I more thoroughly enjoyed; and that, although it was nearly a week before, with my raw hands, I could touch paddle or quant again.

When much molested they are shy and very difficult to work, but fresh fowl, that have not been before shot at that season, can always be easily approached within swivel range, though they usually keep just outside the limits of efficiency of ordinary fowling pieces. There was a deep reach in the Jumna not many miles above its junction with the Chambal, where every year I used to find a good flock of some forty or fifty of these birds. In an ordinary small native ferry boat it was simply impossible, with an ordinary charge in an ordinary double gun, to do anything with these. Up stream or down stream they could swim every bit as fast as it was possible to drive the old tub; and up stream and down stream, as you pressed them, they *would* swim, always keeping as nearly as possible about sixty yards from the boat; but I used each year to get a few by a long shot out of a No. 8 bore, with double B. Eley's green cartridge, and one year I brought the punt down, and coming down stream on them, against wind, bagged nearly half the party. Before the first shot was fired nothing would make them rise; afterwards, for days, they would not let anything approach within a hundred yards of them without rising.

Dresser tells us that "*it does not dive*,* but like the Mallard, when feeding in shallow water, it turns end up, and stretching down its neck, reaches and plucks up the water plants on which it feeds." I should like to know where he obtained this valuable information. The fact is, that though you *may*, at times, see it dibbling about the water like Teal and Shovellers, or again feeding as he describes, its normal habit and practice *is* to dive, and I have watched flocks of them, scores of times, diving, for an hour at a time, with a pertinacity and energy unsurpassed by any other wild fowl. Examine closely their favorite haunts, and you will find these to be almost invariably just those waters in which they *must* dive for their food. Deep broads, where the feathery water-weed beds do not reach within several feet of the surface, not the comparatively shallow ones, where the same weeds (the character of their leaves, however, changed by emergence) lie in thick masses coiled along the surface.

Although mainly vegetarians, they indulge more in animal food than the Pochard. I have found small frogs, fish-spawn, shells, both land and water, insects, grubs, worms, *and on three or four occasions tiny fish*, mixed with the vegetable matter, sand and pebbles that their stomachs contained. Usually at least two-thirds of their food is vegetable, leaves, stems, fleshy rhizomes, rootlets, &c., of arrow grasses, Sagittarias, Horn Worts, and the like; but at times they feed largely on the animal substances above enumerated, and I examined one male that had entirely gorged itself on fishes about an inch in length. Probably it is owing to this that these ducks vary so in quality as comestibles; sometimes they are really first-rate, (they are almost always very fat), while at others they have a rank, marshy, froggy flavour, that it requires lemon and red pepper in abundance to neutralize.

Though constantly seen feeding by day, when in suitable situations, they also feed a good deal during the night, and those whose day quarters happen for the time to be waters that yield little food, leave these at dusk for more prolific haunts. Perhaps they mostly move at that time; certainly you very commonly shoot them when out flighting, and at that time they are usually in pairs or small parties, very rarely in large flocks.

They are strong but heavy fliers, and they are slow in getting under weigh; but for some reason, which I have failed to discover, (for in daylight they do not rise very perpendicularly), they are very seldom caught in the standing net.

---

* The italics are mine.

Jerdon, quoting a writer in the *Indian Sporting Review*, says that "during the day they are constantly on the move, now pursuing one another, now screaming, all up at once, then down again." This, however, I have never observed, except on very cold, or dull, cloudy days. On bright sunny days—and we have few but these during the season in which they visit us—their habit is to feed energetically, from about 8 to 10 A.M., and from 10 A.M. to 3 P.M. to rest either on some shallow or floating in deep water, half the flock often asleep, well out in the middle of the lake or stream. Now and again there may be a little skirmishing and play, or washing and diving, accompanied by a few calls and a little chattering; but during the midday hours, quiescence is their characteristic.

On the whole, taking them all round, they are perhaps the most troublesome* fowl to work, as they are certainly, in my opinion, the handsomest that we have much to do with in India; and there is no species that I have more often watched or more closely studied.

I have sometimes found them out of the water, on the land a yard or two from the water's edge, grazing and picking up small shells and insects, and they then walk better than the other Pochards; but it is rare to *see* them thus, though from the frequency with which they are caught along with Gadwall and other ducks by fall-nets on baited sward, it is probable that during the night they more readily leave the water.

Their call-note, not very often heard by day unless they are alarmed, is quite of the Pochard character—not the quack of a duck, but a deep grating "*kurr*." Occasionally the males only, I think, emit a sharp sibilant note—a sort of whistle, quite different from that of the Wigeon, and yet somewhat reminding one of that. I have never *seen* them do this, but I have on two or three occasions heard the note from parties of them when no other fowl were near; and once, when there were only drakes, and I have repeatedly heard it at night, and once by the Ana Sagur at Ajmere, three ducks came over me in the dark, uttering this sound, and two that I dropped proved to be Red-crests.

As a rule, these birds are always in mixed flocks, and I have never seen any party consisting only of females; but I have, perhaps a dozen times in my life, come across flocks, (one of them numbering fully fifty individuals) composed of adult males only.

I have forgotten to notice their very characteristic wing rustle, which, though resembling that of the Pochard, is louder

---

* Capt. E. A. Butler, no mean authority on such matters, remarks: "The Red-crested Pochard is another of those wary birds that severely tries the sportsman's patience, taking wing on the slightest indication of danger, and flying up and down the tanks invariably out of gunshot. It is not very common, but occurs on most of the large tanks."

and harsher; their wings are short, and rapidly agitated make a very distinct, palpitating, rushing sound, by which even a single bird, passing anywhere near one in the stillness of the night, can generally be recognized. I say generally, and I have often so identified them, but one makes at times very erroneous guesses. This last cold season, coming down the Jumna at night, a bunch of fowl swept over us from astern, and as I fired I set them down by the sound as Red-crests. The night was stormy, the lightning was flashing incessantly, and there was a head wind with drizzling rain. One bird dropped dead (two others fell but disappeared), and proved to be a Common Pochard. The fact is, that the wing rustle varies a good deal according to whether fowl are going with or against the wind, and whether the air is dry and clear, or loaded with mist or drizzle; and only a very practised fen-man can always be quite sure of every bird, at all times, by the sound of its wings.

THERE IS nothing as yet on record to lead to the belief that the Red-crested Pochard breeds within our limits, though it certainly does breed in Algiers very nearly, if not quite, as far south as Kashmir and at Shiraz, which is further south than Mooltan.

Dr. Baldamus, who has taken many nests in Central Germany, all however on "a pond overgrown with reeds, flags, and other aquatic plants, close to the Mansfelder Salt Lake," tells us that they are "always placed in the rushes or flags, usually on a small island in the pond or on the flags; and, like all ducks' nests, they have a foundation of rotten stems of rushes or dead leaves on which a warm bed of down, plucked from the breast of the female, is placed. When the female leaves the nest quietly she covers her eggs, as do all ducks. The eggs vary from eight to nine, ten being the exception, and seven only in late settings." All his nests were taken between the 12th of May and the 1st July, the later nests being much incubated, so that in this locality they probably lay from the 1st May to the 15th of June.

The eggs are only moderately broad ovals, without gloss, a bright, somewhat olive green when fresh and unblown* (fading to a dull greyish olive or greenish grey when blown,) and measure about 2·3 by 1·6.

---

* Salvin, in his "Five Months Birds-nesting in the Eastern Atlas," remarks:—"In the open pools at the upper end of the marsh of Zana, I used frequently to see several pairs of the Red-crested Duck. Two nests only were obtained. The second lot, consisting of seven eggs, were of a most brilliant fresh green colour when unblown; the contents were no sooner expelled, and the egg dry, than the delicate tints were gone, and their beauty sadly diminished."

ALTHOUGH SOME males are very much heavier than any females, there is not much difference in the size of the sexes. Adults measure:—

Males.—Length, 20·5 to 22·1; expanse, 34·0 to 38·2; wing, 10·0 to 10·75; tail from vent, 3·0 to 4·2; tarsus, 1·5 to 1·7; bill from gape, 2·3 to 2·42; weight, 1 lb. 12 ozs. to 2 lbs. 14 ozs.

Females.—Length, 20·1 to 22·0; expanse, 33·75 to 37·0; wing, 9·6 to 10·25; tail from vent, 3·5 to 3·8; tarsus, 1·5 to 1·75; bill from gape, 2·25 to 2·4; weight, 1 lb. 10 ozs. to 2 lbs. 6 ozs.

In the adult male the bill is a brilliant crimson, sometimes a little inclining to vermilion; the nail brown, or white tinged with brownish horn, or pink horny brown or yellow at tip. There is often a dusky shade round the nostrils; the gape is often blackish, as is likewise the base of the lower mandible and the basal portion of the membrane between its rami; but these are all traces, I think, of immaturity.

In the female (and young males) the bill is black, reddish or orange towards the tip, and more or less so along the sides of the lower, and edges of the upper, mandible.

The legs and feet are dingy salmon colour or reddish orange, dusky on the joints and blackish on the webs; but in slightly younger, though full plumaged birds, the legs and feet will be olivaceous orange, pale olive yellow, dingy buffy yellow, reddish brown, or lastly dusky with a reddish tinge.

The irides vary from brown to red (this latter being the colour in the old adult), and are, at different ages, brown, brownish yellow, reddish brown, orange, orange red, and bright red.

Dr. Scully gives the following particulars of a quite young bird:—

"♀. *Juv. Yárkand, 29th July.*—Length, 19·4; expanse, 33; wing, 8·9; tarsus, 1·4; bill from gape, 2·1; weight, 1 lb. 4·75 ozs.

Bill dusky above, brownish below; legs and feet dusky, yellowish green in parts."

THE PLATE is, on the whole, satisfactory, but the male figured was not a very full plumaged adult, and the barring about the white flank patch is a trace of immaturity. Moreover both the scapulars and the shoulder of the wing are somewhat too rufescent; they should be greyer. In some of the plates there are certain small black streaks on the head of the male; this is, I believe, a defect in the printing; nothing like it is observable in any specimen I possess.

In fine adult males the feathers of the crown and occiput are even more developed than is shown in the plate, and are of a conspicuously yellower and paler colour than the sides of the head.

The picture of the female is fairly good, but the under surface is rarely quite as white as is therein depicted ; it is generally a greyish whitey brown. The white margins to the feathers of the interscapulary region and upper back are traces of immaturity, entirely wanting in the old adult.

During the cold weather young males may be met with in every stage of plumage between that of the female and the old drake.

In the spring the white thigh patch and wing lining of the old male are often strongly tinged with a delicate salmon-rosy hue, which, however, almost entirely fades out of skins.

AYTHYA NYROCA

THE WHITE-EYED POCHARD.

—o—

Fuligula nyroca, *Güldenstädt.*

—o—

Vernacular Names.—[Karchiya, Boorar-mada, (Hindee), *N. W. Provinces;* Lal-bigri, Bhooti-hans, *Bengal;* Burnu, *Sindh;* Malac, *Nepal Terai;* Chiki (or Chikit,) Kanat Aurdak, (Turki.), *Yarkand;*]

—o—

COMMMON as is this little species, its distribution in India has been as yet by no means satisfactorily determined.

It is common in the Himalayas during the cold season, *in suitable localities*, from Gilgit to, at any rate, Sikhim, and in Kashmir many are permanent residents and breed there.

In the winter it is more or less common throughout the Punjab and Sindh, (where possibly some few may remain to breed,) in Káthiáwar, Rajputana, the Central India Agency and Khandesh, the Central Provinces, the North-Western Provinces and Oudh, Bengal west of the Brahmaputra, and Chota Nagpur. It is less common in Cutch, the Nizam's Territories, the Northern Circars, the Deccan, and the Pánch Máhals, and is very rare in the Southern Konkan. Southwards I have failed to trace it ; it is not recorded from Mysore, the Malabar Coast, Travancore, Ceylon, or any of the Madras districts south of Mysore and the town of Madras, though it must needs straggle into some, if not all, of these localities. Eastward of the Brahmaputra, the only record I have of it is of a single specimen procured by Mr. Inglis in Cachar. Mr. Damant did not notice it from Manipur, or Colonel Graham from Dibrugarh or Assam generally, and none of Godwin-Austen's or my collectors have apparently met with it in that province. In Chittagong, from what Mr. Fasson* says, it probably does occur. Blyth records it from Arakan, but gives no authority, and I have received no intimation of its having been procured there of late years, and no one has reported it from either Pegu or Tenasserim.

---

* "I cannot speak from my own knowledge, but Mr. Lowis tells me that the Ferruginous (or White-eyed) Pochard occurs here.

"But all wild ducks are rare in Chittagong, and confined to two localities only—the Island of Kutubdia, and a series of jhils amongst low scrub-grown hills near Fenna in Futikcheri. I have been able to visit neither place this season."—H. FASSON.

All this negative evidence is only recorded *quantum valeat* which is, perhaps, not much; but it will, at any rate, show how imperfect our knowledge of the distribution of this species still remains.

Outside our limits, though never noted by Swinhoe, Pére David tells us that this species is *common* in the spring in the Pekin Province. Westwards, however, Prjevalski never seems to have met with it, in his explorations of the valley of the Hoango-ho, or even at the Koko-Nor, several degrees further south than Pekin. Westwards again it is common in summer, and breeds both in Eastern (Yárkand), and Western Turkestan. It has now been recorded or sent from several places in Afghanistan and Beluchistan during the cold season; was procured by Blanford near Ispahan in Persia in March, but at an elevation of 7,500 feet; and is included in various Caspian lists. It is equally found, and breeds, in Asia Minor, in Palestine where but few breed, but where, in winter, it is extremely abundant, as it is in Lower Egypt, extending up-country along the Nile, &c., to Nubia.

It occurs pretty well throughout Southern and Central Europe, not, however, I believe getting anywhere much north of the 57° North Latitude, though it *has*, no doubt, been alleged to occur both near Archangel and in Iceland. It has only once or twice been recorded from Scotland—never from Ireland, Sweden, Norway, or Finland.

They are occasionally seen at the Canaries,* and are abundant in Morocco and Algiers, in both which latter, as also in Southern Spain, Denmark, Germany, Russia, Hungary, Greece, &c., they remain to breed in greater or lesser numbers.

IN KASHMIR the majority are permanent residents; to the major portion, if not the whole of the rest of its Indian range, it is only a winter migrant, arriving in Northern India about the last week in October (though somewhat earlier in the submontane tracts) and a little later further south. Mr. Doig, indeed, writes that they only arrive on the Eastern Narra in December, but I think there must be some mistake here.

Unquestionably weedy lakes and broads, containing moderately deep water, are its favourite haunts in this country; but I have occasionally met with it on river banks, small ponds, and even utterly bare shallow sheets of water, like the Sámbhar Lake.

It is seldom *seen* in the open water, and I have never seen any very huge flocks; but while I have often met with pairs and small parties of from three to seven on small tarns and ponds, I have put up successively many hundreds from different parts of large rushy reedy lakes. Not *en masse*, but successively,

* It may possibly stray, as has now been more than once asserted, to Jamaica. A bird of this kind, that certainly occurs on the Canaries (and probably the Azores also) may well be occasionally blown over to the West Indies; but these are clearly outside its normal range.

for it is a characteristic of this duck to cling to cover and rise singly or in twos and threes, and only when compelled to do so. As I said in my Sindh paper: "It is very indifferent eating, and it *may* be a cognizance of this fact, and that sportsmen generally disdain its slaughter, that leads it to remain tranquilly in amongst the rushes while heavy firing is going on all round, often not taking the trouble to rise till the boat is within twenty yards of it. Anyhow this is the fact, and I have seen as many as thirty or forty rise singly one after the other, all within easy shot, in a couple of hours punting through the rushes."

I may quote, in confirmation, what Capt. Baldwin published some years later:—

"It is a swift flying bird, occasionally found in flocks, but more often singly or in pairs. It loves to frequent jhíls with plenty of cover. I have met with capital shooting about mid-day in tanks bordered with high reeds, with every here and there open pieces of water. Here, when the sun becomes powerful, the White-eyed Duck retires; and a sportsman, seated in a boat, and noiselessly punted by a couple of natives, will, unless the birds have been much bullied and shot at previously, meet with good sport—the ducks rising one or two at a time, and offering capital chances as they top the cover. I have noticed that on these occasions Teal, Gadwall, and other kinds of fowl at once rise and make off on the report of a gun anywhere near, but that the little brown White-eyed Duck does not take alarm. The plumage of this bird is very thick and close, and, though small, it takes a severe blow to bring it down, and unless dead, like all the Pochard tribe, often gives great trouble to recover. I have frequently, at Jhánsi, lost the half of my winged birds in a day's sport. I have already mentioned, when speaking of the Wigeon, that the White-eyed Duck is often erroneously so termed, though it does not resemble a Wigeon at all, either in shape or colour.

"I have noticed a rather remarkable fact in connection with this bird: on three different occasions I have shot specimens *minus* their feet, which, I believe, had been frozen off in some far distant country. On all three occasions both feet were missing, so that it would appear improbable that a trap or gun had been the cause of the missing members in every instance; but I came to the conclusion that the birds had lost their feet by visiting some very cold clime, and that the webbed portion had become frozen and dropped off. If this was the true reason, it would appear that the little Pochard migrates to colder regions than other wild fowl, or why should this one species be affected in such an extraordinary manner?

"It is only a tolerable bird for the table, not to be compared in this respect with the Gadwall, Teal, and others."

Of course, as I have already shown, this bird is *not* a migrant to the Arctic regions, but the point raised is an important one. Not only of this species (and certainly not more commonly in this than in many others), but of nearly all our ducks, I have from time to time shot specimens, *minus* part or the whole of one or both feet. The missing portions always seem to have been cut clean off. The cicatrised portions are always fleshy coloured. I am sure that in the course of my shooting I have killed more than fifty birds thus maimed, and some of them—like the Marbled Teal—birds that never go near freezing or nearly freezing water. What causes these mutilations ? They do not occur, I think, in India ; without exception all I have thus seen have had the wounds perfectly healed. Steel traps are not generally in use in Central or Northern Asia. What takes off the feet ? Do any kinds of pike or other predaceous fish snap them off ? Obliged as I am to reject the frost-bite and steel-trap theories, I can offer no more plausible solution ; but I confess that it by no means satisfies even my own mind, and in default of corroborative evidence I cannot expect others to accept it.

When on the wing the flight of this species is fairly, but by no means very rapid. They rise with some little difficulty, and always by preference against the wind (indeed when there is no wind they are slow in getting under weigh.) If flushed from water, they strike it repeatedly as they rise with their feet, much after the fashion of Coots, but in a less exaggerated style. Rising out of the reeds, they fluster up and go off much like Partridges with a low, straight flight, often dropping suddenly, almost Quail-like, after a short flight.

On land, one never sees them many paces distant from the water's edge, and running down to it, they shuffle along most clumsily.

In the water they are at home ; they swim with great rapidity and dive like the......I was going to use an inappropriate simile, but they dive marvellously. Indeed what becomes of them is often a puzzle ; the instant that, wounded, they touch the water, they disappear, and not unfrequently that is the last you see of them ; at most they only rise once or twice, and then disappear for good. It is a waste of time to pursue them ; if they do rise, give them instantly a second barrel. If not, you must trust to the dogs picking them up in the rushes near the margin later in the day when all is quiet. But even the best dogs will be baffled, and I have seen a well-trained retriever, after skirmishing in weeds and water for several minutes in pursuit of a wounded White-eye, come out with his tail between his legs and a general crest-fallen appearance, clearly under the impression that, in consequence of some delusion, he had been beguiled into hunting a Dabchick—a bird that from his earliest puppyhood he had been taught to consider altogether beneath his notice.

They are with us quite omnivorous; no doubt their food chiefly consists of vegetable matter—leaves, stems, roots and seeds of grass, rush, sedge and all kinds of aquatic herbage; but besides this I have noted at different times, amongst the contents of their stomachs, delicate fresh-water shells and shrimps, insects (including several species of Neuroptera and Lepidoptera!) and their larva, worms, grubs and small fishes.

I have often, when lying up hid in the reeds, waiting for more valuable fowl to come over, watched little parties of them feeding in some tiny, weedy, reed-hedged opening. Part of the time they swim about nibbling at the herbage or picking shells or insects off the lotus leaves; but they are continually disappearing below the surface, often re-appearing with a whole bunch of feathery, slimy weed, which all present join in gobbling up. Sometimes they remain a very long time out of sight, I should guess nearly two minutes (it seems an age); but generally they do not, when thus feeding, keep under more than say from forty to fifty seconds.

I fancy that they feed preferentially by day; first, because when in their favourite haunts I have invariably found them, when I have had opportunities of watching them unperceived, busy feeding at all hours, and never asleep as night-feeding ducks so constantly are between 11 A.M. and 3 P.M.; and, secondly, because I have so rarely killed them when flight shooting. When settled on some comfortable, rush-embosomed, weed-interwoven broad, I am pretty certain that they do not change their quarters at night-fall, as when encamped near any of their chosen day-haunts I have heard their harsh familiar call at intervals throughout the midnight hours; but of course in the less common case, when they affect bare-shored lakes or rivers by day, and some few *do* do this, they must needs go elsewhere to feed during the night, and in such situations I have once or twice seen them at midday snoozing at the water's edge.

Their quack or note is peculiar, though something like that of the Pochard, a harsh kirr, kere, kirr, with which one soon becomes acquainted as they invariably utter it, "*staccato*," as they bustle up from the rushes, often within a few yards of the boat.

What a difference a change of scene and fortunes makes in birds as well as men. The White-eye is not the only class of old Indians that improves vastly by a sojourn in Europe! *Here*, this duck is very inferior eating, *very* fat no doubt at times, but almost always tainted by a certain marshy twang, but in Spain Colonel Irby tells us that "its flesh is not only like that of the Red-headed and Red-crested Pochards excellent eating, but far surpasses either in that respect."

Here, my advice to persons thinking of eating them, when any other wholesome food is available, must be Punch's, to those contemplating matrimony, "DON'T!"

THE WHITE-EYE breeds possibly in some localities in the plains of India, and in Sindh, where it swarms during the cold weather, and where I was informed that in some broads it remains during the whole year. I have never, however, succeeded in finding a nest, or obtaining any reliable information as to one being found in the plains.

In the lakes of Kashmir they breed most abundantly, so abundantly that boat-loads of their eggs are brought into the Srinugger market during the season.

They lay in June, and, according to my native collector, who examined a vast number of their nests, build a moderate-sized nest of dry rush and sedge in amongst rushes, reeds, and water-weeds, sometimes on the ground, and sometimes more or less floating, and supported on masses of water-plants. The interior of the nest is composed of rather finer materials, and the eggs are generally more or less intermixed with feathers and down.

Ten was the largest number of eggs found in any nest, but in Europe they are said to lay as many as twelve.

Writing from Southern Spain, Lord Lilford says:—

"We obtained a nest of nine eggs, from which I shot the female bird. The nest was at a short distance from the water, in high rushes, and was composed of dead, dry water-plants, flags, &c., and lined with thick brownish white down and a few white feathers."

The eggs of this species are at once distinguished from those of most other ducks laying within our limits, by their well-marked, though delicate, *cafe au lait* tint, which, however, has often a faint greenish tinge. In shape they are commonly very regular and perfect ovals, moderately broad as a rule, but occasionally considerably elongated and slightly compressed towards one end. The shell is very smooth and fine, but it has very little gloss.

In length the eggs vary from 1·9 to 2·2 in length, and from 1·4 to 1·54 in breadth; but the average of a large series is 2·1 by 1·49.

SOMEHOW I have but few measurements by me of this species. I have measured numbers, but the paper is not forthcoming. Six measured this last cold season varied as follows:—

Males.—Length, 16·0 to 17·1; expanse, 24·5 to 27·3; wing, 6·8 to 7·45; tail from vent, 3·1 to 3·5; tarsus, 1·1 to 1·3; bill from gape, 1·9 to 2·1; weight, 1 lb. 2 ozs. to 1 lb. 9 ozs.

Females.—Length, 15·9 to 16·5; expanse, 24·0 to 26·5; wing, 6·8 to 7·4; tail from vent, 3·0 to 3·4; tarsus, 1·0 to 1·25; bill from gape, 1·9 to 2·05; weight, 1 lb. 3 ozs. to 1 lb. 6 ozs.

The bill is black, bluish black, and dark leaden, often browner below; the irides white, or greyish white; the legs and toes slate colour, leaden, or dusky grey; the tarsi often with a greenish tinge; the claws and webs dusky to black.

These were all adults; the birds of the year are notably smaller, and have the irides differently coloured, but never, I think, yellow as in the Scaup, the young of which are likely to be confounded with females of this species.

Scully gives the following details of two very young birds:—

♂. *Juv., 30th July.*—Length, 16·1; expanse, 21; wing, 5·1; tail, 2·4; tarsus, 1·1; bill from gape, 1·75; weight, 15·5 ozs. Bill, dusky, livid below; irides dark brown; legs and feet mottled dusky; claws black.

♀. *Juv., 18th July.*—Length, 15·7; expanse, 26·2; wing, 7·05; tail, 2·1; tarsus, 1·2; bill from gape, 1·9; weight, 15·4 ozs. Bill black above, grey slaty below; irides brownish grey; legs and toes dusky plumbeous; webs greyish black; claws black.

THE PLATE is not happy; we have been unfortunate in the particular specimens figured. The male in the foreground was not a perfect adult. In the adult male the whole back, scapulars, and tertiaries are much darker and more uniformly coloured. They are a blackish brown with a decided greenish sheen and with no pale tippings to any of the feathers. Moreover, the abdomen is, in the old male, pure white and unmarked. The adult female (the nearer of the two birds in the background) should also have the back somewhat darker and more uniform, and the head and neck a shade browner and less rufous. The little bird in the background fairly enough represents a young bird, but even this is somewhat too orange on the breast, and should be a little browner. Old females are sometimes quite as white on the abdomen as old males.

The males are immediately distinguishable from every other species ever here procured; the females, when not quite mature, are very like the young of the Scaup, which also sometimes have only a white spot at the chin (in younger birds still the throat also is white), and which closely resemble them in plumage, but which always show some white about the lores where these abut on the sides of the upper mandible, have a broader bill and yellow irides, besides having in birds of like ages longer wings.

FULIGULA MARILA

THE SCAUP.

Fuligula marila, *Linné.*

Vernacular Names.—[None.]

FEW of the wild fowl known to occur within our limits are apparently of rarer occurrence than the Scaup Pochard. Nor, considering that this is pre-eminently a littoral species, that its normal range is the entire northern temperate zone, (its only recorded occurrence within the tropics being that of a pair which Heuglin says he saw in Abyssinia), and that almost our entire coast line is outside that zone, can this be a matter for much surprise.

My only Indian-killed specimens are a quite young female, shot near Srinugger on the 1st of August, and an immature male, shot at the Wooller Lake (also in Kashmir) on the 5th of November.

Mr. A. Grahame Young writes to me that he has shot this species in Kullu, in winter. Hodgson sent home specimens from Nepal, and one of his drawings of a duck obtained in the valley on the 21st of October, though labelled a female of *F. nyroca*, is clearly, by the broad bill, yellow iris, and broad white lore patch (not as yet meeting on the forehead), an immature Scaup. Colonel McMaster is of opinion that one year, in January, he saw several birds of this species, on marshes and salt lakes between Chicacole and Berhampore in the Northern Circars (say 19° N. Lat.,) and the male is a bird that so experienced a sportsman could hardly mistake for any other species that could occur there.

I have no further information as to the occurrence of this species within our limits, but it may prove to be in reality less rare than we now suppose; and immature birds, which are most likely to wander farthest south, may often have been put aside as the young or females of the White-eye.

Outside our limits, the Scaup has been sent from Japan, and is common on the Chinese coasts in winter as far south, at any rate, as Formosa, but is much rarer in the interior of the Empire. Prjevalski appears never to have met with it in Mongolia or the valley of the Hoang-ho, or those portions of Chinese Tibet which he visited. Neither was it observed by any of our Yárkand Expeditions, nor does Severtzoff record it from Western Turkestan. As yet we have no knowledge of its occurrence in Afghanistan, Beluchistan or the interior of Persia; but it certainly occurs in the Caspian, was found breeding commonly on the Boganida* (N. Lat. 70°), and has been observed or procured in winter or in passage in various parts of South-east Siberia, at Lake Baikal, in Darasun, and in the Sea of Ochotsk. In winter it is common on the coasts of Asia Minor, Palestine, the northern extremity of the Red Sea and Lower Egypt, and has been observed on the coast of Algiers.

Everywhere, almost, on the coasts of Europe, (including those of Iceland, the British and intervening islands) the Scaup occurs, rare as a rule, on the Southern or Mediterranean coast, very common on the north-western and Baltic coasts;—breeding in abundance in Iceland, almost throughout Scandinavia, and in Northern Russia, and seen commonly or occasionally, chiefly on passage only, inland in many, if not most, parts of that Continent.

It is found along the entire west coast of North America, so far as this lies within the temperate zone; it breeds in the Hudson's Bay territory, at the Great Slave Lake and in other parts of Northern America; and has been met with in winter on the east coast as far south as Texas and at the Bermudas.

Coincident with this species in North America is a smaller, barely separable form, the Lesser Scaup or little Black-head, *F. affinis*, Eyton, which, while breeding quite as far north, pushes in winter much further south, *i.e.*, to the West Indies and Guatemala, to which *marila* does not, it is believed, extend. This lesser species has also straggled to Great Britain.

OF THE habits of this species in India there is naturally as yet nothing to record. Dresser says:—"It frequents the sea coast, and is but rarely met with on inland waters, being found in bays and estuaries, frequently in large flocks. It dives with ease, obtaining its food chiefly by diving, and is often seen in company with the true diving ducks. It swims fast, and often sits deep in the water; and it flies with tolerable speed, usually at no great altitude above the surface of the water, and alights abruptly, as do most of the ducks, on its hind parts. Mr. Cordeaux says, the Scaups are 'usually the last ducks to leave our waters in the spring. I have seen them off the coast in this parish late in May, the very latest occurrence being a single bird, an old male, on the 24th of that month. These ducks appear to keep in pairs, male and female,

---

* Many species that elsewhere scarcely enter the Arctic regions appear to range well within them in the great Northern Asiatic promontory.

throughout the winter, as we invariably find them in mixed flocks composed of about equal numbers of males and females. The Scaup swims high on the water. They are very expert divers, remaining immersed even longer than the Golden-eye; and I have frequently known them to continue underneath from fifty to sixty seconds. In the evening at dusk and on moon-light nights, Scaups leave the water and fly up on the flats to feed; they are then often killed by our gunners who are lying in wait on the muds for Widgeon and Mallard.' Montagu says that both the male and female have a peculiar habit of tossing up their heads and opening their bills, which in spring is continued for a considerable time, while they are swimming and sporting on the water, and they emit a grunting sort of cry. When caught and kept in confinement, the Scaup soon becomes quite tame; and, although in a wild state, it feeds chiefly on marine mollusca, yet it soon accustoms itself to feeding on vegetable matter, and will freely eat grain, especially barley.

"When feeding, the Scaup is, as a rule, very easy of approach; for it is far less suspicious than most of its allies, and will frequently allow a boat to come within gun-shot-range without taking wing."

"Although it rises," Macgillivray says, "without difficulty, it usually prefers diving to escape pursuit, and is so expert in this that it is very difficult to shoot on the water. Though common in the markets, it is not thought much of for the table, its flesh being rather rank."

BREEDING HABITUALLY so far north as this species does, it is, *prima facie*, highly improbable that it should ever breed within our limits. Still our having procured a young bird of this species, only (apparently) just able to fly, on the lake near Srinugger in Kashmir, on the 1st of August, does awaken the suspicion that a pair or two may occasionally linger to breed in the comparatively elevated lakes of that state. Anyhow no one has yet found a nest there, and for the nidification of this species we must refer to European writers.

Yarrell says:—"Mr. Proctor sent me word that the Scaup Duck is a very common species in Iceland, where it breeds either among the aquatic herbage or the large stones, near the edge of fresh water, making little or no nest, but a quantity of down covering the eggs, which are from five to eight in number. An egg brought from Iceland by Mr. Proctor, and figured in Mr. Hewitson's work, is of a uniform clay brown colour, 2·37 inches in length by 1·62 in breadth."

Dresser again tells us that:—"This species breeds in the northern portions of both the Palæarctic and Nearctic regions. The nest is placed on the ground under a bush, or well concealed amongst high grass, more seldom in a hole or under a stone.

Not unfrequently several females deposit their eggs in the same nest; and Dr. Krüper states that in Iceland he once found twenty-two eggs in one nest. The eggs are deposited from the early part of June to the middle of July; and when the female commences to incubate, she sits very close, not leaving the nest until the intruder is close to it. The normal number of eggs appears to be eight or nine. I possess a nest and seven eggs of this duck, taken by Mr. Meves on Oland, on the 5th July 1871. The nest consists only of grasses, without any down as lining; and the eggs are uniform greyish stone buff in colour, and vary in size from 2·45 by 1·67 to 2·5 by 1·77 inches."

I CAN give no original particulars of this species. I take the following from Macgillivray:—

Male.—Length, 20·0; expanse, 32·0; wing, 9·0; tail from insertion of feathers, 2·75; tarsus, 1·42; bill along ridge, 2·0.

The bill is light greyish blue, or dull lead colour, with the nail blackish; the iris rich yellow; the edges of the eyelids dusky; the feet pale greyish blue, darker on the joints; the membranes dusky; the claws black.

Female.—Length, 18·0; expanse, 28·0; wing, 8·75; tail (as above,) 2·5; tarsus, 1·33; bill along ridge, 1·83.

Bill as in the male, but darker; the feet dull leaden grey with the webs dusky.

Doubtless a series of careful measurements in the flesh, such as we in India always record, would show considerable variations. Specimens now before me measure:—

	Wing.	Bill, straight from margin of feathers to point.	Bill, greatest width.
♂ adult, England	8·0	1·85	0·88
♀ adult, England	8·0	1·9	0·85
♂ *juv.*, Wooller Lake	7·9	1·7	0·87
♀ *juv.*, Srinugger	7·1	1·6	0·78

THE PLATE is very satisfactory, though, if my memory serves me correctly, Scaup swim rather deeper in the water. It has to be borne in mind that in many lights the sheen on the head of the male is purple and not green. Also that in many specimens the black zig-zag barring of the mantle is denser and more decided than in the specimen figured. Some females have the white band broader both on the forehead and lores, than in the specimen figured. In younger birds it does not extend to the forehead at all. My young male is very like the female figured, but is rather browner, no grey stippling on the mantle, a white chin (as in *nyroca*), and the white band at the base of the upper mandible only just beginning to show. But for this, the yellow iris, the broad bill, and the white satin sheen of the abdomen, it might well be mistaken for *nyroca*, under which name it stood for years in our museum. The very young female is equally like the very young *nyroca*, but it has the chin, throat, a portion of the lores white, only a little speckled with rufous brown, (which white is not exhibited by any of my young White-eyes), besides the characteristic bill so much broader than those of young *nyroca* of the same age and sex.

I dwell specially on these points, because, having myself for years passed over these specimens as White-eyes, I cannot help suspecting that others may have done the same. If this species does visit the plains—and I am inclined to believe that it probably will prove to do so in the Punjab and Sindh on its way to the Kurrachee coast, (which lies within its normal range, and where about the mouths of the Indus it would find most congenial haunts)—it will probably be chiefly the birds of the year that will occur, and for these a sharp look-out should be kept.

FULIGULA ½ CRISTATA

THE TUFTED POCHARD.*

Fuligula cristata, *Leach.*

Vernacular Names.—[Dubaru, Ablac, *N.-W. Provinces;* Málac, *Nepal Terai;* Turándo. *Sindh;* Nella chilluwa, (Telegu); Neer-bathoo, (Tamil); Neer-kolee, (Canarese); Sonah, Ablak, *Kabul;*]

VERY rarely seen in the Himalayas,† the Tufted Pochard is rather thinly distributed in the cold season over the Punjab and the Doab, is scarce in Rajputana, more common in Rohilkhand and Oudh, and less so again in the Central Provinces and Bundelkhand.

In Sindh it is not very abundant; in Cutch rare; in Káthiáwar and Gujerat, in the Central India Agency, Khandesh and the Deccan fairly common.

In Bengal, Cis-Brahmaputra, it has been noticed in many districts, but I believe it to be rather scarce there, though my information on the subject is scant. Damant records it, and some of Godwin-Austen's people procured it from Manipur; but I have no other information as to its occurrence east of the Brahmaputra, whether in Assam, Cachar, Sylhet, Tipperah, Chittagong or any portion of British Burma. I do not doubt that it straggles into many of these, but the fact has yet to be ascertained.

It occurs, in places in very large flocks, in Chota Nagpur, the Northern Circars and the Nizam's Dominions, straggling by the way at times into the Southern Konkan. It has been shot near Bellary, and certainly though rare there, visits Mysore; but south of this I have heard of it nowhere in the Peninsula,

* On account of its bright yellow iris, this species is often called "THE GOLDEN-EYE or "THE INDIAN GOLDEN-EYE;" but the *true* Golden-Eye, (the species to be next dealt with), belongs to a quite distinct genus, and this name, commonly as it is applied out here, should be dropped in favour of the old-established English name, "The Tufted Pochard." No doubt in Europe they call it the "The Tufted *Duck*," but it is a true Pochard, and I have therefore modified the name accordingly.

† This species has not been recorded from Kashmir (though I should expect it to occur there). I have never myself met with it in, or received it from any part of, these mountains. Hodgson only got it in the Nepal *Terai*. Scully never saw it in the hill portion of Nepal. But Mandelli obtained several specimens in the interior of Native Sikhim in the course of ten years' collecting.

except in the north of the Coimbatore* district, nor has it been yet recorded from Ceylon. Here too, however, our information is very imperfect, and stragglers will probably turn up in many districts whence the species has not yet been noticed.

Outside our limits, this species is said to be common in China, as far south as Formosa at any rate, (and doubtless it goes further south), from October to March, and it has likewise been obtained in Japan.

It is not scarce on the spring migration in Mongolia and at the Koko-Nor, and some few remain to breed at Lake Hanka. It is common and breeds in Dauria, arriving about the middle of May and leaving towards the close of October. Similarly it is common in South-eastern Siberia in summer. But Middendorff did not apparently meet with it in Northern Siberia, nor have our explorers met with it in Eastern Turkestan. In Western Turkestan,† however, it occurs on passage throughout and remains in some districts the whole winter. In this season, too, it is not uncommon in Afghanistan, both Northern and Southern, and has been sent from Beluchistan. It is abundant on the Caspian, and will probably prove to occur in suitable localities throughout Persia, in winter, since besides occurring in Beluchistan and on the Caspian, it has been sent from Mesopotamia, and is not uncommon at that season in Asia Minor and Palestine. In Lower Egypt it is very common, extending southwards along the Nile into Nubia, and Blanford found it in pairs, in May, on Lake Ashangi in Abyssinia in about 12° 30′ North Latitude (about the same latitude as Madras), but, be it remembered, at an elevation of 8,500 feet.

Westwards it is a winter visitant to the rest of Northern Africa, and it seems to occur throughout Europe (excluding Iceland), to the major portion of the Continent as a cold weather visitant only, but breeding in England occasionally, and more regularly in Norway (to the extreme north), Northern Sweden, Finland, Northern and Central Russia and Northern Germany.

---

* Mr. Albert Theobald, who has collected for years, in the southernmost districts of the Madras Presidency, writes :—

"I have only seen this duck in the northern part of Coimbatore and in the Mysore country; they come in at the latter end of November and leave about April or May. They are not very common and keep in small flocks of four to six.

"It prefers large open tanks or lakes, keeping to the middle. I am not certain if they resort to the fields at nights, as I have not shot them in such localities.

"The best way to shoot them is to have a small punt or canvas canoe disguised with green boughs tied to the prow, and gently propelled by paddling, or by a man swimming behind with his hands on the stern of the boat."

† No. 376.—ŒDEMIA CRISTATA (L.) of Dresser's notes on Severtzoff's Fauna of Turkestan. *Ibis*, 1876, p. 420, can only be meant for this species, though Linné (and L. only stands for the great Swedish Naturalist) never called *any* duck *cristata*, and the present species can, in no possible manner, be classed as a Scotter.

I HAVE seen this Pochard as early as the 12th of October in Etáwah (Doab, North-West Provinces), and again in this same district as late as the 9th of April; but taking Northern India generally, the mass of the birds do not arrive before the second week of November and leave about the close of March. They arrive later, and perhaps linger later in the south. Jerdon notes that he killed one in June in Hyderabad (Nizam's Dominions), and I have had several notes of single birds being seen in the Deccan, Gujerat and the Central India Agency in May; but these are certainly abnormal occurrences, and I believe that even in the south it is very rare to see them after the 15th of April.

Large, fairly deep sheets of open water, surrounded however with rushes or reed beds, and with plenty of weeds in parts, are what the Tufted Duck prefers. On huge bare-shored lakes, like the Sámbhar, they are scarcely ever seen, and one very seldom meets with them on rivers. Single birds or small parties may be found on almost any broad in which the water is tolerably deep in some places, but the huge flocks in which they love to congregate are only met with on large lakes, such as I have above referred to.

At the Manchar Lake I saw two enormous flocks. I have repeatedly seen similar flocks in old times at the Najjafgarh and other vast jhíls in the Punjab, the North-West Provinces and Oudh; and I should guess that at the Kunkrowli Lake in Oodeypore there must have been nearly ten thousand, covering the whole centre of the lake.

These birds are shy, and keep during the day as a rule so constantly in the middle of bright water, and so far from any position in which one can watch them closely, that I know but little of their habits. I fancy that they feed chiefly by day, partly because they are so constantly at work diving, both in the mornings and afternoons, and partly because I have never once shot them in India (I have in England) when flight-shooting. In places where they are unmolested you may pick up a few by long shots from an ordinary boat, or even a good number by sailing down through them; but it is impossible here, except under special conditions, to make any real bag of them without a regular gun-punt and swivel.

This species has, I think, an easier, smoother and more rapid flight than most of the other Pochards, and rises much more rapidly and with less fluster than these; but still like these it strikes the water once or twice with its feet, and makes a loud splashing sound when rising in numbers. It swims rather deep in the water and very rapidly, and dives constantly, keeping under water for a surprising time. When you try to get near them in any slow native boat, the fresh fowl seldom think of rising, but swim and dive away from you quite as quickly as the boat can go. Even when a gun is fired they do not always fly; indeed I have seen a large flock of several hundred birds disappear as if by magic; all having dived as if by one consent. If your boat can go, and you are very sharp, you may in such cases have great fun; a tremendous spurt is put on in the direction in which the mass of the ducks seemed heading as they dived. In a minute they begin to pop up round you within shot; they come up with a regular jerk, generally showing little more than their heads and necks, and there are just about three seconds during which you *can* shoot them, before realizing the circumstances they again disappear. I was once one of a party of ten guns in five boats, that got right in amongst a large flock of these Pochards that wouldn't rise, and kept them diving for, I suppose, ten minutes, during which a fusilade, such as I have seldom heard, was energetically kept up. The result was five birds killed, and three of the party and two boatmen hit (but not badly) with shot which had glanced up off the water. Four out of the five I killed, though several better shots were present, and this by a simple expedient that is worth knowing—I had a few cartridges for Pelicans containing each eight, eighty to the lb. bullets; and, finding I could not shoot quick enough to catch the birds before they got under water, I used these slug cartridges, fired only at those birds which rose close to the boat, and shot well under them.

At other times they will rise before you are within a hundred yards, and taking short flights, plump down again suddenly into the water, stern first, as if shot. In such cases you may at times work them very satisfactorily, if you chance to have a considerable party and several boats, and the lake is long and comparatively narrow. If they are comfortably settled on a sheet of water that suits them and where they have sojourned in peace for a mouth or two, it is scarcely possible to drive them away from it the first day. Next day, after they have been *thoroughly* harried, not a bird is sometimes to be seen, but they will scarcely quit till after dark. In this respect they are like Coots, and if means and appliances are available, they may be worked just as we work these towards the close of autumn at home. The day after the failure above related, (we spent the rest of the day snipe-shooting, killing a good many teal and other ducks round the margin), we found, directly we got on the water, that all the Tufted Pochards, instead of diving, kept rising as we approached. Then I bethought me of our Norfolk Coot-shootings, formed line, boats about 80 yards apart (this was too far, but we had to cover the breadth of the jhil), put a gun on the shore on each side and went straight at them. At first they only rose and flew ahead of us, but as we got nearer the end they began to come back over the line, pretty high, but many of them well within shot. When all were up, we turned and worked backwards, in the same order, and then back again, and so on five or six times getting amongst us sixty or seventy Pochards, besides other things, and yet when we left off at dusk, the flock was there all the same. Next morning not a Pochard was to be seen, whereas the Gadwall, Teal, and other ducks that had left before our third or fourth turn was completed were all back, famously on the *qui vive*, but in their wonted numbers.

Though noisy enough as they splash up in a crowd out of the water, and recognizable at any time by the sharp whistling of their wings as they pass over head, they are, in winter at any rate, singularly silent birds when let alone. When alarmed and flushed they occasionally emit the regular grating Pochard call, kurr, kurr, but not so loudly, I think, as some of the other species.

On land I have never once seen them, but I should expect them to be clumsy walkers like most of the other Pochards.

Their food is perhaps more animal than vegetable. They constantly devour small fish, and one finds every kind of water-insect, worm, grub, and shells, small lizards, frogs, spawn, &c., in their stomachs. Still like the rest they eat the leaves, stems and roots of water plants freely, and I have several notes of birds which had dined (or breakfasted) entirely off some white shining onion-like bulb.

As a rule, they are not, I think, good ducks for the table. I have occasionally found them good enough; but in earlier times they proved so often rank, or froggy or fishy, that of late years I have never cooked them when anything else was procurable; and where you get these you are so certain to get Teal, or Gadwall, or Snipe, or Godwit, or Ruffs and Reeves—all first-rate birds—that I have not perhaps given them a sufficient trial, and I have heard some sportsmen declare them excellent.

CONSIDERING WHERE Blanford met with this species in May, and presumably about to breed, we might well expect to find them breeding in the lakes of Kashmir, in 34° North Latitude, and at an elevation of between 4,000 and 5,000 feet. But so far as is yet known, this species does not even occur in Kashmir, and for all particulars of its nidification we must refer to European writers.

Dresser says:—"The Tufted Duck breeds in the northern portions of Europe, the eggs being deposited early in June. The nest is placed on the ground, not far from or even close to the water. A nest, sent to me by Mr. Meves, taken at Muoniovaara, in Lapland, on the 20th June, consists of grass bents and a few leaves felted together with a mass of sooty brownish-black down, having dull greyish-white centres; and the eggs, eight in number, are uniform pale olive-green or greenish buff in colour, smooth and polished in texture of shell, and in size average about 2·3 by 1·65 inch;" and these are precisely the dimensions of the egg taken by Wolley and figured by Mr. Hewitson in the 3rd edition of his well-known work.

OF THIS species likewise my old paper of measurements has been mislaid, and I have only particulars of seven birds. I fear, therefore, that the subjoined will only imperfectly represent the limits within which the species really varies.

Males.—Length, 16·6 to 17·2; expanse, 27·5 to 30·3; wing, 7·8 to 8·5; tail from vent, 2·5 to 3·25; tarsus, 1·3 to 1·4; bill from gape, 1·85 to 2·0; weight, 1 lb. 8 ozs, to 2 lbs. ½ oz.

Females.—Length, 15·2 to 16·75; expanse, 26·7 to 28·7; wing, 7·6 to 8·0; tail from vent, 2·6 to 3·0; tarsus, 1·2 to 1·4; bill from gape, 1·81 to 2·0; weight 1 lb. 5 ozs. to 1lb. 12 ozs.

In adults the bills vary from dull leaden to light greyish blue, the nail and extreme tip being black; the irides golden yellow; the legs and feet vary like the bill, and there is often an olivaceous tinge, especially on the tarsi; the joints have usually a dusky tinge; the webs vary from dusky to almost black and the claws from deep brown to black. As a rule, the colours of the bill, legs and feet are rather duller and duskier in the female than the male.

In young birds also these parts are duskier, and the irides are brown, brownish white, to almost white and brownish yellow.

THE PLATE, so far as the male is concerned, is very good, but the green on the tertiaries is a little too bright. Moreover in a really old fully-plumaged male, there is none of that brown speckling at the base of the throat shown in the plate; the back is a shade blacker, and the crest much longer. I have a male before me in which it is exactly two and a half inches long.

The female is much too light and rufous a brown; she should be a darker brown, (though rufous brown is at times mingled with this) on the breast and interscapulary region; a much darker brown on the mantle, and a *very* much darker brown, almost a blackish brown, on the head. No doubt immature birds are lighter coloured, but I have never yet met with one in India altogether so light and rufescent as the plate.

There is some difficulty in discriminating the young and females of the White-eye, Scaup and Tufted Pochard.

In the old females, the White-eye has the chin white and the irides white, while those of the other two species have no white chin and yellow irides. The Scaup again has no crest and a broad white band margining the upper mandible, while the Tufted Pochard has no white on the face, and a distinct, though short, crest of narrow recurved feathers.

But in the younger birds all these distinctions do not always hold good. Young Scaup often have a white chin, and very little, a mere speckling, of white at the base of the upper mandible; and the young Tufted Ducks at times have the irides nearly white or brownish white, and have white about the face.

The youngest specimens, however, of the Tufted Pochard that I have seen, have always exhibited the crest which characterizes the species, short no doubt, but of the peculiar linear feathers, so greatly developed in the old adult males; and this is the best practical diagnosis of doubtful birds of this species, though there are other differences in shape and colour of bills, &c.

The White-eye and Scaup can be separated, *I believe* (but am not positive) at any age, by the colour of the irides, and *certainly* by the shape of the bills, which, age for age and sex for sex, are longer and broader in the Scaup, and less spatulate, *i.e.*, more of the same breadth throughout and less compressed or pinched in towards the base, than those of the White-eye.

TRUE POCHARDS of the same types as some of those above dealt with occur throughout the world. The Canvas-back from North America I have already noticed, and there are other species from South America, South Africa, Australia and New Zealand.

CLANGULA ⅓ GLAUCION

THE GOLDEN-EYE OR GARROT.

Clangula glaucium, *Linné.*

Vernacular Names.—[None.]

ALTHOUGH it is quite possible that the Golden-eye may prove a less rare visitant to our Empire, than is at present supposed, all we *now* know in regard to its occurrence here, is, that Sir A. Burnes procured it on the Indus (probably about the mouths of this river, where wild fowl swarm in countless myriads during the winter,) in Sindh, forty odd years ago, and that Dr. Bonavia obtained a fine male some ten years ago, captured by fowlers in the neighbourhood of Lucknow, which is now in our museum.

In China this species is common about Pekin and Shanghai in winter, and has been observed as far south as Amoy, in, say, about 24°30' North Latitude, about the same latitude as Kurrachee and Manipur.

Prjevalski says that this species is "tolerably common at the Dalai-Nor (43° *North Latitude*) at the end of March and beginning of April, on those parts of the lake which are free from ice; and when shot at they rise, but very soon settle down again.

"At Koko-Nor (37° *North Latitude, elevation* 10,000 *feet*) they arrive about the 4th of March, and get rather numerous towards the middle of that month, but are only singly distributed in Kan-su, at the sources of the Tetunga.

"We found them wintering at Lake Hanka (*about* 44° *North Latitude*) on the open parts of the river Sungatch, in small numbers; but in spring, late in March and early in April, they are very plentiful, but always in small flocks of from five to twenty birds, and never mixed with other species.

"The autumnal migration from the Ussuri country occurs in September and October; and in the latter month we often saw flocks of these ducks on the Japanese Sea; and in December some wintering ones came under our observation at the port of St. Olga (*about* 140 *miles east of Lake Hanka.*)"

It occurs in Japan, where Whitley shot a pair in December at Hakodadi. In Southern and South-Eastern Siberia, Dauria and the Amoor region it is found in winter or seen on passage extending to Saghalien and Kamschatka. A certain number probably breed in Southern Siberia, but the majority go further north, though probably scarcely crossing the 70th degree North Latitude. It was not one of the species seen on the Boganida by Middendorff.

In winter it is rare about Kashghar. Stoliczka obtained a single specimen there in February, but neither Henderson nor Scully met with it. In Western Turkestan, however, it is more common, and was observed by Severtzoff both in winter and during passage in many places. Stoliczka found numbers early in May at Lake Sirikul on the Pamir (Lake Victoria of Woods), elevation over 10,000 feet, waiting according to the people of the neighbourhood until the lake, then mostly frozen over, was clear of ice, to breed. It is often seen near Cabul and in Northern Afghanistan generally, during the winter, but has not yet been observed about Kandahar, in Beluchistan or Persia, though it certainly occurs on the Persian shores of the Caspian and eleswhere in that sea. It is common at the same season in the Black Sea, and on the northern coasts of Asia Minor; but there is no reliable record of its occurrence elsewhere in Asia Minor, or in Palestine or Egypt, or anywhere in Northern Africa, except in Algiers, to which it is a rare straggler.

The whole of Europe, including the Islands of the Mediterranean, but excluding Iceland (where, as in Greenland, it is replaced by a *very* closely allied form) falls within its range; but though it may occasionally have bred in Scotland, Shetland and elsewhere, it may, broadly speaking, be said to be only a winter migrant or bird of passage everywhere except in Norway, Sweden, Finland, Northern and Central Russia and the provinces lying along the southern coast of the Baltic, in almost all of which it breeds, more or less regularly, though its main breeding zone is perhaps between the 62nd and 68th degrees of North Latitude.

Again, in the New World, it may be said to extend over the whole of North America, wandering as far south as Mexico and Cuba; but throughout the northern portion of this range the form already alluded to (*C. islandica*), and through its entirety, the little Buffle-head (*C. albeola*), also occur.

THERE IS nothing to record of its habits here, where at present it can only rank as a rare and accidental winter straggler, and I shall therefore quote a part of what Macgillivray tells us about its mode of life. He says:—

"It is chiefly to lakes, pools, and rivers, that they resort, generally in small flocks, but sometimes in great numbers, and their food consists principally of the larvæ of aquatic insects, for which they dive in the clear water...........They also feed on small fresh-water mollusca; but I have not observed any vegetable substances in their œsophagus or stomach... ....In one instance I have seen remains of small fishes in the gizzard.

"But, although essentially lake ducks, they often, especially in frosty weather, resort to estuaries, as well as the open coasts, where they procure testaceous mollusca, crustacea, and fishes. Their flesh is very dark coloured, and, although savoury, not at all pleasant, unless its natural fishy flavour be concealed by arts known to the cook and the epicure...........

"When undisturbed they float lightly; but, if alarmed, have the faculty of sinking deeper. They swim with great speed, dive instantaneously, and are active and lively in all their movements, unless, as some say, when on land, where, however, I have never seen them walking. They fly with rapidity, in a direct manner, their small, stiff, sharp-pointed wings, producing a whistling sound, which in calm weather may be heard at a considerable distance. At night they repose chiefly on the water, but sometimes on points of land. If shot at while feeding, they dive, and appear after a considerable interval, at a great distance; but owing to their vigilance and activity, it is difficult to get near them, although, when without a gun, I have several times been allowed to approach within shooting distance, and on such occasions they merely swim slowly away. In rising from the water, they strike it with their feet and wings, to the distance of several yards, but, on occasion, they can rise at a single effort, especially when there is a breeze...........

"The cry of this bird is a mere grunting croak, and is never heard to any considerable distance; the epithet *clangula* given to it by the earlier ornithologists had reference not to its voice, but to the whistling of its wings."

Yarrell remarks:—"They are active in the water, swimming and diving with great rapidity, when in pursuit of their food, which consists principally of small fishes; if five or six of these ducks are together, they do not all dive at the same time, but some of them remain on the surface, as sentinels, where they keep a good look-out to prevent being approached and surprised by an enemy."

Although it may be found anywhere, even in the heart of a vast Continent, as in Yárkand, in small numbers or on passage, I think we may conclude that it prefers coasts, estuaries and lakes within a moderate distance of seas; and that, except perhaps in places like the mouths of the Indus, we are not likely to see many of them at any time in India.

OF THE nidification of this species, Dresser says:—

"So far as my own experience goes, the Golden-eye always

deposits its eggs in a hollow tree, at some height above the ground; but Naumann says that it frequently breeds in the reeds or rushes close to the edge of the water. In the north of Finland, in Sweden, and in Norway it nests in hollow trees, either near to or at some distance from the water, and very frequently in the nest-boxes which the peasants hang up for water-fowl to breed in. These are frequently hung up close to the peasants' huts; and even then the Golden-eye will nest in them. The bottom of the hollow tree or nest-box is neatly lined by the old bird with down; and on this soft bed the eggs, which vary in number from ten or twelve to seventeen or even nineteen, are deposited. When hatched, the young birds are carried by the female in her beak down to the ground or to the water, one after another being taken down until the entire brood is taken in safety from the elevated nesting place; and I have been assured by the peasants that this always takes place in the dead of the night. The eggs of this duck are dull greyish green, uniform in tinge and rather glossy in texture of shell, oval in shape, and in size average about 2·4 by 1·55 inch; and the down with which the nest is lined is sooty greyish white, the tips of the down being rather darker than the central portion."

THE ONLY original measurements in the flesh that I have of this species, are those taken by Stoliczka of his Pamir and Kashghar birds, but I have collated these with Macgillivray's, and where this was possible, *i.e.*, in the case of wings, &c., with measurements from the skin of my Lucknow and several English specimens, and I give the result, *quantum valeat*:—

Males.—Length, 16·5 to 19·0; expanse, 28·0 to 32·0; wing, 8·6 to 9·35; tail from vent, 3·3 to 4·1; tarsus, 1·41 to 1·65; bill from gape, 1·2 to 1·4; weight, 2 lbs. to 2 lbs. 10 ozs.

Females.—Length, 15·7 to 16·5; expanse, 26·3 to 28·0; wing, 7·5 to 8·25; tail from vent, 3·0 to 3·4; tarsus, 1·22 to 1·35; bill from gape, 1·12 to 1·19; weight, 1 lb. 7 ozs. to 1 lb. 14 ozs.

The irides are bright yellow in females and young males, reddish or orange yellow in old males, white or very pale yellow in the quite young birds. The naked edges of the eyelids reddish dusky; the legs and feet vary from pale yellow in the young to intense orange in the old; the colour is always bright and pure; the webs (including that of the hind toe), nails, and a spot on each of the toe joints, black or dusky; the bill in the old males is bluish or greenish black, rather duskier and duller coloured in the old females and young, and occasionally in these latter, often in the former, and very rarely*

* No European writer notices this, but I have a full-plumaged and clearly old male, with the uniform white wing and scapulars, showing the orange band strongly on the bill. As a rule, however, this is only seen in young males and females, by no means always in these latter, and less commonly still in the former.

in the old males, with a larger or smaller yellowish red or orange spot or bar near the tip of the upper mandible, which in some forms a terminal band at the tips of *both* mandibles, never, however, including the nail, which always remains black or dusky.

THE PLATE gives a good idea of the species, but the bills are wrongly coloured. The male figured is not an old adult; in these the scapulars and the greater part of the wings become uniform white without any of the markings shown in the plate. The figure of the female also is good, but does not represent an old bird; in this the head is darker and browner; the base of the neck all round is greyer; the back is darker and the pale margins to the feathers more or less obsolete.

NEITHER SEX of this species can well be mistaken for that of any other that visits us, as independent of the very characteristic plumage, the bills are peculiarly shaped; short, much higher than broad at the base, and narrowed off towards the point like a Wigeon's.

THERE ARE only two other known species properly referable, in my opinion, to this genus, both of which belong to North America (though straggling within European limits), and these have already been referred to above when speaking of the distribution of the present species.

THERE IS yet another species of which we have given no figure, as when our plates were prepared, no one had any idea that it occurred within a thousand miles of our Empire, but which having now been procured at Khelat-i-Ghilzai in Southern Afghanistan, will probably also occur as a straggler in the Punjab and Sindh, and, therefore, requires some notice here. That is

THE WHITE-FACED STIFF-TAIL DUCK.*

Erismatura leucocephala, *Scopoli.*

On the 20th October 1879, Colonel O. B. St. John, R. E., at that time, I think, Governor of Kandahar, shot a couple of ducks, of a type quite unknown to him, in the Jameh river near Khelat-i-Ghilzai, which he kindly forwarded to me with other specimens.

---

* This is commonly called "The White-headed Duck." But the name, a mere translation of the scientfic one, is incorrect; the bird is White-faced. not White-headed, and it belongs to a distinct section of the ducks, characterized *inter alia* but specially, by their stiff tails.

These ducks proved to be an immature pair of the White-headed Duck.

No one had observed it in Mesopotamia or Persia, and its occurrence, therefore, near Khelat-i-Ghilzai, so much to the south and east of the previously known limits of its range, was most unexpected.

In Southern Europe, the south of France, Spain, Italy, Austria, Greece, Turkey, and the larger islands of the Mediterranean, it occurs, though nowhere apparently in great numbers ; but it is more plentiful in Southern Russia, especially on the Lower Volga.

It is also found in Asia Minor and Palestine, throughout the north of Africa, (Tangiers, Algeria, and Lower Egypt,) on the Caspian, and lastly in Western Turkestan, where Severtzoff says that it is seen on passage, and even breeds.

OF ALL the Old World ducks there is perhaps no more remarkable form than the present species, with its very broad base-swollen bill and lengthened, stiff, pointed, almost Woodpecker-like tail.

It is said to be entirely a fresh-water species, frequenting, as a rule, the larger lakes.

It is apparently very much of a diving duck, often preferring to seek safety under water rather than by flight ; and Tristram tells us that both in flight and habit it more resembles a Grebe than a true Duck.

Personally, of course, I know nothing of this species ; but in order to give some idea of its habits, I may quote from the *Ibis* of 1875, Messrs. Danford and Harvie-Brown's remarks in regard to it, the result of their observations in Transylvania :—

"This curious bird, which we found in the Mezöség, is not very common. We met with a flock of nine or ten birds at a small reedy lake near Záh ; but, owing to the difficulty of paddling the wretched square-ended canoes or punts *(csónak)*, the only substitutes for boats in the country, we found great difficulty in getting near them, and for some days only succeeded in shooting one male, and that at a very long range. A couple of days before our departure, however, we were more fortunate ; the birds were tamer, and let us get a number of long shots, by which we killed three more males and a female. They never attempted to leave the lake, but after a short rapid flight pitched again, generally about the same place. They swam very fast, keeping their stiff Woodpecker-like tails erect at right angles with the body, and when wounded, though they dived constantly, showed no disposition to escape, like other ducks, by hiding among the reeds, but on the contrary avoided them."

Naumann says that they swim very low in the water, something like a Cormorant, showing only head and neck, and a small portion of the rump, and the tail above water. They are most expert divers, keeping several minutes under water. They keep in pairs or small parties, rarely associating with any other species of fowl. Their call is a grating, quacking note, much like that of the Pochards.

They are said to feed upon water insects, small fishes, and shells, as well as vegetable matter; but I suspect that this is rather conjectural.

THE NEST, composed of dry grass, rushes and the like, is built in amongst reeds and sedges, in lakes, marshes or sluggish rivers; and in it the female, towards the end of May, lays from seven to ten eggs, which are said to be a dull white in colour, large for the size of the bird, and characterized by the peculiarly rough and coarse texture of their shells.

THE FOLLOWING was Colonel St. John's note on the two young birds, male and female, which he shot:—

"Length, 16·5; wing, 6·12; bill, length at front, 2·0; breadth, 0·9.

Irides brown; bill and legs (which were very large and stout) dark plumbeous; tail cuneate, of 18 long, rigid feathers.

"Colour above hair brown, minutely speckled fulvous; below bright orange fulvous; the bases of the feathers dark ash; head dark brown; white stripe from base of upper mandible to nape; below the eye a dark stripe separating the white stripe from the pure white chin and throat; male and female precisely similar."

These birds are immature, and I may further quote Dresser's detailed description of the adults and young:—

"*Adult Male (Záh, Transylvania, 16th May).*—Crown black; forehead, sides of the head, including the space above the eye, chin, and nape pure white; below this white the neck is black, with a few buffy brown dots on the forepart; lower neck to the forepart of the back, except in the centre, chestnut-red; this colour extending to the foreneck and upper breast, where it is delicately marked with buffy white; back and scapulars ochreous or reddish buff; rump darker, brownish, all finely vermiculated with blackish; lower rump and upper tail-coverts chestnut-red; quills greyish black, the secondaries externally and the larger wing-coverts greyish buff, vermiculated with blackish grey; lesser coverts dull ashy, but slightly vermiculated; tail long and stiff and blackish in colour; underparts below the breast buffy white, obscurely marked with reddish brown; flanks dull chestnut brown, tinged with warm buff, and vermiculated with darker brown; bill much swollen at the base, pale ultramarine-blue in colour; iris dark brown; legs dull blackish plumbeous. Total length about 17·5 inches; culmen, 1·9; gape, 1·82; wing, 6·3; tail, 4·3; tarsus, 1·35.

"*Adult Female (Záh, 16th May).*—Differs from the male in lacking the clear white on the head, and in being much more rufous in plumage; crown and nape blackish brown, with a chestnut tinge; sides of the head similarly coloured, but marked with white; a white streak passes below the eye nearly to the nape; and the chin and upper throat are white, slightly dotted with blackish brown; general colour of the upper parts darker than in the male, being deep chestnut-red; underparts as in the male; bill dull plumbeous; iris dark brown; legs plumbeous black.

"*Young* (*vide H. Otto, 'Ibis,'* 1875, *p.* 428).—Beak bluish black, with a swelling at the base; feet of a similar colour; plumage brown-black; from the base of the bill, under the eye, and continued over the ear, a white stripe; chin, with a broad outward curve back under the cheek, white, so that the brown cheek appears bordered underneath by this curve, and above by the eye-stripe; belly dirty white, which colour loses itself in the sides; under the shoulder a light spot on both sides, which hardly shines through, and in many specimens is wanting; tail-feathers slit up and spread out like a fan."

♂ MERGELLUS ALBELLUS.

THE SMEW.

Mergellus* albellus, *Linné.*

Vernacular Names.—[Nihenne, *Etáwah, N. W. Provinces;* Ghotye, Chota-Khoruk, *Cabul;* Boz-aurdak, (Turki) *Yárkand;*]

OUR information as to the distribution of this species is very defective. In the Himalayas it doubtless occurs in many localities on passage; but the only place from which it has been actually recorded is Kullu, where Mr. A. Grahame Young writes that it is common about the end of winter, and early in the spring. It is, as Adams correctly states, fairly common in winter on the lakes and rivers of the Punjab, from the Peshawer valley to the Jumna. Great numbers used in old days to haunt the Najjafgarh Jhíl, near Delhi, and they still occur there yearly, though in greatly diminished numbers, since the completion of the drainage works. It is comparatively rare in Sindh, (except perhaps on the Indus, and at the Manchar Lake,) and scarcely less so in Northern Gujerat. I have no record of its occurrence in Cutch, Káthiáwar, Rajputana, Khandesh, the Central India Agency, the Central Provinces, or the North-West Provinces south of the Jumna; but in the Doab, Rohilkhand and Oudh it is a regular, but scarce, visitant. I have no record of its occurrence anywhere else within the limits of the Empire, save Jerdon's statement that it has been killed at Cuttack, where, however, it can scarcely have been more than an accidental straggler.

It is said to be very common in winter on the lakes and rivers of Central China (it does not appear to occur far south), and to pass Pekin in spring in very large numbers. Prjevalski met with it on passage at the end of March, and during the early part of April at the Dalai-Nor and Lake Hanka, but did

---

* I cannot follow those authorities who treat this species as congeneric with the Mergansers. The much shorter, stouter and differently shaped bill, the different dentition (if I may apply this term to the arrangement of the lamellæ) and the tail of 16 instead of 18 feathers, seem to me to justify generic separation.

Since this was written I find that Naumann asserts that the tail, as often as not contains 18 feathers. I have only noted the number from six fresh specimens, and in all of these it was 16; but in over 30 specimens in our Museum, not one has more than this number. Still Naumann is a great authority. and probably had good grounds for what he wrote.

not notice it further south at the Koko-Nor. It is common in winter in Japan, and in Eastern and South-Eastern Siberia on passage, and some certainly breed there as Middendorff had evidence of this at Udskoj and the Shantar Islands (in about 55 degrees, North Latitude); and Radde also says that some few remain to breed in the south of East Siberia, but where the bulk of the birds, seen in winter in China and India, breed, is still uncertain. In Eastern Turkestan they are merely winter visitants, and apparently pretty common, as everyone who has been at Yárkand at that season has procured or noticed them. In Western Turkestan it is also common in winter, (except in the south-eastern districts,) and occurs in lakes up to an elevation of 4,000 feet. It has been observed in Afghanistan near Cabul, Ghazni, Khelat-i-Ghilzai and Kandahar, but not as yet in Beluchistan. St. John shot it at Teheran, and as it breeds in the neighbourhood of Astrachan, there can be no doubt that, though not included by either Ménétries or Eichwald in their lists, it does really occur on the Caspian. It appears to be found on the coasts of Asia Minor, and has been procured on that of Palestine. No one has yet observed it in Egypt, or anywhere in Northern Africa, except in Algeria and Tangiers,* where it is *said* to occur as a rare winter visitant.

It occurs in winter as a straggler in Great Britain and Ireland, and is found at that season, or on passage, pretty well all over Europe, though chiefly near the coasts; but it only appears to breed in Northern and Eastern Finland and Northern and Eastern Russia, in the latter as far south as Astrachan.

THE SMEW arrives late even in Upper India, and the earliest date on which I have noted having seen it, and that near Jhelum in the North-West Punjab, is the 3rd of November. It also, I think, leaves early, as the latest date on which I have killed it is the 27th of March. But it is, comparatively speaking, rare and very irregular in its migrations, there being scarcely a dozen places, that I know of, where you are always sure of finding it, even between the 1st December and the end of February, so that I cannot speak with any great certainty.

Comparatively few old males are seen in India. I have numbers of notes like the following:—"Soj *(south of the Mainpuri District).*—February 3rd, one adult, three young males, two females, out of a flock containing three adult males and twenty or more females and young."—*Najjafgarh Jhil,* 30th December 1867. —"A large flock, between thirty and forty, but containing only four black and white males. Had only a common heavy native "*doongah*" (row-boat), and could never get within one hundred

---

* *Vide* Dresser, who says that Irby records it thence; but Irby says nothing about it in his Orn. S. of Gib., p. 206.

yards, though I followed them about for an hour. At last fired a 2¼oz. B. B. wire cartridge out of my long No. 8 bore with seven drams of powder as the flock turned sideways, and killed one and crippled two others, all young birds, distance *over* one hundred yards," and so on; and only once have I noted. "Strange to say, seven out of the twelve were old males, and as I worked up to the flock, I noticed that, for once, fully half the birds were black and white."

Of many migratory species, the mass of those that go farthest south are birds of the year,* and the great prevalence of these amongst the flocks of this species that are met with here may be explained by the fact that Upper India is the southernmost region which this species regularly visits.

They are eminently gregarious, and are always seen in flocks of from seven to forty, and rarely in larger or smaller parties than from about a dozen to about twenty. Large rivers, like the Indus, (I have never seen them on the Jumna or Ganges) or large lakes covering 20 square miles and upwards of country, are what they chiefly affect; and on these, even though shot at repeatedly, they will remain for months. I have, however, in unfrequented localities, occasionally seen them on ordinary good-sized jhíls, covering, perhaps, barely a single square mile, but these they desert directly they are at all worried.

As a rule, they are wary birds, and difficult to approach. They keep in deep water, far away from any cover, and you can only shoot them from a boat. They can swim faster than any ordinary up-country native boat can be propelled, and faster than one can paddle a punt when lying down. They keep a very sharp look-out, never diving *en masse*, but some always watching, whilst the rest are under water, and, as a rule, the moment they see *any* boat they swim away. In the grey of the morning, when a light stratum of mist lies along the surface of the water, you may creep up in a punt within shot, unnoticed; but then one is very apt, peering through the mist in the twilight, to misjudge distances, and generally make a mess of the matter. Once knowing of a large party of Smews, I went after them early, and as I thought found and fired at them, to find directly I stood up, that I had killed half a boat-load of stilts, small paddy birds, and all kinds of useless waders, standing up to their bellies in the water on a hidden shoal, which, as they loomed through the mist, I could have sworn were the Smews. If you wait, as one does with most other fowl, till you can make certain what they are, they see you, and away they go swimming with little, but their heads and necks visible, faster than you can paddle. But at times, I presume when they have

* Mr. Wallace (Geog. Dist. An., p. 26) seems to take an opposite view, and holds that the young birds do not go as far as the old; but I can only say, that here in India, it is the young birds that straggle, in the case of many species, *furthest* south.

never previously been fired at, you can get within shot without difficulty in a punt, and even by a little management in a common native boat, and you can always get a shot by sailing past them at about 40 yards distance.

They swim and dive splendidly, and if only a single boat is after them, they will constantly stick to the water even after being fired at, rising perhaps at the moment, but dropping within 50 yards, and instantly diving to re-appear from fifty to a hundred yards beyond the place at which they vanished. They come up scattered, but all swim converging on one point, and in a few minutes are swimming away in a close lump, just as before you fired. But if two or three boats hem them in, they generally rise, and, if the place is small, disappear—if large, circle round and light again a couple of miles off. They spring out of the water with ease, and fly with great rapidity, quite as quickly and easily as the Common Teal, but almost silently, and with less of a perceptible wing rustle than any species I know. This is probably due to their very narrow, pointed, somewhat curved wings, by which they can be instantly recognized when flying. They are very active, restless birds, almost always busy swimming and diving. I have never seen one on land, but I once saw a number asleep on the water about midday in March.

They feed entirely under water. I have examined many without ever finding any vegetable matter in their gizzards, or anything but small fish and water-insects, chiefly a kind of cricket (?), and these they pursue under water with astonishing rapidity, as may be guessed by watching in clear water a hard-pressed, slightly-winged bird, when turning it dives under the boat. No duck can touch them at diving, even Grebes and Cormorant, and I have watched both perform the same manœuvre, are scarcely so rapid in their movements under water. They use their wings in diving, though they do not spread them fully, so that you must not judge of their performance by birds with wings injured above the carpal joint, but where the injury is merely on the carpus, sufficient to prevent flight, but not otherwise serious, their diving is a thing to watch.

"During flight," says Jerdon, quoting I know not whom, Pallas probably, "it continually utters its peculiar bell-like call; hence it is called the Bell-duck in Northern Asia." If this is correct, this call must be peculiar to the breeding season. Here its call, seldom heard except when the bird is disturbed, is a short grating cry, about intermediate between the caw of a rook and the quack of a duck, not very unlike that of the Pochard, but less deep, and sharper.

VERY LITTLE is known of the nidification of this species beyond what Wolley gathered from the people of Finland through whom he procured the eggs. Apparently they nest in holes in trees, which they line with their own down, and in which, during the latter part of May and the first-half of June, they lay seven or more eggs.

The eggs are extremely like those of the Wigeon, but rather smaller on the average, smoother and more polished, more as regards texture like those of the Goosander. The eggs seem also to be often characterized by a thin calcareous coating outside the egg-shell proper, of the same nature as that so conspicuous, in some eggs of the Common Swan. Four of Wolley's eggs measure 2·04 to 2·05 by 1·42 to 1·52.

It is quite *possible* that in other places it may, as stated by Temminck and others, breed on the ground or over the water in thick rushes on the borders of lakes and rivers.

THE FOLLOWING is a *resumé of* a large series of measurements in the flesh:—

Males.—Length, 17·0 to 18·1; expanse, 26·3 to 28·7; wing, 7·55 to 8·32; tail from vent, 3·3 to 4·1; tarsus, 1·2 to 1·31; bill from gape, 1·63 to 1·72; weight, 1 lb. 4 ozs. to 1 lb. 12 ozs.

Females.—Length, 15·5 to 16·75; expanse, 23·75 to 26·25; wing, 7·01 to 7·3; tail from vent, 3·3 to 3·9; tarsus, 1·11 to 1·19; bill from gape, 1·48 to 1·6; weight, 1 lb. to 1 lb. 6½ ozs.

In fourteen specimens I have recorded the irides as brown or deep brown, in one as red brown, and *I* have observed no other colour. Macgillivray records it from fresh specimens examined by himself as red and bright red. Naumann says that in the young it is dark brown, (but many of my specimens were full-plumaged males,) then, (and permanently in the females,) dark nut brown, in males of the second year brownish grey, later light ash grey, and in very old males a pure pearl colour or bluish white.

The bill is, as a rule, a delicate pale plumbeous, sometimes a clearer and bluer tint, sometimes duskier, and in some specimens, young of both sexes and old females, it has been almost black.

The nail is generally brownish, horny whitish at the extreme tip, but in some it has been bluish white throughout, and in some almost black throughout.

The legs and feet vary from pale blue grey to plumbeous and dark lavender; the webs, except just where they join the toes, being dusky to black, and the claws brownish black. Often there is an olive tinge on the tarsi, and occasionally, in the young only I think, both these and the toes exhibit small dusky spots and patches.

THE PLATE is, on the whole, good, but the female figured is immature. In the really old female the entire loral region is blackish brown, and in no female is the head quite so red as in the plate; it should be browner. In the old female too the base of the neck all round and back are greyer, and the latter more uniform, the paler margins to the feathers being nearly obsolete. Some males show rather more white on the wing and scapulars than the specimen figured, and the vermiculated feathers shown at the side of the rump belong to the flanks, and would hardly, in the live bird, show up in the position in which they are shown, though they did so, being slightly displaced, in the skin from which the drawing was made.

In India we get many most interesting and beautiful specimens of young males changing from the female to the adult male garb. Dresser's supposed old female from Moscow is clearly one of these.

NO OTHER species of this genus, which is a purely Palæarctic one, (whether one straggler has or has not occurred in America,) is at present known to exist.

MERGUS CASTOR

THE GOOSANDER OR MERGANSER.

Mergus merganser, *Linné.*

Vernacular Names.—[? ; Ala ghaz aurdak, (*Turki,*) Yárkand.]

THE Goosander is a permanent resident of the Himalayas from Gilgit to Sadiya, breeding in the higher valleys, and in the winter making its appearance in every considerable river near its debouch from the mountains, wandering pretty generally well down into the submontane tracts, and straying eastwards, at any rate, to the southernmost limits of the temperate zone, or even just inside the Tropics.

In the larger rivers of the Himalayas, though nowhere numerically very abundant, they are so universally distributed high up in summer, low down in winter, that it is needless to specify the particular localities, over 70 in number, whence I have received them, or where they have been reported to have been obtained.

Outside the Himalayas, I have received them, or know for certain of their having been obtained from the Peshawar Valley in the Cabul River; near Attock, Kalabagh, and just above Dera Ismail Khan in the Indus; near Sealkot in the Chenab and smaller streams; the Kangra Valley; below Roopur in the Sutlej; Dehra Dún, not only in the Ganges from Rukikes to below Hardwar, but in the interior; Pilibhit in the Sardeh; the Sandi Jhíl, near Hurdui (*Irby*); the Kosi River towards the north of the Purneah district; the Western Doars (where they appear to be extremely numerous)*; the Monas in the Kamrup

* Mr. J. R. Cripps writes:—"In the Western Doars I have seen numbers of this species in flocks of from 50 to 200 The furthest point from the hills that I have seen them has been at Ram Sahai Hât, which is thirteen miles from the nearest range of hills, and past which the 'Juldoka' river flows. This river has a sandy and pebbly bottom, and these birds were to be seen feeding along its course during the early forenoon only. They appeared to stick to the spots where the stream ran over a bank of pebbles, and their manner of fishing was exactly as described by Mr. Ball, who says: "In the Subanrika they may be seen in parties swimming against the stream, and all diving together, apparently to catch fish. The sudden disappearance of the whole flock at the same moment gives the idea that they work in concert in hunting the fish which are coming down with the stream. Their flight is very rapid. They arrived in November and left in March."

District; some stream north of Lakhimpur; close to Sadiya; numerous localities near the bases of the Gáro and Khasi Hills, on both their northern and southern faces and well inside them;* near Jamtara about 156 miles from Calcutta on the E. I. line of Railway (*Brooks*); at a large lake seven miles from Burrakur, on the Grand Trunk Road where there were some hundreds (*Parker*); on the Damuda in Bankurah and Bardwan; in Manbhum and Dhalbhum on the Subanrika; Lohardugga (*Ball*); Singhbhum, (Chaibassa, *Tickell*); the Rer River, Sirguja (*Ball*); the Mahanadi, near Arung (Raipur), and further down almost to Sambalpur, (*Blewitt*); this latter district north of the Mahanadi, (*Ball*); Palamow, (*Money*); and the Sone River near Dehree-on-Sone (*E. Stewart, C.S.—W. Forsyth*). Lastly† Ajmere, near which place Major O'Moore Creagh, V.C., shot a fine male in a large tank.

Of course the record is still most imperfect, and I have little doubt that the Merganser will prove to straggle during the cold season, one year or another, to most *suitable* localities in the Empire, north of say the 22nd degree North Latitude. South of this (except, as already mentioned, on the Mahanadi) we have as yet no reason to believe that it ever occurs.

Outside our limits we know it to be common in China, extending as far south as Amoy, and visiting Japan also. Prjevalski found it in Mongolia, in Kansu, and down at the Koko-Nor, but it does not appear to breed in any of these localities. Throughout Southern and South-eastern Siberia it is common, breeding in many places. In winter it is not uncommon in the streams about Kashgar in Eastern Turkestan, whence it was said to migrate in summer, and breed about Lake Lob; and it appears to occur throughout Western Turkestan, breeding in the eastern districts up to an elevation of 8,500 feet. Stoliczka found it at Lake Sirikul (Lake Victoria of Woods) on the Pamir (elevation 10,000 to 11,000 feet) early in May, where also it was said to breed. It is not uncommon in the larger streams of Afghanistan, and is a regular visitant to the Mekran Coast, where Bishop observed it for three successive years at Chabour and Jask.‡

Beyond this we have no record of its occurrence in Asia or any part of Africa, except Algeria and Tangiers, to which it straggles in severe winters.

Excepting Iceland, it occurs pretty well throughout Europe (south of the Arctic Circle) summering and breeding (probably, except in Denmark and Northern Germany, scarcely south of the 55th degree North Latitude) in the north and wintering in

* Davison found a pair on a large stream between Shillong and Chirapunji, at an elevation of about 5,000 feet, in December.

† No doubt the occurrence of this species at Kurrachee, where one was shot at Manoura Point by Captain Bishop, was announced in STRAY FEATHERS. But an examination of this specimen, which was kindly sent me, proves it to be female of *Mergus serrator*, the Red-breasted Merganser.

‡ It is quite possible, however, that these were referable to the next species.

the south. Throughout the temperate zone of North America it occurs similarly, wintering as far south as Northern Mexico and California, and breeding northwards to places little south of the Arctic Circle.

Broadly speaking its range is the temperate zone of the Northern Hemisphere.

IN THE Himalayas you meet with the Merganser at all seasons; in summer in the higher valleys and fresh-water lakes, at 10,000 feet elevation and upwards; in winter in the low river valleys at elevations of 700 to 2,000 feet; and in spring and autumn at intermediate elevations. Outside these mountains you seldom, if ever, see them before December or later than March. You meet them most commonly, I think, in small parties of seven to twenty; but I have seen single birds at times, not unfrequently pairs, and twice large flocks.

As far as I can judge they almost exclusively frequent rivers or lakes, carrying a good head of water, and with more or less rocky, pebbly, or coarse sandy bottoms. I have never yet seen one in any river where it flowed through clay, mud, or alluvial soil. I have never myself seen them in any lake, but they do occur in such, and out at sea, on rocky coasts—further out, or closer in, according to the weather.

On rivers, as on the Ganges above Hurdwar, they will float down with the stream for a couple of miles, and if not hungry, they rise and fly back again; but more commonly they fish their way back, diving incessantly the whole way; and despite their activity, taking a long time to make their way back to where they started from. When gorged they often sit on some rock in the middle of the water, sitting very upright and Cormorant-like, often half-opening their wings to the sun. In the interior, where you find them in smaller streams, they are rarely in parties of more than three or four—most generally at that time in pairs—and then they are either flying up stream, or floating down, twisting round and round in the rapids, or fishing vigorously in some deep pool near the foot of some waterfall or rapid.

When floating down stream they are often nearly as high out of the water as a common duck; but when swimming—and especially swimming against stream—they sit very deep in the water much like Cormorants; and if wounded and pursued, never raise more than the head and neck above the surface. They are famous divers, quite Cormorant-like in this matter, though I think hardly so agile as the Smew. On land one only sees them resting near the water's edge, and when disturbed they shuffle on their breasts into the river. I do not think that they can walk at all. Anyhow I have always seen them just half-glide, half-wriggle, breast foremost, and I think touching the rock, into the water. They rise heavily from the water, taking many yards, during which they flap along the surface before they get clear of it; and many more (unless when rising against a strong wind) before they get up about ten or fifteen yards, at which height they commonly fly up stream. When once on the wing their flight is strong and fairly rapid, though not to compare with that of the Smew.

The great bulk of their food is fish, good-sized ones, often five and six inches long, and, as in the case of the Smew, there are always plenty of pebbles in their gizzards. I have found a kind of cray-fish and water-insects in some I have examined; but mostly they had fed only on fishes from three to six, or nearly six inches in length.

Of course they catch these entirely by diving, and while at times where there has been a good-sized party, I have seen them all disappear *en masse*. I have more often seen several diving quite independently of each other, and it seemed to me some keeping watch while the others dived.

They are very wary birds, and in large rivers (I never myself saw them on any lake) scarcely approachable; and yet, if you are drifting down in a boat trolling and apparently paying no attention to them, they will often fly over within easy shot, until, at any rate, you have thus fired at them once or twice.

In the interior, in comparatively narrow streams, it is often easy to stalk them; and when thus suddenly surprised at close quarters, they emit a harsh croaking cry, rarely heard at other times, which rings out loudly, even amidst the roar of the rushing waters.

Only once or twice have I tried to eat them. They are generally very fat, and the fat is abominably fishy and rank; but if they are *skinned*, soaked in two or three waters, and then stewed with onions and a little Worcester sauce, they will furnish an abundant meal to a hungry man—a thing worth knowing, as one occasionally gets them on a blank day in places where nothing is to be got within fifty miles, and when you cannot afford to kill one of the baggage sheep. However let no one try to eat them when anything better is to be got, as only necessity renders them tolerable.

As yet no one seems to have taken their eggs within our limits, though they breed in numbers, in our larger rivers, at elevations of 10,000 feet and upwards (and perhaps even lower), and in some of the elevated lakes, as the young, from nestlings to nearly fully-fledged birds, have been occasionally shot and caught, in such places between the middle of June and the end of July.

I do not know for certain how long they incubate, but I should guess that with us they lay from about the last week in April to the middle of May, but some may lay earlier and later according to elevation.

"The nest, according to Mr. Selby," to quote Yarrell, "is constructed near to the edge of the water, of a mass of grass, roots, and other materials, mixed and lined with down. It is placed sometimes among stones, sometimes in long grass, or under the cover of bushes, and when the locality affords them in the stumps or hollows of decayed trees."

Acerbi, also quoted by Yarrell, says :—

"The *Mergus merganser*, instead of building a small nest like the ducks, on the banks, or among the reeds and rushes, chooses to lay her eggs in the trunk of an old tree, in which time, or the hand of man, has made such an excavation as she can conveniently enter. The person that waylays the bird for her eggs places against a fir or pine tree, somewhere near the bank of the river, a decayed trunk, with a hole in its middle; the bird enters and lays her eggs in it; presently the peasant comes, and takes away the eggs, leaving, however, one or two. The bird returns, and, finding but a single egg, lays two or three more. She is again robbed as before, but a few are left at last for the increase of her family. As soon as the eggs are hatched, the mother takes the chicks gently in her bill, carries and lays them down at the foot of the tree, when she teaches them the way to the river, in which they instantly swim with an astonishing facility."

And Dresser tells us that "it breeds late in April or early in May, and makes its nest in the vicinity of water, either on the ground, or else it uses the hollow of a tree, the latter being, so far as I know, the usual place selected by this species for the purposes of nidification; and it frequently deposits its eggs in the nest-boxes hung up by the peasantry in the north of Scandinavia and Russia. When at Uleaborg, however, I obtained eggs from nests on the ground, in a hollow scratched out and filled with down. When it nests in a tree it frequently makes use of a suitable hollow at some altitude from the ground, and fills it with a considerable quantity of down, on which the eggs are deposited; when the young are hatched they are carefully carried by the female bird in her bill down to the water; and these young birds are able at once to swim, and even dive, with ease."

Dybowski, writing of this species in Southern Siberia, says :—

"It nests on the ground, amongst the grass, building with dry grass and lining the interior thoroughly with down. The female lays nine eggs and sits close. They arrive about the middle of April, and remain until Lake Baikal freezes towards the end of December."

In the treeless and grassless localities in which we mostly see them in summer, I should not be surprised if they bred like the Brahminy in holes in rocks, but holes near to and not very high above the water.

The eggs are said to vary in number from seven to twelve They are broad, regular ovals, with very fine, smooth, satiny shells of a uniform buffy white or creamy yellow. They vary from 2·5 to 2·9 in length, and from 1·66 to 1·9 in breadth, but the average of eleven is 2·7 by 1·8 nearly.

THE MALES are considerably larger and heavier than the females. The following are the usual particulars of adults of both sexes :—

Males.—Length, 25·0 to 28·1 ; expanse, 35·6 to 40·8 ; wing, 10·95 to 12·1 ; tail from vent, 4·8 to 5·9 ; tarsus, 1·81 to 2·03 ; bill from gape, 2·77 to 2·93 ; weight, 2 lbs. 12 ozs. to 3 lbs. 5 ozs.

Females.—Length, 22·9 to 25·0 ; expanse, 34·5 to 37·8 ; wing, 9·8 to 10·95 ; tail from vent, 4·6 to 5·65 ; tarsus, 1·68 to 1·83 ; bill from gape, 2·25 to 2·6 ; weight, 2lbs. to 2 lbs. 10 ozs.

The bill is, according to age, a brighter or duller, lighter or deeper red, almost vermilion in some, a cinnabar or deep blood red in others. The nail, and a broader or narrower stripe along the culmen, from the nail to the forehead, brownish black, dusky or black. In some this stripe is only indicated. There is often more or less of dusky on the lower mandible, which in some is entirely of this colour, but in others almost wholly orange.

The irides, brown in the young, grow redder with age, and in old males become a deep red with scarcely a tinge of brown.

The legs and feet, including the webs, are bright vermilion in the old of both sexes, perhaps rather duller in the females, and reddish orange in younger birds. The claws greyish or horny white, brownish or reddish towards their bases.

THE PLATE is on the whole fair, but the rufous on the side of the female's head wants toning down a shade with brown. The pale yellow tinting on the upper part of the wing of the male, which should be pure white, is a too faithful, truly Chinese, copy of grease stains on the specimen sent to be figured.

In life, when at rest, the male never shows so much of the grey of the lower back and rump as the picture does. The young birds are like the female, but have rather smaller crests. The plate does scant justice to the crest of the adult female, which is *far* longer than in the adult male, and in one specimen now before me fully three inches in length.

We get in February young males just like old females, and with comparatively long crests, but with velvet black feathers, breaking out in the interscapulary region and tiny black feathers beginning to peep out on the throat.

In July and August the old males have assumed a dress very like that of the female, but they are distinguishable at once by their greater size, white wings, much as in their normal plumage, much darker interscapulary region, dusky lores, and a dark band round the base of the neck immediately below the chestnut of the upper neck.

In fresh specimens the whole white plumage of the neck and lower parts of the male is often overspread with a beautiful salmon, at times pinker, at times more buffy, but this almost wholly disappears in skins.

THE RED-BREASTED MERGANSER.

Mergus serrator, *Linné.*

Vernacular Names.—[None.]

ON the 24th of November 1875, Captain Bishop shot a female Merganser, at Manoura Point, Kurrachee. The specimen was preserved, and some years later kindly sent to me by Mr. Murray, of the Kurrachee Museum. I did not examine it closely at the time, and it was only, when writing my article on the preceding species, and closely scrutinizing our large series of the Goosander, that I discovered that Captain Bishop's bird was unmistakably a female of the Red-breasted Merganser.

No other instance of its occurrence within our limits is known.

It is common in winter throughout China (as it likewise is in Japan), but Pére David tells us that he never succeeded in procuring an adult male there. Probably chiefly the birds of the year visit China. At Lake Hanka, Prjevalski found it scarce. In Mongolia he only saw it at the Dalai-Nor, and in Kansu he met with only a single specimen, a young one. Throughout Southern and South-eastern Siberia, where it breeds freely, it is more common than the preceding species. It has not yet been recorded from Yárkand, Western Turkestan, Afghanistan or Beluchistan (unless, as is possible, the birds observed by Bishop at Chabour and Jask on the Mekran Coast belonged to *this*, and not, as he believed, the preceding species,) nor even in Persia, the Caspian or Asia Minor ; but I suspect it will prove to occur as a rare straggler in severe winters to most, if not all, of these localities.

On the coasts of Palestine it is common ; it has been observed in the Sinaitic Peninsula, and has occurred accidentally in Egypt and Algeria.

It occurs throughout Europe, elsewhere on passage or as a winter visitant only, but breeding in Scotland, the Shetland and Færoe Islands, very abundantly in Iceland, in Denmark, Sweden and Norway right up to the North Cape, the southern littoral of the Baltic, Finland and Northern Russia. On the whole perhaps it is more common in the north, and less so in the south than the Goosander.

In North America its range is similar to that of the preceding species, but it occurs in Greenland, which the Goosander does not; and, though recorded from California, hardly travels quite so far south in winter.

Generally, I think, it may be said to have a rather more northerly range, to extend and breed further north, and to straggle less frequently far south than the Goosander; and it is a species which I should only expect to meet with, within our limits, as a rare straggler.

THE HABITS of this species seem to differ little from those of the Goosander, but they are said to fly with great swiftness, and make a well-marked whistling sound with the wings, barely perceptible, according to my experience, even when quite close in the case of the Smew, and very faint even in that of the Goosander.

Au reste, it will be sufficient to reproduce some remarks of Macgillivray's on this species:—

"In the outer Hebrides, in March, April, and part of May, and again in autumn, I have seen very large flocks in the small sandy bays, fishing day after day for sand eels. They sit in the water much in the manner of the Cormorants, but without sinking so deep, unless when alarmed, and advance with great speed....You may suppose us to be jammed into the crack of a rock, with our hats off, and we peeping cunningly at the advanced guard of the squadron which is rounding the point at no great distance. There they glide along, and now, coming into shallow water, they poke their heads into it, raise them, and seem to look around, lest some masked battery should open upon them unawares. Now, one has plunged with a jerk, another, one here, one there—at length the whole flock. Now start up, and if you wish a shot, run to the water's edge and get down among the sea-weed behind a stone, while I from this eminence survey the submersed flock. How smartly they shoot along under the water, with partially outspread wings, some darting right forward, others wheeling or winding, most of them close to the sandy bottom, but a few near the surface. Some flounders, startled by the hurricane, shoot right out to sea, without being pursued. But there, one is up, another, and I must sink to repose in some hole. How prettily they rise to the surface—one here, another there, a whole covey at once emerging, and all without the least noise or splutter. But they are far beyond shot range. However, having come near the next rocky point, they now turn, dive in succession, and will scour the little bay until arriving here, at hand, they will be liable to receive a salute that will astonish them. A whole minute has elapsed, half another; but now one appears, two, many, the whole flock, and into the midst of them pours the duck shot, while the noise of the explosion seems to roll along the hill side. In a twinkling all are down, save six that float on the water, four dead, one spinning round, and the other striving in vain to dive. In less than two minutes they are seen emerging, more than a quarter of a mile out at sea, and presently again they are out of sight. On such occasions they seldom fly."

According to Naumann their cry is a loudly resounding guttural koerrr or gerrr, heard chiefly during flight, occasionally on rising, and more often from females and young than males, which latter in the pairing season often only emit a single peculiarly hollow low note.

THEY BREED, speaking generally, from about the 50th degree North Latitude to, in places, well within the Arctic Circle. They nest sometimes on the ground, in grass or other low cover, or at the base of small low-boughed trees, sometimes in hollows of trees, or fallen trunks, and sometimes in clefts of rocks *(Dybowski)*; when on the ground the nest is composed of tiny twigs, or fine grass stems, or moss and lichen, or all these mixed, more or less intermingled and well lined with down. When placed in holes there is usually only a bed of down. They lay in May or June, (early or late according to season and locality) eight to twelve or more eggs, which are creamy yellow, more or less tinged with green or grey, or greyish green; moderately broad, very regular ovals, smooth to the touch, though less so than those of the Goosander, varying from 2·45 to 2·8 in length and from 1·68 to 1·82 in breadth, and averaging about 2·57 by 1·75.

I HAVE no original particulars to furnish of this species; the following I compile from European and American specimens and sources:—

Males.—Length, 24·0 to 26·0; expanse, 29·0 to 32·5; wing, 9·0 to 10·0; tail, from insertion of feathers, 3·1 to 4·2; tarsus, 1·8 to 2·05; bill at front, along culmen, 2·4 to 2·5; weight, *(Naumann)* a little over 2lbs.

Females.—Length, 22·0 to 23·5; expanse, 28·0 to 31·0; wing, 8·5 to 9·3; tail, from insertion of feathers, 2·7 to 3·6; tarsus, 1·66 to 1·83; bill, as above, 2·1 to 2·3.

In the male, the bill varies from orange red to deep vermilion, is more or less dusky on the ridge, and has the nail varying from pale yellowish grey to almost black; the feet vary similarly to the bill, and are brighter externally, paler internally, and duller on the webs; the claws are light grey, duller, and browner or redder towards their bases.

In the young and females there is more dusky on the upper mandible, where the red is often only a lateral band, and the feet are duller coloured than in the adult male.

THE PLATE.—The occurrence of this species within, or within a thousand miles of, our limits was not suspected till long after all the plates had been executed, and far too late to enable us to furnish one.

Both sexes resemble those of the Goosander, but may be distinguished by their smaller size, and bills much thinner in proportion to their length, especially at the base.

The adult males, moreover, are at once to be recognized by the conspicuous light brownish rufous band round the base of the neck, narrow behind, broadening out in front into a crop-patch, which band is everywhere adorned by black streaks; by a narrow black band stretching down the back of the neck, a greater length of which is white than in the Goosander: by the flanks (pure white in this latter) strongly vermiculated with greyish black in the present species, and by the much longer and differently shaped crest and other minor differences.

But we are very unlikely to get adult males in this country, and the young and females far more closely resemble those of the Goosander.

They may, however, be distinguished by their smaller size, (they weigh about two-thirds of what the others do,) and differently shaped bills; by their browner crowns and crests; by their entire upper surface being a tolerably dark brown, or ashy brown, or dusky slatey with a brownish tinge instead of the clear, light blue grey of the Goosander, and by the white wing patch composed of the terminal portions of the secondaries and their greater coverts, which in the Goosander forms a single patch, but in the present species (the white tips of the coverts not quite extending to where the white tippings of the quills commence,) is crossed by a dark bar, broader anteriorly, narrower posteriorly, dividing it into two.

With this explanation of the leading differences between this and the preceding species, it seems needless to trouble my readers with any further detailed description.

BESIDES THESE two species of Merganser there is the North American *M. cucullatus*, which has straggled to England, the South American *M. braziliensis*, and one from the Auckland Islands, to say nothing of a supposed species, *M. squamatus*, described from China by Gould, which is, I believe, still held to be of somewhat doubtful validity.

SCALOPAX ½ RUSTICOLA

THE WOODCOCK.

———o———

Scolopax rusticola, *Linné.*

———o———

Vernacular Names.—[Sim-titar, Tutatar? (Jerdon); Sham-titar, Sham-kukra, *Kumaun;* Chinjarol, *Chamba;* Kangtruk, *Manipur;* Wilati-chaha, *Chittagong;* Murgh-i-zerak, *Persia;*]

———o———

A RESIDENT during the summer of the higher wooded ranges of the Himalayas at elevations of ten thousand feet and upwards, from Gilgit* to the western borders of Bhútan (and probably much further east), the Woodcock retreats in autumn to the lower valleys; and while some spend the winter there, and in the Dúns, Terais, Bhaburs, and similar submontane tracts that skirt the bases of these mountains,

---

* I select a few out of the mass of notes I have accumulated in regard to the occurrence of this species in the Himalayas.

Amongst the birds found by him in Kashmir west of the Indus which Major J. Biddulph enumerates in a letter to me, is included the Woodcock.

"Generally distributed over the Kashmir Mountains in woods and forests where it breeds."—*A. Leith Adams.*

"Woodcock come down to Chamba, which is in the valley of the Ravi, about 8,000 feet high, whenever there is severe weather in the higher hills. They do not remain here for the winter, but keep coming and going. After snow and rain they are to be found in good numbers in the gardens and low lands by the river, but if it clears up they disappear again. This winter, for instance, they came down at Christmas time and disappeared early in January, not coming back till the middle of February, when there was a great deal of snow. They are very tame and not easy to flush. They allow the natives to come very near them, without rising. I have shot them in my own garden in the middle of the town. They breed of course in the higher wooded hills, but I have not yet tracked them to any of their breeding haunts."—*C. H. T. Marshall.*

"Pretty common throughout the year, at one elevation or another in Kullu, and the valley of the Beas.

"They breed in the Tos Forests near the limits of vegetation; in the summer they come flitting round the camp fires at night, like great bats. They descend into the upper valley about November, and the first general snowfall sends them down into the lower valley. The end of January is about the best time for them. The largest bag that I know of was 33 to two guns between Nuggur and Ryson; a good many others were missed. If the season be at all favourable, one is pretty sùre of flushing a dozen or so in the course of a day in their especial haunts. I have often come across them squatted beside the streams like frogs, and flushed them within a dozen yards or so, more particularly in a hard frost.

"A portion of those seen in the Kullu Valley during the winter may be migrants from further north, but great numbers breed with us."—*A. Grahame Young.*

"About the end of November I have shot them in several of the valleys below Simla, and in the Sutlej below Kotgarh. During the winter, they are constantly

considerable numbers migrate during the colder months to hilly, well-wooded and watered regions all over the Empire, as far south as Ceylon on the one hand, and Tavoy (at least and probably much further) on the other.

It does not appear to be common in Ceylon, but has been shot there on the higher hills; in the Assamboo Hills* it is fairly common; on the Palnis† rare. It is pretty abundant on the Nílgiris‡ and on the higher hills of Coorg, and occurs, though

---

brought in for sale to Simla, one man sometimes bringing in three or four."—*A. O. Hume.*

"The Woodcock is rather common in the Upper Sutlej valley in the forests of the lesser ranges between four thousand and ten thousand feet; it breeds at and above Chini, and I think I have also seen it in Western Thibet."—*F. Stoliczka.*

"I have killed many in the lower valleys below Mussooree during the cold season, and a few in the Dún, in the *Siwaliks*, and I once bagged five in a single morning along the Lat-ka-pani below Almorah."—*A. O. Hume.*

"They are to be seen in summer in considerable numbers in all the higher hills north of Mussooree, where they breed near the snows. I have repeatedly seen their nests and eggs in former times. Later in the year they descend into the lower valleys, and may occasionally be shot anywhere in suitable places, right down to the plains."—*Frederick Wilson.*

"I took the nest, as mentioned in my paper, on the 2nd of July, in Kumaon near Kemo, elevation 10,000 to 11,000 feet, which is opposite the Namick Salt Springs."—*A. Anderson.*

"Common in Kumaun, resorting to the lower hills and valleys in the cold season. In May I have seen a Woodcock and a Moonal on the wing at the same time." —*L. H. Irby.*

"In June 1855 I got a Woodcock, with nest and eggs, in Nepal at about 11,000 feet elevation. It is usual to find the breeding birds further up and more out of the influence of the tropical rains in scrub rhododendron. I never before got one so near rain or the central region."—*B. Hodgson.*

"The Woodcock arrives in the valley of Nepal early in November, and leaves at the end of February. It frequents most of the small woods in the central part of the valley, and may be found along the foot of the hills, where damp thin tree forest occurs. Its favourite haunts are the boggy bits of ground at the edge of woods. and in such a spot I shot a Woodcock in the Residency grounds within a few yards of some houses. It is not at all common in the valley, and can only be obtained by hard work and with the aid of many beaters."—*J. Scully.*

"The Woodcock breeds in the higher hills in Native Sikhim where my hunters have shot them in summer, though they have as yet failed to secure the eggs. During the winter they are not very rare in the lower valleys, and many specimens have been brought me. They go down right to the plains. I have had two or three killed in the Terai and one in the Bhútan Duars."—*L. Mandelli.*

"I myself saw them regularly every evening at Rinchingpoon, in Sikhim, in November 1860."—*R. C. Beavan.*

* "Woodcock are pretty common in the Assamboo Hills, but only at the highest elevations from November to March."—*Frank W. Bourdillon.*

† "I flushed a Woodcock in the Kodaikánal in 1867. Afterwards one was obtained there by Mr. Levinge; but they are certainly rare on the Palnis."—*S. B. Fairbank.*

‡ "The Woodcock arrives later and leaves earlier than the Snipe on the Nílgiris, coming in late in October or early in November, and departing again at the latest by the end of February. They are never very abundant, but with the aid of a couple or more of bustling spaniels and a few beaters, a few can almost always be had, when they are in season.

"They frequent marshy ground and the banks of streamlets in forest. Though occasionally one is met with in the depths of the larger extents of forest, yet, as a rule, I think that they confine themselves to the outskirts and to the narrow strips of jungle running down the ravines between the hills, and which (the jungles and not hills) are always more or less marshy towards their bases.

perhaps in smaller numbers, in the Sheveroy and Javadi* Hills in the Salem District, in the Anamalis, and in the Burghur and Hosenúr Hills in the Coimbatore District. To the Western Ghats, as near Kanara,† and again to the Eastern Ghats,‡ a few only seem to resort; but it is more numerous in the Gáro, Khási, and Naga Hills, in Manipur § and Sylhet, || and in the Tippera¶ and Chittagong** Hills.

But while these, and possibly other localities, in regard to which I have no information, such as the Vindya, Satpura, Aracan and higher Tenasserim ranges, constitute its regular

---

"When driven they break cover either as soon as flushed, or else keep taking short flights in front of the men and dogs till they reach the foot of the shola, when they fly rapidly off to the next, or back towards the head of the jungle. When they have been much disturbed, they become very cunning, and will not show themselves outside of the cover, but keep flying back over the heads of the beaters, and on one occasion I saw one bird that had been flushed by a dog, rise a few feet in the air, where it hovered till the dog had passed on, and then drop into the same place again."—*W. Davison.*

* "I have shot them on the Sheveroy and Javadi Hills in the Salem district, also on the Anamali, Nilgiri, Burghoor, and Husinoor Hills in the Coimbatore district. I have also heard of their being shot in the Wynád.

"It is a cold weather visitant, arriving about the middle of November and leaving again in February or March. As a rule they are rare, a few only being found in suitable localities."—*Albert G. Theobald.*

† "Colonel Peyton informed me that he had only seen four during a long residence in Kanara (10—12 years), but I don't think any one in these parts ever thinks of regularly searching for the birds."—*H. S. Laird.*

‡ "The Woodcock, I am informed by Captain Blaxland, has several times been seen, and on one occasion shot, on the higher plateaux of Jaipur."—*V. Ball.*

§ "I have shot the Woodcock in Manipur, the Khási Hills, near Shillong, and the Naga Hills near Kohima, and I have seen it in the Gáro Hills. In all these districts it appears to be a migrant, appearing about the end of October, and leaving at the end of March. In Manipur I once shot two in the same day from the howdah in heavy grass jungle while beating for deer; in other places I have generally seen them on the banks of running streams in heavy tree jungle. The localities they affect may easily be discovered by noticing the borings which they make in searching for worms. In the Naga Hills it is common. The Angami Nagas snare them by marking the spots, generally an open glade in a wood, where they come out to feed; they surround the place with bushes leaving two or three runs, in each of which they place two sticks arranged like an inverted V, and from the apex suspend a fine noose. The bird is caught by the neck."—*G. Damant.*

|| During the cold weather a few brace of this species are procurable in suitable localities in the Sylhet district. They frequent the small rivulets that run amongst the densely-wooded *teelahs*, which cover a good part of the northern portion of that district. The sportsman walks up the bed of a rivulet with a few beaters on each side, and gets a snap shot occasionally. I have known of four brace being got in a forenoon, but a brace now and again is the general outturn of cock-shooting in those parts. They arrive in November and leave in February."—*J. R. Cripps.*

¶ The late Mr. Valentine Irwin sent me a Woodcock killed in the Tippera Hills, where he told me that it was not very uncommon in winter.

**"It is a rather noticable fact that the Woodcock is found, though rarely, along the hill margins of the eastern side of this District (Chittagong). We put up one at Puttia one day in March 1878. Mr. Lowis shot two near the Mahamani in January 1878, and two others in 1877 at Fenna. In the same year a Woodcock killed itself here in the station by flying against the telegraph wires. Mr. Martin put up a brace of Woodcock from a *teelah* near Kutubcherra in December 1876, and flushed others in the same locality on three subsequent occasions, namely in December 1877, and in March and June 1878. Again Mr. Lowis shot another last month, and saw a second."—*H. Fasson.*

winter quarters outside the Himalayas, there is not, I believe,* a single district, intervening between these letter and the former, where single birds have not now and then occurred on migration.

Outside our limits Swinhoe tells us that it occurs throughout China during the winter, but Pére David says that in the Northern Provinces at least it is almost unknown, though he found it breeding in Ourato in Mongolia, at Sichan near Pekin, and in Moupin. It does not seem uncommon in Japan. Prjevalskí met with it in April on the Murni-ul Mounts in Mongolia, and tells us that they breed in the Ussuri country, and are very numerous there during migration. In Southern and South-eastern Siberia it appears in summer, and breeds in many places. In Yárkand it must be scarce, as neither Henderson nor Scully saw or heard of it, but Stoliczka procured one near Yárkand itself on the 11th of November. In Western Turkestan it is also somewhat rare, and seems only to have been noticed there on passage. Hutton told us more than thirty years ago that the Woodcock was very common at Quetta and Kandahar, arriving in November and departing in May; but, though a few have been noticed, and a very few killed both in Northern and Southern Afghanistan and Northern Beluchistan during the late war, no one seems to have found them common anywhere. In many parts of Persia they do seem very common during the

---

* I may extract a few notices of localities whence Woodcock have been procured.

In a cocoanut garden on the Mysore Plateau, 65 miles east of Bangalore.—*(C. McInroy)*. Seventeen miles south-west of Belgaum, when Snipe-shooting in some rice fields about X'mas time. The fields were surrounded by jungle.—*(J.S. Laird)*. Masulipatam.—*(Jerdon)*. Guddam, in the Golconda Zemindari.—*(McMaster)*.

A Woodcock was shot last Christmas day, about two miles from Tanna, by R. D. Cairns, of the Oriental Bank, here. It was flushed in some bushes at the foot of some low hills near some marshy ground.—*(J. D. Inverarity.)*

I was taking a stroll yesterday morning (4th November) through the Lyarree Gardens, about two miles from Kurrachee when a Woodcock flopped lazily past me. and settled in a field of lucerne grass about ten yards from where I was standing. After turning round and round two or three times, as if trying to get out of the sun, it rose and flew towards some Guava trees about twenty yards off, sitting under one of them. There was no cover, except some short grass insufficient to hide the bird, and I walked up and shot it.—*(E. A. Butler.)*

Aligarh, Sitapur in Oudh.—*(A. Anderson)*. Bulandshahr, Agra, Mynpuri, Cawnpore *(Hume)* Fyzabad and Kheri.—*(G. Reid)*. Berhampur, Noakhali, Dacca, Tippera.—*(Jerdon)*.

To my knowledge three veritable Woodcocks have been killed in Cachar.—*(J. Inglis)*.

Colonel Graham, Deputy Commissioner, Dibrugarh, writes that a few are always to be seen during the cold season, in suitable localities towards the head of the Assam Valley.—Calcutta Market.—*(Blyth, Hume, Parker)*. Thyetmyo, Bassein, Karenee Hills north-east of Shwaygeen.—*(McMaster)*. Thatone —*(J. C. Davis)*. Kyekagaw, twenty-two miles from Rangoon, February 1865.—*(H. B. Davidson)*. Moulmein.—*(David Brown, Colonel)*. Just under the cone of Mooleyit.—*(W. Davison)*.

On the 28th April 1879, I flushed an undoubted Woodcock, among some willows on the bank of the Gyne River —*(C. Bingham.)*

Mamogan, about 10 miles from Tavoy.—*(H. B. Davidson)*.

Dr. Armstrong caught one in the *Bay of Bengal* in Latitude 18° 40′ North, and Longitude 92° 28′ East, on the 18th November 1875.

cold season, and Colonel St. John has shot numbers there, five one morning, out of a single small rose garden at Firuzabad.

Captain Bishop informs me that in January 1873, whilst shooting near Baghdad in Turkish Mesopotamia, his party bagged five Woodcocks in the date groves skirting the town, so that here also they are probably pretty common, as they are likewise in Armenia, Asia Minor, and Palestine.

To Lower Egypt it is a rather rare straggler, but further west in Algeria and Morocco it appears to be more or less common during the winter. Curiously enough it is a permanent resident in the Canaries, Madeira, and the Azores. Excluding Iceland, it is met with at one season or another throughout Europe and the islands of the Mediterranean, mostly breeding in the north (though probably not within the Arctic Circle), but some few breeding in most countries north of the 45th degree of North Latitude. A straggler or two have undoubtedly occurred in the eastern portions of North America, and Coues thinks that such chance visitations are commoner than is usually supposed, but the Neartic region is clearly outside its normal range.

In the Himalayas they begin to descend, earlier or later, in October, according to the season, and I have shot one at only about 7,000 feet elevation in the valley of the Sutlej as early as the 8th of October. Outside the Himalayas, (as at the Nílgiris,) they appear earlier or later in November, and leave earlier or later in March, according to locality or season.

But all do not migrate at the same time; on the Nílgiris fresh birds are continually dropping in at any rate throughout November and December, and this continued migration is also proved by the occurrence of specimens in the plains as late as the end of December. It is curious that in all the cases in which I have been able to ascertain the exact dates, birds killed in the plains of Upper India have been obtained prior to the 3rd of January, thus apparently proving that it is only on their southward journey, and not on the return trip, that they linger by the way.

Whether all the birds visiting the Empire south of the Himalayas are natives of those mountains, or whether a portion are migrants from more northern regions, is a problem that has yet perhaps to be solved; although, for reasons to be explained further on, I do not believe in many foreign birds reaching us.

Cover and running water are what in India the Woodcock most affects; you may find them alike in the middle of deep forest or thick ringal jungle near the banks of some rushing hill streamlet, foaming and sparkling in its rocky bed, where, save a few tiny velvety corners, there seems no single spot in the neighbourhood where they can possibly feed; and again in clumps of low scrub in a treeless opening, where some stream debouching on a clayey basin converts this into a mossy swamp, through which its movement is only to be detected at the further end where, as if ashamed of its late sluggishness, it gushes out to resume its brawling descent. But swamp or stream, the water must be moving to please the Woodcock; and, though there are exceptions to the rule, you will generally hunt in vain, mountain swamps and tarns, where there is no outlet and the water is stagnant, though all the surroundings and adjuncts be everything, apparently, that the heart of Woodcock can desire. In England we find them beside little stagnant ditches and pools in covers; but in India I have seldom so seen them, having almost always flushed them in the neighbourhood of running water.

They are almost invariably solitary. I have flushed three or four out of one and the same clump of holly bushes not thirty yards in diameter; but it is far more common to pick them up one by one along the course of some cover embowered stream at some distance from each other. At the same time, though thus *living* alone, they *travel* in parties. To-day there will not be a Woodcock anywhere in the valley; next morning there are a dozen scattered about all over the place, at distances of two to four hundred yards from each other; unless indeed there be some enclosed garden or tempting patch of low thick prickly cover, where they think themselves safe from hostile birds and beasts, in which, though still keeping each other as much as may be at arm's length, several will gather. A few days later and not a bird is to be found. They have disappeared, as they arrived, *en masse*. They certainly always move by night, and for the most part feed chiefly during the hours of darkness; and, though they may sometimes be seen feeding in the afternoon, I have never myself witnessed this.

Colonel Tickell says:—" The Woodcock, it is well known, returns year after year, like the Chimney Swallow, to the same spot. One or two of them had thus for several winters attracted attention at the Residency, (Kathmandu, Nepal), and one afternoon, in October 1840, whilst seated lounging near an open window or glass door in that building, I descried a fine specimen, looking very smooth and fat, with his rich chestnut plumage and pretty black bars strongly contrasted against the green turf, run along from under a species of lignum vitæ bush, and begin pecking and boring about in the grass. But pecking is not quite an applicable term to the movements of the bird, which appeared at every two or three steps to plunge his bill into the herbage and hold it there for a second or so, giving his head a quick shaking to right and left, as if endeavouring to pierce the ground, and now and then looking up and allowing me to see his large black eye. Occasionally it appeared to nibble up and swallow some small object; but its powers of deglutition are considerable, and the Woodcock will bolt a whole lobworm as one of the Lazzaroni at Naples takes in a yard or so of maccaroni, or a Madras juggler, a sword. It appeared to me rather a clumsy bird, not nimble and sprightly like the Sandpipers, but somewhat lumpy in its gait, and the large, round, head and perpendicular forehead of the bird gave it an air more of the dove than of the serpent. If alarmed it would run under cover, and squat, its long bill resting on the ground ; but on finding all quiet, would soon rise and glide out. On none of these occasions did it take wing, nor fairly proceed into the open, never straying further than seven or eight yards from a bush."

They are with us very tame and confiding birds ; it is not merely that they, as a rule, only rise when you are quite close to them, and then, if not fired at, only flap a dozen yards or so away behind some bush before they drop again. This might be due to the fact that, being chiefly nocturnal in their habits, they do not see over well in daylight ; are confused by the glare, and conceive concealment more likely to conduce to their safety than flight ; but they really affect rather than shun the neighbourhood of mankind. In a huge valley, containing thousands of charming haunts, if there be a single village in it near a stream, you are more likely to meet with Woodcock in any little garden plots or enclosures on its outskirts than anywhere else. And they are not afraid of men, and if you do not fire at them, you may put them up two or three times in a day, day after day, from the same place ; and after a few days they will scarcely take the trouble to flap ten yards away when you do rouse them up, and will even, squatting by the trunk of some low tree, sit and blink at you with their large eyes only half open in a sort of reproachful half-disgusted way. "That fellow bothering here again ; it is too bad that one can't get a single good day's rest !" And then when a dog bustles in, he is in no hurry, but just flutters noiselessly up a few feet as Dash approaches, and as soon as convinced the bird has flown, the dog rushes off, scouring round and round in large circles hoping to pick up the scent again, down pops the Woodcock placidly in its old place, not apparently at all frightened, only very much dissatisfied. Day after day in the Sewaliks of the Eastern Dún for nearly a fortnight, when after a Sámbhar with fabulously large antlers, never alas ! destined to become trophies of mine, I used to see, and my dogs used to put up the same three Woodcock in the same spots, until we all knew each other perfectly, so well that when having to return to work, I was compelled to give up the Phantom Deer, I parted with those Woodcocks in peace, and believe that for that season, at any rate, they escaped molestation.

No European writer notices their tameness and confidingness, which has so much struck me here ; but that may be because they are such delicious eating—to my mind the king of all birds,—that every one shoots them on the first opportunity, and gives no scope for the development of their amiable qualities. But from what I have myself seen, I cannot help thinking that with a little trouble it would not be difficult to domesticate them. Their mode of feeding has been already described above; and, though I have never seen them at work, I have hundreds of times seen the little, rather funnel-shaped holes that they bore in the mud and turf alongside the streams where they reside; and, as you work up or down these latter, these holes furnish certain indications as to whether there are or are not Woodcock about, and where to look for them if there are. If they have not been disturbed they will be found squatting within a stone's throw of their feeding place.

I have found worms of all sizes and shapes, grubs, larvæ, fragments of black coleoptera, tiny scraps of grass, and a sticky glutinous animal substance which I could not identify in those I have examined. Besides which their gizzards always contain a quantity of gravel.

When migrating they are said to fly strongly and well, but when flushed, the flight is at first slow, uncertain and Owl-like, and ceases suddenly, the bird dropping instantaneously behind some bush. I have never had any sport with Woodcock in Northern India. I have often shot them, rarely more than three in a day; but they gave no sort of sport. They fluttered up flushed by the dogs or some beater within twenty yards, and were knocked over by a snap shot as they hung wavering on first rising. One shot them because they were so good to eat; in every other respect they were not worth shooting. They don't seem to fly a bit as Woodcock do in covers at home, where even a good shot is at times baulked; but, like Snipe, and almost every living thing domiciled in this "clime of the sun," they seem to have become listless and sluggish. And certainly, though markedly smaller and lighter birds, they are very much fatter—balls of fat in many of them, which, unless special measures are adopted, it is impossible to turn into good specimens.

Tickell gives a very good description of Woodcock-shooting in Nepal, which is somewhat different to what we in the North-West are accustomed to. He says:—"Woodcock-shooting in Nepal is laborious work from the steepness of the hills and the spongy nature of the ground which the bird frequents. We found them on light rich mould, thickly matted with grasses, ferns, and other weeds, and everywhere furrowed by little rills of water trickling through the tangle, or here and there stagnating in little pools or 'bog-holes' concealed under a layer of vegetation, which formed tolerable pitfalls to the unwary intruder, receiving him sometimes up to the hip. The jungle on these hills is pretty thick, but not lofty, consisting mostly of briars and thicket; and it would have been impossible to get a fair shot within it, were it not that some of the largest rills (perhaps a yard broad) bordered with mossy turf, formed narrow vistas through the tangle, up and down which the birds when flushed would fly, giving some chance to a snap shot. We had no dogs—a luxury known to very few Indian sportsmen, but employed beaters to find the game. I had never even seen cock-shooting in England, and my first day's experience of it in Nepal surprised me not a little. I was a good Snipe shot in those days, and, imagining from the general resemblance of the two birds that a Woodcock must fly like a Snipe, I was much taken aback, when hailed to 'look out,' at perceiving what appeared like a large bat coming with a wavering, flagging flight along the little lane-like opening in the wood where I was posted; but in an instant, ere I had made up my mind to fire, the apparition made a dart to one side, topped the bordering thicket, and seemed to fall like a stone into the covert beyond. These sudden jerks and zigzags, in the midst of its otherwise dilatory flight, are terribly puzzling to a novice. The bird alights also in the same fashion, dropping at once down as if it had flown against a wall. They were not numerous in Nepal, and two couple bagged to one gun during the afternoon was considered very fair sport. We found them only on the low spurs bordering the open valley of Kathmandu, on its northern side—on such slopes as were of the description above given, looking more like the copses and hazel woods of England than the forests of India."

On the Nílgiris Woodcock do afford some sport; there you have nearly bare comparatively softly undulating hills, covered with fine close turf; their sides and flanks furrowed by narrow ravines traversed by a streamlet, and filled with ilex and wild cinnamon trees, at whose bases grows a dense undergrowth of *Strobilanthes*, brambles, or a grass like bamboo, &c. These narrow strips of jungle, locally termed *sholas*, are on these hills the *favourite* haunts (you *will* find them in many other places) of the Woodcock. Broad sholas, over a hundred yards in breadth, are rarely beaten for cock, as these only fly about inside such and will not come out, and it is vile work struggling through the interior of these jungle patches; but into those which are from twenty to one hundred yards in width, a number of beaters and a pack of dogs, mostly nondescript curs, are turned at the top, and they are then beaten straight down, a shooter walking on each side. Then the Woodcock get well on the wing before you see them, and dart out from the trees flying pretty sharp, affording very pretty, if not difficult, shots. Sometimes, if there is any other *shola* running down not far from the one that is being beaten, they make straight for that; more often they fly a short distance down the outside, and again turn in suddenly. Sometimes, if much pressed, they will work quite down to the far end before you see them;

and there rising higher than usual, turn back over the trees and again drop in them higher up. Ten or twelve birds to two guns in a morning is quite an unusually fine bag, so it must not be supposed that they lie thick as a rule, and yet in particular parts of the hills five or six are at times shot out of one tiny "shola," not perhaps above thirty yards wide, and not a quarter of a mile in length. In thus beating, numbers of hares (the large *Lepus nigricollis*,) Wood-Pigeon (*Palumbus elphinstonii*) and Quail are also flushed, and not unfrequently Grey Jungle-Fowl and a few Wood-Snipe, the latter specially towards the bottom, where almost all these *sholas* end in more or less of a swamp in which both Common and Pintail Snipe are very often also found, so that a beat for Woodcock of this kind does afford very pretty sport.

During the cold season the Woodcock is, I think, mute. At no time have I ever heard it utter any cry that I can remember; but Mr. Frederic Wilson, writing of them in their summer haunts, in the higher ranges near the snow, where they breed, remarks :—

"At this season they are seen towards dusk about the open glades and borders of the forest on the higher ridges, flying rather high in the air in various directions, and uttering a loud wailing cry."

According to European authors, the Woodcock in the summer, during its morning and evening flights, utters a very peculiar call-note, first one or two snorts, "a hollow, coarse, somewhat lengthened nasal sound, followed by a short, fine sharp sort of whistle, which, when one is accustomed to it, may be heard to a considerable distance."

In winter one sees and hears little of these flights at dusk, and just before daylight which characterise the species in the summer. As a rule they lie hid all day within fifty yards of their feeding ground, to which towards dusk they toddle down, as far as I have been able to see, never flying a yard for weeks together unless disturbed ; but though I have never myself seen it, I have been told, by reliable persons, of Woodcock at Simla flying up in certain years, regularly every evening in November or December from the valleys below, towards the top of the highest hill (Jakko), though what they wanted in the absolutely dry scrub there no one can guess. Still quite at the top I have known of ten or eleven (possibly a flight that had just alighted) being found, and five killed.

OF THE nidification of this species in the Himalayas, though Hodgson, Wilson, Duff and many others have found the nests, the only account on record is that by my friend the late Mr. A. Anderson. He says, writing of a trip in Kumaun :—

"On the 30th of June I turned my face towards the snows in another direction, determined to consider my expedition a failure so long as the discovery of the breeding haunts of the Woodcock, which was one of its chief objects, still remained unachieved. After two days' stiff marching I pitched camp at a place called Kemo, at an elevation of some 10,000 feet over and against Namick, which is celebrated for its salt springs.

"We were following up a huge wounded *Presbytis schistaceus* through a dense undergrowth of ringals, when a Woodcock rose close to us, dropping again almost immediately, and disappearing in the cover. A diligent search revealed the long-looked-for prize—four eggs, which were deposited in a slight depression in the damp soil, and embedded amongst a lot of wet leaves, the *thin ends* pointing *inwards* and *downwards* into the ground.

"The eggs found (I could see they were hard-set), I told Triphook I had no intention of leaving the place without bagging the bird. It was raining heavily and bitterly cold with the thermometer down to 40°; but, fortunately for us, before we had had time to make ourselves comfortable under an adjoining tree, the bird flew back in a sort of semicircle, alighted, and ran on to her nest. No sooner down than she was off again, frightened, as I subsequently learnt, at one of our dogs, but which at first thought alarmed me not a little as I imagined she was removing her eggs. After having satisfied myself that my suspicions were unfounded, it was decided that, as I had done my duty in finding the nest, shooting the bird should devolve on Triphook, and right well he did it, considering all the disadvantages which militate against having a snap shot in dense cover and in a thick mist. I never do anything but miss on such critical occasions; at any rate I would rather some one else made a *mull* of it than myself.

"The eggs were a most beautiful set; in consequence of the advanced state of incubation it was a full month before they were made into good specimens; a week later and the chicks would have been hatched. They are far *darker* and *redder* than the usual run of Woodcocks' eggs, all four resembling the *second* figure in Hewitson's work, and in the character of their markings they are not *unlike richly* coloured specimens of some Terns' eggs. They are remarkable for the roundness of their form, and in having none of the pyriform or pear-shaped character which distinguished the eggs of all the allied species."

Whether the Woodcock ever does remove its eggs, as has been asserted, or not, it certainly does carry its young about, one at a time, grasped between the two thighs and pressed against the lower part of the breast.

English writers have all a good deal to say about the nidification of this species, which breeds occasionally almost throughout the British Isles.

Hewitson says:—"The Woodcock lays its eggs amongst the dry grass or dead leaves which form the surface of the woods and plantations which it frequents. It is an early breeder, frequently having young ones in the middle of April. The eggs do not vary much, except in contour. They have none of the pear-shaped character which distinguishes those of all the allied species; on the contrary, they are sometimes more remarkable for the roundness of their form. They are four in number.

Yarrell again remarks:—"They (the nests) were all in dry warm situations, amongst dead grass and leaves, without any attempt at concealment. The nest sent was wholly composed of dead leaves, chiefly of the common fern, loosely laid together, and without any lining.

"It would, however, be more proper to say *beds* than *nests*; for, like those of the Plover, they are merely slight hollows formed by the nestling of the birds in dry soft spots, or on the fallen leaves."

Mr. C. St. John obtained a nest of the Woodcock in Scotland as early as the 9th of March, and he says that there they breed again in July and August. Anderson got his nest, eggs hard set, on the 2nd of July, and was of opinion that this was a first laying and that the hen would soon have laid again. "The ovarium of my specimen contained three impregnated eggs, the largest being about the size of an ordinary pill, so that the present brood would hardly have been able to shift for themselves before the mother would be incubating again; it is evident, therefore, that in India, as in Europe, the Woodcock has a double brood."

But such eggs are often found in birds that do not lay a second time normally, a mere natural reserve to provide against the contingencies of the destruction of the first clutch, and which, if the first brood be reared, are never matured, but passed in an incipient form. And I am by no means certain that Woodcock *any* where, normally, have and rear a double brood, and I very much doubt their doing this in the Himalayas.

The eggs are always four in number. They are typically very broad ovals, but generally slightly compressed near the small end; the ground colour varies from pale yellowish white, through various shades of buff and buffy stone colour, to a reddish *café au lait*. The markings, never very densely set, and at times very sparse, consist of different shades of brown, brownish yellow and brownish red on the one hand, and greys, from sepia to purple on the other. The former occur in moderate-sized blotches, spots and specks, as primary markings. Often these are more numerous in a cap or zone about the large end. Occasionally not a single blotch or spot is one-tenth of an inch in diameter, and nine out of ten are little more than specks; but in other eggs many of the blotches, especially about the large end, are a quarter of an inch and upwards in length. The greys, pinkish, lavender, sepia occur as small clouds, spots and smears, secondary sub-surface-looking markings, rarely either large or thickly set, except when amongst the blotches of a zone or cap, when the egg exhibits such.

The eggs vary a great deal in size and shape, some being much more round than others—indeed, almost spherical, the major axis only exceeding the minor by one-eighth, and others comparatively elongated, the major axis exceeding the minor by nearly one-fourth.

A large series, chiefly Northern European, vary from 1·5 to 1·8 in length, and from 1·3 to 1·5 in breadth. I have no Himalayan eggs, but I suspect that, like the birds, they would average smaller than European specimens.

ACCORDING TO European writers, age for age, the females are larger than the males, and the youngest birds have the shortest bills; the latter is undoubted. As to the former, my measurements do not establish any constant difference between the sexes. I have the exact measurements recorded in the flesh of over fifty Indian-killed specimens, carefully noted by Hodgson, Scully, C. H. T. Marshall, Butler and myself; and these, I think, show our birds to be smaller than European ones, and they show absolutely no constant difference in the size of the sexes. The following is an abstract of all these measurements :—

Length, 13 to 15·0; expanse, 23·0 to 25·5; wing, 7·2 to 8·0; tail from vent, 3·0 to 3·85; tarsus, 1·35 to 1·57; bill from gape, 2·8 to 3·3; weight, 7 ozs. to 12·5 ozs.

In not one out of 53 birds has the wing exceeded 8 inches. In my only Yárkand specimen it is 8·5, and it exceeds 8 inches in every one of five English specimens.

In only five out of 53 birds has the weight exceeded 10 ozs., and these five the weights were—10·5, 11·5, 12·0, 12·0, and 12·5 ozs. Out of 53½ couple shot during three days, at the late Mr. O'Leary's place, at Cool Mountain,* near the Inchigeela Lakes, between Macroom and Bantry (South-West Ireland), 27 weighed between 12 and 14 ozs., six weighed between 14 and 15 ozs., and one between 15 and 16 ozs. Dresser again says that, in a large series shot between 1860 and 1870 at Gartincaber in Perthshire, most of the birds varied in weight between 11 and 12 ozs. Our 53 birds weighed—between 7 and 8 ozs., fourteen—between 8 and 9 ozs., eighteen—9 and 10 ozs., sixteen—above 10 ozs., five. There is an undoubted instance on record of a Woodcock in England weighing 27 ozs.

Our only Yárkand bird has the wing 8·5, and it seems to me therefore, probable, that if India was visited by many Central

---

* People rave about the cock-shooting on the coast opposite to Corfu, and thirty to forty years ago it used to be, and, for all I know still is, very fine; but every bit as good cock-shooting was to be had, as late at any rate as 1861, at Eve Leary in county "Kark"!

or Northern Asiatic migrants of this species, we should get some large and heavy birds, and all our Indian-killed birds would not be so persistently small and light. Certainly, our Himalayan birds do run much smaller and lighter than British ones; but I am far from asserting that this could justify their separation, as a distinct species, as suggested by Hodgson. The Afghan birds are perhaps larger again. Hutton gives the length of one as 16 inches, and the weight 13 ozs.

The legs and feet are pale bluish, brown or drab, or fleshy plumbeous or grey, or livid grey, or bluish fleshy grey, generally more or less shaded dusky on the joints, and the claws are fleshy brown, pale brown, blackish brown, or dusky.

The irides are always dark brown, but in one cream coloured albino they were pale brownish red.

The bill is dusky to blackish brown at tip; the rest pale drab brown, fleshy brown, fleshy brown with a bluish tinge, or almost plumbeous, often nearly white, or pale fleshy at the base of the lower mandible.

THE PLATE is fairly good, but I do not think the legs are ever quite so pink as are represented; there is always a bluish or plumbeous or grey shade over them. The species is an extremely variable one—some are much darker, some are almost white below,—some have a conspicuous blackish brown patch on the upper throat, some have no trace of this; some are much redder, some much greyer above; some have the chin and upper throat quite white, in others it is a warm buff. In some the rump and upper tail-coverts are quite red, as shown in the plate, in others these parts are quite grey.

Mr. Yarrell says:—"Males have the forehead more inclined to grey, with the chin white; and the space above and below the decided dark brown mark from the beak to the eye much lighter in colour, almost white, with the small dark triangular specks, at the end of these light coloured feathers better defined; the back has more of the pale brown and grey, and the rump less red than the female."

Not one of these supposed sexual distinctions hold good in our Indian birds, nor do I even believe that they hold good in English ones. Anyhow, they certainly do not hold good in India.

The absence or presence of triangular marks on the outer web of the first quill feather has also been supposed to have a sexual significance. But of this Yarrell says: —"These marks are indications of youth rather than of sex, and are obliterated by degrees, and in succession from the base to the end of the feather."

It is a curious thing that out of 27 Indian-killed specimens now before me, these triangular marks are present in every specimen. Only in two or three they have disappeared from the basal half of the feather. Our museum does not contain a single Indian-killed specimen with the whole of the outer web of the first quill entirely plain.

In the Woodcock the tail, which is well rounded, consists of only twelve rather soft feathers.

In the Dún, I shot one abnormal bird, which had the entire ground colour creamy yellow, and the markings a sort of sepia grey; white, yellow, and even blackish varieties have been noticed in Europe.

BESIDES THE present species only two other Woodcocks appear to be known. One, the smaller, proportionally longer billed and plainer plumaged, *S. saturata* from Java, and the other (separated by many writers under the generic name *Philohela* on account of its narrow scythe-shaped, three first primaries,) *S. minor*, of the Eastern United States, (extending as far west as Kansas and Nebraska,) and adjoining portions of Canada and Nova-Scotia.

GALLINAGO NEMORICOLA

THE WOOD-SNIPE.

Gallinago nemoricola, *Hodgson.*

Vernacular Names.—[Ban-chaha, *Nepal.*]

EVERYWHERE, in the better known portions at any rate of the Empire, even in those localities it regularly visits, a scarce bird, the distribution of the Wood-Snipe is still most imperfectly known.

In the Himalayas, its home, I only know for certain of its occurrence from near Dalhousie on the west to Native Sikhim on the east. Adams does not include it in his Kashmir list,* though he knew the bird and recorded having killed it further east in the Himalayas ; and I have never yet seen a Kashmir-killed specimen. Very possibly however it may straggle into the realm of the Happy Valley, I can only record that, thus far, this is "not proven." On the other hand it must be rare in both British and Native Sikhim, and in the Terai below these. During ten years in which he collected in these localities in the most exhaustive manner, (obtaining numbers of birds previously fabulously rare, indeed every species ever thence recorded by any one else,) the late Mr. Mandelli only once obtained the Wood Snipe there, when it was brought in to him along with four nests of its eggs, his men having discovered a breeding colony of it in a locality in the interior which they had not before visited.

In the winter, it occurs (though everywhere very sparsely distributed) in the Kangra Valley, in the Dún, and in the north-east of the Saharunpore district in the Siwaliks.

It has been shot in the Kumaon Bhabur two or three times. I had one specimen sent me from a place 40 miles north-west

* Though Adams does not include it in his Kashmir list, he speaks of it as follows in his Punjab and North-West Himalayan list :—

"In the lonely glens by the side of some mountain stream, where the pine grows tall and dense, and the sun's rays rarely penetrate, there we meet the solitary Snipe (*G. nemoricola*) from the lowest range of the Himalayas to the limits of forest."

On the other hand in his Kashmir list he does include *G. solitaria*, which we independently know to occur there.

Colonel Irby says that he "saw several couples of this fine Snipe at Moonsheyaree in Kumaon, at an elevation of about 6,000 or 7,000 feet in May 1859. Those I found were in little rushy patches of bog on the sides of hills, never on streams."

of Lakhimpur in the Kheri district, and it has been obtained in the Nepal (formerly Oudh) Terai, further east. Beyond this I have no record of its occurrence, till we come to the Gáro and Khási Hills, where many have been shot; and again a blank till we reach the far end of the Assam valley, where in the Dibrugarh district Colonel Graham tells me he used yearly to kill a few. Strange to say in Manipur * they appear to be more common than in any other part of the Empire.

To the Nílgiris, Coorg, the Wynád, the Pulneys, Anamallis†, Sheveroys, and hilly parts of the Coimbatore District, they appear as numerically scarce, but regular, visitants during the cold season; but neither Mr. Bourdillon nor any of his friends, whom he consulted, seem to have met with it on the Assamboo Hills, and its occurrence in Ceylon, though possible, indeed probable, has not, I believe, been satisfactorily established.

Between its northern summer and southern winter homes, it has, unlike the Woodcock, been very rarely met with; but Colonel McMaster tells us that he twice shot it at Russelconda in Gúmsur. Blyth once obtained it in the Calcutta market, and Ball met with it once in South Sirguja, (Chota Nagpur ‡).

To Burmah it also straggles. Colonel McMaster saw one killed a few miles from Rangoon, and Davison flushed one near Malewoon, at the extreme south of Tenasserim. Doubtless, as time runs on, we shall learn more of this species, and it will prove to occur in many localities, such as Cachar, Sylhet, Tippera, Chittagong, and Arakan, &c., where, up till now, it has remained unobserved. It has not yet been found, so far as I can learn, anywhere outside our limits.

THE WOOD-SNIPE does not, I think, as a rule, range nearly so high as the Woodcock in the Himalayas; in the summer even it is to be found as low as an elevation of six or seven thousand

* My poor friend Damant wrote to me as follows:—"This bird I have only seen in Manipur, where I shot several specimens; all were killed in grass jungle from the howdah. It seems to be common there, as I killed five in one morning. It has a very slow heavy flight and is easy to shoot. On the wing it is much more like a Woodcock than a Snipe. It appears earlier than the Woodcock; the first I killed was on the 14th September."

† Mr. Albert Theobald says:—

"I have shot this Snipe on the higher elevations of the Sheveroy Hills in the Salem District, and on the Nílgiris, Annamallis, and Guddasal Hills in the Coimbatore District. I have also heard of its being shot in the Wynád. It is a winter visitant, coming and going at the same time as the Woodcock and is decidedly rare.

"It affects swampy and boggy grounds covered with grass, and the moist and damp sholas or belts of trees bordering the perennial streams, running down the bottoms of ravines.

"They are best flushed by good dogs, and are always seen singly; seldom more than four or five can be shot in a day even in the most favorable situation."

‡ Note also that Burgess, P. Z. S., 1855, p. 80, expresses a belief that Lieutenant Boddam of the Engineers shot a specimen of this Snipe at Nassick, 90 miles or so north-east of Bombay, on the 5th of January 1847.

feet, and I do not know that it is ever found much, if at all, above 10,000 feet.

It is so scarce and so accidentally met with that it is impossible to say when exactly it migrates; but I cannot learn that it has been killed either on the Nílgiris or in the Sub-Himalayan tracts earlier than the 1st of November. But Damant shot one in Manipur on the 14th of September, and I have a specimen killed in the Khási Hills a little later in September. Perhaps these eastern birds are not migrants from the Himalayas at all, but breed in some of the hills there.

I have never seen two birds of this species within a quarter of a mile of each other; and though, having seen comparatively so few, this goes for little, every sportsman I have consulted tells me the same thing, *viz.*, that, except in the breeding season, when on rare occasions a pair have been flushed together, it is quite unusual to meet with more than a single bird in the same place.

When down in the plains country their habits seem to be different to what they are in the Himalayas, Nílgiris, &c. Damant mentions (note p. 326) that he shot five from the howdah in one morning, and the following remarks by Captain Baldwin show that in the plains they become at times gregarious:—

"I have known," he says, "old sportsmen who have shot all over the country, and have not seen, much less killed, one of these birds. I have twice been fortunate enough to meet with this Snipe: once near the foot of the Himalayas I flushed one from the corner of a marshy pool, but so suddenly that I was unprepared, and before I could get my gun up he was gone. I did not see another *nemoricola* for many years, till when shooting in the Philibhít District in January 1872, I came across not one, but over a dozen of these birds; they were close to one another. I was with my brother-in-law at the time; we had gone out one morning to shoot Snipe from off the back of a pair of elephants we had with us, each in a howdah. The marsh was covered with a very high kind of rush, so that it would have been impossible to see sufficiently well to shoot on foot.

"We soon put up several Common Snipe, and presently my companion fired at one, and I then saw a large dark bird, which I thought at the time was a solitary Snipe, rise with a croak, and after curving about, drop close by. We went up, and not one, but three rose—two of which fell to our shots. We soon found several more, and nine were killed altogether; they offered the easiest of shots, and did not rise till the elephants were close on them. They were particularly fine gamey birds, and proved most excellent for the table."

They affect tiny swamps and morasses, on the hill sides or in narrow valleys, but only those close to, or surrounded by, tree or high bush or ringal jungle, and in which there is at least some small patch of good cover of rushes, bushes, or the like.

They are very shy retiring birds, much more so than the Woodcock, and are never seen like these on the outskirts of villages. They are always near the edge of the jungle, at some swampy patch, never like the Woodcock often is, a mile inside the forest, alongside some rocky torrent which at most only boasts here and there a tiny corner, between two great rocks, of spongy turf. Nor do you find them even in the most suitable looking patches of mossy swamp, if these are on a bare hill side a quarter of a mile even away from forest or jungle.

This at least is my (limited) experience of the species on the Himalayas. Davison says :—" The Wood-Snipe is a rare bird on the Nílgiris, coming in, I think, later than the Pintail, and leaving earlier. They are usually found singly (though on one occasion I flushed two out of a clump of brambles about ten feet across.) They frequent the outskirts of the *sholas* where these are marshy—never, as far as I am aware, being found any distance in the inside of the jungles as the Woodcock occasionally is. Scrub-clad ravines through which a stream flows is also a favorite resort, and on one or two occasions I have flushed them from under small isolated bushes growing in marshy ground. They rise silently, fly rather lazily, and for only a short distance, and then drop again into cover."

As to this latter there can be no doubt. They rise in the same, dazed, hesitating, blundering owl-like way, as the Woodcock often does when first flushed, and like it generally drop abruptly behind the first convenient bush. Very likely when well on the wing they may, as does the Woodcock, when emerging from a cover to dart in again a few yards lower down, fly pretty smartly; but I have never happened to see a Wood-Snipe with steam up.

From their dazed appearance and sleepy flight, when flushed in bright sunlight, I should imagine them to be nocturnal in their habits. Certainly during the brighter hours of the day they are very unwilling to rise, allowing you almost to tread on them before they do so, and being thus very likely to escape notice, unless dogs are used. But in the early morning and evening they will rise spontaneously like Common Snipe (though even then sluggishly) when you are still twenty yards distant from them.

In the day time they certainly dislike being disturbed, and one can imagine them addressing the intruder in the words of the Prophetic Maid to Odin :—

> " Unwilling, I my *eyes* unclose,
> Leave me, leave me to repose !"

One cannot help feeling a sort of sympathy for these shy, meek, inoffensive birdies, who only ask to be left in peace in their pet little swampy corners; but in this peculiarly constituted universe, one must it seems "*amboss oder hammer seyn*," and the more you shrink from interfering with others, the more earnest they become in meddling with you.

The Wood-Snipe does not seem to be such a great worm devourer as the Woodcock. I have only a record of the contents of the stomachs of a few, but these were only large naked soft grubs, small aquatic insects and remains of insects, especially tiny black *coleoptera*, small hard black seeds, and gravel. Whether the black seeds were eaten by mistake for tiny beetles, I cannot say; but they were not merely accidental, for they occurred in two out of five specimens, and Hodgson also notes having found them in one bird that he examined.

They are very silent birds. I have never heard them utter any sound, nor have I met with any one who has, except Captain Baldwin, who says that they utter a hoarse croak on rising. Still in the breeding season they must have some call-note, probably not unlike that of the Woodcock.

OF THEIR nidification little is as yet known. That they breed in the Himalayas between elevations of about seven and ten thousand feet (and perhaps, though I doubt it, considerably higher,) is certain. That they begin to lay early too is probable. Hodgson notes that on the 10th of March the eggs in the ovary of a female were swelling, and another shot early in April contained a nearly full-sized but unshelled egg. But no European, I believe, has ever yet taken the nest, though Mr. A. G. Young writes that he *knows* that they *do* breed in Kullu.

But, as already mentioned, Mr. Mandelli's native shikaris did once come upon several pairs breeding, and brought in four clutches of their eggs; and in regard to these Herr Otto Möller sends me the following particulars:—

"The eggs were found in Native Sikhim, just opposite Darjeeling. Mandelli several times pointed out to me the spur where they were found, the elevation of which is, I should say, between eight and nine thousand feet. The eggs, eleven in number, were procured during the latter part of June, and the men brought with them the skin of a Wood Snipe, which they said they had shot from one of the nests; but the eggs, though clearly all belonging to the same species, equally clearly belonged to four different nests, and the men could not point out the clutch to which the skin belonged.

"I know by my own experience that our European Great Snipe (*G. major*), commonly thus breeds in company, *i.e.*, where you find one nest, there in the immediate neighbourhood you find several others, and probably this is the case with the present species also."

Judging by these eggs, some of which Mandelli gave me (the rest of them have been kindly lent me by Herr Möller) they lay four eggs, a good deal recalling some varieties of those of the Great and Common Snipe.

In shape they are broad at one end, very narrow at the other, almost hemispherical, in the larger half, and abruptly compressed from the middle and pointed towards the small end.

The shell is stout but very compact in texture, and has occasionally a just perceptible, though always faint, gloss.

The ground is a pale, pinky stone colour of varying shades, sometimes almost white, sometimes browner, sometimes more decidedly pink, densely and boldly blotched (the blotches often longitudinal in their character, and radiating in curved lines from the broad apex) with a rich, at times brownish, maroon, almost black in some spots, browner in some eggs, redder in others, this blotching being generally intermingled with very similarly shaped, subsurface-looking pale grey or inky purple patches and clouds.

In some eggs the markings are almost entirely confined to the upper one-third of the egg, where they are in places all but confluent. In others the markings, though in such cases often less densely set, extend over the entire upper half of the egg; but as a rule but few markings, and these much reduced in size, extend over the lower half of the egg.

The eggs I have measured varied from 1·66 to 1·76 in length, and from 1·2 to 1·28 in breadth, but the average of ten eggs is 1·71 by 1·24.

IN THIS species, so far as my measurements go, I can discover no constant difference in the size of the sexes; for, although the two largest and heaviest birds were both females, there are two other females smaller than one of the males. Perhaps these are younger birds, and perhaps, age for age, the females *may* run larger. I have only a record of seven specimens, however, far too small a number to generalize from. The seven measured in the flesh :—

Length, 11·0 to 12·5; expanse, 18·0 to 19·75; wing, 5·4 to 5·7; tail from vent, 2·5 to 2·9; tarsus, 1·41 to 1·49; bill from gape, 2·41 to 2·62; weight, 4·9 to 6·1 ozs.

Jerdon, following Hodgson's paper, J. A. S. B., 1837, 490, gives the weight up to 7 ozs., but as his MSS. notes show, Hodgson, who weighed about twenty, got only one above 6 ozs., and that one 6·75 ozs., and he says :—"The young of the year weigh from 4 to 4¼ ozs.; adults rarely less than 5 ozs."

The irides are hazel to deep brown; the front of the legs and toes are grey, sometimes, perhaps commonly, bluish, sometimes more plumbeous or slatey, and sometimes with a drabby shade, or again greenish,* and generally everywhere paler

* In one specimen I have recorded the legs and feet as simply greenish brown.

in the female; the back of the legs and soles fleshy, sometimes pinky, sometimes bluish or dusky; the claws horny brown to almost black; of the bill nearly the terminal one-third is brown to blackish brown; the basal two-thirds much paler and with a tinge sometimes reddish fleshy, sometimes yellowish fleshy, sometimes livid, sometimes drab.

THE PLATE is a very fair picture of the specimen figured, but the legs are not correctly coloured, and the bill is quite wrongly drawn; it should be much higher at the base, and thick at the point, like those of all Snipe, and not skewer-like.

But the species is a very variable one; in the majority of specimens the barring on the lower surface is broader, more uniform and continuous, and less crescentic and patchy than in the specimen figured. On the wings the pale barring is often greyer and less rufous; the back and scapulars are often much less cut up with rufous bands than would appear from the figure. In one specimen these parts are plain black, without a single cross bar, only each feather very broadly margined with greyish rufous; the amount and colour of the markings on the upper surface vary much, being sometimes much more profuse, sometimes much greyer, sometimes much more rufous.

One other mistake I notice in the plate; the second dark face stripe should be lower down and further apart from the upper or eye stripe, and should not have been made to join this.

This species seems to be generally confounded by sportsmen with the next, the Eastern Solitary Snipe. But they are really very different looking birds, this being more of the Woodcock, that more of the Snipe. A few of the more conspicuous differences may be pointed out:—

WOOD SNIPE.	EASTERN SOLITARY SNIPE.
Wing, 5·4 to 5·7.	Wing, 6·25 to 6·8.
Bill deep and Woodcock-like at base.	Bill less deep and more Snipe-like at base.
Height of upper mandible at margin of feathers, fully 0·3.	Height of upper mandible at margin of feathers, barely 0·2.
Outer margins of first three primaries nearly uniform with rest of feather.	Outer margins of first three primaries pure white.
Abdomen, vent, and lower tail-coverts *closely barred.*	Abdomem, vent, and lower tail-coverts, *almost unbarred.*
Margins of scapulars *rufous.*	Margins of scapulars *white.*
General aspect darker and duller; back with few broad, dull rufous markings.	General aspect lighter and brighter; back with numerous bright rufous and white markings.

In this species the tail is usually composed of sixteen or eighteen feathers, with the four or five outer feathers on each side narrowed and stiff, and of a nearly uniform grey brown.

In the plate,* given at the close of this article, we have endeavoured to exhibit, in juxtaposition, characteristic representations of the lower tail-coverts, tail-feathers, and wing-linings of this present species, the Eastern Solitary Snipe, and the Common and Pintail Snipes. The figure of these parts in the Wood-Snipe is very good and characteristic, but specimens do vary so *inter se* that it is difficult to make much of such plates.

* This Plate is partly compiled from Mr. Hodgson's drawings.

GALLINAGO ½ SOLITARIA

THE EASTERN SOLITARY SNIPE.

Gallinago solitaria, *Hodgson.*

Vernacular Names.—[Bharka (for all Snipes,) *Nepal.*]

THE Solitary Snipe occurs right through the Himalayas, from Gilgit on the west to Central Bhûtan on the east, and probably quite as far east as Sadiya in these mountains.

During the summer it is confined to the higher ranges from elevations of 9,000 feet and upwards to at least 15,000 feet. In the autumn it descends lower, and during the winter is found in most of the lower valleys, right down to where these debouch on the plains, and in all the Dúns, Terais, Bhaburs, and the like that lie about the bases of the hills; a few also straggle into the submontane districts, and occasionally far away into the plains, as when Mr. A. Guthrie met with one on the 14th of September 1879 near Benares. In the central portion of the Empire they do not normally get far south of the mountain skirts, nor have they ever been observed in any of the hills of Southern or Central India; but on the west they have been obtained in the neighbourhood of Cabul, and one specimen has been sent me, which was shot by Captain Scott of the 4th Sikhs, in December 1877 as far south as Kelat, (elevation 6,700 feet). On the east again they have been procured both in the Gáro and Khási Hills, and towards the head of the Assam Valley, Colonel Graham tells me that he has seen a few above Dibrugarh.

Unlike the Wood-Snipe, bare treeless districts are quite as attractive as better-wooded regions, and I found them almost common on many of the streams in Ládakh, Lahoul and Spiti, where the Wood-Snipe is quite unknown.

In Japan, and according to Pére David in Northern China and Mongolia, and Moupin, and according to Prjevalskí in South-East Mongolia, Northern Tibet, Kansu, and about the Koko-Nor, and in the Ussuri country, this species occurs. But then throughout Southern and South-Eastern Siberia, certain authorities affirm that it is not *solitaria* that is found, but a certain nearly allied species *hyemalis*, of Eversmann, and that Prjevalskí's birds belong to this latter. So too in Western Turkestan, Severtzoff affirms that it is *hyemalis* that occurs, and that this is a good species. I cannot discover where any description of this supposed species has been published. I doubt the Northern Chinese, and South-Eastern Siberian species being distinct, and I believe that the Japanese, Chinese, Mongolian, Siberian, Tibetan, Eastern and Western Turkestan birds are *all* either *solitaria* or *hyemalis*, and I incline to the former alternative; *firstly*, because, years ago, I examined Pekinese and Japanese specimens (one of each) sent to me by Mr. Swinhoe, which, though differing slightly in tints and proportions from the Himalayan specimens I then had, seemed to me to be specifically identical; *secondly*, because Stoliczka obtained a pair of veritable *solitaria*, on the 1st of November at Sanju, on the other side of the Himalayas, in the south of Eastern Turkestan, and Major Biddulph procured it between Sarhad and Punja in Wakhan, and it is extremely unlikely that the Western Turkestan birds should be different from these; and, *thirdly*, because *solitaria* is a species that varies very considerably in colour, size, and markings, as well as in number of tail feathers; and Mr. Bogandoff, on whose authority, apparently, the distinctness of *hyemalis* rests, and who is said to have compared Siberian with Indian specimens, cannot possibly be in a position, (they have only three specimens, I think, at Leyden) to know the extent to which *solitaria* does vary.

Of course this is merely argument. As a fact *hyemalis* may prove to be a good species, but for the present my readers may, I think, assume that it is probably *solitaria* that extends to all the countries above enumerated.

ALTHOUGH THE Eastern Solitary Snipe may be met with at great elevations,—I have myself seen it as high as 14,000 feet, and I believe considerably higher; Henderson shot one on the Chagra Stream, above the Pangong (elevation 15,000 feet) as late as the 8th of October; and Major Biddulph writes that several were shot by his party in the narrow valley, (elevation 13,500 feet), leading from Tanksi to this same lake,—still even in June I have found them as low as 9,000 feet, and the great majority of the birds descend early, so that some are to be found in all the low valleys by the first week in October, and in early seasons by the middle of September. I have no record of any being shot in the Dún or other similar submontane tracts before the middle of November; but these are such frightfully feverish localities in the autumn, that no one shoots there before that time, and from Mr. Guthrie's experience at Benares, I dare say some begin to arrive in all these places much about the same time as they appear in the lower Himalayan valleys, well inside the hills.

They do not seem to care much for cover. I have constantly seen them along the margins of little streams, in bare rocky ravines and valleys, where there were only small corners and nooks of turf and mossy swamp, and no cover a foot high. I have no doubt found them in small open swamps in the middle of jungle, but they stick to the grass and low rushes, and I never myself observed them in scrub or ringal jungle. I have known Wood-Snipe and the Eastern Solitary Snipe flushed within a short distance of each other; but, as a rule, the Wood-Snipe is to be seen only in tiny swamps or morasses, partly or wholly surrounded by thick cover—the Solitary Snipe in little swampy places on open grassy hill sides, or along the margins of rocky-bedded, bare-banked streams.

The Solitary Snipe has a much higher range in summer, and does not go nearly so far south in winter. In the Himalayas at all seasons it is at least ten times as numerous as the Wood-Snipe. It is just as commonly met with in two's and three's as singly whereas (in the hills at any rate) the Wood-Snipe is always solitary.

The flight of the Wood-Snipe, and the shape of its bill, are "wood-cocky," of the Solitary Snipe, both are "snipey."

The latter rises, flies, twists, and pitches precisely like a Pintail Snipe, but is somewhat less rapid and agile in all its movements than this, and *à fortiori* than the Common Snipe.

The Wood-Snipe, so far as my experience goes, rises invariably silently; the Solitary Snipe goes off with a loud "pwich"—a harsh screeching imitation of the note of the Common Snipe.

They feed, to judge from those that I have examined, chiefly on small insects and tiny grubs. I have found a mass of minute black *coleoptera* in the stomachs of two or three; of one I find noted "minute shells." There is always a quantity of gravel or coarse sand in the gizzard.

They are excellent eating, but not I think quite equal to any of the other Snipes, the best of which are certainly the Jacks. There is not much on these latter, but what there is, is delicious.

THE BREEDING season commences in May, when the males are to be often heard and seen in the higher portions of the hills soaring to a considerable height, repeatedly uttering a loud, sharp, jerky call, and then descending rapidly with quivering wings and outspread tail, producing a harsh buzzing sound something like, but shriller and louder than, that produced by the Common Snipe, and this though they do not descend as rapidly as this latter.

The nest, such as it is, is usually placed on grass or moss, close to some stream, often more or less overhung by some tuft of grass or rushes. It consists at most of a few dead rushes or scraps of dry moss or grass, surrounding and at times lining a little depression in the moss, turf or ground. In one case I was told that there was no nest at all, the eggs being laid simply in a shallow, circular depression in deep, spongy club moss, apparently merely hollowed by the pressure of the bird's body.

I have never myself seen a nest, but have this information from natives who have repeatedly seen the eggs, always at places high up on snow-capped ranges, and on snow-fed streams.

I have never succeeded in securing, or even getting sight of, the eggs though on one occasion several (subsequently unfortunately destroyed,) were collected for me in Cashmere.

THE SEXES do not, judged by my measurements, appear to differ appreciably in size, but the three largest birds measured were females, and the two smallest males, so that probably, age for age, if one could make sure of this, the females are the largest. The difference, however, is very small, and in twenty out of twenty-five specimens, males and females are equally larger and smaller than others of the opposite sex, so that I see no use in separating the dimensions.

Length, 12·0 to 12·96; expanse, 19·75 to 21·92; wing, 6·25 to 6·8; tail from vent, 3·1 to 3·45; tarsus, 1·25 to 1·37; bill from gape, 2·52 to 2·87, (no male above 2·77); weight, 5 ozs. to 8 ozs. Several young birds weighed less, one only 4·25 ozs.

The irides are dark brown; the legs and feet in adults are dull olive or yellowish green, or greenish or dull pale yellow—in young birds ashy, with a greenish tinge; the claws black or brownish black; the terminal one-third of the bill is black or brownish black; the basal portions generally yellowish brown, bluish along commissure; but the upper mandible often has a greenish ashy or plumbeous, or vinous or fleshy tinge, and sometimes is plumbeous everywhere except at the dark tip

---

THE PLATE is really a singularly good and faithful picture of the specimens figured, though how the bird in the foreground has succeeded in getting both its legs on the off side, no one who has not mastered space of four dimensions, can hope to explain.

But this species is very variable. In many specimens, perhaps the majority, the white margins to the scapulars are broader and more strongly marked, (in some very much so) than in the plate; often there is much more white spotting or speckling on the wing. The terminal portions of the tertiaries are often very distinctly barred with white; often there is a great deal of pure white dotted about the sides of the head and upper neck. The second, lower, face band, barely indicated in the plate, and in most specimens, is in a few very strongly marked. In some birds the brown is darker and descends much lower on the breast than in others, and this brown is much more uniform in some, and more white spotted in others. There is much more and more distinct barring on the sides and flanks in some specimens than in others. In one specimen before me only the centre of the lower abdomen remains entirely unbarred. Some birds have a well-marked broad median white line on the crown ; in the majority this is barely indicated. Some birds are altogether darker, some lighter, some duller and greyer, some brighter and more rufous, some show no more white than the plate, many have the whole mantle dashed and splashed, and spotted all about with white.

The figure of tail, lower tail-coverts, and wing-lining (see the plate at the end of the last article) is very fair ; but the barring on the five outer laterals on each side should be more distinct.

Typically this species has twenty tail feathers—the six outer ones on each side stiff, narrow and acuminate, white, closely and strongly barred with blackish brown ; the eight central ones, of the ordinary shape, black, with a broad, subterminal bright chestnut band, and tipped with white preceded by a black line.

But the tail varies from sixteen feathers, with four pairs of stiff laterals, to twenty-four (Jerdon says twenty-eight, but I have never found more than twenty-four) with eight such pairs.

F. Waller, Chromo Lith. 48 Hatton Garden, London

½
GALLINAGO STENURA

THE PINTAIL SNIPE.

Gallinago sthenura,* *Bonaparte.*

Vernacular Names.†—[Chaha, *N. W. Provinces, Oudh;* Bharka, Bharak, (Hindee), *Central Himalayas, Nepal, &c.;* Chegga, Cheyga. *Lower Bengal;* Cherayga, *Dibrugarh, Assam;* Check lonbi, *Manipur;* Tibud, Pán-lawa, (Mahrati), *Ratnagiri;* More-oolan, Oolan (Tamil), Muku-puredi, (Telegu), *Southern India;* Kada-kecho. *Orissa;* Ket-batta, (Lurka Koles), Birkú, *Malay Peninsula;* Kas-watua, *Ceylon;*]

I HAVE no authentic record of the occurrence of this species in the Himalayas west of the Jumna, nor in the Punjab, Trans-Sutlej, (though stragglers may prove to occur there), and it is *excessively* rare in the Punjab, Cis-Sutlej, in the N. W. Provinces ‡ and Oudh§ (except in Gorakhpur, Basti, and the submontane tracts of Oudh and Rohilkhand), in Rajputana, Sindh,‖ Cutch and Káthiáwar. Indeed, from the two latter, though doubtless straggling thither also, it has not yet been recorded.

---

* Although this name was written from the first *sthenura*, modern writers take it upon themselves to change it to *stenura*, on the ground that it *must* have been intended to refer to the narrowness of the lateral tail feathers, and must hence have been derived from στενος, 'narrow,' and cannot have been derived from σθενος, 'strength.' To me this appears a wholly unwarrantable assumption. There is nothing to show that the stiffness or strength of the tail feathers was not the point indicated by the name, and I shall certainly continue to spell this in the manner adopted by the authority (Bonaparte) who first published it.

† All these names appear to be indifferently applied to this and the next species.

‡ "During fifteen years, spent chiefly in the Mírat, Aligarh, Mainpuri and Etáwah districts of the N. W. Provinces, I never once came across this species. To my knowledge, however, two or three have been killed in the Doab, and I myself obtained one in the Dún. But this species is a mere chance straggler to the N. W. Provinces, north of the Jumna; in Jhánsi and Bundelkhand it is less rare."—*A. O. Hume.*

"An Eastern species, *and possibly unknown in the Doab;* fairly common in rank high grass, along the watercourses in Northern Oudh, and occasionally met with further south. I got one at Sitapur."—*A. Anderson.*

§ "It is possible that I may have overlooked this species, before special attention was directed to it in *Stray Feathers* in 1873. Since then, however, shooting constantly as I do, and giving Snipe a full share of attention, I have only met with a single specimen in the Lucknow Division, and that in too mangled a condition to be worth preserving."—*George Reid.*

‖ Very few Pintails, indeed, have been observed in Sindh. Colonel Lemesurier, an enthusiastic Snipe shot, wrote to me from Sindh:—"I have not shot a Pin-tailed Snipe since 1872. I have the side tail feathers still by me. They are 1⅝ long, stiff and curved, six on each side, of a dusky colour, with yellow tips."

In Gujerat* the Pintail is more common, occurring, perhaps, in the proportion of one to five of the Common Snipe, and this is about the proportion in Khandesh,† but it is rarer still in the Pánch Máhals.

In the Central India Agency (excluding the Bundelkhand states,) and the western portions of the Central Provinces‡ it is, if anything, less common than in Khandesh; but in Berar, though still in a decided minority as compared with the Fantail, it is somewhat more common.

About Bombay,§ the Pintail is as common as the other, and in the Southern Konkan,|| if anything, more plentiful.

In the Nizam's Dominions, the Deccan¶ and the Belgaum** district the two species are about in equal force, but in Mysore†† the Pintail immensely predominates.

Further south also, though both species occur in every district and in Ceylon, (rare in some places, common in others) I believe that the Pintail is, as a rule, most numerous, though on some of the higher ‡‡ ranges, the Fantail may perhaps be commonest.

---

* "In Gujerat the Pintail is not nearly so common, but this Christmas I found that in a bag of nineteen couple of Snipe there were five couple of Pintails, an unusually large proportion I think in Gujerat."—*J. D. Inverarity.*

† "This Snipe is rarer than the Common Snipe in Khandesh, perhaps one out of five or six being Pintails.

In the Pánch Máhals *G. sthenura* was still rarer, and I did not shoot one for every ten of the Common Snipe."—*J. Davidson.*

‡ "I think that at Kamptee we get only the Common Snipe."—*A. McMaster.*

W. Blanford also says "that about Chanda, Nagpur and the Upper Gódavarí, he never met with this species, though for two or three years he examined every bird he shot."

§ About Bombay the Pintail Snipe is quite as common as the Fantail. Indeed about Tanna, and in the Snipe grounds across the Bombay Harbour, you will get more of the Pintail Snipe than of the other."—*J. D. Inverarity.*

|| "Pintails are abundant throughout the Ratnagiri district, and as far as my experience goes are, if anything, rather more plentiful than the Common Snipe."—*G. Vidal.*

¶ "In the Deccan where Snipe ground and Snipe are scarce, I have always found the two kinds nearly equally divided in a day's bag."—*J. Davidson.*

But note that McMaster says:—"At Secunderabad about five, and at Bellary fifteen, or perhaps twenty per cent. only were Pintails."

** "The Pintail Snipe is very common in the neighbourhood of Belgaum;—in fact about one-half the birds in every bag that I have examined have been Pintails."—*E. A. Butler.*

†† "In Tumkur, Mysore, where there are many tanks and a good many Snipe, seven or eight Pin-tails would be shot for one Common Snipe."—*J. Davidson.*

"Out of 315 Snipe lately examined by me and shot in the Mysore, Hassan, Tumkur, Chitaldrug and Kadur districts of the Province of Mysore—

255,	or	80·95 per cent.	were Pintails,
42,	or	13·34 ,,	,, Fantails,
3,	or	0·95 ,,	,, Jacks, and
15,	or	4·76 ,,	,, Painters."—*C. McInroy, Major.*

‡‡ Mr. Bourdillon remarks:—"The specimen was obtained by Mr. Ferguson at 4,000 feet. The Pintail Snipe occurs in the cold season, at all elevations; it is very scarce at the higher elevations, and most abundant in the rice fields in the plains. About Trevandrum they are much more abundant than *G. scolopacinus.*

On the Palnis Mr. Fairbank only procured the Fantail. On the Nilgíris, however, Colonel McMaster says that the Pintail is almost the only Snipe seen.

Further north on the eastern side of the Peninsula,* in the Northern Circars, the eastern portions of the Central Provinces, Orissa, the Tributary Máhals, Chota Nagpur, Gya—in fact the country between the Ganges and the Gódavarí *apud* Ball—it is difficult to make out (so discrepant† are the accounts) in what proportion the two species occur; but I gather that in the level, low-lying, rice-growing tracts, the Pintail predominates, while in the hilly, jungly portions of this vast area the Common Snipe is much more numerous.

In Lower Bengal, west of the Brahmaputra, I believe, that both species are, taking the whole season round, about equally plentiful; but at any rate about Calcutta, and probably generally in Lower Bengal, this species greatly predominates towards the commencement of the season. In Bengal, east of the Brahmaputra, in Assam, right up to Sadiya, and in Cachar and Sylhet, I gather‡ that, though both species are found everywhere, the Pintail is on the whole decidedly the most common.

In Arakan, Pegu, Tenasserim, the Andamans and Nicobars,

---

* Colonel McMaster writes that out of a bag of 38 couple made near Madras, which he examined carefully, exactly half were Pin and half Fantails.

† According to Ball, S. F., II., 431, while the Common Snipe is common in Chota Nagpur, he personally never met with the Pintail; and from his general *résumé* of the Avifauna of the entire tract lying between the Ganges and the Gódavarí, it is to be gathered that he considers the Fantail the common universally distributed species, and the Pintail only of occasional occurrence in a few localities. But from Cuttack, Ganjam and Vizagapatam, I am informed that the Pintail is the Common Snipe. From Raipore, Blewitt wrote: "Out one day towards the end of April, shooting with Colonel Fullerton and Captain Sherman, we found numbers of Snipe in a plot of low-lying, swampy rice ground some six acres in extent, and I noted that out of 47 couple, which we killed, all but five and a half were Pintails." And again of the northern part of the tract, of which Gya may be taken as the centre, Brooks writes: "On the whole the Pintail is more frequently met with along the Chord Line than the Common Snipe." The fact is, Ball's geological work kept him, I fancy, mostly in the hilly portions of the vast area about which he writes, where the strata are exposed, and took him comparatively little into the level, low-lying, alluvial tracts, and hence perhaps the great discrepancy between his view of the relative abundance of this species and those of other observers.

‡ The most opposite opinions, however, are expressed; and the above is only my *ad-interim* conclusion based on a mass of very discrepant evidence. In weighing this I have had to make the best estimate I can of the relative value of opposing statements, and therefore my conclusions based on it may prove to be erroneous. No one can ever know the trouble I have taken to work out this question, or the difficulties that I have met with in so doing. I will give an instance: A and B, both gentlemen, in every way entitled to credence, but both personally unknown to me, wrote from the same station. A said: "The Pintail is *the* Snipe of the district; we kill five of these at least to every Fantail." B wrote: "The Common Snipe is very common here: not so the Pintail, which I have rarely met with." What was one to do? I sent A's letter to B, B's to A, and begged both to work the question out on the spot. A like a sensible man set to work and registered all his own and friend's kills; B wrote me an ill-considered letter, asking if I meant to impugn his word, and refusing to have anything more to say to me. A's figures, though not so large as I should have wished, bore out his assertions; and (though I may have erred in so doing), looking to the conduct of both, I conceived A to be the most reliable witness, and accepted his view.

I may add in regard to Assam that my collectors have sent me altogether ten Pintails, collected partly on the Khási Hills, partly about Sibságar, Dibrugarh and Sadíya, but not one Fantail, which looks as if the latter were greatly in the minority.

this is undoubtedly *the* Snipe—in most of these localities, (except perhaps about Moulmein just towards the close of the season), not one Fantail being met with to every ten Pintail.

Outside* our limits this species is common in Independent Burma and throughout the Malay Peninsula, and occurs, not only in the Siamese portion of the Peninsula, but also in Continental Siam, both at Bankok and far north at Zimmay. It has been recorded as common in Sumatra, Banka, Java and Borneo, and the whole of China, including the islands of Formosa and Hainan; but in none of these localities does it appear to remain during the summer. It is also said by Taczanowski to be common in the southern portions of Eastern Siberia and in the Amoor and Ussuri regions; and here it has been presumed that the majority breed. Doubtless it occurs in Tonquin, Cochin China, Anam and Cambodia; but of the Avifauna of these provinces I have no record. It has not been observed in either Eastern or Western Turkestan, and this helps to explain why it is so rare in the western half of Continental India.

ALTHOUGH it is possible that some few birds remain throughout the year within our limits in the Eastern Himalayas, the hilly portions of Assam, Chittagong,† Burma, the Andamans,‡

---

* Some difficulty exists in determining the real range of this species, because it was for long confounded with *G. megala* of Swinhoe. For instance, it has been recorded from the Philippines, but the Marquis of Tweeddale's investigations make it certain that *megala* does occur there, and probable that our bird does not. It has been also recorded from Timor, but this seems clearly outside its range, and the bird that really occurs there (as also in Celebes, &c.) must be *megala*. Again the Pintail is said to occur in Japan; but here too the species that really occurs is most probably *megala*, plenty of which have been sent thence, while Schlegel says he has never seen *sthenura* from Japan.

† See the latter part, for instance, of the following interesting note. Mr. H. Fasson says:—"Snipe are common in Chittagong, but not extremely plentiful. Ten or twelve couple is an unusually large bag in a day's shooting. One of the best localities for them is a large swamp, called Dum-Duma, near Fenna; but throughout the district they more commonly occur scattered in twos and threes, especially in the marshy heads of valleys running up amongst the hills. They feed in the rice-fields in the early mornings and evenings; but during the day have a rather strange habit of going up into the dry, thorny jungle that covers the hills, and lying there amongst the bushes. On one occasion, after walking up a lot of promising rice swamp without seeing a bird, a native, whom we asked, offered to show us Snipe, and forthwith took us, with beaters, a scramble up the steep slope of a range of hills covered with thorny jungle about four feet high. Out of this jungle, quite away from any springs or moisture, we put up five Snipe, the last one almost on the summit of the range, some 100 feet above the rice-fields. The Snipe, for the most part, come to the district about the latter part of August, and leave towards the end of March. At those times I have seen great numbers crowded together. Martin speaks of having seen three flights arrive at Fenna on the 30th August 1878. They came flying in large flocks, about 100 yards above the ground; and, after circling several times, all settled in patches of grass jungle surrounded by wooded hills. I believe, however, that a certain number of Snipe are to be found here all the year round. I have flushed Snipe up in the hill jungle, in June; and Jarbo, up at Rungumati in the Hill Tracts, shot half a dozen couple on the 31st July last—a bet had been made that no Snipe were to be found at that time of the year, but they were."

‡ We procured numerous specimens in the Andamans in June and July which bore no signs of immaturity.

&c., the great majority of the Pintail Snipe are in all parts of the Empire migrants. They begin to arrive during the latter half of August* throughout Continental India and Burma (and I may add the Malay Peninsula); but they are somewhat later in the Indian Peninsula†; and even further north and east, though some arrive earlier, the main army of the birds does not appear until September, and it is detachments and divisions of this which mainly, I believe, later invade the Indian Peninsula. And this accounts for the fact that, throughout those parts of Continental India where they are common, alike in the hills and plains,‡ they are much more numerous at the commencement and close of the season, and much less so from the 15th of October to the 15th of March, whereas this is just the period when they are uniformly most common in the Peninsula. In Burma and the Malay Peninsula I

---

* A few notes bearing on this point may be quoted:—"Snipe appeared here (18 miles from Gauhati), yesterday, the 1st of September, in great numbers. The natives said they came a fortnight earlier, but yesterday was the first day I saw them myself."

"Pintailed Snipe, first seen by me this year (1879) at Khulna, District Jessore, Lower Bengal, on the 22nd August, when I bagged it, and thus obtained my first Snipe of the season."—*H. J. Rainey*.

"*G. sthenura* comes in about the middle of August around Moulmein. A register, kept by Captain Dodd, the Master Attendant of Moulmein, a keen sportsman, showed the 17th August as the earliest date on which he has shot his first Snipe, during the last seven or eight years.

"In 1878, he and I procured four couple between us on the 17th August."—*C. T. Bingham*.

"Excessively common in Lower Pegu from the end of August to February, after which period it becomes rare. I have shot specimens up to the end of April."—*Eugene W. Oates*.

"I have shot the Pintail at Deesa, as early as the 24th of August. I sent you the head, neck and tail of one shot on the 29th of that month."—*E. A. Butler*.

Writing from Klang, in Malay Peninsula, about 3° 10′ North Lat. under date 2nd of August, Mr. H. C. Syers, Superintendent of Police, says: "The Snipe have not yet appeared, but we are expecting them every day as they come in by the middle of August."

† In the Southern Konkan they first arrive in October. The earliest date on which I have ever shot them was the 2nd of October."—*G. Vidal*.

"The Pintail is, I consider, our commonest Snipe in Belgaum, and it arrives about the end of September or the beginning of October."—*J. S. Laird*.

"I have shot the Pintail all over Southern India (south of about the 12° North Lat.); they come in about October or November just as the paddy crop is sown."—*Albert G. Theobald*.

‡ "The Pintailed Snipe is exceedingly common in the valley of Nepal, in winter, arriving at the end of August and migrating northwards about the beginning of May; it is most abundant in September and October, and again in March and April."—*J. Scully*.

"In a paper elsewhere published (P. Z. S., 1865, pp. 692-695), I have given some particulars of the occurrence of this Snipe about Barrackpore, where it is very plentiful, more so than the next species, arriving in September, and being replaced by that about the end of October or beginning of November."—*C. Beavan*.

"*G. sthenura* is certainly the earliest to arrive in any numbers in Bengal. About Calcutta, *G. sthenura* seems to disappear in December and January, doubtless migrating further to the south-east," (really to the *south-west*). "I have lately in those months examined bags of 30 to 50 birds without finding one specimen. It abounds again, I believe, in February and March."—*W. Blanford*.

cannot learn that anything similar has been observed,*—indeed the birds arrive, if anything, earlier in the extreme south than in the north. And this is in no way surprising, for the migration is not a north and south, but a north-east and south-west one; and it is not the birds from Pegu and Moulmein, but from countries north-east of it that supply the Malay Peninsula, just as Bombay is supplied, not by birds crossing the Himalayas due north of it (where this species is unknown), but due north-east of it, *viâ* Nepal and Kumaun, or further east still.

The time of their departure varies a good deal according to season and locality; but I believe that in Peninsular India in average years the majority leave before the middle of March,† and in Continental India before the middle of April, but in some years they are earlier and in some later; and alike in north and south some remain always much later, in some places well into May, and in a good many hilly localities a very few seem not to migrate at all.

Like the Common Snipe, the Pintail is sometimes met with in twos, threes or single birds; but in all favourable localities, it is met with in considerable numbers, which, though feeding and, as a rule, rising when disturbed separately, are all obviously acting in concert, arriving and leaving any feeding ground *en masse*. At the beginning of the season, in Lower

---

* It is true that Bingham says, writing from Moulmein: "It is very strange that, at the beginning of the Snipe season, one gets only the Pintail, and at the end chiefly the Fantail, with only one or two perhaps of the former."

But this requires a little qualification, according to others; and if actually about Moulmein, Pintail are scarcer about the middle of the cold season, this does not appear to be at all the rule inland in Tenasserim or Pegu; and if it be so at Moulmein, it is probably due to the fact that the majority of the birds seen in the Andamans and Nicobars, would naturally arrive *viâ* that portion of Tenasserim.

† Theobald, already quoted, (note p. 343), says that in the Peninsula south of the 12° North Lat., "they leave in March, though some stragglers are shot in April."

Again others say:—

"In Belgaum the Pintail appears to stay on through the hot weather until the thunderstorms come. Of course after February it is confined to the patches (chiefly found in jungles) of irrigated rice-land, and on being '*shikared*' soon takes refuge in the jungle. Most of the birds probably leave about the end of February when the country begins to get very dry; but I have found that in jungle tracts some stick to the irrigated rice until the hot weather storms come. These are very uncertain—sometimes commencing in March, sometimes in April or even the end of May. Probably a few birds stay on during the rains."—*J. S. Laird.*

"On the 22nd April this season I bagged four and a half couple, and saw several others. They were in excellent condition and showed no signs of breeding."—*E. A. Butler.*

"The majority of the Snipe leave the Southern Konkan in March; but a few hang about the neighbourhood of the tidal creeks till April and even May."—*G. Vidal.*

"In Mysore, Snipe remained common till the month of April."—*J. Davidson.*

But Major Charles McInroy, in a note quoted a little further on (note, p. 345), shows that, on the 26th of March 1878, they had mostly left Mysore.

In the Calcutta market these Snipe are generally common up to the 15th of April; after this they are scarce in some years. In others they are common, quite up to the close of that month. A few may be seen in some years in May, but never, I am told, more than a few.

Bengal, when the birds are arriving and moving on, you may visit a haunt, well known as a favourite one at that season, morning after morning without seeing a bird. Suddenly one morning the place is alive with them ; next day, and perhaps for two or three more, again not a single Snipe—then again numbers, for a day or two, and so on, until the whole country is thoroughly filled with them.

Great difference of opinion exists even amongst those best qualified to judge as to the habits, flight, and voice of the Pintail ; and I can only, with all diffidence, submit my own views on these matters—the result of a somewhat extended experience,—referring my readers at the same time to the opinions (some of which I quote below*) expressd by others.

---

* "It rises with a sharp, loud cry, unlike the ordinary Snipe, and its flight is heavier. Found in green grass, under a grove of trees, on the margin of the lake."—*J. V. Sturt.*

"*Sthenura*, according to my experience, does not frequent the same ground as the common species ; grass land, interspersed with rushes, is its favorite retreat. Its flights, too, are more laboured than in the other species ; it can at once be distinguished on the wing from this circumstance alone."—*J. C. Parker.*

"The birds obtained by me were not only shot upon the same ground as *scolopacinus, viz.*, along the edges of rice fields, but, in many instances, the two species rose simultaneously, and it was not, until I had shot the birds and examined them, that I distinguished the species. As regards the flight, I must admit that, occasionally when solitary individuals of *sthenura* have risen, the flight has struck me as being more laboured and heavier than in *scolopacinus ;* but then again, when the two species were on the wing at the same time, I did not observe any difference in their flight. As to the call I have never noticed any difference in the 'sca-a-ape,' of the two species."—*E. A. Butler.*

"It frequents rather drier ground than the Common Snipe, being often found in fields grown with potatoes, mustard, radishes, &c.; and it proclaims its affinity to *G. solitaria* by occasionally associating with it, in the colder months, about the grassy ground at the foot of the hills. But it is also constantly found in company with the Common Snipe. Its flight may be slightly heavier than that of the latter species, but where both birds occur in numbers, I believe the most experienced sportsman will be quite unable to distinguish *gallinaria* from *sthenura* on the wing."—*J. Scully.*

"A cold weather visitant to Furreedpore ; common ; it is frequently found in dry places, such as dry paddy fields, drains and the like, which *gallinaria* never is. One that I shot on the borders of a mustard field in the factory compound had about a dozen caterpillars, from 0·5 to 1·25 inch long, in its gizzard ; this bird was very dark coloured on its lower parts I shot a female, the last of the season, on the 24th April 1878 ; she was flushed from a perfectly dry ditch at the back of my house."—*J. R. Cripps.*

"I have arrived at the following conclusions :—

"*First.*—That the Common Snipe remains in Mysore considerably after most Pintails have left ; and

"*Secondly.*—That this is due to the difference in their habits of feeding.

"Pintails affect short grass, paddy fields after the crop is taken off, and so on, whereas Common Snipe are always to be found in *exceedingly muddy* ground—the banks of drying-up tanks, &c. On shooting them their bills will almost invariably be found covered with mud, whilst the Pintails appear to be able (I suppose from the nature of the ground which they frequent) to keep their's comparatively clean. The Pintail will be found round tanks, where the grass reaches to the water's edge—the Fantail, when the water recedes and reaches mud, pure and simple. And this accounts for the Common Snipe remaining longer ; the habitat of the Pintail dries up in this part of the country by the end of February or so.

"I will give one or two proofs of what I have advanced :—

"I.—On the 26th of March 1878, I shot round the edge of a tank in which the

Both the Pintail and Fantail affect cover and moist ground, so that, where both these luxuries exist, you will continually flush both species at the same spot; but the difference between them is that, while the Pintail if unable to get both his requirements will stick to grass and such-like cover, even if there be little perceptible moisture in the ground, the Common Snipe in such a case will stick to the wet ground, even though there be little perceptible cover there. The consequence is that, while you often get both birds in precisely the same ground, you will often find the Pintail apparently quite at home in dry grass lands, stubbles and scrub jungle, where the Common Snipe would never, except accidentally, occur, and again you find the Fantail on almost bare mud banks of rivers and tanks, where it is the rarest thing in the world to meet a Pintail.

Of course, I am well aware that, when much shot at and occasionally, but rarely, at other times, the Common Snipe will be found in dry cover some distance from water; but this is exceptional, whereas the Pintail is commonly and constantly flushed in such localities.

If the bills of the two birds be carefully examined, I think that this difference in habit will be better understood. The Fantail has the end of the bill more or less spatulate, that is to say, dilated and widened out; and in the dry skin it will be seen that the terminal inch of the upper, and even a greater length of the lower mandible is closely pitted with small semi-circular cavities. These are not visible in the freshly-killed bird, because, in life, these cavities are all filled up with nervous matter—nerve knots terminating delicate thread nerves permeating the bill and leading up to and joining the brain.

---

greater part of the basin had dried so as to expose the mud. Although the general average (including this day) is in these parts nearly 86 per cent. of Pintails to 14 per cent. of Fantails, on this occasion I shot 75 per cent. of Fans to 25 per cent. of Pins! My bag was not a large one, but it consisted of nearly all the Snipe remaining at the above date.

"II.—This year I was, with a companion, encamped from 1st to 4th February at a place in the Kadur district. We had only, on the evening of the 1st, time for a short stroll by the edge of a drying-up tank, and in the mud we killed three couple, *all* common. On Monday morning, 3rd, we were below a tank, some two miles off, in grass, where we got five couple, *all* Pintail. In the evening got two couple more off the mud—all Fantail."—*Charles McInroy, Major.*

"In the southern portions of the Peninsula, they chiefly affect swampy ground and young paddy fields; and when these become dry and cut, they keep to dry grass ground, with scrub jungle. I have frequently shot them in sugarcane fields by keeping outside and sending in men and dogs to make them rise."—*A. Theobald.*

"I have included under one head the Common and Pintailed species of Snipe; they are so very similar in general appearance that it is only by very close inspection one observes that they differ at all one from the other." —*J. H. Baldwin.*

"Its note is quite different from that of the Common Snipe, and the flight is rather slower and not so zig-zag.

"During the heat of the day, and sometimes when much shot at, it settles in dry tracts of jungle, some hundreds of yards from the water (I have also seen this habit occasionally in the Common Snipe); and in hot days I have found them in high crops, probably on account of the shade."—*W. E. Brooks.*

It is the drying-up of this nerve matter that reveals these cavities. Clearly this elaborate nervous plexus, calculated to make the end of the bill extremely sensitive, and this widening out of the bill, so as to increase the size of the sensitive area, point to a habit of obtaining the food almost entirely in situations where the sense of sight will not avail; in the case of this bird deep in the mud, where the bill has to do the work of both eyes and hands. But the bill of the Pintail is quite different; there is no dilation towards the tip and a mere trace of the pits so conspicuous in the Fantail; they exist, but are very much smaller, involving a greatly diminished sensitiveness, and cover a materially smaller area. Moreover, the tip of the bill is stronger, the knob on the lower surface of the tip of the upper mandible being thicker and larger, and altogether the extreme tip of the mandible stronger. Clearly this points to feeding habitually in harder ground, and where the eyes can more materially assist in discovering food, *i.e.*, in drier places.

Nor is this a mere hypothesis; the contents of the stomachs sufficiently confirm this *à priori* argument. In the Pintail you find all kinds of *land* organisms, grubs, caterpillars, small insects, crustacea, shells and *grass*, as well as and more frequently than worms, water grubs, aquatic insects, and tiny water-shells and crustacea, which constitute the entire food (in this country at any rate) of the Fantail.

Then as to the flight, I personally am perfectly certain that, as a general rule, and under like conditions, the flight of the Pintail is heavier and more direct than that of the Common Snipe; and in nine cases out of ten, you can, if due allowance be made for existing conditions, tell at once the species of the bird, before you draw trigger, simply by the flight. Of course if you flush Pintail in a cold morning with a good wind, they fly infinitely smarter than Fantail, rising in a dead calm under a hot, mid-day sun; or if you work Pintail on a wind they will go off sharper and twisting more than Fantail worked off the wind; but I individually am certain that all conditions being identical, the flight of the Pintail is more laboured, more direct, and less zig-zaggy than that of the Fantail.

As to the notes of the two birds, I am at a loss to understand how *any* one can assert that they are identical. To my ears they are as distinct as two sounds of the same class can well be—that of the Pintail being sharper, and more screechy. With birds flushed singly, within 25 yards, I would undertake, with my eyes shut, to identify every bird that rose correctly. Of course where half a dozen birds of each species are rising at varying distances all round one, at the same time, or where birds rise at long distances, no one, probably, could certainly discriminate the sounds.

I do not think that, as a rule, Pintail afford the chance for such heavy bags as the Common Snipe. I know a good many places in the North-West Provinces where a good shot could, to this day, easily, with a breech-loader and light charges, bag his seventy-five couple between 10 A.M. and 4 P.M., and a good many places where he could go on doing this for several successive days, and yet not exhaust the ground. In my time I have visited all the best grounds within twenty miles of Calcutta. When Mr. Russell was Collector of Jessore, (and India has seen few better or more persevering Snipe-shots) I visited, under his guidance, most of the best Snipe grounds in that neighbourhood; and in Dacca, too, I shot for nearly a month in the best Snipe swamps, but I have never anywhere seen anything like the masses of Pintail gathered into one neighbourhood that I have of Common Snipe in parts of the Doab.

A recent writer gave a diary of the results of eighteen days' Snipe-shooting about Calcutta between the 14th of September and the 21st of March, showing a daily average of 33 couple to two guns. There is a single locality in the Meerut, two in the Bulandshahr, two in the Aligarh district, &c., where two good shots, shooting thus once a week through the best part of the season, would certainly average eighty, and probably more, nearly one hundred couple per diem. Of course these are out-of-the-way places, far from the head-quarters of the district, and unlikely to be visited by other sportsmen; but in one single spot in the Meerut district, on the Boorha Gunga, in the neighbourhood of Hastinapur, to my certain knowledge, over 700 couple of Common Snipe were bagged during December 1850 by different parties who visited the place. Of course, there were many guns out—some good, some bad, some days as few as two, some days as many as seven. And there was shooting on ten different days, and the average per gun per diem was considerably less than twenty couple. But I have never even heard of any *one* place in Bengal, Burma or Southern India* where anything like this bag of Pintail could have been made by any number of guns. And I think I am correct in saying that the Pintail never masses in such enormous numbers as the Common Snipe not unfrequently does in favorable situations in Upper India.

It is not much use giving sportsmen in India advice as to how to wind and work Snipe; here where every one shoots Snipe, and where Snipe afford so often the chief available sport, every man has his own opinion as to the vexed ques-

---

* For instance Major C. McInroy writes: "The largest bags I know of in the Mysore Province within the last 25 years have not exceeded 60 couple to two guns; but I do not give this as necessarily correct, for many bags may have been made of which I have not heard. I once, shooting badly, bagged 20 couple in about three and a half or four hours, but was unable to go on for I had to move camp."

Again Mr. Oates says: "The largest bag made in Lower Pegu does not often exceed 20 couple."

tion of working on or off a wind, and really with Snipe massed, as ours so commonly are, and lying as they do lie in the Indian noontide glare, and with the almost entire absence of wind during the middle of most cold-season days inland, it matters very little, if you only hold the gun straight, ho.v you work them.

But on one or two points a word of caution may not be out of place.

As a rule men waste an incredible amount of ammunition and tire themselves out by using too heavy charges. In the old muzzle-loader days, with 12 and even 10 bore guns, I have often and often, after completing my fifty couple *with difficulty*, had to leave off, solely owing to the terrible headache induced by the repeated discharges of the gun, and that perhaps before 2 o'clock, whilst half the ground or more remained utterly untouched. Had I then known what I know now, and had the guns now available been so then, I could often have certainly bagged a hundred couple. A twenty or twenty-four bore breech-loader, with the left barrel half choke, rather heavy in metal, is best I think for Snipe. With this have two sizes of cartridges, one dram of powder and half an ounce of No. 10 shot, and one and a half drams of powder and three-fourths of an ounce of No. 7 shot. With these charges, if the gun is a good one, you can kill Snipe as well, and as far as is ever necessary, and you may fire off such cartridges out of such a gun two or three hundred times in a day without the smallest inconvenience.

Wild buffalo have grown rarer during the last thirty years, but when I as a youngster shot Snipe in the Dacca district, it was no very uncommon incident to be suddenly charged out of a mass of bulrushes by a cantankerous old Urna, and we always kept a rifle close behind us in localities where such mar-sports were rumoured to abide. Probably much the same is the case to this day in many parts of Assam.

Once, when four of us had gathered together for a moment close to a dense clump of rush, without warning, from the very edge of the cover, not thirty yards distant from us, out charged an Urna. Our men were all with us ; our rifles were in our hands in a second ; six shots were fired almost simultaneously, and the great mud-coated brute fell on his knees almost within touching distance, and rolled over dead. The curious thing was, that only one ball had taken any real effect ; one had missed altogether, one had lodged in the right side of the neck, one in the ribs, and three had struck the forehead. All the balls, but one, had been about No. 12 round leaden bullets fired from six-groove barrels ; the sixth was a clumsy three-ounce cone, hardened with type metal fired from a two-groove rifle, and this one had gone straight into the brain, the other two flattening themselves under the skin on the skull.

Tickell gives another instance of a similar unprovoked attack. He says :—

"While shooting in those wild morasses, which in India are called "jhils" and in Eastern Bengal "bhíls," it is as well to be provided with a spare double-barrel loaded with ball; for the thick beds of reeds often harbour wild buffaloes, dangerous customers to deal with in such localities. I was one day (in 1843) exploring a marsh of this description near Dhobra, in the Malda District, seated in a "sarunga," a species of dug-out, propelled by punting from the stern. A dense tangle of rushes, reeds, and all kinds of water-plants extended for about two miles in length and a mile in breadth, here and there opening out into pools of deep, clear water, covered with the wide leaves of water-lily, and everywhere pierced by narrow channels, through which the little canoe was propelled, occasionally being shoved through the herbage to pick up some bird which had fallen to my gun. I had just shot a specimen of *Ardetta sinensis*—a beautiful bird, very like in size and colour our little Bittern of Europe—and we were forcing the boat through the reeds to get at it, when a loud plunge and rush in the tangle close by put us on the *qui vive;* and in another moment I perceived through the tall stems of the grass, first the huge back, and then, as he turned, the broad front and horns, of an Urna or wild buffalo. The brute immediately advanced on us, but in so doing got off the hammock he had been lying on, and plunged up to his jowl in the weeds and water. To turn our boat was impossible; so, putting down my gun, I ordered the man to pass me over his "luggee" or bamboo pole, and with it I began vigorously punting "bock agen," as they say in Cumberland. The canoe retraced its course more easily than it had advanced, as the way had been partly cleared by our entrance, and as the native, who appeared to understand thoroughly the character of our pursuer, hauled strenuously at every rush and reed within his grasp; and so, what with warping ahead and poling astern, we made good progress—the plunging and snorting of our friend in the rear, as he struggled after us, allowing of no "lingerings by the way." The chase was exciting, and its result for a time doubtful. When we reached a clearer space the sarunga would slip along, leaving Bubalus well astern; but when we were jammed in the reeds he would come up uncomfortably near; and once, when plunging my pole into an unexpectedly deep hole, I nearly toppled overboard, I gave myself up for lost. I do not know what a buffalo would do with a gentleman in the water: he could not well toss him, nor gore him; perhaps he would trample him under and drown him? Can anybody enlighten us on the point? Thank heaven, it was not my fate to solve this problem by an *experimentum crucis;* for about ten minutes struggle brought us into a stretch of clear deep water, and then it was "Lombard-street to a Chainy orange" in favour of your humble servant and his sable gondolier. The buffalo, perceiving it was a decided case of *nolle prosequi*, and that we could go three yards to his one, desisted from further efforts; and, giving us the welcome view of his stern, regained the reeds, and was heard to plunge and flounder away—so far, indeed, that we noiselessly returned to the spot of our first encounter, and triumphantly carried off *Ardetta sinensis*."

I have known one or two people seriously injured in such untoward *rencontres*, and it is "just as well," as Tickell truly says, not to overlook their possibility when Snipe or Wild Fowl shooting in buffalo-haunted swamps.

The places in which to seek for Snipe vary, even in the case of the same species, in almost every district; and I do not know that I can usefully say more in regard to the probable general whereabouts of the Pintails than that they love good cover of rice, rice stubble, high grass, rush, reed or scrub, in damp ground, whether in fields or swamps, on hill-sides or along the margins of lakes and rivers, but that they will cling to cover of this nature long after the ground in which it grows has become comparatively dry.

Davison writes: "On the plateau of the Nílgiris the Pintail Snipe frequent the swamps or marshes that lie at the bases of the hills. These swamps vary a good deal in the degrees of 'bogginess,' some being comparatively smooth and dry, (though sufficiently wet for this Snipe) and are easily got over; others, again, are either very soft and slushy, or else closely dotted over with dry, rough, irregular mounds, surrounded in every direction by little canals of water;—these last are the worst to get over. You have to step carefully or jump, from mound to mound, taking care before you leave one to make sure that the next will bear you. If you had merely to pick your way over such ground it would be bad enough, but when you have to keep a sharp and constant look-out for any bird that may rise in front, to the side, or even occasionally behind you, it makes matters a good deal worse. Suddenly, just as you have accomplished a particularly nasty jump, before you have had time to settle firmly on your feet, you hear the contemptuous sneer of a departing Snipe, one of your beaters screams out *Isnope* (shikarees and beaters on the Nílgiris always call Snipe, *Isnope*, or *Isnipe*); you whisk round to get a shot, see the bird just within range, raise your gun, feeling happy at the prospect of adding one more to the bag, when, before you know exactly how it has happened, you find yourself up to your waist in a nice soft black ooze. Your gun has gone off, and so has your bird, and you have to wait till you are helped out by a couple of your beaters, who, as they approach you, are trying to look sympathetic while it is all they can do to avoid laughing outright at your mishap.

However, after having been well scraped, you start again, and if you are fortunate and know your ground well, or have a shikaree who does, and knows when to look for the birds—for these Snipe, though found about the body of the swamp, in the morning and afternoon, generally retire during the day, (unless it is cloudy) to the edge of the *shola* which usually heads every swamp, or to the cover of the andromeda bushes which fringe its edges—you may succeed in bagging half a dozen couple; and if you are not solely intent on the long bills, may have added a couple of Hares, a brace of Spur Fowl, a few Bush Quail, and perhaps even a Grey Jungle Cock, to the bag.

"Snipe shooting on the Nílgiris is generally accomplished with the aid of beaters, more or less numerous according to taste and resources, and perhaps a few dogs; but a very effective and very economical way—and one to which the swamps about Ooty are particularly adapted—is to have, say only two men, and twenty or thirty yards of rope, about the thickness of a lead pencil. To the rope should be attached, at distances of two or three feet, tags about a foot long of white cloth. On coming to a swamp, one man goes to either side, each holding one end of the rope which they drag over the swamp, occasionally flapping it up and down. If the swamp is a narrow one you skirt it; if a broad one, you walk down the middle, but in either case a few feet behind the rope, and you will thus obtain a good many shots.

"When disturbed, the Pintail will, on being flushed, often settle on grassy hill-sides far away from water, or take refuge in a *shola*, and often, when they first come in, they will alight on bare hills where they will remain the whole day."

Again, I may quote my friend Mr. Vidal's remarks on Snipe-shooting in the Southern Konkan, though these apply equally to both species:—

"Snipe-shooting in Ratnagiri can seldom be had before the first or second week in November, after the monsoon rice has been harvested. Even then the birds are so scattered and uncertain in their choice of grounds that a great deal of heavy walking is necessary to get a moderate bag. The best grounds are the low-lying khárvat rice fields, on the banks of the tidal creeks, and reclaimed from the salt water, by earthen embankments. But in shooting over such grounds it is well, if possible, to choose your time so as to have two or three hours of the highest tide. For all round the paddy fields are acres and acres of mud swamps with stunted thorny bushes, in which many of the birds lie at low tide until they are driven up to the fields by the flood. These mud swamps, intersected by numerous deep channels, and full of pit-falls and sticky black slush, are too nasty walking to tempt even the most enthusiastic sportsman. But as the Snipes themselves are driven from these pestilent strongholds by the tide, there is happily no necessity to venture into them.

"The best Snipe-shooting is to be had near the coast in the vicinity of the large rivers; but inland there are many snug little grounds formed by terraced rice fields at the foot of the hills, and here and there a low-lying tank, where the monsoon water, rapidly receding, leaves an oozy bed of rushes and sedge, where a few Pintails are always at home. December and January are the best months for Snipe-shooting, as by that time the superfluous rain water has all evaporated, and the birds are concentrated in all their regular legitimate haunts, whereas earlier in the season the area of wet ground is so large that there is no knowing where to look for them."

All Snipe seem to affect particular spots; there may be fifty localities within a radius of a few miles, all, so far as any human being can judge, equally likely to attract the birds, and yet in practice there always prove to be two or three corners possessing such irresistible attractions for them that year after year, and week after week, whether the other likely spots are blank or not, *they* are sure to contain Snipe if there be any in the country. There used to be, and probably is still, a small swampy pond on the road-side, between Maipuri and Bhongaon, a trumpery little place skirting a much frequented high road, to which one year, that I was detained in the station, I drove every morning, but Sundays, during the greater portion of November and December, and where I each day killed every Snipe on the pool, from two to, I think, on one occasion six couple without once finding less than four birds. These were Common Snipe, but I know that the same precisely is the case with Pintails; and Mr. Fasson alludes to an instance of this kind in Chittagong. He says: "There is a tank near Chukurea, by the road side, which we have frequently noticed as *always* containing a couple of Snipe. I and others have, during the past three years, gone by that road some fifteen or twenty times, and have never failed to shoot a Snipe in that tank, sometimes a couple, and have always found it re-occupied even if we visited it again the next day. It is a smallish tank with low, reedy grass edges, in which edges the Snipe lie."

Davison writes to me of a curious trait observed by him of this species, which, so far as I am aware, has never been noticed in the case of the Common Snipe. He says: "At Klang, in the Selangore District, (Malay Peninsula) I noticed that the Snipe *(G. sthenura)* instead of remaining in the paddy flats and other similar low-lying places (which they frequented during the day) all resorted for the night to two comparatively elevated spots. One, and the favorite one apparently, was a grassy tract lying between the Klang fort at the top of the first rise of the hill, and the Resident's house which is a little higher up. This bit of ground was very dry and covered with a short, stiff, turf grass. The birds, as soon as it began to get dark (which was soon after 6 P.M.), began to arrive from all directions, singly, in couples, or in wisps, each one, as it alighted, uttering its characteristic cry. The birds remained all night, but dispersed as soon as the morning gun was fired from the fort at 5 A.M., when it was still quite dark. Their other nightly resort was a small bit of ground, also on the hill, that had been recently cleared of brushwood to make a garden. This place, situated at the foot of a small rise, was rather marshy. All the Snipe in the neighbourhood flocked to these two places at night, the former, where I should say several hundred Snipe congregated every evening, being the most frequented. But although I frequently went after them, yet, on the whole, I was not successful, owing to the difficulty of seeing the birds well enough to make sure of them, when flushed or even when first alighting. I found that the only plan was to go some little way down the slope of the hill and take my chance of a bird or birds passing immediately over head. No doubt when the birds first began to arrive there was generally light enough to see them, though indistinctly; but within a quarter of an hour (Klang is not a hundred miles from the equator) it becomes too dark to see to shoot."

OF THE nidification of the Pintail Snipe absolutely nothing certain is known, though Hodgson records that in females, obtained by him on the 4th of May, the eggs were still small. No doubt some few birds do remain all the year in the Andamans, the Chittagong Hill Tracts, and other hilly tracts; but whether birds thus remaining breed there, is as yet uncertain. Possibly this bird does not breed until the second year, and these birds and the late stayers generally may be birds of the year. Even, however, if some do breed here, the great majority doubtless breed elsewhere, and it has been supposed that they breed in South-Eastern Siberia; but Dybowski, who gives a full account of the breeding of *G. megala (heterocerca*, Cab., *apud* Cabanis, *hodie**) in Darasun, leads us to infer that this species breeds further north, as he says, "not uncommon *on passage*, arrives in the spring early in May, remains in autumn till October."

* Or at any rate of J. F. O., 1873, 104. I personally cannot help suspecting that the specimen *originally* described as *heterocerca* (J. F. O., 1870, 235) was merely *sthenura*, and that Cabanis' *heteroearca*, from Luzon (J. F. O., 1872, 317) was *megala*. According to the passage first referred to, however, *heterocerca* is affirmed by Cabanis to be equivalent to the species we English now call *megala*.

As to *megala*, Cabanis believes that Swinhoe really first applied this name to specimens of *solitaria* (a bird Swinhoe never obtained, unless a bird he sent to Blyth, and which was lost, belonged to this species), and that the name *megala* was later wrongly transferred to his *heterocerca*. This hypothesis is absolutely untenable since Swinhoe *had* no specimens of *solitaria*, to which to apply the name, until several years later when he got one or more (he sent me one of each) from Pekin and Japan, and his name *megala* was applied to the *Common* Great Snipe of China, of which he had numbers of specimens, and which is unquestionably the bird we now call *megala*.

But I have discussed this question more fully in the out-coming November 1880 number of *Stray Feathers*, to which I must refer any chance reader who may care to investigate further this barren question of nomenclature.

It is true that Swinhoe, writing (*Ibis*, 1863, 415) on Formosan Ornithology remarked, that "a few stay to breed in our marshes." But later, in his revised list of the Birds of China (P. Z. S., 1871, 497) he seems to have changed his opinion and says, "probably goes north to breed." And we gather from Pére David that even at Pekin, in Northern China, it only occurs on passage.

If, as I believe, *heterocerca* of Cabanis, *apud* Prjevalski, (which he keeps separate from *megala* of Swinhoe) is really *sthenura*, then he gives us the following in regard to its breeding:—

"It breeds in tolerable numbers on the Ussuri, but is still more plentiful during migration, about the 10th of April and in the end of August.

"In the latter half of April the birds choose their nesting localities in the thinly overgrown marshes, and their peculiar courting commences. Rising into the air, similar to our *G. scolopacina*, and describing large circles above the spot where the female is sitting, it suddenly dashes downwards with great noise (which is most likely produced by the tail-feathers, like that made by our species, and somewhat resembles the noise of a broken rocket). As the bird approaches the ground the noise increases, until it has got within a hundred yards, when it suddenly stops the sound and quietly flies on, uttering a note something like "*tiric, tiric, tiric.*" Courtship lasts until the middle of June, and is mostly heard or seen in the mornings and evenings, but occasionally in the day time, and even at night in clear weather." He adds that "it was not seen in the Hoang-ho Valley where *megala* breeds numerously."

Middendorff never seems to have met with this species, and the *G. sthenura*, Temminck, of Radde, is clearly not our bird, but probably *megala*.

Now countless myriads of this species visit this Empire (and the other countries already mentioned when describing its range) during the winter. If only half of these bred in Southern or South-Eastern Siberia, one would think that every collector, Radde, Middendorff, Schrenk, Dybowski, would have found them breeding; and unless we suppose that, as a rule, this species has not been discriminated from the Fantail, we must admit that its breeding head-quarters are still somewhat of a mystery.

THE FEMALES in this species average larger and heavier than the males; but the dimensions and weights of both sexes are very variable, according doubtless to age, and the weights vary also materially according to season; birds shot in the latter part of March and in April, running, as a body, heavier than those shot from October to the end of January.

The following is the *resumé* of the dimensions and weights

of nearly one hundred specimens of each sex, killed between the 20th August and the 27th April:—

Males.—Length, 9·75 to 10·9; expanse, 15·5 to 17·4; wing, 4·95 to 5·42; tail from vent, 2·0 to 2·57; tarsus, 1·19 to 1·27; bill from gape, 2·12 to 2·5; bill at front, 2·2 to 2·6; weight, 3·3 ozs. to 4·75 ozs. Average, 3·91 ozs.

Females.—Length, 10·0 to 11·17; expanse, 16·1 to 18·25; wing, 5·0 to 5·58; tail from vent, 2·0 to 2·67; tarsus, 1·2 to 1·35; bill from gape, 2·38 to 2·62; bill at front, 2·45 to 2·7; weight, 3·75 ozs. to 5·1 ozs. Average, 4·2 ozs. Average of both sexes, 4·06 ozs.

The legs and feet are greenish or greenish leaden, but especially late in the spring these parts exhibit, in some birds, a distinct olive yellow tinge; the irides are deep brown; the bill generally has the gape, the extreme base and margins of the upper mandible greenish, or olive, but sometimes some or all of these are unicolorous with the rest of the basal four-sevenths of the upper mandible, which are usually pale horny brown; on the other hand even these at times show a greenish tinge; the terminal three-sevenths of the bill are deep brown, blackish horny towards the tip, and paling towards the opposite direction.

THE PLATE is not good. I do not mean to assert that no *sthenura* was ever like the plate, because the species is so extremely variable that this would be rash; but it does not at all accurately represent an average specimen. If the white margins of the *scapulars* had been given a fawny tinge, if the breast had been made browner, and the markings continued over it, and if the second face band, which is about a quarter of an inch below the eye had been shown instead of being absolutely ignored, the picture of the standing bird would have been fair. As for the picture of the bird flying away, which has the entire lower parts from chin to vent white, and the entire lower back and rump unmarked grey, it is purely an effort of the artist's imagination. In every specimen of this species that I have ever seen, the front of the neck and the upper breast at least have been pale brown or fawny, mottled, streaked or barred with dark brown. In every specimen the lower back is regularly bared, in some greyish white and blackish brown, in others fawn colour and brown, &c.; but it is invariably barred, never uniform.

Again, the rump and upper tail-coverts are never grey, but always a sort of olivaceous or rufescent brown, often well barrred, always showing traces of this.

The species is an excessively variable one. I have specimens now before me with the entire lower breast, abdomen, and vent pure white and unmarked. I have others with the whole of these parts barred, almost as strongly and regularly as in *nemoricola.* There are some in which the front of the throat and upper breast are fawn coloured, blurred with numerous ill-defined spots and streaks of dark brown, and others in which the upper breast is strongly and distinctly, though rather irregularly, *barred.* Many birds have less barring even on the flank than is shown in the plate; in others it is far more profuse, narrower, and closer set. Most specimens have two dark streaks down the throat, one starting from either base of the lower mandible, which is about in the same line as the front of the eye; sometimes these are only indicated and occasionally entirely wanting. The upper surfaces differ widely—some are altogether brighter, the black more intense, the markings on the scapulars are more intense rusty, their pale margins a brighter and richer buff. In some few birds, almost exclusively Andaman specimens, the back and wing markings are almost as white as in the plate; but, as a rule, they vary from pale fawny white to rufous buff.

The plate of the wing-lining and tail of this species (*vide* plate, *ante*, facing page 332,) is on the whole very fair; but as a rule the lower tail-coverts, &c., are a paler and more fawny buff than in the specimen figured.

I cannot say that Mr. Neale's plates will help any one materially in distinguishing between the Pintail and Fantail, but still there ought to be no difficulty in discriminating them.

In the first place there is the difference in the shape of the bill (*vide* ante, p. 346) by which you can distinguish the two, even when served up dressed for dinner.

Then there is the difference in the barring of the under surface of the wing. In the Pintail the axillaries and the entire wing-lining, except the lower greater coverts, are invariably strongly and distinctly barred with blackish brown. This, according to my experience, is *never* the case in the Common Snipe. In many specimens of this latter there is no barring at all, properly speaking, on the lower surface of the wing; but even where the axillaries and some of the coverts *are* strongly barred, *the median secondary lower coverts are always unbarred,* forming a white unbarred patch in the centre of the upper portion of the lower surface of the closed wing.

Then there is the difference in the tail feathers. These, in the Common Snipe, are fourteen, occasionally sixteen, very rarely twelve in number—all ordinary shaped and soft. In the Pintail there are only ten such feathers, but on either side of these ten, are from five to nine, very narrow, rather rigid, feathers, making up a total of from twenty to twenty-eight feathers. There are not always the same number of these on each side. I have often found, in apparently uninjured tails, one more on one side than another. These narrow feathers are generally completely hidden by the lower tail-coverts; occasionally I have found them entirely wanting, and I have repeatedly seen them just sprouting, and in every stage between that and full development. But even where they are entirely wanting, the presence of only ten ordinary tail feathers, the tail being perfect and symmetrical, is sufficient to distinguish this species from the Common Snipe.

In the Common Snipe the outer web of the first primary is white or nearly so ; in the present species it is unicolorous with the inner web, *i.e.*, a rather pale brown. Again, in the Common Snipe, all the secondaries are pretty broadly and very conspicuously tipped with pure white, while in the Pintail they are at most only margined with albescent or brownish white.

There are many other minor and more or less constant differences, but the above are amply sufficient to enable any one to distinguish the two species at a glanee.

Melanoid and albinoid varieties of this species are occasionally met with. Of the latter I have a fine example now before me, procured by my friend Mr. J. C. Parker near Calcutta. The lower surface does not differ much from the normal type, except that the markings on the breast and flanks are pale brownish grey, but the entire upper surface is a mixture of pale cream colour and pale brownish grey. I have seen at least half a dozen similar creamy-coloured birds in the course of the last thirty years. I also once shot one that was snow-white everywhere, with only faint traces of grey markings. Before the mutiny, I had a specimen procured near Dacca, which was everywhere blackish dusky, darker than either of the only two Sabine's snipe I ever saw, but very similar to these ; but alike in this and in all the albinoid specimens I have seen, the wing-lining and axillaries differed but little from the normal type, and had not participated, at any rate to the same extent, in the general change or loss of colour. I do not know whether this is always so, but it has been the case in all the instances that have come under my personal observation.

GALLINAGO GALLINULA ½ GALLINAGO SCOLOPACINUS.

THE COMMON OR FANTAIL SNIPE.

Gallinago cœlestis, *Frenzel.*

Vernacular Names.—[Chaha, *N. W. Provinces, Oudh;* Bharka, Bharak, (Hindee), *Central Himalayas, Nepal, &c.;* Chegga, Cheyga, *Lower Bengal;* Cheryga, *Dibrugarh, Assam;* Check lonbi, *Manipur;* Tibud, Pán-láwa, (Mahrati), *Ratnagiri;* More-oolan, Oolan, (Tamil), Muku-puredi, (Telegu), *Southern India;* Kadakecho, *Orissa;* Ket-batta, (Lurka-Koles); Kas-watua, *Ceylon;* Pashálek, *Afghanistan;* Maharamche, (Turki), *Yárkand;*]

THERE is no corner of the Empire, from Ceylon, the Nicobars, and the Pakchan on the south to the Habb river and Gilgit on the west, and Manipur and Sadiya on the east, in which the Common Snipe does not occur, as a commoner or rarer visitant, or at any rate straggler, during the winter, and some few at least breed in Kashmir.

In describing the distribution of the Pintail, I have said so much of that of the present species that I need not now enter into any great detail—suffice it to say that the two species are, to a great extent, complementary to each other in their ranges, the one being most abundant where the other is rarest, and *vice versâ;* that in Oudh, the N.-W. Provinces, the Punjab, and the Himalayas west of the Jumna, in Sindh, Rajputana, Cutch, Káthiáwar, the Central India Agency (excluding the Bondela States), and the western portions of the Central Provinces, this is *the* Snipe, and in all suitable localities very plentiful. That again in the hilly country between the Ganges and the Gódavarí, Chota Nagpur, the Tributary Máhals, &c., this is the predominant form, while in the Andamans and Nicobars, and Tenasserim Proper it is extremely rare, and in the rest of British Burma,* Bengal, east of the Brahmaputra, and Assam, decidedly less common than the Pintail and in many districts quite scarce.

In Independent or Upper Burma this species is fairly abundant in suitable localities during the cold season. In the

* "The Common English Snipe is everywhere rare in Pegu, compared with the Pintail. It does not appear to arrive so early. It is found in much the same places, and bags almost always contain one or two specimens of this species."—*Eugene W. Oates.*

Malay Peninsula it is rare to a degree. Out of several hundred Snipe carefully examined by Davison, only two, one shot near Malacca (2° North Latitude), and one in the island of Tonka (8° North Latitude), proved to belong to the present species. It has not been recorded or sent, so far as I know, from Continental Siam, or the countries eastwards of this, (though it probably straggles to most or all of these) or from Sumatra, Java, or Borneo; but it seems not uncommon in the Philippines (where it has been procured in the islands of Luzon, Bohol, Leyte, &c.,) and Japan, and is common in Hainan, Formosa, and throughout China during the cooler half of the year. Prjevalski met with it at Lake Hanka in the Ussuri country, where some few breed, in the valley of the Hoang-ho and South-East Mongolia, in the former of which it is a rare breeder, as also probably in the latter, and at the Koko-Nor in Chinese Tibet. It is a summer visitant throughout Siberia, breeding commonly as far north as the 70th degree North Latitude, on the Boganida. In Eastern Turkestan it is similarly a common summer visitant,* as it is likewise in Western Turkestan where some, however, also remain in winter. Stoliczka obtained it at Punja in Wakhan in April. To Afghanistan and Beluchistan it is a winter visitant only, widely and universally distributed, but owing to the nature of the country nowhere met with as yet in large numbers. Throughout Persia it appears to be common in winter in suitable localities, and some *may* breed there as it was observed in May near Karman, at an elevation of some 8,000 feet. Westward it abounds in Turkish Arabia (Mesopotamia), Armenia, and parts of Asia Minor, and occurs also in Palestine.

Throughout the north of Africa, as far south at any rate as the highlands of Abyssinia on the east and the Gambia river on the west (say approximately the 12th degree North Latitude), the Canaries and Madeira, the whole of Europe, including the islands of the Mediterranean, the Azores and Iceland, and the southern portions of Greenland, the Fantail occurs in suitable localities at one season or another, breeding for the most part north of the 50th degree North Latitude to well within the Arctic Circle, but occasionally further south, as in Algeria, the Atlantic Islands and perhaps even Abyssinia,

* "The Common Snipe was tolerably numerous in the neighbourhood of Yárkand in summer, where it was ascertained to breed. The bird was never observed in winter. It was found in the neighbourhood of marshy ground and inundated fields. This species breeds in May and June: the eggs—a good deal incubated—were obtained on the 12th June, and two young nestlings on the 16th of the same month.

"Two eggs measured 1·58 in length by 1·11 in breadth, and 1·55 by 1·13. In form they are like a broad oval, suddenly pinched and pulled out to form the small end of the egg. They have a slight gloss, and the ground colour is dirty olive green. The small end is unspotted, the constricted portion of the egg has some largish spots of brownish, and the large end is nearly covered with confused blotches of brown and brownish black."—*J. Scully.*

where at Lake Ashangi (elevation 8,500 feet, 12° 30′ North Latitude), Blanford found it still common in the beginning of May.

THE COMMON SNIPE, I am disposed to think, arrives, broadly speaking, from three weeks to a fortnight later than the Pintail. There is no general arrival of even the advanced guard of the Fantail until quite the end of August, while the Pintail constantly appear in considerable numbers with the third week of that month. The question is complicated by the fact that individual stragglers of the Common Snipe often appear along with the first Pintail detachments. Thus Butler shot both species at Deesa on the 24th of August; but, as a rule, they only begin to arrive in appreciable numbers in September*; they are not well in until the close of the month, and are even later in South† and in Burma.‡

They mostly leave the plains before the close of March§, but some linger everywhere much later, especially in the Sub-Himalayan and similar well-watered and well-wooded tracts, and

* "The Common Snipe arrives in the valley of Nepal about the 1st of September, and retires early in May. Although it may be shot in the valley in any month between the dates above indicated, it is most numerous on its migrations, being more common from September to about the middle of November, and in March and April. I found it rather scarce in the Nawakot district in November. It is always found in the wet fields and swampy grounds in the central parts of the valley, and seems to avoid the crop fields and the ground at the foot of the hills. It occurs in the valley in about one-third of the numbers of *sthenura*."—*J. Scully.*

"The Common Snipe begins to make its appearance towards the end of September, but it is not until the end of October that it appears in any numbers in the Lucknow Division."—*Geo. Reid.*

"On the Eastern Narra (South-East Sindh) they begin to arrive in September, and leave in April."—*Scrope B. Doig.*

"The first full Snipe was shot here (Jacobabad) this year on the 28th of August. but it was some time later before any considerable numbers appeared."—*P. J. Maitland.*

"Snipe migrate from colder climates to the plains of India about the first week in October."—*J. H. Baldwin.*

† "I have shot them all over Southern India south of the 12th degree North Latitude; they are cold-weather visitants, arriving about October, and leaving again during March and April, some few remaining until May or even later. They are quite common."—*A. Theobald.*

‡ "The Common Snipe is comparatively rare; *the* Snipe of Burma is the Pin, tail. The Fantail does not appear till the cold weather is well in. say in December- and then but few will be found in even a large bag of Snipe. It stays till late. I have shot them in March."—*Eugene Oates.*

"The Common Snipe comes in about the end of September. I note that the first I shot near Moulmein were a couple on the 23rd September 1878."—*T. C. Bingham.*

§ "Very common in Faridpur in suitable localities; for the first half of the season, October to December, they are a good deal scattered about, and are found in standing paddy, marshes and such like places; but from January they are only to be found in "bhils" and marshy hollows, if these have grass growing over them. By the end of March very few birds are to be seen."—*J. R. Cripps.*

"The majority leave (the Lucknow Division) again about the middle of March, though some may still be found up to, if not later than, the 15th April. On that date, this year, while birds-nesting along the banks of the Goomtee, I was surprised to find a number of them frequenting patches of rice cultivation all along the river margin."—*Geo. Reid.*

in the North-West Punjab; and in some seasons a good many are to be met with up to the 15th of April almost everywhere, and individuals may at times be seen alike in the north and south* of India, in May or even June. Of these late stayers, a few may be birds hatched late in the previous year, that would not breed that year, and that feeling no sexual impulse to migrate linger in comfortable quarters, but the majority I suspect are sickly or injured birds incapable of undertaking the long journey.

On the whole my experience and inquiries lead me to believe that there are *far* fewer lingerers of this species than of the Pintail; and that on the average, taking the country as a whole and a series of seasons, the Common Snipe both leaves slightly earlier and arrives somewhat later than the Pintail.

Such at least is the conclusion I arrive at after prolonged enquiries, continued throughout many years. It will be distinctly understood that I am quite aware that individuals, and even small parties of both species, may be, and have been, met with almost everywhere, where the species is common, equally early and equally late. What I mean is, that if the exact dates of the arrival and departure of every Snipe visiting the Empire for a series of years were recorded, the average date of the arrival and departure of the Fantails would prove, the former fully three weeks later, the latter a fortnight earlier than that of the Pintails.

For the benefit of those disposed to aid in further elucidating this question, it should be noticed that the nature of the season greatly affects the question; that Pintails seem less subject to the influences of excessive or deficient rainfall; that a bumper rainy season in the north, while it brings in the Fantails earlier there, certainly delays their arrival in the south; that such a season, followed as it generally is by a prolonged cold weather, detains all Snipe beyond their average dates; that the early setting in of the south-east monsoon takes them away earlier; and that the prevalence of southerly winds, towards the latter half of the rains, in Upper India at any rate, delays their appearance,

---

*"I have shot them on dry, grassy plains, and also once in a young tope in front of the Vellore Railway Station in May and June, and at another time in a babool (*Acacia arabica*) plantation in Palamcottoh in April and May; but the birds were in all these cases in very poor condition, and hardly able to fly. At the latter place I saw them for the first time sitting on ground, which had not sufficient grass to give them cover."—*A. Theobald.*

"About the middle of March Snipe begin again to collect in whisps, and by April 1st, warned by the first blasts of the hot winds, they are away to other climes. I find a note in my game-book of a strange occurrence. On May 2nd, 1871, when out tiger-shooting, and when the hot weather had regularly set in, I shot seven Snipe, and flushed several more on the edge of a tank near a village named Goorsora in the Lullutpore District. What had caused these birds to delay their departure so late I cannot imagine. I remember that, when cooked, they appeared to be thin, and wanting the flavour for which Snipe are so justly famed."—*J. H. Baldwin.*

and generally, that just conclusions can only be arrived at in this matter, after analysing a large body of facts collected all over the country, in the light of the various seasonal conditions under which they occurred.

The Common Snipe is eminently gregarious, and, like the Pintail, it arrives and departs *en masse.* True that early and late in the season, single birds or couples are often met with, and that this is common enough even in the height of the season, in localities furnishing little cover or scanty nutriment; but where these are abundant, and Snipe are *in*, you invariably find several in the same locality. Not that when feeding, or rising when disturbed, they mass in flocks like Ruffs and Reeves or Sand-pipers. On the contrary, although, when wild, they may rise in whisps and occasionally two, three, or four may be flushed from the same spot, where all must have been feeding together, as a rule they feed, no matter how numerous they be, a few yards apart, and rise independently of each other.

You find them in Upper India, in every swamp or marsh on the margins of ponds, lakes and rivers, wherever there is a more or less muddy foreshore protected by low grass rush or reed. Of all things they seem to love a kind of rush with a circular stem (*Scirpus carinatus*, I think) which is common about the edges of ponds and jhíls in the North-West Provinces, and which is a sure find for them. In the heat of the day, where *urher* and similar crops run down to near the water's edge, alongside some jhíl, you will often find many Snipe in these; and when a good deal shot at, especially about mid-day in bright hot weather, they will constantly drop in young wheat and the like.

One peculiarity of the Snipe is correctly pointed out by Mr. Reid. He says: "Although Snipe frequent wet places they never, *when resting*, allow their breasts to be in contact with water. Where the water is therefore at all general—no matter how shallow it may be—it is hopeless to expect these birds to lie close; this is only possible where suitable resting places are abundant."

But true as this is, you will constantly, at mid-day, find numbers of Snipe resting on thin layers of water weed, half a mile away from any firm dry land, floating in water several feet in depth. In such situations, softly and silently punted from one weed bed to another, in a stable flat-bottomed boat, you may enjoy perhaps the best Snipe-shooting in the world. Each little patch contains two or three Snipe, which only rise when the prow grates on the edges of the floating mass. The birds when shot all drop in the water; any that are missed drop on a neighbouring patch, and without the smallest exertion, without soiling your boots even, you may thus shoot in some large jhíls, from 11 A.M. to 3 P.M., almost as rapidly as you could load and fire in muzzle-loading days.

I need not, I think, offer any instructions of my own as to how Snipe should be shot, the more so that my advice would mainly consist in getting a good gun, loading it lightly and *holding it straight*; but I subjoin* very useful hints on the subject by Captain Baldwin and Mr. Reid. Both these gentlemen, however, are staunch "off-the-wind" workers, that is to say, they advocate always working down with the wind (in accordance with the accepted English method) on to Snipe, and it is therefore only right to note that here, in India, in shooting vast flooded tracts, where nothing rises above the level of your waist, it is very questionable whether it is not often better to shoot them "on the wind," *i.e.*, advancing on them *against* this latter. True they go straight away, and twist a good deal at starting, but they will lie much closer, and if you only let him get his distance a Snipe's twisting at mid-day in India does not matter much, and I have "many a time and oft" made good bags, by working against the wind, amongst Snipe too wild to let you get within shot, when worked with the wind.

And Snipe out here are *not*, as a rule, the birds they are at home. A very fair Snipe-shot as a boy, (having been at

* "Always walk deliberately and slowly, taking short paces; be ever at the ready; learn to fire quickly and sharply, with both eyes open and well in front of the object, as soon as the gun can be brought up to the shoulder; and always fire at a bird within distance, however difficult and twisting a chance it may offer. Never speak yourself, or allow your attendants to talk, and make as little noise, or splashing in walking, as possible. Try and mark where birds pitch that have risen some distance off, and if a Snipe drops to your shot in thick grass or rushes on walking up, throw your handkerchief as nearly as possible over the spot where you think the bird fell, before beginning to search; without such a mark, one is liable unwittingly to wander from the vicinity of the lost bird.

"Walk down wind, with the sun at your back, if possible. As a rule do not begin your shooting till the sun is well up, and the air warm. Early in the morning the birds will seldom lie well, and by following them about from one spot to another you may drive them away altogether; whereas, if you wait till later, say 10 o'clock, these same Snipe will afford you excellent sport. Employ the early hours of a cold weather morning in Duck-shooting—good Snipe jhils generally hold Duck as well. If by yourself, four attendants or coolies are generally sufficient to take the field with; if possible place them all on one flank, so that your attention is fixed in one direction, and you are prepared to turn that way only; whereas if your men walk on either side of you, it is doubtful on which side a Snipe may rise, and your attention is divided."—*J. H. Baldwin.* (In 'Large and Small Game of Bengal.')

"I have noticed that many young sportsmen, and even some old ones, make a sad mistake when going after Snipe in pouncing upon the birds in the early morning; nothing spoils a day's sport like this. The birds are then as wild as they can be; every shot puts them up in whisps, and, favored by the cool morning breeze, they will very likely leave the ground altogether. To avoid this, and to secure a good bag, it is only necessary to ascertain, first, that birds are abundant, and then to leave them in peace and quietness until 10 or 11 A.M. They will then have separated and settled down for the day, will lie close and seldom rise more than two or three at a time, and what is of equal importance will rarely fly far on being disturbed. This is all that sportsmen need to know to have fair sport, but a knowledge of the habits of the bird will often be of use. One *constant* peculiarity in the bird is that it *invariably flies against the wind*; in the hurry scurry of rising it may start off in any direction, but once fairly on the wing it will face the wind. Sportsmen, therefore, who are good at side or cross shots, may have them to their heart's content by *walking down the wind.* When Snipe are wild, and the day is windy, this is in fact the only way of securing even a decent bag."—*George Reid.*

it in our Norfolk marshes, from the time I was twelve years old,) I flattered myself after the first few seasons here that my shooting had vastly improved ; and when later I was returning hugged myself in secret with the idea that I would now rather show my friends at home how Snipe *should* be shot. Vain delusion !—the very first day on the ronds showed me the difference between a Snipe rising in a cold climate, on a dull drizzly day with a strong wind blowing, and one rising here in India in the hot noontide glare of a still cold season day. There, shoot as well as you might, you were bound to miss a lot of shots ; continually as you pulled the trigger, just as you thought he had settled into the straight running, you saw too late to hold your hand, friend Snipe dart off a good yard at right angles to his course. Moreover, the pace they go at there is far greater than what we are accustomed to see here. If any one, who is beginning to think himself a grand Snipe-shot out here, wishes to test his probable success at home, let him choose some very cold day about X'mas just after the winter rains, when there is a sharp, cold wind blowing, dense cloud over head and mist around, and shoot his best from 7 to 10 A.M. He will then vividly recall the difficulties of Snipe-shooting in our beloved native land !

As a whole, my experience is, that even in India the Fantail not only flies somewhat faster and habitually twists more than the Pintail, but also that, as a rule, all conditions being equal, it lies less close and well. On several occasions near Calcutta, where the two species were mixed—and there were only a few birds of each—I noticed that the Fantails mostly rose long shots, while the Pintails rose within thirty yards ; as also that, when I fired, all the Fantails near me rose, off ground on which, having re-loaded, I still picked up a Pintail or two. It does not do to generalize positively from one's own limited experience ; but I believe that, if the point be closely looked into, and due allowance made for the ever-varying conditions under which one is always meeting the two species, the facts will be found to be as I say.

Colonel Tickell says : "Snipe-shooting in Burma or Arakan is a pursuit of pleasure under considerable difficulties. The sport is in its prime long before the country has emerged from the floods of the rainy monsoon ; so that Auceps has to wade through paddy fields up to his middle (if not haply higher,) and under a sun which blisters his back, before he can make a good bag. To a full-blooded man the cold water below, and the hot sun above, are a severe trial, especially as full-blooded men are generally short-legged. It must be remembered, too, that wading in a paddy "khet" is not like wading in a clear salmon stream with a smooth, sandy bottom, but demands a struggle at each step to wrench your foot out of several inches of mud, and another struggle to force your way through the paddy itself ;

and, at least I know in *my* case, a frantic rush now and then to avoid a monstrous horse leech, which animals in these paddy swamps abound, and eagerly follow man, horse, or cattle to 'drink their blood,' like our old friend Fi-Fo-Fum in 'Jack the Giant Killer.'

"In the Bengal Presidency the shooting is far more agreeable than in Burma. There is seldom need to wade at all, or at most not above the ankles. By the time the Snipe are abundant and in good condition, the paddy has been reaped, and the fields are nearly dry, and walking over them is easy and pleasant. The swampy margins of 'jhíls' are also a favourite resort of these birds, as also open patches in forest, where springs of water well out through moss-like turf and weeds, and keep ever moist and soft the rich black soil.

"It takes some time to understand Snipe ground, and many a fruitless weary hour has been passed by novices in India plunging and splashing, and labouring and wading through rank herbage, coarse grass and reeds, or beds of rushes, interrupted by pools of water, and such like spots, without seeing a Snipe probably all the day. It is not easy to describe the ground this bird selects. In paddy fields I found, where the stubble showed the mud freely—that is, was not too thick—and where *puddles* of water were interspersed, fringed with short, half-dry, curling grass and small weeds, there the Snipe were sure to be if in the country; and note, if these puddles were coated over with a film of irridescent oily matter (the washings of an iron soil) the chances were greatly increased of a find. Off the alluvion, or dead flat country which borders both sides of the Ganges for various distances, the paddy cultivation in Orissa and Bengal is confined to the lower parts of the undulating soil—the ridge and valley being termed in Chota Nagpur the 'tarn' and the 'dhoon' respectively. The dhoons are narrow, and occupied generally by a single row of rice fields, divided by small banks, called 'bunds,' 'als,' or 'arees' in different parts of India. The sportsman can walk on the dry turf along the margin of these 'khets,' and shoot the Snipe as they rise from the muddy stubble, without wetting the sole of his foot. The fields, generally in a single row, are irrigated in dry weather from a tank excavated at the higher end of the valley; through the lower embankment of this reservoir the water slowly percolates, keeping the field next it, and perhaps the next one to that also, perpetually moist. It is to these spots the Snipe are driven as the season advances, and the country dries up, and here may be found perhaps fifty in an acre of ground."

Of the food of this species I have already spoken when dealing with the Pintail, and its familiar note of "psip," uttered as it rises, often looking back as it goes, though sounding apparently (to judge from the very different syllables employed to represent it), very different to different ears, is too well known to require further notice.

Speaking of the bags made, or asserted to be made, of this species, Mr. Reid remarks :—

"I have heard of fabulous bags—ranging from 80 to over 100 couple in a day—being made by a single sportsman ; but the largest I can vouch for is one of 57 couple made by myself in the Lucknow division. It included, however, 11 couple of 'Jacks ;' but, though I was looking for them, not a single specimen of either the Painted or Pintailed Snipes."

Now, though I have never myself made even quite as large a bag as Mr. Reid, as in the days when I mostly shot this present species we used large bore muzzle-loaders, with heavy charges, the rapidly repeated concussions from which always knocked me up both in Quail and Snipe-shooting before the day was much more than half over, I do not consider bags of 100 couple even at all fabulous ; and I am quite sure that any *good* shot, with a rather heavy small bore breech-loader, with small charges, might, to this day, easily bag his hundred couple in the day in many places in Upper India.

I have never myself seen a Snipe perch on either bush or tree ; but sportsmen have assured me that in the hills they have occasionally seen this; and it is a well-ascertained fact that, during the breeding season, they do in Europe often so perch high up upon large trees, as well as on lower perches of a similar nature, and thence emit their well-known nuptial call, tchik-tchak, tchik-tchak.

In many parts of the country, but specially in the neighbourhood of Calcutta, numbers of both kinds of Snipe are caught in horse-hair nooses, thousands of which are set between tufts of grass and in little natural or artificial lanes in the rushes, on favourite and frequented feeding grounds. It is also said that they are caught in nets, but I never was able to learn the *modus operaudi*, and I cannot conceive how this can be done unless possibly with a high standing net at night, the birds being worked against the wind, so that they go straight away without rising high.

ALTHOUGH NO European has, I believe, yet taken the eggs of this species within our limits, a few do certainly breed in Kashmir. Mr. Brooks saw and heard* one drumming (as it is commonly called) in orthodox style over a marsh there, and numerous eggs have been procured by native collectors.

This humming, drumming, neighing, or bleating note, as it is variously designated, a sound quite *sui generis*, and never to be

* Mr. Brooks writes : "I saw a Common Snipe soaring away above the swamp where I took the Mallard's nest ; and, as it was making its breeding, bleating, and drumming noise, doubtless its mate was sitting on its nest below, though I failed to find it."

mistaken after it has once been heard, is peculiar to the breeding season. At this period of the year Snipe may be constantly observed, but especially towards the evening, rising to a great height in the air, often uttering a sharp call sounding something like "tchik-tchak, tchik-tchak." Suddenly, with outspread tail and sharply vibrating wings, they begin to descend with great velocity in a slanting direction, and so long as this descent lasts this peculiar drumming sound is heard. Having thus descended to within from thirty to a hundred yards of the ground, the bird resumes its natural flight, the sound ceases, and away goes Mr. Snipe uttering his "tchik-tchak" louder than ever, as if greatly gratified with the performance with which he has edified his spouse on her nest below. That this drumming was not produced from the throat was proved by the fact that the bird *had* been heard (though this is certainly exceptional) to utter its "tchik-tchak" note whilst still drumming, and subsequently this latter was experimentally demonstrated to be caused by the rapid passage of the air through the outermost tail feathers which, even in this species, have the shafts stiff and sabre shaped, and the laminæ of the web very long and firmly interlinked.

In Europe Dresser, following Herr Meves, seems to assume that it is simply the normal contact with the air of the tail feathers in their rapid downward course that evolves the drumming; but, though this may have some share in producing this sound, this latter is distinctly vibratory while the descent is even, and, as I have repeatedly noticed, the vibration of the wings, which are in constant motion during the descent, is synchronious with the vibration of the sound, so that I have no doubt that both wings and tail play an at least equal part in this remarkable performance. Probably the beats of the pinions force the air against which they strike with increased velocity backwards against the tail feathers. Anyhow of this I am quite certain, *viz.*, that the sonnd actually arises from the tail feathers, and that the beats of the wing impart to it its vibratory character.

The nests found in Kashmir were described* as cup-shaped hollows in soft, mossy, spongy turf, surrounded or overhung by rushes and grass, and sparingly lined with fine grass, and in one case the needle-like leaves of a horse tail (*Equisetum*).

The birds apparently do not commence laying in Kashmir until May, and much incubated eggs have been found late in June. In Europe eggs may, it is said, be found from the first week in April, though the first are generally laid about

* I may also quote what Hewitson says of the nests in England :—

"The Snipe lays its eggs amongst rushes, grass, or heather, making—and this only at times—a slight nest for their reception, by gathering together a few bits of heath and dry grass. The eggs of one bird are, I believe, invariably four in number. The egg is a remarkable production for a bird so small, being as large as that of the Pigeon and of the Rook, and considerably larger than those of the Magpie and Partridge, birds three or four times its own size and weight."

the middle of that month; and I myself have taken eggs in Norfolk as late as the 17th of May.

The eggs, always normally four in number, are nearly hemispherical at the larger end; but from the middle they are compressed and elongated, so that, while one-half of the egg is a half globe, the other is a long cone, abruptly truncated or rounded off at the tip. Sometimes the cone is pinched in near the tip so as to make the egg almost pear-shaped.

The shell is extremely smooth, but has, at most, only a faint gloss. In colour and markings the eggs vary very much. Typically the ground colour varies from a yellow stone to a dark *café au lait*, but not unfrequently it has an olive tinge; and again in some eggs the ground is decidedly green, quite a light bright green in one, and in one or two it is more blue than green. The markings are large blotches, smears, spots, and clouds of brown of varying shades, becoming black in some spots; the brown is very often reddish or purplish, and where pale in some of the sub-surface-looking clouds, is at times a pale purple, at others pure brown, at others a sepia grey. The markings are always densest on the large half of the egg, where they occasionally form a nearly confluent cap, and are generally almost confined to the upper two-thirds of the egg, the conical end exhibiting few markings. Usually the markings are nearly all very large and bold, and comparatively few in number; but occasionally they are much more numerous, smaller in size, and more thickly set.

The eggs, very large for the size of the bird, vary from 1·54 to 1·62 in length, and from 1·1 to 1·23 in breadth.

IN THIS species also the females do average slightly larger, and have longer bills than the males; and so, as I have recorded a huge, series of measurements, I give the weights and dimensions of the sexes separately, although, as a fact, a vast number of each do not differ in size, and all one can say is, that the smallest birds are males, and the very largest always females.

Males.—Length, 9·0 to 11·3; expanse, 15·0 to 17·5; wing, 4·9 to 5·6; tail, from vent, 2·5 to 2·9; tarsus, 1·2 to 1·34; bill, from gape, 2·39 to 2·7; at front, 2·43 to 2·75; weight, 3·3 to 5·1 ozs. Average, 4·15 ozs.

Females.—Length, 9·2 to 12·5; expanse, 16·0 to 18·25; wing, 4·87 to 5·71; tail, from vent, 2·3 to 3·0; tarsus, 1·25 to 1·33; bill, from gape, 2·5 to 2·9; at front, 2·62 to 3·0; weight, 3·1 to 5·5 ozs. Average, 4·27 ozs. Average of both sexes, 4·2 ozs.

Some years ago my friend, Mr. J. C. Parker, writing to *Stray Feathers*, remarked: "I find, from looking over an old diary, that I have recorded the weights of some scores of each species; the average weight of the Pintail is 4 ozs. 3 drams, and of the Fantail only 3 ozs. 3 drams. The heaviest of the former was 4 ozs. 9 drams, of the latter 3 ozs. 13 drams."

I can only say that he must have weighed comparatively few birds, or that he was unlucky in the birds he met with. Of course all my weights were taken from freshly-shot birds, weighed, if not wetted in falling, then and there, or at any rate, if not sooner dry, at the mid-day halt. There is a material loss of weight, especially in Upper India, in the first twelve hours after death. I may add that it is useless to weigh live birds purchased in the market, since astounding as this may appear, these average *nearly* 1 oz. lighter than freshly-shot ones. Indeed I have bought large old females of the present species that certainly in good condition never weighed under 4½ ozs., weighing barely 3 ozs.

The bills have the terminal one-fourth or more deep brown to blackish; the rest pale brown, or horny brown with a yellowish tinge, dark along the edges, often brownish green just at the base of the upper mandible, and generally yellowish or yellowish green or olive, on the basal fourth (more or less) of the lower mandible; the irides are deep brown, almost black; the legs and feet are ordinarily greenish, often pale olive green, or greenish olive, but also at times pale greenish drab and greenish grey, and as the season advances they acquire a stronger yellow tinge—the legs of birds killed in April and May being often a distinct yellow green; there is often a dusky shade over the joints, and the claws are deep brown to black.

THE PLATE, I mean Mr. Neale's plate of our present species (there designated *Gallinago scolopacinus*), might, perhaps, be worse. I cannot say that I ever saw a Fantail, with quite such a huge pure white band down the centre of the forehead, or with quite so much fiery rusty on the back; but with the name clearly written below it, most people will be able to make out what it is intended to represent. This species does not normally vary *very* much, though some are darker, some lighter, some greyer, browner or more rufous everywhere; and in some too the pale margins of the scapulars are very broad and conspicuous, far more so than in the plate; while in others they are nearly obsolete, and again these pale margins vary from a rich rufous buff to pale fawn colour or buffy white.

But abnormal albinoid or fawn-coloured varieties are not very uncommon in India; and besides these a very dark or melanoid form, generally known as Sabine's Snipe (and in former times considered specifically distinct) has been occasionally met with in England and Ireland and once in France (*Harting*).

The plate of the tail and wing lining of this species (*ante p.* 332.) is fairly good, but the lower tail-coverts are usually less brightly tinted, paler and duller coloured in fact.

As mentioned when treating of the Pintail, the Fantail has fourteen to sixteen tail feathers, and occasionally only twelve. At home the sixteen tail feathers appear to be uncommon, but here they are common enough. Kaup elevated the birds possessing sixteen rectrices to the dignity of a distinct species; but the birds are identical, and in this Snipe group the number of the tail feathers is variable in every species with which I am at all well acquainted.

I have already, in the preceding article, fully discussed the differences between the Fantail and Pintail, but there is one point that I have neglected to notice, and that is that, age for age and sex for sex, the present species has an appreciably longer bill. This will appear clearly if we contrast the dimensions already given, the results of careful measurements of over 350 birds :—

		Males.	*Females.*
Length of bill from gape.	FANTAIL	... 2·39 to 2·7	... 2·5 to 2·9.
	PINTAIL	... 2·12 to 2·5	... 2·38 to 2·62.

No doubt a large old female Pintail has a bill longer than most male and a good many young female Fantails; but birds of the same sex and age being compared, the bills of the Fantails are invariably the longest.

ALTHOUGH THERE is no record of the fact, it seems highly probable that the European Great or Solitary Snipe *(Gallinago major)*, which certainly occurs in Persia, will also prove to occur in Sind, the Western Punjab, Afghanistan, and Khelat. Indeed I have heard tales of huge Snipe being shot in these parts, which I am inclined to suspect may refer to this species.

Though much larger than the Common Snipe, weighing from 7 to 9 ozs., or even more, the bill is a trifle shorter and slenderer than in the Common Snipe, and not spatulate, but more like that of the Pintails. The bird is a Fantail, like the Common Snipe, not a Pintail; but it has the axillaries very broadly and regularly barred black and white, as in the Pintail only more broadly.

The upper plumage is very similar to that of the Common Snipe; but all the wing-coverts, especially the primary greater coverts, are much more conspicuously tipped with pure white, and the whole of the front and sides of the neck and entire breast are very distinctly spotted with dark brown, not blurred and clouded, as in the Common Snipe. The spots on the breast moreover are very decidedly sagittate or triangular.

In the fresh bird the weight would generally suffice for the immediate identification of the species; but it may be well to add that the tail in all that I have examined had sixteen feathers (though this number probably varies) with the three outer tail feathers on either side mostly *pure white aud unbarred.*

THE JACK SNIPE.

Gallinago gallinula, *Linné.*

Vernacular Names.—[Chota chaha, (Hindustani); Chota bharca, *Nepal*; Oolan* (Tamil), *Madras*; Tibud, Pan-lawa, (Mahrati), *Ratnagiri* †]

THE Jack Snipe occurs throughout the whole of Continental and Peninsular India, including probably Ceylon, but not the Andamans or Nicobars.

Colonel Graham admits its occurrence in the neighbourhood of Dibrugarh, but it must be very rare in the valley of Assam, as neither Godwin-Austen nor any of his or my collectors appear, as yet, to have met with it there. In Sylhet and Cachar I only know of single specimens having been procured. I have no record of its occurrence in Tipperah or Aracan, and in Chittagong Mr. Fasson tells me that it is decidedly rare. In Pegu it it said to be very rare, and in Tenasserim I only know of its occasional appearance in the neighbourhood of Moulmein. Practically my present information leads me to consider it in the light of a mere straggler to all parts of the Empire east of the Brahmaputra. But I found it myself by no means very rare near Dacca ; and it is quite possible that it is rather the defectiveness of our present knowledge than the real rarity of the bird that has led me to this conclusion ; and I do hope that sportsmen in these eastern portions of our Empire will give some little attention henceforth to the matter.

The distribution, elsewhere, in Asia of this species is rather perplexing. It does not occur, so far as we have been able to ascertain, anywhere in the Malay Peninsula ; the only authentic record of its occurrence anywhere in China is a single specimen sent from Formosa; and a single specimen has similarly been sent from Japan. Prjevalski never met with it in Mongolia, Western China, or Chinese Tibet. Taczanowski, summing up all the records, says that it is found nowhere in Southern or Eastern Siberia, though Middendorff found it breeding in the extreme north on the Boganida (Latitude 70° N.),

* This name, though commonly used for all the Snipe, more properly applies, I believe, to the smaller Sandpipers.

† Probably most of the names applied to the Common and Pintail Snipes are also applied to this with some qualitative term signifying "small."

and as a fact Radde once saw it near Lake Iltschir in the Sajan Mountains. None of our explorers observed it anywhere in Eastern Turkestan (Yárkand), and in Western Turkestan it is only seen on passage. On the other hand, in Afghanistan and Beluchistan and throughout Persia, it is in winter, in proportion to the Common Snipe, quite as common as, or perhaps even commoner than, it is in India, and we might conclude that the migration was a south-easterly and north-westerly one, and that birds reached us from the west and from thence spread over the Empire, were it not that they reach the valley of Nepal, and even the neighbourhood of Calcutta earlier than they reach Jacobabad. We might conclude that the birds breeding in Northern Siberia, west of the 100th parallel of E. Latitude, (east of which it scarcely seems to extend) came down nearly due north and south almost without halting some 2,500 miles to India, much as the Great Snipe of Europe (*G. major*) is supposed to traverse the entire Continent of Africa from north to south; but looking to the comparatively feeble flight of this species, this seems unlikely, and the probability is, that the non-record of the Jack Snipe in Eastern Turkestan is due partly to the very imperfect manner in which our officers have, as yet, been able to work that vast tract, and partly to the birds passing through the country rapidly, and that hereafter it will prove to occur not only there, but at all suitable places in Central Asia on passage to and from India, though it may not usually get quite so far east as the Koko Nor.

Further it occurs in Asia Minor, Palestine, Northern Africa along the Mediterranean, and the whole of Europe (but not extending to any of the Atlantic Islands, the Færoes, or Iceland), being a winter visitant to the greater portion of this whole region, and summering and breeding for the most part only north of the 60° N. Latitude (to far within the Arctic Circle, where indeed it seems most common), but in Central Russia, and possibly in Denmark as far south as the 55th degree.

THE JACK SNIPE is very variable, according to my experience in the North-West Provinces, in its migrations, appearing much earlier in some years, and being much more plentiful in some than in others; but even when most abundant, it is nowhere, in any part of the Empire that I have visited, or from whence I have received accounts, at all common as compared with Fantails or Pintails, within the regular ranges of either of these; and, moreover, the bird lies so close and is so easily overlooked, that it is by no means surprising if accounts as to the times of its arrival and departure differ widely*; and I must

* In the North-Western Provinces, the earliest date on which I have ever shot it has been the 9th of September. In most years I have seen the first birds *just* at the close of September or the very commencement of October. In one year I noted

confess that, not having paid in past times any close attention to the matter, I can now only say that in different seasons, and in different parts of the country, it arrives between the latter end of August and October, but on the whole I believe somewhat earlier in the east than in the west.

As regards its departure, although it does not remain later than *some* of both the other common species, it does certainly, I should say, as a body linger longer; and time after time I have noticed that, when the Common Snipes had been reduced to one-tenth of their former number, or even less, the Jacks were quite as numerous as they had been at any previous period; and, while in Upper India the proportion of Jacks killed to Common Snipe hardly amounts to ten per cent. between the 15th of November and the 15th of March, towards the end of

---

that, although throughout the latter part of October I had been shooting Snipe in likely places, and the Common Snipe was plentiful, the first Jack was seen on the 3rd of November, and that several other men who had been shooting in Etáwah, Mainpuri, and Cawnpore, told me about this time that they had seen no Jacks that season. Later the same year in February, in the same places, they were abundant. The following are some of the notices that I have met with, or that have been sent me as to the times of its arrival, departure, &c.:—

"It makes its appearance later than the Common Snipe and departs earlier."—*T. C. Jerdon.*

"It appears in India and departs about the same time as the Common Snipe; but I have never seen it lingering so late as many stray ones of the latter species are known to do."—*S. R. Tickell.*

"When at Jhánsi, I noticed that, for three successive years, we found and shot the little Judcock before a full Snipe had been seen, and I have been confirmed in this opinion by several experienced sportsmen."—*J. H. Baldwin.*

"The Jack Snipe arrives in the valley of Nepal in the beginning of September, and does not leave until about the middle of April. It is most common in the valley during October, November, and March, and is found in the Nawakot district in November. It was generally found in fields of growing corn or other crops."—*J. Scully.*

"They come in (at Jessore) during the latter half of August."—*H. J. Rainey.*

"Judging by those we see of it, and compared with the Common Snipe, the Jack might be said to be very rare in the Lucknow division; but owing to its skulking habits, it appears to be much rarer than it really is. It would seem to arrive later and to depart earlier than the Common Snipe."—*G. Reid.*

"The first Jack was shot here at Jacobabad this year on the 4th of October; the first full Snipe on the 28th of August."—*P. J Maitland.*

"*Gallinago gallinula*, Lin., arrive in November on the Eastern Narra, and leave by April."—*S. Doig.*

"We shot the first Jack at Deesa, in 1876, on the 23rd of September. This species arrives about a month later than the other two."—*E. A. Butler.*

"Jack Snipe are found, but rather sparingly, in Ratnagiri. Only the larger Snipe grounds attract them, and they are not like the Common and the Pin-tailed Snipe, found in every little patch of inundated rice land. They arrive very early, and have been shot at Dapuli in September."—*G. Vidal.*

"I have shot them all over Southern India, south of the 12th degree North Latitude. They come in late in the year, about the end of November, and leave again before the end of February. They don't appear to be common, except in some parts of Malabar, near Nellamboor and Wondoor, and in some parts of Palghat.

"They appear to prefer the higher standing paddy and tall grass of swamps; they almost rise at the foot, and are not so easy to hit as the others. Very few are snared by the native fowlers, hardly any being brought to the markets for sale."—*A. Theobald.*

"The Jack Snipe is fairly (some say very) common in Southern Travancore, from September to April, or the early part of May."—*Frank W. Bourdillon.*

this latter month and early in April, I have known bags to contain actually *more* Jacks than full Snipe. Tickell says: "On one or two occasions, in very jungly places of bog and rank weeds interspersed among rice cultivation, I have found the "Jacks" almost monopolising the ground, to the exclusion of the Common Snipe; but this is very rare. Commonly they are found in the proportion of one to forty or fifty of the larger kind, and then only in deeper cover." But I cannot say that I have anywhere thus met with Jacks monopolising the ground earlier than the middle of March. Perhaps in Orissa, where I have never shot, it may be different; and Tickell goes on to say: "I think I have met with more to the southward, on the borders of Orissa, than in any part of Central India, on either side the Ganges. In the Calcutta markets, where the Common Snipe is to be seen in heaps, dead and alive, the Jacks are seldom to be met with. They seem to me to take to the more retired parts of the country, such as Singhboom, where, especially in the 'gât parrum' (beyond the Ghauts), the rice cultivation struggles for mastery with the swampy jungle."

He is quite wrong, however, about the Calcutta market, to which thousands are yearly brought.

As a rule, Jacks are eminently solitary birds; once in a way two or three will be found together in the same corner, but except quite towards the close of the season, when it is not unusual to find them in parties collecting, I suppose, preparatory to migration, even if there be half a dozen on a huge marsh, they are all far apart.

They affect particular spots more even than do Common Snipe. You cannot shoot continuously over any tract without getting to know two or three places bound to hold a Jack. You may shoot the tenant of to-day, but a week later the place is again occupied, and so you may go on through a whole season, finding one Jack in the self-same spot, whenever you visit it—nay at times you may kill one bird in the morning at one of these pet haunts, and find another there waiting to be bagged as you return in the evening. Granted, that you find many more Jacks lying about in chance places, where you have not before seen one, and where, probably, you do not again find one, or at any rate till long afterwards, but my belief is, that these outlying Snipes know, in some way of their own, of all these "eminently desirable residences," and are always on the look-out to pop into any one of them the moment it becomes vacant.

Now, these pet abodes have a character of their own; they may always be correctly described as *corners;* sometimes they are corners of paddy fields surrounded, on two out of three sides, by a low, earthen embankment; sometimes they are in an angle formed by a little scrub, or a couple of bushes, often just at the corner of a bed of bulrushes or high reed;

they are always sheltered and secluded spots, where the ground is thoroughly moist or marshy, and where the cover is pretty high. It is just the same at home as here, and I used to know a particular corner in an osier bed in Sommerton, where, if there were any Jack in the county, one was certain to be found.

At all times, Jack are much more attached to good cover than the Common Snipe, and to good, wet, marshy soil than the Pintail. I never found them on the almost bare mud banks, which constantly attract the former, and *very* rarely in the dry cover, which the latter so often affect. Tickell's remarks on this point are most just. He says: "The Jack Snipe is much less numerous in India than the ordinary Snipe, and appears more restricted in its choice of locality. It is found in much the same haunts as the latter, but always in deeper cover, where grass and weeds, springing up in the semi-fluid mud, intermix with the stubble of the paddy fields."

They lie extremely close, suffering you, at times, almost to crush them with your foot, before they will rise, and very often allowing themselves to be captured by a cunning old retriever. Indeed, without dogs, it is impossible to make sure of getting up all the birds there are; but they have a strong scent, and no good dog will pass one, and it is having shot so much to dogs that makes me assert as above (in opposition to Dresser and his authorities,) that, except towards the close of the season, Jacks in India are normally solitary in their habits.

They rise noiselessly, and as Tickell says: "Its flight is slower than that of the Common Snipe, fluttering and feeble. When flushed, it proceeds at no great height from the ground, and in a vacillating way, as if every moment about to settle. It then either drops suddenly, as if dead, or gives a little shoot into the air first, and then falls, as it were, to the ground. When once alighted it squats, so that no bird is more easy to mark; indeed, one may know almost the very blade of grass it will spring from when flushed again."

But though perhaps its flight may *be* (and it certainly looks) somewhat slower than that of the Pintail, it is so irregular and balking, that, although probably one of the easiest birds in the world to shoot, if you reserve your fire till the proper moment, it is constantly missed through over-eagerness, and all kinds of apocryphal stories are told of gentlemen enjoying a whole season's sport, a dozen or twenty shots daily, off one Jack, until some blundering friend spoilt the arrangement by killing this solitary, but prolific, source of enjoyment. As a matter of fact, no decent shot is likely to miss it twice running; and, as it always drops within a hundred yards, and waits exactly where it drops for you to flush it again within ten yards, very few poor Jacks, once seen by sportsmen, ever survive their first interview with mankind, at any rate in India. Possibly, like the Common Snipe, though I have not particularly noticed this, they also, in colder climes, and beneath cloudier skies, are able to make better use of their wings.

Some sportsmen, it is true, think them hardly worth shooting, but to them I should say, what I once heard an old woman of methodistical tendencies, reply to our Rector, with whom she differed on matters of grace and regeneration, "That comes all along of your ignerence." For of a surety, perfect in their own way, as may be a well-fattened Ortolan in Italy, or Quail in India, delicately enwrapped in their protecting vine leaves, equally perfect though in another way (and far above all plebeian Fantails and Pintails) is a plethoric Jack, who, after glancing at the glowing embers, awaits, enthroned upon a toast, your eager devotion.

It seems to be assumed by European writers that Jacks only feed at night; but such is assuredly not the case here, as I have shot them at 9 A.M., and again at 5 P.M., in the act of feeding, and with half-swallowed food in their throats. I dare say they feed a good deal at night. I know that, during the heat of the day, they lie up, (asleep I fancy, by the way dogs pounce on them), but they also certainly feed both in the mornings and towards evening. Their food, here, consists of grubs, worms, and tiny insects, shells and crustacea, besides which a certain amount of green vegetable matter, minute portions of weed, club moss and grass, as far as I could make out, is occasionally found in their stomachs. I have never chanced to find any seeds, but it seems certain that in Europe they do eat grass seeds at times, and probably they do the same here.

THEY do not breed within our limits. Wolley, the first ornithologist who took their eggs, gives a long account of finding the nests in Finland. One gathers that in the breeding season the males career about at a great pace high in air, giving rise to a peculiar sound, of which Wolley says that he can only liken it to the cantering of a horse in the distance, over a hard, hollow road. Of certain nests, which were found in the great marsh of Muonioniska, he says:—

"The nest of the 17th, and four of the 18th June, were all alike in structure, made loosely of little pieces of grass and equisetum, not at all woven together, with a few old leaves of the dwarf birch, placed in a dry, sedgy or grassy spot close to more open swamp."

The eggs, always four in number, are very large for the size of the bird, so much so that Hewitson, in figuring them, remarked:—

"Were not the eggs verified beyond a doubt, no one would credit that a bird of such small dimensions (not a great deal larger than a Skylark) could produce them, or, having produced them, could keep them warm. They are precisely of the same length as those of the Snipe, but are of less width across the broadest part. The bird weighs about two ounces; the four eggs are more than an ounce and a half. The great egg of the Guillemot is one-eighth of the weight of the bird; the eggs of the Jack Snipe weigh nearly as much as it does itself."

In shape, the eggs are much like those of the Common Snipe,—nearly hemispherical at one end, pulled and pinched out into a cone, with the small end abruptly truncated and rounded off, at the other,—but they are narrower in proportion to their length.

In colour and markings the few I have so closely resemble eggs of the Common Snipe, that it is useless for me to attempt any separate description; but Dresser says that they run into richer (? coloured) varieties than those of this latter species.

Five eggs vary from 1·49 to 1·57 in length, and from 1·05 to 1·13 in breadth, but doubtless both smaller and larger eggs occur.

I CANNOT discover any constant or average difference in the sizes of the two sexes; they vary a great deal according to age, but equally large and small birds of both sexes appear to occur. The following is a *resumé* of my measurements:—

Length, 7·75 to 9·0; expanse, 13·25 to 14·89; wing, 4·1 to 4·67; tail, from vent, 1·87 to 2·5; tarsus, 0·89 to 0·95; bill, from gape, 1·5 to 1·7; at front, 1·57 to 1·74; weight, 1·53 to 2·48 ozs.

The legs and feet are pale greenish, at times with a bluish or a greyish shade, generally more or less olive or yellowish; the claws blackish brown; the irides deep brown; the bill is blackish brown at tip, and darkish brown on nares and along the commissure; the rest paler, sometimes a pale grey brown, sometimes with a fleshy tinge, and sometimes with a dull bluish or slatey tinge, especially towards the base of the lower mandible.

THE PLATE is rather an ideal or Turneresque conception of what a Jack Snipe might be, than a portrait of what a Jack really is; but it would not be so very bad if the red on the crown (the central band on which is almost entirely blackish brown) were removed, if the red on the back and scapulars, so sadly exaggerated, were reduced in extent and toned down, and if a pale buff or stone yellow were substituted for the glaring white margins to the scapulars and tertiaries, and the white tippings of the coverts toned down a little. If, besides this, the whole breast were given a fawny brown shade, and the streaks were rendered a little less harsh and regular, I do not think that there would be much fault to find with the plate. Luckily the species is not one that can be mistaken for any other; but I may note that its tail consists of twelve soft, more or less pointed, feathers, the central pair the most pointed of all, and projecting more than a quarter of an inch beyond the longest of the others.

SNIPE OCCUR all over the world, and besides the five species dealt with, and the two (*major* and *megala*) referred to above, *at least* a dozen others occur in Africa, North and South America, Madagascar, Australia, New Zealand (Chatham Islands), the Auckland Islands, &c.

½
RHYNCHEA BENGALENSIS

THE PAINTED SNIPE.

Rhynchæa capensis, *Linné*.

Vernacular Names.—[Ohari, *Nepal;* Kone, Konebatta (Kole), *Singbhoom;* Tibud, Pan-lawa, (Mahrati), *Ratnagiri;* Mail-ulan, (Tamil) *Madras;* Baggerjee, *L. Bengal;*]

I HAVE no record of the occurrence of this species in Kullu, Kashmir or any part of the Himalayas west of the Satlej, or again in the Peshawar Valley, or the extreme north-west portions of the Punjab.

It is found throughout the rest of the Empire, including Ceylon, but excluding the Andamans and Nicobars. But to the drier portions of the North-West Provinces and Oudh, the Punjab, Rajputana and many parts of the Central India Agency and portions of the Central Provinces, it is practically only a rainy season visitant; and, while it is by no means common in Pegu,* it is so rare in Tenasserim Proper†, that, although we know that it has been shot near Moulmein, and have received a specimen thence, we have never, in all the years during which we collected in that province, ourselves met with a single specimen.

In the Malay Peninsula it is equally rare; indeed the only specimen we certainly know to have been obtained there was one shot at Perak, by Lt. Kelham, of the 72nd Highlanders. It occurs in Upper or Independent Burma, but is apparently rare there, and Anderson obtained a single specimen at Momien. It is said to have occurred in Siam, and probably does, but I have seen no specimen thence, nor do I know the authority on which Tickell asserts its occurrence there.

It has been recorded from Sumatra, Java, Borneo, and many islands of the Philippine group, and occurs as a summer visitant in Formosa, and throughout the eastern half, at any rate, of China, as far north as Pekin. Prjevalski found it in South-East

---

* "The Painted Snipe is a constant resident in all Pegu. It is nowhere common, and four birds is the largest number I have seen together."—*Eugene W. Oates.*

† It appears to be rare in some others of the Eastern Districts also. Thus, writing from North-East Cachar, Mr. John Inglis says:—

"The Painted Snipe is rarely obtained here. Out of some 500 Snipe which I shot last autumn, I only obtained two female painted ones."

But in the valley of Assam, especially the eastern end, Colonel Graham writes to me that it is common.

Mongolia, and breeding at Lake Tsaidamin Nor, which is in about the same latitude as Pekin, being 40° North Latitude, but it does not go north into South-East Siberia, or the Ussuri country, nor he says into Kansu of Western China, nor to the Koko Nor in Chinese Tibet. It has not been observed in either Eastern or Western Turkestan, or towards the Pamir, or in Northern Afghanistan; but Captain Cook, R.E., of the 5th Goorkas, shot a specimen in January, in Central Afghanistan, in the Kurrum Valley, and Hutton procured it near Kandahar in the south. From Beluchistan it has not been recorded, nor from any part of Persia, but Antinori gives it from Asia Minor, and it occurs throughout the better known portions of Africa, including Madagascar, except only in the northern and north-western portions lying between Egypt and the mouth of the Senegal. In the Berlin Museum list it is recorded as coming from Arabia also, but *v.* Heuglin doubts the fact.

The above review proceeds on the assumption, now generally admitted to be correct (though Swinhoe affirmed that the African species differed in having the chin bare) that *R. capensis* and *R. bengalensis* are identical. There is yet another supposed species, *R. australis*, certainly very close to our bird, and perhaps identical, and if so (which, however, I hardly anticipate) Australia also must be included in the range of the Painted Snipe.

ALTHOUGH PERMANENT residents of the major portion of the Empire, and only regular migrants to the drier, north-western regions of India, yet even elsewhere Painted Snipe move about a great deal, and, except perhaps in some exceptional localities, are rarely to be found in exactly the same places at different seasons.

This follows, however, naturally from the character of the localities which they chiefly affect, *viz.*, moist, but not flooded, ground, covered with abundant and thick cover of rush or grass, and if interspersed with bushes and thin scrub so much the better.* Of course you find them in marshes where there is plenty of water lying about, and in flooded land; but you will always, I think, if you look closely, discover that the exact spots whence they are actually flushed are in such cases patches slightly raised above the general level; and, though moist, still free from water. I once found half a dozen of these birds in a particular spot, and saw them there week after week for several weeks. A heavy X'mas shower fell, and the next day not a bird was to be seen, though their favourite haunt was only about two inches under water. Again, later, they (or other birds of this species) returned to this same spot as soon as the water had

---

* Major C. McInroy too writes :—

"I have noticed in Mysore that the Painter is exceedingly partial to longish grass amongst date trees, where the ground is slightly damp."

subsided, and remained there for many weeks until the ground began to dry up.

One week only a pair were left; the next, which was quite at the close of February, none were to be seen. The ground had become too dry, and thereafter, though the rush and grass still looked green and fresh, not a Painter was ever seen there up to the middle of April when I left.

It follows that with such predelictions they must necessarily change their quarters a great deal. The places are few and far between in India, where ground and cover keep in exactly the condition they prefer throughout the entire year. Not only do they have to move about from place to place within the same district, but whole regions* (like many parts of Lower Bengal) become too water-logged for them during the rains, or (like many parts of the N.-W. Provinces, Oudh, Rajputana, &c.,) too dry for them, a month or so after the rains have ceased. People often think that this species does not occur or is rare in their neighbourhoods, simply because they have not looked for them in proper situations, or in situations such as they affect at those particular times when these are in the state essential to attract them.†

When breeding,—and that, as I shall explain further on, they seem to be in one place or another during a great portion of the year—they are always found in pairs, the two birds sticking very close to each other, and to the nest. When not breeding, they are commonly found fairly close together, but hardly in what we should call flocks, in parties consisting of one or more families, these latter comprising, as a rule, two old

---

* "I have seen and shot this bird almost all over Southern India south of the 12° North Latitude. In the dry districts it comes in during the cold weather and remains till all the swamps and fields are dry, but in well-watered portions, like Tinnevelly, Tanjore, Malabar, and parts of Coimbatore, I have shot them throughout the year.

"I have never found the nest, but heard of one being taken near Erode.

"They are common in the inland districts, but rare towards Madras, where they are caught in large numbers for the sake of their skins, which are exported to China. The bird fetches from two to four annas each in the Madras market, while the preserved skins are sold at from eight annas to one rupee.

"They are snared with horse-hair nooses by the Madras fowlers."—*A. Theobald.*

† Thus Mr. Reid at one time wrote to me, speaking of the Lucknow Division :—

"The Painted Snipe is not by any means numerous. I have not seen or killed one for over two years, but before the drought of 1877, I used to shoot them pretty often."

Later again he said : "I write to supplement what I said about the Painted Snipe.

"Yesterday, the 16th of June, I took what I may call my 'usual' trip down the Goomtee, and was very much surprised to find that Painted Snipe were *very* abundant amongst the rushes and weeds all along the sides of the river. They seemed to me to be quite tame and familiar, frequenting patches of cover often quite close to where Dhobies were at work They literally swarmed in quieter nooks. It struck me at the time that they were breeding, but after dissecting six females on the spot with the same result, I came to the conclusion that it was too early (by at least 15 days) to expect to find eggs."

Of course the banks of a stream, like the Gomtee, could never remain long exactly as they like their ground, and these birds soon passed on, doubtless to breed further north.

birds, and three or four (never more) young ones. But I have occasionally seen a dozen or more birds, all apparently adults, in the same patch of cover; and since Captain Butler drew attention to the matter, I have repeatedly seen similar parties, consisting entirely of young birds of both sexes, all of course in the plumage of the male, though in some few of the females signs of the coming adult plumage were appearing.

Painted Snipe, as a rule, lie close and require some hustling to flush them, at least, if met with in the good cover they chiefly affect. Sometimes you *may* find them in thin stuff, such as satisfies the Common Snipe, and then I have known them rise on your approaching within twenty yards. But, as a rule, it is only when you begin to trample through the patch in which they are for the time living that they rise, and I have found them occasionally quite as hard to put up as any Jack. They seem very tame or stupid birds. You may flush them week after week out of the same patch in your quest for Pintails or other snipe, but so long as the spot continues to their liking, they steadily cling to it; and even if, as of late years in view to settling certain questions to be discussed further on I have had to do, you shoot several of the party, following them about to effect this, the remainder are "all there" the next week just as if a gun had never been fired.

They rise silently according to my experience, but I am told that occasionally (I presume during the breeding season) the females utter their characteristic low note when suddenly flushed. The flight is comparatively slow, laboured, and with irregular flappings, and a good deal resembles that of some of the Rails, especially in the way they sometimes hang their legs. They fly low, and soon drop again into cover; but if fired at and missed, or possibly just touched with a grain or two of shot, they sometimes give a little shoot into the air, and put on a spurt, carrying them double the distance they usually go. If the patch into which they drop is small, you will find them much where they dropped, for in daylight they rarely cross the open, even when undisturbed, and never, I think, when alarmed; but if fortune favours them, and they reach a good bed of rushes, they will often make tracks through this in a regular Rail-like fashion, and you may find them fifty yards or more further on.

I said that in the daytime they rarely cross the open, but on one occasion, when lying up in a bed of bulrushes trying to circumvent an Osprey that was hunting about, I saw three running about on a tiny patch of short, close, moist turf just outside the rushes, and not twenty yards from where I was, and picking up something rapidly from the ground. After watching them for several minutes, I made a slight clicking sound, and they instantly sneaked into the cover with lowered heads. In this action, and in their mode of moving about, they reminded me far more of Rails than of Snipe, and certainly alike in all their ways, and even in their note, there is much that recalls the Rails.

Their cry, heard only I believe (but am not certain) when they are breeding, is a single, low, rather deep note, which Wood-Mason calls "a low, regular hoarse, but rich purr," and Tickell describes as "low and mellow, a single soft note frequently repeated, kone, kone, kone," but which, to my ears, most resembles the sound produced by blowing into the neck of a phial. I have heard no second sound, and thought this was produced by both sexes, as two birds are continually heard answering each other; but Mr. Wood-Mason's investigations have shown that the females in this as in the Australian form (though *apparently* to a much less extent) differ from the males in having a more developed windpipe, with a large convolution just where it enters the body, to which development the peculiar call referred to may be assumed to be due. Hence it was probable that the females only would utter it, and Mr. Mason states, as a matter of fact, that, amongst captive birds while the females continually thus called, the males only jerked out a sharp squeak at irregular intervals, and then only apparently in answer to the females.

This squeak of the male I have never heard in the field, but the call now proved to be that of the female I have often heard, most commonly in the morning, not unfrequently towards dusk, and occasionally, but rarely, during the day.

In Southern India the natives call it the "Peacock Snippet," and certainly, when standing at bay, with the breast lowered to the ground, the back raised and tail expanded, and the head with upturned bill surrounded by the spread wings brought round so as almost to meet in front, they present a very striking and beautiful picture; and I cannot but believe that, during the nuptial season, the birds nautch, as natives assert, in some such position opposite each other.

They certainly move about (and probably feed) much more at night than by day. They are very fond apparently of running at night, just as Rails do, along the small, turf-clothed ridges dividing paddy fields, and numbers are caught in horse-hair nooses set along these, together with *Porzana fusca* and *maruetta.*

About their food I regret to say that I can only speak from memory. I kept an exact record of the contents of the stomachs of over fifty specimens, but this is not forthcoming now just when it is required. I remember that insects and tiny crustacea and shells, land and water, predominated, and that there were also grubs and caterpillars, and some admixture of vegetable matter; but I have also an idea that I repeatedly noticed grain and seeds of sedges and grass in their crops. Of this latter I cannot now be sure, but I find that Hodgson notes finding both rice and fragments of mustard seeds in their gizzards, so that my remembrance is probably correct.

For the table the Painted Snipe, for some reason or other, is very inferior ; the flesh has often a sort of muddy taste, and wants entirely that peculiar, and I think delicious, flavour of the true Snipe, which, in its highest perfection, is found only in the Jack.

THE PAINTED SNIPE breeds in almost all the localities in which it occurs ; in humid, well-watered districts, where it is a permanent resident, twice, if not three times, a year ; in dry ones, once during its annual rainy season visit ; and in very low-lying, much-flooded tracts, once, or possibly twice, during the drier portions of the year.

Reviewing the pretty abundant evidence now available, I should say broadly that the majority bred once during the height of the rains, and once during the middle of the cold season ; but practically in one place or another, this species has been found breeding in almost every month in the year ;* and,

---

* I may quote here a few of the notes I have received bearing on this point :—

"I was informed yesterday (11th February 1879), that there were some Snipe seen in the bed of an almost dry river running past my bungalow here (Aurungabad), and went down with my gun to get them. My informant pointed to a spot almost as bare as the palm of my hand, and incredulously I walked up to it, when up got a Painted Snipe at my feet, which I shot, and at the report of the gun another rose close by, which I also knocked over. A lad, who was with me, then pointed out to me what was evidently the nest of the bird, (a lump of mud and slime trodden down in the centre into a hollow) containing one egg, and on my return another egg, precisely similar, was taken out of the female bird."—*C. Gubbins.*

"On the 10th of May 1875, at a swamp, some 40 or 50 miles from Calcutta, whither I took a run up by the E. B. R., I got a nest with four fresh eggs of the Painted Snipe."—*J. C. Parker.*

"Remain all the year round on the Eastern Narra. Breed in May, June, and July, laying four eggs."—*S. Doig.*

"I took one nest near Calcutta towards the end of August."—*A. O. Hume.*

"I took numbers of the Painted Snipe's nests near Deesa in 1876, in August and September."—*E. A. Butler.*

"On the 24th September 1874, I extracted a perfect egg from a female I had shot (near Tonghoo)."—*Wardlaw Ramsay.*

This year (1874) Mr. Rainey took two eggs (which he very kindly sent me) on the 30th September at Khulna. Jessore.

Captain Sheppard obtained a nest with four eggs in September in Raipoor.

"On the 1st December last, at Gorebunder, about twenty miles from here, I caught two young Painted Snipe, about half grown ; they were unable to fly. Is this not rather late to see birds so young?"—*J. D. Inverarity.*

"I have lately found *Rhynchæa bengalensis* breeding in this locality, (Chamrajnugger, 35 miles south-east of Mysore, and 40 miles north of the Nílghiris).

"I shot a male bird on the 5th December, and on dissection found that it was breeding : on 10th December a brace rose from some marshy grass of which I shot one, which proved to be a female. I found a fully formed egg in it, which would have been laid in a day or two, the shell being still soft. I had a long search next day in hopes of finding the nest, but without success. Still I think that I have found enough to warrant my saying that *Rhynchæa bengalensis* breeds in this locality in the month of December."—*M. Forbes Coussmaker.*

Mr. Legge, writing from Ceylon, says of the Painted Snipe : "This species, which is resident in this island (although I have no doubt its numbers are very much increased in the cool season), appears to breed at all times of the year.

"To commence with the evidence of our pioneer, Layard says : 'The season of incubation is from May to July.' That it breeds at or about this season is, I know from personal observation and inquiry, quite correct. The late Mr. Advocate Lorenz, (a much-lamented member of the Ceylon bar), who took a great interest in

while I have no doubt that they have two broods a year, I think it possible that, under favorable conditions, they may have more.

I have only once myself taken a nest, and that was at the end of August, in a small swamp on the Diamond Harbour Road, about six miles from Calcutta. It was on very wet ground in the midst of low rushes, and consisted of half-dry rush twisted round into a tolerably neat and compact nest. It measured six inches in diameter exteriorly, and less than four inches interiorly, and the cavity, which had no lining, was a good inch in depth. It contained two quite fresh eggs.

A nest of this species, sent me by Mr. A. J. Rainey, is a large circular pad of mingled coarse and fine rice-straw, some 6 inches in diameter and about 1·75 in thickness, and with a central depression, perhaps three-quarters of an inch in depth. It was taken on the 22nd September 1871 at Khalispoor, about 1½ miles from Khulna, in Jessore, on rather wet ground, in a bare field from which a crop of rice had been reaped about a month before.

Mr. S. Doig wrote to me some years ago: "I found a nest of the Painted Snipe on the 23rd of June, in a small island in the bed of the Narra. The bird leaving the nest fluttered off as if her wing was broken, and after going some twelve yards, lay with her wings spread out on the top of the weeds near the shore. The nest, which was a slight depression in the ground at the root of a tussock of grass, contained four eggs, very much incubated. On the same island were a lot of young ones just hatched, and on another island I found young birds fully fledged."

Since then he has taken numbers of nests in May, June, and July on the Eastern Narra.

Captain E. A. Butler has also taken many nests, and to supplement my personal want of experience, I shall quote an excellent account he formerly wrote to me of the nidification of this species:—

"At Milana, eighteen miles east of Deesa, I found several Painted Snipe's nests this year (1876.) The dates upon which they were discovered are given below.

"The nests, all of which were in the vicinity of rice fields, were, in most instances, on the ground; but in one or two cases

birds, wrote me shortly before his death that he had once found a nest with young in the month of April in the Western Province. It was situated in the grass of a bank between two paddy fields. Again, a friend of mine observed a pair of old birds in company with two young near a tank in the south of Ceylon. This was in May 1872. On his giving chase, the chicks took to the water and swam like ducklings. In the beginning of September last year, I had several young brought me from Wackweell, near Galle, a locality where I have found them more abundant than anywhere else in Ceylon. These data corroborate Layard's statement, but they testify at the same time to a wider period, commencing a month earlier and ending a month later. With regard to the cool season, I am aware of eggs having been taken perfect from birds in November, and of the young being captured in March. Mr. Holdsworth procured a beautiful egg from a wounded bird on the 31st December (P. Z. S., 1872, p. 473), and I obtained another taken from a dead bird on the 29th March."

they were raised as high as eight or ten inches from ground, and supported by the grass in which they were built.

"Of the various situations they were found in, I may mention as one of the most common the raised footpaths which so often intersect these rice fields. In the rains the sides of the paths become overgrown with grass, and in this grass the nest is often built. Another favourite place is the short, dark green rushy grass that grows by the sides of tanks, and in swampy ground. This, perhaps, is *the* most favourite place of all, and in many of the nests, found in this situation, the blades of grass were drawn together over the top of the nest so as to form a sort of canopy as in some nests of *Porzana akool*. Another favourite spot is a rice field that has been ploughed up and left unplanted for some time until the grass begins to grow over it.

"One nest I discovered was placed under a low bush (about one foot high) growing in short grass in swampy ground by the side of a tank. Another nest I found by the side of a public road on the borders of a rice field. A small pool of water, about twelve feet square, had become almost dry, and some short, dark-green, rushy grass had sprung up. In this grass a pair of Painted Snipe built their nest.

"The nest consists generally of a more or less substantial pad of sedge or wet grass, in a hollow in the ground, sometimes altogether exposed, sometimes under cover of a tussock of grass, or with blades of grass growing over it.

"The old birds are almost always near the nest, and usually lie close, rising heavily when flushed, and settling again after a short flight. I got so accustomed to their mode of rising at last, that I could almost always say, when the birds got up, whether there was a nest or not. They usually run a yard or two from the nest before rising, but on more than one occasion I have seen a bird slip quietly off the nest, and squat by the side of it until flushed.

"The eggs are always, as far as my experience goes, four in number.

"The following is the detail of the nests taken by me this season :—

24th	August	1876,	a nest containing	4	fresh eggs.
26th	"	"	do.	4	do.
"	"	"	do.	4	about to hatch.
12th	September	"	do.	4	fresh eggs.
17th	"	"	do.	4	do.
22nd	"	"	do.	2	do.
23rd	"	"	do.	4	do.
23rd	"	"	do.	4	do.
27th	"	"	do.	4	do.

"In addition to these nests I found young broods, just hatched, on the 26th August, and again on the 26th September. The chicks are buff, striped with dark brown, much in colour like young Pheasants. The bill is also quite short at that age."

I have already mentioned that there is every probability that the female only calls; the female, as will be seen further on, is larger and handsomer than the male; the young of *both* sexes wear the plumage, not of the female, but of the adult male; and in yet one other point does the case of the Painted Snipe resemble that of the Bustard Quails, for in no less than three cases in which old birds have, to my knowledge, been captured on the eggs, such old birds have proved to be males. I do not know that the female never sits; that is a point for future careful investigation. All I know is, that in the only cases in which I have been able to test it, it has been the males who were incubating.

The eggs of this species, almost invariably, I believe, four in number, are of the same type, so far as shape is concerned, as those of the Common Snipe; but they are, as a rule, not quite so pinched out towards the small end as those of that species.

Compared with those of the true Snipe they are very small; the Painted Snipe weighs from two to fully three times what the Jack Snipe does; but the cubic contents of the eggs of the former are less than four-fifths of those of the latter.

In colour and markings the egg has a somewhat Plover-like appearance, but is more glossy.

The shell, very hard and of a very close and compact texture, has generally a very appreciable, and occasionally a great deal of gloss. The ground colour is typically a yellowish stone or *cafe au lait* colour, but in some has a strong olive tinge, and in some again is a very pale, clear, greenish creamy, or even pale greenish drab. The markings consist, as a rule, of a few very large and very irregular-shaped blotches, intermingled with numbers of smaller blotches and irregular streaks, spots and occasionally lines, but sometimes *all* the markings on the egg are *comparatively* small. Some show a very conspicuous broad confluent zone round one end; but the markings are extremely variable in size, shape and arrangement, and all one can say is, that they generally between them cover nearly half the surface of the egg. The markings are intense blackish brown, appearing quite black in some spots, where the colour is most intense, but paling off into sepia in some few sub-surface-looking spots and clouds. In some eggs there are none of these secondary markings, and in none are they very numerous or conspicuous. Occasionally some of the markings verge upon a raw sienna brown. In length the eggs vary from 1·29 to 1·49, and in breadth from 0·89 to 1·05, but the average of 40 eggs is 1·39 by 0·99.

IN THIS species the females are very decidedly larger than the males, birds of the same age of course being compared, since the difference in size between an old male and a young female is not so apparent.

The following is a *resumé* of the dimensions of apparently adult birds only:—

Males.—Length, 9·25 to 10·0; expanse, 16·8 to 18·0; wing, 4·9 to 5·2; tail from vent, 1·5 to 1·8; tarsus, 1·65 to 1·83; bill *at front*, 1·65 to 1·85; weight, 3·5 ozs. to 4·9 ozs.

Females.—Length, 9·75 to 10·89; expanse, 18·0 to 19·25; wing, 5·25 to 5·6; tail from vent, 1·6 to 2·0; tarsus, 1·75 to 1·96; bill *at front*, 1·8 to 2·05; weight, 4·4 ozs to 6·42 ozs.

The legs and feet are generally greenish, usually a pale yellowish green, or greenish yellow, often greyer, or duskier, or somewhat hoary on the joints and toes; sometimes, however, they are a deep olive, sometimes pale bluish overlaid with a greenish tinge, and sometimes simply dull pale green; the claws are brown, sometimes paler, sometimes darker.

The irides vary from hazel to very deep brown, and have sometimes a greenish or olive tinge.

The bill is very variable; typically it is a pale fleshy brown darker or purer brown towards the tip, and with a greenish tinge towards the base; it is subject, however, to a good deal of variation, and I quote in illustration of this a few of my notes:—

♀ 2nd February—bill, reddish brown.
♂ 1st December—bill, pale, rather fleshy, brownish olive, duller towards tips.
♀ 4th ,, ,, culmen, and terminal 3-5ths pale yellowish fleshy; sides of basal 2-5ths with a brownish green tinge.
♀ ,, ,, pale brownish fleshy, olivaceous on basal 2-5th.
♀ 1st ,, ,, pale pinkish brown, deeper horny brown towards tips.
♂ ,, ,, pale brown, with a slight olive tinge, darker towards tips.
♂ ,, ,, pale pinkish or fleshy brown, with more or less of an olive tinge and terminal portions deeper brown.
♀ 21st September—bill, greenish, yellowish fleshy at tip of both mandibles.
♀ 10th June—bill, basal 2-5ths greenish blue, pinkish elsewhere.

And Oates says of one, a male, "basal half of bill olivaceous, the terminal half reddish brown, turning to pure brown at the extreme tip."

THE PLATE, as a faithful record of the plumage of the species, is excellent; only the legs are wrongly coloured, and the lores of the right hand figure are too dark. This figure represents an adult male, that on the left an adult female.

Schlegel and others have asserted that the plumage depicted in the latter is that of adults of both sexes. Jerdon pointed out that it was that of the adult *female only.* Then Colonel Tickell, in writing of this species in the *Field*, remarked (the italics are mine):—

"The above descriptions disagree in many points with those given by Jerdon; but they are carefully worded from observation of several fine specimens of both sexes and different ages shot by myself in Tirhoot, Lower Bengal, and Singbhoom. *The colouring ascribed by Jerdon to the adult male is that of an immature bird of either sex, and the description of his female is that of a mature bird of either sex.*"

This determined me to look into the question myself, and I shot and bought and dissected over 100 birds. Of these, nearly fifty were in the plumage depicted in the left hand figure; every one of these proved to be, without exception, females. In this enormous number of birds, examined between the 1st November and 1st April, not one single bird in this plumage was a male.

Moreover, I found that (I speak of birds sexed by dissection) in the *females* the wings varied from 5·25 to 5·6, and the bills at front from 1·8 to 2·05, while in the males the wings varied from 4·9 to 5·2, and the bills from 1·65 to 1·85, and out of all the birds examined, in what had thus been proved to be the adult female plumage, only one single specimen, but what would have been recognized to be a female merely by its dimensions. This one, a female by dissection, with comparatively large eggs in the ovary, and in the full female plumage, had a wing of only 5·03 and a bill at front of only 1·73. It was in fact a dwarf female, a female by dissection, a female in plumage, but of dimensions rather less than those of an average male. It has occurred to me that similar dwarf females may have led Schlegel, Tickell and others into the error above referred to.

One thing is certain—besides the large series of this bird examined and sexed specially for this enquiry, I possess twenty-three specimens sexed at other times by myself and others in the adult female plumage. Every one of these has been sexed female by dissection. This makes seventy birds in which the plumage, attributed by Jerdon to the adult female, has proved on dissection to pertain to that sex, without *one single instance* in which it has proved on dissection to pertain to the male.

To me this seems to prove the rule, but there *may* be exceptions. It seems to me *possible* that, as in many species females with diseased ovaries assume a *quasi*-male plumage, so in this species, in which ordinary sexual relations are reversed, males with diseased generative organs *may* assume a *quasi*-female plumage. I hope every one will try whether it is possible to find a single male in the plumage depicted in the left hand figure of the plate, and if they ever find such, examine carefully the generative organs and preserve the specimen, so that we may see whether in such exceptional cases the identical plumage of the female is assumed, or only something approaching or mimicking it.

The young of *both* sexes resemble the male, *i.e.*, the plumage depicted in the right hand figure, but the young females soon begin to show signs of the adult plumage; they get the dark pectoral band more strongly marked, and the wing-coverts begin to show the green, crossed by narrow, dark, transverse bars characteristic of the adult female garb.

Some years ago Captain E. A. Butler raised the question as to whether the plumage depicted in the left hand figure was not merely seasonal, assumed only when the birds were breeding, and whether, at other times, even adult females did not wear the same livery as the males.

At the time, not having then specially investigated the plumage of this species, I was inclined to agree with him in this suggestion, which was apparently supported by the specimens (then far from numerous) in our museum.

Now, however, I entirely disbelieve this: First, because I have obtained, and have now before me, specimens in full female plumage, shot in January, February, March, May, July, September, November and December; and I have no doubt myself that a little further attention to the subject will yield birds in this plumage in April, June, August, and October also. Secondly (and this is the most important point, seing that it has already been explained that in one place or another the birds lay almost throughout the year), because every one of the apparently full-grown females examined by me in male, or nearly male plumage, exhibited undeveloped virgin ovaries. I failed to find a single female, in this plumage, with an ovary showing that she had ever bred, though I found one in intermediate plumage in which the eggs were just beginning to swell. Even this bird would, I believe, have completed the change of plumage before any of those eggs came to be laid.

I must now again return to the plate; and, admirably as this depicts the plumage of the specimens figured, it is necessary to explain that, in this species too, the plumage varies considerably.

To take the females first. Many birds have the chestnut of the neck lighter coloured and entirely want the blackish shading on the sides of the neck. In some the yellow line caused by the buffy outer margins to the scapulars is very conspicuous; in others these margins are absolutely wanting. In some birds the peculiar elongated, linear-lanceolate pure white feathers that have their origin amongst the bases of the tertiary coverts are much more plainly visible than in the plate, while in many specimens they are much less developed, and are only discovered on raising the feathers. In some birds, those I think in fullest plumage, the back has a regular reddish violet glow, as depicted, but more commonly this part is green, like the coverts. The narrow transverse barrings on the whole of the visible portion of the closed wing are often further apart and more distinctly marked than in the plate, and the tail shows more distinct buff patches on the grey ground than in the specimen figured.

In the male the lores are never so dark as represented. The whole front of the neck is often streaked and spotted with white, and the wing has the buff markings arranged more in lines and not so much like a series of arrow heads as in the plate. The yellow margins to the scapulars are often much more broadly marked, and the feathers of the back are more distinctly tipped with white so as to show a narrow white line along the lower margin of each of the dark bars shown in the plate.

EXCLUDING RHYNCHÆA AUSTRALIS, from Australia, to which allusion has already been made, and which may, or may not, (*non vidi*) be distinct from our Old World form, the only other known species of the genus is *Rhynchæa semicollaris* of South America.

½

PSEUDOSCOLOPAX SEMIPALMATUS.

THE SNIPE-BILLED GODWIT.

—o—

Pseudoscolopax semipalmatus, *Jerd.*

—o—

Vernacular Names.—[None.]

—o—

THE Snipe-billed Godwit has been so seldom observed within our limits that it may be well to mention every instance of its occurrence that has come to my notice.

About the close of 1844 Jerdon procured the type in the Madras market. On December the 12th, 1847, Blyth procured one in the Calcutta market. Colonel McMaster writes: "I have killed it in January, (? 1863) near Rangoon, feeding close to the Whimbrel (*Numenius phæopus*,) and the Stilt (*Himantopus candidus*.)"

On the 28th September (? 1876) Mr. Oates obtained two specimens, a male and a female, near the mouth of the Sitang in Lower Pegu, and on the 13th of December 1878 I purchased three specimens in the flesh (one male and two females) in the Calcutta market, which had been captured in a bird-net thirteen miles south-east of Calcutta.

Besides these instances, Colonel Graham writes that he has shot "a few" in Eastern Assam; but I am by no means sure that my kind friend has correctly identified the species. No one else at any rate has ever met with this species in Assam, but it would be extremely likely to occur there on passage.

Outside our limits it has been procured at *Pontianak* in Borneo (two specimens by Diard), and it has occurred in China, but is probably rare there. I do not gather that Pére David himself ever met with it, but Swinhoe says he procured two specimens—one in partially moulted plumage, in autumn at Hankow, Central China, the other in full summer plumage from the neighbourhood of Tientsin.

Verreaux received a specimen from Dauria, and not recognizing it in its rufous summer garb, renamed it *Micropalma taczanowskia*. For years Dybowski failed to meet with it in Darasun, and the neighbourhood of Lake Baikal; but he notified the existence of one specimen in the Irkutsk Museum, obtained somewhere in the neighbourhood, and of another at Warsaw which had been procured near Chita the capital (?) of

Trans-Baikalia. Later however he found it on the Argun River (which divides Trans-Baikalia from that part of Northern Mongolia, called Kheluntsyan on English Maps) in about 50° North Latitude. It was very plentiful there in the spring, and remained until the females were nearly ready to lay, but did not nest there, probably proceeding further north for that purpose. Prjevalski never appears to have seen this species in all his wanderings in Mongolia, the Valley of the Hoangho, Kansu, &c. Nor did Schrenk, Middendorff, or Radde meet with it apparently anywhere in Northern or Eastern, or South-Eastern Siberia. Indeed the representative American form, the so-called Red-breasted Snipe *(Macrorhamphus griseus)* has been obtained in the extreme east of Siberia. Clearly we have yet to discover both the summer and winter head-quarters of this curious species.

ABSOLUTELY nothing is *known* of the haunts, habits, flight, voice, or food of this species; but we may surmise that, during the non-breeding season, it is chiefly to be found on or in the neighbourhood of sea coasts, as is the case with the Red-breasted Snipe of America. From its bill conspicuously spatulate, and covered for the terminal inch with nerve pits and channels, indicating a bill more sensitive even than that of the Common Snipe, we may infer that it frequents soft mud flats and oozy ground. Its comparatively long and very pointed wings, together with the ample development of the pectoral muscles, indicate a rapid and powerful flight; while as to its food the sensitive character of the bill shows that this is almost exclusively sought for beneath the surface, and will probably consist of worms, small sand-eels and soft-bodied crustacea.

In shooting birds like the present species, Godwits, Curlew, Whimbrel and many others, along the mud flats that fringe our coasts, and almost fill many of our harbours, sportsmen should never forget the extremely treacherous character of these banks, and the dangers that attend incautious attempts to retrieve wounded birds. I have several times myself, when walking on what appeared to be sound ground, with only about a foot of mud over it, suddenly sunk another foot or more, and once I went in right to my waist, and so remained helpless until dragged out, (leaving my boots behind) by the united efforts of two boats' crews. But I might just as well have lit upon some deeper mud hole, where I should probably have sunk before aid could have reached me.

Tickell tells how a boatman of his was all but lost on one of the mud banks in the Roopnarain, near the junction of that river with the Hooghly, and in my coast shootings I have had many stories told me of men who have thus perished. Tickell had dropped a bird on one of these banks. "The tide had turned to rise. I was much averse to the man getting out of the boat to fetch the bird, but the others seemed to think the mud just there was safe, and it certainly was, so far that the man did not sink higher than his knees, and would have reached the bird safely; but it fluttered a few yards further on his approach, and thus led him plunging and labouring on, till in a moment, to my horror, he sank up to his waist. He had come suddenly on a spring or percolation of water, which rendered the mud perfectly quick or semi-fluid. His ghastly look, as he writhed round towards us, in a vain attempt to reach the boat, I shall never forget to the last day of my life. The men with me were fishermen of those parts, and pretty well accustomed to accidents of the kind; but even they seemed to think this a bad case. They shouted to the sinking man to keep perfectly still, and with strenuous efforts we managed to pole and push the *dingey* to within three yards of him. They then threw the large steering oar and a spare bamboo sideways over and beyond the man, and on these rested another bamboo, the near end of which was over the *dingey's* gunnel. On this bamboo the man rested by his arms and chest, and ceased to sink deeper. As the tide rose we drifted near enough to touch him; but all our efforts were unequal to extricate him from the mud, and as the water began to mount to his shoulders I was in unspeakable dread of what would follow in five minutes more if we could not get help. Happily, the young flood was bringing up, as usual, a perfect fleet of boats, hastening to the various market towns up the Roopnarain; and after much shouting and offers of 'bucksheesh' two boats were induced to come to our assistance, and by crowding their beaks or prows together with ours, four or five men were able to grasp the unfortunate fellow and regularly "man-handle" him out, *quitte pour le peur*. But what *peur!* Of all the ghastly deaths that imagination can conjure up, sure none can be so horrible as smothering, by inches, in the mud! It made me think then, and often years afterwards, what an exquisite luxury, did we but appreciate it, is that of simply breathing!"

This treacherous character of mud banks is a very real and ever present danger, and the not-unheard-of practice amongst some European sportsmen, of *compelling* their boatmen, *vi et armis*, to retrieve wounded birds off mud-banks, cannot be too strongly deprecated. In one instance, to my knowledge, it resulted in the loss of two lives.

In *no* case, no matter how thin the mud appears in the place first tried, should any man be allowed to plunge into one of these banks without a good long thick bamboo in his hands.

Not only on the coast, but in many of the larger rivers hundreds of miles from the sea, most dangerous *dul-duls* or quick sands occur; indeed are in the Ganges most common.

Only the other day, old and practised hand as I am at this work, I suddenly sank in above my waist, when hunting for Tern's eggs, in the Ganges a few miles below Allahabad.

The young sportsman should never, therefore, forget that mud-flats, whether by the sea or inland, are places to be only ventured on with great care.

OF THE NIDIFICATION of this species, we are as ignorant as of its haunts and habits. Schlegel says that it nests in Northern China and Mongolia, and quotes Swinhoe as the authority for this assertion. But Swinhoe, I believe, never stated anything of the kind, and, as a matter of fact, we know that a good deal further north, in North Latitude 50 degrees, the bird only halted during the spring and passed on to breed. Probably their summer head-quarters are in Northern Yakutsk, in the lower valleys of the Lena and other rivers, emptying themselves into the Arctic Ocean between the 120th and 170th degrees East Longitude.

THERE SEEMS to be little difference in the size of the sexes. The following are the exact dimensions recorded in the flesh of six birds, two males and three females, and one, sex unrecorded. The first three sets of dimensions, recorded by myself, the next two by Mr. Oates, the last by Blyth :—

	Female.	*Male.*	*Female.*	*Male.*	*Female.*	?
Length	13·0	13·3	13·3	13·5	13·4	13·0
Expanse	22·5	23·0	23·5	23·0	21·5	21·0
Wing	6·75	6·8	7·1	7·0	6·8	6·5
Tail, from vent	2·6	2·4	2·5	2·9	2·5	2·5
Tarsus	2·1	2·0	2·2	2·05	2·05	?1·75
Mid-toe and claw ...	1·55	1·58	1·48	1·5	1·52	1·5
Hind-toe and claw ...	0·58	0·6	0·6	—	—	0·56
Bill, at front, from margin of feathers	2·88	3·15	3·12	—	—	2·87
Bill, from gape	2·89	3·1	3·07	2·9	3·25	—
Height of both mandibles—at base, at margin of feathers	0·45	0·45	0·47	—	—	—
Bare portion of tibia ...	1·16	1·2	1·32	—	—	—
Weight	3.9 ozs.	4·0 ozs.	4·1 ozs.	—	—	—

In my specimens the bill was deep brown, pinkish fleshy towards base of lower mandible; the legs and feet were pure dull lead colour, a little dusky at the joints, and in one specimen on the toes; the claws were deep brown; the irides were also deep brown.

In Mr. Oates' birds "the bill was black, turning to plumbeous at the gape; iris dark brown; claws black; legs and toes dark plumbeous."

Blyth says: "Bill dusky, dull carneous towards the base of the lower mandible; legs and toes lead coloured."

THE PLATE would be an exact representation of the winter plumage, if the brownish fulvous shade which overlies the head, neck, back, breast, and sides were replaced by grey. This is *not* the fault of the artist. The only specimen available, when our plate was prepared, nearly three years ago, was Mr. Blyth's old specimen which did exhibit this fulvous shade, which latter, as we now know by comparison with fresh birds, was only what is technically called "museum brown," due to long exposure in Calcutta to damp, heat, dust and light; the bill should be blackish dusky or deep brown, except just towards the base; the legs and feet should be lead coloured instead of green as in the plate.

The breeding plumage is widely different, and, like that of the true Godwits, very rufous. I have never myself seen this species in summer plumage, but this latter is thus described by David and Oustalet:—

"The upper parts bright rufous with brown streaks on the middle of the crown, on the lores, and down the back of the neck, and large spots of the same colour on the dorsal feathers; the lower parts of a more uniform rufous; the feathers of the abdomen margined a little with white, and the flanks and lower tail-coverts marked with a few irregular brown streaks; wing-coverts, secondaries and tertiaries a greyish brown, margined with white; primaries brown, with white shafts; the tail feathers transversely rayed with white upon a brown ground."

Probably this plumage is entirely lost by the end of October, but Mr. Oates says of one of his specimens shot on the 29th of September:—

"The male is still partially in summer plumage; the breast is ferruginous, and the tertials are edged with the same."

Doubtless the great mass of the specimens met with in India will be in winter plumage, and the bird is so rare, and it is so desirable that it should be certainly identified wherever met with, that I subjoin a more detailed account of this plumage, recorded by myself from fresh specimens:—

The wings, when closed, reach 0·2 beyond the end of the tail; the first quill is the longest, the second a trifle shorter; the elongated tertials are nearly equal to the third quill; the outer toe to second joint is connected by a web to half way between first and second joint of the mid-toe; the mid-toe from between first and second joint is connected by a web to the first joint of inner toe; the hind toe is long, thin, free, considerably raised above the sole. There is a conspicuous groove on each side of bill from the forehead over the nares, almost to the point; the point of the bill is much dilated, not showing reticulations or pittings in the *fresh* specimen, (though these are very conspicuous in dry ones), but with a deep central groove; the inner surface of the upper mandible or palate, exhibits a double row of sharp, thorn-like, recurved papillæ* ; the tongue is long, simple, sharp-pointed and membraneous towards the tip.

The lower wing-coverts are much developed, the greater ones of the hinder secondaries being almost as long as the quills themselves.

There is a conspicuous dark line from the eye to the nostrils ; a broad, not very regular dull white, or brownish white, band above this line, extending backwards, diminished in breadth, as a supercilium ; the chin, cheeks, throat, and front and sides of neck are white, with a brownish tinge, thickly streaked, longitudinally, with little brown lines, short and more or less speck-like about the chin, throat and face, longer, broader, more pronounced, lower down ; the few last feathers at the base of the neck, on the sides, and at front, with traces of arrow-head, subterminal brown bars ; the feathers at the extreme sides of the breast with these well marked.

The breast, abdomen, sides, flanks, vent, lower tail-coverts, tibial plumes, axillaries, and wing-lining, in *some* specimens all pure white and unmarked, in others with a few spots, traces of obsolete bars, on some of the feathers of the sides, flanks and lower tail-coverts.

The variation in the amount of barring at the base of the neck, on the extreme sides of the breast and elsewhere, is probably seasonal.

The lesser lower coverts everywhere just inside the edge of the wing, brown centred.

The forehead between the dull white bands, the crown and occiput, moderately dark, slightly sooty brown, with just a trace of paler margins to the feathers.

The nape, back of neck, and interscapulary region similar, but the brown somewhat lighter, and the pale brown margins to the feathers more conspicuous ; the scapulars similar, but most of them rather darker ; the lesser wing-coverts generally decidedly darker, with the pale margins obsolete or nearly so, while in the median coverts these are more conspicuous and white or albescent ; the winglet and primary greater coverts very dark brown ; the coverts, more especially the hinder ones, tipped white ; the rest of the greater coverts a lighter brown, often greyer, tipped, margined, and more or less imperfectly barred towards the tips with pure white, most conspicuously so on the inner webs ; the earliest primaries deep brown, growing less deep as they recede towards the secondaries, which are a rather light, in some birds decidedly grey, brown ; all the quills with much white and white mottling on the inner webs, the amount of which increases as the feathers recede from the outside of the wing ; all but the first five or six primaries more or less conspicuously margined, often in a mottled fashion,

* This also characterizes *Pseudototanus haughtoni.*

on the outer web, and at the tips also, with white; the secondaries more strongly so, and these, and the later primaries, with more or less of a mottled-white shaft-streak.

The rump and upper tail-coverts white, conspicuously barred with black, the terminal bar more or less following the curve of the feather; the tail feathers white, with regular, rather broad, transverse blackish brown and black bars; the central feathers always, the next one or two pairs often, and sometimes nearly the whole tail, with an ashy brown shade over the whole terminal portions of the feather, alike over white and black, both of which it obscures and dulls.

As Swinhoe observed, but for the bill, this species closely resembles the Eastern Bar-tailed Godwit, *Limosa baueri*, Naumann, (novæ-zelandiæ, *Gray;* uropygialis, *Gould.*), but this latter is a larger bird with a wing longer by a full inch and a quarter, and with the bills there is no mistaking this present species, in which the bill widens out towards the point where it is comparatively soft and fleshy, while in the Godwit referred to, it gradually narrows to the point, which is hard, polished and horny.

NO OTHER species of this peculiar genus is known to exist, but the genus *Macrorhamphus* is very close to *Pseudoscolopax*, and by some considered inseparable, and one species (the only* known one) of that genus, the Red-breasted Snipe *(M. griseus)* inhabits the whole of North America, and Greenland, wandering in winter to Mexico, Central America, the West Indies, Brazil, and many parts of South America.

---

* Some authors have divided this species into two, but the best authorities seem to be agreed that the second supposed species is not even entitled to rank as a variety.

½
TOTANUS HAUGHTONI

ARMSTRONG'S YELLOW-SHANKS.

Pseudototanus* haughtoni, *Armstrong*.

Vernacular Names.—[None.]

THIS rare, or at any rate hitherto little noticed species, was first obtained by Dr. Armstrong on the 18th of December 1875, near the mouth of the Rangoon River, between Elephant Point and China Bakeer. At that time he only secured two specimens. In December 1876 and January 1877 he succeeded in shooting four more specimens in the neighbourhood of Amherst. In December 1877, I procured one mangled specimen in the Calcutta market.

No other instances of the occurrence of this species within our limits, or elsewhere, have, so far as I know, as yet been recorded.

LITTLE PRACTICALLY is known of the habits of this species. The specimens obtained were found feeding on extensive sand banks in company with large flocks of Sand Plovers and other waders, and the hard-pointed, non-sensitive bill indicates sufficiently a habit of surface feeding, as opposed to the mud-boring of the last species.

Dr. Armstrong writes to me: " With regard to the habits of the species all that have been killed by me both at China, Be-keer, Beloo Gyoon, and Amherst, have been upon

* I established this genus for the reception of this species, S. F., VII., 488, (December 1st, 1878). The following is my definition of the genus which I reproduce (*vide, loc. cit. sup.* et S. F., IV., 1876, 347) :—

Bill considerably longer than the head, stout, nearly straight, but the culmen perceptibly recurved, tapering quite at the base, after that of nearly uniform width throughout, rather obtusely pointed just at the tip, which is bent down over the lower mandible ; culmen broad, slightly flattened towards the tip ; nostrils, lateral, sub-basal (commencing nearly a quarter of an inch from the base) placed in a membraneous groove which extends rather beyond half the length of the bill (say 11-20ths.) ; palate armed with a double row of recurved horny papillæ ; the wings reaching considerably beyond the end of the tail and pointed ; the first quill longest ; tail moderate and nearly even ; tarsi slender, one-fifth longer than mid-toe and claw, covered in front by numerous narrow faintly marked scales ; toes slender, moderately long ; anterior toes united by a membrane, which extends from the first joint of the middle toe to the first joint of the inner, and nearly, if not quite, to the second joint of the outer one ; hind toe long, slender, somewhat elevated.

extensive sand and mud flats *fully exposed to the sea.* I have *never* seen a *single* specimen on the numerous smaller flats forming the banks of the rivers and creeks in the vicinity of these localities, and where its near allies, the Green and Red-Shanks, are so abundant.

"I have never seen them solitary; they appear to seek their food sometimes in couples, but more usually in small parties of 3 or 4 or 5, and are often associated with large flocks of Stints or Green-Shanks, with whom however, they do not appear to mingle. They are much more wary than their companions, and it requires much caution to get within shooting distance of them. They are always the first to rise, so that in order to obtain specimens, I made it a rule to fire at the first birds of the flock that rose.

"In other respects their habits are similar to those of the other '*Shanks*,' Green, Red and Yellow; but I have often noticed that they like to dabble with their bills in the mud or sand like ducks in a puddle of water.

"The stomachs of some I killed contained small mud-fish and crustacea, while those of others were crammed with larvæ and small molluscs."

I only know of eight specimens of this bird, four in our museum and three in that of Trinity College, Dublin, all shot and preserved by Dr. Amrstrong, and one mutilated specimen bought in the Calcutta market.

THE FOLLOWING are the dimensions of six specimens, five recorded by Dr. Armstrong; one by myself:—

	♂	♂	♀	♂	♂	♀
Length	12·45	13·2	12.9	11·75	12·16	—*
Expanse	23·0	23·25	22·3	20·5	23·0	—†
Wing	6·9	7·3	7·0	6·7	7·05	—†
Tail from vent	2·95	3·0	3 0	2·09	2·8	2 9
Tarsus	1·79	1·85	1·65	1·72	1·82	1·7
Bare portion of tibia	—	0·95	0·86	—	—	0·89
Mid-toe and claw	1·45	1·5	1·4	1·6	1·51	1·47
Hind-toe and claw	0·45	0·52	0·5	0·4	0·45	0·47
Bill from gape	2·4	2·5	2·2	2·23	2·45	—*
,, at front	2·15	2·1	1·93	2·1	2·3	—*
Weight	—	—	—	—	—	3·3ozs.

I am not sure that these have all been correctly sexed, if so, the fourth must have been a young bird, as, judging from the analogy of the Green-Shanks, in the adults, the males should be appreciably larger than the females.

The irides are deep brown; the bill is dusky on the terminal half, blackish towards the tip; the basal half is paler, varying from yellowish horny to greenish plumbeous, growing

* Bill broken off short at base; length from forehead to tip of tail, 10·85.

† All the earlier primaries pulled out.

yellowish near the gape; the legs and feet vary from greenish yellow to dull ochreous, and have more or less of a dusky shade over the joints.

THE PLATE exhibits fairly enough the shape and proportions of the species, but as to the colouration Mr. Neale may be able to explain it—*I* cannot.

The plate professes to exhibit the *summer* and winter plumage. The former, which I presume the figure in the foreground, is intended to depict is, to the best of my knowledge, purely imaginary. *Possibly*, Mr. Neale obtained a specimen in summer plumage elsewhere, but if so, I have never been informed of the fact, and none of the six specimens that I have seen were in the slightest degree like the figure in the foreground. Failing more definite information, I can only conclude that, seeing that the winter plumage a good deal resembled that of the Common Green-Shank, a summer plumage also has been invented for our bird on the model of that of the Green-Shank. This, though creditable to some one's ingenuity, is a proceeding hardly conducive to scientific accuracy, and scarcely to be commended. The guess *may* prove a lucky one, but nature is so full of surprises that I should not be in the least astonished if it proved wholly erroneous.

Anyhow, my readers will kindly remember that, so far as I know, there is at present no foundation in fact, for the handsome bird in the foreground with its extraordinary, patchy, vivid green legs.

The ticket on the specimen sent to Mr. Neale to figure says distinctly: "Legs and feet greenish ochreous yellow, somewhat dusky over phalangeal joints." *De coloribus non est disputandum* with an eminent artist; but still I believe that the general sense of the public will be with me when I say, that our artist's rendering of this description is decidedly "out of the common." Except for the bright green feet, the figure in the background does approximately represent our bird, in the sole garb in which (to the best of my belief) it has ever as yet been met with; but to make it really correct, the very dark brown marks on the crown, and the dark brown lunules on the back, must be entirely removed, since crown and mantle are alike a pale greyish or ashy brown, each feather very narrowly margined with white.

The plate being such as it is, I am compelled to subjoin an exact description of our specimens.

A broad stripe from the forehead (on which it forms a band) to just over the eye, the feathers about the gape, chin, throat and front of the neck, breast, abdomen, vent, lower tail-coverts, sides of the body and flanks, axillaries, and wing-lining, lower back and rump, pure white; crown, back of the neck, interscapulary region, scapulars, secondaries, and tertiaries, and most of their coverts, pale ashy, in some feathers browner, and more drabby, in others greyer, each feather narrowly, more or less obsoletely, margined with white or albescent; all the lesser coverts about the shoulder of the wing moderately dark hair brown; primaries and their greater coverts dark hair brown, almost black on the outermost feathers, paling as they recede towards the secondaries, and with a certain amount of white or greyish white on the inner webs; the later shorter primaries margined at the tips with white; the shaft of the first primary very broad and pure white; the shafts of the succeeding primaries narrower and brown, darkest towards their bases, palest, an inch or so, from their tips; upper tail-coverts white, showing traces of narrow, scratchy, imperfect, zig-zag or arrow-head bars; tail feathers all margined with white; the rest of the feather grey or ashy, slightly darkest just inside the white margin, and with more or less white freckling towards the shafts, especially on the outer feathers; the feathers of the crown, occiput, back of the neck and interscapulary region, and sometimes the scapulars, just perceptibly darker shafted; a band from the gape under the eye and the sides of the neck and of the breast, white, with dark shafts to the feathers, and in the case of the sides of the neck and breast with here and there tiny, pale, ashy brown shaft patches also.

I dare say specimens of this species have often been passed over as Common Green-Shanks, but it has a much broader culmen, and rather more massive bill; the webs between the three anterior toes are very much more developed, and the tarsi are much shorter; moreover, the winter plumage, though bearing a strong superficial resemblance to that of the Green-Shanks, is yet altogether more uniformly coloured. There is none of the *marked* dark striation of the crown, and there are none of the dusky spots and markings just inside the edges of the feathers which characterise the entire mantle of the Green-Shanks, even in mid-winter. The whole mantle in our bird is a nearly uniform, mingled brownish and greyish ashy, the uniformity scarcely broken by the somewhat darker shafts of some of the feathers, and the very narrow, albescent edgings of some or most of these feathers.

Although presenting this superficial resemblance to the Green-Shanks, our bird could scarcely stand as a *Totanus*; indeed its short tarsi and much webbed feet rather recall *Pseudoscolopax semipalmatus*, but then the bill is much shorter and of a different character, wholly wanting the tumid multi-pitted ends of that species, and the membrane between the outer and middle toes is also proportionately larger.

The bill is something like that of *Tringa crassirostris*, but stouter, broader, and longer, and with the lateral grooves extending only for 11-20ths of the length of the bill, and this peculiarity, of course, with the comparative shortness of the bill, equally separates it from the Godwits, in which the lateral grooves run quite, or very nearly, to the point.

Again the webbing of the feet reminds one of *T. semipalmatus*, Gmel.; but that is altogether a larger bird, (wing, 8·25), with a longer and much slenderer bill (at front, 2·42) with very much longer tarsi (2·58), and a huge, unmistakeable, white patch on the wing.

In the short tarsus and stout bill this species is allied to *T. incanus*, Gmelin, but that is decidedly a smaller bird, with as *extreme* dimensions, wing, 6·95; tarsus, 1·37; and bill at front, 1·55, with a proportionally longer and more rounded tail, and shorter mid-toe, with a less stout bill, and scarcely any webbing to the feet. The plumage further of our birds (at any rate in winter, for we know as yet nothing of the summer garb) differs entirely from that of the Ash-coloured Yellow-Shanks.

AS YET no other species has been recognized as belonging to this new genus.

LIMOSA ÆGOCEPALA
SUMMER & WINTER PLUMAGE

THE BLACK-TAILED GODWIT.

Limosa ægocephala, *Linné.*

Vernacular Names.—[Goodera, Gairiya, Jangral, Burra chaha. *N. W. Provinces*; Malgujha, *Nepal*; Jaurali, *L. Bengal*; Susling, *Sindh*; Tondu ulanka (Telegu).]

THROUGHOUT the Himalayas, at any rate from Kashmir to Sikhim, the Black-tailed Godwit has been met with, but chiefly, if not solely on passage, in autumn and spring.

During the cold season it is pretty common, though rather locally distributed, throughout the Punjab, Sind, Rajputana, * Cutch, Káthiáwar, Northern Guzerat, the North Western Provinces and Oudh, and the plains portion of Bengal west of the Brahmaputra.

Southwards of this tract it must be very rare in India. It does occur in Southern India, for Jerdon, in his Catalogue, distinctly states that, though rare, he has seen it there, and Layard records it from Ceylon, but Davidson has not yet met with it in Khandesh. Blanford does not include it in his list of birds either of Central and Western India, or of the Wardha Valley, nor McMaster, in his Nagpore and Berar List, nor King in his Goona List, nor have I myself seen it, or received it from any of my collectors, in the southern or eastern portions of the Central Provinces. Ball does not include it in his Lists of the Birds of Chota Nagpore, or the country southwards to the Gódavarí. Again neither does Lloyd include it in his Konkan List, nor Vidal in his of Ratnagiri, nor Fairbank in his Lists of the Birds of the Mahrathi country, and of Khandala, Mahableshwar, and Ahmednagar, nor Davidson and Wenden in their Deccan List. McInroy does not mention it as observed in Mysore, nor apparently has Theobald ever shot it in Southern India, south of the 12th degree North Latitude, most parts of which he has worked over during the last ten years. Nor has Mr. Bourdillon obtained it in Southern Travancore.

This is all negative, but, while Jerdon's statement proves that the bird does occur, all this evidence shows that it must be very rare in India south of the 20th degree North Latitude.

West of the Brahmaputra, again, it seems to be rare. Colonel Graham writes that he has seen a few in Upper Assam; but I

* I have myself shot it as far south as the Kunkrowli Lake in Oodeypore.

am not sure that he could distinguish between this and the representative eastern species, which would be the one most likely to occur at Dibrugarh, and neither Godwin-Austen, nor any of his or my collectors, have yet procured it anywhere in Assam, Sylhet, or Cachar, nor, though I found it not rare about Dacca, has it been sent or recorded from Tipperah or Chittagong. Blyth notes it from Arakan, but I have seen no specimen thence. In Lower Pegu it is found, Oates says, on all the tidal rivers, and is particularly common about the mouths of the Sitang. Ramsay, however, says that he only once saw the bird in Burma, and in all our collecting in Tenasserim we only once met with a single bird, and that near Moulmein. It has never been procured at the Andamans or Nicobars.

Outside our limits, in the Malay Peninsula, China, Chinese Tibet, Mongolia, Southern and Eastern Siberia, it is replaced by the smaller eastern representative species (of which more anon) *L. melanuroides*, Gould. Neither species occurs, so far as we know, in Eastern Turkestan, but in Western Turkestan the present species has been observed on passage, and some may breed there. It has been procured at Cabul and Kandahar, in Beluchistan, in Persia, on the Caspian, near Shiraz, and at the mouths of the Euphrates. Again, it has been sent from Mesopotamia, and occurs in Asia Minor and on the coast of Palestine and throughout Northern Africa from Abyssinia to Morocco.

Though extending rarely within the Arctic Circle, it occurs on passage or as a summer or winter visitant, in most parts of Europe, including the Islands of the Mediterranean, the Canaries, the Færoes and Iceland, and has twice been recorded from Greenland.

IN THE plains of Upper India, the earliest date on which I have ever shot the Black-tailed Godwit, is the 5th of October, and the latest the 9th April. But, as a rule, it is quite the end of October before they are well in, and almost all have left by the close of March. In Nepal Hodgson notes that they "arrive in flocks of from ten to fifteen from the north in September, and then feed in the newly cut rice fields. They stay about a month. Ere they depart, they have separated into pairs, and then often stray into the later uncut rice. They return in March and April, mostly in pairs, but usually only remain for a few days then as the valley is too dry."

These birds must come from Northern and Western Siberia, where the species occurs, and it will doubtless hereafter prove to occur in Eastern Turkestan also, on passage.

In Lower Bengal they arrive about the end of October and leave towards the close of March. Writing from Farídpur, Cripps says:—

"To the south of my factory was a large expanse of paddy field, in the centre of which was a sheet of water of about 20 acres in extent. In the hot weather the water was reduced to about 18 inches in depth, and this place for the latter half of March used to swarm with these birds. From about 9 to 2 in the day, the whole of the birds used to go away somewhere, evidently to feed. They used to allow me to approach within gunshot, and on the report of a gun would fly to the other end of the "bhíl," when they could not be so easily shot. By the beginning of April not a bird was to be seen."

They are very locally distributed; in one part of a division or even district they may be very plentiful, in another quite scarce. Where plentiful, you will find them in flocks of from ten to a hundred or more, and then, as a rule, comparatively tame. Where scarce, you see them singly, in pairs, or in parties of three or four, and then they are generally shy, wary, difficult to circumvent, and fully deserving of the title, bestowed on them by our ancestors, of "Goodwits."

Inland you more commonly find them about the margins of broads and swamps, (though even there it is not rare to find them on the banks of our larger rivers,) but towards the coast they chiefly affect the vast, sandy and muddy flats that characterize the estuaries of our larger rivers.

Their habits vary a good deal according to season and locality. They feed largely, when this is available, on rice, both wild and cultivated. In India this is, to judge from many examinations I have made, their favourite food. But they also eat seeds of some of the millets, of grass, sedges, and the like, numbers of small insects, tiny shells, and occasionally worms and grubs, and soft-bodied crustacea. Their diet, however, depends upon what is available, and you may kill birds with their gizzards entirely crammed with any one of these, to the exclusion of the others.

Where recently cut or nearly ripe rice fields are at hand, they feed in these, by day if they are little frequented, but by night if there liable to disturbance. Thus, while at some places you will find them standing the whole day in the grassy shallows of some broad, generally just outside the grass, or where it is very sparse and low, in others they leave these places entirely during the greater part of the day, and are only to be seen there in the mornings and evenings. In such cases you may generally (for they will, unless very much persecuted, visit the same places for weeks together) track them to their feeding grounds, often close at hand, rarely more than a couple of miles from the water they frequent. Such feeding grounds may be recently-cut rice fields, or nearly ripe standing rice, wild or cultivated, or very often stretches of spongy sward, interspersed with patches of low rush. But, though they generally have regular feeding grounds, which they visit for some hours once in the twenty-four hours, they also feed at other times, and you may see them stalking about in water, three to five inches deep, picking small insects off the surface with their long bills; or again walking along the water's edge on sands or mud banks, picking up small shells and shrimps.

Selby says that this species may be "frequently seen wading tolerably deep in water, *immersing the head at intervals and searching the deposit beneath.*" This may be a fact, but I can only say that I have often watched this species, and yet have never noticed that it *immersed the head.*

They are not birds that court concealment. They are often, when in ones or twos, difficult enough to get near, but they are usually easy enough to see, as they always, or almost always, keep out in the open, whether they be walking or wading, or asleep on one leg in water just up to their breasts, and their necks, heads, and long bills nestled into their backs.

On land, where a large party is feeding, they alternately stalk about with much dignity, and make rapid and easy little runs, accompanied often by flutterings of the wings to pounce on some tid-bit. When thus occupied, and in force, they are at times ridiculously tame, and I have stood watching a flock for several minutes, on a low earthen ridge overlooking their feeding ground, and within thirty yards of the nearest birds, without their taking the smallest notice of me. Of course they are easy to shoot at such times, and in two shots, fired at such flocks, whilst I was at the Manchar Lake, twenty-two were procured at one time, and eighteen the other. This sounds like very unsportsmanlike butchery, but then they are one of the very best birds for the table with which India presents us. They are always nice; even those that I have shot close to the sea were entirely free from any unpleasant flavour, while when really fat and in good condition, well fed on rice, they are, in my opinion, though very differently flavoured, quite equal to either Woodcock or Jack, and far superior to Fantail or even Common Snipe.* Of course they must be properly cooked, only plucked and cleaned the moment before they are put to the fire, only cooked *just* sufficiently and served up at once. I can't help dwelling upon this because all game is, as a rule, utterly spoilt in India by our native cooks. First they pluck and clean birds hours before they are wanted, the result being that, in the extremely dry atmosphere of Upper India, the flesh is half-dried up before the cooking commences. Then the bird, instead of being roasted lightly, is stuck in a cooking pot and steamed at leisure, at times, for hours, very often when cooked, taken off and allowed to cool, and always only taken out to brown for a few minutes, just before being

---

* Our forefathers fully appreciated this bird, which less than one hundred years ago bred *plentifully* in England, and Yarrell tells us that—

"Thomas Muffet, that ever famous doctor in physick, as he is called in his title-page, says in Health's Improvement, page 99. 'but a fat *Godwit* is so fine and light meat, that noblemen, yea and merchants too, by your leave, stick not to buy them at four nobles a dozen.'"

served. Of course, thus treated, even Woodcock are dry and tasteless.

Though they rise rather clumsily, these Godwit have a strong, rapid, and very direct flight when well on the wing; and as they fly rather high, almost out of shot, when passing from one broad to another, or when coming from or going to their feeding grounds, they often afford very pretty overhead shots. When rising or fluttering about feeding, the white wing bar is very conspicuous, and by this, like the lesser Red-Shanks (*Totanus calidris*) they may always be distinguished at a glance.

I cannot remember often hearing this bird utter any sound, but during the breeding season, at any rate, they are represented as being very vociferous when their nests are invaded, and at other seasons they occasionally emit a clear whistled-call repeated two or three times in rapid succession as they rise. But, as a rule, I should call them eminently silent birds during the non-breeding season.

SO FAR as is yet known this species does not breed within our limits. In Western Europe, although some few may breed in Iceland, and even well within the Arctic Circle in Finmark, and again in the Balearic Isles south of the 40th degree North Latitude, its normal breeding zone seems to be between 50° and 55° North Latitude. In Russia it breeds nearly as far north as the 60th, and as far south as the 45° North Latitude.

As to their nidification I may quote what has been said of it in Holland and Poland. Yarrell says: "Mr. Hewitson says the Black-tailed Godwits commence laying their eggs early in in May. The nest is composed of dry grass and other vegetables, and is concealed amongst the coarse herbage of the swamps and low meadows. Mr. Hoy mentions that, when disturbed, they are clamorous, flying round and vociferating the cry of *grutto, grutto, grutto,* by which name the bird is known among the country people in Holland."

Of their nidification in Poland, Taczanowski says: "Usually they begin breeding early in May, and about the middle of June young may be found fully fledged. They generally breed in large societies, in tolerably damp places covered with high, thin herbage, where there are tussocks or small dry places, but also in the fields (in scattered pairs or small colonies), and in small marshes covered with grass and bushes. On the top of a tussock or dry place they make a depression about three inches deep, and line it carefully and neatly with dry grass, depositing four eggs, on which both male and female sit. If a human being approach their nesting-colony, they meet him when some distance from it, uttering loud cries, and returning again and again in larger numbers as he comes nearer to their nests. When he is amongst the nests, all the birds fly overhead, uttering a continual lamentation. If the intruder remains there any time, they become tamer, and a few return to their eggs, especially if the latter are hard-set. Before they have eggs they are very shy, rarely approaching within gunshot; but when the young are hatched, they are most courageous, and will come within a few feet of the intruder, not even retreating when fired at, and dozens may be killed. They will attack a cow or horse if they approach their breeding places, and attack and pursue any bird of prey or crow that may pass near."

The eggs are rather broad ovals, pulled out and pointed towards the small end after the fashion of Snipe's eggs, but usually in a less conspicuous degree. The eggs vary much both in size and colouring. The ground colour varies from pale brownish or greenish white, through various shades of greenish olive and yellowish stone colour; but probably a dull, not very pale greenish tint, is most common. The markings, generally most numerous about the large end, never very thickly set, and sometimes extremely sparse, consist of larger or smaller blotches, spots, and smears of varying shades of brown (redder in some, more olivaceous in others) and of a greater or lesser number of underlying grey clouds and spots, more violet in some eggs, more lavender in others, and occasionally dull sepia.

In length the eggs seem to vary from 1·9 to 2·35, and in breadth 1·35 to 1·52; but Dr. Rey gives the average of fifty eggs as 2·15 by 1·5 nearly.

IN THIS species, if birds of the same age are compared, the females are very decidedly larger. Quite young birds are very much smaller. I propose to give only dimensions of birds which showed no signs of nonage, but even these included birds of very different ages, and, I suspect, that for at least the first three years, these Godwits go on under favourable conditions, steadily increasing in size and weight.

The following is a *résumé* of the measurements of over fifty individuals, all of which were apparently adults, *i.e.*, showed no signs of nonage :—

Males.—Length, 16·0 to 18·1; expanse, 25·0 to 29·8; wing, 7·5 to 8·81; tail, from vent, 3·12 to 3·5; tarsus, 2·85 to 3·35; bill, at front, (which in *this* species is precisely the same as from gape,) 3·65 to 4·5; weight, 7·8 to 12·0 ozs.

Females.—Length, 18·3 to 20·2; expanse, 28·0 to 31·3; wing, 8·4 to 9·25; tail, from vent, 3·25 to 3·94; tarsus, 3·3 to 3·7; bill, at front, 4·5 to 5·1; weight, 9 ozs. to 15 ozs.

Mr. Cripps and others have kindly furnished me with elaborate measurements, some of which do not agree over well with mine. I can only say that mine include over fifty individuals, and have been most carefully made; and that, where others disagree with these, I can only suppose that in some cases quite young birds must have been measured, and that in others the birds must have been missexed.

The legs and feet are always dark coloured, but they vary in shade and are blackish plumbeous, blackish green, very dark olivaceous, dusky with a greenish tinge, deep leaden brown, sooty brown, dark greenish brown, dusky brown, dull greyish brown, etc., but the greenish tinge is the most common. The claws are black. Note that the mid-toe claw is long, much dilated on the inner side, more or less delicately serrated there, and when perfect (the tips are very commonly much worn away or broken) more or less distinctly *recurved*.

The irides are dark brown. Normally the basal three-fifths of the bill are fleshy livid, or reddish pink, more or less brownish on the culmen, while the terminal two-fifths are brown to blackish brown, darkest, at times almost black, towards the tip.

Sometimes the basal portions of the bill are more of a yellowish horny, though still with a faint fleshy tinge, or a fleshy cream colour, and at times there is but little of this lighter colour on the upper mandible, it being replaced by brown, though not nearly so dark as the brown of the terminal portion. Occasionally the basal portions might be best described as a mixture of dingy orange and pink.

As a rule, about the basal three-fifths of the bill are of these clearer and lighter tints, but sometimes these extend for two-thirds of its length, and at others for barely more than one-half.

THE PLATE represents both the summer plumage (the figure in the foreground) and the winter plumage (the hind figure). Both are very fair, though the irides are wrongly coloured in both, and the bills of both should be darker towards the tips. As a rule, the brown of the winter plumage is of a rather paler and of a greyer and more earthy tint than is depicted, and unfortunately the most characteristic features in that plumage, the pure white rump and upper tail-coverts (except the longest) and jet black, narrowly pale-tipped tail, are hidden in the drawing.

We never, I think, or *very* seldom, see birds in *quite* the full summer plumage here depicted ; but by the close of March they have assumed a good deal of the barring on the lower surface and of the rufous colouration that characterize this stage, and the commencement of the change (which is effected *not* by a moult, but by a change in the colour of the existing feathers) may be observed in some birds as early as the middle of February and in almost all (all in fact I think, except birds in their first year) by the middle of March.

A SMALL representative race of this species, the Eastern Black-tailed Godwit (*L. melanuroides*, Gould; *L. brevipes*, Gray), occurs in the Malay Peninsula, China, Japan, Mongolia, Chinese Tibet, Eastern and Southern Siberia, and extends through Sumatra, Borneo, the Philippines. (P. Z. S., 1878, 288) Ceram, and probably all or most of the islands of the Archipelago to Australia.

Many authorities deny specific rank to this form, and if specific rank were never accorded on the score of difference in size, I might agree in this view, for there appears to be absolutely no difference in plumage; but the difference in size seems very great. The smallest male of *ægocephala*, not manifestly by the plumage a *quite* young bird, that I have ever been able to meet with, had the following dimensions:—

Wing, 7·5; tarsus, 2·85; bill at front, 3·65.

This was an exceptionally small bird. Contrast this with the similar dimensions of an old male *melanuroides*, which we shot near Malacca.

Wing, 7·41; tarsus, 2·59; bill at front, 2·9.

No one ever saw anything like a perfect adult of *ægocephala*, let alone an old bird with worn claws, approaching even these dimensions. And the bill is not only so much shorter, it is altogether slenderer and more delicate.

I think it probable that stragglers of this small form may appear in Eastern Assam and on the Southern Tenasserim coast, and hence my particular notice of it.

LIMOSA RUFA
SUMMER & WINTER PLUMAGE

THE BAR-TAILED GODWIT.

Limosa lapponica, *Linné*.

Vernacular Names.—[None.]

I FOUND this species fairly common in February 1872, in the Kurrachee Harbour, and ascertained its occurrence further east about the mouths of the Indus. Subsequently Captain Butler procured a few specimens at Kurrachee. There is no other authentic instance of its occurrence within our limits.

No doubt Blyth says (*Ibis*, 1865, p. 36, n.) : "There is an Himalayan example in the Derby Museum, Liverpool, presented by Colonel Everest. Mr. Hodgson also obtained the species in Nepal." Colonel Everest, at one time or another, worked almost all over India, but no doubt much of his time was spent in the Himalayas, and this specimen *may* have been obtained there, or it may not have been obtained in India at all. As for its alleged occurrence in Nepal, Hodgson does not figure the species, nor mention it in any of his notes, nor is it included in any of his, or Mr. Gray's, lists of his collections to which I have access. Dresser calmly states that "Captain Bulger records it as not uncommon at Mulcivon, Selham and Ras Dowra in Sikhim!" It seems almost needless to say that Captain Bulger does nothing of the kind. Of course these places could *not* be in Sikhim, but *must* be in some country where Arabic is spoken, and accordingly I find that it is Mr. C. F. Tyrwhitt Drake who makes the above-quoted remark in his Birds of *Morocco*, (*Ibis*, 1869, 154).

Outside our limits it has been shot near Ormarra on the Mekran Coast, but I have no record of its occurrence elsewhere in Beluchistan, nor in Afghanistan, nor Eastern or Western Turkestan, nor in Persia ; but as both Pallas and Eichwald say, it is common on the Caspian, and I know it to occur on the Mekran Coast, it most probably also visits both the Northern and Southern Coasts of Persia. It is rare on the Black Sea, and the islands of the eastern portion of the Mediterranean, and it does not seem to have been as yet observed in either Asia Minor or Palestine.

Brehm says it occurs in Egypt and Nubia, but neither Shelley nor Heuglin ever met with it there ; the latter, however, shot it along the Red Sea Coasts, and also on the Northern Somali Coasts *i.e.*, the southern shores of the Gulf of Aden, from September to December. In Algiers it is common in winter, as it is also about Tangiers and other places in Morocco, and it is said to have occurred on the Western Coast of Africa as far south as the Gambia River, and occasionally to have straggled to the Canaries.

Excluding the Azores, the Færoe Islands and Iceland, it appears to have occurred in most of the countries and islands of Europe breeding apparently for the most part between the 60th and 70th degrees North Latitude.

THE EARLIEST occurrence of this species, of which I know was, when one was killed by Captain Butler at Kurrachee, on the 29th of September. The latest was the specimen (just beginning to show signs of the summer plumage) shot on the 23rd of March at or near Ormarra.

I know but little of the habits of this species. I found them frequenting the vast mud banks of the Kurrachee harbour, in company with Stints, Snippets, Curlew, Whimbrel, Shore and Grey Plovers, Oyster-catchers, and the like. They fed scattered about amongst a crowd of these other species, but, on being disturbed, rose and flew off in flock of from six or seven to twenty. They were often in large numbers, say as many as a hundred feeding on the same bank, but they flew off in different directions in comparatively small parties. They were excessively wary, and the few specimens (six) that I obtained, were all chance hits at seventy or eighty yards and upwards, with large shot and wire cartridges out of a heavy gun.

They rise more easily and rapidly than their larger congeners but their flight is less rapid though equally direct. Winged birds falling into the water swim well, jerking the head and neck forward at each stroke. Their call, even less frequently heard than that of the black-tailed species, is a rather low, piping note.

So far as our experience here extends, they are essentially coast birds, frequenting banks in harbours, bays, and the tidal estuaries of large rivers. Common as they are in places along the Sindh coast, they have never yet been observed any distance inland.

The few birds I examined had fed chiefly on tiny shrimp-like things, small mollusca, sand worms and insects, but most of their stomachs contained matter that I took to be minute acephalæ, or jelly fish. I found no vegetable matter in any of their gizzards, and the flesh of two or three that we cooked, hoping to find them as good as the other species, was by no means well flavoured. It was not fishy, but it had a faint, froggy, flavour, and reminded me of that of eels caught in muddy broads and dykes at home.

THIS SPECIES breeds in the far north; it is said to have bred in Holland, but if so, this is considerably south of its normal breeding zone.

No reliable accounts of its nidification seem to exist, but it is said to lay in May and June, depositing two or three eggs (why not four?) in a depression in the soil or in mossy tussocks in the northern morasses.

Wolley says that this species breeds in marshes, chiefly in the neighbourhood of mountains, and gets up so warily from its nest, that it is difficult to find the eggs.

The eggs appear to resemble, closely, those of the Black-tailed Godwit (already fully described) both in shape and colouration, but to average smaller, varying in length from 1·9 to 2·12, and in breadth from 1·4 to 1·53. But it is by no means certain that any of the eggs of this species, common enough in European collections, are authentic.

IN THIS species likewise adult females (to judge from our measurements) exceed the males in size, and specially in length of bill; but I have the measurements in the flesh of only eight birds, (six of my own and two of Butler's recording) so that I cannot pretend to say that the following figures at all exhaust the limits within which the species may vary:—

Males (6).—Length, 13·5 to 14·8; expanse, 25·5 to 27·75; wing, 7·8 to 8·4; tail from vent, 2·7 to 3·3; tarsus, 1·95 to 2·06; bill, at front, (which in this species also is the same as from gape,) 2·75 to 3·12; weight, 7·7 to 10 ozs.

Females (2).—Length, 15·75; expanse, 28·0 to 28·5; wing, 8·2 to 8·4; tail from vent, 2·75 to 3·0; tarsus, 2·1; bill at front, 3·61 to 3·75; weight, 9 ozs to 11·3 ozs.

The legs and feet, in some almost black, are in others plumbeous or dusky plumbeous; the irides are deep brown; the bill is deep brown to blackish on the terminal half, darkest near the tip, and pinkish fleshy, more or less brownish on the culmen, on the basal half.

THE PLATE represents this species in both summer and winter plumage, the latter being depicted in the sitting figure. In both figures the terminal portions of the bills and the irides are too light coloured.

Here too the tail of the bird in winter plumage is hidden, but it is typically regularly barred, pure white and brown, much as depicted in the summer plumage, though in that stage the white interspaces have more or less of a rufous tinge. But in one or two of our birds, which I take to be young ones, the tail is *not* barred; the feathers are a grey or grey brown, white tipped, with dark shafts, and only traces of a single darker antepenultimate bar. In another the exterior pair *are* barred white and brown, but all the rest are still grey, with only indications of coming darker bands.

I have no specimen at hand in full summer plumage; one killed (as above) late in March, has a reddish buffy tinge over the breast and front of the neck, and one or two red and black feathers on the head. It is only, therefore, just commencing to put on the summer plumage, which is, I believe, fairly correctly depicted in the standing figure of the plate.

THERE IS another closely allied species, (if indeed it merits specific rank)—the Eastern Bar-tailed Godwit, which we have shot in the Malay Peninsula, and which may hereafter appear in Burma and Eastern Assam on passage. This race (*L. baueri*, Naumann; *L. uropygialis*, Gould; *L. novæ-zealandiæ*, Gray) is distinguished first, *possibly*, by its slightly larger size and longer bill, (birds of the same age and sex being compared); secondly, by having the lower back and rump, which in the western bird are mostly white, much blotched or barred with brown; indeed in many specimens the entire lower back (not rump) is brown, the feathers being only narrowly margined with white; thirdly, by the much more profuse markings and barrings of its wing lining and axillaries.

I have, however, English specimens of *lapponica* making a considerable approach in the matter of rump and wing lining markings to some of my New Zealand, Malayan, and Japanese specimens of *baueri*, and a very large series of both will require careful consideration, before the specific validity of the eastern race can be finally accepted.

This species or race occurs in the Malay Peninsula and Sumatra to our knowledge, possibly in Borneo, certainly in Java, Celebes, Timor, and other islands of the Archipelago, Australia, including Van Diemen's Land, New Zealand, New Hebrides, Norfolk Island, and other islands of Central Polynesia. It also occurs in the Philippines (P. Z. S., 1878, 711), Japan and along the entire Chinese Coast, including those of Hainan and Formosa. But in all these countries the bird is a winter, or at any rate non-breeding visitant, for some young and weakly birds *may*, in places, remain the whole year.

It is said to have occurred in Mongolia, Eastern and South-Eastern Siberia, and Alaska.* To the latter it is extremely unlikely that it should extend, and as regards the others, though it doubtless must traverse them on passage, neither Radde, Schrenk, Dybowski or Prjevalski ever appear to have met with it. But in the extreme north of Siberia, Middendorff found this species breeding in great numbers on the Taimyr River, in 74° North Latitude. This is in about 100° East Longitude,

* Swinhoe says, P. Z S. 1871, 406: "Breeds in Amoor land and Alaska," but this appears to be entirely groundless.

and birds coming thence due south would hit the coast first about Bankok, and next about the middle of the Malay Peninsula, while birds breeding further west (up to the 90th degree East Longitude) in that great Northern Siberian Promontory, would similarly reach the Eastern Coasts of the Bay of Bengal. There are no grounds, however, for concluding that these birds do migrate due north and south, and we know nothing, moreover, of the effect of the lagging of the atmosphere in the diurnal revolution of the earth on the course of birds thus migrating, so that, while it is quite possible that this species will prove to occur on the Arakan, Pegu, and Tenasserim Coasts, it is impossible to predicate that they will. On the coasts of Siam, Cambodia, Cochin China, and Tonquin, we may be quite sure that they do occur.

BESIDES THE four species or races of Godwits noticed above, *viz.*, the Black-tailed and Eastern Black-tailed, both of which at all seasons have the axillaries pure white, and the Bar-tailed and Eastern Bar-tailed, both of which at all seasons have the axillaries, white, barred or spotted or marked with brown (varying from greyish to blackish) America has two other species—the American Black-tailed (*L. hudsonica*, Latham) distinguished by its black axillaries, and the Great Marbled Godwit, (*L. fedoa*, Linné), which equally, at all seasons, has rufous axillaries, barred or marked with black.

STRAY FEATHERS.

UNDER this title has been published for many years a magazine devoted entirely to the ORNITHOLOGY of the BRITISH ASIAN EMPIRE and the circumjacent countries.

No one can make any satisfactory progress in the Ornithology of India without the assistance of this magazine, which is strongly recommended to all who may be led by a perusal of "THE GAME BIRDS," to desire to know something about the multitudinous other families, genera and species of Birds that inhabit this Empire.

The magazine for the current year, and its volumes for most of the past years, may be procured from

THE CENTRAL PRESS,

5, COUNCIL HOUSE ST., CALCUTTA.

APPENDIX.

SUBSEQUENT to the publication of Volumes I. and II. and the printing off of Volume III., a few notes have been received in regard to some of the species therein treated of. Another Tragopan has been added to our Avifauna, and the female of the Crestless Moonal, unknown when Volume I. was published, has been procured.

The additional information thus made available is reproduced below.

THE GREAT INDIAN BUSTARD. (Vol. I., pp. 7, *et seq.*)—

In the first place I was wrong in supposing that this species does not cross the Jumna northwards, and eastwards into the North-Western Provinces. It is shown that it is a permanent resident of parts of the Mozuffernuggur district, occurs in Saharanpur, and probably in Meerut likewise.

Mr. Frederic Wilson writes: "There are always, at this time of the year (November 10th), a few of the Great Indian Bustard east of Mozuffernuggur, on the high ground just before the dip into the Ganges Kadir. My son had a rifle shot at one, and so had my assistant, both missing. I myself came across a flock of sixteen one day, but did not get a shot. I shall probably go down in that direction this cold weather, and will try and send you one."

And Mr. F. W. Butler says: "You say that the Great Indian Bustard does not occur in the North-Western Provinces, north and east of the Jumna, but some few birds of this species are really always to be found in the Mozuffernuggur district all through the year.

"I yesterday put one up about six miles from my house, a cock. I saw a dead bird some years ago, that had been killed for Mr. George Palmer, C.S. An inspector of mine wounded a cock badly last January. Some years ago, while riding across from Roorkee to Bijnour, I saw a number of birds on some sandhills, which I then believed to be Vultures. I had then never seen the Great Bustard. I was struck by the birds, and watched them for some time. Eventually I rode into them, and put them up; this was during the rains. I have no doubt now, especially after reading your remarks (p. 11,) that these birds were Bustards.

"Between the line of the railway and the Ganges canal, from near Roorkee to, I believe, Ghazeeabad, there runs a broken range of sandhills. Along this tract, right and left of the range, the land is high and sandy (*bhoor*), and here Bustards are to be found. I cannot positively assert that they extend into the Meerut district, but I believe such to be the case; and certainly a bird is to be occasionally seen during the rains in the Saharanpur district, east of Deobund.

"In this district (Mozuffernuggur) they are to be found all the year round, and one was caught alive here some years ago for Mr. Craigie Halket by some *bahelias*.

"The Bustard I saw yesterday, I flushed within a quarter of a mile of the Grand Trunk Road, (Meerut to Roorkee) on some *bhoor* land close to a police outpost.

"In 1871, I was in the Mirzapur district. I was told by natives, and also I think by Mr. Pollock, C.S., that both Bustard and Florican were to be found some miles from the station, along the great Deccan road.

"Mr. Ward Smith, an Assistant Engineer, D. P. W., stationed here, tells me he frequently sees Bustard about Jowlee in the Mozuffurnugger district."

I wrote somewhat doubtfully of the occurrence of this species in Mirzapur and Rewah. As to the former Mr. Butler, as above, confirms what I had heard, and as to Rewah, Major McInroy writes: "I do not know why the Bustard should *not* be found in Rewah, for it is, or used to be, exceedingly common all round Nagode.

"I cannot say whether *any* of the Bustard, found there during the cold season, migrate from Mysore; but some, at all events, breed there, as in the Tumkur district, to my certain knowledge, and I believe in other districts too."

This also confirms their breeding in Mysore, of which, when I wrote, I had no certainty.

I mentioned that they occurred, in suitable localities of course, throughout the Central Provinces, and several gentlemen write to confirm this. Mr. J. A. Betham says: "I have seen Bustard in the Betul district between Badnur and Muttaie, and once near Satna (between Jabalpur and Allahabad); in the latter instance the bird was close to the Railway when the train passed, and did not appear to mind the rattle and noise. I was surprised, for I had always imagined them to be very shy birds."

Another gentleman writes that he has seen them on several occasions near or within a few miles of the Bargash Railway Station of the Jabalpur line.

It appears that in the Nerbudda valley the Vernacular (Hindee) name for these Bustards is, *Serailoo.*

Two eggs of this species will be found very fairly figured on the first of the four plates of eggs that follow this Appendix.

THE BENGAL FLORICAN. (VOL. I., pp. 23, *et seq.*)—

In speaking of this species as occurring in the North-Western Provinces, north of the Ganges, and mentioning that I had never met with it west of the Kadir of the Ganges, I did not perhaps make it sufficiently clear that I was aware that in that Kadir, alike on the left and right banks, it occurred in the cold season. I did not know, however, that it was really *common* anywhere on the right bank, but Mr. A. M. Markham says: "The Bengal Florican is very common in the Kadir of the Ganges (right bank) in the Mozuffurnuggur and Saharanpur districts, especially the former."

I was not moreover aware that this species ever straggled far into the Doab, and well away from the Ganges, but that it does so is now certain. Mr. C. E. Yeatman informs me that in 1865 (cold season) he saw a pair and shot one, a fine cock, in a small dâk jungle, near Secunderabad, in the Bulundshahr district; that again he met with one, in the winter of 1874, in some high sandy ground near Shekoabad in the Mainpuri district; and that lastly, on the 11th of December 1879, he shot a hen just above the Jumna ravines in the south-west corner of the same district. Again Mr. Markham writes: "On the 5th of February, at Mahewa close to the Jumna, in the extreme west of this, the Allahabad district, I twice put up a hen Florican (*S. bengalensis*, of Jerdon), not the small Likh Florican (*S. auritus*, of Jerdon) of Central India, but the large Florican which we meet with in the grass plains of Rohilkhand and Northern Oudh. Most unfortunately I had only Quail shot in my gun when she first got up, and I only tickled her, and when I put her up the second time, she was out of shot. I could not put her up again, and next day had to leave the locality. I never heard of a Florican here, and am curious to know what you think of the occurrence. It most certainly was a *Florican*, and not a *Bustard* I have seen hundreds and shot scores of them."

We must therefore now admit this species as a rare straggler to the Doab and extend its range as far west as the Jumna.*

When I wrote I had never seen an egg, but I have since been presented with one by Mr. F. A. Shillingford, who says: "The Florican's egg I myself picked up in June last. The female bird was seated on it when I first saw her about five yards distant; when she rose I found one egg. There was no attempt at a nest; the egg was lying on damp mud with the few blades of grass that were growing near trodden down. Young birds have several times been caught in this district."

This egg is of the same type as regards texture and colouration as many of those which I possess of the Great Indian Bustard and Lesser Florican, but is intermediate in size, and conspicuously more elongated than those of either of the others. It is more of the shape of a hen's egg, but rather more elongated than this even, and decidedly more compressed towards the small end. The shell is firm and strong, smooth and compact, but has little gloss. The pore-pittings are very inconspicuous.

---

* Mr. Fasson says: "It may be worth noting that I have seen and shot Florican in the Mymensingh district, as I see you do not mention that as a known locality. It occurs not unfrequently along the skirts of the Mudhopore jungle." But Mymensing is of course in Eastern Bengal, the whole of which I explicitly included in its range.

The ground colour is a dull, pale green stone colour, and it is rather sparingly streaked and blotched with dull, rather pale brown, somewhat greyer in some spots, more olivaceous in others.

It measures 2·6 inches in length by 1·76 in breadth.

I hope other correspondents will send me more of these rare eggs, as eggs of these Bustards vary so much that, without a good series, one cannot properly describe them.

THE LESSER FLORICAN OR LIKH. (Vol. I., pp. 33, *et seq.*)—

At page 36 I quoted a remark of Mr. Davidson's that this species was only found sparingly in Mysore. It appears however that in some parts of that province, at any rate, they are very abundant. Major McInroy says: "I think I am within the mark when I say that near Mallur, a station on the Bangalore-Madras line of rail, and 25 miles from Bangalore, thirty birds were shot in one day by two officers of the Forest Department. Several good bags have been made in that neighbourhood. Florican are pretty numerous throughout East Mysore, but, for some reason which I cannot divine, are not nearly so common in the western division of the Province.

"I have known four or five killed of a morning within a few miles of Samulcottah, a now deserted military cantonment seven miles from Coconada."

Two eggs of this species are figured on the first of the four egg plates which follow this Appendix.

THE LARGE OR BLACK-BELLIED SAND-GROUSE. (Vol. I., pp. 47, *et seq.*)—

When Volume I. was published, I had no detailed information of the nidification of this species in Kabul or Beluchistan. But it was found breeding in numbers not ten miles from Kandahar during our recent occupation of that place, and in the neighbourhood of Chaman (also in Southern Afghanistan) Mr. H. E. Barnes found them breeding plentifully in May and June.

They lay in slight depressions in the soil similar and similarly situated to those in which the Common Sand-Grouse lays. Mr. Barnes says: "The eggs, three in number, are, as regards shape and colour, exact counterparts of those of *Pterocles exustus*, but are of course larger. They average 1·8 by 1·35."

An egg sent me by that gentleman, the parents of which he shot and identified, is a very elongated, cylindrical, dumpy, sausage-like egg; the shell is extremely fine and compact, and has a fine gloss. The ground colour is a very pale green or greenish white, and it is moderately thickly studded with irregular spots, and small blotches more or less streaky in shape, of a rather pale yellowish brown and very pale, slightly purplish, grey. It measures 1·84 by 1·2.

Another egg, very kindly sent me by Mr. James Murray of the Kurrachee museum, taken near the Jeempir Railway station, Sind, on the 10th of July, and sent to him along with a pair of birds of this species, is very different in appearance, and is really, I believe, an egg of *P. alchata*.

It is a decidedly shorter egg; it has much less gloss, the ground colour is a pale *cafe au lait*, the markings are of the same colours as on the other egg, but they are more thinly set, and the bulk of them much smaller; but then there are a couple of great large splashes of both the yellowish brown and the purplish grey, which far exceed in size anything on the other egg. This egg measures only 1·7 by 1·2.

It is just *possible*, though I doubt the fact, that some few *P. arenarius* may breed in the desert country about the estuary of the Loonee, and eastwards in the Thurr and Pakur, north of the Runn of Cutch. Mr. R. H. C. Tufnell writes: "The late General McMaster killed a bird of this species, (a male), on the plains near Sirhpoor (? between Ahmedabad and Deesa) on the *7th May*, but it may have been a chance or wounded bird, though apparently strong and quite at home. (I take the above from a note made by General McMaster in the margin of his Jerdon.)"

THE SPOTTED SAND-GROUSE. (Vol. I., pp. 53, *et seq.*)—

I said that this species was only common in Sind and Jeysulmir, but it appears that it is also common in the southern portion of the Dhera Ghází Khan district (Punjab.); Mr. Tufnell writes: "Near Rajanpur, on the Punjab Frontier, these birds were extremely plentiful in August last, running about on the open 'pat,' or among the stunted tamarisk bushes."

An egg of this species is figured on the third of the plates of eggs which follow this Appendix.

THE CORONETTED SAND-GROUSE. (Vol. I., p. 57.)—

I stupidly said that I could find *nothing* recorded of the habits of this species, when in reality years ago I had put the following on record :—

"Sir William Merewether tells me that the flight and cry of *P. coronatus* are both quite different from those of all the other species. They have a curious fluttering flight, and appear often to hover in the air, especially before settling, and their cry is a twittering one."

Mr. Tufnell writes that he procured several specimens of this species when at Vitakri, in Beluchistan.

The occasional range of this species within our limits is considerably more extensive than I suspected. Lieut. W. W. Lean writes to me, under date the 7th of October:—

"Two males of the Coronetted Sand-Grouse were shot within three miles of this post, (Fort Jumrood, near the mouth of the Khyber Pass,) this morning by Dr. Julian Smith. The flock (some twenty in number) was first seen flying from the direction of the Khyber, uttering their peculiar cry. Suddenly they separated, preparatory to alighting along a nullah, which crosses a very stony plain, to drink.

"The largest of the two birds measures 12 inches in length and 23·25 in expanse, and weighs 23 rupees say 8½ ozs.

"The colouring of the plate is, as you say, defective. The occiput is really cinnamon and not burnt sienna. The blue grey superciliary stripe forms a complete ring, a little white intervening between it and the eye. The orange of the plate should be more of a yellow ochre, which goes rather lower down than is shown in the plate, and is continued on across the back of the neck, thus forming a ring. The yellow tinge of the plate is replaced by stone grey or rather a mixture of cinnamon and grey stone, and the burnt sienna and sepia shades are replaced by stone and brown.

"The neck is not thick, but dove-like, in fact in shape exactly like that of the male Spotted Sand-Grouse as depicted in the plate.

"I can only find small seeds and gravel in their crops."

Since I wrote Mr. H. E. Barnes found one or two nests of this species near Chaman (South Afghanistan) ; they contained three (in one case *very*) hard set eggs, of the usual elongated cylindrical shape, one of which measured 1·5 by 1·06.

One of these eggs, taken on the 27th of May, for which I am indebted to this gentleman, has a fine and compact shell, and a moderate amount of gloss; the ground colour is a pale creamy white, the markings, spots, moderate-sized blotches and streaks are, as usual, of two colours,—a pale, rather washed-out yellowish brown, and a very pale, almost sepia grey. This egg measures 1·63 by 1·07.

THE PAINTED SAND-GROUSE (Vol I., pp. 59, *et seq.*)—

I mentioned that this species extended to Mysore, but I had no details of its distribution. It would now appear that in the Province, as a whole, it is extremely rare, but that there are some few localities in which it is pretty abundant. Thus Major McInroy, than whom no sportsman is better acquainted with Mysore, as a whole, writes: "You mention that this species does extend to Mysore, but it is extremely rare there. The following are the only two instances in which I have met with it during five years of travelling in all parts of the province, whilst especially in the Chitaldroog District, the Common Sand-Grouse is in legions :—

"*23rd January* 1879.—Two brace near Ramgherry, Hosdurga taluk, Chitaldroog district, Mysore. One brace in hilly jungly ground ; the other brace on the plain within a quarter mile of the village of Ramgherry, still there were a few bushes. I shot a brace of the Common Sand-Grouse within a *few yards* of these. In the first case there were three birds, in the other a pair only.

"*1st February* 1879—Bukambídí, Tarikere taluk, Kadur district, Mysore. One brace out of three birds. Scrub jungle at foot of a hill."

On the other hand Mr. Tufnell says : "As regards the occurrence of this bird in the Mysore province I can speak, from experience, of its being anything but rare on the wooded islands of the Cauvery, near Seringapatam. The largest bag I can remember making in that part of the country was thirteen birds, killed near French Rocks on 17th October 1878, by Major St. John and myself. They breed in the same place."

In corroboration of my account of the kind of localities affected by this species Captain Heaviside, R.E., writes: "The country in which I have found these most abundant consists of low, flat-topped hills, such as are found in the Nerbudda valley, south of Mhow. These hill-tops have patches of black soil on them, and are covered with thin tree jungle. This year, in Khandesh, I have found these birds common on the same sort of ground, and have noticed them in the evening on the cart tracks. where they were probably dusting themselves, as there is no grain traffic on these roads. In both places, but more specially in the Nerbudda valley, I generally got about a brace whenever I went out shooting for an hour or two. I agree with Jerdon in thinking they have crepuscular or nocturnal habits, as I have seen them flitting round when it was practically dark."

An egg of this species has been figured on the second of the egg plates that follow this Appendix.

THE CLOSE-BARRED SAND-GROUSE (VOL. I., pp. 65, *et seq.*)—

When writing of this species I remarked that, although never recorded from Beluchistan, it must needs occur there. This has since proved to be the case. Mr. Tufnell writes: "Two specimens of the Close-barred Sand-Grouse were procured last November on the Bhor plain in Beluchistan, and the officer who killed and gave them to me told me that he saw many more of the same species on this plain. I think I saw a small flock of these birds near the same place in the beginning of January, but could not be certain."

THE COMMON PEA-FOWL (VOL. I ., pp. 81, *et seq.*)—

I gave from June to October as the laying season of this species, but it appears that both in the Sub-Himalayan tracts and in Southern India some birds, at any rate, begin laying in April. Thus my old friend Mr. Frederic Wilson says: "You say, page 90, that Pea-Fowl breed in June, July, and August; but in the Dún here we find the eggs about the end of April, and early in May they are plentiful enough."

And Major McInroy writes: "*Hoonsoor, Mysore, 25th April.*—Took a Pea-Fowl's nest containing four fresh eggs. One of my men first found it about a week ago; it then contained only one egg. This seems to be an early date for Pea-Fowl to lay in the *South*, though I see that some are said to lay in April in the *North*."

In Ceylon, I learn that they begin laying as early as X'mas, and that fresh eggs may still be found well into April.

At page 89, I referred to the albino varieties of this speices that are occasionally met with. Mr. F. W. Butler now writes: "It may interest you to know that I lately shot a Pea-Fowl in the Mozuffurnuggur district, similar to the one described by you in your book, as being 'a hen of a uniform dirty yellow colour.' My bird, however, was more white than yellow. I flushed the bird in a cotton field at dusk, and at the moment believed I had put up a Turkey."

THE EASTERN OR BURMESE PEA-FOWL (Vol. I., pp. 93, *et seq.*)—

When I wrote I was not aware that this species extended anywhere within our limits northwards of Arakan, but it now appears that, though very locally distributed, it is the only Pea-Fowl met with in Chittagong, extending quite to the north of that district.

Mr. H. Fasson, to whom I am indebted for this information, remarks:—

"The Peacock found in this, the Chittagong district, is the Eastern or Burmese Pea-Fowl, (*Pavo muticus.*)

"I have seen a live specimen, and have heard of small flocks at Jooykhola in Fatikchiri, the extreme north of the district, at Gurjunia, and at Ramoo in the south, and at Rangunia on the Kurnafoolee, where one was shot the other day. These small parties, of four or five birds each, are the only ones I have had *khabar* of, and they seem to stick a good deal to those neighbourhoods, so that, when I asked in various parts of the district if there were any Pea-Fowl about, I used to get the answer, 'There are none here, but there are some near Gurjunia, or at Ramoo, &c.' as the case might be. I saw the place they frequent at Gurjunia ; it is a great stretch of high reed jungle and elephant grass, filling a wide valley between forest clad hills."

Extending thus to the extreme north of Chittagong it is probable that this species will also prove to occur in Hill Tipperah and Southern Cachar.

THE ARGUS PHEASANT. (Vol. I, pp. 99, *et seq.*)—

According to the experience of the officers in charge of the London Zoological Society, this species only lays two eggs at a setting, the two eggs being laid at an interval of two days. They have laid in March, May, and July. One hen, which had lost her first setting, laid later a second, so perhaps they have more than one brood in the year. Incubation, in which the male took no part, lasted twenty-four days.

The egg is figured and described as a moderately elongated and regular oval, sligthly compressed towards one end, of a "rich coffee colour" (I should call it a rich reddish *cafe au lait—a very* different thing to *coffee* colour), "minutely punctured throughout" (what with is not said, but *apparently* brown) "with a darker blotch at the large end." One egg (as if eggs did not vary in size, and the measurement of one egg could ever suffice) is said to measure 2·6 by 1·9.

It is a pity that English writers, as a rule, have no conception of describing eggs thoroughly and accurately, still the above may be accepted, until better information is available, it being borne in mind, that experience gained from birds long captive as to number of eggs laid, and even as to the colour and markings of eggs, does not always hold good with the same birds in a wild state, and that it is therefore quite possible that the information furnished as to these latter, by natives, to Davison (Vol. I., 101) may yet prove to have been correct.

THE GREY PEACOCK-PHEASANT. (Vol. I., pp 105, *et seq.*)—

Some little additional information in regard to this species has reached me from Chittagong.

Mr. H. Fasson writes: "The Polyplectron of this district (Chittagong) is undoubtedly, as you say, *Polyplectrum tibetanum*, and the *Mathura*, *Euplocamus horsfieldi.*

"They are both very common in all the heavy jungles of the district. The Polyplectron rarely to be seen or shot, but not infrequently snared with horse-hair by the village boys—the *Mathura* often put up and shot when beating for Jungle-Fowl.

"The Polyplectron is in this district invariably called 'katmoir'; and is not known by any of the vernacular names given in your book. I do not know what 'kat' is intended to signify ; 'moir' is of course Peacock."

Mr. J. Jarbo again says: "Polyplectrons are very early birds, and in this, the Chittagong, district very shy. As far as I can learn they never leave the bank of a stream very far ; they are found in the deep, cool and secluded nooks near streams, may be at the edge of the main jungle, bnt never in isolated pieces of jungle. I have never, by any chance, seen one after 7 o' clock A.M.

"When I was at a garden called Boorooncherra in Southern Cachar, I remember constantly picking up feathers belonging to this bird, and always in the same, or near the same place. I never could account for this except by thinking that some knowing animal, finding out that this was their favourite haunt, laid in wait and daily carried off a victim."

THE NICOBAR MEGAPODE. (Vol. I., pp. 119, *et seq.*)—

An egg of this species is figured on the second of the plates of eggs.

THE MOONAL. (Vol. I., pp. 125, *et seq.*)—

When Vol. I. was published I was not aware that this species extended westwards beyond Chitral, but during the late war, it was found to be common in Afghanistan on the Sufaid Koh.

Lieut. W. S. Fairbrother (29th P. N. I.). amongst others, writes: "I see that you are not aware of the Moonal being found out of the Himalayas, or westward of Kashmir. So you may be glad to hear that it is common in the Sufaid Koh here (Kurum, Afghanistan). Freshly-killed birds were brought in by the natives to Shalozan last winter. The natives here (Turies) all call the Moonal, *Kukur*, but I cannot say whether this is its specific name, or applied to all Pheasants indiscriminately."

Major C. H. T. Marshall says: "Here, in Chamba, they call the male *Nilgur*, and the female *Nulwai.*"

THE CRESTLESS MOONAL. (Vol. I., pp. 135, *et seq.*)—

For a magnificent male of this species (the first and only specimen that I have as yet succeeded in procuring) I have been indebted to Sir S. C. Bayley.

Looking through my former description, I find that I have omitted one important point, and that is, that the basal portions of the tail feathers (completely hidden by the upper and under tail-coverts) are black, with a few imperfect narrow white bars.

The dimensions of this specimen do not differ materially from those given at p. 135, but there is a strong spur, 0·61 in length, on each leg.

A female of this species has also at last been obtained from the Mishmis, who brought it down to Sadiya, and a description and plate of it have been given in the P. Z. S.

The female differs from that of the Common Moonal in having the ground colour of the whole lower back, rump, and upper tail-coverts creamy, profusely variegated by dark brown, and in having the tail feathers (which are black) broadly tipped with this same creamy colour, and crossed higher up with numerous, narrow, transverse, zig-zaggy bars of the same colour.

The general style of colouration, too, is much more uniform, and the bird is smaller. The following is the published description of this female:—

"*Description.*—Head and (upper) back very rich dark umber-brown, each feather of the former with a V-shaped pale ochre mark; each of the latter has a centre line of a richer brown, finely mottled towards the margins; a broad extent of the rump and upper tail-coverts are pale ochraceous white, very finely and delicately mottled with dark brown; tail above rich black, with six or seven narrow whitish bars, and tipped with the same (the counter-colouring of the male); shoulder of wing very rich dark chestnut brown; the shafts pale ochraceous; primaries rich dark umber; secondaries slightly mottled with brown; cheeks and throat dark umber, markings like those on the head; chin white; breast, abdomen, and thighs dull umber, most delicately and finely mottled with pale ochre; underside of tail black, with narrow white bars; the legs appear to have been of a pale grey, and the bill whitish.

"Wing, 11·5; tail, about 8; tarsus, 3; bill at front, 1·75." I have not as yet myself seen a female.

THE WESTERN TRAGOPAN. (Vol. I., pp. 143, *et seq.*)—

An egg of this species will be found figured on the third egg plate at the end of this Vol.

THE CHINESE CRIMSON TRAGOPAN. (Vol. I., p. 154.)—

When our first volume was published, the occurrence of this species, within our limits, was quite unsuspected.

Capt. H. Stevens, of the 42nd N. I., was the first to procure and recognize the distinctness of a specimen of this species brought down to Sadiya by some Mishmis.

There is no certainty of course that the Mishmis, who brought down this specimen, procured it in their own hills; but there is good reason to believe that they did so. In the first place, the species is known to occur in Central China, from near Hankow to the Eastern hills of Setchuen; these latter extend to within probably 200 miles of the Mishmi Hills, and though believed to be divided from them by at least two, if not three, profound river valleys, there would be nothing *primâ facie* to lead us to disbelieve in this south-western extension of the bird's range.

But in the second place, the specimens of this species, observed by Mr. Bennett in Mr. Beale's Aviary at Macao, had been procured in Yunan, the north-western portions of which almost meet the Mishmi Hills, so that there can be no reason to doubt that this bird did really come, as supposed, from these latter.

The Chinese Crimson Tragopan greatly resembles the Indian Crimson Tragopan (Vol. I., pp. 137, *et seq*), but may be distinguished at once by having the inter-scapulary region, scapulars, back, rump, and upper tail-coverts, of the same rich maroon red as the lower part of the back of the neck, thickly dotted with circular or oval, pearly grey or greyish white, spots, more or less completely encircled by a narrowish black band. Also by having the breast and under parts all thickly set with huge, oval, pearly grey spots, occupying more than half the visible terminal portions of the feathers, spots *not* surrounded by a black line as *are* the much smaller ones on the breast of *satyra*.

The following are the dimensions taken from this Mishmi skin, which is that of an adult male :—Length. about 23·0 ; wing, 10·3 ; tail, from the *os coccygis*, 9·0; tarsus, 3·2 ; mid toe and claw, 3·0 ; bill from gape, 1·5. The bird is, therefore, much about the same size as *satyra*.

The colours of the soft parts I quote from Père David : "Irides chestnut ; bill white ; culmen and base brownish ; legs and feet of a rosy flesh colour, inclining to red ; horns of a bluish green, indigo blue at base ; naked skin round the eye indigo blue, with the lores and eyebrows green ; gular apron indigo blue, passing to greenish blue on the edges, which are ornamented with *square* patches of purplish red." Gould figures these patches as oval and crimson, and Captain Stevens writes :—

"I kept the bird for over a year in a cage in my verandah. It had light blue horns and dark blue wattles, with crimson bars."

The forehead and anterior portion of the crown, (the central feathers of which are elongated and form the anterior portions of the crest), the sides of the head, including the ear-coverts and a band round the margin of the gular skin, black ; the posterior portion of the crown and occiput, (the feathers of which are elongated and form the central and posterior portions of the crest), and the feathers of the upper part of the neck all round immediately adjoining the black already referred to, a sort of orange yellow at their bases, becoming a ferruginous maroon towards the tips.

The lower part of the back of the neck, interscapulary region, scapulars, back, rump, and all but the longest row of upper tail-coverts a rather dull maroon red, the feathers with numerous, small, circular or oval, greyish white to pearly grey spots, surrounded by a black band, more or less imperfect in some, and showing here and there, where the feathers are slightly disturbed, a tongue-shaped black band running up from this black frame which encircles the spot, and with a zig-zaggy whitish line inside the margin of this tongue. The longest upper tail-coverts are grey brown, washed towards their margins with rusty maroon. In the next row of tail-coverts above these the greyish white spots are very much larger than in the smaller upper tail-coverts, and almost entirely want the black encircling band ; the tail is black, the basal three-fourths are more or less profusely variegated with irregular, transverse, zig-zaggy bars, of a warm buff colour, more or less ferruginous on the lateral tail feathers ; the exterior tail feathers of all are fully two inches shorter than the rest, and are only blackish brown, and show a dull, imperfect, rufous buff tipping ; a faint trace of the same on the next pair ; the primaries and their greater coverts and the secondaries are black, variegated like the tail ; the markings on the secondaries being, however, paler and yellower ; the winglet, the two longest feathers of which are longer than the primary greater coverts, and have the outer webs a uniform rich ferruginous orange buff, form a conspicuous longitudinal band on the anterior portion of the wing—a feature common to *Ceriornis satyra ;* the shoulder of the wing a sort of orange maroon ; the tertiaries and the rest of the coverts much like the back, except that the pearly grey spots are larger, and that the feathers are here and there variegated with zig-zaggy irregular spots, patches or bars, of yellowish white to ferruginous buff, set in black, which, however, are only conspicuous on the tertiaries ; the edge of the wing and the smaller lower wing-coverts orange buff, the feathers washed at the tips with maroon.

The breast and entire lower parts, except the tibial plumes and the longest lower tail-coverts, mingled rich maroon and delicate French grey ; the feathers of the breast and upper abdomen being maroon, with a huge, terminal, oval grey spot, which, in all the feathers of the breast, goes quite, or almost quite, to the end of the feathers, while, in the feathers of the lower abdomen and flanks, there is a perceptible, though narrow, maroon fringe left beyond the grey spot, and in the lesser and median lower tail-coverts this fringe is so much more developed that the grey spots are only subterminal; the longest lower tail-coverts are blackish brown, with a rufous ferruginous shaft and traces of imperfect bars of the same colour, and washed towards the margins and tips with rusty maroon. On the sides of the body, opposite the breast, and again in places on the flanks, traces of the basal portions of the feathers, black, variegated with irregular zig-zaggy transverse bars of white, or buffy white, are visible where the feathers are disturbed; whether they would be so in life I cannot say. The tibial plumes are orange ferruginous, tinged with maroon.

The size of the grey or greyish white spots on the lower surface, and the width of the maroon fringe extending beyond these, seem to vary a good deal (to judge from the different plates I have examined) in different specimens.

I have seen no specimen of the female, but figures show that she is very similar in marking to that of *satyra*, but altogether paler coloured and greyer.

In the Zoological Gardens at home it has been observed that this species begins to lay in April, and lays seven or eight eggs, making its nest, if possible, off the ground.

An egg there laid is figured as a broad oval, with no gloss, of a clear buff colour, freckled with reddish spots, and measuring 2·05 by about 1·6.

Our other two Tragopans lay in a wild state much *longer* eggs, but the eggs laid in captivity often differ perceptibly both in size and shade of colour from those laid by the same species in a wild state.

THE KOKLASS (Vol. I., pp. 159, *et seq*)—

Major C. H. T. Marshall writes: "In Chamba the people call this species the *Kukrola*, or simply '*Kuk.*'"

THE BLACK-BREASTED KALIJ. (Vol. I., pp. 197, *et seq.*)—

About this species also some further information has reached me from Chittagong. Mr. H. Fasson says: "I notice you say that you have no certain information of the *Mathura* Pheasant (*Euplocamus horsfieldi*) occurring in Southern Chittagong. I can speak distinctly to this, as I have seen and shot *Mathuras* on several occasions in Thanna Chukurea, near Doolochazara. I have also twice seen them put up when beating for Jungle-Fowl in Thanna Puttea."

Mr. J. Jarbo writes: "Like the Polyplectrons the Black-breasted Kalij have a habit of frequenting streams overhung and darkened by jungle, during the heat of the day.

"The Mathura I have often seen driven out of the jungle during beats, but never the Polyplectron. The former I have even seen feeding along the banks of the Kurnafoolee river during noon-tide, but this only where some overhanging rock or jungle made a deep, cool shade. In the cool of the afternoon and evening I have often and often seen them feeding on the upper banks of the river in bands of from two to six or eight, but this only from November till May. During all months of the year when I have been travelling, marching up some dark secluded stream, I have very frequently come across them in the heat of the day, perched on some low branch overhanging the water, or paddling and walking about on the damp sand. These birds are not nearly so wary as the Common Jungle-Fowl. When surprised in the open they will make for the jungle, and will then halt a few yards inside the edge, while the Jungle-Fowl, on the contrary, having once (pretending all the while not to see you) gained shelter, will, in nine cases out of ten, run for forty or fifty yards into the interior of the cover."

THE ARACAN SILVER-PHEASANT. (Vol. I., pp. 201, *et seq.*)—

It seems now probable that this species extends outside the Aracan Yoma, along the great range, which is a continuation of this, and which divides Chittagong from various feudatory states of Upper or Independent Burma.

Mr. G. P. Sanderson writes: "I am as certain as it is possible to be, without having procured the specimen, that I saw this bird in the extreme north of the Changree valley (N. L 23° 17′) in Chittagong. I emerged suddenly upon the river one evening whilst shooting, and saw a beautiful Pheasant run from the water's edge on the far side into a thicket. It was only about thirty yards distant. I have been puzzled ever since to know what it could have been, until your 'Game Birds' appeared, when I recognized the description at once. The Black-breasted Kalij was common, and I had shot numbers of them in the same locality, so there is no chance of my having mistaken the Aracan Silver Pheasant for the Kalij. The splendid blue of the bird I saw was very striking. It was of slender make, and very shy, and quick in its movements. I only had a rifle in hand or could have secured it."

THE RED JUNGLE-FOWL. (Vol. I., pp. 217, *et seq.*)—

Mr. H. Fasson says: "Jungle-Fowl, which the people call *Kura*, afford very fine sport here in Chittagong. The low hills which fringe the bases of the various ranges are divided by numerous narrow valleys, which have been now converted into long winding strips of paddy cultivation, while the hills themselves still remain clothed with scrub jungle and forest. The birds attracted to the cover these more or less isolated hills afford, by the rice in the intervening valleys, may be flushed, in great numbers, by coolies beating through the scrub, and afford fine shooting to sportsmen posted in the valleys, as the birds cross these, seeking new cover in the next of these low hills. They fly under these conditions very fast, and take hard hitting to bring them down."

THE GREY JUNGLE-FOWL. (Vol. I., pp. 231, *et seq.*)—

There is a great difference of opinion as to the value of this species for the table. Major McInroy writes: "Mr. Davison says (Vol. I., p. 235): The Grey Jungle-Cock, even at the best, is very dry and hard. This is correct literally as to the old cock, but most people would suppose it to apply to the species, and if so, it cannot be said to be so everywhere, as a young bird of either sex is most palatable and gamey, when hung for a day or two. This applies to Mysore."

To whom replies Captain E. A. Butler as follows: "Adverting to the remarks of Mr. Davison and Major McInroy on the Grey Jungle-Fowl, as a bird for table, I beg to record my experience:—

"When living at Mount Aboo some years ago, I shot numerous Jungle-Fowl at the foot of the hill, in the *cold* weather, and always found them (old and young of both sexes) excellent eating, reminding one of the flavour of an English Pheasant. On turning to the account of the bird in the first volume of the GAME BIRDS, I was surprised to find it cried down as an article of food, and intended writing to you before; however, perhaps it is as well I delayed doing so, as my opinion now is changed from the following circumstance: At the beginning of March, this year, I shot a pair of Jungle-Fowl *(male and female)* near Belgaum, in the afternoon, and in the evening, after returning home, my butler said they smelt so strong that he did not consider them fit for table. Having decided upon skinning them, I had them put upon one side till the following day, when I discovered that the strong odour, referred to by the butler, arose from the crops of the birds being charged to the muzzle with human excrement.

"This may be an exceptional case, but as food is scarce in the hot weather, I have no doubt myself that, at that season, they feed constantly upon the filth I have mentioned, so recommend those who regard the flesh as 'palatable and gamey' to satisfy themselves in future before ordering them for table as to the source from which that 'gamey' flavour is produced.

"I may add that two Pea-Fowl, shot the same day, had their crops also bulged with the same disgusting food, and yet all of the birds were shot in a wild jungle far away from any village, and where only a few wood-cutters existed. In the cold weather and in the rains, when food is abundant, I dare say they may be fit for table, and indeed I know from experience that they are excellent eating; but in the hot weather, when their natural food is scarce, there can be no doubt, from the above facts, that they are the foulest of feeders, as also are the Grey and Black Partridges, some of the Button-Quails, and numerous other species of so-called Game Birds that I could mention."

THE PAINTED SPUR-FOWL. (Vol. I., pp. 255, *et seq.*)—

Several correspondents note additional localities where this species has been observed. Mr. A. M. Markham says: "I have shot the Painted Spur-Fowl in the wooded rocky hills in the south of the Allahabad district. They are fairly common there."

Mr. W. Forsyth remarks: "I have shot the Painted Spur-Fowl at Rhotas, a place 30 or 40 miles up the Sone from Dehree, where the Grand Trunk Road crosses that river. It is common in the hills on the Gya and Shahabad sides of the river."

And Captain E. A. Butler writes: "I have just examined a skin of this species shot near Gokak, about 40 miles north-north-west of Belgaum. The man who shot it told me that he saw five or six more at the same time, and that he fancied it was not uncommon about the hills in that neighbourhood."

THE HIMALAYAN SNOW-COCK. (Vol. I., pp. 268, *et seq.*)—

Speaking of this species I said that it probably extended west of Kashmir into Afghanistan. Lieutenant Fairbrother, of the 29th P. N. I., writing from Kurrum, 29th June 1880, says: "A party which ascended the highest peak (Seetaram, 15.000 feet) a week ago, came across a brood of Snow-Cock, and captured all the chicks (nine I think), but later released them. The parents were not obtained, though fired at with a small rifle, the party having no gun." As no specimens were preserved, we cannot even yet be quite *positive* what the species is that inhabits the Sufaid Koh, but there is little doubt that it is the same as the Himalayan one.

In speaking of the habits of this species, I remarked that, although I had always found them wild and wary, I had *heard* that in some parts of the hills they were extremely tame. Lt. A. C. Bruce, R.E., confirms the accounts I had received from others of their tameness. He says:—

"In 1875, I myself shot the Himalayan Snow-Cock, about 13.000 feet above sea level, above the Neelni Nulla in Kashmir. The best description of the place where I actually shot these birds, will be to say that I found them on high ridges above the Upper Trisangum Nulla, about four easy marches from Bundypur on the Wooller Lake. I myself only found them in this particular place, but I have no doubt that there are plenty of them scattered over the district surrounding Gurais and Tilail; subject to the condition they would not be found lower down than about 13,000 feet, at any rate prior to the end of September.

"Above this altitude I believe they occur throughout the higher spurs of the Haramook mountain, &c.

"Where I shot the birds I could have killed a good many as there was a large pack thereabouts, and *they were certainly the tamest game birds I ever came across.* The largest of the two I shot was a male; it weighed 8lbs., and measured over 30 inches in length, and 44 in expanse. The other was a female not very much smaller, but wanting the blunt spurs. What struck me particularly about these birds was their tameness and singularly musical call. When walking they carry their tails like an ordinary hen."

Major C. H. T. Marshall writes: "Here, in Chamba, they call the Snow-Cock *Galound.*"

An egg of this species will be found figured at the bottom of the third of the plates of eggs that follow this Appendix.

THE PAINTED PARTRIDGE OR SOUTHERN FRANCOLIN. (Vol. II., pp. 19, *et seq.*)—

In describing the distribution of this species I included the Kistnah district within its range. A Reviewer, with the usual self-complacent ignorance of his class, asserted that I was wrong, and that it was the Black Partridge that occurred there. This was palpably absurd to any one who had studied the distribution of the two species, but yet it may be as well to state that Mr. J. G. Horsfall has kindly sent me a specimen of the Partridge found in parts of the upland taluks of the Masulipatam (Kistnah) district, and this proves to be, as I said, *Francolinus pictus*, the Painted Partridge or Southern Francolin.

When Vol. II. was written I was unable to ascertain on any good authority that this species occurred in Ceylon. Neither Layard nor Holdsworth had ever met with it, though the latter had heard that it did occur. Two or three residents of the island, whom I consulted, denied its occurrence; and, as I had good reason to believe that it did not, in the Peninsula, range further south than 11°30′ North Latitude, I had no difficulty in accepting their statements. I have now, however, ascertained that a small outlying colony of this, or a very closely allied species, exists in the centre of the southern portion of the Island, in about 5°50′ North Latitude. and a little north and south of this in the country south of Newara-Eliya and about Haputale. The tract occupied by them is very limited. and even in this tract they are said to be very sparsely distributed. I have hitherto failed to procure a specimen, and though the Ceylon bird is most probably. as asserted, identical with our Indian birds, I should not be surprised if this isolated colony proved to be at any rate a recognizably distinct race. Very possibly, however, the bird may have been at some time artificially introduced. Quail and many other kinds of Indian birds have, we know, been repeatedly turned loose in Ceylon.

The Grey Partridge. (Vol. II., pp. 51, *et seq.*)—

Captain W. S. Heaviside, R.E., speaks up for the Greys. He says: "This despised bird is common in Shekawattee and Bikanir, and appears to me to be very good eating there. The flesh was more tender and juicy than usual, owing, I believe. to their feeding on white-ants: these insects are easily got at in that sandy country, as they work very much on the surface of the ground."

The Thibetan Partridge. (Vol. II., pp. 65, *et seq.*)—

We have figured an egg of this species on the third of the plates of eggs with which this volume concludes.

The Black-Throated Hill Partridge. (Vol. II., pp. 79, *et seq.*)—

On the fourth of the plates of eggs which follow this Appendix, a figure of the egg of this species is given.

The Black-Breasted or Rain Quail. (Vol. II., pp. 151, *et seq.*)—

Three eggs of this species are figured on the fourth of the egg plates with which this volume concludes.

The Blue-Breasted or Painted Quail. (Vol. II., pp. 161, *et seq.*)—

Mr. Laird writes to say that he had confounded two species, and that the birds he got ten miles south of Belgaum proved to have been the Painted *Bush Quail*, and not this present species.

At the same time I notice that Jerdon says that he recorded one specimen in his Catalogue from Belgaum. So that possibly a straggler may occur in this district occasionally. though hitherto neither Mr. Laird nor Captain Butler (who first drew attention to the matter) have met with it there.

With reference to the distribution of this species Dr. Bidie, of the Madras Central Museum, writes: In December last I shot a pair of this species, near Goodavancherrie, Chingleput district, some 20 miles from Madras. I was shooting Snipe at the time, and got the cock, but lost the female amongst the long grass."

An egg of this species has been figured on the third of the plates of eggs which follow this Appendix.

The Burmo-Malayan Button-Quail. (Vol. II., pp. 183, *et seq.*)—

I stated that this species occurred in Aracan and Hill Tipperah. It might therefore naturally be expected to occur in the intervening district of Chittagong. Accordingly Mr, H. Fasson has sent me a fine specimen shot on the 13th December, at Jooykhola, Thanna Fatikchiri, in the northern part of this district.

BAILLON'S CRAKE. (Vol. II., pp. 203, *et seq.*)—

An egg of this species is figured on the second of the plates of eggs which follow this Appendix.

THE BROWN AND ASHY CRAKE. (Vol. II., pp. 225, *et seq.*)—

An egg of this species has been figured on Plate III.

THE BLUE-BREASTED BANDED RAIL. (Vol. II., pp. 245, *et seq.*)—

On Plate II will be found a figure of an egg of this species.

THE SARUS. (Vol. III, pp. 1, *et seq.*)—

An egg of this species is figured on the fourth of the plates of eggs with which this volume concludes.

THE PINK-HEADED DUCK. (Vol. III., pp. 173, *et seq.*)—

An anonymous writer in the *Asian* furnishes the following additional information as to the distribution, &c., of this species. He says :—

"The Pink-headed Duck is not very rare in the trans-Gangetic pergunnahs of the Allahabad district.

"In 1873 a friend purchased three living specimens of the Pink-headed Duck, from a fowler at Allahabad. This was in the hot weather, and the birds were stuffed and mounted with my assistance, so that I can vouch for the species. These birds were taken somewhere in the north-east portion of the Allahabad district.

"On the 25th of May 1876 I saw and fired at a flock of twelve of these birds, on the Ganges, only about two miles north of Newton's Hotel. The exact spot was a point on the river due north of the centre of the Allahabad Race Course.

"Some days after I fired at another pair on the river some few hundred yards lower down, but again failed to bag one.

"A certain find, however, for the Pink-headed Duck, in the hot weather, is a large weedy jhíl near the village of Mukoondpur, somewhere about the north-west corner of the Allahabad district.

"I have, on two or three occasions, seen small flights of *R. caryophyllacea* in various parts of the Allahabad district, and recognized them by their black colour and the pink they showed on the under side of the wing, particularly when they turned side on, in flight.

"As the migratory ducks have all left the country by April, the permanent residents then become conspicuous by their absence ; and the only bird for which it is then possible to mistake the Pink-headed Duck, is the Grey Duck, *Anas poecilorhyncha*. From this bird the Pink-head should be easily distinguished by its nearly uniform black (at a distance) plumage, by its pink and angular head, with its remarkably straight profile, and by the pink it shows under the wing. Any flight of black ducks, about the size of a Mallard seen during the hot weather, or rains, will probably prove to be this species. And if sportsmen will please bear this in mind we shall soon hear something more about the Pink-headed Duck.

"As it would be hardly possible to mistake either the Whistling Teal or Comb Duck for this bird, I do not think any further remarks necessary; but I may mention that the season in which I found the Pink-headed Ducks on the river was a very dry one, and the jhíls for miles around to my knowledge were dry.

"Among other birds, I found pheasant-tailed Jacanas, fairly common along the sandbanks of the Ganges ; having no doubt been compelled to take to this disreputable sandpiper mode of life by the dryness of the jhíls and the absence of their beloved water plants."

At page 178, I quoted Mr. Shillingford's weight in *Troy* lbs. and ozs. of a Pink-headed Duck. It may be well to note that the pound *Troy* is equal to, or contains 5.760 grains, (the same as grains *Avoirdupois*) and is divided into 12 ozs. each of 480 such grains The pound *Avoirdupois* contains 7,000 grains, and is divided into 16 ozs, each of 437.5 grains, so that 2 lbs. 8 ozs. Troy, the weight given by Mr. Shillingford for one of his ducks, is equivalent to about 2 lbs. 3.14 ozs *Avoirdupois*.

The following additional measurements of the Pink-headed Duck I owe to Mr. F. A. Shillingford :—

Sex.	*Length.*	*Expanse.*	*Wing.*	*Tail.*	*Tarsus.*	*Bill at front.*	*Weight.*
♂	23·5	38·0	10·75	5·0	2·0	2·25	1 lb. 14 ozs.
♂	23·5	38·5	11·0	4·5	2·0	2·25	2 lbs.
♂	23·0	37·5	10·75	4·5	1·87	2·25	1 lb. 13 ozs.
♂	24·0	38·0	10·75	5·0	2·0	2·12	1 lb. 12 ozs.
♀	23·0	37·0	10·5	4·5	2·0	2·25	1 lb. 15 ozs.

Of the female he furnishes the following description, noting that the specimen described was an adult shot on the 15th of June, and then contained one fully-formed white egg.

"Bill pinkish brown ; cere (?) dull white ; irides dull orange ; tarsi, toes, webs and nails purplish slate.

"Head, chin and upper portion of throat dull ashy pink ; crown and back of neck light brown ; the rest of the body lighter brown than the male ; interscapular feathers edged with light brown, and abdominal feathers edged with pinkish brown ; primaries and all but the last five secondaries light rufescent brown ; the inner webs and portions covered by the coverts and winglets pinkish white ; upper wing and winglet light brown ; upper margin of wing white. Last row of greater coverts edged with white ; tertiaries and scapulars dark brown ; under side of entire wing dull lustrous white ; speculum whitish brown, with a very slight tinge of rufous."

THE WHITE-EYED POCHARD (Vol. III, pp. 263, *et seq.*)—

Of this species also an egg has been figured on Plate IV.

THE WHITE-FACED STIFF-TAIL DUCK. (Vol. III., pp. 289, *et seq.*)—

My prediction, p. 289, (as to the occurrence of this species within our limits.) had not been two months in type, when Mr. F. Field, U. C. S., Punjab, most kindly sent me a specimen of a Duck, that he was unable to identify, which proved to be a young bird of this present species. He said : "I shot this bird on the 28th of October at the "Old Nullah" about a mile from the Civil Station of Loodhiana, Punjab. It was sitting alone in a pool. I stalked up close behind some reeds, and then showed myself, expecting to see it fly. All it did was to cock its little stiff, thin, pointed tail, and swim off in a quiet way for some ten yards. Its appearance, while swimming with its tail turned upwards, was most peculiar. I tried to frighten it into flying, but it would not rise, so I shot it while swimming. Unfortunately I did not sex it. It measured in the flesh :—Length, 18·0 ; wing, 6·1 ; tail from vent, 3·5 ; tarsus, 1·3 ; bill at front, straight from margin of feathers to point, 1·7 ; from gape, 2·0 ; mid-toe and claw, 2·8.

"The irides were brown ; the bill very dark grey, almost black ; the legs and feet grey, with blackish webs and joints."

This species may be recognized at any age by the *tail*, composed of 18 narrow spine-like feathers, with scanty, stiff, disunited, narrow webs, quite worn off towards the tips, which exhibit only the bare shafts. The lateral feathers are successively shorter and shorter, so that the whole tail is sharply wedge-shaped, and owing to the nature of the feathers, which are only covered for about half an inch at their bases by the upper and under tail-coverts, looks poor and scraggy, much of the cormorant type, but much feebler, thinner, barer and poorer in appearance. Still, though the tail will suffice for identification, it may be well to add to Mr. Field's remarks a detailed description of his bird, as young birds like this are the most likely to occur in India.

The lores, forehead, crown and upper part of the occiput are a dark brown, the feathers barely perceptibly margined at the tips with yellowish brown. The rest of the occiput and nape are nearly similar, but the pale margins of the feathers are broader and more conspicuous. A broad, dull, white stripe, (a little speckled with brown) runs from the base of the upper mandible on either side to near the base of the occiput, but does not quite meet behind. Below this, from the gape, runs a broad dark brown stripe, also feebly freckled with pale buffy. Below this again, the rest of the cheeks, as well as the chin and throat, are dull white. The neck all round is grey brown, freckled with yellowish white.

The interscapulary region, scapulars, tertiaries, upper tail-coverts, back and rump except the central portions of the two latter, are a dull, pale, brownish yellow or dull buff, freckled and obsoletely vermicellated with darkish brown. The central portions of the back and rump are dark brown, narrowly and imperfectly barred with dull buff. The tail is a dull rather pale brown, earthy in places and in places with a rusty tinge. The wings, a grey brown; primaries and their greater coverts plain; the rest more or less freckled towards the tips of the feathers with dull buff.

On the breast and the rest of the lower parts the basal portions of the feathers are brown, and the tips dull brownish yellow on the breast, passing to buffy white lower down; there is a little nearly pure white about the vent. The brown bases show through more or less everywhere, least on the upper breast, most on the lower abdomen. The wing-lining is mingled French grey and white; the axillaries are pure white.

Captain Elwes informed me that he once received a skin, which he had good grounds for believing came from the Malay Peninsula, and which he had come to the conclusion belonged to this present species. This, *quantum valeat;* possibly his skin may have first come from elsewhere to Singapore, or may belong to some other species of the genus of which there are several. Amongst these are *E. moccoa*, Smith, of Southern Africa, (the female of which much resembles that of our bird,) *E. australis* of Western Australia, and *E. rubida, ferruginea* and *dominica* from America.

THE COMMON SNIPE. (Vol. III., pp. 359, *et seq.*)—

Since my remarks (p. 368) on the manner in which the drumming sound is produced were printed, the following explanation of the matter (entirely confirming my view) by Captain Legge has appeared in "The Birds of Ceylon:—"

"It is a pity that Mr. Dresser adopts Herr Meves's tail theory of the Snipe's drumming after what has been written by Mr. Hancock and others. In my article on this species, printed on the 13th January last, and written after I had myself carried out the experiments on which Herr Meves's hypothesis was based, I showed that the conditions under which the tail feather is moved with the stick and wire on the one hand, and with the caudal vertebræ of the bird on the other, are totally different, and that though a noise may be produced like the Snipe's drumming with the one means, it cannot possibly be by the other. With the intention of referring again to the matter in the appendix, after I should have had an opportunity of observing for myself, I repaired this season to the breeding grounds of the Snipe in Mid-Wales, and there had an admirable opportunity of verifying Mr. Hancock's theory that the sound is chiefly made by the wings; and I am now perfectly satisfied that this is the case, notwithstanding that the tail is spread during the performance. I went there, partly convinced in my own mind that the sound was a vocal and at the same time a mechanical one—that is, that it was made in the same manner as has been observed in the case of the Great Snipe, with the bill and throat; but it only requires close, very close, observation, and good hearing to come to a right conclusion in the matter. The most favourable occasion I had for observation was on the evening of the 10th June, when the same Snipe, having young near where I was standing, drummed over my head, flying backwards and forward in the manner now to be described, without cessation, for a period of fifty-two minutes, timed by my watch? It was a calm evening on an immense bog, with the sun gradually sinking behind the wild surrounding hills; and, as I stood, binoculars in hand, and with my wire and tail-feather for purposes of comparison of sound, intently watching the remarkable performance of the interesting bird, the time flew rapidly by, and I do not think I ever spent a more pleasant hour in the observation of nature. There were other birds drumming all round me, for the evening is *the* time for this performance; but I gave my undivided attention to the one, which I had particularly alarmed by my proximity to her young.

"The aerial course taken by the bird was an ellipse, of the average length of a quarter of a mile, described over where I stood; but it was sometimes varied by her making a figure of "8" above my head, the bird always returning to its original starting-point in the air, and again making the same tour. The movement for the purpose of drumming was generally performed twice, but sometimes thrice, going and coming, making from four to six times in each figure described. It flew at a height of about 100 yards with a quick and regular movement of the wings, and drummed in this wise :—The body was suddenly turned on one side, and the bird descended rapidly for about 100 feet at an angle of 45° degrees, moving its wings with very rapid and powerful strokes, its tail being at the same time opened to the utmost; having arrived at the lowest point of its descent it suddenly turned its body in the reverse direction, that is, elevated the wing, which had been before depressed, and with a short upward sweep ceased the drumming noise and rose to its original position, continued its course for a short distance, and then descended with the same rush again. The movement was always performed with the same wing pointed downwards throughout one-half of the bird's course; that is, if it commenced to drum with the left wing down, when flying from east to west, that wing was inclined downwards the next time it descended, until the course was altered, and the bird flew back from west to east, when usually the other wing was inclined towards the earth.

"The instant the bird commenced its descent the drumming noise was heard, and it continued till it finished off with a sort of whiz directly the upward sweep, by which the bird recovered itself, was performed. By closely watching the bird it could be distinctly *seen* that the vibrations falling on the ear *coincided exactly with the beat of wings*, which, assisted with the downward rush through the air, were the *primary* cause of the sound. The tail, however, was spread, as I have already remarked, and to such an extent that it took the form of a fan, the lateral feathers being at right angles to the centre; and herein lies the *secondary* cause of the sound. During the drumming beats of the wing the quills are more drawn back than in the ordinary strokes (this can be observed if the bird be closely watched), so that the atmospheric wave or air propelled by the powerful stroke of the wing is driven through the rigid, sabre-shaped, and opened-out feathers of the tail, thus making the peculiar noise. If a succession of quick puffs emitted from the lips be brought to bear upon the opened-out tail of a Snipe, a peculiar noise is produced, which is analogous to that made by the much more powerful agency of the wings of the bird during the rapid downward rush through the air which it resorts to when drumming; and as the peculiar sound is unquestionably coincident with the beating of the wings, it can only be accounted for on the hypothesis here set forward."

THE PAINTED SNIPE. (Vol. III., pp. 381, *et seq.*)—

On Plate III. will be found the figure of an egg of this species, there designated *Rhynchæa bengalensis*, the name used for this species, until its identity with the African bird being generally acknowledged the older name *R. capensis* had to be adopted.

GALLINAGO NEMORICOLA

GALLINAGO SOLITARIA

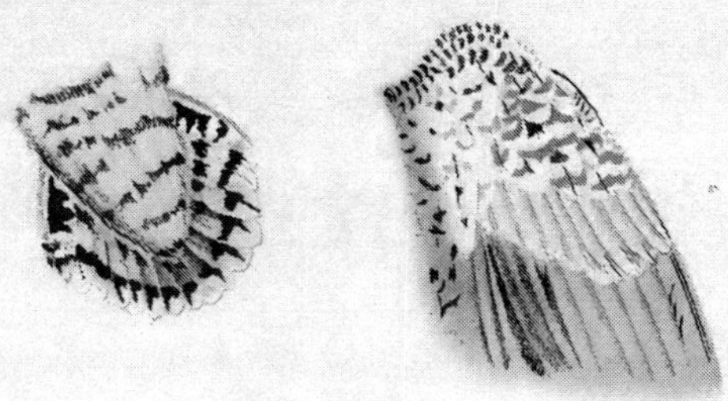

GALLINAGO SCOLOPACINUS

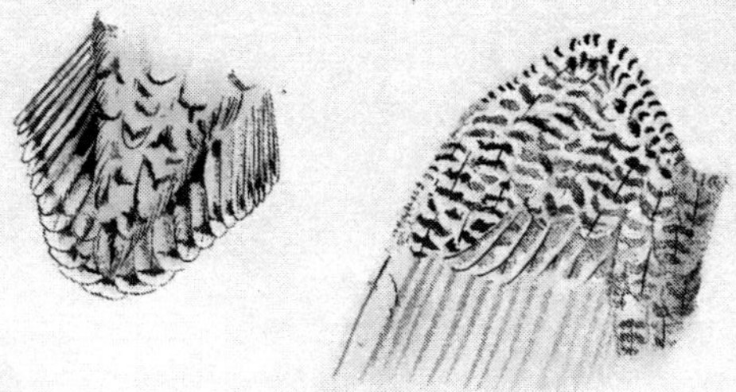

GALLINAGO STENURA

Pl.I.

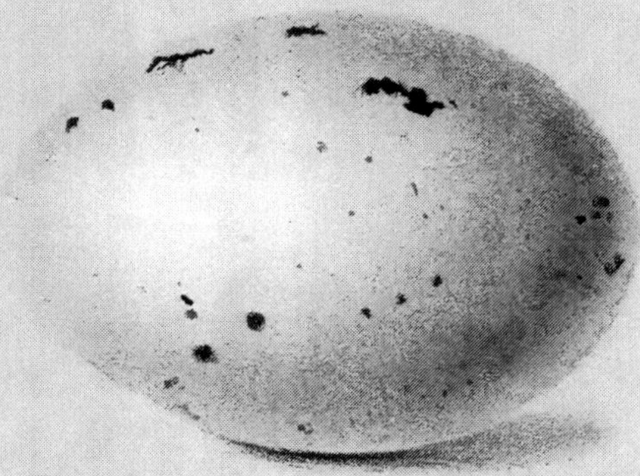

Eupodotis edwardsi.

Syphеotides aurita

Sypheotides aurita

Eupodotis edwardsi

Pl. II.

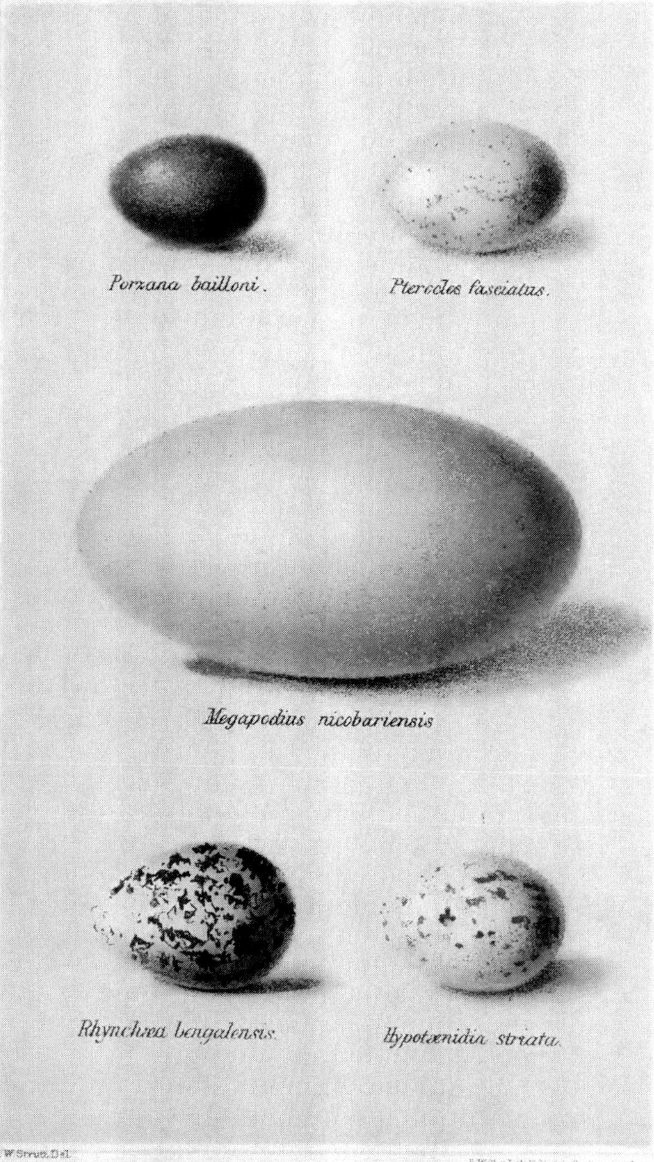

A. W. Strutt, Del.

E. Weller Lith. 17, Hatton Garden, London.

Pl. III.

A. W. Strutt. Del.

Pl IV.

A.W. Stuart Del

INDEX.

PRINTED BY A. ACTON, CALCUTTA CENTRAL PRESS CO., LD., 5, COUNCIL HOUSE STREET.